The Palgrave Handbook of Populism

Michael Oswald
Editor

The Palgrave Handbook of Populism

Editor
Michael Oswald
Political Science
University of Passau
Passau, Bayern, Germany

ISBN 978-3-030-80802-0   ISBN 978-3-030-80803-7 (eBook)
https://doi.org/10.1007/978-3-030-80803-7

© The Editor(s) (if applicable) and The Author(s), under exclusive license to Springer Nature Switzerland AG 2022
This work is subject to copyright. All rights are solely and exclusively licensed by the Publisher, whether the whole or part of the material is concerned, specifically the rights of translation, reprinting, reuse of illustrations, recitation, broadcasting, reproduction on microfilms or in any other physical way, and transmission or information storage and retrieval, electronic adaptation, computer software, or by similar or dissimilar methodology now known or hereafter developed.
The use of general descriptive names, registered names, trademarks, service marks, etc. in this publication does not imply, even in the absence of a specific statement, that such names are exempt from the relevant protective laws and regulations and therefore free for general use.
The publisher, the authors and the editors are safe to assume that the advice and information in this book are believed to be true and accurate at the date of publication. Neither the publisher nor the authors or the editors give a warranty, expressed or implied, with respect to the material contained herein or for any errors or omissions that may have been made. The publisher remains neutral with regard to jurisdictional claims in published maps and institutional affiliations.

Cover illustration: Agata Gładykowska/Alamy Stock Photo

This Palgrave Macmillan imprint is published by the registered company Springer Nature Switzerland AG
The registered company address is: Gewerbestrasse 11, 6330 Cham, Switzerland

Preface

Handbooks are intended to give a systematic overview of a subject and its most important sub-areas. This volume is not intended to compete with other handbooks dealing with populism already on the market—there are excellent handbooks. And, although this handbook is a stand-alone publication, its value lies in how far it extends the discussions on important topics that are either not covered in other volumes or not adequately represented. Of particular note here are the highly important topics such as 'Populism & Gender' or 'The Psychology of Populism'. This handbook offers insight into some of the most potent and relevant dimensions of populism's expressions and thereby extending our understanding and appreciation of the concept's significance within our contemporary political world.

Many thanks go out to not only the many authors of this volume who have labored so diligently and tenaciously to draw out the many aspects and implications of populism and have sought to enlighten us about the less than obvious hues and tomes of one of social science's most compelling and demanding subjects, but to those research assistants as well who have so generously and selflessly devoted their time and dedication to this project's progress and completion, without whom this volume would not have been possible. First and foremost, among those are Elena Broda and Mario Schäfer who assisted with editing and the essential task of careful and diligent communication with the volume's authors. I could not have done it without you! Also, many thanks to my wife Valentina, and above all to my children, Ava and Levi.

Passau, Germany
March 2021

Dr. Michael Oswald

Contents

Part I Populism–Introduction to & Some Reflections on the Concept

1. The New Age of Populism: Reapproaching a Diffuse Concept — 3
   Michael Oswald, Mario Schäfer, and Elena Broda

Part II Theoretical Critique

2. The Past and Present of American Populism — 31
   Anton Jäger

3. Populism Is Hegemony Is Politics? Ernesto Laclau's Theory of Populism — 49
   Benjamin Arditi

4. "An Antipodean Populism? Winston Peters, New Zealand First, and the Problems of Misclassification" — 69
   David B. MacDonald

5. A Critique of Left-Wing Populism: Critical Materialist and Social-Psychological Perspectives — 85
   Helge Petersen and Hannah Hecker

Part III The Political Psychology of Populism & its Affective Underpinnings

6. The Psychology of Populism — 103
   Darren G. Lilleker and Nathalie Weidhase

7. Emotional Mobilization: The Affective Underpinnings of Right-Wing Populist Party Support — 115
   Hans-Georg Betz and Michael Oswald

8   From Specific Worries to Generalized Anger: The
    Emotional Dynamics of Right-Wing Political Populism   145
    Christoph Giang Nguyen, Mikko Salmela,
    and Christian von Scheve

Part IV Authoritarian Populism & Fascism

9   Fascism and Populism   163
    Carlos de la Torre

10 Populism and Authoritarianism   177
    Gabriella Gricius

11 Authoritarian Populism and Collective Memory
    Manipulation   195
    Rafał Riedel

12 The (Almost) Forgotten Elitist Sources of Right-Wing
    Populism Kaltenbrunner, Höcke and the Distaste
    for the Masses   213
    Phillip Becher

Part V Economic Populism, Inequality & Crises

13 Populism and the Economics of Antitrust   227
    Aurelien Portuese

14 The Red Herring of Economic Populism   245
    Paris Aslanidis

15 Populist Mobilization in the United States: Adding
    Political Economy to Cultural Explanations   263
    Christian Lammert and Boris Vormann

Part VI Populism & Gender

16 Right-Wing Populism and Gender   277
    Gabriele Dietze

17 'The Gendered Politics of Right-Wing Populism
    and Instersectional Feminist Contestations'   291
    Julia Roth

18 Popular Sovereignty and (Non)recognition in Venezuela:
    On the Coming into Political Being of 'el *Pueblo*'   303
    Sara C. Motta and Ybiskay Gonzalez Torres

Part VII New Populisms and Cleavages

19 Environmental Populism — 321
Aron Buzogány and Christoph Mohamad-Klotzbach

20 Medical Populism — 341
Gideon Lasco

21 Global Populism — 351
Daniel F. Wajner

22 Populism and the Cosmopolitan–Communitarian Divide — 369
Frank Decker

23 Populism and the Recasting of the Ideological Landscape of Liberal Democracies — 379
Albena Azmanova

Part VIII Populism Discourses

24 Meaning Matters: The Political Language of Islamic Populism — 389
Inaya Rakhmani and Vedi Hadiz

25 Populism, Anti-populism and Post-truth — 407
Antonis Galanopoulos and Yannis Stavrakakis

26 Experience Narratives and Populist Rhetoric in U.S. House Primaries — 421
Mike Cowburn

27 The Framing of Right-Wing Populism: Intricacies of 'Populist' Narratives, Emotions, and Resonance — 437
Julia Leser and Rebecca Pates

28 Populism and Collective Memory — 451
Luca Manucci

Part IX Populists in Office

29 Populism in Southeast Asia — 471
Paul D. Kenny

30 Populism in Africa and the Anti-Corruption Trope in Nigeria's Politics — 485
Sylvester Odion Akhaine

31 Populism in Southern Africa Under Liberation Movements as Governments: The Cases of Namibia, South Africa and Zimbabwe — 497
Henning Melber

32 Venezuela: The Institutionalization of Authoritarian
    Populism   511
    Thomas Kestler and Miguel Latouche

33 Populist Neo-Imperialism: A New Take on Populist
    Foreign Policy   527
    Ole Frahm and Dirk Lehmkuhl

Part X Strategic Populism & Societal Support

34 Populism as an Implementation of National Biopolitics:
    The Case of Poland   545
    Szymon Wróbel

35 Understanding the Support of Right-Wing Populist
    Positions Within Unsuspected Groups: The Case
    of Professional Social Workers in Italy   563
    Luca Fazzi and Urban Nothdurfter

36 Clarifying Our Populist Moment(s): Right-Wing
    and Left-Wing Populism in the 2016 Presidential Election   579
    Edward G. Carmines, Eric R. Schmidt,
    and Matthew R. Fowler

Part XI Consequences of Populism & Anti-Populist
         Discourse

37 New Parties, Populism, and Parliamentary Polarization:
    Evidence from Plenary Debates in the German *Bundestag*   611
    Marcel Lewandowsky, Julia Schwanholz,
    Christoph Leonhardt, and Andreas Blätte

38 The Enemy in My House: How Right-Wing Populism
    Radicalized the Debate About Citizenship in France   629
    Elena Dück and Sebastian Glassner

39 Can Right-Wing Populist Parties Solve the "Democratic
    Dilemma"?   649
    Martin Althoff

40 Searching for the Philosopher's Stone: Counterstrategies
    Against Populism   665
    Mario Schäfer and Florian Hartleb

Index   687

NOTES ON CONTRIBUTORS

Sylvester Odion Akhaine is a Professor of Political Science at the Department of Political Science, Lagos State University, Nigeria.

Martin Althoff Dipl.-Soz.-Wiss. Martin Althoff studied political science at the University of Duisburg-Essen from 2005 to 2012. After graduation, he worked from 2013 to 2017 as a research assistant at the Institute for Political Science at the University of Münster. Since 2017 he has been working as a Lecturer and research assistant at the NSI-University of Applied Sciences in Hannover. He is currently working on his Ph.D. thesis, researches and publishes on the subject of political participation and works primarily with quantitative methods.

Benjamin Arditi is a Professor of Politics at UNAM, the National University of Mexico. He is the author of *Politics on the edges of liberalism: difference, populism, revolution, emancipation* (Edinburgh University Press, 2007, 2008; Spanish translation in Gedisa 2010, 2014, 2017). He co-edits the book series Taking on the Political published by Edinburgh University Press. His research focuses on networked political insurgencies, populism and illiberal and postliberal politics.

Paris Aslanidis is a Lecturer of Political Science at Yale University, Department of Political Science and Hellenic Studies Program, MacMillan Center for International and Area Studies. His work focuses on populism from the perspectives of party politics, social mobilization and intellectual history. He has published with *Political Studies, Democratization, Sociological Forum, Mobilization, Quality & Quantity*, among other journals, and his chapter on 'Populism and Social Movements' appears in the *Oxford Handbook of Populism*.

Albena Azmanova is an Associate Professor of Political Theory at the University of Kent's Brussels School of International Studies. Her research spans justice and judgment, democratic theory and social transformation and critique of contemporary capitalism. She is the author, most recently, of Capitalism on Edge: How Fighting Precarity Can Achieve Radical Change Without Crisis Or Utopia (Columbia University Press, 2020). She holds a Ph.D. from the New School for Social Research (New York) and has held teaching or research positions at Sciences Po. (Paris), the New School (New York), the Max-Planck-Institute for the Study of Societies (Cologne), Harvard University, and UC Berkeley.

Phillip Becher (b. 1987) is a social scientist and currently working at the University of Siegen. He has recently published his Ph.D. thesis on the work of American fascism scholar A. James Gregor as a monograph. His research interests include political theory, the history of political ideas, political parties and social movements. Becher's publications, papers and presentations deal inter alia with Italian neo-fascism, contemporary German right-wing populism and the intellectual new right.

Hans-Georg Betz is a leading expert on populism and the radical right in affluent liberal democracies. He has written several seminal books and articles on radical right-wing populism, nativism and Islamophobia. He currently serves as an adjunct professor in the institute of political science at the University of Zürich where he teaches advanced courses on populism and globalization. Before coming to Switzerland, he taught at York University in Toronto, The Paul H. Nitze School of Advanced International Studies (SAIS) in Washington, DC, and the Loyola University Rome Center in Italy. He also held a joint visiting chair at Columbia University/New York University in New York City. He currently lives near Lausanne in the French part of Switzerland. Hans-Georg Betz has written extensively on populism, the radical right, and nativism, both past and contemporary.

Andreas Blätte is a Professor of Public Policy and Regional Politics at the University of Duisburg-Essen. He received his doctoral degree from the University of Erfurt and studied Political Science, European Law and Economics at the LMU Munich and the University of Aberystwyth, Wales. His research combines a focus on policies and politics in immigrant societies with the use of large-scale corpora and computational social science approaches. His published work includes several R packages and corpora that were developed in the context of the PolMine Project that he has established.

Elena Broda is a Ph.D. candidate at the Department of Journalism, Media and Communication at the University of Gothenburg. She studied Political Science at the University of Hamburg and the University of Passau. Her research focuses on political communication in transforming information environments, and she writes her dissertation on the role of misinformation regarding the development of misperceptions and knowledge resistance in online issue publics.

Aron Buzogány works at the University of Natural Resources and Life Sciences (BOKU) in Vienna, Austria. He holds a Ph.D. in political science from Freie Universität Berlin and has held academic or visiting positions at Yale University, the German Public Administration Research Institute in Speyer, the University of Munich, Freie Universität Berlin and Johns Hopkins University SAIS in Washington, D.C. His work is within comparative politics and touches on different aspects of environmental, energy and climate policy in the European Union, including its contestation by political parties and social movements.

Edward G. Carmines is a Distinguished Professor, Warner O. Chapman Professor of Political Science, and Rudy Professor at Indiana University. At IU, he serves as Director for the Center on American Politics and Director of Research for the Center on Representative Government. He is the co-author of six books, including Issue Evolution: Race and the Transformation of American Politics (with James A. Stimson; Princeton University Press, 1989) and Reaching Beyond Race (with Paul M. Sniderman; Harvard University Press 1997)—both of which won the American Political Science Association's Gladys M. Kammerer Award for the best book in the field of U.S. national policy.

Mike Cowburn is a Ph.D. candidate in political science at the Graduate School of North American Studies of the Freie Universität Berlin. His research interests include Congress, political parties, elections, intra-party factions, polarization, and candidate nomination systems. His Ph.D. project examines congressional primary competitions in the twenty-first century, considering their role in nominating experienced candidates and whether contests have contributed to partisan polarization in Congress.

Carlos de la Torre is Director of the UF Center for Latin American Studies. He has a Ph.D. from the New School for Social Research. He was a fellow at the Simon Guggenheim Foundation, and the Woodrow Wilson Center for Scholars. His most recent books are *The Routledge Handbook of Global Populism,* (Routlege, 2019); *Populisms a Quick Immersion,* (Tibidabo Editions, 2019), *De Velasco a Correa: Insurreciones, populismo y elecciones en Ecuador,* (Universidad Andina Simón Bolívar, 2015), *The Promise and Perils of Populism,* (The University Press of Kentucky, 2015), *Latin American Populism of the Twenty-First Century,* co-edited with Cynthia Arnson, (The Johns Hopkins University Press and the Woodrow Wilson Center Press, 2013), and *Populist Seduction in Latin America,* (Ohio University Press, second edition 2010).

Frank Decker is a Professor of Political Science at the University of Bonn. He has published widely on problems of institutional reform in Western democracies (including the EU), party systems and right-wing populism. Recent books include *Die Zukunft der Demokratie,* co-edited with Thomas Hartmann and Jochen Dahm (Bonn 2019), *Ausstieg, Souveränität, Isolation,* co-edited with Ursula Bitzegeio and Philipp Adorf (Bonn 2019), *Die USA—eine scheiternde*

Demokratie?, co-edited with Patrick Horst and Philipp Adorf (Frankfurt a.M. 2018), *Parteiendemokratie im Wandel*, 2nd. ed. (Baden-Baden 2018).

Gabriele Dietze (P.D., Dr.) conducts research from a cultural and media studies perspective on racism, sexism, migration and right-wing populism. She is a member of the Center for Transdisciplinary Gender Studies at Humboldt University Berlin (ZtG). Among other positions, she is currently Harris Professor for gender studies at Dartmouth College (Hanover, NH) and was visiting fellow at the DuBois Institute at Harvard University (Cambridge, MA). Some of her recent publications include *Sexualpolitik. Verflechtungen von Race und Gender* (Campus 2017) and *Sexueller Exzeptionalismus. Überlegenheitsnarrative in Migrationsabwehr und Rechtspopulismus* (transcript 2019) and together with Julia Roth (Eds.) *Right-Wing Populism and Gender in Europe and Beyond* (transcript 2020).

Elena Dück is a Mercator-IPC research fellow at the Istanbul Policy Center at Sabancı University. She holds a Master's degree in 'International Cultural and Business Studies' and a Ph.D. in 'International Relations' from the University of Passau. Her research focuses on social-constructivist approaches to foreign policy analysis and security discourses. She has published articles on French security discourses and on Canadian and U.S. foreign policy. Her current project explores the role of international educational cooperation in German–Turkish relations.

Luca Fazzi is a full Professor of Sociology and Social Work at the University of Trento (Italy) where he is head of the degree program in Social Work. His teaching and research interest focus on third sector organizations, participation and engagement in social work practice. He has published extensively in international journals and international handbooks. Current projects include identifying strategies of local development and the political role of social work.

Matthew R. Fowler is a postdoctoral scholar at the University of Chicago's Center for the Study of Race, Politics, and Culture and GenForward Project. His research involves group consciousness and intergroup attitudes—applied to white identity and racial attitudes, affective political polarization, and public opinion in American politics. His work has been published in P.S: Political Science & Politics, American Review of Politics, and the Indiana Journal of Global & Legal Studies.

Ole Frahm is visiting scholar at Freie Universität Berlin and Lecturer at the University of St Gallenwherehe researched Turkey's relations with the post-Soviet space as part of the Horizon 2020 project EU-STRAT. He has studied politics, philosophy, economics and European studies at the universities of Oxford, Bath, Paris (Sciences Po) and Berlin where he completed his Ph.D. on state building and nation building in Sub-Saharan Africa at the Humboldt Universität. Frahm has teaching experience in Germany, Algeria and Turkey, has published and presented his research widely and worked at think tanks and in political consultancy.

Antonis Galanopoulos is a Ph.D. candidate at the School of Political Sciences, Aristotle University of Thessaloniki, Greece. He holds a Bachelor degree in Psychology and a Master's degree in Political Theory and Philosophy. His doctoral research is financially supported by the General Secretariat for Research and Technology (GRST) and the Hellenic Foundation for Research and Innovation (HFRI) (Scholarship Code: 2552).

Sebastian Glassner is a research associate and Lecturer at the Professorship of International Politics at the University of Passau. He holds a Master's degree in 'Governance and Public Policy' from the University of Passau. Furthermore, Mr. Glassner studied at the Sciences Po Toulouse. His research interests include foreign policy analysis, as well as discourse theory and populism. He focuses in particular on France, Italy and the UK.

Gabriella Gricius is a Ph.D. student and Graduate Teaching Assistant at Colorado State University and Graduate Fellow at the North American and Arctic Defense and Security Network (NAADSN). She received her Master's degree in International Security from the University of Groningen.

Her interests are focused on the Arctic region, particularly as it concerns Russian policy and the risk of securitizing the region. She is also a freelance journalist and has published in Foreign Policy, Bear Market Brief, CSIS, Responsible Statecraft, Global Security Review, and Riddle Russia as well as the academic journals including the Asian Journal of Peacebuilding, Sicherheit und Frieden, the Kyiv-Mohyla Law & Politics Journal, and the Canadian Naval Review.

Vedi Hadiz is a Professor of Asian Studies and Director of the Asia Institute at the University of Melbourne. He is a recent Australian Research Council Future Fellow and an elected Fellow of the Academy of the Social Sciences in Australia. He is the author of Islamic Populism in Indonesia and the Middle East (Cambridge University Press, 2016), among other books.

Florian Hartleb (born 1979 in Passau/Germany) is a political scientist and Managing Director at Hanse Advice in Tallinn, Estonia. He conducts research with a global focus on right-wing and left-wing extremism and terrorism, as well as on digitalization. In 2004, his thesis subject was left- and right-wing populism. In the past, he worked for the German Parliament, the Konrad-Adenauer-Stiftung and the Estonian Office for equality. He is currently lecturing at Catholic University Eichstätt and University for Police Saxony-Anhalt and author of various books. In addition, he is a research associate at the Brussels-based Wilfried-Martens-Centre for European Studies. Recent Publications: Lone Wolves. The New Terrorism of Right-Wing Actors, Springer Nature, Cham/Schweiz u.a., 2020; e-Estonia. Europe´s Silicon Valley or a new 1984? in: Denise Feldner (ed.): Redesigning Institutions: Consequences of and Concepts for the Digital Transformation, Springer Nature: Heidelberg et al. 2020, pp. 215–228.

Hannah Hecker studied social sciences at Goethe University Frankfurt. Her main focus is on social-psychological perspectives on group-oriented misanthropy, antiziganism and anti-feminism. She works as a research secretary at the Fritz Bauer Institute for the Study of the History and Impact of the Holocaust based in Frankfurt am Main.

Anton Jäger is a Wiener-Anspach postdoctoral fellow at the Université libre de Bruxelles and University of Cambridge. His writings have appeared in outlets such as *Jacobin*, *LSE Review of Books*, *Los Angeles Review of Books*, *nonsite*, *The Guardian*, *De Groene Amsterdammer*, *London Review of Books*, among others. Together with Daniel Zamora (Université Libre de Bruxelles) he is currently working on an intellectual history of basic income, under contract with the University of Chicago Press.

Paul D. Kenny is a Professor of Political Science in the Institute for Humanities and Social Sciences at Australian Catholic University and a visiting fellow at the Australian National University. Specializing in comparative political economy, he is an award-winning author of two books on populism, *Populism and Patronage: Why Populist Win Elections in India, Asia, and Beyond* (Oxford, 2017) and *Populism in Southeast Asia* (Cambridge, 2019).

Thomas Kestler is an Associate Professor at the Institute of Political Science and Sociology at the University of Würzburg. He earned his Ph.D. in 2008 from the Catholic University of Eichstätt with a dissertation on political parties in Venezuela. His main research areas are political systems and institutions in Latin America.

Christian Lammert is a political scientist and Professor at the John F. Kennedy Institute (FU Berlin) with a special focus on political systems in North America. His recent research interests include economic inequality and redistribution, tax and transfer systems and crises phenomena of democracy in the transatlantic region. Among his recent publications is (together with Markus B. Siewert und Boris Vormann) the second edition of the 'Handbuch Politik USA' (Springer Verlag 2020) and (together with Boris Vormann) 'Democracy in Crisis. The neoliberal roots of popular unrest' (Pennsylvania University Press 2020).

Gideon Lasco is a physician, medical anthropologist and writer. Based in Manila, he is a Senior Lecturer at the University of the Philippines Diliman Department of Anthropology and research fellow at the Ateneo de Manila University Development Studies Program. He obtained his medical (MD) and Master's degrees (M.Sc. in Medical Anthropology) from the UP College of Medicine, and his Ph.D. in Anthropology from the University of Amsterdam. His researches focus on contemporary health-related crises, from the drug wars in Asia to vaccine controversies around the world.

Miguel Latouche is a Venezuelan writer and an Associate Professor at the Central University of Venezuela (UCV). He did his Master's studies at Syracuse University as a recipient of the Fulbright Program and received his Ph.D. in Political Science from the UCV. From 2009 to 2017 he was director of the UCV School of Social Communication. In 2018 and 2019 he did postdoctoral studies at the University of Bamberg and the Goethe University Frankfurt (Germany). Currently, he is a Guest Professor and Philipp Schwartz fellow at the University of Rostock (Germany). He is also a columnist for *The Wynwood Times*.

Dirk Lehmkuhl is a Professor for European Politics at the University of St. Gallen. He studied at the University of Konstanz, was a Ph.D. candidate at the University of Bielefeld and completed his Ph.D. at the European University Institute in Fiesole. Thereafter he was a postdoc at the Max-Planck Institute for Common Goods and completed his Habilitation at the University of Zurich. His research includes studies at the interface between international relations and international law, various topics of European public policy, external governance of the EU. Over the past years he was involved in two EU-sponsored research projects as coordinator and investigator on the Eastern partnership (EU FP7 project ISSICEU; www.issiceu.eu; EU H2020 project EU-STRAT; www.eu-strat-eu).

Christoph Leonhardt studied Political Science in Leipzig and works as a research associate at the Institute of Political Science of the University of Duisburg-Essen. His current research interests include the relationship between political discourse and institutional change, in particular combining perspectives of Political Science and Computational Social Science.

Julia Leser is a political anthropologist and a postdoctoral researcher at Humboldt University Berlin, where she is currently working on the research project 'Challenging Populist Truth-Making in Europe (CHAPTER)'. She is co-author of the book *The Wolves are Coming Back: The Politics of Fear in Eastern Germany* (with Rebecca Pates, 2021) and official speaker of the German Political Science Association (GPSA) working group 'Political Ethnography'. Her fields of interest include political anthropology, political ethnography and affect studies, and further include national security and migration control, nationalism, populism and political theory.

Marcel Lewandowsky is a political scientist and currently a DAAD visiting Assistant Professor at the Center for European Studies, University of Florida. He received his doctoral degree with a study on German regional election campaigns from the University of Bonn, Germany, where he had studied Political Science, Public Law and Modern History. His current research focuses on comparative politics with special regard to the stability of democratic regimes, parties and party systems as well as populism in Europe.

Darren G. Lilleker is Head of the Centre for Comparative Politics and Media Research and Professor of Political Communication at Bournemouth University. Dr Lilleker's interests are in political communication, with particular focus on the use of digital environments and the impact upon citizen cognition and engagement. He has published over 100 journal articles and book chapters, his most relevant work on this topic being *Political Communication and Cognition* (Palgrave, 2014).

David B. MacDonald is a full Professor in the political science department at the University of Guelph, Canada, and recently completed a three year appointment as the Guelph Research Leadership Chair for the College of Social and Applied Human Sciences. He has previously been on faculty at the University of Otago, New Zealand, and the École Supérieure de Commerce de Paris (ESCP-Europe). He has an SSHRC grant with co-researcher Shery Lightfoot entitled 'Complex Sovereignties: Theory and Practice of Indigenous-Self Determination in Settler States and the International System'. His research focuses on Global Populisms, Comparative Indigenous Politics in Canada, Aotearoa New Zealand, Australia and United States, and he also works in the areas of International Relations, genocide studies, and critical race theory. Recent publications are The Sleeping Giant Awakens: Genocide, Indian Residential Schools, and the Challenge of Conciliation (University of Toronto Press, 2019), and Populism and World Politics: Exploring Inter and Transnational Dimensions Co-Edited with D Nabers and F Stengel (Palgrave Macmillan, 2019). He has a Ph.D. in International Relations from the London School of Economics. This chapter was supported by SSHRC Insight Grant 430413.

Luca Manucci is a post-doc researcher at the University of Lisbon. He received a Ph.D. in comparative politics from the University of Zurich, and his research focuses on populism, political parties and the media. He currently works at a project on Iberian populism titled Populus: Rethinking populism, financed by national funds from the FCT- Foundation for Science and Technology, within the project PDTC/SOC-OC/28524/2017.

Henning Melber is an Extraordinary Professor at the Department of Political Sciences/University of Pretoria and the Centre for Gender and Africa Studies/University of the Free State in Bloemfontein, a senior research associate with the Nordic Africa Institute in Uppsala and a senior research fellow with the Centre for Commonwealth Studies/Centre for Advanced Study at the University of London. He is the Director Emeritus of the Dag Hammarskjöld Foundation in Uppsala and the current President of the European Association of Development Research and Training Institutes (EADI). As a political scientist and sociologist in African and Development Studies his research includes a regional focus on Southern Africa (in particular Namibia).

Christoph Mohamad-Klotzbach works at the University of Würzburg, where he has gained his Ph.D. He is currently a postdoc at the Institute of Political Science and Sociology and the general coordinator of the DFG Research Unit FOR2757 on 'Local Self-Governance in the context of Weak Statehood in Antiquity and the Modern Era (LoSAM)'. His work is within comparative politics where he focuses on fields like democracy and democratization, political culture and social capital, weak statehood, political parties and voting behavior.

Sara C. Motta is a mother, storyteller, poet, critical theorist and popular educator and currently Associate Professor at the University of Newcastle, Australia. Her scholarly practice transgresses borders-epistemological, social and spatial-as a means to co-construct with communities in struggle a critical political science practice for and of the subaltern. She has published widely in journals including Political Studies, Latin American Perspectives, Antipode, Historical Materialism and produced a number of books including (co-edited with Alf Nilsen) *Social Movements in the Global South: Dispossession, Development and Resistance* (Palgrave Macmillan), (co-edited with Mike Cole) *Education and Social Change in Latin America* (Palgrave Macmillan) and *Constructing 21st Century Socialism in Latin America: The Role of Radical Education* (Palgrave Macmillan). Her most recent book is *Liminal Subjects: Weaving (our) Liberations* (Rowman & Littlefield International), winner of the 2019 best Feminist Theory and Gender Studies Book Award, International Studies

Christoph Giang Nguyen is a Lecturer at the Otto-Suhr Institute at the Freie Universität Berlin. He holds a Ph.D. in political science from Northwestern University. His work focuses on the way insecurity and disadvantage shape political attitudes and the way that emotions such as anger, anxiety, and disgust translate general grievances into specific political attitudes. He is also interested in research methods and research design, with a focus on experimental methods, large-N observational data, but also mixed-methods and qualitative research designs.

Urban Nothdurfter is an Associate Professor in Social Work and Social Policy at the Free University of Bozen/Bolzano (Italy) where he is head of the degree program in Social Work. His research interests focus on the connections between social policy development and social work practice, the street-level delivery of social policies and on issues of gender and sexuality in social work. Recent projects deal with LGBT+ parenting and the political role of social work.

Michael Oswald is an Assistant Professor of political science at the University of Passau, associate research fellow and lecturer at the John F. Kennedy Institute of the Free University of Berlin and faculty member at International Center for European Education. His main interest lies in Political Communication, Populism and Extremism research. He wrote his dissertation on the Tea Party movement and has held visiting scholarships at Texas A&M and Harvard University.

Rebecca Pates is a Professor of Political Theory at Leipzig University and member of the Academia Europae, has managed a number of research grants on the governmentality of sex work and on trafficking for sexual exploitation, funded by the EU and the German Research Council. Her most recent research is on the malleability of nationalism in the German context.

Helge Petersen is a Ph.D. student at the University of Glasgow, School of Social and Political Sciences. His Ph.D. project examines the history of political struggles over racist violence and state racism in the British post-war period. His research interests include critical racism, nationalism and antisemitism studies, critical state theory, historical and political sociology.

Aurelien Portuese is Director of Antitrust and Innovation Policy at the Information Technology and Innovation Foundation, the world's top think tank on science and technology. He is also an Adjunct Professor of Law at the George Mason University and at the Catholic University of Paris. Aurelien Portuese has 10 years of academic experience where he specialized in antitrust law and innovation. He has published extensively and presented articles in international conferences.

Inaya Rakhmani is an Assistant Professor and Head of the Asia Research Centre, Universitas Indonesia, and the Deputy Director (Science and Education working group) of the Indonesian Young Academy of Sciences (ALMI). She has had 20 years experience in academic and applied research in higher education and social science research reform, as well as the role of media in democratic processes. Inaya's academic interest that underlies her applied research practices focuses on understanding how culture can hinder and enable the redistribution of wealth and access to many. She is the author of 'Mainstreaming Islam in Indonesia' published by Palgrave MacMillan.

Rafał Riedel is Professor at the University in Opole (Poland), Ph.D. holder in Political Science, Jean Monnet Professor, habilitated (in EU Studies) at the University of Wrocław, graduated at the Silesian University and Economic University in Katowice; Professor at the Political Science Institute of the Opole University, earlier also: guest researcher at ARENA (Centre for European Studies) at the University of Oslo, Gastdozent at TUC and Wissenschaftslische Mitarbeiter w ETH Zurich. Previously engaged in educational and research programs, as a scholar, co-organizer or fellow at European University Institute, Open Society Institute, Deutscher Akademischer Austauschdienst, Marie Curie Fellowship Programme, Max Planck Institute, European Values Network, Fundacji Rozwoju Systemu Edukacji—EEA/Norway Grants.

Scientific interests: European integration process, democratic deficit, populism, transitology, considology and other problematic in the field of political science, European studies and economy.

Julia Roth is a Professor of American Studies with a focus on Gender Studies and InterAmerican Studies at Bielefeld University, Germany. Prior to this position, she was a postdoctoral fellow at the research project 'The Americas as Space of Entanglements' in Bielefeld and at the interdisciplinary network 'desiguALdades.net- Interdependent Inequalities in Latin America' at Freie Universität Berlin as well as a Lecturer at Humboldt University Berlin, the University of Potsdam and the Universidad de Guadalajara, Mexico. Her research focuses on postcolonial, decolonial and gender approaches, intersectionality and global inequalities, anti-racist feminist knowledge from the Caribbean and the Americas, citizenships and gender, right-wing populism and gender. From 2020 to 2021, she was co-convenor of the ZiF research group 'Global Contestations of Women's and Gender Rights' at the Center for Interdisciplinary Research, Bielefeld.

Mikko Salmela is an Adjunct Professor of Practical Philosophy and a Member of the Helsinki Hub on Emotions, Populism, and Polarisation (HEPP) at the University of Helsinki. He is also Associate Professor at the Centre for Subjectivity Research, University of Copenhagen. His main research interests are in empirically informed philosophy of emotion, philosophical and political psychology, and philosophy of sociality.

Mario Schäfer is a doctoral candidate in International Politics at the University of Passau. He studies European Studies and Governance and Public Policy in Passau, Germany and Ljubljana, Slovenia. Prior to that he studies history with minor subject Political Science in Mainz, Germany and Siena, Italy. He conducts research on European Enlargement Policy, Conflict management and Border Conflicts. His doctoral thesis concerns the EU's approach to settle border conflicts during accession processes with special focus on Cyprus and Croatia/Slovenia. Additionally, he published two reviews—one of them about Chantal Mouffe's Für einen Linken Populismus/For a Left Populism (2019), representing other research topics of his such as populism, collective memory and identity politics.

Eric R. Schmidt is a Ph.D. candidate in Political Science at Indiana University. His dissertation, Voting in Groups, Thinking Like Ideologues: The Paradox of Partisan Conflict in the United States documents one of the most insidious consequences of polarization: disconnect between the issue conflict that helps citizens make sense of politics, and the intergroup conflict that helps parties mobilize winning coalitions. His peer-reviewed work has been published in Political Behavior, P.S.: Political Science & Politics, and the Journal of Political Institutions & Political Economy.

Julia Schwanholz is a political scientist and Senior Lecturer at the University of Duisburg-Essen. Previously, she represented interim professorships for democracy research as well as comparative politics and ethics in politics at different German Universities. She received her Ph.D. at the University of

Göttingen. Her expertise lies in parliaments, democracy and public policy research with an emphasis on digital transformation.

Yannis Stavrakakis is a Professor of Political Discourse Analysis at the School of Political Sciences, Aristotle University of Thessaloniki, Greece. He is the editor of the *Routledge Handbook of Psychoanalytic Political Theory* (New York: Routledge, 2020). His current research focuses on the discursive study of populism and especially on the analysis of populist and anti-populist discourses. He is the director of the POPULISMUS Observatory: www.populismus.gr.

Ybiskay Gonzalez Torres is a sociologist from Venezuela and completed her Ph.D. in Politics at the University of Newcastle, Australia. She is currently a casual academic staff at the University of Newcastle, Australia. She has published about Venezuela in the Bulletin of Latin America, and in the book Populismus. Diskurs–Hegemonie–Staat, edited by Kim and Agridopoulos (forthcoming Nomos, 2020). Her book entitled Polarised Politics: The Confrontational "Us and Them" between Chavistas and the Opposition in Venezuela will be published by Rowman & Littlefield International in 2021.

Christian von Scheve is Professor of Sociology at Freie Universität Berlin. He is a Member of the Executive Board of the DFG Collaborative Research Centre 'Affective Societies' and Research Fellow at the German Institute of Economic Research (DIW) Berlin. His main research fields are economic sociology, social psychology, and cultural sociology with a special interest in emotion, social interaction, and stratification.

Boris Vormann is a Professor of Politics and Director of the Politics Concentration at Bard College Berlin. His research focuses on the role of the state in globalization and urbanization processes; nations and nationalism; and the crisis of democracy. His most recent books are the co-edited volume The Emergence of Illiberalism: Understanding a Global Phenomenon (Routledge, 2021; coedited with Michael Weinman) and a handbook on politics and policy in the United States for a German-speaking audience (Handbuch Politik USA; Springer VS, 2020; coedited with Christian Lammert and Markus Siewert).

Daniel F. Wajner is a postdoctoral fellow at the Leonard Davis Institute for International Relations at the Hebrew University of Jerusalem, while teaching at the Department of International Relations and the Rothberg International School. His main areas of research are international legitimacy, conflict resolution, regional cooperation and populist foreign policies, particularly focusing on their interplay in the realm of Middle East and Latin American politics.

Nathalie Weidhase is a postdoctoral researcher in Media, Culture and Communication at Bournemouth University. She has published on women in popular music, celebrity feminism, and Brexit and the royal family. Her current work is concerned with the intersections of populism and gender in popular culture and media.

Szymon Wróbel is a full Professor of philosophy at the Faculty of Artes Liberales at the University of Warsaw and the Institute of Philosophy and Sociology of the Polish Academy of Sciences. He is the author of numerous books and articles scattered in various scientific journals. His books in English include: Deferring the Self, The Animals in Us—We in Animal and Grammar and Glamor of Cooperation, published in 2013, 2014 and 2015 by Peter Lang Publishing. In Polish: Ćwiczenia z przyjaźni (Exercises in Friendship), Lektury retroaktywne (Retroactive Readings) and Polska pozycja depresyjna (Polish Depressive Position) published by Kraków Publishing House Universitas in 2012, 2014, 2015. In 2016, IFiS PAN Institute published his book, Filozof i terytorium (Philosopher and Territory) on the Warsaw School of Historians of Ideas. His last book, Atheism Revisited. Rethinking Modernity and Inventing New Modes of Life has been published by Palgrave Macmillan in 2020. Currently, he is the head of the experimental Laboratory of Techno-Humanities at the Faculty of Artes Liberales where for several years he realizes the 'Technology and Socialization' project.

List of Figures

Fig. 8.1	Simplified cross-lagged, autoregressive model between generalized emotions, specific worries, and support for (right-wing) populist parties (*Note* Simplified generalized model of generalized emotion, populist support, and specific worries in a cross-lagged, autoregressive panel setting)	153
Fig. 22.1	Placement of right-wing populism within the conflict line model of contemporary party systems (*Own illustration* The big circle marks the sphere of constitutionality)	374
Fig. 23.1	Ideological landscape twentieth century (*Source* Azmanova, 2020)	382
Fig. 23.2	Ideological landscape twenty-first century (*Source* Azmanova, 2020)	384
Fig. 26.1	% primaries competence based	428
Fig. 26.2	Candidate quality	429
Fig. 28.1	How the authoritarian past shapes the populist present	454
Fig. 36.1	Right-wing and left-wing populism by party identification 2017 cooperative congressional election study	590
Fig. 36.2	Predicted effects of right and left-wing populism on Trump or Clinton voting in 2016, by partisan subgroup	602
Fig. 37.1	Salience of selected issues in *Bundestag* speeches	618
Fig. 37.2	Polarization in selected issues in *Bundestag* speeches	619
Fig. 37.3	Polarization in policy field 'environment' and populism	620
Fig. 37.4	Polarization in policy field 'reunification' and populism	621
Fig. 37.5	Polarization in policy field 'welfare state' and populism	622
Fig. 37.6	Polarization in policy field 'immigration' and populism	623
Fig. 38.1	Interaction between right-wing populism and Securitization Theory. (*Source* Own illustration)	633

Fig. 39.1 Relationship between the electoral success of right-wing populist parties and the level of voter turnout in Western European countries   656
Fig. 39.2 Relationship between the electoral success of right-wing populist parties and the level of voter turnout in Eastern European countries   657

List of Tables

Table 1.1	Perspectives on populism	6
Table 8.1	CLP model regressing AFD support on specific worries and fear and anger	155
Table 10.1	Hungary V-DEM scores and IDEA indices	183
Table 10.2	Philippines V-DEM scores and IDEA indices	186
Table 10.3	USA V-DEM scores and IDEA indices	189
Table 11.1	Authoritarian populists' framing of memory	207
Table 17.1	Right-wing populist patterns of gendering	294
Table 19.1	Three kinds of populism and their relationship concerning environmental policies	325
Table 36.1	Exploratory factor analysis with two retained factors, eight initial items in populism index	587
Table 36.2	Exploratory factor analysis with two retained factors, six items (Dropping *Traditionalism* and *Manufacturing Jobs*)	588
Table 36.3	Confirmatory factor analysis, right-wing populism and left-wing populism, 2017 cooperative congressional election study	590
Table 36.4	Republican identifiers: Determinants of right-wing and left-wing populism	592
Table 36.5	Democratic identifiers: Determinants of right-wing and left-wing populism	593
Table 36.6	Partisan independents: Determinants of right-wing and left-wing populism	594
Table 36.7	Republican identifiers: determinants of voting for Donald Trump in 2016	597
Table 36.8	Democratic identifiers: determinants of voting for Hillary Clinton in 2016	598
Table 36.9	Partisan independents: determinants of voting for Donald Trump in 2016	599
Table 36.10	Partisan independents: determinants of voting for Hillary Clinton in 2016	600

Table 39.1	Voter turnout and vote shares for right-wing populist parties in European Countries	654
Table 39.2	Regression models (dependent variable: voter turnout)	658
Table 40.1	The three dimensions of populism	666
Table 40.2	The exclusionary–inclusionary axis of counterstrategies actor-related (Combating the symptoms)	669
Table 40.3	Countering the roots of populism—supporter-related	675

Part I

Populism–Introduction to & Some Reflections on the Concept

CHAPTER 1

The New Age of Populism: Reapproaching a Diffuse Concept

Michael Oswald, Mario Schäfer, and Elena Broda

POPULISM AS A CONCEPT

Populism has become one of the most frequently researched topics in political science and its different conceptualizations are used in many other disciplines such as communication, sociology, economics and its mother discipline history. The dedication of whole conferences and journal issues to just one aspect of populism—e.g. environmental populism—is a testimony to this development, let alone the sheer numbers of publications: Google scholar lists just under 20.000 hits for populism in the year 2020 alone. The recent success stories of populists, especially in Europe and the United States, have added to this interest.

Researchers have conceptualized and defined populism since the term evolved into an analytical tool in the 1950s but despite this large research agenda, populism remains a contested concept. In fact, there are at least three

M. Oswald (✉)
Political Science, University of Passau, Passau, Germany
e-mail: michael.oswald@uni-passau.de

M. Schäfer
International Politics, University of Passau, Passau, Germany
e-mail: mario.schaefer@uni-passau.de

E. Broda
Department of Journalism, Media and Communication JMG, University of Gothenburg, Gothenburg, Sweden
e-mail: elena.broda@jmg.gu.se

© The Author(s), under exclusive license to Springer Nature Switzerland AG 2022
M. Oswald (ed.), *The Palgrave Handbook of Populism*,
https://doi.org/10.1007/978-3-030-80803-7_1

different strands of populism research: populism as political strategy, ideology, and as discursive style. This alone makes the field of populism fragmented thus rendering the term less clear today than at any other point in time. In fact, an extensive amount of literature has been devoted to this problematic nature of populism in the first place. Much more than there is regarding possible synergies among the different strands of research. Additionally, each generation of researchers slightly varied the focus of populism research and thus the meaning of populism itself.

Consequently, the term is used in and beyond science to refer to a myriad of regionally different phenomena throughout varying historical periods. As such, scholars have analyzed an agrarian movement in the United States during the late nineteenth century, the evolvement of Latin American populism during the twentieth century, and the current resurgence of populism in Europe all under the same cloak (see for instance Betz, 1994; Dornbusch & Edwards, 1991; Jagers & Walgrave, 2007; Kazin, 1995; Mudde, 2007; Mudde & Kaltwasser, 2017; Norris & Inglehart, 2019; Roberts, 1995; Taggart, 2002).

Moreover, the term is utilized to characterize parties, movements, supporters of certain policies, attitudes and much more—sometimes even for mainstream politicians if they imply to speak for the common people. On top of that, some researchers apply a normative presumption—be it positively or negatively—to the term. And in political discussions it is often utilized as a means to defame people or issues. This broad span of populism research, the different approaches, the pejorative connotation, and the arbitrary use of the term leaves the analytical value of the concept slim. And yet, populism research has made great progress identifying issues around populist attitudes and how they can affect voters (e.g. Van Hauwaert & Van Kessel, 2018), the psychological roots of populism (Lilleker and Weidehase in this volume) as well as the role of emotions (see Betz and Oswald in this volume), just to name a few. These accomplishments show that we cannot just retire the term. After all, it continues to be ubiquitous in research and politics. Therefore, we need to ask what populism can mean today, especially regarding its suitability for the scientific debate.

To that end, we briefly dip into the past, assess the historic roots of the concept and identify common conceptual elements as well as elements that are not constitutive from a conceptual point of view. We also discuss the relation between populism and democracy further, especially in terms of the relation between populism and extremism. Finally, we offer an eclectic definition and propose a six-step orientation that should be viewed as an axiom as a means to re-assert the scientific value of the concept of populism as well as populism research writ large.

Definitions, Perspectives and Strands of Populism

The ambiguity of populism begins with a lack of consistency inasmuch as the variety of definitions ranging from an interpretation as discourse over one as style to its strategic use. We have delineated nine different theoretical perspectives which harbor commonalities but also, at times, contradict one another. These perspectives are presented in Table 1.1, alongside a short definition and exemplary authors.

There are certainly more viable approaches, like understanding populism as a 'Collective Action Master Frame for Transnational Mobilization' (Aslanidis, 2018), so the list presented here is non-exhaustive. Yet, it goes to show just how dispersed populism research has become. One of the major issues with these different approaches concerns what populism actually constitutes and what categories should subsequently be used for its analysis. Relatedly, it is questionable if all of these approaches are suited to grasp the entire span of populist phenomena within some 130 years.

In practice, it seems, we tend to go with an 'you know it when you see it' approach when it comes to identifying populist phenomena, much like Supreme Court Justice Potter Stewart's comparison to a definition of pornography. This analogy is not that farfetched if we think about the fact that some people despise nude magazines and others would reserve the word strictly for more explicit material. Some would argue that the world needs pornography while others warn of its dangers. Still, it is there and efforts to inhibit it are futile. The same applies to populism.

Populism today is largely determined by a similar subjectivity and therefore what people we want to perceive as such—from establishment politicians to extremists. Both are concerning: using the term for extremists is belittlement; using it for politicians who might suggest a simple policy appealing to a large segment of society can be distortive. A real 'voice' for the people against unpopular policies can be denigrated if labeled populist even though some see populist movements as a cure (Mudde & Rovira Kaltwasser, 2017, cf. Huber & Schimpf, 2016; Ostiguy, 2017). Further, the lack of anything resembling a conceptual consensus in addition to the widened gap between perspectives may sometimes lead to an increasingly ideological or normative stance on the issue even within science. This fragmentation impacts operationalization, analytical approaches as well as the quality of and trust in science.

In addition to conceptual challenges, populism became a 'Kampfbegriff' ('*battle word*') within media discourse and political practice: a means to defame policies that seem disagreeable, or to attack politicians, not necessarily for policy content, rather categorically. It therefore attaches a stigma to political movements or personalities—deserving or undeserving—and is often more a means to lead a political battle than for scientific analysis. This pejorative character of populism and the normative attachment that many add to the concept gives rise to the assumption that populism either encompasses a derogation from democratic norms or that it is a means to revive democracy for the people. This sets the focus on both normative ends neglecting the more relevant part for democracy that may lie in between.

The imbalance of today's populism research is also found in the fact that the term seems to imply right-wing populism (RWP) to some, inasmuch that even

Table 1.1 Perspectives on populism

Perspective	Short definition	Authors (examples)
Populism as a strategy of mobilization, or mode of organization	'[P]opulism is best defined as a political strategy through which a personalistic leader seeks or exercises government power based on direct, unmediated, uninstitutionalized support from large numbers of mostly unorganized followers' (Weyland, 2001) '[A] mass movement led by an outsider or maverick seeking to gain or maintain power by using anti-establishment appeals and plebiscitarian linkages' (Barr, 2009, p. 38)	Brubaker (2017), Jansen (2011), Weyland (2001), Barr (2009) and Betz (2002)
Populism as a practice of discourse	Populism is 'a dichotomic discourse in which "the people" are juxtaposed to "the elite" along the lines of a down/up antagonism in which "the people" is discursively constructed as a large powerless group through opposition to "the elite" conceived as a small and illegitimately powerful group. Populist politics thus claim to represent "the people" against an "elite" that frustrates their legitimate demands, and presents these demands as expressions of the will of "the people"' (De Cleen & Stavrakakis, 2017, p. 310)	(Laclau (1985), Laclau and Torfing (1995), Howarth and Stavrakakis (2000) and Aslanidis (2016)

Perspective	Short definition	Authors (examples)
Populism as a socio-cultural approach	'Populism is characterized by a particular form of political relationship between political leaders and a social basis, one established and articulated through "low" appeals which resonate and receive positive reception within particular sectors of society for social-cultural historical reasons. We define populism, in very few words, as the "flaunting of the low"' (Ostiguy, 2017, p. 73)	Ostiguy (1998, 2009, 2014, 2017) and Aslanidis (2020) (populism as a cultural phenomenon)
Populism as a political style (mostly of political communication)	'[W]e define the concept of political style as the repertoires of performance that are used to create political relations Appeal to "the people", Crisis, Breakdown, Threat; "Bad Manners" "use of slang, swearing, political incorrectness and being overly demonstrative and "colourful", as opposed to the "high" behaviours of rigidity, rationality, composure and technocratic language' (Moffitt & Tormey, 2014, p. 392)	Moffitt and Tormey (2014), Block and Negrine (2017) and Bonikowski and Gidron (2016)
Populism as 'political opportunism'	'[P]olitical ideas and activities that are intended to get the support of ordinary people by giving them what they want' (Cambridge, 2014)	Betz (1994), Nkrumah (2021) and Cambridge (2014)

(continued)

Table 1.1 (continued)

Perspective	Short definition	Authors (examples)
Populism as an 'anti-incumbent', 'anti-establishment' or 'anti-mainstream' attitude	Populism 'is a mass movement led by an outsider or maverick seeking to gain or maintain power by using anti-establishment appeals and plebiscitarian linkages. To be clear, one cannot reduce populism to the use of fiery, antielite rhetoric, nor to the rise of demagogic outsiders, nor even to highly vertical connections between leader and followers. Rather, the specific combination of these factors defines populism' (Barr, 2009, p. 44)	Sikk (2009) and Barr (2009)
Populism as a 'thin centered ideology' as 'a set of ideas'	'Thin-centered ideology that considers society to be ultimately separated into two homogeneous and antagonistic camps, "the pure people" versus "the corrupt elite", and which argues that politics should be an expression of the volonté Générale (general will) of the people' (Mudde & Kaltwasser, 2017, p. 6)	Canovan (2002), Freeden (2017), Mudde (2004) and Shils (1954, 1956, 1960)
An attempt of persuasion	'[P]oliticians employ populism as a flexible mode of persuasion' (Kazin, 1995, p. 3) It can be used anywhere politicians want to persuade advocating a conflict between the oppressors and the suppressed	Kazin (1995)

Perspective	Short definition	Authors (examples)
Logic (Logic is often seen as a part of the category 'discourse'. But not all approaches do not strictly fit in that category)	'[I]f populism consists in postulating a radical alternative within the communitarian space, a choice in the crossroads on which the future of a given society hinges, does not populism become synonymous with politics? The answer can only be affirmative' (Laclau, 2005a, p. 47)	Da Silva and Vieira (2019), De Cleen (2019), Laclau (2005a), Judis (2016) and Müller (2016)

specific RWP characteristics become elevated to general characteristics. Even though RWP is at the political forefront, populism can occur in any political spectrum, and it often does in left-wing discourses. According to Matthijs Rooduijn and Tjitske Akkerman, the French PCF and the Italian PRC are just as populist as the *Sozialdemokratische Partei der Schweiz* and Germany's *Die Linke* for instance (Rooduijn & Akkerman, 2017). This renders the question: if the (democratic) left and the (democratic) right are nearly all 'populist', what can the term 'populism' deliver in terms of understanding the political landscape? Because this would mean we have a 'non-populist' political center—even though mainstream politicians often are accused of 'populists moves'—populists to the left and right, and extremists on both fringes. The ongoing difficulty of uniformly defining and conceptualizing populism is reflected in this question and adds to the term's scientific disvalue and its character as a *Kampfbegriff*.

Despite these glaring issues, the populism concept is still of importance—not just as a social phenomenon but also from a research perspective. On the one hand, this is evidenced by the consistently high occurrence of populist parties, social movements and related phenomena. On the other hand, the sizeable research shows that the concept provides important, promising, and resonant explanations. In any case, reflections on the origins of populism should provide some interesting insights. A brief historical perspective allows us to distinguish populism from other concepts and to develop some common characteristics of populist strands.

THE NORMATIVE ATTACHMENT TO POPULISM

In the past years, there is a mainstreaming in populism research to measure if and to what degree populism poses a threat to liberal democracy. This carries the undertone that populism is per definition bad, partially arrived through looking at all forms of populism and a broad time span with the same perspective.

Generally speaking, the first forms of populism appeared in the United States as early as the seventeenth century. Conflicts between government and farmers, small business owners and miners occurred left those groups with the feeling they had been cheated out of their political influence (Oswald, 2020). Farmers, in particular, complained of low prices for their products and high tax burdens. If uprisings such as the Shays Rebellion in Massachusetts or even the French Revolution are counted—just think of Marat's newspaper *L'Ami du peuple* (The people's friend)—populism has even contributed to the formation or improvement of democracy. Also, the Chartists as a working-class male suffrage movement for political reform and the Narodnik revolutionaries in Tsarist Russia were essentially populist movements in the nineteenth century. Still, we believe one can only speak about a path dependent populism that we can use in today's understanding if we look at representative institutions as a yardstick. Based on this, we can date the populism we talk about today to the Populist Movement and the People's Party in the United States.[1]

The United States People's Party was founded in 1892 and it initiated impulses to social change (Clanton, 1984, p. 148). They called for unemployment benefits, women's suffrage and the direct election of senators, strengthening the belief that Senate should be accountable to the people. Overall, due to their commitment at the municipal, state and national level, many regulations came into force, such as protective requirements for jobs or innovations in health and housing policy. In many cases, these initiatives laid the foundations for the far-reaching social reforms of the twentieth century. At the federal level they were able to push for a reform of the public service as well as some monopoly and railway regulations (Freidel, 1973, p. 84). Despite these leading impulses, the party gradually became insignificant at the beginning of the twentieth century, mainly because its demands were finally adapted by the two major parties (Clanton, 1984, p. 142). Richard Hofstadter aptly described the People 's Party's fate with an analogy of a bee: it died after it had stung the political establishment (Hofstadter, 1955).

The People's Party and the populist movement nevertheless left a legacy: until the 2000s, populism in the United States was rather positively connotated—and it still is more so than in other Western democracies. It is sometimes even given a cultural value, since many citizens understand that populists, as representatives of the 'forgotten people', fulfill the task of a corrective. After all, not only the farmer's protest in the late nineteenth century but also impulses for the New Deal and the Civil Rights Movement were populist struggles.

Nevertheless, the view on populism has changed quite a bit over the last 130 years. Until the mid-1950s, populism as a scientific term was used almost exclusively by historians. And until then, the populist movement was mostly described as a noble cause. Especially John D. Hicks's *Populist Revolt* (1931) made a large contribution in the sense that populists were understood as fighters against an unbridled power of the economy and the political elite. Since the 1950s, however, the paradigm changed, and populism has increasingly been discussed critically—at least in academia (Oswald, 2020). Parts of the populist movement were suspected to have been anti-Semitic (aversion to Jewish bankers) and nativistic, plus it was increasingly seen as a forerunner of the Coughlin movement and McCarthyism (Freidel, 1973, p. 83, see also Anton Jäger in this volume). Although some of those theses are disputed, they still defined the connotation of populism in most academic circles until today.

Even though the negative effects of populism are much more part of the discourse, there is still a tradition that defends its positive effects: 'Populists aim to channel [an] authenticity and speak truth to power, bringing about positive change on behalf of the people' states Margaret Canovan (1999, pp. 2–3). And Chantal Mouffe's call *For a Left Populism* (2018) is just one prominent example for a theoretical strand that makes a case for a 'good populism' and calls to put an end to the liberal and elitist denigration of populism (Laclau, 2005a). This tradition sees populism as a means for emancipation and to cope with right-wing populism. Granted, populism can give a voice to those who do not feel represented and therefore, populism offers perceivably 'forgotten' parts of the electorate a political home, improving political responsiveness (Mudde & Kaltwasser, 2017). Furthermore 'Populist parties can shake up party systems where government has long been dominated by the same (combination of) parties" (Verbeek & Zaslove, 2019, p. 8). Thus, populism diversifies a rather homogenous political landscape without any relevant alternative. As such, populist movements force governments or traditional political parties to reflect on themselves and their positions.

In this sense, Cas Mudde and Cristóbal Kaltwasser describe populists as the '(bad) consciousness of liberal [democracies]' (Mudde & Kaltwasser, 2017, p. 116). They raise their voices to criticize multilateral organizations 'limiting the power of elected politicians' (p. 117) to conduct the will of 'the people' or to criticize the power of non-elected and non-responsive technocratic institutions, such as constitutional courts or the European Central Bank. And 'Populist actors revitalize social movements as well as public opinion by emphasizing a conflictive dimension of politics' (Huber & Schimpf, 2016, p. 874). This became clear during the presidency of Donald Trump in which a couple of social movements have been revitalized and had a strong impact on society. This also affected the 2020 voter turnout. The prospect of Trump's second term as President pushed more people to the ballot boxes than ever—on both sides. Even though populism does not increase voter turnout per se, populist parties characterize a self-protecting democracy to promote competition and set a new strung of political thoughts to established parties. Additionally, populists can bring already salient topics to the fore on the agenda (Huber & Schimpf, 2016, p. 874). Still, populists often show disregard toward democratic institutions such as systems of checks and balances as well as the separation of powers (Huber & Schimpf, 2016, p. 875; Hawkins, 2003)—Donald Trump being a case in point. Even though, he complied with court decisions and the checks and balances provided a stable foundation, the disregard for institutions that perceivably distort the people's will must be eyed critically.

But instead of focusing on the 'good' or 'bad' character of populism we should rather see it as a symptom of a political system's graver problems. And in light of the either too abstract definitions or concreter ones that in return cannot account for all populist phenomena as well as the either positive or negative connotation of populism, it is still necessary to find a more concise, rigid and meaningful definition. If some elements do not match, logic requires that we steer back to the lowest common denominator and take it from there. We agree with Rooduijn when he suggests, we should 'carefully conceptualise populism, building on existing studies, and distinguishing it from related concepts" (Rooduijn, 2019, p. 366). Furthermore, he cautions to employ precision, distinctiveness and a rather narrow framework but remains open-minded exploring the literature and formulating novel hypotheses (Rooduijn, 2019, p. 362). However, it is not even clear which criteria are widely accepted and why some approaches prioritize certain categories over others. In the following we thus set out to identify several 'core elements' that most conceptual approaches to populism have in common.

Six categories can be reconstructed deductively from mostly accepted cross-range populism definitions, which gives an opportunity to conceptualize populism, building on existing studies. Therefore, we are not focusing on the perspectives but the elements.

CORE ELEMENTS OF POPULISM

Anti-establishment, 'for the People' and Projection on Out-Groups

First and foremost, researchers generally share the understanding of populism as a dualism of 'the elite' vs. 'the people' (Comaroff, 2011, p. 104; Rooduijn, 2019, p. 364). This dichotomy is the central message of populists that claim to represent and speak in the name of the 'people' on the one hand, and an outgroup which is very often named the 'elite'. As part of the populist mindset, the elite harm the people, either economically or culturally.

Yves Mény and Yves Surel see three essential aspects at the core of populism in terms of this relationship: (1) The role of the people and their fundamental position not only in society, but in the structure and functioning of the entire political system. In this view, there is a discrepancy between the 'privileged few' and the 'underdogs'. (2) Thus, there is a betrayal by those who should represent the people. (3) Lastly, there is the demand to restore the primacy of the people and their place in society, replacing the elite by leaders who govern for the good of the people (Mény & Surel, 2000, 2002b). In this sense, anti-establishment politics refer to rhetorical appeals based on an opposition to those in power (Barr, 2009, p. 44). These appeals also involve specific corrections to remedy the shortcomings of the nation's representative democracy. This can range from simple demands to a replacement of the government by those who supposedly embody the will of the people (Barr, 2009, p. 44).

Elites are also thought to look down on the common people who allegedly do not understand the complexity of society or politics. This implies that expertism is flawed and we should rather 'rely on ordinary citizens' common sense' (Galston et al., 2018, p. 34). Consequently, it is not necessarily an external designation but an internal one of the disenfranchised, forgotten, powerless group themselves.

It is noteworthy that 'the elite' and 'the people' can be viewed as empty signifiers, meaning it is largely a matter of interpretation who specifically forms part of either category. For instance, 'the elite' can refer to establishment parties, the media, international businesses or international organizations. Similarly, 'the people' can refer to a population based on a specific perception of class or culture, as long as it remains a homogenous character of some sort. Consequently, both terms can be more or less exclusive, depending on the respective interpretation. The terns 'the people' has taken on varying meanings—in RWP it is typically constructed along cultural or ethnic dimensions, whereas left-wing populism has generally taken a civic approach. What 'the elite' is somewhat less clear. The term remains vague and appears to mostly be constructed in its opposition to 'the people' (whatever the term may refer to in any given context) rather than on a substantive basis of any elite group. It is also noteworthy, however, that populist audiences often do not take issue with the fact that their populist leaders often are part of some kind of elite. Finally, in relation to the elite-people dichotomy, certain out-groups may emerge that are blamed for perceived problems within society (Salmela & Scheve, 2017, p. 574). Again, any group could be constructed as such but especially affected are perhaps societal minorities.

Anti-status Quo (Protest Attitude) and Relative Deprivation

One notion, that was of importance in the past but appears to be sometimes neglected nowadays is that there must be a disbalance in what a part of the population wants and what the government does. Simply put: citizens who are completely satisfied would probably not protest. Even though a utopian status of contentment for all cannot be achieved, it is striking that dissatisfaction, anti-elitism, the global rise of populism and globalization go hand in hand ever since populist movements started in the late nineteenth century. Populism therefore is often seen as 'the product of a failure of the existing system of political parties to provide credible representation for "neglected" groups of citizens' (Schmitter, 2019, p. 76). Still, many right-wing populist parties fared best in some of the wealthiest countries in Europe such as Austria, Denmark or Germany and they did so in the most affluent country-regions: the German-language cantons of Switzerland, the Flemish part of Belgium and northern Italy. Populism might be 'closely linked to growing distrust of the formal institutions that organise social, economic and political power within individual countries' (Hadiz & Chryssogelos, 2017, p. 400) but one of the 'neglected' groups of citizens might also be affluent und decently represented. Thus, we believe it is important to understand the neglect foremost as perception of neglect or fear thereof.

One important typical aspect of this anti-status-quo-sentiment is ‚feelings of relative deprivation, referring to a perception of one's own—or one's group's—disadvantage in relation to others, and thus relative deprivation should be seen as a favorable indicator of populism (Pettigrew, 2017). Relative deprivation can occur with loss of status or fear thereof. This includes resentments against those who supposedly caused a personally disadvantageous situation, but also those who stand for progressive change that, from such a vantage point, leads to the loss of one's own lifestyle. Interestingly, positional deprivation in relation to the wealthiest deciles enhances support for the radical left, whereas positional deprivation in relation to the poorest deciles causes support for the radical right (Burgoon et al., 2019, p. 84). The anti-status-quo-sentiment and the perception that the country is on a losing track, create the fear of loss, be it economically or culturally.

There certainly are neglected societal groups—and to some extent also those that have been labeled losers of globalization. But the 'modernization loser thesis' as an explanatory model for populism is obsolete since those groups account for a rather small share of the vote. Overall, a frustration over economic and cultural concerns might well be a better explanation than just looking at 'neglected groups'. There is more to the protest attitudes toward the political leadership and their ideas of a society, which might even be just a fear of loss.

Loss (Fear) Economic-Cultural
Anti-status quo (virulent protest attitude) and relative deprivation go hand in hand with existing or perceived problems within specific segments of society. Therefore, populism must always be viewed in the context of interaction and social background.

Loss aversion is a powerful driver for both economic and cultural issues. Populists from the left mostly use terms like 'neoliberal reforms' or 'neoliberal politics' and thereby insinuate that the government and financial elites are using 'the people' for their own financial gain or implementing their vision of a society over the people's will. In the right-populist sphere often both cultural and economic issues are seen as problematic. This particularly encompasses immigration where populists claim to speak for the forgotten and disadvantaged people in terms of leveraging alleged favorable socio-economic conditions for migrants in comparison to their own. Due to this alleged primacy given to migrants they feel unacknowledged. This also extends to debates around free speech which is, accordingly, denied as a means of maintaining the status quo, in particular by means of enforcing political correctness.

The populist sentiment extends to taxation as well—opposition to taxes being the original claim by populists from the nineteenth century. In the same manner (though due to different reasons) left- and right-wing populists position themselves against globalization since it is perceived as one of the main reasons for the loss of manufacturing and lower skilled employment in many Western countries, but also culture. Similar to the fear of job loss, populists raise the issue of losing one's social standing in society. By blaming globally acting 'elites' who themselves enjoy favorable jobs and status advantages, populists channel their anger.

Unimodality and Anti-pluralism
Anti-pluralism is an essential part of populism because of its homogeneous conception of 'the people' and the idea of a uniform popular will. Though, populists do understand that they are not speaking for society as a whole, they

rather see the will of 'the people' as a majority rule representation of what the 'ordinary people' want.

This elevation of the will of a segment of the population as the one of 'the people' per se renders 'the people' to be a monolithic group. This is considered to be one of the major issues with populism from a democracy perspective (Jagers & Walgrave, 2007, p. 322). As such, populism is often characterized as anti-pluralist and as a counter-concept to liberalism, some even argue contrary to democracy (Caramani, 2017; Müller, 2016; Pappas, 2019; Riker, 1982):

> [D]ividing a country's population into the people and the others suggests that some parts of the population are not really part of the people and do not deserve to share in self-government. Individuals outside the charmed circle of the people may therefore be excluded from equal citizenship, violating the principle of inclusion that is part of Dahl's definition of democracy. [...]. Imposing the assumption of uniformity on the reality of diversity not only distorts the facts but also elevates the characteristics of some social groups over others. To the extent that this occurs, populism becomes a threat to democracy. (Vgl. Galston, 2018, pp. 37–38)

Taking a less pessimistic stance, Takis Pappas (2019) understands populism as democratic illiberalism; as the opposite of political liberalism. This democratic illiberalism puts populism on the same level as other ideologies (Pappas, 2013, p. 33). Pappas therefore looks at populism in a reductionist way:

> [M]odern populism is better understood as a novel political system that maintains electoral democracy while also working against the principles of political liberalism. [...] [W]e may define populism simply as 'democratic illiberalism' [...]. (Pappas, 2019, p. 19)

Indeed, the exclusionary approach to populism may give way for more radical and fundamental opposition in a Manichean 'who-is-not-with-us-is-naturally-against-us' stance. This approach is sometimes extended to populism as overall anti-democratic. Though, this is criticized by Yannis Stavrakakis and Anton Jäger because of its 'essentialist rigidity' which reduces 'democracy to liberalism'; they see it as 'maybe fitting for a polemical pamphlet; yet one quickly realizes what is at stake here' (Stavrakakis & Jäger, 2018, p. 552). This is certainly true considering the equation of liberalism and democracy, plus the idea of majority rule representation is by definition not anti-democratic. Plus, we must not forget that the idea of populism is that the will of the movement is not represented. Certainly, the protest focuses on *the issues* this particular group wants to see represented. This seems to be very important—but also neglected by theorists—since the anti-pluralism of issues might just be a consequence of the perception that their issues are not represented.

Ultimately, the Manichean generalization might rather be described as a political difference between diametrically opposed factions as Filipe da Silva and Mónica Vieira suggest:

> Populism, we contend, is not synonymous with politics as such, but an outgrowth of popular sovereignty and its egalitarian promise. Its primary logic is not an oppositional logic of friend versus enemy, but a logic of resentment between fellow citizens. (Da Silva & Vieira, 2019, p. 6)

There are indeed advantages of such minimal definitions and Pappas' claim that populism can serve as a means to dismantle liberal institutions is surely right. But the generalization that populism is per se anti-democratic, cannot be upheld. It can even be a means to make grievances and issues which are vital to a segment of society salient in the first place. The shortcomings of the definition as anti-democratic is often a theoretical fuzziness because the conception of populism thereby stretches into other illiberal currents such as authoritarianism or even extremism (see discussion on conceptual flaws & distinguishment from other concepts).

In this context, we need to touch upon the diverging perspectives on left- and right-wing populism and their relation to democracy. Left-wing populism is often described as inclusionary and right-wing populism as exclusionary. Granted, left-wing populist attitudes are directed primarily against economic and political elites but mostly inclusive regarding other out-groups; right-wing populists' anti-elitism is directed against political elites, with lower tolerance values for out-groups (Andreadis et al., 2018, pp. 33–34). Still, left-wing populism cannot be labeled entirely inclusionary since the anti-pluralistic stance is also advocated in the agitation against the elite out-group.

Adversity to Political Mediation and the Volonté Générale

Populism in most definitions is seen as adverse to political mediation. Populist parties are often 'anti-party-parties' and usually there are calls to strengthen direct democratic institutions such as referenda. This is part of the claim to represent the majority of the people who are either silent or cannot project the popular will into politics. From this perspective, representative politics are perceived as being distortive. In some cases, there is an immediate contact between the (charismatic) leader of the populist movement and the people without intermediary institutions. Although we regard adversity to political mediation as only being a minor characteristic usually, they simultaneously demand to strengthen the *Volonté Générale*.

The *Volonté Générale* (popular will) is understood as being more than the sum of all particular interests (*volonté de tous*; will of all). It is the articulation of common interests within a community that serves the benefit of this community as a whole. Thus, individuals on their own might err but 'the people' who articulate a common will of what's normatively desirable within a society cannot. The vox populi is the 'common sense' which constantly challenges the status quo by criticizing complex issues by more simple answers which can be deducted from simplistic assumptions. This general will can, however, only be achieved by restoring a popular government in the sense that it acts for the people and not for a corrupted elite. Therefore, populists often promote more 'self-government' and reject representative democracy (Mudde & Kaltwasser, 2017, p. 17). Thus, populism is perceived to be an empowering force to give the people their voice back. The assumption of any popular will is problematic, though. Surely, it would be impossible to even come close to it within any pluralistic society due to the variety of different interests. Elevating one will above others may thus serve to alienate in particular minorities. Further, it might very well justify illiberal tendencies (Huber & Schimpf, 2016, p. 875).

Simplification
Most populist communication is shaped by what Canovan calls a "simple and direct style" (Canovan, 1999, p. 3). Many populism definitions include this simplification of complex issues and some of them cite it as a central feature: Complex political issues are broken down in a simplified way and portrayed as monocausal so that equally simple solutions can be formulated as answers. This often results in policies that resonate with the population but often are only geared toward short-term gains.

However, not just the communication style is characterized as simplistic but the underlying assumptions as well. This does not only refer to how populists frame political issues but to the very nature of the populist concept: The dichotomization between 'the people' and 'the elite' is an example of this. However, these clear and simplistic lines of argumentation reduce the world's complexity into general—albeit more feasible—categories. That being said, breaking political issues down to simple categories to render them more comprehensible is not always a sufficient condition for being labeled a populist. The first chancellor of the Germany's Federal Republic, Konrad Adenauer, is famous for his ability of simplification, yet few would label him as such.

CONCEPTUAL FLAWS AND DISTINGUISHMENT FROM OTHER CONCEPTS

There are a couple of features in populism definitions that are not generally valid in the sense that they are constitutive elements of the concept of populism. We thus proceed with a non-exhaustive discussion of elements that should not be included in definitions of populism.

Firstly, charismatic leaders are one such feature. Granted, in many cases, strong leadership is conducive to the functioning of a populist project but not all populist movements and parties do have a charismatic leader—at least not always more than other parties and movements do. Thus, it should not be regarded as a main characteristic even though populist movements favor tendentially strong charismatic leaders.

Furthermore, the moralization and moralism approach is certainly interesting but probably not a defining criterion. From a populist perspective, moral virtues are mostly present among the people, not among the elites. Therefore, they see a moral renewal of politics necessary. Jan-Werner Müller observes that populists claim to represent the authentic people exclusively morally, which is certainly a valid observation; but he even goes this far to say that '[t]he core claim of populism is [a] moralized form of antipluralism' (Müller, 2016, p. 20). We certainly talk about moral categories since the mere accusation of governing not in the people's interest as their representators is a moral flaw. But this is problematic as Stavrakakis and Jäger pointed out:

> the *essentially moralistic* (i. O.) profile of populist reasoning – the idea that 'the key distinction in populism is moral' (Mudde & Kaltwasser, 2017, p. 14), that it involves a predominantly 'moralistic imagination' (Müller, 2016, p. 19) – bears striking resemblances to the stereotypical treatments of populism first offered in the pluralist canon [...]. [T]he crucial problem with the criterion of moralization is not its origins and/or is dubious intellectual trajectory; it is its precise status as one of the minimal criteria for the differential identification of populism. Indeed, one is left wondering what such a criterion really means and how it could be effectively deployed. A series of interrelated questions seem pertinent here: How exactly is the moralistic stress of populism to be defined? Does moralization affect only populist discourse? Is it something unequivocally dangerous? (Stavrakakis & Jäger, 2018, pp. 558–559)

These are important questions (to which Stavrakakis and Jäger give answers). We cut it short and simply state if anything is moralistic, it is much of the political mainstream in Western democracies.

As mentioned before, many people refer to right-wing populism in relation to political mobilization of mass constituencies against established elites, and some even count nationalistic exclusionism as a key characteristic of populism. However, populism can be used to further any political project regardless of the ideological outlook. Thus, right-wing populism is more of a sub-type of populism rather than embodying the concept as such. In order to evaluate movements, parties or single actors, the underlying ideologies need to be scrutinized, not just the populism they use.

It is generally problematic that the term populism is used all too frequently, and even more so if it is used for clearly authoritarian, demagogic or extremist phenomena. This creates an overall vagueness in addition to rendering authoritarianism, for instance, more harmless than it actually is.[2] Both authoritarians and extremists might use populist methods and stylistic devices since populist techniques generally deliver a means for all kinds of demagogues in order to activate people's emotions, especially their hopes and fears (Galston, 2014, p. 18). But that does not mean one should conflate populism with these more extreme phenomena, even if they bare resemblance. It very much depends on the relation of parties and movements with democratic institutions, norms and processes. Authoritarians and extremists are anti-democratic, and their goal is to scrap democracy and install an authoritarian or even totalitarian regime; populism's relationship with democracy is more ambiguous as stated earlier in this chapter. Sheri Berman, for instance, suggests that right-wing extremists should be labeled as populists:

> Current right-wing extremists are thus better characterized as populist rather than fascist, since they claim to speak for everyday men and women against corrupt, debased, and out-of-touch elites and institutions. (Berman, 2016, p. 43)

We, however, believe this to be wrong as measuring everything by the same yardstick would render the term populism useless, and the belittlement of grave anti-democratic tendencies frankly poses a danger itself. After all, we would not categorize dictators as (just) populists, even if they use parts of the populist playbook. And suppressing the feeling that the political game is rigged against a part of society by labeling all populism extremism would not make the phenomenon vanish. The issue of distinction from other concepts is not exhausted with extremism or authoritarianism, of course. Rooduijn (2019), for instance, discusses 'nativism' and 'Euroscepticism'.

Even though it is important to distinguish populism from other (especially graver) concepts, it should not be viewed as completely harmless either. The question of the extent to which populist attitudes and actors pose a threat to liberal democracies is very relevant. But this question can only be answered within specific contexts and using correct terminology may actually be of help as terminological precision renders the concept itself more meaningful for scientific endeavor, ridding it of its current arbitrariness.

Naturally, terminological precision is only possible when there is conceptual clarity in the first place. Having touched upon both constitutive and non-constitutive elements of current conceptualizations of populism, we now turn toward synthesizing the more constitutive elements into a definition.

Defining Populism

Canovan stated in 1981 that an all-encompassing definition of populism cannot be formulated (Canovan, 1981). She might be right taking into account the current developments in science, the media and general discussions on politics. Nevertheless, we have an abundant collection of definitions. An evaluation of the saliency by the currently most used populism definition revealed that beneath the rich literature, few of the definitions are used. Among the most salient are older ones like Edward Shils (1960), Margaret Canovan (1999), Cas Mudde (2004) and Ernesto Laclau (2005a, 2005b) as well as recent publications such as Jan-Werner Müller (2016) and Cas Mudde and Cristóbal Rovira Kaltwasser (2017).[3]

Müller built on a vast conceptualization of political logic tradition. Still, he states we do not 'have anything like a theory of populism, and we seem to lack coherent criteria for deciding when political actors turn populist in some meaningful sense' (Müller, 2016, p. 2). We second that there are not cohesive

1 THE NEW AGE OF POPULISM: REAPPROACHING A DIFFUSE CONCEPT 21

theoretical accounts, we rather deal with approaches and conceptualizations to populism. Still, it is striking how close Müller's definition of populism is on what has been around for more than 50 years:

> The core claim of populism is [...] a moralized form of antipluralism. Populist actors not committed to this claim are simply not populists. Populism requires a *pars pro toto* [i.O.] argument and a claim to exclusive representation, with both understood in a moral, as opposed to empirical, sense. There can be no populism, in other words, without someone speaking in the name of the people as a whole. (Müller, 2016, p. 20)

For comparison, Shils (1956) definition is eerily similar in some aspects:

> Populism proclaims that the will of the people as such is supreme over every other standard, over the standards of traditional institutions, over the autonomy of institutions and over the will of other strata. Populism identifies the will of the people with justice and morality [...] and in the ‚direct' relationship of the people and their leader unmediated by institutions. Populism is not confined to the ‚left' and is not confined to the lower classes. (Shils, 1956 [1996], p. 98)

Shils emphasizes the primacy of the people's will and a direct relationship between the people and the government whereas Müller highlights an exclusionary and anti-pluralistic core of populism (Müller, 2016, p. 20). Still, we certainly see strong overlaps. This holds especially true if we boil down Müller's approach to its essentials: His criteria for populism as a 'political logic' comprises the monist sentiment, the moralistic issue and the anti-pluralist as a 'danger to democracy' (p. 3). All of those were already evident in 1956 albeit described in different terms. Shils' and Müller's approaches are even similar in the sense that there is no clear distinction to extremism; Shils does not even discriminate between dictators and populists.

Roughly ten years after Shils formulated his approach, George Hall made an attempt of eclectically defining populism at the London Conference on Populism in 1967:

> Populist movements are movements aimed at power for the benefit of the people as a whole which result from the reaction of those, usually intellectuals, alienated from the existing power structure, to the stresses of rapid economic, social, cultural or political change. These movements are characterized by a belief in a return to, or adaptation of, more simple and traditional forms and values emanating from the people, particularly the more archaic sections of the people who are taken to be the repository of virtue. (Hall, 1967, p. 145)

Much like Shils definition it is also quite comparable to today's conceptualizations, albeit perhaps a little too positive for today's mainstream. But it has the advantage that it adds a perspective of the origins of populism.[4] Still, both definitions show that not that much has changed in populism theory. This begs the question why we haven't made adequate theoretical progress in the last 55 years but instead have rather witnessed a fragmentation into different approaches.

The prominence of the Mudde and Kaltwasser publication reveals that there is a trend to understand populism as 'a set of ideas that, [that] in the real world, appears in combination with quite different, and sometimes contradictory, ideologies' (Mudde & Kaltwasser, 2017).[5] Much like the critique of Paris Aslanidis (2016) concerning the 'thin ideology' concept as such, these conceptualizations bear the risk of being a little undifferentiated which may lead to both 'false positives' as well as an over-stretching of the concept into other phenomena. For example, from such a perspective, extremists could fall into the populism category but also some legitimate critiques of an administration governing against a large share of the population's interest. Furthermore, conceiving populism as a 'set of ideas' basically renders the term useless since everything in political thought can be viewed as a set of ideas. Put differently: It is a very vague common denominator. Another issue is the sheer ‚thickness[6] of the term ‚ideology itself, which overstretches its use for this phenomenon. We understand ideology as a perspective of political reality based on values and opinions that define a certain *Weltanschauung* (world view). Perceiving ideas stemming from this world view as not implemented or even threatened, would result in opposition to the respective cause. In case the perceived threat is the elite and this dichotomy can be put in terms of the people vs. the establishment while operating within democratic norms, we would rather call it a populist attitude than 'ideology'.

To remedy some of the conceptual issues mentioned throughout this piece, we provide a nine-fold definition of populism, which consists of the seven operationalizable elements:

1. Anti-status quo attitude because specific interests are not met
2. A resulting dualism between 'the people' and 'the elite'
3. Representation of the 'disenfranchised', often coupled with perceived relative deprivation
4. Simplified solutions
5. Anti-mediated politics/direct democracy
6. Anti-pluralism
7. Simplification
8. Projection on an out-group
9. Working within democratic boundaries.

In accordance with the elements, we propose the following working definition which provides a frame for the different variations of populism:

> Populism is a mode of political identification which gives rise to negatives attitudes towards the country's stewardship, claiming a neglect of the 'common people' by 'distant elites'. This resulting dualism is mostly a symptom of a

deeper dissonance within political systems, championing simple – often curtailed – solutions with a preference for direct democratic elements over political mediation. Populist protests or politics are often illiberal based on a majoritarian claim, an anti-pluralist outlook and a problem attribution to out-groups. Still, populism is not necessarily anti-democratic and it can give voice to those who feel unrepresented or affected by (relative) deprivation.

However, we also want to stress again what populism is decidedly *not*. This particularly refers to distantly similar but distinct phenomena such as extremism. In conjunction with this approach, we recommend using a six-step orientation that can re-assert the scientific value of the populism concept and populism research.

- First, do not overstress the issue of a specific perspective.
- Second, separate populist actors and movements/followers (attitudes vs. messages) but look at both.
- Third, drop the normative attachment.
- Fourth, go back to the roots and use widely accepted categories.
- Fifth, use it with a clear distinction from other especially graver concepts.
- Sixth, conceptually distinguish between populism and other phenomena such as extremism.

Even if populism is a fragmented field today, it continues to play an important role both in science and politics. And populist phenomena will not simply evaporate any time soon. Re-asserting the scientific value of populism is thus imperative in regard to the future study of populism. With this chapter we have sketched out what such a re-assertion might look like.

Notes

1. Jan-Werner Müller (2016) claims that those were not populists but we beg to differ as they have clearly embraced a populist discourse.
2. One can claim that populism is harmful to democracy but just thinking about the effects of a label makes one wonder: Would more people vote with more ease for a populist or an extremist? In this perspective the answer to the issue of harm seems obvious.
3. Hanna Pitkin's 1967 book ‚The Concept of Representation 'was the most cited reference we found during our search. Pitkin did not address populism as a concept but for populism research most relevant, she thoroughly elaborated a philosophical discussion about representation and how to define it. One whole chapter is dedicated to political representation, an aspect highly salient in populism research. Although she does not mention populism per se, she deals with populists' sense of entitlement, namely to advocate for the vox populi and represent the authentic people not the elite who should have done so.
4. Also in 1967 one of the first scales to identify populism were developed (Axelrod, 1967).

5. This is limited to the fact that it is not clear how many citations use the definition critically.
6. The theoretizations of the term ‚ideology ' might be able to fill a whole library; adding this baggage to the populism-debate is another reason to refrain from integrating the concept into the ‚ideology '-debate.

Literature

Andreadis, I., Stavrakakis, Y., & Demertzis, N. (2018). Populism, ethnic nationalism and xenophobia. *Επιστήμη Και Κοινωνία: Επιθεώρηση Πολιτικής Και Ηθικής Θεωρίας, 37*, 11–40.

Aslanidis, P. (2016). Is populism an ideology? *Political Studies, 64*, 1–16.

Aslanidis, P. (2018), Populism as a collective action master frame for transnational mobilization. *Sociological Forum, 33*(2), 443–464.

Aslanidis, P. (2020). Major directions in populism studies: Is there room for culture? *Partecipazione e Conflitto, 13*(1), 59–82.

Axelrod, R. (1967). The structure of public opinion on policy issues. *Public Opinion Quarterly, 31*(1), 51–60.

Barr, R. R. (2009). Populists, outsiders and anti-establishment politics. *Party Politics, 15*(1), 29–48.

Berman, Sheri (2016, November–December). Populism is not fascism: But it could be a harbinger. *Foreign Affairs*, pp. 39–44.

Betz, H. G. (1994). *Radical right-wing populism in Western Europe.* Springer.

Betz, H.-G. (2002). Conditions favouring the success and failure of radical right-wing populist partiesin contemporary democracies. In Y. Mény & Y. Surel (Eds.), *Democracies and the populist challenge* (pp. 197–213). Palgrave Macmillan.

Block, E., & Negrine, R. (2017). The populist communication style: Toward a critical framework. *International Journal of Communication Systems, 11*, 178–197.

Bonikowski, B., & Gidron, N. (2016). The populist style in American politics: Presidential campaign discourse, 1952–1996. *Social Forces, 94*(4), 1593–1621.

Burgoon, B., van Noort, S., Rooduijn, M., & Underhill, G. (2019). Positional deprivation and support for radical right and radical left parties. *Economic Policy, 39*(97), 49–93.

Brubaker, R. (2017). Why populism? *Theory and Society, 46*(5), 357–385.

Canovan, M. (1981). *Populism*. Junction Books.

Canovan, M. (1999). Trust the people! Populism and the two faces of democracy. *Political Studies, 47*, 2–16.

Canovan, M. (2002). Taking politics to the people. In Y. Mény & Y. Surel (Eds.), *Democracies and the populist challenge* (pp. 25–44). Palgrave Macmillan.

Canovan, M. (2004). Populism for political theorists? *Journal of Political Ideologies, 9*(3), 241–252.

Caramani, D. (2017). Will vs. reason: The populist and technocratic forms of political representation and their critique to party government. *The American Political Science Review, 111*(1), 54.

Clanton, G. (1984). 'Hayseed Socialism' on the Hill: Congressional populism, 1891–1895. *Western Historical Quarterly, 15*(2), 139–162.

Comaroff, J. (2011). Populism and late liberalism: A special affinity? *The Annals of the American Academy of Political and Social Science, 637*, 99–111.

Da Silva, F. C., & Vieira, M. B. (2019). Populism as a logic of political action. *European Journal of Social Theory, 22*(4), 497–512. https://doi.org/10.1177/136843 1018762540

De Cleen, B. (2019). The populist political logic and the analysis of the discursive construction of 'the people' and 'the elite'. In *Imagining the Peoples of Europe. Populist discourses across the political spectrum* (pp. 19–42). John Benjamins Publishing Company.

De Cleen, B., & Stavrakakis, Y. (2017). Distinctions and articulations: A discourse theoretical framework for the study of populism and nationalism. *Javnost-the Public, 24*(4), 301–319.

Dornbusch, R., & Edwards, S. (1991). The macroeconomics of populism. In *The macroeconomics of populism in Latin America* (pp. 7–13). University of Chicago Press.

Freeden, M. (2017). After the Brexit referendum: Revisiting populism as an ideology.

Freidel, F. (1973). The old populism and the new. *Proceedings of the Massachusetts Historical Society*. Third Series *85*, 78–90.

Galston, W. (2014). *The new challenge to market democracies: The political and social costs of economic stagnation*. Brookings Institution Press. Retrieved January 5, 2021, from http://www.jstor.org/stable/https://doi.org/10.7864/j.ctt1hfr137.

Galston, W., Hunter, J., & Owen, J. (2018). *Anti-pluralism: The populist threat to liberal democracy*. Yale University Press. doi:https://doi.org/10.2307/j.ctt216 68rd.

Hadiz, V. R., & Chryssogelos, A. (2017). Populism in world politics: A comparative cross-regional perspective. *International Political Science Review, 38*(4), 399–411. https://doi.org/10.1177/0192512117693908.

Hall, G (1967). Attempt of definition. In D. MacRae, L. Schapiro, F. W. Deakin, H. Seton-Watson, P. Worsley, E. Gellner, & I. Berlin (Eds.), *Conference on populism: Verbatim report*. London School of Economics and Political Science.

Hawkins, K. A. (2003). Populism in Venezuela: The rise of Chavismo. *Third World Quarterly, 24*(6), 1137–1160.

Hofstadter, R. (1955). *The age of reform: From Bryan to F.D.R.* Vintage Books.

Howarth, D., & Stavrakakis, Y. (2000). Introducing discourse theory and political analysis. In D. Howarth, A. J. Norval, & Y. Stavrakakis (Eds.), *Discourse theory and political analysis* (pp. 1–23). Manchester University Press.

Huber, R. A., & Schimpf, C. H. (2016). Friend or foe? Testing the influence of populism on democratic quality in Latin America. *Political Studies, 64*(4), 872–889. https://doi.org/10.1111/1467-9248.12219.

Jagers, J., & Walgrave, S. (2007). Populism as political communication style: An empirical study of political parties' discourse in Belgium. *European Journal of Political Research, 46*(3), 319–345.

Jansen, R. S. (2011). Populist mobilization. *Sociological Theory, 29*, 75–96.

Judis, J. B. (2016). Rethinking populism. *Dissent, 63*(4), 116–122.

Kazin, M. (1995). *The populist Persuasion*. Basic Books.

Laclau, E. (1985). *Hegemony and socialist strategy: Towards a radical democratic politics*. Verso.

Laclau, E. (2005a). On populist reason. Verso.

Laclau, E. (2005b). Populism: What's in a name? *Populism and the Mirror of Democracy, 48*.

Mény, Y., & Surel, Y. (2000). *Par le Peuple, Pour le Peuple. Le Populisme et les Démocraties*. Fayard.Mény.
Mény, Y., & Surel, Y. (2002a). *Democracies and the populist challenge*. Palgrave Macmillan.
Mény, Y., & Surel, Y. (2002b). The constitutive ambiguity of populism. In Y. Mény & Y. Surel (Eds.), *Democracies and the populist challenge*. Palgrave.
Mouffe, C. (2018). *For a left populism*. Verso.
Mudde, C. (2004). The populist Zeitgeist. *Government and Opposition, 39*(4), 541–563.
Mudde, C. (2007). *Populist radical right parties in Europe*. Cambridge University Press.
Mudde, C., & Kaltwasser, C. R. (2017). *Populism: A very short Introduction*. Oxford University Press.
Müller, J.-W. (2016). *What is populism?* Penn State University Press.
Nkrumah, B. (2021). Political opportunism: Populism as a new political tactic in South Africa. In *Africa's radicalisms and conservatisms* (pp. 117–140). Brill.
Norris, P., & Inglehart, R. (2019). *Cultural backlash: Trump, Brexit, and authoritarian populism*. Cambridge University Press.
Populism. (2014). *Cambridge*. https://dictionary.cambridge.org/de/worterbuch/englisch/populism.
Ostiguy, P. (1998). *Peronism and anti-Peronism: Class-cultural cleavages and political identity in Argentina* (Ph.D. dissertation). Department of Political Science, University of California, Berkeley.
Ostiguy, P. (2009). *The high and the low in politics: A two-dimensional political space for comparative analysis and electoral studies* (Kellogg Institute Working Paper #360), Notre Dame: Kellogg Institute for International Studies.
Ostiguy, P. (2014). *Flaunting 'low' appeals: A cultural-relational approach to populism*. Paper prepared for the conference "A New Critical Juncture? Changing Patterns of Interest Representation and Regime Politics in Contemporary Latin America", Kellogg Institute of International Studies, University of Notre Dame.
Ostiguy, P. (2017). Populism: A socio-cultural approach. In C. Rovira, P. Taggart, P. Ochoa & P. Ostiguy (Eds.), *The Oxford handbook of populism* (pp. 73–97). Oxford University Press.
Oswald, M. (2020). Der Populismus in den USA. In C. Lammert, M. Siewert, & B. Vormann (Hrsg.), *Handbuch Politik USA* (pp. 55–72). Wiesbaden.
Pappas, T. S. (2013). Why Greece failed. *Journal of Democracy, 24*(2), 31–45.
Pappas, T. S. (2019). On populism, planets, and why concepts should precede definitions and theory-seeking. *Sociologica, 13*(2), 19–22.
Pettigrew, T. F. (2017). Social psychological perspectives on Trump supporters. *Journal of Social and Political Psychology, 5*, 107–116. https://doi.org/10.5964/jspp.v5i1.750.
Riker, W. H. (1982). *Liberalism against populism* (Vol. 34). WH Freeman.
Roberts, K. M. (1995). Neoliberalism and the transformation of populism in Latin America: The Peruvian case. *World Politics*, 82–116.
Rooduijn, M. (2019). State of the field: How to study populism and adjacent topics? A plea for both more and less focus. *European Journal of Political Research, 58*, 362–372. https://doi.org/10.1111/1475-6765.12314.

Rooduijn, M., & Akkerman, T. (2017). Flank attacks: Populism and left-right radicalism in Western Europe. *Party Politics, 23*(3), 193–204. https://doi.org/10.1177/1354068815596514.

Salmela, M., & von Scheve, C. (2017). Emotional roots of right-wing political populism. *Social Science Information, 56*(4), 567–595. https://doi.org/10.1177/0539018417734419.

Schmitter, P. C. (2019). The vices and virtues of "populisms." *Sociologica, 13*(1), 75–81. https://doi.org/10.6092/issn.1971-8853/9391.

Shils, E. A. (1954). *Populism and the rule of law.* University of Chicago.

Shils, E. (1956). *The torment of secrecy: The background and consequences of American security policies.* Elephant Paperbacks.

Shils, E. (1960). The intellectuals in the political development of the new states. *World Politics, 12*(3), 329–368.

Sikk, A. (2009). *Parties and populism* (Centre for European Politics, Security and Integration (CEPSI) Working Papers 1). Centre for European Politics, Security and Integration (CEPSI), SSEES, UCL: London, UK.

Stavrakakis, Y., & Jäger, A. (2018). Accomplishments and limitations of the 'new' mainstream in contemporary populism studies. *European Journal of Social Theory., 21*(4), 547–565. https://doi.org/10.1177/1368431017723337.

Taggart, P. (2002). Populism and the pathology of representative politics. In *Democracies and the populist challenge* (pp. 62–80). Palgrave Macmillan, London.

Torfing, J. (1995). *New theories of discourse.* Blackwell.

Van Hauwaert, S. M., & Van Kessel, S. (2018). Beyond protest and discontent: A cross-national analysis of the effect of populist attitudes and issue positions on populist party support. *European Journal of Political Research, 57*(1), 68–92.

Verbeek, B., & Zaslove, A. (2019). Contested issues surrounding populism in public and academic debates. *The International Spectator, 54*(2), 1–16. https://doi.org/10.1080/03932729.2019.1606513.

Weyland, K. (2001). Clarifying a contested concept. *Comparative Politics, 34*, 1–22.

Part II

Theoretical Critique

CHAPTER 2

The Past and Present of American Populism

Anton Jäger

* * *

What is the greatest threat to Europe today? In April 2010, a journalist put that question to one of the EU's leading officials, Belgian euro-president Herman van Rompuy. It was a crisis moment for Europe: just weeks earlier, anti-austerity insurrections had broken out in Greece and Spain, while in Italy an elected government had been replaced by technocrats. In his conversation with the German daily *Frankfurter Allgemeine*, the former offered a succinct answer—'the greatest danger to the contemporary West' he told German colleagues, 'is populism' (Staubenow, 2010; Stavrakakis, 2013, p. 27). Curiously, however, 'populism' was publicly embraced a few years later by none other than the then undisputed leader of the West: Barack Obama. Speaking to journalists in 2016, the American president addressed the advent of Donald Trump, a figure regularly portrayed in the press as an avatar of 'Populist' politics. Obama took a different view, however:

> I'm not prepared to say that some of the rhetoric that's been popping up is populist. You know, the reason I ran in 2008, and the reason I ran again, and the reason even after I leave this office I will continue to work in some capacity in public office is because I care about people and want to make sure every kid in America has the same opportunities I had....Now I suppose that makes me a 'populist." 'Now, somebody else, who has never shown any regard for workers,

A. Jäger (✉)
History Department, University of Cambridge, Cambridge, UK

© The Author(s), under exclusive license to Springer Nature Switzerland AG 2022
M. Oswald (ed.), *The Palgrave Handbook of Populism*,
https://doi.org/10.1007/978-3-030-80803-7_2

has never fought on behalf of social justice issues, who has, in fact, worked against economic opportunity for workers, for ordinary people — they don't suddenly become 'populist' because they say something controversial in order to win votes. That's not the measure of populism. (Obama, 2016, no page)

The two examples illustrate longstanding and essential differences between European and American understanding of populism. While the former tends to associate the term with everything politically odious, the latter attaches a rather different set of associations to it: memories of the Civil Rights movement, late nineteenth-century farmer agitation, New Deal radicalism. This culture shock has not stopped the rise of the global populism industry in the last ten years, however, further encouraged by the 2016 Trump and Brexit votes as instances of 'populism'. The statistics speak for themselves: from 1970 to 2010, the number of Anglophone publications containing the term rose from 300 to more than 800. In the 2010s they jumped over 1000 (Mauger, 2014, p. 4; Mudde et al., 2017, p. 9). In English, just over 500 academic publications have appeared on the topic in the past year, while newspapers are currently running special series on it (Eklundh & Knott, 2020; Finchelstein & Urbinati, 2018; Goodwin and Eatwell, 2018; Judis, 2016; Moffitt, 2017; Mounk, 2018).

In Europe, two disciplines have proven particularly prominent in this recent surge: political science and political theory. The first is based mainly in politics departments and offers quantitative and qualitative insights into the recent changes in mainly, but not exclusively, European party systems signaled by the rise of 'populism'. These traditions encompass research on Populist voting patterns, party behavior, electoral bases, and policy platforms. Although empirically rich and variegated, its grasp of the term 'populism' can sometimes appear under-resourced, unable to fully pinpoint the phenomenon it is seeking to trace. Political philosophy offers a welcome back-up here. This second discipline's work now spans a rich plethora of research traditions, ranging from the 'ideational' to the 'discursive' to the 'strategic'. As the most prominent tradition represented by Cas Mudde and Jan-Werner Müller, this first opts for a 'thin ideological' approach, seeing populism as an ideology dividing a population into two opposing camps: the people and the elite, both taken as perfectly homogeneous, with politicians and government expected to enact this 'will of the people' (Abts & Rummens, 2007; Mudde, 2016; Mudde & Kaltwasser, 2013). The second, discursive or performative tradition represented by writers such as Yannis Stavrakakis, Mark Devenney, Benjamin Moffit, and Ernesto Laclau sees populism neither as ideology nor as strategy but rather as a 'political logic'. In this view, a 'populism' is latently present in every political space, seeking to build 'fronts of equivalence' against a 'constitutive outside' (Csigo, 2017; Laclau, 2005, pp. 17–18; Ostiguy, 2017; Rummens, 2016). A third, strategic tradition not the political strategy mobilizes a 'people' against an elite and solidifies its grip on state power through patrimonial networks, based on 'direct, quasi-personal contact, not on organizational intermediation' (Weyland, 2017, pp. 48, 56–58).

Each of these traditions shares their own points of convergence and divergence. Taken together, however, they also exhibit a covert *consensus* on the nature of populism past and present. Firstly, all see populism as essentially opposed to political mediation and hostile to intermediary bodies such as parties, unions, or parliaments. This feature implies that Populists prefer direct or plebiscitary democracy over parliaments or parties, which are seen as distortions of popular power. Secondly, populists are said to privilege a politics of identity over a politics of 'interests' or 'issues', preferring to unite a people around cultural rather than economic markers. Thirdly, today's populism is cast as *monistic*. Populists adhere to a homogeneous vision of the people which is uniquely deserving of representation on a state level. Fourthly, populism is seen as more concerned with politics rather than policy. Fifthly, in all traditions, populism appears as particularly *leader centric* (Breiner, 1996). Populism is dependent on leadership for its functioning, in keeping with its distaste for mediating structures. Its preconditions are tailored to this character: historically, this new mode of politics is said to arise out of the decomposition of party democracy in Europe in the last thirty years, with declining membership rates, increased volatility, and falling voter participation as its most acute symptoms. All in all, populism thus appears as the ideology of an increasingly 'disorganized' or 'desociologized' democracy, as Pierre Rosanvallon has recently termed it (Rosanvallon, 2020; Selinger & Conti, 2016, pp. 548–562).

The literature surveyed offers powerful perspective on the transformations of (mainly European) party democracy in the last decades (Bickerton, 2012; Bickerton & Invernizzi, 2021; Mair, 2013). Three problems still persist within it, however. The first is a question of *definitional adequacy*. In short, do all of the movements classified as 'Populist' throughout history fit the characteristics set out by different traditions? The question whether such variegated movements as the Spanish Podemos, the French Front National, the Argentinian Peron movement, the American People's Party, or the Italian Five Start Movement fit under the same rubric is hard to answer. A second, related problem remains a lack of *historical perspective*. Although writers such as Federico Finchelstein and Jason Frank have worked to remedy populism studies' historical deficit, further work in this area still remains outstanding (Finchelstein, 2014; Frank, 2017). Theorists of populism simply know too little about previous movements in history classified as 'Populists', often extrapolating from the present into the past, or effacing qualitative differences between time periods. A final and third issue remains one of *normative bias*. Most populist theorists remain vulnerable to the accusation that they presuppose a particular order as normatively desirable, seeing 'populism' either as a supposed derivation from liberal-democratic norms (as in Cas Mudde or Jan-Werner Müller's work) or as a redemptive solution for the current democratic malaise (as in the left populism of Chantal Mouffe and Ernesto Laclau) (Arditi, 2005; Mouffe, 2018). Both historically and normatively, the contemporary populism literature still shows some conspicuous gaps.

A recent wave of scholarship has now sought to grant populism studies greater historical depth. This has mainly involved discussions in the history of political thought, a field in which the work of Pierre Rosanvallon and Nadia Urbinati occupies a prominent place (Rosanvallon, 2006, 2019; Urbinati, 2019). To both scholars, the most suitable historical precedents for the current Populist discussion are nineteenth-century discussions on French Bonapartism. In these cases, a strong leader unified an atomized (peasant) population against a liberal, parliamentary bloc. This populist solution was the outcome of a specific dialectic between democracy and liberalism in the nineteenth century. While French liberals desired an 'undemocratic liberalism' with checks and balances, new 'illiberal democrats' sought to maintain the elections and popular sovereignty of French Revolution but openly disregarded liberal norms. Like Populists today, Bonapartism accepted the necessity of general suffrage and democratic authorization. But it sought to recast these ideals into an increasingly anti-pluralist direction, turning democracy against itself. The connection with today's Populist discussion is intuitive and clear. Built on an atrophied civil society, Bonapartism constructed its regime of Weberian leadership democracy with voting bases mobilized in plebiscites—much like Salvini, Orban, and Trump today (Körösényi et al., 2020). For its enemies, the movement suffocated association, press freedom, and negated the idea of a legitimate opposition. Although not a direct road to a totalitarian party dictatorship, this pre-history gives a sharply authoritarian frame to the current discussion—as Herman Van Rompuy's statement also exemplifies.

Urbinati and Rosanvallon's recasting of the contemporary discussion is also conspicuous for what it leaves out—the late nineteenth-century American Populist movement of the 1880s and 1890s, the activists who first introduced the term 'populism' into our political language. These original Populists also hardly fit their Bonapartist story. Very wary of strong presidential power and executives, they first looked to civil society organizations for relief in the 1880s and then began to construct a legislative route to reform. In the 1880s and 1890s, Populists hoped that co-operative organizing, constitutional reform, and parliamentary pressure could save the farmers' republic. Along the way, they also rethought the fundamentals of the American republican tradition, from concepts of federalism to parliamentary power to its definition of the 'people'. And although they ran into the same problems as Rosanvallon and Urbinati's 'Populists'—issues of democratic representation, complexity, the exact boundaries of the 'people'—they took their answer in a distinctly different direction.

All of these characteristics make American 'big p' Populism somewhat of a black swan event for the current literature. Contemporary researchers have sought to deal with this problem in a variety of ways. Some exclude the late nineteenth century from their theory and state that they restrict their investigation to populism in the last thirty years—a radically historicist option. Others have bit the analytical bullet, among which Jan-Werner Müller, whose *What is Populism?* claims that 'counterintuitive as it might seem... bitten the one party in US history that explicitly called itself "populist" was in fact not populist' (Müller, 2016, p. 81). On the other side of the disciplinary fence, no rapprochement is incoming either. Historians of the late nineteenth-century Populist movement have been hesitant to connect their research with existing, twenty-first-century debates, struck by a sense of (American) culture shock. But what would it mean to connect these two conversations and grant 'big p' American Populism a place in the 'small p' Populist debate?

* * *

In June 1892, a group of radical farmers gathered in the city of Omaha, Nebraska to found a movement that was to run in elections the following year. In the months before, their formation had morphed into a fully-fledged party—the People's Party—based on a vast and intricate network of Farmers' Alliances and producer co-operatives, and in the early 1890s these Alliances crystallized into the newly formed Party which gave the word the term 'Populist' (D'Eramo, 2013, pp. 5–28; Houwen, 2011; Stavrakakis, 2017).

The American Populists of the late nineteenth century stand out as one of the most formidable social movements in American history—and uncomfortable outliers amidst today's anti-populist consensus. From the 1870s to the 1900s, white and black Populists built movements which knit workers and farmers together in a broad 'producerist' coalition. This coalition was represented by organizations such as the Farmers' Alliance, the Grange, the Colored Farmers' Alliance, and the 1891 People's Party. This coalition remade their country's republican tradition through the notion of a 'co-operative commonwealth', temporarily uniting black and white farmers in a common cause. They also broke with the individualism that had previously characterized American agrarianism, building a parallel co-operative economy in farmers' clubs, agricultural brotherhoods, and labor unions. Unsurprisingly, some of the most celebrated works of American history have been produced on this Populist moment, from Charles Beard to Richard Hofstadter to C. Vann Woodward to Charles Postel (McMath, 2008, pp. 209–217; Sanders, 2009, pp. 149–150; McMath et al., 2008, pp. 1–35).

What—and, most importantly, *who*—did this original Populist movement stand for? Its progenitors included agrarian co-operatives, trade unions, and Granger clubs, can be traced back to at least 1877. Drawing on the Greenback and Jeffersonian strands in American political thought, they revolted against low grain prices and currency scarcity, while also defending the cause of industrial workers. The movement rapidly gained traction in the last twenty years of the century. In the 1880s, American farmers developed a vast and intricate social movement organized around the Farmers' Alliances, and in the early 1890s these Alliances crystallized into the newly formed People's Party. Its 1892 Omaha Platform called for the nationalization of the American railroad system, the centralization of federal monetary policy, and the burial of postbellum rivalries. It also advocated the 'democratization' of the federal government, in which the state apparatus would be handed back to who Populists considered to be its legitimate owner—the people. As their Omaha platform declared:

> We meet in the midst of a nation brought to the verge of moral, political, and material ruin. Corruption dominates the ballot-box, the Legislatures, the Congress, and touches even the ermine of the bench.... The fruits of the toil of millions are boldly stolen to build up colossal fortunes for a few, unprecedented in the history of mankind; and the possessors of those, in turn, despise the republic and endanger liberty. From the same prolific womb of governmental injustice we breed the two great classes — tramps and millionaires. (Pollack, 1967, p. 60)

For a while in the early 1890s, American history seemed to be moving in the Populists' direction. Their presidential candidate James B. Weaver achieved a respectable 14% in the 1892 presidential election; in 1894, they captured a sizeable number of legislative seats in Western and Southern states.

At the heart of the Populist story stands the Populist reinvention of America's ideal of republican democracy in the later nineteenth century. This was an ideal first designed by a founding generation of American revolutionaries such as Jefferson, Franklin, and Paine in the 1780s and 1790s. Until the 1870s, this ideal possessed a number of clearly identifiable components. It relied on the ideal of a self-sufficient, male and white farmer who owned a plot of land in a country of 'small but universal landownership'. Reliant on the forced labor of women in the household and the expropriation of indigenous peoples, it derived the notion of an independent will from the propertied independence of male farmers. These farmers assured the latter's status as productive and, therefore, full citizens. These individuals would express their vote in regular elections and without interference from parties or other intermediary institutions, preferably on a state and not a federal level—a terrain which opened the door to tyranny. In this sense, Jeffersonian republicanism relied on the imaginary of a proprietary individual for its own regime of unmediated, direct democracy. As an ideal, however, Jeffersonian democracy also barred women, indigenous, and black subjects from full citizenship. It also shunned the necessity for large-scale institutions between individuals and states. Instead, Jeffersonians hoped that farmers could maintain their special influence on a small state. This state would not take on any bureaucratic burdens, plan production, or redistribute existing property patterns. From its inception in the eighteenth century, Jefferson's tradition thus insisted on the importance of the small, male, white farmer to a political economy oriented toward agriculture. At times hostile to political institutions, this vision was strengthened by the settler expansion of the Jackson presidency, which widened Jefferson's 'empire of liberty' across the West and strengthened the Southern slaveholding system (Belich, 2013; Wood, 2009).

In the late 1870s, however, this Jeffersonian vision of America faced three enduring challenges. First, corporations emerged as the primary actors in a new capitalist economy. Spurred by new 'general incorporation laws' decreed at the close of the Civil War, thousands of new companies sprung up and began to dominate a new commercial landscape. Their prominence undermined the belief that only 'natural' individuals like small farmers could count as citizens and indicated that America had drifted away from its status as a farmers' republic. They also created new forms of mediation between citizens and states, making previous direct democratic mechanisms unworkable. Second, and together with this corporate perversion of citizenship, the emergence of a host of new actors inevitably expanded and burst open previous definitions of the 'producer': ex-slaves in a post-Reconstruction South, women's clubs, workers in the West's new industrial theater. Although potential allies, their claims on a newly activist state also threatened established privileges in existing farmer communities. They also burst open the Jeffersonian notion of a propertied and ethnically homogeneous people. Third, the dissolution of the Western frontier and a tightening Southern land supply removed the last safety valves that had shielded farmers from the market economy before. This left America's farming class entirely dependent on commerce. A reckoning between smallholders and a new corporate class was poised to come, enabled by the might of a rapidly growing federal government (Zavodnyik, 2011).

Populists proposed a specific problem to this vision. First, they began by reclaiming the artificial person of the corporation to combat existing monopolies in railroads, credit provision, and banking in the 1870s and 1880s. In this earlier period, the rural radicals put forward ideals of co-operative association as new safeguards for republican government, relying on French theorists such as Pierre-Joseph Proudhon, Alexis de Tocqueville, and Saint-Simon. By relying on these thinkers of democratic association and pluralism, Populists were able to reintegrate mediation into their democratic vision and reinvent a more inclusive version of the 'people'. When these efforts ground to a halt in the late 1880s, Populists increasingly turned their eyes to the state. There they hoped to expand state capacity without increasing administrative privileges and hoped to engineer a public money supply. At this level they also faced the original problem of Jefferson's original anti-federalism: although large corporations could only be tamed with federal power, the expansion of this federal power contained a potentially tyrannical seed.

To counter this problem Populists went for a 'statutory' rather than a 'discretionary' state, in which legislatures would remain the most powerful entities (Novak, 1996, 2010, pp. 377–405; Sanders, 1999, p. 8). Legislatures would here write 'statutes' which would allow farmers to take specific action against corporations, rather than handing control to administrators which would control prices. More than any of their contemporaries, the Populists also obsessed over questions of monetary centralization and control. This tradition was not without precedent. Since the 1860s, when President Lincoln introduced greenbacks to remedy the Civil War's deflationary dynamics, the idea that the American state might use its authority to control the money supply from private banks had already stirred the radical imagination.

Populists extended these greenback efforts into the 1880s. One of the most pressing problems of the decade was the scarcity of credit and currency in rural areas, which drove an infernal spiral of deflation and price depression. Loosening and widening the base of currency, Populists claimed, would fuel productive investment, raise the price of agricultural produce, and break the power of established merchants, whose hold on currency often went hand in hand with price gouging. The most recurrent Populist response—pushed by businessmen, small farmers, and intellectuals alike—to the problem of deflation was a more elastic money supply and so-called fiat currency, terminating America's attachment to the gold standard. Once this 'sound' money dogma was broken and the monopoly of private banks was brought to an end, a fully public bank could freely issue currency and lessen the stringent credit conditions of merchants and corporations. The most interesting of these was developed by Texas businessman and self-taught heterodox economist Charles Macune. In the late 1880s, faced with the failure of a more voluntary approach that relied on farmers' co-operatives, Macune began to rethink the American state's role as a provider of credit in what he called a 'subtreasury' plan. The plan's set up was as radical as it was simple: the subtreasury would allow American farmers to store their grain and other commodities in government-tended warehouses and grant them interest-denoted vouchers, valid for up to a full year, based on the amount of grain they stored. These vouchers would circulate as money—not unlike gold—releasing farmers from costly borrowing and freeing them to wait for opportune times to sell their crops. The plan implied a system of state banks that could tend this deposit system and redirect capital into agrarian communities (Macune partly drew on the French socialist Pierre-Joseph Proudhon's proposals for a 'people's bank' in these writings, which had also sought to facilitate credit creation across society) (Carruthers & Babb, 1996; Destler, 1946, pp. 338–365; Macune, 1889, p. 166; Ritter, 1993, pp. 139–140). Envisioning a democratic credit system, Macune hoped to update Jefferson's vision of a community of smallholders to a corporate era.

This was a clear difference with contemporary populisms. Rather than conquering the executive or supporting a Bonapartist president, parliaments were the best conduit for the exercise of popular sovereignty. In the 1890s such Populist calls for strong parliaments were increasingly coupled with plebiscitary measures. These included 1892 pleas for referenda, popular initiative, and direct election of federal judges and senators. Populist theorists thereby expounded a vision of association and centralization that remained thoroughly 'pluralist' by the standards of today's discussion. They embraced parliamentary representation, recognized the need for bureaucratic expansion and affirmed the basic tripartite structure of American government. Although they did advocate the 'democratization' of some federal organs (visible, for example, in their 1890s proposals to make Supreme Court judges subject to popular recall), they never questioned the legitimacy of checks and balances itself, most visible in their preference for legislatures as the ultimate sites for popular power.

Even this moderate program was not accepted kindly in the United States of the late nineteenth century. The Eastern bourgeoisie, for instance, was terrified by the agrarian jacquerie coming from the West. In his private diaries, future president Theodore Roosevelt wrote that the Populists 'should be put up against the wall and shot', since their campaign was nothing less 'than an appeal to the torch' (cited in Hesseltine, 1962, p. 71). Yet it was in the Southern states that the Populists faced their mightiest and most ruthless opposition. Their efforts to unite black and white tenant farmers against local landlords and merchants were met with violent resistance on behalf of the landed elite, which had a stranglehold over Southern commodity markets. Anti-Populist tactics were not particularly sophisticated, in any region. In the 1896 election, for example, Eastern banks sent representatives into Midwestern towns, warning farmers that their homes would be foreclosed on if they dared elect Populist lawmakers (Durden, 1963, pp. 397–423). In the South, even more primitive instruments were used: Southern Democrats fought off the Populist threat with physical intimidation, alcoholic bribes, and stuffed ballot boxes.

Nonetheless, the Populists performed relatively well. Their candidate James B. Weaver achieved a respectable 14 percent in the 1892 presidential election; in 1894, Populists captured a sizeable number of seats in Western and Southern states. In the South, however, Democrats escalated their attack on Populist threat with full Klan terror, burning and looting houses, and killing activists. The rest of the country in the meantime remained loyal to old party machines. In desperation, Populists started looking for help within the established parties themselves. In 1896, the Democratic Party co-opted the Populist platform by nominating William Jennings Bryan as proponent of 'free silver' and a moderately inflationary policy for president (DeCanio, 2011; Nugent, 2015). After a bitter debate, the Populists decided to relegate Bryan's name on their own ticket rather than run a candidate against him. Bryan lost his election to the Republican McKinley, however, and by 1897 the former Populist party was disbanding across the spectrum. With it also went the last hopes of enacting the 1892 Populist plans in their original form.

1896—the year in which the People's Party lost its final presidential battle— did not herald the official end of the 'Populist vision', however. As scholars such as Elizabeth Sanders, Matthew Hild, and Charles Postel have shown, the efforts of the Farmers' Alliances continued to weigh on the legislative activity in the Progressive era, with farmers making up constituencies for the Clayton Antitrust Act of 1914, the 1913 Federal Reserve Act and 1914 Federal Trade Commission Act. In all these cases, echoes of the Populist movement informed state action in the Progressive Age. Nonetheless, the ambitious scope of the Alliance effort faded from view, and by 1900 the dispersion of the Populist coalition had become a *fait accompli*. A sizeable number of ex-members had joined the new Socialist Party, while a majority deserted the reform cause altogether.

To these Populist survivors, the Progressive era yielded a peculiar and painful paradox. While Populism had lost its battle at the ballot box, many of its proposals found a way into Progressive platforms. The 1906 Hepburn Act regulated railroad power. The 1914 Cotton Futures Act enacted some of the market control proposed by Populists. The 1914 Federal Trade Commission Act, in turn, owed much to Populist agitation, while the 1913 Income Tax and the 1916 Revenue Act appeared as replicas of the Omaha proposals (Nadav, 2018; Sanders, 2019; Schlozman, 2015, pp. 110–115). American banking and credit provision also lived in a Populist shadow. The 1913 Federal Reserve Act was pushed through with farmer bases, while the 1916 Federal Farm Credit Act resembled the sub-treasury's proposal for credit injections. The party itself declined, however; 'as I write', the political theorist Walter Lippmann noted in 1913, 'a convention of the Populist Party has just taken place. Eight delegates attended the meeting, which was held in a parlor' (Lippmann, 1913, p. 275). As the historian Elizabeth Sanders summarizes this paradoxical development:

> The periphery agrarians worked to expand the power of the national state and provided the political muscle for enacting the progressive legislative agenda of 1909-17. The roots of their statism lay not in the writings of the new social intelligentsia but in the antimonopoly agitation of the 1870s, the Greenback movement of the 1880s, the populism of the 1890s, and William Jennings Bryan's Democracy of 1896-1908... Here, then lies the paradox of Progressive era state expansion: driven by social movements deeply hostile to bureaucracy, it produced a great bureaucratic expansion. (Sanders, 1999, p. 389)

This partial adoption also explains why so many Populists could move into unpredictable directions. The Southern Tenant Farmers' Union extended Populist efforts into a careful assault on the Southern planter system. Father Coughlin and Huey Long channeled farmer unrest in the New Deal years, openly deploying Populist rhetoric. In the 1940s, however, memories of Populism drove Martin Luther King's first civil rights efforts in the South, who claimed he had always 'identified with populism' as reminiscent of 'a time when Negroes and whites found common ground' (Rieder, 2009, p. 171). In the 1960s, 'Populist' rhetoric (but not necessarily policy) could be found in the campaigns of segregationists such as Barry Goldwater or George Wallace, who supposedly drew on the Populist precedents in this region—even though their Democratic forefathers had crushed the Populist movement itself (Postel, 2016, p. 81).

This Populist dispersal can also explain the differences in understanding between Van Rompuy and Obama a hundred years later, however. The Populist coalition of the 1890s had always been a rather broad church, attracting political cranks of all stripes, such as the Minnesota writer Ignatius Donnelly, who claimed that the unacknowledged author of Shakespeare's plays was, in fact, Francis Bacon and who firmly believed in the existence of a land named Atlantis. But Populist eccentricity could also assume more sinister forms. The most explicit case was that of the Georgia Populist Thomas E. Watson. Watson's biography always read like a quintessential Southern epic. The son of a Southern slave owner, the young Watson had spent his youthful years in dire poverty due to the devastation wrought by the Civil War. His father lost his plantation and spent the rest of his days mired in depression and paralysis. Predictably, Watson's youth was suffused with talk of the Lost Cause and haunted by the memory of great Southern statesmen: John Calhoun, Robert E. Lee, Thomas Jefferson.

But Watson was no ordinary apologist for the plantocracy. Like his hero Thomas Jefferson, Watson was fascinated by the French Revolution and saw himself as a defender of the commonwealth against aristocratic privilege. Although a proud Southern secessionist, he later abandoned the Democratic Party because of its collusion with the 'moneyed interests' and joined the third-party crusade in the late 1880s. As a Populist organizer, Watson helped broaden the Populist appeal across race and gender lines. In the 1890s, he came out as an opponent of lynch laws, championed black voting rights, and lauded the influx of women in the movement.

This more inclusive Populism was not viewed kindly in a South riven by racial animosity. The year 1892 witnessed some of the most vicious campaigns of racist violence in Southern history, many of them directed at Populist organizers. In May 1892, for example, Watson had to rally his supporters to ride to the protection of the black Populist preacher H. S. Doyle, who had received threats from Democratic opponents in the run-up to the presidential election. His call was swiftly heeded. Over two thousand agrarian followers congregated at Watson's Georgia mansion, staying the night to fend off possible Democratic attacks. The Democratic press was apoplectic. Southern newspapers exclaimed that the South was 'threatened with anarchy and communism', because of 'the direful teachings of Thomas E. Watson' (Hamilton, 1972, p. 489). (The incident was recounted by the great Southern historian C. Vann Woodward, who wrote laconically that 'the spectacle of white farmers riding all night to save a Negro from lynchers was rather rare in Georgia' [Woodward, 1938, p. 21]). But Watson's racial liberalism was not to last. A fervent supporter of black voting rights and progressive political causes in the 1890s, Watson morphed into a race-baiting fanatic after Populism's defeat in 1896. In the 1910s, he fulminated against 'Jewish billionaires' in his magazine *The Jeffersonian* and openly advocated the disfranchisement of blacks in Southern states (Evans, 2006, pp. 238–239; Schmier, 1986, pp. 433–455). As such, he helped to codify the new Jim Crow.

Watson's temperament soured even further as the twentieth century progressed. In the notorious Leo Frank case of 1913, he played an instrumental role in summoning Southern mobs to lynch the Georgia businessman, who had been unjustly accused of murdering one of his underage hirelings, the thirteen-year-old factory girl Mary Phagan. Watson's anticapitalism now assumed an overtly reactionary form. While he himself had pleaded for several Jewish clients in the early 1900s—even claiming, as a public defender, that 'no Jew can do murder'—he now came to identify the 'Hebrew menace' as a threat to his republican vision. Even in the darkest days of his political career Watson showed flashes of his earlier radicalism, however. In the wake of Woodrow Wilson's anti-communist witch hunt, Watson called Eugene V. Debs 'one of the greatest, truest, purest Americans now alive' (Woodward, 1938, p. 463). He even voiced support for the Bolshevik government. To Watson, Wilson's US war plans were a conspiracy 'to prevent Russia from showing the world how a democracy may be established — thus setting a bad example that may "infect" other submerged masses'. In a further twist, Watson defended Rosa Luxemburg and her comrades in the German Revolution and opposed a bid by Henry Ford for the US Senate on the grounds of the latter's antisemitism. A similar story played out in in the Scopes 'Monkey Trial' of 1925, in which former Populists played the starring roles for both the defense and the prosecution: William Jennings Bryan of Nebraska, who defended Tennessee's ban on teaching evolution, and Clarence Darrow of Illinois, who opposed it (Mencken, 2006; Tontonoz, 2008). Again, former allies now found themselves on the opposite sides of the spectrum.

Historians have repeatedly found themselves perplexed by the Jekyll-and-Hyde-like paradoxes of Populist thought. How could a man committed to biracial organizing in the 1890s turn into a racist patriarch in the 1910s? And how could Populists both become creationists and evolutionists? European interpreters have here tended to focus exclusively on populism's darker side. In his latest book on populism, for instance, Jan-Werner Müller relies on Watson to construct a story of 'exclusionary' Populist logics. 'Populism', Müller notes, 'is always and everywhere antipluralist' and 'always ends in exclusion' (Müller, 2016, p. 20). Although several hypotheses have been put forward, by far the most plausible traces this negativity to the rather partial readings of the original Populist movement offered by American historians of the 1950s—and one major historian in particular: Richard Hofstadter. These Cold War-era accounts painted a picture of Populism as inherently conspiratorial and totalitarian. As Hofstadter saw it, Populists exemplified the 'paranoid style in American politics', with mad ravings against the 'money power' and a proclivity for racial phobias (Hofstadter, 1963). Together with Cold War intellectuals like Daniel Bell and Seymour Martin Lipset, Hofstadter drew a straight line from big-P Populism to American McCarthyism, arguing that both traditions share the same pedigree (Brinkley, 1998, pp. 137–140; Hofstadter, 1955; Ostler, 1995, p. 1; Ross, 2018, p. 85).

Hofstadter's vision is best understood in context. For a long time, American historians had looked fondly on the Populist episode. In the 1920s, Progressive historians like John Hicks and Vernon Parrington cast the Populists as the last representatives of the great Jeffersonian tradition (Parrington, 1927). In these accounts, the Populists were the last bulwark against corporate capitalism, maintaining the settler spirit and fighting the United States' drift from republic to empire (Destler, 1963). In the 1940s, this vision still reigned supreme. Marxist historians like Anne Rochester and Chester McArthur Destler, for example, found a distinct brand of American radicalism in populism: the socialist movement the United States never had (Destler, 1963).

Hofstadter and his colleagues disagreed. To them, the Populists were not benevolent reformists or the last small-d democrats. Rather, they were the forebears of figures like Joseph McCarthy and a host of other far-right cranks who populated the postwar political landscape. According to Hofstadter, commercially ambitious yet culturally nostalgic farmers wanted the new economy's benefits but could not live with its consequences. He contrasted the Populist 'agrarian myth' with the commercial realities of the late nineteenth century, castigating farmers for engaging in pastoral posturing while also seeking the benefits of market society. Their difficulty squaring the capitalist circle produced a kind of political nostalgia. This nostalgia could also take far less innocent forms. Hofstadter claimed the Populists were essentially antisemitic and had activated much of the anti-Jewish sentiment in the Gilded Age. In their ravings against the 'money power', they often slid into racial stereotyping, blaming the United States' financial ills on the 'evil Rothschilds' (Bell, 1944, p. 15). The fact that Tom Watson himself became the main instigator in the Leo Frank case only further proved his point.

Hofstadter's thesis immediately faced objections. The debate, often referred to as 'one of the bloodiest episodes in American historiography', lasted over twenty years, eventually involving historians such as Walter Nugent, John Hicks, and Comer Vann Woodward, all of whom wrote passionate defenses of the Populist movement (Hicks, 1955; Woodward, 1972, 1960, 2012). This quickly led to some embarrassing conclusions. Many of Hofstadter's claims—that the Populists were antisemitic; that they provided the social basis for McCarthyism—turned out to be empirically unjustifiable. Nor could Hofstadter explain the career of many later Populists, who joined European Jews in the American Socialist Party and became fierce critics of Henry Ford. The claim that most former Populist states had become seedbeds of McCarthyism—one of Hofstadter's key arguments—also turned out to be false. Hofstadter and his colleagues saw that most ex-Populist states strongly supported the Wisconsin Senator. By the end of the 1960s, Hofstadter's thesis was in tatters (Goodwyn, 1991).

Yet while Hofstadter began to admit mistakes, European political scientists became even more enthused with his version of small-p populism. In the 1980s, Hofstadter's thesis gained further traction in European political science departments, most interestingly in France. In 1984, for instance, in a text called 'La rhétorique du national-populisme', the French political scientist Pierre-André Tagueiff introduced the term 'national-populism' to describe the far-right National Front (FN) (Taguieff, 1984, 2013, p. 70). Swiftly, Taguieff's neologism established itself in media circles—accordingly, the original Populists were quickly buried under three decades of ideology. Americans now find it difficult to convince Europeans that it once signified something other than pure demagoguery and protofascism. One need only look to the most recent literature on populism to confirm this trend. Jan-Werner Müller's aptly titled *What is Populism?* declares it a political philosophy that's not only anti-elitist, but also anti-democratic, anti-pluralist, and moralistic, all in extremely dangerous ways. As he writes:

> The core claim of populism is thus a moralized form of antipluralism... Populism requires a pars pro toto argument and a claim to exclusive representation, with both understood in a moral, as opposed to empirical, sense. There can be no populism, in other words, without someone speaking in the name of the people as a whole. (Müller, 2016, p. 20)

Perhaps the most interesting features of Müller's book come to the fore when comparing it to the work of his pluralist predecessors. Here is Hofstadter's colleague Edward Shils in 1956:

> Populism proclaims that the will of the people as such is supreme over every other standard, over the standards of traditional institutions, over the autonomy of institutions and over the will of other strata. Populism identifies the will of the people with justice and morality. (Shils, 1956, p. 98)

These similarities throw up an interesting question: why has so little changed in populism studies? Although some later Alliance members such as Watson definitely fit the bill of populism as anti-pluralist authoritarians, this history hardly comprises their whole legacy. Today Donald Trump might count as a 'Populist', with compatriots such as Vladimir Putin, Viktor Orban, or Marine Le Pen. Seen in light of original American history, however—as Obama pointed out in 2016—that ascription feels far more fraught (Frank, 2020). Involving original, 'big p' Populisms in the current discussion would have at least three unsettling advantages. Firstly, it would inject a degree of historical consciousness into the contemporary populism literature and expand its range of possibilities, beyond the Bonapartism now centered by writers. Secondly, it would impose some definitional accuracy on existing definitions, forcing scholars to account for an interesting outlier to the literature—thereby destabilizing suppositions governing the current populism debate. Thirdly, it would enrich the range of concepts and sources available to political philosophers working on populism, pointing out alternative trajectories for the Populist 'people' beyond the exclusionary versions familiar to us today. Not all 'populisms' scorned foreigners, loathed mediation, conducted culture wars, or sought direct democracy in a presidential leader. In fact, most of history shows that the original American Populists were hardly 'Populist' at all.

Literature

Abts, K., & Rummens, S. (2007). Populism versus democracy. *Political Studies, 55,* 405–424.
Arditi, B. (2005). Populism as an internal periphery of democratic politics. In F. Panizza (Ed.), *Populism and the mirror of democracy* (pp. 72–98). Verso Books.
Belich, J. (2013). *Replenishing the Earth: The Settler Revolution and the birth of the Anglo-world, 1783–1939.* Oxford University Press.
Bell, D. (1944), 'The Grass Roots of American Jew Hatred', *Jewish Frontier,* 15–20.
Bickerton, C. (2012). *European integration: From nation states to member states.* Oxford University Press.
Bickerton, C., & Invernizzi, C. A. (2021). *Technopopulism: The new logic of democratic politics.* Oxford University Press.
Breiner, P. (1996). *Max Weber & democratic politics.* Cornell University Press.
Brinkley, A. (1998). *Liberalism and its discontents.* Harvard University Press.
Carruthers, B. G., & Babb, S. (1996, May). The color of money and the nature of value: Greenbacks and gold in postbellum America. *American Journal of Sociology, 101*(6), 1556–1591.
Csigo, P. (2017). *The neopopular bubble: Speculating on "the people" in late modern democracy.* Central European University Press.
DeCanio, S. (2011). Populism, paranoia, and the politics of free silver. *Studies in American Political Development, 25*(April), 1–26.
D'Eramo, M. (2013, July–August). Populism and the new oligarchy. *New Left Review, 82,* 5–28.
Destler, C. M. (1946). *American radicalism, 1865–1901; essays and documents.* Octagon Books.
Destler, C. M. (1963). *Henry Demarest Lloyd and the empire of reform.* University of Pennsylvania Press.
Durden, R. F. (1963, December). The "cowbird" grounded: The populist nomination of Bryan and Tom Watson in 1896. *The Mississippi Valley Historical Review, 50*(3), 397–423.
Eklundh, E., & Knott, A. (Eds.) (2020). *The populist manifesto.* Rowman & Littlefield.
Evans, E. (2006). *The provincials: A personal history of Jews in the South.* University of North Carolina Press.
Finchelstein, F. (2014). Returning populism to history. *Constellations,* 467–482.
Finchelstein, F., & Urbinati, N. (2018). On Populism and democracy. *Populism, 1*(1), 15–37.
Frank, J. (2017). Populism and praxis. In P. Taggart et al. (Eds.), *Oxford handbook of populism* (pp. 629–643). Oxford University Press.
Goodwin, M., & Eatwell, R. (2018). *National populism and the revolt against liberal democracy.* Penguin Books.
Goodwyn, L. (1991). Rethinking "populism": Paradoxes of historiography and democracy. *Telos, 88,* 37–56.
Hamilton, R. F. (1972). *Class and politics in the United States.* Wiley.
Hesseltine, W. B. (1962). *Third-party movements in the United States.* Van Nostrand.
Hicks, J. (1955, October 22). Politics in pattern. *Saturday Review,* 12.
Hofstadter, R. (1955). *The age of reform.* Knopf.
Houwen, T. (2011). The non-European roots of the concept of populism. *Sussex European Institute, 120,* 1–52.

Judis, J. B. (2016). *The populist explosion: How the great recession transformed American and European politics*. Columbia Global Reports.
Körösényi, A., Illés, G., & Gyulai, A. (2020). *The Orbán regime: Plebiscitary leader democracy in the making*. Routledge.
Laclau, E. (2005). *On populist reason*. Verso Books.
Lippmann, W. (1913). *A preface to politics*. Mitchell Kennerley.
Macune, C. (1889). A review of modern political Isms: Anarchism, socialism and communism. *National Economist*, 1(11), 166–170.
Mair, P. (2013). *Ruling the void*. Verso Books.
Mauger, G. (2014). «Populisme», itinéraire d'un mot voyageur, *Le monde diplomatique*, 4.
Mudde, C., & Kaltwasser, C. R. (2013). Exclusionary vs. inclusionary populism: Comparing contemporary Europe and Latin America. *Government and Opposition*, 48(2), 147–174.
Mencken, H. L. (2006). *A religious orgy in Tennessee: A reporter's account of the scopes monkey trial*. Melville.
Moffitt, B. (2017). *The global rise of populism: Performance, political style, and representation*. Stanford University Press.
Mouffe, C. (2018). *For a left populism*. Verso Books.
Mounk, Y. (2018). *The people vs. democracy: Why our freedom is in danger and how to save it*. Harvard University Press.
Mudde, C. (2016). *Syriza: The failure of the populist promise*. Springer.
Müller, J. (2016). *What is populism?* University of Pennsylvania Press.
Nadav, P. (2018). Negotiating the lender-of-last-resort: The 1913 Fed Act as a debate over credit distribution. *Tulane Public Law Research Paper*, 1–62.
Novak, W. J. (1996). *The people's welfare: Law and regulation in nineteenth-century America*. University of North Carolina Press.
Nugent, W. (2015). Comments on Wyatt Wells, "rhetoric of the standards: The debate over gold and silver in the 1890s". *The Journal of the Gilded Age and Progressive Era*, 14, 69–76.
Obama, B. (2016, September 29). Remarks by President Obama, Prime Minister Trudeau of Canada, and President Peña Nieto of Mexico in North American Leaders' Summit Press Conference, *White House, Office of the Press Secretary*.
Ostiguy, P. (2017). Populism: A socio-cultural approach. In *The Oxford handbook of populism* (pp. 73–100).
Ostler, J. (1995). The rhetoric of conspiracy and the formation of Kansas populism. *Agricultural History*, 69(1, Winter), 1–25.
Parrington, V. (1927). *Main currents in American thought, vol. 3. The beginnings of critical realism in America, 1860–1920*. Harcourt.
Pollack, N. (Ed.). (1967). *The populist mind*. The Bobbs-Merrill Company.
Postel, C. (2016). The American populist and anti-populist legacy. In P. Taggart & J. Abromeit (Eds.), *Transformations of populism in Europe and the Americas: history and recent tendencies* (pp. 105–116). Bloomsbury Academic.
Rieder, J. (2009). *The word of the Lord Is Upon Me: The righteous performance of Martin Luther King, Jr*. Harvard University Press.
Ritter, G. (1993). *Goldbugs and greenbackers: The antimonopoly tradition and the politics of finance in America, 1865–1896*. Cambridge University Press.
Rosanvallon, P. (2006). *Democracy past and future*. Columbia University Press.
Rosanvallon, P. (2019). *Le siècle du populisme*. Seuil.

Rosanvallon, P. (2020). *Le siècle du populisme*. Seuil.
Ross, D. (2018). The new and newer histories: Social theory and historiography in an American Key. In G. S. Wood (Ed.), *Imagined histories: American historians interpret the past* (pp. 60–85). Princeton University Press.
Rummens, S. (2016). *Wat een theater! Politiek in tijden van populisme en technocratie*. Pelckmans.
Sanders, E. (1999). *Roots of reform: Farmers, workers and the American state, 1877–1917*. University of Chicago Press.
Sanders, E. (2009). "Horny-handed sons of toil"—R.I.P. *Historical Methods, 42*, 149–150.
Sanders, E. (2019). The midwest and reform (Unpublished manuscript), pp. 1–30.
Schlozman, D. (2015). *When movements anchor parties: Electoral alignments in American history*. Princeton University Press.
Schmier, L. (1986). No Jew can murder: Memories of Tom Watson and the Lichtenstein murder case of 1901. *Georgia Historical Society, 70*(Fall), 433–455.
Selinger, W., & Conti, G. (2016). The other side of representation: The history and theory of representative government in Pierre Rosanvallon. *Constellations*, 548–562.
Shils, E. (1956). *The torment of secrecy: The background and consequences of American security policies*. Elephant Paperbacks.
Staubenow, M. (2010, April 4). Anlaufstelle für Merkel und Sarkozy. *Frankfurter Allgemeine*.
Stavrakakis, Y. (2013). Populism, anti-populism and European democracy: A view from the South, *openDemocracy Working Papers*, 1–6.
Stavrakakis, Y. (2017). How did 'populism' become a pejorative concept? And why is this important today? A genealogy of double hermeneutics. *Populismus Working Papers, 6*, 1–28.
Taguieff, P. (1984). La rhétorique du national-populisme. *Mots, 9*, 112–139.
Taguieff, P. (2013). *Le nouveau national-populisme*. CNRS Editions.
Tontonoz, M. (2008). The Scopes Monkey trial revisited: Social Darwinism versus social gospel. *Science as Culture, 17*(2), 121–143.
Urbinati, N. (2019). *Me the people: how populism transforms democracy*. Harvard University Press.
Weyland, K. (2017). Populism: A political-strategic approach. In P. Taggart et al. (Eds.), *The Oxford handbook of populism* (pp. 48–58). Oxford University Press.
Wood, G. S. (2009). *Empire of liberty: A history of the early Republic, 1789–1815*. Oxford University Press.
Woodward, C. V. (1938). Tom Watson and the Negro in agrarian politics. *The Journal of Southern History, 4*, 15–30.
Woodward, C. V. (1951). *Origins of the new south*. Louisiana State University Press.
Woodward, C. V. (1972, June 4). 'The ghost of populism walks again. *The New York Times Magazine*, pp. 6–17, 60–69.
Woodward, C. V. (1960). The populist heritage and the intellectual. In *The burden of southern history* (pp. 141–166). Louisiana State University Press.
Zavodnyik, P. (2011). *The rise of the federal Colossus: The growth of federal power from Lincoln to F.D.R.* ABC-CLIO.

CHAPTER 3

Populism Is Hegemony Is Politics? Ernesto Laclau's Theory of Populism

Benjamin Arditi

Introduction

Ernesto Laclau was one of the most gifted political thinkers of his generation. The work of many of us would not have been the same without his intellectual influence. It is difficult not to be bowled over by the elegance of his writing—the turns of phrases, the conceptual wizardry, the frequent use of examples, the ease with which he weaves his arguments by drawing from the work of philosophers, linguists, psychoanalysts, or historians.

He also had a knack for luring critics into his conceptual territory by reading their work through the lens of his own terminology. When this was not a viable option, he was equally skillful at undermining or dismissing criticism with responses that were meant to have the force of syllogisms. On both counts Laclau followed in the footsteps of Louis Althusser, who was also comfortable with intertextuality and always strived to present his arguments as if they were self-evident. Althusser was no stranger to him given that his theories framed his first book of essays, *Politics and Ideology in Marxist Theory* (1977).

An earlier version of this chapter was published in *Constellations*, 17(3): 488–497. This is an expanded and more developed take on Laclau's theory of populism.

B. Arditi (✉)
Faculty of Politics and Social Sciences, National University of Mexico (UNAM), Mexico City, Mexico
e-mail: arditi@unam.mx

© The Author(s), under exclusive license to Springer Nature Switzerland AG 2022
M. Oswald (ed.), *The Palgrave Handbook of Populism*,
https://doi.org/10.1007/978-3-030-80803-7_3

Laclau parted ways with the thought of the relative autonomy of the superstructures and the determination in the last instance by the economy in the writings leading to the publication of *Hegemony and Socialist Strategy* (1985). What still resonated there as well as in *New Reflections* (1990) and On *Populist Reason* (2005) is Althusser's talent for giving a semblance of seamlessness to his discourse.

On Populist Reason (hereafter *OPR*) is a fascinating read. It is written in a way that renders the subject matter a continuation, enhancement and confirmation of his post-Gramscian theory of hegemony. Hegemony is the medium through which populism unfolds and, as we will see, it is often difficult to tell them apart except for the fact that populism emphasizes the splitting of political space into two antagonistic camps. Laclau addresses the theories of Margaret Canovan, Kenneth Minogue and various contributors to the Ghita Ionescu and Ernest Gellner book on populism. He also discusses what Gustave Le Bon, Gabriel Tarde, William McDougall and Sigmund Freud have to say about groups, crowds and leaders. This prepares the reader for his own interpretation of populism.

I won't distract readers with a summary of Laclau's thoughts on Canovan et al., or with didactic explanations of discourse, equivalence, articulation, antagonism and other terms of his lexicon. I will go directly to his theory of politics-as-populism, highlighting things he did not perceive or did not want to see.

DEMANDS AND THE PEOPLE

Laclau develops his argument in two stages. He first uses a series of simplifying assumptions that he will abandon gradually to deliver what he calls his "fully fledged notion of populism" (Laclau, 2005a, p. 159). The passage from one stage to the other involves the introduction of floating signifiers in a discourse that until then had relied on empty signifiers. The latter serves him for explaining the construction of popular identities when frontiers between a collective and its surroundings are stable. Floating signifiers allow him to contemplate the displacement of those frontiers when populist forces are engaged with their adversaries. Yet the impression one gets from reading *OPR* is that instead of two versions of his theory of populism we have different tonalities of the same conceptual core. This is because the ideas—and often the structure of sentences as well as the theoretical summaries Laclau himself provides from time to time—are similar in both accounts, the simplified and the fully fledged ones.

He develops his theory of populism in six steps that apply to any of the two stages of the argument. These are: (1) when a series of social demands cannot be absorbed differentially by institutional channels (2) they become unsatisfied demands that enter into a relationship of solidarity or equivalence with one another and (3) crystallize around common symbols that (4) can be capitalized by leaders who interpellate the frustrated masses and thus begin to incarnate a process of popular identification that (5) constructs the people as a collective actor to confront the existing regime with the purpose of (6) demanding regime change. This narrative is governed by the claim that politics-as-populism divides the social scene into two camps and produces an antagonistic relation between them. Also, by recurrent references to empty and floating signifiers, the idea of a constitutive lack he borrowed from psychoanalysis, heterogeneity, the distinction between naming and concepts, and the primacy of representation.

Demands, or more precisely, *social* demands, function as his minimal unit of analysis. The term signifies both a request and a claim. The passage from the first to the second provides one of the defining features of populism, which conceives all requests as claims (Laclau, 2005a, p. 73). Laclau then distinguishes between intra- and anti-systemic demands, or those that can be accommodated within the existing order and those that challenge it. He calls the former democratic demands, and those against the system popular ones.

When democratic demands are fulfilled, they become absorbed and positioned as differences within the institutional ensemble. For example, workers' suffrage: it was initially rejected by the liberal state, but after decades of labor mobilizations, liberals relented and praised it as a sign of institutional strength. In the terminology of Antonio Gramsci that Laclau used in the 1980s, democratic demands are characteristic of transformism, that is, of a hegemony that seeks to absorb dissent as internal differences within its discursive space. Transformism is a kind of *gatopardismo*, an expression coined by Giuseppe di Lampedusa in his novel *The Leopard* to indicate that something must change for everything to remain the same: transformism deactivates a radical questioning of the institutional system.

In contrast, popular demands are those that remain unfulfilled. These are the ones that interest Laclau because they are the embryo of populism, the starting point for the constitution of the people that will confront the status quo (Laclau, 2005a, pp. 74, 127). The key operation in this process is the convergence of multiple unfulfilled social demands into a chain of equivalence and the concomitant division of society into two antagonistic camps. The identity resulting from this relation of equivalence is wider than the particularisms that make up that chain, but it does not annul the differential nature of each discrete demand or group linked together in the popular camp. The shared identity constitutes their common denominator. This is consistent with how Gramsci conceived hegemony: a circumstantial political alliance like an electoral coalition leaves the identity of the intervening forces untouched, whereas hegemony modifies them by virtue of the ensemble of shared values and ideas that bring them together in a historic bloc. This is how hegemony produces a superordinate identity, something in excess of the participating individual entities.

The construction of the popular camp is intimately connected with how Laclau understands the "people": both as *plebs* and *populus*. He borrows his distinction from Roman thought, although he also praises the notion of demos of Jacques Rancière and compares it to his own notion of the people. For Rancière, the demos are not a preexisting sociological category but the name of an outcast, "of those who are denied an identity in a given order" (Rancière, 1992, p. 61). The demos appear in the interval that opens between their de-classification from the place they occupy in the existing order and their simultaneous identification with an equality that is not properly theirs yet (61). Demos is the part of those who have no part in the community and identifies its name with the name of the community (Rancière, 1998, pp. 8–9; 2010, pp. 33–34). Rancière's ideas reverberate in Laclau's account of the people. On the one hand, because he sees the construction of the people as a political task and not a fact of the social structure (Laclau, 2005a, p. 224), which echoes Rancière's distinction between the demos and a preexisting and counted sociological group. On the other hand, like the demos, Laclau's people is internally split between *populus* and *plebs*, whole and part, the sum of citizens and the underprivileged, and the populist construction of the people requires an operation that presents the *plebs* as the totality of the *populus* (81, 93 ff.).

But they differ, among other things, on the role of legitimacy. For Rancière, politics arises when the people appear as a supplement of all empirical counts of the parts of the community (Rancière, 2010, Thesis 6). Legitimacy is not part of how he conceptualizes the noise introduced by the demos into the partition of the sensible. The legitimacy of this disruptive noise is either one of the stakes of a disagreement or is simply not relevant for the emergence of the "outline of a vanishing difference" he calls politics (Rancière, 2010, p. 35). For Laclau, however, "in order to have the 'people' of populism, we need something more: we need a *plebs* who claims to be the only legitimate *populus*" (Laclau, 2005a, p. 81). The quote is eloquent: Laclau sees legitimacy as a constitutive feature of the populist *plebs*. But it is difficult to tell how we are to understand the role legitimacy plays in a populist challenge, or what is it that enables a set of demands to generate a legitimate claimant. Laclau introduces this qualifier of the *plebs* without developing it, maybe because he thought it was self-explanatory or wanted to leave it vague on purpose.

Legitimacy is implicit in the classic distinction between the real and the legal country: populists invariably assume that genuine legitimacy lies in the former. But claiming that populism involves "a *plebs* that claims to be the only legitimate *populus*" is troubling for democratic politics. Nadia Urbinati (2019) reminds us that populism is not simply a *pars pro toto*, for then it would be a commonplace occurrence: this is how political representation works. Laclau's populist *plebs* functions differently: it challenges the establishment and declares itself deserving of supremacy because it is the good part, the *only* legitimate one (Urbinati, 2019, pp. 70, 79, 80). This turns populism into a potentially disruptive force for democracy as it opens the door for it to govern only for that special part (80, 95).

Laclau's silence about the source of legitimacy pushes his theory in the direction of formalism and reveals a normative deficit like the one in Carl

Schmitt's decisionism. For Schmitt, a norm is only valid in a normal situation, and the sovereign is whoever makes the decision about whether to call for a state of exception to restore it when compromised (Schmitt, 1988, p. 13). Given his endorsement of Hobbes' theory of political obligation, *protecto ergo obligo*, he claimed that whoever could guarantee a normal situation had to be obeyed, even if it meant obeying the Nazi authorities. The corollary is that order, no matter what kind, is always preferable to disorder, so legitimacy ends up resting on the ability to maintain it. Laclau describes the populist *plebs* as the one that challenges order, but he doesn't provide criteria to identify who can lay claim to the title of legitimate *populus*, or why. Does it refer to any collection of unfulfilled demands that coalesce in a *plebs* that challenges the institutional system, whether they want more social justice or ethnic homogeneity? Is success the measure of legitimacy? If it is, what would deter the triumphant *plebs* from treating the opposition, or at least some of it as illegitimate through an inverted image of the internal enemy of the national security doctrine advocated by the U.S. during the Cold War? For this doctrine, the armed forces are meant to combat a country's external threats, but when these arise from within as a bad part defined as Marxist political formations, the military is authorized to treat groupings of their own nationals as enemy combatants. Latin American military regimes invoked it to justify the repression of those they defined as subversives. Laclau talks of a good part authorized to overturn the institutional system because it is the legitimate *populus* but is mum about what makes it legitimate.

THE UNIFICATION OF THE *Plebs* AS AN EFFECT OF ITS IDENTIFICATION WITH A LEADER

Laclau links the role of the leader in unifying a *plebs* to naming and singularity. His starting point is that a chain of equivalence exists if one of its links condenses all the others. In situations in which the institutional system is shaken and fails to fulfill the task of keeping society together, "the name becomes the ground of the thing", to which he adds: "[A]n assemblage of heterogeneous elements kept equivalentially together only by a name is, however, necessarily a *singularity*" (Laclau, 2005a, p. 100). Singularity is whatever functions as the principle of unity of an assemblage of groups and demands.

This is the prelude to a sequence that takes him from equivalence to the name of the leader. Says Laclau: "the equivalential logic leads to singularity, and singularity to the identification of the unity of the group with the name of the leader" (Laclau, 2005a, 100). He is not referring to actual persons but to the *name* of the leader as a structural function, an empty or pure signifier of unity. Yet when he invokes two stalwarts of the Western canon to shore up this idea, he quickly shifts from the name to actual individuals. First Hobbes, for whom only an individual can really incarnate the indivisible nature of sovereignty, and then Freud, who says that "the symbolic unification of the group around an individuality [...] is inherent in the formation of a 'people'" (100). The corollary of this personalization of the principle of unity is that without a leader there can be no people and therefore no politics either. Readers of Laclau in Argentina, Bolivia, Spain, Venezuela and elsewhere took the centrality of the leader as an axiom, either when writing on populism or embarking in politics.

Those closer to Gilles Deleuze and Felix Guattari would balk at this by recalling a provocative passage in *A Thousand Plateaus*: "is a general necessary for n individuals to manage to fire in unison?" (1987, p. 17). Deleuze and Guattari say that *there can* be action in concert without a master of ceremony because they think in terms of rhizomes or systems that do not require an articulatory center. Rhizomes resemble the distributed communications systems of network theory. Some have built on this to propose the multitude, not the populist *plebs*, as the subject of emancipatory politics. Paolo Virno depicts it as "a *plurality which persists as such in the public scene*, in collective action, in the handling of communal affairs, without converging into a One, without evaporating within a centripetal form of motion. Multitude is the form of social and political existence for the many, seen as being many" (Virno, 2004, p. 21). The multitude embraces the n of the many without the $+1$ of identity found in chains of equivalence. This is how many saw the cycle of protest inaugurated in 2011 with the occupation of Tahrir Square in Egypt and followed by the Spanish *indignados* of the 15M movement, Occupy Wall Street (OWS) in the United States, #YoSoy132 in Mexico, or the Chilean protests of 2019 for a new constitution. These insurgencies refused to build their unity in the way Laclau proposes, i.e., they were not a singularity kept together through an identification with a leader.

The strong attachment to a leader is an issue even if one is not prepared to endorse the notion of multitude or succumb to the fascination of the general assemblies of OWS or 15M. This is because the leader is not only an empty signifier but also a person, so Laclau's endorsement of the Freudian "symbolic unification of the group around an individuality" (Laclau, 2005a, p. 100) must address the underside of the argument. He focuses on the mechanics of the populist mode of unification of the people without examining the objections of those who worry about walking the line between following a leader and the cult of personality. He does not discuss unedifying traits such as the infallibility of the leader, her being beyond good and evil, her role as indisputable broker among factions, the suppression of dissent in the name of the unity of the people, the belief that challenges to the leader means treason or that criticism is a virtual *casus belli*. Hugo Chávez was undoubtedly a great political leader who attempted a re-foundation of the Venezuelan republic based on social justice. Yet he kept a tight control of his movement: followers who strayed from his views were criticized and marginalized. This underside of a personalist leadership turns the populist empowerment of the *plebs* into something fragile. It lasts while people don't dispute the dictates of a leader and is often diluted with the death of the leader or her departure from power.

The problem of succession in highly personalistic systems is not trivial. The *plebs* identifies with the name of the leader, which is a signifier of unity, but we have seen that she is also an actual person. If populism mounts a challenge to the institutional system with the purpose of re-instituting it, and if the new is always born with traces of whatever forces brought it to life, then those new institutions will bear the marks of those forces, and of the leader with whom the *plebs* identify. Who can fill the shoes of whoever led the populist challenge when she's gone? Who can measure up to an institutional setting that has been made to suit its original and "natural" dweller? How to prevent the outgoing leader from maneuvering to appoint her successor, like when Chávez designated Nicolás Maduro? In Latin America strong leaders like Alberto Fujimori of Peru, Evo Morales of Bolivia, and even Chavez tried to lift constitutional limits to reelection. When this is not an option, their departure from the government (think of Rafael Correa in Ecuador and Morales, although in the case of Bolivia things turned out better than expected) puts their achievements at risk and reveals the fragility of Laclau's model of a populist construction of order.

Progressive governments are equally marred by personalism and the temptation to characterize their critics as virtual enemies of the people. Podemos in Spain is a textbook example. Pablo Iglesias and Iñigo Errejón, two of the founders of the party, took their inspiration from Laclau to build a political project around what they called the populist hypothesis. After a meteoric rise in polls and parliamentary seats, Podemos stalled and started to reduce its political footprint even being part of a center-left governing coalition. For Samuele Mazzolini and Arthus Borriello (2021, p. 13), "an excessive dependence on the leader and the presence of a vertical and centralist structure made Podemos more exposed to electoral volatility and prone to disregard the work of construction of organization and insertion in different spaces of society". Lluis de Nadal (2020) says that Secretary General Iglesias referred to himself as "signifier Pablo Iglesias" (5). He describes the vertical and personalist decision-making structure promoted by Errejón, then Podemos' organization secretary, as one with limited checks and balances to protect dissident groups and contain the concentration of decision-making in the leader (13–15). Errejón discovered the perils of this structure when he clashed with Iglesias: he was ostracized and eventually quit Podemos.

This casts doubts on whether politics-as-populism can really give rise to what Laclau calls "forms of democracy outside the liberal symbolic framework" (Laclau, 2005a, p. 167). He says nothing more about it, so readers have no way of knowing what he meant by non-liberal democracy. The worrying signs appear when one puts together the role of the leader with the claim that the people of populism are the sole legitimate *plebs*. Urbinati (2019, pp. 79–80) reminds us that then the legitimacy of other *plebs* flounders. Claude Lefort questions any symbiosis of leaders, people and power. For him democracy is a regime in which the space of power must remain empty. This is not because it entails a power vacuum but because the site of power can be occupied by anyone and none can embody it—not a person, a group, a party or a social class (Lefort, 1988, p. 17). The role Laclau assigns to the leader in politics-as-populism contradicts the emptiness of the space of power. In successful populist challenges to the status quo the leader is the architect and tenant of power in institutions that will be tailor-made for her.

Laclau does not have to conceive democracy in Lefort's terms, but his theory should not dodge the problem of personalism either. One must ask whether the democracy he associated with politics-as-populism is preferable to the liberal one, if it expands participatory mechanisms beyond elections, or even if it can be considered a priori democratic.

HEGEMONY IS POPULISM IS POLITICS

In Laclau's understanding of politics, the frontiers between hegemony, politics and populism are fuzzy. This is because he construes the subject matter of *OPR* with conceptual building blocks that are similar and often identical to those he used to develop his post-Gramscian theory of hegemony with Chantal Mouffe in *Hegemony and Socialist Strategy* (hereafter *HSS*). Both refer to articulation, difference, equivalence, frontiers, antagonism, and many other familiar terms of Laclau's vocabulary. One noticeable absence is dislocation, which in *New Reflections* functions as a central category and in *OPR* is used so sparingly that it is not even worthy of an entry in the index. If in *HSS* he tends to equate politics with hegemony, in *OPR* it is populism that blends with politics (or at least with radical politics) through the language and practice of hegemony. Populism becomes the truth of the political or the privileged road to comprehend it. I want to look at this convergence of politics-as-hegemony with politics-as-populism.

In *HSS* hegemony "is, quite simply, a political *type of relation*, a *form*, if one wishes, of politics" (Laclau & Mouffe, 1985, 139). This is a way of saying that the hegemonic form of politics has an ontic, not an ontological status. Yet in the closing lines of the book Laclau and Mouffe describe "the field of the political as the space for a game which is never "zero-sum", because the rules and the players are never fully explicit. This game, which eludes the concept, does at least have a name: hegemony" (Laclau & Mouffe, 1985, 193). The quote leaves little to the imagination: if the political is a field for a game called hegemony, then the semantic territory of politics and hegemony overlap. This might explain why Laclau is critical of a politics of the multitude. The cohesiveness of the multitude does not require, and even rejects, the chains of equivalence and the superordinate identity of hegemony. It is a mode of collective action outside the hegemonic form of politics outlined in *HSS*.

In *OPR* the argumentative sequence also takes us from a form of politics to politics proper. Laclau begins by saying that "Populism is, quite simply, a way of constructing the political" (Laclau, 2005a, p. xi). Later he adds that "populism is the royal road to understanding something about the ontological constitution of the political as such" (67), and that "by 'populism' we do not understand a *type* of movement ... but a *political logic*" (117). I will let the casual reference to "the ontological constitution of the political" pass for now to highlight that all three passages depict populism as one possibility of politics, leaving the door open for non-populist ways of constructing the political. Populism has an ontic status. Yet its distance from politics begins to shrink when one reads that "there is no political intervention which is not populistic to some extent" (Laclau, 2005a, p. 154), a claim he reiterates almost verbatim when referring approvingly to Meny and Surel's assertion that there is no politics that does not have a populist streak (Laclau, 2006b, p. 57). Populism is a component *of all* politics. Whatever distance exists between them disappears when Laclau states that populist reason, insofar as it is the very logic of construction of the people, "amounts ... to *political* reason *tout court*" (Laclau, 2005a, p. 225). At this point populism ceases to be a way of understanding the political or of constructing the people: it has become the analog of both.[1]

It might seem unreasonable to infer so much from these remarks, but Laclau reiterates the point elsewhere when he says: "If populism consists in postulating a radical alternative within the communitarian space, a choice in the crossroads on which the future of a given society hinges, does not populism become synonymous with politics? The answer can only be affirmative" (Laclau, 2005b, p. 47). Given this synonymy, one wonders why we need two words, populism and politics, to describe the same class of phenomena—primarily the construction of the people—or why Laclau chose to call his book *On Populist Reason* if the subject matter is political reason or the type of reason operating in radical variants of politics.

In *OPR* one also finds the construction of the relation between hegemony and populism as one of genus to species. Laclau does so through the rhetorical figure of catachresis, "a rhetorical displacement [occurring] whenever a literal term is substituted by a figural one" (Laclau, 2005a, p. 71). He uses catachresis as a way of naming an absent fullness—in this case, the absent fullness of community. This absence is not an empirical deficiency but a constitutive lack in the Lacanian sense of "a void in being" or "deficient being" (Laclau, 2005a, pp. 112, 116) like the one experienced whenever a demand is not met (85).

Lack and catachresis work together as two aspects of the same argument. First, if catachresis refers to "a *constitutive* blockage in language which requires naming something that is *essentially* unnameable as a condition for language functioning" (Laclau, 2005a, p. 71), then hegemony is a catachresical operation because it consists of the "operation of taking up, by a particularity, of an incommensurable universal signification" (70). The hegemonic identity resulting from this operation will be of the order of an empty signifier because the particularity in question seeks to embody a totality/universality: in a word, to embody an impossible object. Hence Laclau's paradoxical formula: fullness is unachievable yet necessary (Laclau, 2005a, pp. 70–71). And second, he describes the lack by following Joan Copjec's characterization of the Lacanian *objet petit a*: it is a partial object that elevates the external object of the drive to the dignity of the Thing (Laclau, 2005a, pp. 119–120; also, 2006a, p. 671). Laclau draws a strong conclusion from this. He says: "[I]n political terms, that is exactly what I have called a hegemonic relation: a certain particularity which assumes the role of an impossible universality", and "[T]he logic of the *objet petit a* and the hegemonic logic are not just similar: they are identical" (Laclau, 2005a, pp. 115–116; also 226). This three-fold identity results in the formula hegemony = catachresis = logic of the *objet petit a*. All three are interchangeable insofar as they are ways of dealing with a constitutive lack and producing that impossible yet necessary object, the fullness of community.

Populism replicates this scheme. Its construction of the people is catachresical because it attempts to give a name to the absent fullness of community (Laclau, 2005a, p. 85). The populist *plebs* (a part) aspires to become the sole legitimate *populus* (the whole) and handles the question of deficient being by "introducing 'ordering' where there is basic dislocation" (Laclau, 2005a, p. 122). Following Copjec's psychoanalytical narrative, the populist construction of the people elevates a partial object to the dignity of the Thing/Whole. This partial object is the good part embodied by the chosen *plebs*, which will eventually undermine political representation itself by becoming not just a *primus inter pares* but the only legitimate part.

I mentioned earlier that the specific difference that populism introduces vis-à-vis hegemony is the division of society into two camps. The purpose of this is to produce a relation of equivalence among demands and construe an antagonistic relation with those in the other camp. Thus, populism can be said to be a species of the genus hegemony, the species that calls into question the existing order with the purpose of constructing another (Laclau, 2005a, pp. 122–123). This genus has one other species, institutionalist discourse, whose essence is to maintain the status quo and functions as the target of populist politics.

Laclau's Second Thoughts About Popular Subject Positions

This reinforces the lingering suspicion that Laclau's intellectual itinerary from his first essay on populism in *Politics and Ideology* in 1977 to OPR in 2005 could be read as a continual rewriting of the theory of politics-as-hegemony or as an intellectual enterprise where populism is less a subject matter than the cognitive backdrop or even the unacknowledged instigator of his political thinking.

Laclau readers will also notice that in the interval between the publication of *HSS* and *OPR* there was a change in his position about the desirability of splitting the political arena in two. In *HSS* this is the effect of a popular subject: "We shall use the term *popular subject position* to refer to the position that is constituted on the basis of dividing the political space into two antagonistic camps; and *democratic subject position* to refer to the locus of a clearly delimited antagonism which does not divide society in that way" (Laclau & Mouffe, 1985, p. 131). Laclau and Mouffe did not generalize the explanatory validity of these struggles because they associated the popular subject position with the Third World. Advanced capitalism was dominated by democratic subject positions that multiplied the points of antagonism and prevented the dichotomous division of the field of conflict (Laclau & Mouffe, 1985, p. 131). These antagonisms arose from class divisions, as well as from gender, racial, ethnic, religious and other cleavages without aiming to split the political space in two.

This is partly because Laclau abandons the opposition between advanced and peripheral capitalism and because what *HSS* described as an unacceptable aspect of the Gramscian conception of hegemony is brought back in politics-as-populism. We see this when Laclau maintains that "populism requires the dichotomic division of society into two camps—one presenting itself as a part which claims to be the whole; that this dichotomy involves the antagonistic division of the social field; and that the popular camp presupposes, as a condition of its constitution, the construction of a global identity out of the equivalence of a plurality of social demands" (Laclau, 2005a, p. 83). He is not referring to something that happens in "specific conjunctures": he is saying that populism *requires* such division. A few pages later he reiterates this: "populism involves the division of the social scene into two camps" (Laclau, 2005a, p. 87). The division of society into two antagonistic fields, which is what popular subject positions do, is now generalized as constitutive of populism. The latter becomes the basis for an emancipatory politics that subverts the institutional order to create a new one. Laclau's theorization of politics-as-populism becomes an ad hoc revision and re-elaboration of the narrative of hegemony to adjust it to the subject matter of *OPR*. This creates a continuous slippage between populism and hegemony, and between these and politics.

Is a Crisis a Condition or an Effect of Politics-as-Populism?

Laclau portrays institutionalist discourse as "one that attempts to make the limits of the discursive formation coincide with the limits of community" (Laclau, 2005a, p. 81). It aims for a coincidence of the inscription with the inscribed, or the institution with the instituted. The instituted is the given, the site of the populist challenge and the target of its interruptive drive. In populism, a part identifies itself with the whole—the *plebs* that presents itself as the sole legitimate *populus*. It disputes the claim of institutionalist discourse of having achieved a coincidence between the discursive formation (the institution) and the community (the instituted). The populist interruption of the given would appear to confirm the constitutive role of the political. But is this really the case?

Another comparison with Rancière can be revealing. For him, political agency or, more precisely, political subjectification, consists of naming a subject to reveal a wrong and creating a community around a dispute. Politics *is* a practice of dissensus; all it requires is a mode of subjectification, "the production through a series of actions of a body and a capacity for enunciation not previously identifiable within a given field of experience, whose identification is thus part of the reconfiguration of the field of experience" (Rancière, 1998, p. 35). The de- and re-structuration the field of experience occur through subjectification, regardless of whether the given has been unsettled beforehand.

Laclau concurs with Rancière that the political is constitutive: "the political has a primary structuring role because social relations are ultimately contingent, and any prevailing articulation results from an antagonistic confrontation whose outcome is not decided beforehand" (Laclau, 2006a: 664). He reiterates this in *OPR*: populism interrupts the given by presenting itself "both as *subversive* of the existing state of things and as the starting point for a more or less radical *reconstruction* of a new order wherever the previous one has been shaken" (Laclau, 2005a, p. 177, his italics).

If the order was shaken by the subversive practice of populism, then there is no doubt that populist politics seeks to undo the given and to rebuild it. But textual evidence suggests that for Laclau a situation of disorganization is more of a prerequisite than an effect of populist politics. This is clear in his distinction between the ontological function of producing order and its ontic fulfillment. Says Laclau: "when people are confronted with radical *anomie*, the need for *some kind* of order becomes more important than the actual ontic order that brings it about" (Laclau, 2005a, p. 88). He does not explain why there is this need. He lets the evocative force of *anomie* (a breakdown of social norms, the crisis of belief systems) do the legwork of persuading us. The word conjures images of disorder like hyperinflation, lines in front of supermarkets, uncontrollable criminality, an inoperative judiciary, an incompetent political class insensitive to people's needs, corruption, ungovernability and, at the limit, being caught in the chaos of failed states.

There is a subtext behind the descriptive tone he uses to outline the relationship between *anomie* and order. First the need for order, which might simply be a criterion of practical reason. But a text that introduces the relation between *anomie* and order as part of a theory must explain why there is such need. Second, the idea of order as a psychological need, something inherent in our human nature, turns order into an ontological fetish that subverts the contingency of what it means to be human. This is because in situations of radical *anomie* "the need for *some kind* of order becomes more important than the actual ontic order that brings it about" (Laclau, 2005a, p. 88). But then the desire for order becomes a pre- and extra-discursive assumption. Order would turn out to be a necessary feature of what it means to be human, which might be true, but it is an untheorized ontological claim.

The third observation about the subtext is the absence of normative criteria. If Laclau is serious about the claim that people prefer an order regardless of the content of that order, then in principle, they are indifferent to whether that order promotes ethnic cleansing or the respect for human rights and the democratic process. Such indifference makes the theory ethically and morally suspicious and moves it away from emancipatory thought. Enrique Peruzzotti raises the question of the normative deficit in Laclau's theory by reference to the subversive role of populism. He says that for Laclau, "The creative force of populism is linked to its desire to transcend the status quo, indistinctively of the order that might result from such intervention", which ultimately leaves us with "a theory predicated on a transcendental politics that nevertheless is devoid of clear normative horizon" (Peruzzotti, 2019, p. 40). And again: "If the theory cannot account for the normative and institutional order to which a populist intervention gives rise, how can its democratic status be defended?" (Peruzzotti, 2017, p. 218). I think that Peruzzotti is right on both counts.

This again brings Laclau's arguments closer to Schmitt's, as we saw in the analogy between decisionism and the formalistic assumptions about the legitimacy of the *plebs*. Both take for granted the goodness of order. Yet Schmitt saw crises as signs of danger to the existing order and proposed the state of exception to restore a threatened status quo. Laclau, in contrast, *welcomes* crises or moments of radical *anomie* because they are an opportunity for a populist mobilization: crises, as situations in which the community has been shaken, are conditions of possibility for the occurrence of populist challenges to the institutional order.

The role of *anomie* resurfaces when Laclau states that "some degree of crisis in the old structure is a necessary precondition of populism" (Laclau, 2005a, p. 177) and *contrario* sensu, "when we have a highly institutionalized society, equivalential logics have less terrain on which to operate; as a result, populist rhetoric becomes a commodity lacking any sort of hegemonic depth" (Laclau, 2005a, p. 191). He is quite explicit about a crisis being a precondition of populism: when the institutional order is successful, populism is reduced to "a commodity lacking any sort of hegemonic depth". He considers this as a virtual axiom: equivalential logics cannot flourish unless there is some de-institutionalization that unsettles the old order. Without such disturbance, populism cannot rise above "petty demagoguery" (Laclau, 2005a, p. 191). The conclusion is that critical junctures are windows of opportunity for developing a relation of equivalence among unsatisfied demands, and thus for the emergence of populism.

The link between crisis and populism is recurrent in the literature. Margaret Canovan (1999) speaks of how the widening of the gap between pragmatic and redemptive politics increases the chances of success of populism. There is also a host of writers who see populism as a response to the breakdown of political representation (Weyland, 2018), to a social and political crisis (Levitsky & Loxton, 2018), to the failure of public policies due to the incompetence of elites (Hawkins, 2018), or as a politics of the extraordinary (de la Torre, 2016). Anomalous situations create a fertile terrain for political impresarios to mount a challenge.

So Laclau is not alone with respect to the role of crises. I can sympathize with his argument, but it is difficult to argue that politics-as-populism has a constitutive force—that it subverts and reconstructs the given—and at the same time claim that populist interventions are dependent on a prior crisis of the existing order. This dependency subordinates the political to critical junctures and renders its status derivative instead of constitutive. One might object by saying that this problem is more imaginary than real, for in politics some conditions are more propitious than others for the success of an endeavor. This is true, and it would be absurd to deny it. But the facticity of unsatisfied demands says nothing about the strength of the institutional system, and Laclau is not describing a populist practice: he is assembling a theory of politics-as-populism. If politics has a structuring role, then it must aim to trigger a de-institutionalization of the given instead of hoping for a crisis to generate its subversive effects.

For Rancière there are no preconditions. Those who embark in politics disidentify themselves from their subordinate place and begin to act as equals to others even though they are still the part that has no part. Subjectivization is a practice that aims to modify the institutional system, with or without a previous crisis. It is what people have always done to change the status quo, whether the African National Congress' efforts to dismantle apartheid or the Chileans who fought for a constitution. They looked for favorable circumstances, but did not wait to find cracks in the system to mount their challenges. In Laclau's theory of populism, if the political remains subservient to the opportunities opened by de-institutionalization—whose emergence he does not explain but simply depicts as something that happens—then it cannot have the primary structuring role that he assigns to it.

This requisite of a previous crisis exposes him to the kind of criticism he and Mouffe made of the Second International in *HSS*. There they argued that by the time Marxism had become a dogmatic theory, the International's belief in laws of history led it to privilege a logic of necessity at the expense of the contingency that characterizes political action. Socialist politics languished by subordinating the opportunity for radical change to the arrival of objective conditions specified by the doctrine (Laclau & Mouffe, 1985, pp. 20–26). We can say something similar about Laclau: his politics-as-populism cannot prosper without a previous crisis in the institutional system. One would have to wait for systemic *anomie* before embarking in radical politics, in which case populism becomes a reactive or parasitic politics, even an opportunist one, feeding off a prior crisis in the institutional system that is its condition of possibility. This contradicts Laclau's efforts to make populism a proactive politics.

Do All Politics Require Demands?

We have seen that Laclau understands a demand in the sense of a request and a claim, and that for populism it means the latter. He also distinguishes between democratic or intra-systemic demands, which can be solved by means of transformism, and social demands, which question the institutional system when left unsatisfied (Laclau, 2005a, p. 73). The latter are his minimal unit of analysis for populism and politics (74, 127). Readers of Laclau take this to be self-evident: if people mobilize without saying what they want, why call them protesters and not simply revelers, performance artists or whatever? Because this is not as obvious as it seems. The criterion of unsatisfied demands prevents us from describing the insurgencies of the Spanish *indignados* and Occupy Wall Street as political. Yet we do, and they are. Participants talked about real democracy, wanted to get rid of corrupt politicians that did not represent them, called themselves the 99%, and invoked another way of being together without really defining what they meant by such things. What motivated people to participate in those protests was their unhappiness with the existing state of things, not the system's inability to satisfy a non-existing list of demands.

Manuel Castells understood this when he said that the strength of protests like OWS was that "the movement demanded everything and nothing at the same time" because they were mobilizations for which the very idea of negotiating points was not applicable (Castells, 2012, p. 185). OWS expressed a desire for something different to come, but was not a platform for channeling unsatisfied demands, at least not at first. Many politicians and commentators criticized it for this, but OWS "was popular and attractive to many precisely because it remained open to all kinds of proposals and did not present specific policy positions" (Castells, 2012, p. 185). Something similar happened with the Spanish *indignados*. They did not have a program because the radical transformation of society would not arise from programmatic objectives but from the experiences of its actors (Castells, 2012, pp. 143–144).

Having formulated demands might strengthen a mobilization, but their absence is not an impediment for politics, especially radical politics that seeks to change the world. Is this not what Laclau expects from populist politics? Subverting and changing how we relate to one another is the core of emancipatory politics. OWS and the *indignados* sought this *without* formulating social demands: their dissatisfaction did not fit in a list of demands. To borrow a line from Marina Sitrin (2014), these insurgencies had goals without demands.

Slavoj Žižek moves this critique in a different direction by saying that demands are not a prelude for a radical transformation but a sign of conventional politics "The term *demand* involves a whole theatrical scene in which a subject is addressing his demand to an Other presupposed to be able to meet it. Does the proper revolutionary or emancipatory political act not move beyond this horizon of demands? The revolutionary subject no longer operates at the level of demanding something from those in power; he wants to destroy them" (Žižek, 2006, p. 558). This means that a (populist) politics built around social demands, regardless of whether these are satisfied or not, involves a relationship of interlocution between recognized parties within the institutional system.

Followers of Laclau may ask if there can be a radical politics that is *not* contaminated by the order it seeks to change. They would be right, of course: a relation of pure exteriority with whatever one opposes is metaphysics, not politics. The *plebs* that challenges the institutional system is always born with traces of that system, and this does not make it a mere internal effect of the system. But Žižek's point is not about exteriority versus interiority. He is simply using Laclau's premises to argue that a politics based on mutually recognized interlocutors undermines the radicalism of the subversive and reconstructive aims of populism. If the *plebs* make demands to the institutional order, it does not really matter whether these are satisfied or not: demanding already blunts the edge of radical politics.

FROM A VAGUE SENSE OF SOLIDARITY TO STABLE IDENTITIES

Laclau says that one of the structural preconditions for populism is "the unification of these various demands—whose equivalence, up to that point, had not gone beyond a feeling of vague solidarity—into a stable system of signification" (Laclau, 2005a, p. 74). He reiterates this a few pages later by speaking of "the consolidation of the equivalential chain through the construction of a popular identity which is something qualitatively more than the simple summation of the equivalential links" (Laclau, 2005a, p. 77).

Let us examine this passage from a feeling of vague solidarity to a stable system of signification that turns popular identity into something that is qualitatively more than a sum of the intervening links. The latter resonates with the structuralist claim that the whole is more than the sum of its parts. Like in his theory of hegemony, the constitution of the popular camp involves the creation of a superordinate identity shared by the groups and demands that partake in a chain of equivalence. We take for granted that difference and equivalence intermingle and that no equivalence ever manages to efface the differential element of the participating demands. Laclau also warns us that his narrative of populism unfolds in two stages and that the simplifying assumptions about empty signifiers recede once his fully fledged theory of populism is in place. This happens when floating signifiers and something like a Gramscian war of position starts to destabilize the neatness of antagonistic frontiers.

What he does not mention is how stable must a system of signification be in order to speak of a proper popular identity, or how to know if we have met this condition of stability. There is a similar silence about a popular identity which is "qualitatively more" than the sum of its links. When is it licit to say that the passage to a qualitatively different form of solidarity has occurred? We might want to respond by using Laclau's fuzzy qualifiers, like "more or less" (Laclau, 2005a, p. 177) and "beyond a certain point" (162, 200), but this is an ad hoc solution to circumvent these issues, not to settle them.

The absence of arguments to support the distinction blurs the line that separates Michael Hardt and Antonio Negri's multitude from the chain of equivalence among unsatisfied demands required for the populist construction of the people.[2] Laclau's criticism of the theory and politics of the multitude would then become less credible as the people would resemble the singularities of the multitude. He might have responded that there cannot be a convergence of the multitude and equivalence because Negri and other theorists insist on immanence, and thus sacrifice the moment of negativity characteristic of politics (Laclau, 2001). Chains of equivalence do not operate through immanence due to an antagonism that separates an "us" from an adversarial "them" seen as an obstacle and negation of our identity. Be it as it may, we have no way to assess the passage from a vague feeling of solidarity to a stable popular identity.

Laclau's Self-Referential Bias

Žižek suggests there is some circularity in Laclau's reasoning: "For Laclau, in a nice case of self-reference, the very logic of hegemonic articulation applies also to the conceptual opposition between populism and politics: populism is the Lacanian *objet petit a* of politics, the particular figure which stands for the universal dimension of the political, which is why it is the royal road to understanding the political" (Žižek, 2006, p. 553). Hegemony becomes the bridge between populism and politics and the device Laclau uses to turn populism into the analog of politics.

Self-referentiality often comes with the territory of academic success. Yet it is difficult to dismiss the problem altogether. When he assesses Yves Surel and Andreas Schedler's work on populism Laclau is sympathetic to what they say but claims that the system of alternatives they propose is too narrow. This is because their theory emphasizes the subversive aspects of populism at the expense of the task of reconstructing an order, and because their arguments are limited to populist experiences in Western Europe. What Laclau means by a wider system of alternatives is his own theory.

Take his brief discussion of General Georges Boulanger's failed populist project in nineteenth-century France. Laclau begins by outlining the four politico-ideological features of Boulangism. These are: the aggregation of heterogeneous forces and demands that exceed the institutional system, the equivalential link between these demands by virtue of sharing the same enemy, the crystallization of this chain around the empty signifier "Boulanger", and the reduction of "Boulanger" to a name that grounds the unity of the object (Laclau, 2005a, pp. 180–181). The language he uses to spell out the experience of Boulangism (chain of equivalence, empty signifier, a name that founds the unity of the group) is the one of his theory of populism outlined in previous pages. It is no surprise, then, that Laclau concludes that the four characteristics of Boulangism "reproduce, almost point by point, the defining dimensions of populism which we have established in the theoretical part of this book" (Laclau, 2005a, p. 181).

Laclau reinforces this "almost point by point" when contrasting the populism of Boulanger with the one of Italy's Silvio Berlusconi. He says that the latter could act with some ambivalence, operating within the institutional order while using populist language as a political tool. Boulanger, however, could not afford to simply subvert the existing order. He had to try to create a new one because he was being pushed out of the institutional system, and for this he had to seize the Élysée Palace, something he did not dare to do (Laclau, 2005a, p. 180). The argumentative sequence is classical Laclau: he outlines a theoretical framework, introduces an example using the categories he proposed earlier, and draws consequences from the example that match "almost point by point" what his theory had already predicted.

A More Cautious Reception of OPR

Like Canovan and others, Laclau wanted to avoid casting populism as the mere opportunism of demagogues who promise heaven and earth to their followers. His readers welcomed the conceptual apparatus of OPR that weaved hegemony, empty signifiers, *objet petit a*, the people and so on into a narrative about populism as a solid tool to understand radical politics and assemble a Left alternative. I have tried to show that his theory can also blind us to the dangers of a politics that splits society into two antagonistic camps and builds the cohesion of a movement around the singularity of a name. The latter is not only an empty signifier of unity but also the name of a strong leader.

I do not say this out of an antipolitical celebration of consensus. Strife is inevitable in projects of radical change, as these will face resistance from those weary of losing privileges derived from economic power, positions of authority, the color of their skin, family connections and so on. My reservations have to do with tensions in his theory. I mentioned that a politics founded on demands leaves many insurgencies outside the realm of politics, and the requirement of crises as a precondition for change undercuts the constitutive role Laclau assigns to politics. I also referred to the underside of the theory: taking the populist *plebs* as the only legitimate *populus*, splitting society into two antagonistic camps and focusing so much on a leader is likely to have a bearing on the practices, laws and institutions of a winning coalition. The narrative of populism he proposes can then mutate from an emancipatory project to something more ominous through a permanent creation of enemies that entrenches the new leadership and puts critics under suspicion of treason.

Borrowing a trope from Walter Benjamin's negative utopia, one must be prepared to pull the emergency brakes of the locomotive of politics-as-populism when instead of the promised land it heads towards the abyss.

NOTES

1. Laclau is aware of the distinction between politics and the political but often uses them interchangeably, and so do I.
2. This last point was suggested to me by Guillermo Pereyra in a conversation about multitude and the "people" of populism.

LITERATURE

Canovan, M. (1999). Trust the people! Populism and the two faces of democracy. *Political Studies, 47*(1), 2–16.

Castells, M. (2012). *Networks of outrage and hope: Social movements in the internet age*. Polity.

Deleuze, G., & Guattari, F. (1987). *A thousand plateaus*. The Athlone Press.

de la Torre, C. (2016). Populism and the politics of the extraordinary in Latin America. *Journal of Political Ideologies, 21*(2), 121–139.

de Nadal, L. (2020). On populism and social movements: From the Indignados to Podemos. *Social Movement Studies*. https://doi.org/10.1080/14742837.2020.1722626.

Hawkins, K. (2018). The ideational approach. In C. de la Torre (Ed.), *Routledge handbook of global populism* (pp. 57–71).

Lacan, J. (1977). The mirror stage as formative of the *I* function. *Ecrits* (pp. 1–7). W. W. Norton.

Laclau, E. (1977). *Politics and ideology in Marxist Theory*. New Left Books.

Laclau, E. (1990). *New reflections on the revolution of our time*. Verso.

Laclau, E. (2001). Can immanence explain social struggles? *Diacritics, 31*(4), 3–10.

Laclau, E. (2005a). *On populist reason*. Verso.

Laclau, E. (2005b). Populism: What's in a name? In F Panizza (Ed.), *Populism and the mirror of democracy* (pp. 32–49). Verso.

Laclau, E. (2006a). Why constructing a people is the main task of radical politics. *Critical Inquiry, 32*, 646–680.

Laclau, E. (2006b). La deriva populista y la centroizquierda latinoamericana. *Nueva Sociedad, 205*, 56–61.

Laclau, E., & Mouffe, C. (1985). *Hegemony and socialist strategy*. Verso.

Lefort, C. (1988). The question of democracy. In *The political forms of modern democracy* (pp. 9–20). Polity.

Levitsky, S., & Loxton, J. (2018). Populism and competitive authoritarianism in Latin America. In C. de la Torre (Ed.), *Routledge handbook of global populism* (pp. 334–350).

Mazzolini, S., & Borriello, A. (2021). The normalization of left populism? The paradigmatic case of Podemos. *European Politics and Society*. https://doi.org/10.1080/23745118.2020.1868849.

Peruzzotti, E. (2017). El populismo como ejercicio de poder gubernamental y la amenaza de hibridación de la democracia liberal. *Revista SAAP, 11*(2), 213–225.

Peruzzotti, E. (2019). Laclau's theory of populism. A critical review. In C. de la Torre (Ed.), *Routledge handbook of global populism* (pp. 33–43).

Rancière, J. (1992). Politics, identification, and subjectivization. *October, 61*, 58–64.

Rancière, J. (1998). *Disagreement: Politics and philosophy*. The University of Minnesota Press.

Rancière, J. (2010). Ten theses on politics. In S. Corcoran (Ed.), *Dissensus. On politics and aesthetics* (pp. 27–44). Continuum.

Schmitt, C. (1988 [1922]). *Political theology: Four chapters on the concept of sovereignty* (G. Schwab, trans.). MIT Press

Sitrin, M. (2014). Goals without demands: The new movements for real democracy. *South Atlantic Quarterly, 113*(2), 245–258.

Urbinati, N. (2019). Antiestablishment and the substitution of the whole with one of its parts. In C. de la Torre (Ed.), *Routledge handbook of global populism* (pp. 77–97).

Virno, P. (2004). *A grammar of the multitude*. Semiotext(e).

Weyland, K. (2018). Populism and authoritarianism. In C. de la Torre (Ed.), *Routledge handbook of global populism* (pp. 319–333).

Žižek, S. (2006). Against the populist temptation. *Critical Inquiry, 32*, 551–574.

CHAPTER 4

"An Antipodean Populism? Winston Peters, New Zealand First, and the Problems of Misclassification"

David B. MacDonald

Introduction

This chapter problematizes claims by Cas Mudde and Cristóbal Rovira Kaltwasser (2017) and Benjamin Moffitt (2017) that there is a coherent "Antipodean populism" in which Pauline Hanson's One Nation (ON) and Winston Peters' New Zealand First (NZF) can be paralleled in terms of a range of characteristics, which collectively distinguish them from their populist counterparts in Western Europe or the Americas.

The primary focus here is on NZF rather than ON. I critique Moffitt's paralleling of the two parties based on his "three enemies argument," which sees Antipodean populism as being anti-elitist, anti-immigrant, and anti-Indigenous. My analysis is aimed less at Moffitt's presentation of Australia, but on his deployment of a Hanson-centric lens to interpret the policies and motivations of NZF. I divide this chapter into four sections. First, I provide an overview of how populism has been defined, before then turning to an analysis of how Moffitt advances a distinct Antipodean form of populism. Second, I follow this with a brief discussion of NZ's settler context before moving in the third part to a brief discussion of how Hanson's ON ably adheres to Moffitt's understanding of the Antipodean style. In the final, I focus on Peters and the NZF. I note that on the surface, Moffitt's triple enemy approach would seem

D. B. MacDonald (✉)
College of Social and Applied Human Science, University of Guelph, Guelph, ON, Canada
e-mail: dmacdo03@uoguelph.ca

to apply to NZF, with its focus on anti-elitism, criticism of high immigration, and critique of supposed favoritism for Indigenous Maori.

However, using a more critical lens, I argue that Moffitt's approach ignores the settler nature of New Zealand society and the growing development of a bicultural ethos over the past four decades. Because of this misclassification, Moffitt largely ignores that Peters focuses on delivering benefits to Maori as a key part of his political platform. Even his anti-immigration stance parallels some debates within Maori communities, while also displaying notable differences. Further, as an insider to Indigenous politics in contradistinction to Hanson's outsider status, Peters' critique is qualitatively different and is interpreted in a different way by both Maori and immigrant communities alike because he is part Maori and has many Maori MPs in his caucus. Finally, as someone who has served in government on four occasions, Peters and his party have toned down their populism when in office, enhancing the theory that populism is a style that can be performed or not performed, as the occasion requires.

An Antipodean Populism?

Populism has recently been described as a mode of representation, as Moffitt puts it, "a political style that is performed, embodied and enacted across a variety of political and cultural contexts" (2016, p. 4). Despite regional and other differences in populism, populist parties often (although not always) share certain characteristics. One commonality is a discourse of society divided between a pure and moral people possessed of some form of authenticity, facing an out of touch, corrupted elite (Mudde, 2017). Populists aim to channel this authenticity and speak truth to power, bringing about positive change on behalf of the people (Canovan, 1999, pp. 2–3). A charismatic leader can bring success to populist parties (Mudde & Kaltwasser, 2017, p. 43), seeking to "establish emotional connectivity with the audience" and securing the party's electoral prospects on this basis (Lavin, 2017).

On the social conservative right, some populist parties within European or Western settler states target ethnic minorities and/or Indigenous peoples, claiming to speak for a silent majority, by breaking taboos, denouncing identity politics, and political correctness (Grevin, 2016, p. 1). Populist leaders can also bring followers together around what has been called "the solidarity of the dirty secret," reframing aspects of the mainstream political agenda by plainly stating what "we all secretly think but feel guilty about" (Panizza, 2005, p. 27).

Comparative work on populism between Australia and New Zealand is in its infancy, which is surprising considering that both One Nation and New Zealand First are several decades old. In their recent *Oxford Handbook of Populism*, Mudde and Kaltwasser identify a "clear" form of Antipodean populism common to both ON and NZF. Both parties are seen to be "right-wing populist parties," and "very similar to the parties of that period in western Europe." Both are seen to develop from a common base of "growing frustration with increased immigration and with neoliberal welfare state reforms." The difference lies in the base constituency, with ON defending the "interests of the descendent of the white settlers," while being "critical of the indigenous Aboriginals," where by contrast, "NZF presents itself primarily as the voice of the indigenous Maori people" (Mudde & Kaltwasser, 2017, p. 38).

These different support bases, however, merit little further discussion in their analysis, and virtually none in Moffitt's work in the same volume, which seeks to align these two parties as closely as possible, highlighting similarities while downplaying differences. In his identification of an Antipodean populism, Moffitt deploys ON as the lens through which to approach NZF. Both parties, he argues, exhibit a clear "regional subtype of populism," which "mixes the general ethno-exclusivism and nativism of Western European populism with the more producerist and protectionist aspects of North American populism" (Moffitt, 2017, p. 130).

What also makes this Antipodean style unique is its positioning against a "triple enemy," comprised of elites, immigrant "others" and Indigenous Peoples. The elite as enemy includes the typical stock targets of populist attention: politicians, bankers, the media, academics, and urban professionals. Elites are strongly associated with globalization and are thus seen as economic and cultural threats to an authentic people. The second enemy is the "figure of the immigrant Other," first Asians, then followed more recently by Muslims (Moffitt, 2017, p. 133).

Anti-Indigenous sentiments form the third aspect of this focus, with Moffitt claiming that this "is where antipodean populists truly differ from their European counterparts." Here, both Hanson and Peters attack programs for Indigenous peoples as "forms of 'reverse racism' and 'preferential treatment' that discriminate against non-native Australians and New Zealanders." Both leaders rail against similar threats: an "Aboriginal industry" in Australia or a "Treaty Grievance Industry" in New Zealand (Moffitt, 2017, p. 133). In a larger context, both Hanson and Peters are lumped together with each other as well as with Western European populisms in terms of being "generally located on the right side of the ideological spectrum." Both leaders as well, "broadly fit the mold of the anti-immigrant radical right populists of Western Europe" (Moffitt, 2017, p. 134).

Moffitt does note several caveats about Peters—that he is "of Maori heritage" which complicates his "attacks against pro-Māori policies and the Treaty of Waitangi settlement process" (2017, p. 128). How this might "complicate" his critique is not explained, and seems largely irrelevant to his dyadic comparison. Further, Peters sells his policy "in a smoother package," and "his tone is not outrageous," nor "particularly coarse," but expresses "a tendency to go 'straight for the jugular' in a sardonic and exasperated manner" (Moffitt, 2017, p. 129). Why is Peters more successful electorally than Hanson? Moffitt avers that this is reducible to New Zealand's Mixed Member Proportional electoral system as well as some differences in Peters' style, but not content (Moffitt, 2017, p. 130).

THE SETTLER COLONIAL CONTEXT OF AOTEAROA NEW ZEALAND

In what follows I offer a comparison of Hanson and Peters and their respective parties along the lines sketched out by Moffitt, arguing that while Moffitt is relatively accurate in his analysis of Hanson, he is on weaker ground with Peters. This is so in part because Peters and his party have strong Indigenous elements, with many Maori MPs. Their concerns as *tangata whenua* (people of the land) are of a qualitatively different order than those of white settlers militating against immigrants of color and Indigenous peoples. While some aspects of the discourse are comparable, the context and significance of the discourses are different. Moffitt briefly but inadequately acknowledges settler colonialism in both countries, yet does not operationalize this as a key lens through which to draw distinctions. Settler colonialism, however, is not incidental, nor are the clear differences between a relatively monocultural society like Australia with a veneer of multiculturalism (Hage, 2006), and an (albeit imperfect and imbalanced) Indigenous-settler bicultural society like New Zealand, mediated through an evolving treaty relationship which sees the Maori-Pakeha (Indigenous-settler) relationship as crucial to national identity. A key distinction between these settler states lies in the divergent social experiments of the 1970s; in Australia, forms of multiculturalism were pursued while NZ saw the development of an official biculturalism. Both societies moved from an overt and very public white monoculture to views of the nation that were more open to change (Smits, 2011, p. 88).

These political trajectories can in part be explained by the different demographic, social, and legal histories. NZ was settled much later than Australia, and the relationship between Maori and Pakeha would be embedded in the 1840 Treaty of Waitangi, which was supposed to guarantee power-sharing and co-governance (working group on constitutional transformation, 2016; Jones, 2016). This was in part reflected Maori numerical and military superiority at the time, a situation which changed over the nineteenth century, as Maori lost most of their land, their political and economic power, and their demographic majority.[1]

This dynamic began to shift in the 1970s and 1980s, and de facto forms of biculturalism grew out of Māori protest. A Maori renaissance was epitomized through such signposts as the 1975 Waitangi Tribunal to settle breaches to the Treaty, and the introduction of Te Reo Māori as an official language in 1987. Māori educational systems were promoted, there was widespread introduction of Māori names for institutions, and a reinvigoration of Māori culture. This was accompanied by Crown settlements to Māori iwi (tribal nations) wronged by breaches of the Treaty.

Since the 1980s, Māori have achieved parliamentary representation higher than their percentage of the overall population. In the 2017 elections, 28 Māori MPs were elected in a House of 120: eight from the National Party, thirteen from the Labour Party (including all seven Maori seats), five from New Zealand First, one from the Green Party, and one from the ACT Party. This is a rate of 23% Indigenous representation (Koti, 2017). In the October 2020 election, the rate was similar.

Changes since the 1980s have resulted in a rise of symbolic biculturalism and a Māori resurgence. This has also been accompanied by numerous settlements for iwi (roughly 1–2% of the value of what was taken), which have helped generate a growing Māori economy worth $50 billion annually investing in housing, dairy, fishing, forestry, geothermal energy and many other areas (McNicol, 2017).

This is a different context from what Hanson is describing in her policies and speeches, because Indigenous peoples do not have any access to political power—there are no seats in Parliament, no Treaty, no myths or institutional structures of biculturalism. Sarah Maddison thus notes that "Australia's parliaments remain fundamentally white institutions", where Indigenous peoples are poorly represented (2010, p. 664). In the most recent elections, only five Indigenous people were elected at the federal level (Gobbett, 2017).

Australia is rarely seen as an Indigenous-settler bicultural society and does not embed Indigenous ways of being and knowing as foundational to the nation and its political culture. Indeed, some present Australia as marked by a "culture of disrespect" that freezes out Indigenous worldviews, values, legal and governance traditions, and "results in legislation and policy that operates to deny Indigenous rights" (Hobbs, 2018, pp. 176–177). Talk of constitutional and other reforms in Australia rarely addresses the loss of Indigenous sovereignty as a result of colonization, and reconciliation talk is often framed in terms of national unity, not Indigenous rights (Maddison, 2017, pp. 4–5). The bar is comparatively low for Indigenous issues in Australia, so to compare abstract discourse from two different parties is to decontextualize any comparative study.

Moffitt's Model and Pauline Hanson

Formed in 1996 by a former Liberal MP Pauline Hanson, One Nation has seen electoral success in Senate and state elections (Queensland, New South Wales and Western Australia), notably with Hanson being elected to the Senate in 2016. Hanson began her populist career by tilting against a "danger of being swamped by Asians," stoking fears that "the yellow race will rule the world" (Aly & Walker, 2007, p. 205). Her anti-Aboriginal sentiments tapped into a wellspring of negative views disguised under a mantra of combating "reverse racism" and "preferential treatment" (Deutchman, 2000, pp. 58–60). At the 2018 Commonwealth games, Hanson derided the Aboriginal content of the ceremonies as "disgusting," and declared herself Indigenous for having been born in Australia (Bickers, 2018). Islamophobia is perhaps her most obvious feature, with her latest book (2018) depicting Hanson gleefully disrobing from a black burqa on the Senate floor. Recent policies now include "A Government inquiry or Royal Commission into Islam" to see if it is an ideology in disguise and opposition to "Further Muslim immigration" (One Nation, 2018).

Hanson has sought to portray herself as an authentic socially conservative (white settler) Australian, and race and color go unremarked in her discourse, other than as a backdrop for her claims that everyone should live under the same law and abide by the same rules (McSwiney & Cottle, 2017, p. 91). Hanson's rhetoric also evokes comparisons with former Alaskan governor Sarah Palin, in their myths of the settler frontier, marked by hard work, community spirit and rugged individualism, and opposed to the establishment, identity politics, and political correctness (Mason, 2010, pp. 188–189).

Overall, Moffitt's analysis of Hanson is consistent with much of the academic material, highlighting her anti-elitism, her critique of globalization, her staunch anti-Muslim and anti-Asian rhetoric, her attacks on political correctness and any sort of recognition or rights for Aboriginal peoples (Goot, 2005, p. 112).

Moffitt's Model and Peters

Wynston Raymond Peters was born in 1945, the sixth of eleven children, and raised by a Maori father and a Scottish mother. As a Maori from rural Northland, Peters overcame considerable structural racism and poverty, eventually standing for election for the center-right National Party. Peters was first elected to Parliament in 1979, lost his seat in 1981, and returned in 1984, with a safer seat that he would keep as a National, independent, and New Zealand First MP until 2005 (Gustafson, 2006, p. 63).

NZF was formed in 1992 after Peters fell afoul of National over its economic shift to the right. From 1984, economic reforms under the Labour Party moved NZ from a highly regulated and protectionist economy to one of the most open and market-oriented in the world, with major cuts to protection for domestic industry. This strengthened the overall prospects for the economy but led to a massive decline in manufacturing, while property prices soared and the gap between rich and poor rose exponentially (Smith, 2005, p. 181). Peters publicly stood against the selling of state assets, the increase in foreign investment, and the changing nature of immigration, which shifted from privileging Europeans to a points system which increased the number of Asian immigrants (Liu & Mills, 2006, pp. 87–88).

In 1992, Peters broke ranks with his party over their support for neoliberalism and was dismissed from caucus, forming his own party soon after. NZF has since enjoyed a level of electoral success that has eluded ON. NZF has polled between 4 and 13.3% of the popular vote since 1993 and has only been out of Parliament between 2008 and 2011. Three times they have been involved in governing the country, through a coalition with National in 1996–1998; a confidence and supply agreement with Labour in 2005 and a coalition with Labour in 2017. This has been beneficial to Peters, who has secured numerous cabinet positions including in the most recent coalition: Deputy Prime Minister, Foreign Affairs, State-Owned Enterprises, Racing, Minister for Disarmament and Arms Control, and acting Prime Minister in 2019. Others within the party have also gained cabinet level positions including Defense, Infrastructure, and Internal Affairs.

Policies: Peters and Hanson

On the surface, some aspects of NZF's platform appear similar to ON. Peters has typically described the party promoting "the very traditional New Zealand values that once saw this great country among the world's leaders—hard work, fair pay, valuing our citizenship and building a sense of community" (Peters, 2010). Nostalgia for a mythical golden age of community and prosperity formed a central part of the party's campaign message in 2017: to "change New Zealand back to the way it used to perform" (Peters, 2017a). Like ON, anti-elitism has always been a staple of NZF discourse, particularly surrounding globalization and the selling of state assets to government supporters and foreign elites. The National government was a particular focus of attack in the last election and stood accused of "always put[ting] the short-term profits and greed of its cronies ahead of the interests of New Zealanders as a whole" (Peters, 2017b).

Peters has also denounced political correctness, lamenting how hypersensitivity, claims of offense and hurt feeling by "the 'PC brigade'" have stifled meaningful debate on immigration and Indigenous issues. Elites have taken the lion's share of the blame, whether they be bureaucratic "shiny bums" in Wellington or corporate-oriented "latte sippers in Auckland," those who think themselves better than rural, middle class, and blue collar voters (Peters, 2017b).

Moffitt's Model and Maori Issues

Moffitt notes of Peters: "heritage does not necessarily equal empathy," and "while Peters is of Māori heritage, he has been one of New Zealand's most prominent critics of Māori 'special treatment'" (Moffitt, 2017, p. 133). This quick dismissal of Peters' allows Moffitt to draw close parallels between NZF and ON. On the surface, it may appear like such comparisons are justified. For example, Peters has consistently attacked what he sees as government handouts to Maori on the basis of ethnicity and overcompensation for Treaty grievances. Peters however largely focuses his attacks on Maori elites rather than Maori people themselves, what he has called a "Maori grievance industry" (TVNZ, 2002), or "a burgeoning treaty industry preoccupied with an elite group of Maori who have secured their own futures while the great majority of Maori continue to struggle" (Radio Live, 2017). Indeed, he sees the Maori people as one of the people who are suffering from elite corruption and foreign interference. This is a very different positioning from that of Hanson.

NZF's critique of neoliberalism and the rise of Maori elites has some basis in fact, although there is also distortion here. Maori and Pacifika people were disproportionately affected with manufacturing job losses when free trade with Asian countries was introduced in the late 2000s. Māori unemployment as well as the percentage of Māori living below the poverty line rose significantly. Similarly, access to housing plummeted (Poata-Smith, 2013, pp. 150–155).

While this would seem to buttress Peters' condemnation of a supposed "grievance industry", contra Peters, Poata-Smith notes a clear double standard when evaluating Maori versus Pakeha companies. Treaty settlements represent only a small percentage of the value of land and resources stolen by the state, and the settlement process forces them to play by settler rules, and effectively "locks Maori self-determination into a free-market, capitalist economic framework" (Poata-Smith, 2013, pp. 155–156). And yet while economic reforms have grown some iwi capital bases, they have also created unreasonable expectations that iwi should be funding basic health, welfare, and education for their iwi members, something well beyond their financial capacity (Poata-Smith, 2013, p. 157). This is the larger context within which Peters operates—one where neoliberalism has resulted in specific problems for Maori which his party seeks to address.

Moffitt's Model and Immigration

Is Peters comparable to Hanson in his xenophobic stance against non-European immigration? At a surface level, this may seem to be the case. After all, Peters has maintained anti-Chinese rhetoric for well over two decades, as it has played well with his many Pakeha supporters. One of his signature policy demands (although never applied in practice) has been to reduce annual immigration to a 10,000-person maximum (Wong & Ritchie, 2017). This rhetoric began in 1996, when Peters campaigned on the fear that NZ was becoming "a paradise for foreign take-over merchants" (Gustafson, 2006, p. 63). In 2005, the NZF, in a press release entitled "New Zealand—The Last Asian Colony" warned that "Maori will be disturbed to know that in 17 years' time they will be outnumbered by Asians".

Islamophobia has not played a major role in NZF's policy making nor in its electoral appeal although Peters is no stranger to this brand of xenophobic politics. Peters has historically drawn contrasts between peaceful and tolerant traditions of western democracy and the "anti-Semitic, anti-Christian, and anti-gay (...) intolerance" of fundamentalist Islam (Myles, 2016, pp. 144–145). Islamophobia reached a crescendo after the 2005 London terrorist bombings. In an infamous speech, Peters warned that NZ's culture of tolerance was under threat from "radical Islam," from "fanatics for whom that tradition is alien." Peters also cautioned that within moderate Muslim communities was "a militant underbelly," and indeed both "moderate and militant, fit hand and glove," both being part of "the agenda is to promote fundamentalist Islam" (Peters, 2005a). Views such as this did not prevent Peters from becoming foreign minister in 2008 and again in 2017, and his Islamophobia has declined since that time, perhaps since Islamic countries are key consumers of NZ lamb and dairy products. Unlike ON, NZF's anti-Islamic sentiments are inconsistent and have been primarily reactionary—xenophobic characterizations of Islam after terror attacks involving Muslims.

Throughout his career, Peters has denied that NZF is a racist party or has ever promoted racist immigration policies, arguing instead that the issue has always been about numbers and the ability of the economy to sustain them (Peters, 2002). As foreign minister he has also overseen a dramatic increase in trade with China and his line appears to have softened in many ways. By late 2017, he went so far as to chide critics of China's human rights, instead focusing on the ability of the Chinese economy to lift millions out of poverty and urged western commentators to focus on these achievements instead of "constantly harping on about the romance of 'freedom'" (Cooke, 2017).

PETERS AND INSIDER POLITICS

Peters' xenophobic and anti-Treaty language have been important ingredients in his electoral appeal since the 1990s. Do they make him comparable to Hanson as part of an Antipodean populism? There are a number of reasons to question this claim.

The neoliberal, pro-business, and "dole bludger" rhetoric of Hanson (Gillespie, 2017), is not on display here, instead, Peters has claimed that NZF is on a mission to "restore moderate capitalism with a kind, responsible face." While ensuring the productivity of business, Peters has also stressed the centrality of the country's "long established social contract of caring for the young and the old and those who were down on their luck through no fault of their own." In terms of policies, Peters has promoted a large variety of center-left policies which have little in common with Hanson's approach (Peters, 2010).

Additionally, Peters has a different relationship with both the established Pakeha-centered and Maori political orders. Mudde and Kaltwasser usefully distinguish between three types of populist: "outsiders, insider-outsiders, and insiders." Most populists fall into the middle camp—they have some experience and connections within the establishment, but are perceived or are able to portray themselves as outsiders (Mudde & Kaltwasser, 2017, pp. 74–75). Peters would arguably be a typical insider–outsider within the political system, given that he was first elected as a National MP, and served in cabinet before being ejected and consequently forming his own party.

With a contingent of Indigenous supporters, Peters as an Indigenous person also presents himself as an insider in the world of Maori politics. During an interview with the author in late 2013, Peters was clear that "my ancestry goes back in this country a thousand years, I'm not going to have anyone come back and in five minutes tell me: I care more about NZ than you do." When we discussed NZF's social conservatism, Peters argued: "Yes, well Maori are inherently conservative, that's why we've been popular with Maori" (Peters, 2013).

Peters does enjoy some support from Maori communities. NZF secured two important constituencies which it has maintained on and off for the past two and a half decades—poorer older Pakeha and young Maori, both of whom have disproportionately suffered from neoliberal policies (Liu & Mills, 2006, p. 91). In 1996, NZF gained all five Maori seats and has maintained a significant share of the Maori vote. In the 2017 election, NZF polled well in the northern part of the country, where statistically voters "are less likely to have attended university, more likely to have been born in New Zealand, more likely to be Māori and have lower household incomes, on average" (Fyers, 2017).

Peters certainly has a bifurcated view of Maori issues, and while he does not deny the history of colonization, he argues that NZ has done relatively well compared with other settler states, "better than most colonised nations." He took particular aim at the Maori Party for promoting a "separatist agenda," claiming that Maori tribes or iwi are nations. He has described this as "imported nonsense" (Peters, 2010). Maori sovereignty for Peters impedes the proper functioning of a unitary state. As he articulated to the author, the signing of the Treaty against the idea of any partnership: "well if no one on the 5th of February 1840, in the whole British Empire including all the inhabitants in the UK weren't in partnership with the Queen Victoria, then how come the Maori were? I've never had an answer in all these years" (Peters, 2013).

In 2005, Peters has sought to steer toward what he sees as a middle path between the major parties, recognizing the Treaty "as a significant historical document, but not the panacea for Maori development." As well: "We believe Maori culture and language must be preserved and enhanced because of its inherent place in New Zealand culture. You see we recognise that nobody else in the world will protect Maori culture and language, and nor should they" (Peters, 2005b).

This recognition however takes second place to what Peters sees as larger economic concerns and a sense of individual responsibility for personal success. As such: "the key to Maori success, just like non-Maori, is for government services to be based on needs and not race" (Peters, 2005b). He also advances economic arguments against devolving too much centralized power to iwi. Peters put this in 2013: "So instead of having pan-Maori operations to solve Maori problems they're trying to do it through this Iwi and this Iwi and this Iwi, the multiplicity and duplication of the services and personnel. It means a serious dilution of the quality of people and inevitably, corruption" (Peters, 2013).

Peters departs significantly from mainstream Maori views of the Treaty and the role of iwi in Maori identity. As a non-Te Reo speaker as well as someone not closely tied to his traditional iwi (Ngāti Wai) he has not focused on this aspect of his identity in public life. Indeed, Peters exemplifies a traditional Pakeha view that the Treaty extinguished the sovereignty of iwi, while most Maori leaders as well as the Waitangi Tribunal (Māori Law Review, 2014) have articulated the opposite conclusion—that sovereignty was not relinquished. Indeed, such an act on the part of the Maori signatories to the Treaty was entirely dissonant with their existing legal orders. The Treaty initiated a process through which the Crown arrogated for itself sovereignty over Maori and all the lands of Aotearoa New Zealand, but the Treaty was not in and of itself some sort of legal contract ceding the authority of Maori leaders and iwi to a foreign power (Jones, 2016, pp. 8–9).

While Peters is arguably on the right-wing end of Maori debates on these issues, he is debating within a Maori context and is not an outsider in the way that Hanson clearly is. Context is crucial, and the context is very different. It is difficult to disaggregate NZF's views on Maori issues sufficiently to break them down into themes that can be readily compared with white nativist parties in other countries. This is because Peters is not a white settler and does not present himself as such.

It is also worth considering that Peter's rhetoric against the Treaty and Maori elites does not translate into policies against Maori as a people, a group he claims to represent in contradistinction to Hanson's approach. On two occasions he has rejected the more anti-Maori pro-business National Party in favor of Labour. In 2017, National gained over 44% of the vote and 58 of 120 seats in the House of Representatives. By choosing a coalition with Labour, a party with more pro-iwi policies and a confidence and supply agreement with the Green Party, Peters enhanced Maori political power and representation. Labour won all seven Maori seats, while the Maori Party (formerly in coalition with National) disappeared from the electoral map. In aligning with Labour, Peters secured the representation in government of not only his own Maori MPs, but those of Labour and the Greens as well.

Conclusions

NZF presents many unique aspects for a populist party, not least its ability to function successfully within an established democratic system and to form an integral part of government. While Moffitt has chosen to parallel NZF and ON, they are notably different in terms of tone, policy, style, electoral success rates, support base, and many other salient issues. All of these raise serious doubts about any study which seeks to identify an Antipodean populism without clearly analyzing the broader context.

Peters' criticism of iwi elites is largely based on neoliberalism and the rise of inequality rather than anti-Indigenous sentiments per se. This is clear when we see the support base for his party and his caucus. This marks an obvious difference from Hanson, as does Peters' take on Asian immigration. Both forms of discourse are partially rooted within some Maori debates over what the Treaty of Waitangi represents, and how the neoliberal turn has impacted on New Zealanders. This is in marked contrast to the sorts of white nativism we see in Australia, or in Western Europe. When we compare these two cases, there are few salient similarities that would warrant using a term like "Antipodean populism" to join Australia and New Zealand together. This makes NZF a phenomenon, worthy of more detailed study and comparison with other populisms worldwide.

NOTES

1. While Maori were still presented in colonial narratives as racially inferior to Europeans, they were nevertheless afforded a political role within the colonial system that was explicitly denied to Aboriginal and Torres Straight Islanders. This was reflecting in some Maori males gaining the vote by 1867, as well as designated Maori seats in parliament and roles for Maori leaders in cabinet in the late nineteenth and early twentieth centuries (Murphy, 2009, p. 63). Myths of partnership never implied equality, and the government engaged in widespread land theft, the denial of Maori language and cultural rights and many other matters. As well, political assimilation within settler dominated political systems acted to marginalize and impoverish Maori (Bargh, 2013).

LITERATURE

Aly, A., & Walker, D. (2007). Veiled threats: Recurrent cultural anxieties in Australia. *Journal of Muslim Minority Affairs, 27*(2), 203–214. https://doi.org/10.1080/13602000701536141.

Bargh, M. (2013). Multiple sites of Māori political participation. *Australian Journal of Political Science, 48*(4), 445–455. https://doi.org/10.1080/10361146.2013.841123.

Bickers, C. (2018, April 6). 'Disgusting': Pauline Hanson blasts Commonwealth Games ceremony's focus on Indigenous culture. *Gold Coast Bulletin*. Retrieved from https://www.goldcoastbulletin.com.au/sport/commonwealth-games/disgusting-pauling-hanson-blasts-commonwealth-games-ceremonys-focus-on-indigenous-culture/news-story/94e28bad13233bf0836c19fddb0bb8a3.

Canovan, M. (1999). Trust the people! Populism and the two faces of democracy. *Political Studies, 47*(1), 2–16. https://doi.org/10.1111/1467-9248.00184.

Cooke, H. (2017, December 5). Winston Peters says western world is too hard on China over freedom issues. *Stuff*. Retrieved from https://www.stuff.co.nz/national/politics/99542129/winston-peters-says-western-world-is-too-hard-on-china-over-human-rights-issues.

Deutchman, I. E. (2000). Pauline Hanson and the rise and fall of the radical right in Australia. *Patterns of Justice, 34*(1), 49–62. https://doi.org/10.1080/00313220008559135.

Fyers, A. (2017, October 17). These are the NZ First voters who gave Winston Peters the keys to power. *Stuff*. https://www.stuff.co.nz/national/politics/97917491/these-are-the-voters-who-gave-winston-the-keys-to-power.

Gillespie, K. (2017, October 31). We need to talk about the dole. *Vice.* https://www.vice.com/en_au/article/pa3abv/we-need-to-talk-about-the-dole.

Grevin, T. (2016, May). The rise of right-wing populism in Europe and the United States: A comparative perspective. *Friedrich Ebert Stiftung.* www.fesdc.org/fileadmin/user_upload/publications/RightwingPopulism.pdf.

Gobbett, Hannah. (2017). *Indigenous parliamentarians, federal and state: A quick guide.* https://www.aph.gov.au/About_Parliament/Parliamentary_Departments/Parliamentary_Library/pubs/rp/rp1718/Quick_Guides/IndigenousParliamentarians.

Goot, M. (2005). Pauline Hanson's One Nation: Extreme right, centre party or extreme left?. *Labour History, 89*, 101–119. https://doi.org/10.2307/27516078.

Gustafson, B. (2006). Populist roots of political leadership in New Zealand. In R. Millar & M. Mintrom (Eds.), *Political leadership in New Zealand* (pp. 51–69). Auckland University Press.

Hage, G. (2006). *White nation: Fantasies of white supremacy in a multicultural society.* Pluto Press.

Hobbs, H. (2018). Constitutional recognition and reform: Developing an inclusive Australian citizenship through treaty. *Australian Journal of Political Science, 53*(2), 176–194. https://doi.org/10.1080/10361146.2018.1449801.

Jones, C. (2016). *New treaty, new tradition: Reconciling New Zealand and Maori law.* UBC Press.

Koti, T. (2017, September 24). Who are our Māori Members of Parliament now? *Maori Television.* http://www.maoritelevision.com/news/politics/who-are-our-maori-members-parliament-now.

Lavin, F. (2017, October 20). Things fall apart: Populism and foreign policy. *Georgetown Journal of International Affairs.* https://www.georgetownjournalofinternationalaffairs.org/online-edition/2017/10/20/things-fall-apart-populism-and-foreign-policy.

Liu, J. H., & Mills, D. (2006). Modern racism and neoliberal globalization: The discourses of plausible deniability and their multiple functions. *Journal of Community & Applied Social Psychology, 16*(2), 83–99. https://doi.org/10.1002/casp.847.

Maddison, S. (2010). White parliament, black politics: The dilemmas of Indigenous parliamentary representation. *Australian Journal of Political Science, 45*(4), 663–680. https://doi.org/10.1080/10361146.2010.517180.

Maddison, S. (2017). Recognise what? The limitations of settler colonial constitutional reform. *Australian Journal of Political Science, 52*(1), 3–18. https://doi.org/10.1080/10361146.2016.1260684.

Māori Law Review. (2014). Waitangi Tribunal finds Treaty of Waitangi Signatories did not cede sovereignty in February 1840. *Māori Law Review.* http://maorilawreview.co.nz/2014/11/waitangi-tribunal-finds-treaty-of-waitangi-signatories-did-not-cede-sovereignty-in-february-1840/.

Mason, R. (2010). 'Pitbulls' and populist politicians: Sarah Palin, Pauline Hanson and the use of gendered nostalgia in electoral campaigns. *Comparative American Studies: An International Journal, 8*(3), 185–199. https://doi.org/10.1179/147757010x12773889525867.

McNicol, H. (2017, June 28). The $50 billion Maori economy is poised to get bigger. *Stuff.* https://www.stuff.co.nz/business/94141344/the-50-billion-maori-economy-poised-for-growth-diversification.

McSwiney, J., & Cottle, D. (2017). Unintended consequences: One Nation and neoliberalism in contemporary Australia. *Journal of Australian Political Economy*, *79*(Winter), 87–106.

Moffitt, B. (2016). *The global rise of populism: Performance, political style, and representation*. Stanford University Press. Kindle.

Moffitt, B. (2017). Populism in Australia and New Zealand. In C. R. Kaltwasser, P. Taggart, P. O. Espejo, & P. Ostiguy (Eds.), *The Oxford handbook of populism*. Oxford University Press.

Mudde, C. (2017). Populism: An ideational approach. In C. R. Kaltwasser, P. Taggart, P. O. Espejo, & P. Ostiguy (Eds.), *The Oxford handbook of populism*. Oxford University Press.

Mudde, C. & Kaltwasser, C.R. (2013). Exclusionary vs. inclusionary populism: Comparing contemporary Europe and Latin America. *Government and Opposition*, *48*(2), 147–174. https://doi.org/10.1017/gov.2012.11.

Mudde, C., & Kaltwasser, C. R. (2017). *Populism: A very short introduction*. Oxford University Press.

Murphy, N. (2009). 'Maoriland' and 'Yellow Peril': Discourses of Maori and Chinese in the formation of New Zealand's national identity 1890–1914. In I. Manying (Ed.), *The Dragon & The Taniwha: Maori & Chinese in New Zealand* (pp. 56–88). Auckland University Press.

Myles, R. (2016). Winston Peters "puts his hand to the plow": The Bible in New Zealand political discourse. *Journal of the Bible and Its Reception*, *3*(1), 135–153. https://doi.org/10.1515/jbr-2016-1010.

New Zealand First Party. (2005, April 26). *New Zealand—The last Asian colony* [Press release]. http://www.scoop.co.nz/stories/PA0504/S00527.htm.

New Zealand First Party. (2017). First week of parliament for 2017. We are ready—Winston Peters [Facebook video]. https://www.facebook.com/winstonpeters/videos/1816564408369678/.

Panizza, F. (2005). *Populism and the mirror of democracy*. Verso Books.

Pauline Hanson's One Nation. (2018). *One nation policies*. http://www.onenation.org.au/policies/.

Peters, W. (2002, July 15). One country. Address to Chinese Communities and Associations, Auckland. http://www.scoop.co.nz/stories/PA0207/S00380.htm.

Peters, W. (2005a, July 28). The end of tolerance. Address to members of Far North Grey Power, Kaitaia. http://www.scoop.co.nz/stories/PA0507/S00649.htm.

Peters, W. (2005b, July 5). No re-run of 1996. Address to members of Whangarei Grey Power, Whangarei. http://www.scoop.co.nz/stories/PA0507/S00107.htm.

Peters, W. (2010, January 29). MMP—The inside story. Address to Political Science Students, Auckland University, Auckland. http://www.scoop.co.nz/stories/PO1001/S00116.htm.

Peters, W. (2013, November 13). Interview with Winston Peters, Bowen House, Parliament of New Zealand, Wellington.

Peters, W. (2016, January 26). State of the nation speech. Address to the Orewa Rotary Club. http://www.scoop.co.nz/stories/PA1601/S00115/rt-hon-winston-peters-state-of-the-nation-speech.htm.

Peters, W. (2017a, September 21). Campaign advertisement 2—What you need to know about real change [Facebook video]. https://www.facebook.com/winstonpeters/videos/2137672186258897/.

Peters, W. (2017b, July 16). New Zealand is heading toward political upset. *Indian Newslink*. http://www.indiannewslink.co.nz/new-zealand-is-heading-towards-political-upset/.

Poata-Smith, E. T. A. (2013). Inequality and Maori. In M. Rashbrooke (Ed.), *Inequality: A New Zealand crisis* (pp. 148–158). Bridget Williams Books.

Radio Live. (2017, July 21). Winston Peters: Retain or abolish the Maori seats. *Radio Live*. http://www.radiolive.co.nz/home/opinion/2017/07/winston-peters--retain-or-abolish-the-maori-seats.html.

Smith, P. M. (2005). *A concise history of New Zealand*. Cambridge University Press.

Smits, K. (2011). Justifying multiculturalism: Social justice, diversity and national identity in Australia and New Zealand. *Australian Journal of Political Science, 46*(1), 87–103. https://doi.org/10.1080/10361146.2011.546051.

TVNZ. (2002, April 18). Maori missing out, says Peters. *TVNZ*. http://tvnz.co.nz/content/94957/2483318/article.html.

Wong, S. & Ritchie, O. (2017, April 27). Winston Peters targets students in immigration crackdown. *Newshub*. http://www.newshub.co.nz/home/politics/2017/04/winston-peters-targets-students-in-immigration-crackdown.html.

Working Group on Constitutional Transformation. (2016). Jackson, M. & Mutu, M. *Report of Matike Mai Aotearoa – The Independent Working Group on Constitutional Transformation*. https://nwo.org.nz/resources/report-of-matike-mai-aotearoa-the-independent-working-group-on-constitutionaltransformation/.

CHAPTER 5

A Critique of Left-Wing Populism: Critical Materialist and Social-Psychological Perspectives

Helge Petersen and Hannah Hecker

INTRODUCTION

More than one decade after the major crisis of the capitalist world-economy in 2007/2008, the political landscape in many nation-states has witnessed a significant shift to the right, an increasing attraction to authoritarian forms of conflict resolution and paranoid ideologies such as racism and antisemitism. In a situation of weakness, stagnation, and confusion about the elements, origins, and repercussions of this shift, parts of the political and academic left have begun to fundamentally reconsider the coordinates of their political strategies and visions. It is especially the project of left-wing populism which has gained prominence as a new intellectual and political approach. Its most influential theoretical justification can undoubtedly be found in the collaborative work of Ernesto Laclau and Chantal Mouffe. Instead of rejecting the appeal to "the people", traditionally associated with the right, Laclau and Mouffe make a case for integrating it into a left-wing framework. Challenging the liberal-elitist "denigration of populism" (Laclau, 2005, p. 17) as an irrational aberration or reactionary threat to the democratic order, they argue that populism not only underlies any form of democratic politics but also represents its emancipatory

---

H. Petersen (✉)
School of Social and Political Sciences, University of Glasgow, Glasgow, Scotland, UK
e-mail: h.petersen.1@research.gla.ac.uk

H. Hecker
Fritz Bauer Institut, Goethe University, Frankfurt, Germany
e-mail: hecker@em.uni-frankfurt.de

potential (Laclau, 2005; Mouffe, 2018). Furthermore, developing an alternative notion of "the people" is seen as the only possible way of countering the ongoing rise of the right (Mouffe, 2016).

Laclau and Mouffe's embrace of the "populist moment" has been widely criticized. Various Marxist authors focus on the socio-economic insufficiencies of their approach, including their "hyperdiscursive" ontology (Miklitsch, 1995; see also Boucher, 2008, pp. 93–108), their rejection of class-theoretical perspectives (Bray, 2015, p. 33; Wood, 1998; Žižek, 2008, pp. 305–333), their advocacy of social- and liberal-democratic reformism (Boucher, 2008, pp. 108–124; Žižek, 2008, pp. 305–333), as well as their preservation of the nation-state as the primary theoretical framework (Sotiris, 2017; Sparke, 2005, p. 33). What is missing in these approaches, however, is an explicit problematization of the political-ideological consequences of these insufficiencies. (Left-)liberal authors put a stronger emphasis on the problematic political outcomes of both left-wing and right-wing populisms, focusing especially on their antidemocratic, anti-pluralistic, and anti-liberal features (Arato, 2013; Arato & Cohen, 2017; Cohen, 2019; Fassin, 2019; Müller, 2016). This critique, however, is usually not substantiated by an analysis of the societal conditions of populist ideology, and is further weakened by the tendency to attribute anti-emancipatory tendencies not to the notion of "the people" as such, but only to its authoritarian misappropriation. What links both types of critique is a tendency to evaluate left-wing populism as a political strategy rather than as an ideological worldview (Bray, 2015; Cohen, 2019; Fassin et al., 2018; Žižek, 2006).

The main goal of this paper is to provide a systematic analysis and critique of both the socio-historical conditions and the political-ideological consequences of the left-wing populist dichotomy between "the people" and "the elite" as conceptualized by Laclau and Mouffe. A useful way to critically interrogate this left-wing fascination with populism is to bring in a line of thought which is largely ignored by Laclau and Mouffe: the materialist critical theory and social psychology developed by Max Horkheimer and Theodor W. Adorno (Adorno, 1982; Horkheimer, 2013; Horkheimer & Adorno, 2002). Their works not only point to the repressed content of Laclau and Mouffe's critique of Marxist perspectives, but also provide a methodological approach to the critique of ideology that is most useful in order to point to the theoretical limitations and political pitfalls of Laclau and Mouffe's account of populism.[1] Beginning with a short reconstruction of Laclau and Mouffe's model of left-wing populism, the paper makes use of two modes of critique systematized by Horkheimer and Adorno. In the context of an immanent critique, it is demonstrated that this model is based on a simplistic, personalized worldview that fails to live up to its own emancipatory claims. A social-psychological critique further problematizes Laclau and Mouffe's willingness to even take up distinctly anti-emancipatory notions of collective identity and existential struggle. Against this background, it is concluded that Laclau and Mouffe fail to provide a progressive alternative to the contemporary rise of right-wing politics.

THE POST-MARXIST MODEL OF LEFT-WING POPULISM

Laclau and Mouffe's theorization of left-wing populism is part of their wider intellectual project of developing a post-Marxistvision of political conflicts in late modern societies (Laclau & Mouffe, 1996, 2014; see also Marchart, 2007). Within the confines of this paper, it is not possible to expand on the broad theoretical landscape that has been utilized and reformulated as part of this project, such as Gramsci's theory of hegemony, Freud's and Lacan's psychoanalysis, De Saussure's, Wittgenstein's and Derrida's theory of language, or Schmitt's theory of enmity and antagonism. What needs to be highlighted, however, are two general aspects that underlie their model of left-wing populism. First, Laclau and Mouffe put a strong emphasis on what they regard as the main blind spot of the Marxist tradition: the autonomy of the political and discursive realm of social reality (Laclau & Mouffe, 2014, pp. 91–101). With such an emphasis on political discourse as the "primary terrain of the constitution of objectivity as such" (Laclau, 2005, p. 68), however, Laclau and Mouffe go far beyond a critique of Marxist economic determinism and class reductionism. For the main thrust of their post-Marxism is to dismiss the very notion of an objective, material reality that goes beyond the realm of (inter-)subjective perception and symbolic construction (Laclau & Mouffe, 2014, pp. 65–75). Second, they seek to justify these theoretical assumptions, not based on socio-historical experience, but on strictly ontological grounds. According to Laclau and Mouffe, ontological reasoning is a search for those features that are "inherent to human societies" (Errejón & Mouffe, 2016, p. 38) and therefore need to be acknowledged as ever-present, foundational principles (see also Laclau, 2005, pp. 67–72). Thus, although Laclau and Mouffe dedicate much of their efforts to criticize Marxist and other essentialisms (Laclau, 2005, pp. 67–124; Laclau & Mouffe, 2014, pp. 93–148; Mouffe, 2018, pp. 87–90), the main parameters of their own approach are essentialized as unsurmountable aspects of the human condition.

It is within such an ahistorical and "hyperdiscursive" (Miklitsch, 1995, p. 183) framework that Laclau and Mouffe develop their model of left-wing populism which consists of three main elements: The first element of populist mobilization are "social demands" which Laclau defines as requests or claims based on individual needs that remain unsatisfied within the established order, but, as isolated expressions, do not lead to transformative political action (Laclau, 2005, pp. 73–74). To develop such a politically disruptive effect, different social demands need to intertwine—a process which Laclau and Mouffe call the creation of an "equivalential chain of unsatisfied demands" (Laclau, 2005, p. 74; see also Laclau & Mouffe, 2014, pp. 113–120). To conceptualize this second element, Laclau and Mouffe make use of De Saussure's and Derrida's (post-)structuralist theory of language and discourse (Laclau, 1996, pp. 36–46, 2005, pp. 67–93; Laclau & Mouffe, 2014, pp. 91–101, 113–120). This has two implications: First, Laclau and Mouffe understand social demands as discursive signifiers whose specific meaning results, not from their relation to something in the objective world, such as bodily expressions or societal processes, but only from their relation to other signifiers (Laclau, 2005, pp. 68–69). In this sense, they understand political mobilization as a process of identification between unsatisfied demands, but not as the result of a process of reflection on the societal causes of the experience of dissatisfaction. What is more, it is this dismissal of intellectual practices which leads them to emphasize the "primary role of affect" (Laclau, 2005, p. 169) in the creation of equivalential chains (see also Laclau, 2005, pp. 101–117; Mouffe, 2018, pp. 71–78). Second, they assert that, in order for such an affect-based process to become possible, a common object of identification is needed. Laclau calls this object an "empty signifier" (Laclau, 2005, pp. 69–71), that is, a meta-category which needs to lose its particular content in order to represent what all the other signifiers have in common (see also Laclau, 1996, pp. 36–40). The underlying assumption is that the expression of unsatisfied demands is driven by the desire for a "communitarian fullness" (Laclau, 1996, p. 42) which is absent in the established order. Against this background, they assert that the notion of "the people" is the most appropriate representation of this existential need for collective identity and communitarian harmony: "[T]he construction of the 'people' will be the attempt to give a name to that absent fullness" (Laclau, 2005, p. 85).

The symbolic construction of "the people", however, is not a self-referential process. On the contrary, drawing on the Derridean notion of the "constitutive outside" of signification processes (Mouffe, 2000, pp. 12–13), Laclau and Mouffe assume that the only possible way of constructing "the people" is the exclusion of what is beyond its boundaries. This is where the third element of populist mobilization comes into play: The "radical exclusion" (Laclau, 2005, p. 82) of a common enemy which is made responsible for the disruption of the "harmonious continuity of the social" (Laclau, 2005, p. 85). The question of the enemy is also important for them in order to distinguish between right-wing and left-wing populism: According to Mouffe, right-wing populism promotes the exclusion of "numerous categories, usually immigrants, seen as a threat to the identity and the prosperity of the nation" (Mouffe, 2018, p. 24), whereas left-wing populism is characterized by its opposition to "the elite" or "the oligarchy", usually identified as an alliance of neoliberal forces dominated by "finance capital" (Mouffe, 2018, pp. 17–18).

Immanent Critique: The Contradictory Promises of Left-Wing Populism

Based on this framework, Laclau and Mouffe seek to make a case for left-wing populism not only as the only viable antidote to its right-wing counterpart, but also as a progressive alternative to the established socio-political order.

Indeed, what clearly distinguishes their approach from right-wing populism is a promise of emancipation which, despite their sharp critique of Marxism, still remains embedded within a tradition of left-wing thought and practice (Laclau, 1996). At the same time, however, they strongly reject the notion of a radical emancipation of humanity as a "totalizing aspiration" (Laclau, 1990, p. 215; see also Mouffe, 2018, p. 3). This ambivalence toward the question of emancipation also leads them to a contradictory social and political critique, which is especially evident in their account of capitalism. In her latest work, for instance, Mouffe states that "[t]he process of radicalizing democracy necessarily includes an anti-capitalist dimension as many of the forms of subordination that will need to be challenged are the consequences of capitalist relations of production" (Mouffe, 2018, p. 49). At the same time, however, she strongly rejects those left-wing currents that emphasize the need for theoretical reflection on capitalism as a crucial element of an anti-capitalist practice: "Instead of designating the adversaries in ways that people can identify, they use abstract categories like 'capitalism', thereby failing to mobilize the affective dimension necessary to motivate people to act politically" (Mouffe, 2018, p. 50). It is this paradoxical call for an anti-capitalist practice devoid of a concept of capitalism that is scrutinized in this section. More specifically, it is argued that this contradiction is constitutive of the limitations of the populist worldview. Instead of simply stating these insufficiencies, however, they are developed immanently. Following Adorno, immanent critique is a "process where what is criticized is measured against its own assumptions, its own principles of form" (Adorno, 2017a, p. 32). In this sense, Laclau and Mouffe's own anti-capitalist claims are taken seriously but confronted with the limitations of the actual socio-economic analysis that underlies their model of left-wing populism. More specifically, it is argued that the populist distinction between "the people" and "the elite" is based on a simplified and personalized worldview that tends to reproduce the very status quo it claims to overcome.

To shed light on Laclau and Mouffe's ambivalence toward questions of capitalism and emancipation, it is instructive to go back to the origins of their post-Marxist approach. One of the main starting points for their intellectual endeavor is a critique of Marxist economic determinism and class reductionism (Laclau & Mouffe, 2014, pp. 65–76). This important critique of orthodox Marxism, however, is inseparably connected to the rejection of a much broader horizon of materialist thought (Boucher, 2008, pp. 86–87). The only Marxist approach that is incorporated in their post-Marxist framework is Gramsci's theory of hegemony (Laclau & Mouffe, 2014, pp. 55–61, 120–131). What is relevant for the discussion in this paper, however, is that Laclau und Mouffe's reading of Gramsci is based on the abandonment of two key aspects of his work: First, while Gramsci discovers the concept of hegemony in light of the historically specific context of Western-European capitalist democracies in the early 20th century, Laclau and Mouffe ontologize it as an ahistorical principle. It is therefore unsurprising that those aspects of Gramsci's work that focus on the shifting patterns of industrial capitalism in the early twentieth century are largely disregarded (Gramsci, 1971, pp. 279–318). Second, while Gramsci conceptualizes hegemony as a set of political strategies to domesticate the conflict dynamics inherent to capitalist social formations, Laclau and Mouffe detach the former from the latter. In this sense, Gramsci's reflection on the objective conditions of political action are disregarded (Laclau & Mouffe, 2014, pp. 120–131).[2]

This selective appropriation of Gramsci's theory of hegemony indicates that Laclau and Mouffe are not interested in analyzing the specificity of the capitalist mode of coercion, domination, and exploitation. This stance also leads them to discredit as "pathetic" (Laclau & Mouffe, 2014, p. ix) and "desperate" attempts to "grasp the realities of contemporary capitalism" (Laclau & Mouffe, 2014, p. viii) those critical materialist approaches that reflect on the constitutively impersonal, structural character of capitalist social relations. Beginning with the Marxian critique of political economy and continuing with the works of authors such as Lukács, Pashukanis, Horkheimer, and Adorno, this line of thought argues that the specific feature of capitalist societalization is the increasing dissolution of personal relations of subjugation in favor of a division of labor based on the anonymous processes of competition, accumulation, and bureaucratization.[3] In capitalist societies, Marx argues, "the behaviour of men in the social process of production is purely atomic. Hence their relations to each other in production assume a material character independent of their control and conscious individual action" (Marx & Engels, 1996, p. 103). Adorno and Horkheimer's approach is especially instructive insofar as they develop this argument against the historical background of the massive concentration of wealth and power under monopoly capitalism. Thus, they are indeed attentive to what they call "the power of those whose economic position in society is strongest" (Horkheimer & Adorno, 2002, p. 95). However, these actors are not seen as the origin of societal injustice and misery, but instead as personified manifestations of an "objective social tendency" (Horkheimer & Adorno, 2002, p. 96), that is, a historically specific division and appropriation of labor "that is reified, divested of the immediacy of human relations, dominated by the abstract principle of exchange" (Adorno, 1997, p. 241).

It is this reproduction of coercion and domination "behind the backs" (Marx & Engels, 1996, p. 54) and "over the heads" (Adorno, 2017b, p. 45) of the social actors which eludes Laclau and Mouffe's post-Marxist worldview. What is offered instead is an explanatory framework that confines itself to the intentions and strategies of collective actors. Within this framework, then, the sole object of critique is "the elite", that is, a small group of powerful actors that is imagined not only as the main beneficiary but also as the original architect of social injustice. Moreover, it is assumed that progressive social change does not occur primarily because these "privileged elites [...] are deaf to the demands of the other groups in society" (Mouffe, 2018, p. 18). However, what is not criticized are the objective positions which these elite actors hold, nor the societal processes which underlie the unjust distribution of wealth and power in the first place. Laclau and Mouffe's emancipatory promises thus shrink from the radical transformation of the societal fabric to the replacement of one type of political leadership by another. Furthermore, although the distinction between "the people" and "the elite" vaguely refers to political-economic power imbalances, it is not informed by a systematic analysis of capitalist hierarchies and antagonisms.[4] In class-theoretical terms, for instance, it represents an analytical distortion. According to Laclau and Mouffe, "the elite" or "the oligarchy" is always restricted to certain fractions of capital. It is "the transnational corporations' attempt to impose their power over the entire planet" (Laclau & Mouffe, 2014, p. xix), "the entrenched wealth and power of the new class of managers" (Mouffe, 2000, p. 15), and the "great expansion of the financial sector" (Mouffe, 2018, p. 18) which is seen as the primary cause of social injustice. The "productive economy" (Mouffe, 2018, p. 18), on the other hand, is taken out of the equation (see also Mouffe, 2000, pp. 118–121). Similarly, "the people" is introduced as a collective identity that cuts across—and thus negates the significance of—class-specific lines of demarcation (Mouffe, 2018, p. 24). Moreover, Laclau and Mouffe's repeated advocacy of nationalism demonstrates that this cross-class, anti-plutocratic stance tends to move in the direction of the very denial of socio-economic categories of analysis (Errejón & Mouffe, 2016, p. 69; Laclau, 2005, pp. 182–191; Mouffe, 2018, p. 71).[5] Thus, instead of reflecting on the complexity of social hierarchies and antagonisms in contemporary capitalism, the left-wing populist worldview simplifies and distorts them beyond recognition.

SOCIAL-PSYCHOLOGICAL CRITIQUE: THE REGRESSIVE ENTANGLEMENTS OF LEFT-WING POPULISM

It could be argued that this tendency to promote a simplistic and personalized worldview is mainly due to an insufficient analysis which could easily be overcome in the direction of a more sophisticated critique of capitalism (see for example: Žižek, 2006). However, there is much to suggest that this insufficiency is only an indication of a deeper theoretical and political problematic. The goal of this section is to demonstrate that Laclau and Mouffe justify their populist worldview based on deeply ahistorical assumptions about the nature of identity, collectivity, and affectivity. What is more, these considerations lead them to take up openly anti-emancipatory positions about the relation between individuality and collectivity as well as the necessity of existential struggle.[6]

An instructive way of illustrating these tendencies within Laclau and Mouffe's model of populism is to examine their utilization of the Freudian mass psychology which figures prominently in their justification of populism (Laclau, 2005, pp. 21–64, 101–117; Mouffe, 2000, pp. 137–140, 2005, pp. 25–29, 2018, pp. 70–78).[7] In his work *On Populist Reason*, for instance, Laclau begins with a detailed reconstruction of the pre-Freudian tradition of mass psychology which he rightly criticizes for its "denigration of the masses" (Laclau, 2005, pp. 21–52), that is, its tendency to portray mass formation as an expression of archaic drives and irrational feelings. Freud's *Group Psychology and the Analysis of the Ego* (Freud, 1955), on the other hand, is valued as a "radical breakthrough" (Laclau, 2005, p. 52) that overcomes this elitist perspective. According to Laclau, Freud's most important insight is that "the social bond is a libidinal one" (Laclau, 2005, p. x), that is, that every social bond is sustained by what Laclau calls an affective "investment" (Laclau, 2005, p. 97). More specifically, Laclau asserts that Freud, unlike his predecessors, has discovered that affective expressions are not the opposite of but represent themselves a distinct type of rationality (Laclau, 2005, p. 58). It is therefore unsurprising that Laclau and Mouffe regard Freud's conceptualization of mass formation as an affect-based form of political mobilization as an indispensable source of inspiration. It is especially Freud's notion of collective identification which features in their model of left-wing populism as the "motor of political action" (Mouffe, 2018, p. 74; see also Laclau, 2005, pp. 52–64).

There are various aspects of Freud's mass psychology, however, which are disregarded by Laclau and Mouffe. Most importantly, while they essentialize the principles of mass formation as "inherent to any social identity formation" (Laclau, 2005, p. xi) or "constitutive of the mode of existence of human beings" (Mouffe, 2005, p. 28), Freud points to very specific conditions under which individuals develop the need for collective identification. More precisely, he attributes this need to an inner conflict: Modern individuals, he argues, are confronted with social expectations and constraints which they usually internalize in the form of what Freud calls an "ego ideal" which separates itself from the "ego" (see Freud, 1955, pp. 111–116). The failure to stand these external pressures, however, results in tensions between ego and ego ideal, which creates feelings of dissatisfaction and frustration (Freud, 1955, p. 143). According to Freud, mass formation is nothing but the collective attempt to relieve this unpleasant experience by replacing the ego ideal by a "group ideal" (Freud, 1955, p. 129) that now represents everything the individual desires and strives for. However, he highlights that mass formation does not actually change the causes of the inner conflict (the societal pressure) but only reorganizes its symptoms (the unpleasant feelings). Thus, it is only an unconscious and illusionary response to this conflict, characterized by the "predominance of the life of phantasy and of the illusion born of an unfulfilled wish" (Freud, 1955, p. 80). What is more, he asserts that the political consequences of mass formation are highly problematic: Not only is strong collective identification characterized by "the individual's lack of freedom" (Freud, 1955, p. 95), it can also lead to "cruelty and intolerance towards those who do not belong" (Freud, 1955, p. 98).

In order to fully grasp the socio-historical significance of this conflict between ego and ego ideal, it is worthwhile to look again at the work of Horkheimer and Adorno. It was one of their main achievements to decipher this psychological conflict as a specific symptom of modern, capitalist societies, which has fundamental effects on emancipation processes. As outlined in the *Dialectic of Enlightenment* (Horkheimer & Adorno, 2002, pp. 1–62) and *The Eclipse of Reason* (Horkheimer, 2013, pp. 92–161), the reproduction of these societies depends on the individual's internalization of the social pressures by which it is confronted. The ego ideal, then, comes to represent an aggressive type of subjectivity adapted to the survival within a competitive division of labor and hierarchical distribution of power. As "the children of a liberal, competitive and individualistic society" (Adorno, 1982, p. 121), modern individuals "are continuously admonished to be 'rugged' and warned against surrender" (Adorno, 1982, p. 121; see also Horkheimer, 2013, pp. 105–109). At the same time, Horkheimer and Adorno highlight that this process of internalization is highly precarious: Not only is it based on the strong repression of individual needs and desires, it also confronts the individuals with either the actual experience or the potential threat of failure (Adorno, 1982, p. 126). The immediate psychological expression of this conflict are feelings of unpleasure, dissatisfaction, and frustration which, in a social world of "ruggedness", contain strong aggressive components (Adorno, 1982, p. 123). For Horkheimer and Adorno, these observations have far-reaching consequences for the question of emancipation. Their main argument is that affective dispositions *as such* do not necessarily lead to emancipatory ambitions. In agreement with Freud, they assert that unpleasant affects, as un- and preconscious dispositions, remain ambiguous toward their conditions of emergence. In other words, these affects themselves do not bring to mind the social circumstances in which they have emerged (Horkheimer, 2013, pp. 92–127; Horkheimer & Adorno, 2002, pp. 147–165). According to Adorno, it is especially the impersonal character of modern social relations which tends to remain opaque in everyday life: "Nothing is more difficult for people than to experience and comprehend the anonymous, objective as such" (Adorno, 1971, p. 75, translated by H.P. & H.H.). Against this background, Horkheimer and Adorno conclude that both progressive and regressive responses to those affective dispositions are possible (see especially Horkheimer, 2013, pp. 112–114). A progressive response attempts to transform the spontaneous feelings of unpleasure and aggression into the intellectual critique of and practical resistance against coercion, domination and suffering. They acknowledge that this is a difficult endeavor insofar as it requires strong intellectual and practical resistance against the conformist tendencies within society. For Adorno and Horkheimer, it thus becomes important for any emancipatory project to strengthen practices of "independent thought" (Horkheimer, 2013, p. 127). A regressive response, however, does exactly the opposite: It offers a relief from the difficult and exhausting process of intellectual (self-)reflection and instead advocates the immediate, unregulated mobilization of dissatisfaction and hatred. Instead of strengthening the desire for human emancipation, the regressive response searches for "powerful surrogates" (Horkheimer, 2013, p. 113) which allow for the satisfaction of these aggressive dispositions without actually changing their objective conditions of existence. Most notably, Adorno and Horkheimer distinguish between two types of surrogates which Freud has already identified as key features of mass formation: First, the imagination of a "collective identity" which offers, as a compensation for the unresolved inner conflict, the creation of strong libidinal bonds with other members of the collective—without actually liberating the individuals but only intensifying their state of powerlessness (Horkheimer & Adorno, 2002, p. 9). Second, the imagination of a "common enemy", that is, an easily identifiable object that is falsely blamed for the experienced suffering and thus figures as an ideological substitute for its actual social causes:

> Under the pressure of the superego, the ego projects aggressive urges emanating from the id [...] as malign intentions onto the outside world, and succeeds in ridding itself of them as reactions to that outside world, either in fantasy by identification with the alleged malefactor or in reality by ostensible self-defense. (Horkheimer & Adorno, 2002, p. 158)

As a result, the initial aggressions are not critically transformed but remain intact as an ever-present reservoir of collective violence.

In light of Freud's as well as Adorno and Horkheimer's social psychology, it can be argued that Laclau and Mouffe's model of left-wing populism represents an anti-emancipatory response to the contradictions and dilemmas of modern subjectivity. As discussed above, Laclau and Mouffe fail to take into account Freud's discussion of the inner conflict which underlies the need for collective identification. This is not simply due to an insufficient reading of Freud, but results from their post-Marxist ontology that refuses to acknowledge the distinct impact of objective social relations on the unconscious impulses and affective expressions of modern individuals. However, if the existence of such a conflict is denied, there is no need to further reflect on the problem of either progressive or regressive ways of dealing with it. On the contrary, Laclau and Mouffe assume that affective expressions of dissatisfaction always-already bear an "equalitarian dimension" (Laclau, 2005, p. 125) or "democratic nucleus" (Mouffe, 2018, p. 22). Against this background, it is unsurprising that they do not consider it necessary, let alone desirable, to mediate these expressions by practices of intellectual (self-)reflection. Instead, their model of populism is based on "the predominance of the 'emotive' over the 'rational'" (Laclau, 2005, p. 39; see also Mouffe, 2018, pp. 72–78). The main task of populism, then, is to politically mobilize, but not to critically modify these affects. As Mouffe puts it, a populist strategy "should address people in manner able to reach their affects. It has to be congruent with the values and the identities of those that it seeks to interpellate and must connect with the aspects of popular experience" (Mouffe, 2018, p. 76).

A closer look at Laclau and Mouffe's notions of "the people" and "the elite" shows that such an "exclusion of reflection" (Horkheimer & Adorno, 2002, p. 156) also paves the way for the other anti-emancipatory mechanisms identified by Horkheimer and Adorno. As was discussed above, 'the people' is introduced as a 'collective identity' that promises the individuals to forget their antagonistic and hierarchical social relations and unifies around the desire to establish a harmonious community. This promise, however, is illusionary insofar as it does not encourage its members to critically reflect on and practically change the societal origins of these divisions. Thus, the unsatisfied demands around which "the people" is constructed remain intact and the only psychological substitute which "the people" is able to offer is a *feeling* of collective harmony which needs to be established through relations of identification. Unlike both Freud as well as Adorno and Horkheimer, however, Laclau and Mouffe do not problematize the process of collective identification itself. Although the construction of "the people" begins with an articulation of individual needs, it nonetheless culminates at a point where, as Laclau puts it, the collective identity "develops a logic of its own which can lead to a sacrifice or betrayal of the aims of its individual links" (Laclau, 2005, p. 135). Thus, although Laclau and Mouffe advocate democratic types of political leadership (Laclau, 2005, p. 60; Mouffe, 2018, p. 70), they nonetheless envision an authoritarian relationship in which individual needs are subsumed under the collective will. The introduction of "the elite" as "the common enemy" can also be regarded as an attempt to mobilize affective dispositions for anti-emancipatory purposes. Most notably, the assumption that a small group of elite actors is primarily responsible for all forms of social injustice feeds off the widespread inability to make sense of the specifically impersonal forms of social domination and coercion. What is more, it provides a concrete object on which those unsatisfied feelings of aggression and hatred can be discharged. To justify these acts of aggression, Laclau and Mouffe imagine "the elite" as a clearly identifiable group that abuses its immense power in order to oppress and exploit the "people". Instead of situating elite actors within a societal order that is characterized by the asymmetrical distribution of wealth and power, they are imagined as an invasive, threatening force located outside of the communitarian space. For instance, this leads Laclau to endorse political narratives about the "corrupt" and "parasitic" nature of elite actors as genuine examples of left-wing populism (Laclau, 2005, pp. 89–93, 201–208). He even goes so far as to claim that the enemy always represents "pure threat" (Laclau, 1996, p. 38), "pure anti-community, pure evil and negation" (Laclau, 1996, p. 42).[8]

What makes these remarks especially problematic is that they are largely developed in the context of an ontological justification. Laclau and Mouffe do not spill much ink on the analysis of the actual social and political influence of neoliberal, financial or other elite actors. Instead, they claim that the existential struggle between hostile collective identities triggered by the conspiratorial abuse of power is an unsurmountable feature of *any* social and political life. Thus, despite their anti-essentialist approach to identity formation, they stop short at the key elements of their model of political mobilization. "The people" is characterized not as an historically specific category emerging in the wake of capitalist modernity, but rather as an ontological necessity, a quasi-mythical substance of social life. Similarly, "the enemy" is introduced as the precondition for the formation of any group identity (Mouffe, 2005, pp. 56–57, 2018, pp. 90–93). In this sense, Laclau and Mouffe ambivalence toward emancipatory perspectives does not simply emerge from an insufficient analysis of the contemporary historical conjuncture but is a matter of principle. Instead of reflecting on the condition of possibility of the "individual and social emancipation from domination" (Horkheimer & Adorno, 2002, p. 165) and the "abolition of violence" (Horkheimer & Adorno, 2002, p. 165), the post-Marxistmodel of left-wing populism eventually remains imprisoned within the ontological assumption that "violence is ineradicable" (Mouffe, 2000, p. 132).

Conclusion: The Political Implications of Left-Wing Populism

In this paper, it was demonstrated that Laclau and Mouffe's model of left-wing populism is based on a Manichaean, personalized worldview that fails to take into account the impersonal, anonymous aspects of modern relations of domination and coercion, as well an uncritical politics of affect which, instead of strengthening processes of critical (self-)reflection, reinforces the unconscious experience of suffering and dissatisfaction. Based on a reading of both Freud's as well as Horkheimer and Adorno's social psychology, it was argued that Laclau and Mouffe not only constrain their own emancipatory claims, but also connect these with explicitly anti-emancipatory conceptions of collective identity and existential struggle.

Against this background, it also becomes possible to evaluate the political implications of Laclau and Mouffe's model of left-wing populism. Going back to the social-psychological terrain, it is instructive to look at the main political conclusion which Adorno draws from his reading of Freud. What Freud discovered, Adorno asserts, is nothing less than the socio-psychological foundations of modern fascist movements: "It is not an overstatement if we say that Freud [...] clearly foresaw the rise and nature of fascist mass movements in purely psychological categories" (Adorno, 1982, p. 120). This statement can be read as a warning against the dangerous political consequences resulting from Laclau and Mouffe's essentialization and euphemization of the main insights of the Freudian mass psychology. It would be misleading, however, to accuse Laclau and Mouffe of simply replicating a right-wing approach. For this would ignore that Laclau and Mouffe indeed intend to develop an alternative to right-wing populism. The problem is rather located at another level: Instead of radically transforming the social-psychological foundations of right-wing politics, they take these foundations for granted and only suggest to orientate them "towards more egalitarian objectives" (Mouffe, 2018, p. 22). This emphasis on symptoms rather than causes also leads them to a half-hearted critique of right-wing populism. Mouffe, for instance, suggests that this critique needs to focus on the leaders and organizers, but should not be extended to their supporters. A left-wing populist approach, she asserts, "does not mean condoning the politics of right-wing populist parties, but refusing to attribute to their voters the responsibility for the way their demands are articulated" (Mouffe, 2018, p. 22). This statement puts the problematic political implications of left-wing populism in a nutshell: Not only does left-wing populism fail to develop a critique of the social causes of the mass support for right-wing populist politics, it also reproduces, in inversed form, the elitist assumption that most individuals are incapable of understanding their social circumstances, of finding appropriate political representatives, and of taking responsibility for their own views and actions. Left-wing populism might be an attractive political strategy to win popular support and electoral majorities. In the end, however, it does not support its (potential) supporters in becoming active, conscious, and independent participants in emancipatory processes.

Acknowledgements We would like to thank the organizers of the 2017 Oxford Graduate Political Theory Conference on "Democracy and Dissent: Theorizing Political Agency from Sites of Difference" for the opportunity to present and discuss an early version of our argument developed here.

Notes

1. For an approach that utilizes the early "Frankfurt School" for the critical analysis of contemporary right-wing populism, see Rensmann (2018).
2. For Gramsci's critical engagement with *both* economic determinism and political voluntarism, see Gramsci (1971, pp. 125–205). For a systematic analysis of the historical specificity of Gramsci's theory of hegemony, see Thomas (2010, pp. 220–241).
3. For more contemporary approaches, see Bonefeldt (2016), Gerstenberger (2009), Heinrich (2012), and Postone (1993).
4. In her latest work, Mouffe provides some glimpses of a more structural analysis of the process of neoliberal transformation which, however, remains highly rudimentary and largely irrelevant for her model of political mobilization (Mouffe, 2018, pp. 25–27).
5. Such remarks tend to be disregarded by recent post-Marxist attempts to conceptually detach populism from nationalism (see for example De Cleen, 2017; De Cleen & Stavrakakis, 2017; Stavrakakis et al., 2017).
6. Following Adorno, the limitations of immanent critique are reached if the object of critique does not offer normative claims against which it can be measured and evaluated. In that case, he suggests to examine the conditions under which anti-emancipatory claims become socially and politically attractive (Adorno, 1982, 1996).
7. To shed light on this problematic tendency, it is also possible to examine Mouffe's utilization of the work of Carl Schmitt who developed an ontological justification of relations of enmity (Schmitt, 2007; Mouffe, 2000, pp. 36–59; 2005, pp. 8–19). Various authors convincingly demonstrate Mouffe's failure or unwillingness to take the influence of Schmitt's authoritarian and fascist political positions on his theoretical reasoning seriously (see for example Arato, 2013; Cohen, 2019). This type of critique, however, usually does not explain why

Schmitt is so attractive for Mouffe in the first place. An engagement with the social-psychological underpinnings of her work is a useful starting point in order to illuminate these motives.

8. It should be noted that Mouffe's notion of enmity is less radical: Distinguishing between the concepts of "enemy" and "adversary", she advocates a less militant type of political struggle in which the enemy is at the same time recognized as a legitimate participant in this struggle (Mouffe, 2000, pp. 80–107). However, this does not affect her general agreement with Laclau's notion of "the enemy" as an external force that is "perceived as putting into question *our* identity and threatening *our* existence" (Mouffe, 2013, p. 5, original emphasis).

LITERATURE

Adorno, T. W. (1971). *Kritik. Kleine Schriften zur Gesellschaft*. Suhrkamp.

Adorno, T. W. (1982). Freudian theory and the pattern of Fascist Propaganda. In A. Arato & E. Gebhardt (Eds.), *Essential Frankfurt school reader* (pp. 118–137). Blackwell.

Adorno, T. W. (1997). Opinion delusion society. *The Yale Journal of Criticism, 10*(2), 227–245.

Adorno, T. W. (2017). *An introduction to dialectics*. Polity Press.

Adorno, T. W. (2017). *Soziologische Schriften II*. (2nd ed., Vol. 2). Suhrkamp.

Arato, A. (2013). Political theology and populism. *Social Research, 80*(1), 143–172. Retrieved from http://www.jstor.org/stable/24385712.

Arato, A., & Cohen, J. L. (2017). Civil society, populism and religion. *Constellations, 24*(3), 283–295. https://doi.org/10.1111/1467-8675.12312.

Bonefeldt, W. (2016). Negative dialectics and the critique of economic objectivity. *History of the Human Sciences, 29*(2), 60–76. https://doi.org/10.1177/0952695116637294.

Bray, M. (2015). Rearticulating contemporary populism: Class, state, and neoliberal Society. *Historical Materialism, 23*(2), 27–64. https://doi.org/10.1163/1569206X-12341422

Boucher, G. (2008). *The charmed circle of ideology: A critique of Laclau & Mouffe, Butler & Žižek*. re.press.

Cohen, J. L. (2019). What's wrong with the normative theory (and the actual practice) of left populism. *Constellations, 26*(3), 391–407. https://doi.org/10.1111/1467-8675.12427.

De Cleen, B. (2017). Populism and nationalism. In C. Rovira Kaltwasser, P. Taggart, P. Ochoa Espejo & P. Ostiguy (Eds.), *Oxford Handbook of populism* (pp. 342–362). Oxford University Press.

De Cleen, B., & Stavrakakis, Y. (2017). Distinctions and articulations: A discourse theoretical framework for the study of populism and nationalism. *Javnost - the Public, 24*(4), 301–319. https://doi.org/10.1080/13183222.2017.1330083.

Errejón, I., & Mouffe, C. (2016). *Podemos: In the name of the people*. Lawrence and Wishart.

Fassin, É. (2019). The blind spots of left populism. *Krisis 2019 (1)*, 86–90. Retrieved from https://krisis.eu/wp-content/uploads/2019/10/Krisis-2019-1-Didier-Fassin-The-Blind-Spots-of-Left-Populism.pdf.

Fassin, É., Tazzioli, M., Hallward, P. & Aradau, C. (2018). Left-wing populism: A Legacy of defeat—Interview with Éric Fassin. *Radical Philosophy, 2*(2). Retrieved from https://www.radicalphilosophy.com/article/left-wing-populism.

Freud, S. (1955). Group psychology and the analysis of the ego. 1920–1922. In J. Strachey (Ed.), *The standard edition of the complete psychological works of Sigmund Freud* (Vol. XVIII, pp. 65–142). Hogarth Press.

Gerstenberger, H. (2009). *Impersonal power: History and theory of the Bourgeois State*. Brill.

Gramsci, A. (1971). *Selections from the prison notebooks*. International Publishers.

Heinrich, M. (2012). *An introduction to the three volumes of Karl Marx's capital*. Monthly Review Press.

Horkheimer, M. (2013). *Eclipse of reason*. Martino Publishing.

Horkheimer, M., & Adorno, T. W. (2002). *Dialectics of enlightenment: Philosophical fragments*. Stanford University Press.

Laclau, E. (1990). *New reflections on the revolution of our time*. Verso.

Laclau, E. (1996). *Emancipation(s)*. Verso.

Laclau, E. (2005). *On populist reason*. Verso.

Laclau, E. & Mouffe, C. (1996). Post-marxism without apologies. In E. Laclau (1996). *New reflections on the revolution of our time* (pp. 97–132). Verso.

Laclau, E., & Mouffe, C. (2014). *Hegemony and socialist strategy* (2nd ed.). Verso.

Marchart, O. (2007). *Post-foundational political thought: Political difference in Nancy, Lefort, Badiou and Laclau*. Edinburgh University Press.

Marx, K., & Engels, F. (1996). *Collected works volume 35—Karl Marx capital: Volume 1*. Lawrence & Wishart.

Miklitsch, R. (1995). The rhetoric of post-marxism: Discourse and institutionality in Laclau and Mouffe, Resnick and Wolff. *Social Text, 45*(Winter), 167–196. https://doi.org/10.2307/466680.

Mouffe, C. (2000). *The democratic paradox*. Verso.

Mouffe, C. (2005). *On the political*. Verso.

Mouffe, C. (2013). *Agonistics: Thinking the world politically*. Verso.

Mouffe, C. (2016). The populist moment. *Open Democracy*. Retrieved from https://www.opendemocracy.net/en/democraciaabierta/populist-moment/.

Mouffe, C. (2018). *For a left populism*. Verso.

Müller, J.-W. (2016). *What is populism?* University of Pennsylvania.

Postone, M. (1993). *Time, labour and social domination: A reinterpretation of Marx's critical theory*. Cambridge University Press.

Rensmann, L. (2018). The persistence of the authoritarian appeal: On critical theory as framework for studying populist actors in European democracies. In J. Morelock (Ed.), *Critical theory and authoritarian populism* (pp. 29–48). University of Westminster Press.

Schmitt, C. (2007). *The concept of the political* (expanded). University of Chicago Press.

Sotiris, P. (2017). From the nation to the people of a potential new historical bloc: Rethinking popular sovereignty through Gramsci. *International Gramsci Journal, 2*(2), 52–88. Retrieved from https://ro.uow.edu.au/gramsci/vol2/iss2/6.

Sparke, M. (2005). *In the space of theory: Postfoundational geographies of the nation-state*. University of Minnesota Press.

Stavrakakis, Y., Katsampekis, G., Nikisianis, N., Kioupkiolis, A., & Siomos, T. (2017). Extreme right-wing populism in Europe: Revisiting a reified association. *Critical*

Discourse Studies, 14(4), 420–439. https://doi.org/10.1080/17405904.2017.1309325.

Thomas, P. D. (2010). *The Gramscian moment: Philosophy, hegemony and marxism.* Haymarket Books.

Wood, E. M. (1998). *The retreat from class: A new 'true' socialism.* Verso.

Žižek, S. (2006). Against the populist temptation. *Critical Inquiry, 32*(3), 551–574. https://doi.org/10.1086/505378.

Žižek, S. (2008). *In defense of lost causes.* Verso.

Part III

The Political Psychology of Populism & its Affective Underpinnings

CHAPTER 6

The Psychology of Populism

Darren G. Lilleker and Nathalie Weidhase

Introduction

Populism is defined by Cas Mudde (2004) as a thin or weak ideology: merely an argumentational style that is centered on a set of basic but shared assumptions about the world. The populist politician is likely to invoke images of race and nation, dwelling on juxtaposing the symbolism of historical greatness with a present where the history and culture are under attack from others. Populism thus is more of a rhetorical style than a political program, not only because it has a range of nationally contextualized variants, but also because it promises to return the nation or a people to the status enjoyed in some long past and often mythical golden age. While promoting a people-centered project, populists tend to blame elites for betraying the heritage, culture, and sovereignty of the nation. Hence when scholars talk of populism as more of a communication style, they highlight the anti-elitist and people-centered argumentational tropes. The populists presents themselves as the voice of the 'pure' people whose identity and societal status, often privilege, is being threatened by agents who represent interests that differ from those of the people. The targets for attacks tend to be domestic governments or bureaucracies which

D. G. Lilleker (✉)
Faculty of Media & Communication, Bournemouth University, Poole, UK
e-mail: DLilleker@bournemouth.ac.uk

N. Weidhase
Department of Sociology, University of Surrey, Guildford, UK
e-mail: n.weidhase@surrey.ac.uk

are targeted because they allow a nation to become subjugated by transnational actors such as the EU; defend the rights of outsiders, often migrants or refugees, so undermining the rights of so-called indigenous populations; and so broadly betray the will of the masses. Elsewhere in this handbook one can study differing instances of populism, our interest, however, is understanding the cognitive processes that make individuals susceptible to manipulation by populist political rhetoricians.

We argue that the causes for populism to gain support are underexplored and that often those who attend rallies, pledge support, and lend their votes to populists belong to an underclass who are socially conservative, xenophobic, and lacking the values which democracies espouse. We seek to challenge these assumptions. Firstly, we present evidence that demonstrates that populism appeals most to citizens who feel disenfranchised and marginalized yet belong to the majority ethnic group. These are people who are likely to have serious concerns about their life chances, but yet lack real political representation. While it is true that supporters of populist projects tend to have low educational attainment, lower standards of living and income, low interest and knowledge of politics, and feel increasingly unrepresented by mainstream, centrist political projects (Norris & Inglehart, 2019), this does not necessarily make them backward or stupid. Rather, we argue that there is an appeal of populists among these groups precisely because of the combination of fear and anger they feel due to their socioeconomic conditions. Such individuals seek solutions to the problems they face during their lived experiences, ones which populists hint they offer.

Secondly, we adopt a cognitive approach to explain how populist rhetoric supports the cognitive needs of these individuals. Populism seeks to give the disenfranchised a voice, provides a glimpse of an identity that places the marginalized at the heart of a political project, and speaks in a rhetoric the less politically literate citizen can understand, engage with, and identify with. The appeal of populism, we argue, is its simplicity, a simple narrative which speaks to current lived experiences while offering a glimpse of a better future where the meek can inherit their earth, their land, and reclaim their identity. In building this argument we draw on concepts of identity as well as cognitive psychology, but first, we identify who the populists are.

Who Are the Populists

The finding that voting leave at the UK's 2016 referendum on membership of the European Union was associated with older age, White ethnicity, low educational attainment, infrequent use of smartphones and the internet, receiving benefits, adverse health and low life satisfaction (Alabrese et al., 2019) was used to deride this group. Matthijs Rooduijn's (2018) study shows that many of these characteristics are shared by those with the highest propensity to support populists. In a study of fifteen European nations, those voting for the ten radical right parties tended to be male, of low education, of lower social class, and with lower levels of religious beliefs. However, these demographic variables only tell a partial story and are not significant for every case. The more significant predictors are attitudinal variables, specifically high levels of political distrust and negative attitudes toward immigrants. While this matches the caricature of the low educated xenophobe, the fact that political distrust is the most significant predictive attitude suggests a slightly more complex predictor. Sören Holmberg (1999), writing in one of the first studies that responded to the downturn in trust in political institutions, argued that trust and distrust were factors of partisan support of the government, personal, and national economic security and perceptions of external threats.

Studies over the intervening two decades have shown party convergence over many areas of policy (Holmberg, 2019), increased economic insecurity due to the global financial crisis of 2008 (Muro & Vidal, 2017), and what has been dubbed an immigration crisis (Freitag & Kijewski, 2017), all impacting negatively citizen's feelings of trust and security. Arguably, these factors are cumulative and have come together to decrease public trust in political institutions (Gaina et al., 2020), particularly among those who are most vulnerable to declining socioeconomic conditions. Those within the lower social strata have fewer opportunities for social or employment mobility, they live in more insular communities, and are anchored by traditions of partisanship and social hierarchies (Norris & Inglehart, 2019). As partisan divides become blurred, one anchor becomes seriously eroded. Recession brings job insecurity and fears for the life chances of oneself and one's family. Immigration brings pressures on services and greater competition for jobs. These are real experiences. Jolanda Jetton's research (2019) shows opposition to immigration is founded on perceptions that immigrants are given greater support than the indigenous working class, who feel their rights and status are becoming devalued. Trust in political institutions, seen as distant from these people, declines, particularly as institutions are seen incapable of dealing with either the financial or immigration crises. The tensions felt by these people are only assuaged by the populist who offers to give these marginalized individuals a voice. The following discussions introduce two concepts; the first being identity and the second communication heuristics, to suggest why the people characterized here are more susceptible to populist political rhetoric.

The Psychology of Identity and the Lure of Populism

The populist communication style creates a sense of identity, they give rhetorical substance to an entity called 'the people' a mythical homogenous community which is ill-served by those with power (Moffitt & Tormey, 2014). While a mythical, or at least imagined community, the identity is created within historical and popular culture narratives of nation or race. Giddens (1991) argues that people seek security in a coherent identity with biographical continuity; simply put, people need to know who they are and where they come from. Dmitry Chernobrov (2016, p. 593) argues that where the "self's most valued continuity lies" is in "preserving a positive image of the self." Experiences which question the positive image of the self must therefore be assuaged and external forces are needed on which to pin blame. Here we introduce the notion of the other. Othering is a concept widely used within both sociological, psychological, and communication research to explain the creation of a stereotype, one used to define a group that can be blamed for the ills of a community on the basis of their difference (Dervin, 2012). To 'other' is to define an out-group, those who are not part of the community and differ from the in-group. To other is to view differences through a xenophobic, fearful lens. But othering is also a defense mechanism, it allows blame to be placed on the outsider because the outsider's difference makes them wrong so making the in-group identity's correctness even more immutable (Murer, 2010).

One example would be Germany's Alternative für Deutschland (AfD, Alternative for Germany) and their appeal to a German homeland that needs protection. Robert Grimm noted in 2015 that the AfD began to move toward "a xenophobic, nativist and law and order rhetoric" (p. 265) particularly in East Germany, where the party received 20.5 percent of the vote in 2017 German election—roughly double what it received in the western states with 10.7 percent (Hansen & Olsen, 2018). AfD voters are drawn to the party's anti-immigration stance more than their Eurosceptic ideology, and in fact "the dominant factor by far impacting vote choice for the AfD in 2017 was anti-immigrant sentiment" (Hansen & Olsen, 2018, p. 15). The refugee crisis in the summer of 2015 and the subsequent influx of refugees had a considerable impact on the electoral success of the AfD in national and regional parliaments (Stecker & Debus, 2019). The AfD's anti-immigration rhetoric is embedded in a nativist fantasy of Germany's past that needs resurrecting. Particularly in (relation to) East Germany, the AfD mobilizes a form of nostalgia that both glorifies the Eastern past, and promises a future better than the West German alternative. This is a strategy not unique to the AfD: the right-wing protest movement PEGIDA ("Patriotische Europäer gegen die Islamisierung des Abendlandes", which translates to "Patriotic Europeans against the Islamization of the Occident") used the concept of Monday demonstrations and the Peaceful Revolution slogan "Wir sind das Volk!" ("We are the people!") to legitimize their political claims and activities (Volk, 2020). Slogans like "Vollende die Wende" ("Complete the Turn)," another term for the Peaceful Revolution and fall of the Berlin Wall in 1989) or "Wende 2.0" ("Turning Point 2.0") offer revisionist populist fantasies that tap into a sense of collective identity that can only be understood and realized by those considered 'insiders'.

This insider group is constructed in inherently nativist terms: the people invited to join this mythical future are those of German heritage only. One of the AfD election posters used in the 2017 election featured the image of a non-White pregnant woman's torso with the slogan "'New Germans'?

We prefer making them ourselves!" (Non-White) immigrants (and their children) are not considered German, and thus not part of German history or future. It is noteworthy, however, that this rhetorical appeal to the homeland and native population is not restricted to right-wing parties, as examples from Germany and the UK show. In 2000, then-CDU candidate in the North Rhine Westphalia State Election Jürgen Rüttgers caused controversy when, during his election campaign, he demanded more investment in IT training for the native German youth rather than loosening immigration restrictions with the slogan "Kinder statt Inder!" ("Children instead of Indians!"). This comment was made at the height of the *Leitkultur* ('leading culture') debate, in which German politicians and public intellectuals aimed but struggled to define "the existence of a clearly identifiable spectrum of German cultural values" (Manz, 2004, p. 481) to which immigrants were supposed to adhere. While Germany continues to view its people as being bound together by cultural and especially blood ties (Brubaker, 1992), the Leitkultur debate seemingly aimed to shift questions of (national) belonging away from heritage and toward greater emphasis of common culture and values. Particularly since the 1950s and its increase in 'guest workers' to support post-war economic growth, and the subsequent increase in population share with immigration history, a definition of German citizenship and belonging predominantly based on lineage seems outdated in times of a multicultural German reality. However, based on Bassam Tibi's notion of a European Leitkultur, including values such as "primacy of reason over absolute religious revelation" and "universally acknowledged pluralism" (Tibi, 2000, p. 183), the German version appropriated some of the vagueness of the original and filled in some gaps with demands of cultural assimilation as a condition for national belonging. As such, Tibi's concept was "easily appropriated by the right through an ethnocultural interpretation" (Manz, 2004, p. 485). Rüttgers' campaign, then, marked a stark return to the notion of heritage-based ties that define Germany as a national community, where preference is given to heritage over other forms of belonging.

Similarly, at his first conference speech as Labour leader in 2007, Prime Minister Gordon Brown stated his government would invest in "British jobs for British workers" (Summers, 2009), embracing a rhetoric previously reserved for parties like UKIP. As such, mobilizing a slogan that "resonated with a defensive and fearful nationalist sentiment and a growing resentment about immigration" (Yates, 2015, p. 115) revealed the slow mainstreaming of populist rhetoric in political communication: the same slogan was later repurposed by protesters on the pickets of the Lindsey Oil Refinery Dispute. Three years later, Brown was caught on microphone calling Rochdale pensioner Gillian Duffy a 'bigoted woman' at a campaign event during the 2010 UK General Election after she challenged him on immigration from Eastern Europe (Mullany, 2011). This tension between publicly used slogans and personal conviction further illustrates the instrumental use of populist rhetoric mobilized to connect with voters: simplistic populist messages that identify clear in-groups and out-groups.

Those experiencing high levels of insecurity and perceived marginalization are those most in need of finding an identity to feel secure about. That can be tribal identities around music or football teams or their place within a national identity which Ashley Jardina (2019) argues has emerged in the US as a backlash against Obama's presidency. Populists seek to create the identity of 'pure' people, the ultimate in-group, and characterize them as being in a battle against one or more outgroups (Mudde, 2004). The outgroup may be elites generally, specific politicians or the political class, or insurgent outsiders such as immigrants. While the socioeconomic privations experienced by those who are susceptible to populists may be more due to global market forces, the lack of clear partisan representation combined with austerity policies and competition over jobs and access to welfare allow space for simpler narratives to gain traction (Norris & Inglehart, 2019). Traction can be particularly strong when the populist promises to redress the imbalances that cause grievances, often reporting commonly felt grievances back to their targeted communities. Through the creation of a shared identity of the people, the populist reinforces their own authenticity as one of that community while presenting a Manichean understanding of complex issues: if 'they' are winning, 'we' are losing (Waisbord, 2018). The notion of a shared identity under attack, as well as out-groups towards which to point blame, resonate with the psychological needs of those most likely to support populist projects.

The Power of a Populist Communication Style: Cues, Heuristics and Bias

The insularity of many of these communities means that the notion of a shared identity is powerful, and the notion of a community of the people resonates with narratives of class solidarity as well as a nation being as one in the face of forces of enmity. Such tropes appeal because they resonate with ideas learned through socialization and basic education, history is often taught in ways that instill national values which can remain part of national consciousness among the many who do not progress beyond basic comprehensive education (see Tomlinson, 2019 for example). They are also likely to draw inferences about values and culture from a narrow diet of media and popular culture. Because of these factors as well as lower levels of civic education, the individuals within those demographics who are most likely to find appeal in populist rhetoric are those who are most likely to lack a sophisticated perspective of society and nation. Equally, these individuals are least likely to have high interest in and knowledge of the complex processes by which policies are determined or the constraints which impact upon politicians satisfying the competing demands of various segments of the population. While they have high levels of concern about a whole range of issues, they are likely to find politics a low involvement area of their lives. Low involvement would also be exacerbated by their low trust in those who are seen as being professional politicians: politicians perceived to focus on their careers above the wider interests of society (Jones, 2008).

Individuals who approach an issue with low involvement tend to process political arguments peripherally, applying little or no serious critical attention. Rather than considering arguments carefully they might focus on simple slogans, images, expressions of authenticity, and the charismatic style of the individual populist politician. Such communicational elements are referred to as informational cues. As such, they contain minimal information about the policy or the specifics of a political program.

Slogans like Boris Johnson's 2019 UK General Election rallying cry "Get Brexit Done," Donald Trump's "Make America Great Again," or the AfD's "Vollende die Wende" (complete unification) are examples of low-information political communication: they make emotional appeals rather than policy proposals. These slogans offer simplistic appeals to a supposedly better, more glorious past (as in the case of "Make America Great Again" and "Vollende die Wende"), or promise a better future free of current and past constraints (as is the case with "Get Brexit Done"). "Get Brexit Done" in particular highlights the vacuity of populist slogans: its short appeal to relief from the seemingly endless (but in fact only four years) debates about the meaning of Brexit hides the uncertain future of trade talks and a potential cliff edge at the end of the transition period in January 2021.

This is perhaps why "Get Brexit Done" was a more successful slogan, leading to the election of Boris Johnson, than "Brexit means Brexit," Theresa May's attempt to stake out her Brexit stance to appeal to voters. Even the follow-up, the "red, white and blue Brexit" did not clarify matters much, but did appeal to a vague, perhaps banal (Billig, 1995) sense of Britishness and nationalism. May's 2017 election campaign (or the failure thereof), which centered on the slogan "Strong and Stable" neither of which May was able to embody, ultimately resulted in the loss of a clear Conservative majority and a hung parliament that made the following two years of Brexit policy-making more difficult than perhaps expected. While "Brexit means Brexit" was equally simplistic, its tautological emptiness was devoid of any meaning. "Get Brexit Done" pointed toward an end point in the foreseeable future, whereas "Brexit means Brexit" promised nothing but an eternal rhetorical (and political) circle—the opposite of an escape or successful journey. Delivered in conjunction with Boris Johnson's optimism and populist charisma, "Get Brexit Done" promised voters a move to a brighter future.

What they offer, then, is a cognitive shortcut, if the informational cue resonates it is stored in the memory and if reinforced can form the basis of an attitude, particularly if the cue reinforces existing biases and prejudices the individual holds (Petty & Cacioppo, 1986). A slogan may give an indication of the priorities of one candidate or another, if it resonates it will act as the foundation for a positive attitude. Similarly, pictures of a candidate with ordinary people, or memes which capture public sentiment, can capture attention, aid recall of a slogan, and again inform attitude formation. Informational cues about the character of the candidate, their authenticity and the extent they represent the values of a community can have particular resonance. All these elements, and a range of similar informational cues, are powerful as they have emotional resonance and so affect receivers (Petty et al., 2015).

The populist style of communication is designed precisely to appeal to the individual with low involvement in formal politics. The populist deliberately targets those who are marginalized, feel disenfranchised, and whose life chances are fragile to the vagaries of socioeconomic change. Populists build a persona of authenticity, claim to speak for the pure people while defining those they represent as people for whom they speak and seek opportunities to appear like the woman or man in the street. The populist communication style also means they are likely to stand out within the political communication environment. Benjamin Arditi (2005) likened populists to the drunk at the party, the person who speaks their mind and challenges conventions. Standing out, through the use of controversial claims, slogans, and memes, means populist messages cut through the clutter, reach their audience and have resonance.

It is worth noting that populist communication and performance style in particular is indebted to popular culture, as exemplified by the rise of the celebrity politician. Affinity and connection are built through performance and communication styles not dissimilar to those of celebrities connecting with their fans (Street, 2019). Populist leaders "can become quasi-celebrities, known as much – or sometimes more – for their media performances and stylistic outbursts than for the 'content' of their politics" (Moffitt, 2020, p. 85). As the former host of US reality TV show *The Apprentice*, one such example would be Donald Trump, whose communication style is "characterized by [its] own form of reasoning, one that was more about persona than prose" (Dow, 2017, p. 136). Chants like "Lock her up!" (directed at his 2016 opponent Hillary Rodham Clinton) and "Build the wall!" play up to his (former) role as an entertainer, ultimately pose more questions than they answer, and serve as crowd motivators, rather than serious policy proposals and as such echo Boris Johnson's style of communication.

At the same time, it is a communication style that marks Trump as different from traditional politicians, which is further enforced by the mobilization of his celebrity status. As the star of *The Apprentice*, Trump has been able to craft himself as a 'self-made' millionaire who made his fortunes through hard graft rather than the wealth into which he was born. This marks him as different from traditional career politicians: his ability to "pass as somehow *working class*" despite his upbringing and success, together with his "vulgarian persona" (Biressi, 2020, p. 128, original emphasis) set him apart from dynasty and career politicians. Indeed, for celebrity politicians and populists, "Achieving an image of authenticity may indeed mean defining oneself *against* the traditional politician" (Street, 2019: 10). In the case of Trump, his perceived authenticity, partially constructed through his transgressive verbal style of telling it how it is," enabled a communication style that "effectively distilled the complex reality of neoliberal competition, race and class rivalries and xenophobia into a simple story" (Biressi, 2020, p. 128). It is then this anti-establishment political persona that gives credence and perceived heft to the simplistic messages of the (celebrity) populist.

Yet populist claims seldom truly add up. The inferred connections between migration and the privations experienced by those in fragile economic situations are often spurious at best, other threats from migration are false, similarly there is little chance of going back to the glorious ages that populists invoke to negatively portray the present or a future unless the populist gains power. The populist does not invite critical reflection, they seek visceral reaction, they seek to have an affective response. Psychologists Daniel Kahnemann and Amos Tversky argue that those most susceptible to manipulation, arriving at the wrong but obvious answer, are those least likely to consider issues carefully (Kahneman, 2011). Using the cognitive reflection test alongside a range of other conundrums, they found a strong correlation between a failure to answer logic tests and a failure to overcome other real-world problems. Arguably it may not purely be a lack of cognitive ability, although individuals who do not undertake logic tests a lot may encounter problems as may those with lower educational attainment. However, those with low involvement and under conditions of high affect may also find themselves in a position where affect overrules logic. Arguably populists encourage their targeted communities to use what Daniel Kahnemann and Amos Tversky called system one thinking, where limited processing of information means one arrives at the most obvious, if erroneous, answer (Kahneman, 2011). Acceptance of populist arguments is aided through their use of simple but resonant visuals and slogans which do not require analysis but reinforce extant prejudices (McDermott, 2001). Social media platforms such as Twitter, Facebook, and WhatsApp, all utilized heavily by populists during recent contests, work along communicative norms that elide with the populist style (Engesser et al., 2017). Not only do eye-catching, controversial, and amusing statements gain traction, they encourage the formation of echo chambers where Manichean views can be constantly reinforced. Hence, the modern communication environment supports the rise in support of populist arguments among the sections of national populations most susceptible to their arguments.

Concluding Thoughts

Populist supporters are the citizens most sensitive to change, their economic circumstances make their existence fragile and hostage to global socioeconomic and political forces. Their low education attainment matched with low involvement in politics makes them susceptible to the simplicity of arguments of populists. Populists fill a representational void within communities which party strategies of moving to the center ground have opened. In seeking representation and a voice they find the authentic style, in-touch rhetoric and out-group explanation as one which explains their situation while providing what might seem an easy solution. In emphasizing base identity politics, the populist gives these communities hope as well as a source of blame. But the rise of the populist should not be blamed on the inadequacy of those citizens who are the losers in the neo-liberal globalized economy. These voters have been marginalized by mainstream parties who manage economies to benefit business and not the less privileged. It is this gap which populists successfully exploit and their rise should be a warning to those projects that claim to champion the principles of democracy.

Literature

Alabrese, E., Becker, S. O., Fetzer, T., & Novy, D. (2019). Who voted for Brexit? Individual and regional data combined. *European Journal of Political Economy, 56*, 132–150.

Arditi, B. (2005). Populism as an internal periphery of democratic politics. In F. Panizza (Ed.), *Populism and the mirror of democracy* (pp. 72–99). Verso.

Billig, M. (1995). *Banal nationalism.* Sage.

Biressi, A. (2020). President Trump: Celebrity-in-chief and the desecration of political authority. *Celebrity Studies, 1*(1), 125–139.

Brubaker, R. (1992). *Citizenship and nationhood in France and Germany.* Cambridge University Press.

Chernobrov, D. (2016). Ontological security and public (mis) recognition of international crises: Uncertainty, political imagining, and the self. *Political Psychology, 37*(5), 581–596.

Dervin, F. (2012). Cultural identity, representation and othering. *The Routledge handbook of language and intercultural communication, 2*, 181–194.

Dow, B. J. (2017). Taking Trump seriously: Personal and presidential politics in 2016. *Women's Studies in Communication, 40*(2), 136–139.

Engesser, S., Ernst, N., Esser, F., & Büchel, F. (2017). Populism and social media: How politicians spread a fragmented ideology. *Information, Communication & Society, 20*(8), 1109–1126.

Freitag, M., & Kijewski, S. (2017). Negative experiences and out-group trust: The formation of natives' trust toward immigrants. *International Journal of Intercultural Relations, 59*, 9–18.

Gaina, V., Dimdins, G., Austers, I., Muzikante, I., & Leja, V. (2020). Testing a psychological model of political trust. *International Journal of Smart Education and Urban Society (IJSEUS), 11*(3), 1–10.

Giddens, A. (1991). *Modernity and self-identity: Self and society in the late modern age.* Stanford university press.

Grimm, R. (2015). The rise of the German Eurosceptic party alternative für Deutschland, between ordoliberal critique and popular anxiety. *International Political Science Review, 36*(3), 264–278.

Holmberg, C. (2019). *Convergence, polarization and the rise of radical right parties—The effect of convergence on one dimension on the polarization on another in Western European party systems.* Lund Student Papers. https://lup.lub.lu.se/student-papers/search/publication/8965244.

Holmberg, S. (1999). Down and down we go: Political trust in Sweden. In P. Norris (Ed.), *Critical citizens: Global support for democratic government* (pp. 103–122), Oxford University Press.

Hansen, M. A., & Olsen, J. (2018). Flesh of the same flesh: A study of voters for the Alternative for Germany (AfD) in the 2017 election. *German Politics, 28*(1), 1–19.

Jardina, A. (2019). *White identity politics*. Cambridge University Press.

Jetten, J. (2019). The wealth paradox: Prosperity and opposition to immigration. *European Journal of Social Psychology, 49*(6), 1097–1113.

Jones, K. (2008). Professional politicians as the subjects of moral panic. *Australian Journal of Political Science, 43*(2), 243–258.

Kahneman, D. (2011). *Thinking, fast and slow*. Macmillan.

Manz, S. (2004). Constructing a normative national identity: The *Leitkultur* debate in Germany, 2000/2001. *Journal of Multilingual and Multicultural Development, 25*(5–6), 481–496.

McDermott, R. (2001). The psychological ideas of Amos Tversky and their relevance for political science. *Journal of Theoretical Politics, 13*(1), 5–33.

Moffitt, B. (2020). *The global rise of populism: Performance, political style and representation*. Stanford, CA: Stanford University Press.

Moffitt, B., & Tormey, S. (2014). Rethinking populism: Politics, mediatisation and political style. *Political Studies, 62*(2), 381–397.

Murer, J. S. (2010). Institutionalizing enemies: The consequences of reifying projection in post-conflict environments. *Psychoanalysis, Culture & Society, 15*(1), 1–19.

Mudde, C. (2004). The populist Zeitgeist: *Government and opposition, 39*(4), 541–563.

Mullany, L. (2011). Frontstage and backstage: Gordon Brown, the 'bigoted woman' and im/politeness in the 2010 UK General Election. In S. Mills (Ed.), *Discursive approaches to politeness* (pp. 133–165). De Gruyter.

Muro, D., & Vidal, G. (2017). Political mistrust in southern Europe since the Great Recession. *Mediterranean Politics, 22*(2), 197–217.

Norris, P., & Inglehart, R. (2019). *Cultural backlash: Trump, Brexit, and authoritarian populism*. Cambridge University Press.

Petty, R. E., & Cacioppo, J. T. (1986). The elaboration likelihood model of persuasion. In L. Berkowitz (Ed.), Advances in experimental social psychology (pp. 123–205). New York: Academic Press.

Petty, R. E., Cacioppo, J. T., & Kasmer, J. A. (2015). The role of affect in the elaboration likelihood model of persuasion. In L. Donohew, H. Sypher, & E. T. Higgins (Eds.), Communication, Social Cognition, and Affect (pp. 117-146). Hillsdale, N J: Edbaum.

Rooduijn, M. (2018). What unites the voter bases of populist parties? Comparing the electorates of 15 populist parties. *European Political Science Review, 10*(3), 351–368.

Stecker, C., & Debus, M. (2019). Refugees welcome? Zum Einfluss der Flüchtlingsunterbringung auf den Wahlerfolg der AfD bei der Bundestagswahl 2017 in Bayern. *Politische Vierteljahresschrift, 60*, 299–323.

Street, J. (2019). What is Donald Trump? Forms of 'celebrity' in celebrity politics. *Political Studies Review, 17*(1), 3–13.

Summers, D. (2009, January 30). Brown stands by British jobs for British workers remarks. *The Guardian*. Available online https://www.theguardian.com/politics/2009/jan/30/brown-british-jobs-workers.

Tibi, B. (2000). *Europa ohne Identität? Die Krise der multikulturellen Gesellschaft*. Bertelsmann.

Tomlinson, S. (2019). *Education and race from empire to Brexit*. Policy Press.

Volk, S. (2020). "*Wir sind das Volk!*" Representative Claim-Making and Populist Style in the PEGIDA Movement's Discourse. *German Politics*, online first https://www.tandfonline.com/doi/abs/; https://doi.org/10.1080/09644008.2020.1742325.

Waisbord, S. (2018). The elective affinity between post-truth communication and populist politics. *Communication Research and Practice*, 4(1), 17–34.

Yates, C. (2015). *The play of political culture, emotion and identity*. Palgrave Macmillan.

CHAPTER 7

Emotional Mobilization: The Affective Underpinnings of Right-Wing Populist Party Support

Hans-Georg Betz and Michael Oswald

Forty Years of Radical Right-Wing Populism: An Assessment

In recent years, the academic literature on radical right-wing populism in liberal democracies has grown at an exponential rate. Major political science journals have dedicated special issues to the phenomenon; leading scholars throughout the social sciences—from sociology to economics, from communications to gender studies—have taken note of its importance and made significant contributions to the burgeoning literature; and the media have disseminated their findings among the general public. As a result, radical right-wing populism is currently one of the most closely scrutinized phenomena in contemporary comparative politics.

Several reasons account for this development: Most importantly the presidency of Donald Trump and Brexit; secondly, the upsurge of support for radical right-wing populist parties in the aftermath of the financial crisis of 2008, particularly in France, Italy, Austria, and the Scandinavian countries; thirdly, the emergence of radical right-wing populist parties in Western European countries previously thought to be immune to radical right-wing

H.-G. Betz (✉)
Department of Political Science, University of Zurich, Zurich, Switzerland
e-mail: hans-georg.betz@uzh.ch

M. Oswald
Political Science, University of Passau, Passau, Germany
e-mail: michael.oswald@uni-passau.de

© The Author(s), under exclusive license to Springer Nature Switzerland AG 2022
M. Oswald (ed.), *The Palgrave Handbook of Populism*,
https://doi.org/10.1007/978-3-030-80803-7_7

mobilization, i.e., Germany and Spain. Finally, the diffusion of a political climate of democratic distemper which has become a breeding ground for a 'politics of backlash,' for 'illiberal democracy,' and a yearning for strong leaders.

One of the most important results of this intense academic preoccupation with the populist right has been growing awareness of the complexity and seemingly irreconcilable contradictions inherent in contemporary radical right-wing populism in liberal democracies. This is a far cry from the relatively cursory explanations advanced at the beginning of the first broad-based wave of Western European populist mobilization in the early 1990s. These studies interpreted the radical populist right's success at the polls largely as a response to processes of socioeconomic and/or sociocultural modernization and/or a response to the upsurge of migration starting in the late 1980s (for Austria see Halla et al., 2017; Wodak & Pelinka, 2002).

On this reading, the appeal of radical right-wing populist parties in the 1990s was largely owed to their ability to speak to the "losers of modernization" (Betz, 1994). The explanation appeared plausible and seductive, it had only one flaw: it fundamentally clashed with empirical reality. It turned out that right-wing populist parties did best in some of the most dynamic and affluent countries and regions in Western Europe—Austria, Denmark, the German-speaking cantons of Switzerland, northern Italy, the Flemish part of Belgium, and finally Germany. Their electoral base reached across all social strata; but it was particularly pronounced among various segments of the middle class, such as skilled workers and entrepreneurs of small and medium-sized companies and their staff. Not surprisingly, most of these parties—from the Front national in France to the Freedom Party of Austria (FPÖ) in Austria to the Lega Nord in Italy—promoted a program inspired by economic liberalism.

During the first wave of radical right-wing populist mobilization, parties such as the Danish Fremskrittspartiet and its Norwegian counterpart, the Fremskrittspartiet, were largely dismissed as 'flash parties,' i.e., parties "that come and go" (Lane & Ersson, 2007, p. 95). But the second wave of radical right-wing populist mobilization following the financial crisis of 2008 showed that the populist right has become a permanent fixture in a large number of liberal democracies. It demonstrated once more that these parties were capable of defying all attempts on the part of the political establishment to relegate them to the 'smut' margins of politics. In fact, in a growing number of advanced liberal democracies, some right-wing populist parties have managed to break through the *cordon sanitaire*, they have become *salonfähig*. It was a tacit acknowledgment of the key role radical right-wing populist leaders such as the late Jörg Haider and his successor, the disgraced Heinz-Christian Strache in Austria, Marine Le Pen in France, and Matteo Salvini in Italy have come to play in contemporary Western European politics.

In this paper, we set out to develop a comprehensive analytical/interpretative framework for the study of contemporary right-wing populism in liberal democracies, based on the extant state of the art literature on the subject. In Western Europe, right-wing populism is a relatively new phenomenon. Its genealogy, however, is much longer, going all the way back into the nineteenth century. Historically, instances of radical right-wing populist mobilization have always advanced two ideational narratives—a populist indictment of the elite, however defined, and a nativist claim to stand for the legitimate aspirations of the native-born. It is this ideational amalgam which accounts to a large extent for the success of radical right-wing populism in advanced liberal democracies today.

What sets radical right-wing populist parties and movements apart is their deliberate elicitation of a panoply of emotions, such as anxiety, anger, and nostalgia. Narratives tend to evoke a nostalgic vision of 'the good old days': the years of the postwar economic miracle (the famous German *Wirtschaftswunder*, the French *trente glorieuses* and the Golden Age in the US), marked by rapid economic growth, full (male) employment, expanding welfare programs and growing mass prosperity. These were the years when the belief in progress was still intact and the future was still positively defined. This is certainly no longer the case in contemporary Western Europe. Western European societies today are suffused with a combination of negative emotions, ranging from anxieties, fears, and indignation to outright rage in response to a multitude of crises, threats, and uncertainties, for which the political establishment does not seem to have any realistic and sustainable solutions. For large parts of the population, the future is negatively defined—particularly when it comes to the future prospects. The upsurge of Western European radical right-wing populism in recent years has to be seen in this larger context. It is for that reason that an explanation of the phenomenon needs to consider the whole range of input from across the social sciences, from political science to economics, from sociology and social psychology to cultural studies, from political geography to gender studies and, last but not least, legal studies.

This, however, is only half of the story. Contextual conditions favorable for populist mobilization remain latent if there are no credible and persuasive political entrepreneurs capable of translating vague popular unease and apprehension into a terse, trenchant narrative. This explains, for instance, in part why Germany and Spain for a long time appeared relatively immune to the sirens of right-wing populism—a fact that was erroneously attributed to the lasting impact of the lessons learnt from history. The gains of the Alternative for Germany (AfD) and the sudden upsurge of electoral support for Vox in national and regional elections in Spain have gainsaid this notion. They have demonstrated once again that the political appeal to resentment is a wide-open field ready to welcome any political newcomer savvy enough to take advantage of the opportunities offered by popular political disenchantment, disaffection, and rage. It took the AfD only a few years to pose a serious challenge to Germany's established parties, particularly in the eastern part of the country. The resurgence of the populist right in Flanders (Vlaams Belang) and the sudden upsurge of support for a relative newcomer in the Netherlands (Forum voor Democratie) in the most recent European election are also prominent cases in point.

A comprehensive analysis of contemporary radical right-wing populism has to take account of all of these features. Given the vast amount of literature on the topic—and the sensitive nature of the phenomenon under investigation—any attempt to advance such an analysis obviously poses a particularly significant challenge. The choice of literature, as well as supporting evidence, must necessarily be selective, informed by the idiosyncratic predispositions of the interpreters. We will sketch the outlines of a broad-based interpretative framework for the analysis of contemporary radical right-wing populism in advanced liberal democracies largely based on the extant literature on the topic. The discussion is divided into three parts. The first part addresses questions of taxonomy. It deals with the main features of radical right-wing populism with a particular emphasis on genealogy. The second part addresses the question of what accounts for the protracted staying power of radical right-wing populist parties. The third part briefly addresses the question of what these parties have concretely done when in a position of genuine power to respond to the concerns and interests of the 'ordinary people' they purport to represent.

What Is Right-Wing Populism?

Stripped down to its most basic core, right-wing populism is a fusion of two ideational elements—populism and nativism. Populism as political doctrine holds that society is divided into two antagonistic blocs—the vast majority of ordinary people and a relatively small elite that acts in its own interest. Nativism is informed by the notion that the material and cultural interests of the 'native-born' should be accorded absolute priority over those new to the community—and that solely on the grounds that the former are natives. Politically, it involves a variety of measures on the part of the 'indigenous' population designed to defend, maintain, and revive the cherished heritage of their culture. In the American contest, where the concept originated, it has centered upon the "demand that citizens come before noncitizens, Americans before foreigners, and that we take care of home first before abroad" (Greenberg & Zdunkewicz, 2017, p. 6).

In short, nativism fundamentally rejects the progressive extension of Peter Singer's 'moral circle'—i.e., the distinction between those entities that are deemed worthy of moral consideration and those that are not (Crimston et al., 2016; Singer, 1983). Instead, it advocates a narrow conception of solidarity on the grounds that only a narrow conception will sustain solidarity in an age of progressive individualization (de Beer & Koster, 2009). In practical policy terms, nativist doctrine holds that governments have as their primary duty the promotion and protection of the well-being and welfare of its own citizens, often defined in ethnic terms. At the same time, nativist doctrine demands from governments the active demonstration of a "reasonable partiality towards compatriots" (Miller, 2005)—particularly with regard to employment and social benefits.

In today's right-wing populism, nativism is closely aligned with the notion of national sovereignty. It is this combination, which is at the heart of the radical right's 'neo-nationalist' appeal, which Maureen Eger and Sarah Valdez have shown to constitute the defining characteristic of the contemporary radical right in advanced capitalist democracies (Eger & Valdez, 2015, 2019). At the same time, neo-nationalism represents a certain degree of common ground between the populist right and the populist left. Both are vehemently anti-establishment (take, for instance, Podemos's attacks against *la casta*), both explicitly seek to regain national sovereignty—if for quite different reasons (Eger & Valdez, 2015, p. 127). They usually diverge on the question of nativism, even if the populist left occasionally appears tempted by nativist appeals (a prominent example is Sahra Wagenknecht of *Die Linke* who adopted nativist lingo in an attempt to regain AfD voters).

What Accounts for the Staying Power of Right-Wing Populist Parties?

Much of the current debate on right-wing populism conveys the impression that this is a new phenomenon. Nothing could be further from the truth. Right-wing populist parties have been around for decades. A number of them, such as the FPÖ, the Rassemblement National, the Fremskrittspartiet and the Lega are among the most well-established parties in Western Europe. In fact, the Lega, which was founded in 1991 as Lega Nord, is now the 'oldest' still existing party of the Italian Second Republic, having survived all the ups and downs of almost three decades of Italian politics. This differentiates the contemporary radical populist right from earlier populist movements and parties in liberal democracies (such as the French Poujadists in the 1950s) which mostly had a relatively short shelf life. Granted, most contemporary right-wing populist parties have experienced a series of ups and downs at the polls, in some cases these fluctuations have been quite dramatic. A case in point is the Vlaams Belang (VB, originally Vlaams Blok). After continuously rising in the polls in the first decade of the new century, the party's support base had virtually collapsed by the parliamentary election of 2014, with many of its former voters defecting to the relatively moderate Flemish nationalist Nieuw-Vlaamse Alliantie. Five years later, the VB was back, increasing the number of its seats in the Belgian parliament from 3 (2014) to 18. The resurgence of Pauline Hanson in the Australian parliamentary elections of 2016, after spending almost twenty years in the political wilderness, is an even more striking example (see David B. MacDonald in this volume).

What might explain the resilience of contemporary radical right-wing populist parities over an extended period of time? In general, explanations for the rise and success of these parties have primarily focused on macrostructural factors such as modernization, globalization, economic and financial crises, and more recently, rapid technological innovation. These factors certainly are of prime relevance, particularly for understanding the recent upsurge of right-wing support across advanced liberal democracies. The crucial question is, however, how these macrostructural factors translate into support for the radical populist right. Empirical evidence shows, for instance, that financial crises tend to result in a significant increase in support for far-right political parties (Funke et al., 2016). This was certainly the case in the aftermath of the 'Great Recession' of 2008 which—albeit not across the board and to the same extent—saw a significant upsurge in support for the populist right in a number of countries (Kriesi & Pappas, 2015). Correlation, however, does not explain the mechanisms that link macrostructural factors to electoral outcomes. After all, financial crises do not vote for the radical right. We believe the contemporary radical right's remarkable staying power is their ability to evoke, appeal to, and mobilize a range of primarily negative emotions.

Methodological Individualism and the Crucial Role of Emotions

Ernesto Laclau has argued that the analysis of populism has to start on the individual level (Laclau, 2005). On this view, populism is the result of individuals' demands that remain ignored, dismissed and, as a result, unmet and unsatisfied within the established democratic framework, primarily because of the political establishment's unresponsiveness to these demands. Political space for populist mobilization opens up when individuals come to realize that they are not alone, that their demands and grievances are part of a larger chain of equivalent demands and grievances dismissed by the political establishment as unreasonable and/or politically incorrect. This leads to the constitution of an antagonistic frontier *vis-à-vis* an antagonistic force, aka the elite (Thomassen, 2005, p. 292). As a result, what started as a single, unconnected demand turns into a fundamental populist challenge to the socioeconomic and sociopolitical establishment.

Laclau's individual-level approach helps to set the focus in order to understand a political project that mobilizes ordinary people into contentious political action while "articulating an anti-elite, nationalist rhetoric that *valorizes* ordinary people" (Jansen, 2011, p. 82, italics added). Jansen's formulation makes an important point regarding an essential facet of populism: the fact that populism accords recognition to ordinary people, their anxieties, and concerns. It does this by satisfying the need for psychological compensation via a rhetoric that primarily appeals to a range of primarily negative emotions, such as anger, indignation, and resentment (on the difference see Miceli & Castelfranchi, 2019), but also fears of loss (Oswald & Broda, 2020). In *Strangers in their own land* Arlie Russell Hochschild characterizes Trump supporters as having been "in mourning for a lost way of life." Yearning "to feel pride" they instead "have felt shame. Their land no longer feels their own" (Hochschild, 2006,

225). Kathy J. Cramer makes a similar point in *The Politics of Resentment*, with respect to the mood—which had been building up way before Trump's campaign—that would lead disenchanted rural populations to support Donald Trump (Cramer, 2016).

Arthur C. Brooks noted in an article for *Foreign Affairs* that the United States had a 'dignity deficit.' This was important because "to be treated with dignity means being considered worthy of respect" (Brooks, 2017, p. 108). Individuals gain a sense of dignity, in turn, when they have a feeling that their lives produce value for themselves and others. "Put simply, to feel dignified, one must be needed by others" (Brooks, 2017, p. 108). But delocalization, offshoring, outsourcing, and, as a result, deindustrialization in advanced capitalist countries have made many workers "structurally irrelevant" (Castells, 2004). And often Trump supporters were depicted as ignorant, racist, and misogynist rubes, in need of enlightenment, their awareness raised (Lynch, 2017).

What distinguished Donald Trump from his competitors was his willingness and ability to tap into these sentiments. As Hochschild puts it, Trump.

> is an 'emotions candidate.' More than any other presidential candidate in decades, Trump focuses on eliciting and praising emotional responses from his fans rather than detailed policy prescriptions. His speeches – evoking dominance, bravado, clarity, national pride, and personal uplift – inspire an emotional transformation. (Hochschild, 2006, 225)

His audience, as if 'magically lifted,' no longer feel like strangers in their own land (Hochschild, 2006, p. 226).Trump put a significant emphasis on the concerns of workers in his campaign speeches, according to them some measure of dignity by "raising their moral value" (Lamont et al., 2017, 153). This is where individual-level emotions translate into political support.

Mabel Berezin has noted that emotions "are physical and expressive responses to some sort of destabilization" (Berezin, 2002, 36). Destabilization is closely related to Robert Andrew's notion of 'strains' or 'stressors' which figure prominently in his explanation of the causes of crime and delinquency. Andrew has made a strong case that strains evoke powerful negative emotions, such as anger and fear (Agnew, 2001; Ganem, 2019). Mikko Salmela and Christian von Scheve explicate the link between individual experience, macro-level transformations (social and cultural), and electoral outcomes. This translates into support for right-wing parties at the micro-level via mechanisms that transpose feelings of personal insecurity in the face of macro-level dislocations into emotions (such as resentment, anger, rage) (Salmela & von Scheve, 2017). It is likely that those mechanism trigger actions from penning insulting and denigrating comments on newspaper websites and the social media, to taking part in demonstrations (for instance, Pegida) or voting for a radical right-wing populist party (Heaney, 2019, p. 226).

Anger, rage resentment, and indignation together with anxiety and fear are the most prominent emotions cited in the literature on populism in general and radical right-wing populism in particular. Takis Pappas's study of *Populism and Liberal Democracy* refers to emotions—and here particularly resentment/ressentiment—as a core mechanism fuelling populist rhetoric (Pappas, 2019). For example, fear of globalization is closely associated with support for the radical populist right (de Vries & Hoffmann, 2016). What most of these emotions (anxiety is a notable exception) have in common is that they have negative connotations, as does embitterment, which recently joined the list (Poutvaarna and Steinhardt 2018). What most of them also have in common is the fact that all of them represent reactions to perceived moral injuries, injustices, and insults. Embitterment, for instance, similar to resentment, is characterized as an emotive response to "persistent feelings of being let down, insulted or being a loser" (Linden, 2003, p. 197). A perception of injustice paired with the feeling to be unable to take countermeasures might lead to these severe frustrations.

Anger seems to be particularly conducive and responsive to populist mobilization (Marcus et al., 2019). For one, anger is closely associated with appraisals of unfairness experienced as an undeserved injustice and the perception of having been wronged (Miceli & Castelfranchi, 2019; Mikula et al., 1998). This perception, in turn, is closely associated with 'other-agency,' i.e., the notion that an external agent is responsible for a negative event or condition (Ellsworth & Smith, 1988, 280). In other words, for anger to manifest itself, there has to be an 'appraisal of accountability'—the notion that somebody is to be blamed for the negative event or condition (Smith & Lazarus, 1990, p. 619). The perception of having been wronged, in turn, "renders anger 'legitimate,' that is, it makes anger coincide with *resentment* proper" (Miceli & Castelfranchi, 2019, p. 17). This makes anger an ideal motivating factor for populist mobilization (see also Rico et al., 2017). This also applies to another major emotion associated with populism—nostalgia (Kenny, 2017; Gest et al., 2017; Steenvoorden & Harteveld, 2018).

The Nostalgia Factor

Johannes Hofer coined the term nostalgia in 1688 and defined it as being the "sad mood originating from the desire for the return to one's native land (Anspach [Hofer] 1934, p. 381)." Nostalgia today is no longer a sickness but an emotional state and it has increasingly been brought into a connection with populism (Gest et al., 2017; Kenny, 2017; Polletta & Callahan, 2017; Steenvoorden & Harteveld, 2018; van Tilburg et al., 2019).

Understanding nostalgia as an emotion, it can—when activated—produce images and notions of times when life was 'good' (Wilson, 1999, p. 297). According to Marshall McLuhan, nostalgia is an understanding of the present in a rear-view mirror perspective. He presumes that humans generally perceive the future in relation to the past and that they almost cling to the familiar.

McLuhan cites cars which were initially referred to as "horseless carriages" (McLuhan, 1968, p. 292). This sense of familiarity helps to understand life experiences, especially of the 'common people' (Ylä-Anttila, 2017, p. 342). In economic terms, this experience is often the remembrance of good times with large economic growth, full employment, and a moral society. But it can also be just the idea of a longing for a familiar coziness, which the German origin for nostalgia 'Heimweh' tells. With that rear-view mirror perspective, nostalgia can be defined as a sense of longing for an imagined glorious past (Mols & Jetten, 2014, p. 77). This desire should not be misunderstood as an identification with past times; rather, rear-view mirror nostalgia denotes a flight into an ideal world "of gingerbread and nursery" (McLuhan, 1970, p. 189). This enables the positive reinterpretation of a seemingly past golden age (Naughton & Vlasic, 1998, p. 60) and the term nostalgia transcends mere sentimentality: On the one hand, it can affect human emotion, and on the other, it demands an active re-construction of the past (Wilson, 1990, p. 299).

This kind of retrospection is problematic not only because it is irrational given that the period of time in question cannot be recreated and thus the longing fulfilled (Wilson, 1990, p. 297); nostalgia in this understanding is more than just the longing for a certain time period—this past is the cliché of the look into the past with rose-colored glasses. Therefore, this rear-view does not have to relate to an actual past, it merely has to create the impression among recipients that they were removed from this ideal in their memories (Wilson, 1990, pp. 297, 301). This idealized past offers a perspective where people can long to, especially since nostalgia has at least some roots in dissatisfaction (Natali, 2004, p. 18).

Although nostalgia is not a negative emotion per se, there is a connection to fear, insecurity, longing, and other strong emotions. In right-wing populist rhetoric, emotions, and feelings are important because communicators tap into sentiments of threat and loss. They thus frame policy issues in a way that they evoke emotions like anger, anxiety, fear, and feelings of powerlessness (Salmela & von Scheve, 2017, p. 580). Some of those discourses are more appealing than others but they are all infused with fear, anxiety, desire or hope. These discourses lead to audience identification or relatability (Solomon 2013).

Salmela and Scheve cite two psychological mechanisms as the reasons for the rise of the new populist right: ressentiment and emotional distancing. The mechanism of ressentiment work in a way that negative emotions (fear/insecurity) turn from repressed shame into anger/resentment/hate toward the 'enemies' (political, cultural elites, immigrants, etc.) (Salmela & von Scheve, 2017, p. 580). They see "a common denominator for all social classes affected by precarization is their vulnerability to significant losses, both economically and socially, and their fears of losing their job, social position and standards of living" (Salmela & von Scheve, 2017, p. 580). This fear of declining living conditions caused by an imminent threat along with the resulting dissatisfaction seems to be preconditions which make people susceptible to nostalgia (Mols & Jetten, 2014, p. 77). This can be a sense of cultural loss but also status anxiety.

Status describes the position of an individual in a social group, legally or professionally but it also entails the perception of the position one "deserves by virtue of one's social position" (Busquet, 2011, 70). Since individuals in a meritocratic system are "trapped by a series of structural changes that they cannot control, but which affect them directly [...] [, they] may fall from favor and expose themselves to losing their social position and status" (Busquet, 2011, 70f.). And a fear of precarization or déclassement seems to have a similar or even bigger impact politically than actual déclassement (Salmela & von Scheve, 2017, p. 580).

> [N]ostalgic deprivation mainly stems from a 'discrepancy between individuals' self-reported social, political, or economic status and their perceptions of the past that moderates support [therefore,] Nostalgic deprivation is a measure of how much status has been gained or lost over time (Gest et al., 2017, p. 1712).

When the imagined ideal and the present do not match a sense of loss can ensue (Wilson, 1999, p. 297, 301). In cases like these, "narratives of the past are often used to supply ontological security in the present" (Kinvall, 2014, p. 322). Nostalgia can bring back a certain worth since it "reassures us of past happiness and accomplishment" [...] "irrespective of how present circumstances may seem to question or obscure this" (Davis, 1977, P. 420).

> [A] distinction between emotions and cognition as alternative paths to resonance sheds light on the different mechanisms that account for frame effectiveness. It helps us for example, to make sense of [...] the election of Trump, in which beliefs and understandings did not necessarily align with powerful emotions of discontent with the status quo (Giorgi, 2017, p. 728).

Right-wing populist strategies are also often geared toward strengthening collective fears like the loss of the national identity. In the context of returning to a perceived original state of affairs, nostalgia may serve as a means of attraction (Mols & Jetten, 2014, p. 76f.). According to Wilson, nostalgia becomes relevant in the sense that its strategic use is particularly effective when cultural change is occurring in a society, and some people increasingly feel obsolete (Wilson, 1999, p. 301). Nostalgia seems to be the perfect cope for the new structures through modernization, globalization, and automation. These identity-based strategies often rely upon we vs. them dichotomies as discursive techniques in order to exclude specific groups. Frequently, the goal is a newly defined self-image of the audience as a group (Mols & Jetten, 2014, p. 76). As such, nostalgia is closely linked to identity, both individual and collective. Nostalgia "reassures us of past happiness and accomplishment" and "simultaneously bestows upon us a certain worth, irrespective of how present circumstances may seem to question or obscure this" (Davis, 1977, p. 420).

As Tuukka Ylä-Anttila has argued, nostalgia derives much of its emotional impetus from a sense of familiarity, which "is particularly compatible with the populist valorization of the experience of the common people" (Ylä-Anttila, 2017, p. 342). Or, as GuobinYang in his analysis of Chinese nostalgia in the 1990s observes, nostalgia "affirms identity through articulation" which "makes possible the public sharing of private experiences." It "brings private thoughts and feelings into the public sphere while also helping to transform that sphere by creating or reconstructing collective identities among particular social groups" (Yang, 2002, pp. 278–279). This goes a long way to shed light on the mechanisms informing the contemporary radical populist right's identitarian politics (Betz & Johnson, 2004).

Recent works on emotional effects of specific framing include Rinaldo Kühne's integrative mode. Frames trigger specific anticipated emotions such as anger, sadness, or fear (Kühne, 2013, p. 17f.). Cognitive resonance stems mostly from an appeal to audience's beliefs and understandings. Emotional resonance is based on an appeal to audience's feelings, passions, and inspirations. Identification might be the main mechanism (Giorgi, 2017, p. 728). According to the value function in prospect theory, it is in particular loss frames that have an effect on individuals (Tversky & Kahneman, 1981). This type of communication strategy is often utilized in populist tactics, thereby aiming for perceived dissonance between government and society. Frequently, nostalgia and traditionalism are combined in the process in order to foster fears of the future (Mols & Jetten, 2014, p. 76).

Nostalgia, understood as an emotion, is closely associated with grief over experienced loss, either as an individual confronted with the passing away of a loved one or as a community with the inexorable transformation of a familiar space (such as, for instance, a neighborhood as a result of gentrification). Here nostalgia reflects a yearning for the lost sense of community brought about by the dislocations associated with globalization, financialization, technological innovation, and societal modernization. Examples of this kind of nostalgia abound, from the nostalgia of the Cultural Revolution generation in 1990s China to nostalgia for the Soviet Union in current-day Russia to the nostalgia for the German Democratic Republic (GDR) in the eastern part of Germany—aka *Ostalgie*—which explains, at least in part, why the AfD has been so successful there (Betz & Habersack, 2019; Pourtova, 2013; Yang 2002).

At the same time, however, nostalgia represents a "symptom of the real unease caused by an unjust society, a condition that would disappear as soon as the underlying cause of the dissatisfaction was done away with" (Natali, 2004, 18). This was the case with nineteenth-century American populists' embracing of a bucolic vision of the Jeffersonian republic, directed against bankers and commodity speculators, railroad magnates, grain elevator operators, and local money lenders (Oswald, 2020). This is the case today when Sweden's radical populist right evokes the world of Astrid Lindgren together with the notion of the *folkhemmet* (literally, the people's Home), which defined the golden era of Swedish Social Democracy in the postwar decades—when life was significantly harder but also more 'innocent' and 'simpler' than today (Elgenius & Rydgren, 2019). And it was the case in 2016, when 81% of Trump supporters said their life is worse than it was 50 years ago for people like them (Pew Research Center, 2016). Indeed, trends in absolute income mobility show the percentage of children earning more than their parents has declined drastically in the past 70 years (Chetty et al., 2017).

Since nostalgia is not necessarily negatively defined, unlike anger, rage, resentment, and embitterment, in an age characterized by grand-scale social, economic, and cultural destabilization, the politics of nostalgia can also represent an emotional counterweight providing a positive sense of reassurance and comfort for those profoundly troubled by these developments. Or, as Catarina Kinvall puts it, "narratives of the past are often used to supply ontological security in the present"—i.e., a "sense of biographical continuity in the light of emerging changes" (Kinvall, 2014, p. 322).

All of this, in turn, explains the central position the question of identity holds in the contemporary radical populist right's discourse. In a recent analysis of the rationale behind the recent upsurge of populism cum nativism in India under the banner of Hindu nationalism (promoted by Modi's BJP and affiliated groups), Kinvall lays out the logic of the links between nostalgia, identity, and support for radical right-wing populism. Citing a passage from Anthony Giddens' *The Constitution of Society*, she notes that "ontological security is about having a 'sense of place' as the world is changing, a 'place' that provides 'a psychological tie between the biography of the individual and the locales that are the settings of the time–space paths through which that individual moves'" (Kinvall 2019, 285). With the impact of globalization, rapid technological change, and mass migration, this experienced sense of space—what the Germans call *Heimat*—which provides the individual with meaning with respect to both the past and the present, becomes increasingly disrupted and instable. Individuals feel increasingly "trapped by a series of structural changes that they cannot control, but which affect them directly" (Busquet, 2011, p. 70) leaving them with the sense of having become strangers in their own land.

Catch-All-Parties of Protest and Structural Factors Prone to Engender Strong Emotions

In recent years, students of radical right-wing populism have reached a tentative consensus to separate its causes along economic and cultural lines (Gidron & Hall, 2017). At the same time, there is a strong sense that economic factors might have a smaller effect on support for the radical populist right than do cultural ones (Bornschier, 2010; Bornschier & Kriesi, 2013; Davis et al., 2019; Inglehart & Norris, 2016). Against that, the most recent direction in research on the structural causes of radical right-wing populist support suggests that economics does matter, but in significantly more complex ways than earlier theoretical approaches suggested (see, for instance, Vlandas & Halikiopoulou, 2019). These approaches presumed that support for right-wing populist parties, such as the Rassemblement National or the German Republikaner, was to a large extent the direct result of the inability of certain groups in society to adapt to the risks associated with modernization processes such as individualization or with economic processes such as globalization (the well-known "modernization loser thesis").

The argument had considerable intuitive appeal but failed when empirically tested. In fact, empirical studies have shown that support for radical right-wing populist parties extends across the whole of the social spectrum, with 'modernization loser' groups accounting for only a relatively small share of the vote. The explanation is as straightforward as it is mundane: Unemployed or relatively poor people tend not to vote. Left-wing parties, in return, have little incentive to appeal to these potential voters. And radical right-wing populist parties don't seem to be able to mobilize them either. A case in point is the AfD: typical 'modernization losers' were not significantly more likely to vote for the AfD than was everybody else. Support for the party came largely from individuals with average and/or higher incomes (Lengfeld, 2017; see also Schwander & Manow, 2017).

This is not to deny the importance of the 'proletarization' of the radical populist right over the past few decades. This denotes a gradual shift in the core constituency of successful parties such as the Front national, the FPÖ, the Scandinavian Progress parties, and the Swiss People's Party (SVP) from the old middle class to the popular classes, what in French is known as the *couches populaires*. They are responsible for the "changing face of class politics"—set in motion by the defection of a significant part of the manual working class from the traditional left to the radical populist right (Arzheimer, 2013; Bornschier & Kriesi, 2013). At the same time, however, the populist right has managed to mobilize a remarkably heterogeneous, yet volatile, social coalition with a substantial presence of working-class voters.

In the process, these parties have turned into what one might characterize as catch-all-parties of protest, seeking to appeal to a broad range of potential constituencies without, however, substantially toning down their rhetoric on core issues. The catch-all strategy has been reflected in a broadening of their programmatic offerings as well as intensified efforts on the part of these parties to brush up their image and insert themselves into the mainstream—following Marine le Pen's strategy of *dédiabolisation*. Mainstreaming refers in this context to both "a process of accommodation between the democratic political system and the populist far right" and "the adaptation of mainstream political discourse" to their issues and logic (Feischmidt & Hervik, 2015, pp. 10–11). This has increasingly happened, most recently in Denmark with the social democrats largely adopting the anti-immigrant agenda of the Dansk

Folkeparti—resulting in a drastic drop-in electoral support for the latter, and in Austria, where the center-right ÖVP followed a similar path (Heinisch et al., 2019).

Simon Bornschier and Hanspeter Kriesi maintain that "economic marginalization and job insecurity play no role in determining the vote" for radical right-wing populist parties (Bornschier & Kriesi, 2013, p. 26). The most recent literature on the combined impact of globalization and technological innovation challenges this view. It suggests that globalization and technological innovation have revived traditional political cleavages—particularly center-periphery ones.

Originally, the center-periphery cleavages opened up between the central state seeking to impose a dominant culture across the territory and the periphery seeking to preserve its cultural idiosyncracies. More recently, they involved conflicts between relatively affluent regions, such as Flanders, Scotland, Catalonia, and northern Italy and the rest of the country charged with "living off the hard work of the former." Today, these regional conflicts are overshadowed by a new conflict, engendered by the growing polarization between areas that benefit from the combination of globalization and automation and those that are increasingly falling behind or have been left behind altogether (Rodríguez-Pose, 2018; Wuthnow, 2018). It is these "places that don't matter," as Andrés Rodríguez-Pose (2018) puts it, that voters are "surfing the wave of populism and, through the ballot box or revolt, attacking the very factors on which recent economic growth has been based: open markets, migration, economic integration and globalization" (Rodríguez-Pose, 2018, p. 205).

The growing number of studies addressing this polarization clearly show one thing—geography matters. A recent study on home ownership in the UK shows that disparities in home ownership and real estate values strongly correlate with the results of the Brexit vote (Ansell & Adler, 2019). In Sweden, support for the radical populist right (Sverigedemokraterna) has been concentrated in the south of the country to a degree that defies common social science explanations (Blomqvist et al., 2019, p. 14). With respect to the United States, Trump did particularly well in communities "with more economic distress, worse health, higher drug, alcohol and suicide mortality rates, lower educations attainment, and higher marital separation/divorce rates." These are "places that are generally worse off today than they were a generation or two ago" (Monnat & Brown, 2017, p. 229). Those are particularly rural areas and small towns in the formerly industrial Midwest. Closely associated with this spatial dimension is a second important development—the growing cleavage between cosmopolitanism and parochialism (or, alternatively, communitarianism) characteristic of virtually all advanced liberal capitalist democracies. Both developments are important for the study of the radical populist right because they tend to elicit a range of emotions.

Among the most significant of such emotions are the ones provoked by, and associated with, individual feelings of relative deprivation, both economic (winners vs. losers of globalization and automation) and cultural (cosmopolitan vs. parochial dispositions). Relative deprivation is broadly defined "as a judgment that one or one's ingroup is disadvantaged compared to a relevant referent; this judgment invokes feelings of angry resentment" (Pettigrew, 2016, p. 9). It is an individual experience that "may arise when people compare their socio-economic status with that of others at the same point in time (social comparison) or with their own past or future status" (Chen, 2015, p. 3). This might explain the finding that an increase in aggregate education in non-urban areas is associated with greater support for the radical populist right (Stockemer, 2017). It is at the local level that diverging social trajectories are particularly apparent and observable and the sense of falling behind particularly painfully experienced, potentially leading to resentment. As a number of studies have shown, relative deprivation is associated with a strong sense of injustice with respect to the individual's predicament, giving rise to negative sentiments, such as anger and resentment (Smith et al., 2012, p. 203). Today, the experience of relative deprivation is primarily a result of genuine and/or perceived status loss. Experimental studies suggest that relative deprivation potentially "impacts aggressive behavior" via "increased feelings of disadvantage and aggressive affect" (Greitemeyer & Sagioglou, 2019, p. 515).

Brian Burgoon et al. demonstrate that "positional deprivation relative to the wealthiest deciles (upper-register positional deprivation) tends to spur support for the radical left" while "positional deprivation relative to the poorest deciles (lower-register positional deprivation) spurs support for the radical right" (Burgoon et al., 2019, p. 84). A recent contribution by Sarah Engler and David Weisstanner goes in the same direction. Starting with the observation that relative deprivation "reflects the extent to which citizens fall behind or stagnate even if they retain their job" they argue that relative deprivation makes radical right parties "appealing for voters" because they "use alternative non-economic criteria in their claim to restore status" (Engler & Weisstanner, 2020, p. 383). These and similar findings pair well with studies on the 'squeezing' of the middle class in advanced capitalist democracies. This has to a large extent been the result of technological change which has engendered broad-based increases in employment in both high and low skill occupations to the detriment of middle-skill occupations, resulting in job polarization (Acemoglu & Autor, 2011).

A number of empirical studies have shown that across Europe there has been a trend toward job polarization, with significant increases in the number of highest and lowest skilled jobs concomitant with an equally significant contraction of those in the middle (Goos et al., 2009; Peugny, 2019). Thomas Kurer's exploration of the 'declining middle' goes in the same direction. He argues that it is particularly among those workers who manage to 'survive' in the brave new world of massive economic restructuring that the radical populist right finds fertile ground for its resentment-laden discourse (Kurer, 2020). A comparative study of the sentiments of AfD and RN supporters in the strongholds of these two parties from 2018, for instance, found a widespread sense of unfairness and disadvantage stemming from personal "experiences of devaluation" coupled with a strong belief "that politics has withdrawn from certain social and geographical areas" resulting in an equally "strong sense of abandonment" (Hillje, 2018, p. 2).

Two secular processes account for these fears—globalization and automation. One significant result of automation has been a further acceleration of inequality. As Wolfgang Dauth et al. have shown for Germany, those workers who have retained their jobs—albeit not necessarily performing the same tasks as before the onset of automation—have seen a significant wage decline. Robots "raise labor productivity but not wages" (Dauth et al., 2017). Thus automation is contributing to inequality and its inexorable advance engenders anxiety among those potentially directly affected by it.

Stanley Rachman defines anxiety as "a tense anticipation of a threatening but formless event; a feeling of uneasy suspense" (Rachman, 2013, p. 2). Since anxiety lingers on, it represents a permanent psychological substratum for political mobilization. Thomas Kurer and Bruno Palier, for instance, have recently argued that the anxieties and disaffection on the part of those individuals faced with increasingly bleak employment prospects in the wake of automation represent a significant reservoir for radical right-wing populist mobilization (Kurer & Palier, 2019). A recent study of the impact of 'automation anxiety' on the 2016 Presidential election concludes that U.S. districts exposed to the 'robot revolution' were significantly more disposed to vote for Donald Trump than those less exposed. This suggests that the victims of automation have a considerable propensity to vote for radical political change (Frey et al., 2018, p. 26). In 2018, large majorities of respondents in ten countries (developed and developing) thought automation would not only make it more difficult for people to gain employment but also further increase inequality. Only a small minority said they believed automation would create new, better-paying jobs (Wike & Stokes, 2018).

Economic factors are important to account for a sense of status loss and relative deprivation associated with technological innovation (Alba & Foner, 2017). They are, however, hardly sufficient to explain the depth of resentment prevalent among significant segments of the population of advanced liberal democracies. They are part of a deep split between segments of society which increasingly overlaps with geographical sorting.

Wilkinson notes that urbanization "has sorted and segregated national populations and concentrated economic production in megacities, driving us further apart—culturally, economically, and politically—along the lines of ethnicity, education, and population density." Urbanization "has intensified the self-selection of temperamentally liberal individuals into higher education and big cities while leaving behind a lower-density population that is relatively uniform in white ethnicity, conservative disposition, and lower economic productivity" (Wilkinson, 2018, pp. 4–5). Richard Florida finds that 'bohemians' (characterized as formerly marginalized eccentric and alternative types of individuals with a high level of 'human capital' whose virtues make them particularly valuable in the new 'knowledge economy' where creativity and innovation are highly appreciated) are 'highly concentrated' in spaces which also have a high concentration of 'high-technology industry' (Florida, 2002, p. 67). 'Creative-class workers' tend to settle in cities with tolerant environments, diverse populations, and good jobs.

These arguments, while originally made with respect to the United States, are equally pertinent for current-day Western Europe. As elsewhere in Western Europe, it is the radical populist right, i.e., Salvini's Lega, which has benefited most from this 'problem of dignity.' In the European election, the Lega did very well throughout Lombardy and particularly in the deindustrialized towns in the vicinity of Milan—the only area held by the traditional left. The Lega's strongholds in norther Italy goes a long way to illuminate some of the dynamics which revived the party's electoral fortunes. Concentrated in small communities (15 thousand or less), middle-aged, with a steady job in the private sector, the typical 'leghisti' are "tied to their territorially-based traditions and identity." With a highly negative view of the national public administration and rather pessimistic with respect to the economic development of the country, they "fear of status loss and the associated privileges." For them, the Lega is the only party in Italy that defends their dignity and 'roots' (Rho, 2019).

Rho's account resonates to a large extent with similar accounts found in other Western European countries and in the United States in the wake of radical right-wing populist electoral success. In fact, on both sides of the Atlantic, these dynamics account for what has emerged as the major new political cleavage for the coming decades—cosmopolitanism versus parochialism (see Piketty, 2018). Michael Zürn and Pieter de Wilde have maintained that what is at the core of this divide are concerns "that directly address the core questions of justice in the face of globalization—concerns for redistribution, recognition and representation" (Zürn & de Wilde 2016, p. 293). In other words, these are questions of dignity and social justice.

In the United States, sociopolitical polarization is particularly glaring, driven by the new cleavage: "Democrats have become the party of the multicultural city, Republicans the party of the monocultural exurbs and country—the party of relatively urbanization resistant white people" (Wilkinson, 2018, p. 7). Similar observations have been made by Simon Kiss et al. with respect to Toronto and De Maesschalck in the case of Antwerp, both of them affluent metropolitan cities. Both studies reveal growing center–periphery tensions—reflecting a growing city-peri-urban divide and polarization (De Maesschalck, 2011; Kiss et al., 2020). The case of the Netherlands suggests, however, that the dynamics of this new cleavage are more complex and go beyond a simple urban/rural division. Both Amsterdam and Rotterdam are metropolitan areas. Yet the latter has been a fertile terrain for populists, most famously Pim Fortuyn, whereas in the former, populism has remained marginal. One explanation for these opposing trends lies in the socioeconomic and sociocultural differences between the two cities. Whereas Amsterdam has become an important service sector heavily weighted toward finance, research, and information and communication with a strong international focus. Against that, Rotterdam is dominated by its port, and by a traditional economic structure "that constantly threatens to become obsolete" (Enzinger, 2019).

Similar dynamics have been observed in Western Europe, most notably in France, the UK, Sweden, and the eastern part of Germany. As Christophe Guilluy shows, over the past several decades, France has increasingly been divided between "*la France périphérique* and *métropoles mondialisées*" (Guilluy, 2014, p. 71). Tellingly, Guilly promotes his analysis as a study on "how the popular classes have been sacrificed" on the altar of what he calls '*la mondialisation heureuse*' (happy globalization). At the same time, he shows how the neglect of, if not outright contempt for, the *France populaire* has breathed new life into the Front national under Marine Le Pen, who has successfully promoted herself as the advocate of *la France oubliée*—the forgotten France reflected, for instance, by the decline of public services in these areas, which leave its inhabitants with the impression of being second-class citizens (Fourquet, 2012, pp. 51–52). Similar observations were made by Hervé Le Bras and Emmanuel Todd. They noted as early as 2013 that the FN had become, economically and territorially, the party of the *dominés* (i.e., those lacking agency), "the weak which, as a result of their education and occupation, have been held at a distance from the urban centers of power and privileges, relegated to the peri-urban and rural areas" of the country (Le Bras & Todd, 2013, p. 290).

Similarly, in the UK, support for Brexit was particularly pronounced in lagging areas, which, ironically, have tended to benefit from the EU's support for regional and local economic development (Los et al., 2017). These are areas with very low levels of mobility, where residents feel, to a certain extent at least, trapped, unable to move to places promising greater opportunities. However, as Lee et al. (2018) have recently noted, lack of mobility "only matters for respondents living in places experiencing relative economic decline or those where there have been substantial recent increases in non-white British migrants." Had more of them been in a position to move, had these "left-behind" places done better economically, had they "remained more stable in terms of demographic composition," the Brexit vote might have gone in the other way (Lee et al., 2018).

Echoing observations advanced after the election of Donald Trump, Matthew Goodwin and colleagues have submitted that the most substantial vote for Brexit came from "the least diverse local jurisdictions, or in those with large concentrations of working-class voters and voters with few educational qualifications" (Ford & Goodwin 2017, pp. 25–26). On the whole, the Brexit vote.

> was delivered by the 'left behind'—social groups that are united by a general sense of insecurity, pessimism and marginalisation, who do not feel as though

elites, whether in Brussels or Westminster, share their values, represent their interests and genuinely empathise with their intense angst about rapid social, economic and cultural change" (Godwin and Heath 2016, 331).

In a similar vein, Satnam Virdee and Brendan McGeever have argued that the support of Brexit among working-class voters was informed by "a deep sense of loss of prestige" and an attempt to "retreat from the damaging impact of a globalized world that is no longer recognizable, no longer 'British'" (Virdee & McGeever, 2018, p. 1811). A recent statistical analysis of support for the Swedish radical populist right provides further evidence for the importance of these dynamics. One of the central findings of the analysis is that radical right populist "ideas gave spread faster in rural regions with low population densities" than elsewhere in the country (Blomqvist et al., 2019, p. 14).

Similar dynamics explain the upsurge of radical right-wing populism in the eastern part of Germany. Over the past several years, the AfD has gradually replaced *Die Linke*, giving voice to the resentment of parts of the East German electorate (Betz & Habersack, 2019). The East German region's particularly high support for the AfD is paradigmatic (Salomo, 2019). The impact of regionally idiosyncratic precarious structural conditions on sentiments and, via the resulting grievances, on voting behavior. These conditions are marked by the exodus of a large number of younger and better-educated individuals and particularly young women, especially in rural areas (Bauer et al., 2019, p. 9). The result has been a high level of demographic homogeneity—a disproportionate number of seniors and a disproportionate number of young men (Salomo, 2019). Similar conditions can be found throughout the territory of the former GDR, accounting in part for the gains of the AfD in recent years (Betz & Habersack, 2019).

The case of the eastern part of Germany shows that relative deprivation extends far beyond economics involving as well social and cultural deprivations and grievances. What they have in common is a strong sense on the part of a significant number of individuals of 'falling behind' and/or 'being left behind' profound socioeconomic and sociostructural disruptions that, nevertheless, exert a very direct impact on their life chances. The experience of deprivation is bound to provoke a panoply of negative emotions, such as anxiety, frustration, anger, and resentment. A recent analysis of American responses to automation shows profound worries among respondents with regard to robotization. At the same time, it found considerable differences between educational groups: The highly educated thought that automation made their work more interesting and provided them with opportunities for advancement; those lacking the necessary cultural capital expressed opposite sentiments (Smith & Anderson, 2017).

Recent contributions from economics and political science have started to analyze these dynamics. Autor et al.'s study of the regional effect of Chinese import penetration on the vote for Donald Trump is arguable the most prominent case in point (Autor et al., 2017). So is Colantone and Stanig's work on the impact of trade competition on electoral choice in Europe; Dippel et al.'s study of the impact of trade shocks on electoral choice in Germany and Caselli et al.'s study on Italy (Caselli et al., 2020; Colantone & Stanig, 2018; Dippel et al., 2016). In each of these cases, there is relatively strong evidence that globalization (in the form of Chinese imports) has given a non-negligible boost to right-wing populist candidates and parties. The emerging literature on the impact of automation on voting behavior paints a similar picture. A recent paper by Anelli et al. demonstrates that "higher exposure to automation increases support for nationalist and radical-right parties, both at the regional and at the individual level" (Anelli et al., 2019, p. 35). Along similar lines, Zhen Im et al. find that as the risk of automation increases, the probability a person affected by automation will vote for the radical populist right substantially increases as well (Im et al., 2019). Jane Gringrich's study of the impact of automation goes in the same direction. She finds that voters with negative expose to automation are prone to vote for the radical populist right, even in cases where they are being compensated by the welfare state—as they should according to traditional trade theory (Gingrich, 2019). This suggests that anger and resentment provoked by redundancy associated with automation are not necessarily a question of economics (mitigated by welfare state compensation) but go deeper, involving individual pride, an individual's sense of self-worth, and social status, which are significantly more difficult to resolve politically.

The arguments advanced so far provide a plausible answer to two phenomena associated with the contemporary radical populist right: their staying power over several decades, despite often intense hostility and animosity on the part of the political establishment and the media; and their upsurge in the polls in recent years. Extant empirical evidence suggests that the success of these parties is to a large extent the result of their ability to exploit a range of negative emotions provoked by secular socioeconomic, sociostructural, and sociocultural processes and developments that open up every new fields for populist and nativist mobilization. What mobilizes individuals to vote for the radical populist right are often perceptions of being treated unfairly, of being ignored and dismissed, and, in the worst case, of being disdained and treated with contempt by the 'political class.'

As Houtman et al. have noted, egalitarianism is fundamentally differently understood among the working class than among the middle class. The middle class might be less egalitarian-minded; yet egalitarianism is "nevertheless part and parcel of a progressive political outlook that includes an acceptance of cultural differences and post-traditional identities" and, hence, "a willingness to share the nation's wealth with immigrants from poor third-world countries." Against that, for the working class, albeit being more egalitarian-minded, egalitarianism is "more closely tied to authoritarian rejections of cultural diversity, desires to exclude immigrants from the national welfare system, and rightist political identifications there" (Houtman & Derks 2008, p. 116).

Right-wing populist parties promote themselves as the ultimate defenders of cultural identity, national sovereignty, and the welfare state. Prominent examples are Marine Le Pen's 'social turn' after she took over the reins of the Front National and, more recently, the Sverigedemokraterna's adoption of the *folkhemmet*. At the same time, the radical populist right has used them to launch a frontal attack at the established political parties—and particularly the 'cosmopolitan left'—charging them with having nothing but contempt with their 'own' people, i.e., the native-born. In its most extreme version, the argument goes as far as to charge that the 'cosmopolitan elite' promotes and furthers the 'great replacement' (of the 'indigenous' population by migrants, particularly from Muslim countries) to fulfill its utopian cosmopolitan dreams.

These discursive tropes play to the diffuse fears and anxieties informing recent outbursts of nativism, which, in turn, reflect widespread uneasiness with ethnic diversity and multiculturalism. A significant number of the population in liberal democracies believe that ethnic diversity undermines national culture. Politically, the result has been more polarization and a new cleavage, pitting the advocates of multiculturalism against the defenders of idiosyncratic national identity. Hardly surprising, the radical populist right has promoted itself as the most fervent promoter of the latter. What informs these demands is an illiberal conception of democracy, based on ethnoreligious discrimination and the perpetuation of 'indigenous' privilege—what has come to be known as "ethnocracy" (Anderson, 2016). Ethnocracy fits in well not only with the notion of "our people first" but also with notions prevalent on the radical right that migrants (particularly from predominantly Muslim countries) represent the vanguard of a migratory tsunami which will end in the 'Great Replacement '.

Conclusion: The Need for a Holistic View

Once dismissed as 'flash' parties, right-wing populist parties can now be considered to be a part of the political establishment. Their success has various reasons—social, economic, political, and cultural—and many of them have made a successful transition to "catch-all-parties of protest." Of late, the complexity of contemporary radical right-wing populism in its various permutations has increasingly come to be appreciated and analyzed. A comprehensive analysis of the persistent success of radical right-wing populist parties in contemporary democracies requires a comprehensive approach that addresses all the major elements that have contributed to their remarkable staying power.

The focus of this chapter has been on one element—emotions. Its purpose is to elucidate the crucial role emotions play in populist mobilization. The discussion is based on the assumption that populist mobilization is the end point of a process at the beginning of which stand unmet popular demands and particularly grievances. This is the point Ernesto Laclau has made most forcefully and persuasively in this theory of populism. Grievances provoke and engender a range of emotions, most prominently anger, indignation, and resentment. On this reading, the success of radical right-wing populist discourse depends to a significant degree on the extent to which the radical populist right's rhetoric manages to evoke and appeal to these emotions. This is particularly true for nostalgia, especially group-based nostalgia, defined as the "nostalgic reverie that is contingent upon thinking of oneself in terms of a particular social identity or as a member of a particular group" (Wildschut et al., 2014, p. 845). This is the nativist core of contemporary radical right-wing populism.

The populist right's ideational fusion of anti-establishment and exclusionary rhetoric resonates with perceptions of cultural decline, growing inequality and the prospect of a bleak future, which suffuse large parts of Western publics, on both sides of the Atlantic. They feed into a panoply of fears of irretrievable loss, both economic and cultural, and anxieties and pessimism with respect to the future. Most of these sentiments stem from the large-scale socioeconomic and sociocultural changes modern societies have been forced to confront in recent years, which have left significant sectors of society disoriented and stranded and yearning for meaning and stability. Under the circumstances, it is hardly surprising that seemingly empty and inane slogans such as "our own people first" and "Make American Great Again" appeal to large segments of the population.

This chapter has provided a basic analytical framework for the study of the role of emotions in populist mobilization. What we are still largely missing are discourse-oriented studies that explore how right-wing populist parties concretely appeal to emotions, what tropes and rhetorical devices they use to evoke and elicit an affective response among their target audience. Such an analysis will fill one of the few remaining gaps in the comprehensive approach to the study of the contemporary radical populist right.

Literature

Abou-Chadi, T., & Krause, W. (2020). The causal effect of radical right success on mainstream parties' policy positions: A regression discontinuity approach. *British Journal of Political Science, 50*(3), 829–847.

Acemoglu, D., & Autor, D. H. (2011). Skills, tasks, and technologies: Implications for employment and earnings. In C. Orley C. Ashenfelter & D. Card (Eds.), *Handbook of Labor Economics* (vol. 4, part B, pp. 1043–1171). North-Holland.

Agnew, R. (2001). Building on the foundation of general strain theory: Specifying the types of strain most likely to lead to crime and delinquency. *Journal of Research in Crime and Delinquency, 36*(4), 319–361.

Alba, R., & Foner, N. (2017). Immigration the geography of polarization. *City & Community, 16*(3), 239–243.

Anderson, J. (2016). Ethnocracy: Exploring and extending the concept, cosmopolitan civil societies. *An Interdisciplinary Journal, 8*(3), 1–29.

Anelli, M., Colantone, I., & Stanig, P. (2019, July). *We were the robots: Automation and voting behavior in Western Europe* (Institute of Labor Economics Discussion

Paper 12485). https://www.iza.org/publications/dp/12485/we-were-the-robots-automation-and-voting-behavior-in-western-europe.
Ansell, B., & Adler, D. (2019). Brexit and the politics of housing in Britain. *The Political Quarterly, 90*(S2), 105–116.
Anspach, C. K. (1934). Medical dissertation on Nostalgia by Johannes Hofer, 1688. *Bulletin of the Institute of the History of Medicine, 2*(6), 376–391.
Arzheimer, K. (2013). Working-class parties 2.0? Competition between centre left and extreme right parties. In J. Rydgren (Ed.), *Class politics and the radical right* (pp. 75–90). Routledge.
Autor, D., Dorn, D., & Hanson, G. (2017). *When work disappears: Manufacturing decline and the falling marriage-market value of men* (NBER working paper 23173). https://www.nber.org/papers/w23173.pdf.
Bauer, T. K., Rulff, C., & Tamminga, M. M. (2019). Berlin calling—internal migration in Germany. *Ruhr Economic Papers, #823*. http://www.rwiessen.de/media/content/pages/publikationen/ruhr-economic-papers/rep_19_823.pdf.
Berezin, M. (2002). Secure states: Towards a political sociology of emotion. *The Sociological Review, 50*(S2), 33–52.
Betz, H. G. (1994). *Radical right-wing populism in Western Europe.* St. Martin's Press.
Betz, H. G., & Johnson, C. (2004). Against the current—Stemming the tide: The nostalgic ideology of the contemporary radical populist right. *Journal of Political Ideologies, 9*(3), 311–327.
Betz, H. G., & Habersack, F. (2019). Regional nativism in East Germany: The case of the AfD. In R. Heinisch, E. Massetti & O. Mazzoleni (Eds.), *The people and the nation: Populism and ethno-territorial politics in Europe* (pp. 110–135). Routledge.
Blomqvist, B. R. H., Sumpter, D. J. T., & Mann, R. P. (2019). Inferring the dynamics of rising radical right-wing party support using Gaussian processes. *Philosophical Transactions of the Royal Society A, 377*, 20190145.
Bornschier, S. (2010). *Cleavage politics and the populist right.* Temple University Press.
Bornschier, S., & Kriesi, H. (2013). The populist right, the working class, and the changing face of class politics. In J. Rydgren (Ed.), *Class politics and the radical right* (pp. 10–30). Routledge.
Brooks, A. C. (2017, March/April). The dignity deficit: Reclaiming americans' sense of purpose. *Foreign Affairs.* https://www.foreignaffairs.com/articles/unitedstates/2017-02-13/dignity-deficit.
Burgoon, B., van Noort, S., Rooduijn, M., & Underhill, G. (2019). Positional deprivation and support for radical right and radical left parties. *Economic Policy 39*(97), 49–93.
Busquet, J. (2011). The fear of loss of status. *Transfer: Journal of Contemporary Culture, 6,* 68–77.
Caselli, M., Fracasso, A., & Traverso, S. (2020). Globalization and electoral outcomes: Evidence from Italy. *Economics & Politics, 32* (1), 68–103.
Castells, M. (2004). Informationalism, networks, and the network society: A theoretical blueprint. In M. Castells (Ed.), *The Network Society* (pp. 3–45). Edward Elgar.
Chen, X. (2015, April). *Relative deprivation and individual well-being: Low status and a feeling of relative deprivation are detrimental to health and happiness,* IZA World Labor. https://www.ncbi.nlm.nih.gov/pmc/articles/PMC5638129/pdf/nihms863193.pdf.

Chetty, R., Grusky, D., Hell, M., Hendren, N., Manduca, R., & Narang, J. (2017). The fading American dream: Trends in absolute income mobility since 1940. *Science, 356*(6336), 398–406.

Colantone, I., & Stanig, P. (2018). The trade origins of economic nationalism: Import competition and voting behavior in Western Europe. *American Journal of Political Science Review, 62*(4), 936–953.

Cramer, K. J. (2016). *The politics of resentment: Rural consciousness in Wisconsin and the rise of Scott Walker*. University of Chicago Press.

Crimston, D., Bain, Paul G., Hornsey, M. J., & Brock, B. (2016). Moral expansiveness: Examining variability in the extension of the moral world. *Journal of Personality and Social Psychology, 111*(4), 636–653.

Dauth, W., Findeisen, S., Südekum, J., & Wößner, N. (2017). *German Robots—The impact of industrial robots on workers* (IAB-Discussion Paper 30/2017). http://doku.iab.de/discussionpapers/2017/dp3017.pdf.

Davis, F. (1977). Nostalgia, identity and the current Nostalgia wave, The. *Journal of Popular Culture, 11*(2), 414–424.

Davis, N. T., Goidel, K., Lipsmeyer, C. S., Whitten, G. D., & Young, C. (2019). Economic vulnerability, cultural decline, and nativism: Contingent and indirect effects. *Social Science Quarterly, 100*(2), 430–446.

De Beer, P., & Koster, F. (2009). *Sticking together or falling apart?: Solidarity in an era of individualization and globalization*. Amsterdam University Press.

De Maesschalck, F. (2011). The politicisation of suburbinasation in Belgium: Towards an urban-suburban divide. *Urban Studies, 48*(4), 699–717.

De Vries, C. E. & Hoffmann, I. (2016). *Globalisierungsangst oder Wertekonflikt? Wer in Europa populistische Parteien wählt und warum*. Bertelsmann Stiftung, eupinions #2016/3, https://www.bertelsmann-stiftung.de/fileadmin/files/user_upload/EZ_eupinions_Fear_Studie_2016_DT.pdf.

Dippel, C., Gold, R., & Heblich, S. (2015). *Globalization and its dis-content: Trade shocks and voting behavior* (NBER, Working Paper 21812). https://www.nber.org/papers/w21812.pdf.

Eger, M. A., & Valdez, S. (2015). Neo-nationalism in Western Europe. *European Sociological Review, 31*(1), 115–130.

Eger, M. A., & Valdez, S. (2019). From radical right to neo-nationalist. *European Political Science, 18*(3), 379–399.

Elgenius, G., & Rydgren, J. (2019). Frames of nostalgia and belonging: The resurgence of ethno-nationalism in Sweden. *European Societies, 21*(4), 583–602.

Ellsworth, P. C., & Smith, C. A. (1988). From appraisal to emotion: Differences among unpleasant feelings. *Motivation and Emotion, 12*(3), 271–302.

Engler, S., & Weisstanner, D. (2020). Income inequality, status decline and support for the radical right. In R. Careja, P. Emmenegger, & N. Giger (Eds.), *The European social model under pressure: Liber Amicorum in Honour of Klaus Armingeon* (pp. 383–400). VS Verlag für Sozialwissenschaften.

Enzinger, H. (2019). A tale of two cities: Rotterdam, Amsterdam and their immigrants. In P. Scholten, M. Crul, & P. van de Laar (Eds.), *Coming to terms with superdiversity: The case of Rotterdam* (pp. 173–189). Springer Open.

Feischmidt, M., & Hervik, P. (2015). Mainstreaming the extreme: Intersecting challenges from the far right in Europe. *Intersections, 1*(1), 3–17.

Florida, R. (2002). Bohemia and economic geography. *Journal of Economic Geography, 2*, 55–71.

Ford, R., & Goodwin, M. (2017). A nation divided. *Journal of Democracy, 28*(1), 17–30.

Fourquet, J. (2012). *Le sens des cartes: Analyse sur la géographie des votes à la présidentielle.* Fondation Jean-Jaurès, https://jean-jaures.org/nos-productions/le-sens-des-cartes-analyse-sur-la-geographie-des-votes-a-la-presidentielle.

Frey, C. B., Berger, T., & Chen, C. (2018). Political machinery: Did robots swing the 2016 US presidential election? *Oxford Review of Economic Policy, 34*(3), 418–442.

Funke, M., Schularick, M., & Trebesch, C. (2016). Going to extremes: Politics after financial crises, 1870–2014. *European Economic Review, 88,* 227–260.

Ganem, N. M. (2019). The role of negative emotion in general strain theory. *Journal of Contemporary Criminal Justic, 26*(2), 167–185.

Gest, J., Reny, T., & Mayer, J. (2017). Roots of the radical right: Nostalgic deprivation in the United States and Britain. *Comparative Political Studies, 51*(13), 1694–1719.

Gidron, N., & Hall, P. A. (2017). The politics of social status: Economic and cultural roots of the populist right. *British Journal of Sociology, 68*(S1), S57–S84.

Gingrich, J. (2019, January–March). Did state responses to automaton matter for voters? *Research and Politics,* (January-March), 1–9.

Giorgi, S. (2017). The mind and heart of resonance: The role of cognition and emotions in frame effectiveness. *Journal of Management Studies, 54*(5), 711–738.

Goodwin, M. J., & Oliver H.h. (2016). The 2016 referendum, Brexit and the left behind: An aggregate-level analysis of the result. *Political Science Quarterly, 87*(3), 323–332.

Goos, M., Manning, A., & Salomons, A. (2009). Job polarization in Europe. *The American Economic Review, 99*(2), 58–63.

Greenberg, S., & Zdunkewicz, N. (2017). *Macomb county in the age of trump: Report from focus groups with independent and democratic trump voters in Macomb county.* https://static1.squarespace.com/static/582e1a36e58c62cc076cdc81/t/58c2c5 b53a04110deeef0e3c/1489159605800/Dcor_Macomb_FG+Memo_3.10.2017_F INAL.PDF.

Greitemeyer, T., & Sagioglou, C. (2019). The experience of deprivation: Does relative more than absolute status predict hostility? *British Journal of Social Psychology, 58,* 515–533.

Guilluy, C. (2014). *La France périphérique: Comment on a sacrifié les class populaires.* Flammarion.

Halla, M., Wagner, A. F., & Zweimüller, J. (2017). Immigration and voting for the far right. *Journal of the European Economic Association, 15*(6), 1341–1385.

Heaney, J. G. (2019). Emotion as power: Capital and strategy in the field of politics. *Journal of Political Power, 12*(2), 224–244.

Heinisch, R., Werner, A., & Habersack, F. (2019). Reclaiming national sovereignty: The case of the conservatives and the far right in Austria. *European Politics and Society.* https://doi.org/10.1080/23745118.2019.1632577.

Hillje, J. (2018). *Return to the politically abandoned: Conversations in right-wing populist strongholds in Germany and France.* Das Progressive Zentrum, http://www.progressives-zentrum.org/return-to-the-politically-abandoned/.

Hochschild, A. R. (2006). *Strangers in their own land: Anger and Mourning on the American Right.* New Press.

Houtman, D., & Derks, A. (2008). *Farewell to the Leftist working class.* Routledge.

Im, Z. J., Mayer, N., Palier, B., & Rovny, J. (2019). The "losers of automation": A reservoir of votes for the radical right? *Research and Politics, 6*(1).

Inglehart, R., & Norris, P. (2016). *Trump, Brexit, and the rise of populism: Economic have-nots and cultural backlash* (HKS Working Paper No. RWP16–026). https://papers.ssrn.com/sol3/papers.cfm?abstract_id=2818659.

Jansen, R. S. (2011). Populist mobilization: A new theoretical approach to populism. *Sociological Theory, 29*(2), 75–96.

Kenny, M. (2017). Back to the populist future?: Understanding nostalgia in contemporary ideological discourse. *Journal of Political Ideologies, 22*(3), 256–273.

Kinvall, C. (2014). Fear, insecurity and the (re)emergence of the far right in Europe. In P. Nesbitt-Larking, C. Kinnvall, & T. Capelos with H. Dekker (Eds.), *The Palgrave Handbook of Global Political Psychology (Palgrave Studies in Political Psychology) Houndmills* (pp. 316–334). Palgrave Macmillan.

Kiss, S. J., Perrella, A. M. L., & Spicer, Z. (2020). Right-wing populism in a metropolis: Personal financial stress, conservative attitudes, and Rob Ford's Toronto. *Journal of Urban Affairs, 42*(7), 1028–1046.

Kriesi, H., & Pappas, T. S. (2015). *European populism in the shadow of the great recession*. ECPR Press.

Kühne, R. (2013). Emotionale Framing-Effekte auf Einstellungen: Ein integratives Modell. *Medien & Kommunikationswissenschaft, 61*(1), 5–20.

Kurer, T. (2020). The declining middle: Political reactions to occupational change, 53(10–11), 1798–1835.

Kurer, T., & Palier, B. (2019). Shrinking and shouting: the political revolt of the declining middle in times of employment polarization. *Research and Politics, 6*(1), 1–6.

Laclau, E. (2005). *On populist reason*. Verso.

Lamont, M., Park, B. Y., & Ayala-Hurtado, E. (2017). Trump's electoral speeches and his appeal to the American white working class. *The British Journal of Sociology, 68*(S1), 153–180.

Lane, J. E., & Ersson, S. (2007). Party system instability in Europe: Persistent differences in volatility between West and East? *Democratisation, 14*(1), 92–110.

Le Bras, H., & Todd, E. (2013). *Le mystère français*. Seuil.

Lee, N., Morris, K. & Kemeny T. (2018). Immobility and the brexit vote. *Cambridge Journal of Regions, Economy and Society, 11*(1), 143–163.

Lengfeld, H. (2017). Die „Alternative für Deutschland": Eine Partei für Modernisierungsverlierer? *Köln Zeitschrift f Ür Soziologie Und Sozialpsychologie, 69*, 209–232.

Linden, M. (2003). Postraumatic embitterment disorder. *Psychotherapy and Psychosomatics, 72*(4), 195–202.

Los, B., McCann, P., Springford, J., & Thissen, M. (2017). The mismatch between local voting and the local economic consequences of Brexit. *Regional Studies, 51*(5), 786–799.

Lynch, C. (2017, March 20). *The smug style in American liberalism: It's not helping, folks—But there's a better way*. Salon. https://www.salon.com/2017/03/20/the-smug-style-in-american-liberalism-its-not-helping-folks-but-theres-a-better-way/.

Manow, P., & H. Schwander (2019). *A labor market explanation for right-wing populism—Explaining the electoral success of the AfD in Germany* (Unpublished paper).

Marcus, G. E., Valentino, N. A., Vasilopoulos, P., & Foucault, M. (2019). Applying the theory of affective intelligence to support for authoritarian policies and parties. *Political Psychology, 40*, 109–139.

Mayer, N. (2014). The electoral impact of the crisis on the French working class: More to the right? In L. Bartels & N. Bermeo (Eds.), *Mass politics in tough timesopinions: Votes and protest in the great recession* (pp. 267–296). Oxford University Press.
McLuhan, M. (1968). *Understanding media: The extensions of man*. Latimer Trend & Co. Limited.
McLuhan, M. (1970). *From Cliché to Archetype*. Viking Press.
Miceli, M., & Castelfranchi, C. (2019). Anger and its cousins. *Emotion Review, 11*(1), 13–26. https://doi.org/10.1177/1754073917714870.
Mikula, G., Scherer, K. R., & Athenstaedt, U. (1998). The role of injustice in the elicitation of differential emotional reactions. *Personality and Social Psychology Bulletin, 24*(7), 769–783.
Miller, D. (2005). Reasonable partiality towards compatriots. *Ethical Theory and Moral Practice, 8*(1/2), 63–81.
Mols, F., & Jetten, J. (2014). No guts, no glory: How framing the collective past paves the way for anti-immigrant sentiments. *International Journal of Intercultural Relations, 43*(Part A), 74–86.
Monnat, S. M., & Brown, D. L. (2017). More than a rural revolt: Landscapes of despair and the 2016 Presidential election. *Journal of Rural Studies, 55*(October), 227–236.
Müller, J. W. (2016). *What is populism?* University of Pennsylvania Press.
Natali, M. P. (2004). History and the politics of Nostalgia. *Iowa Journal of Cultural Studies, 5*(Fall), 10–25.
Naughton, K., & Vlasic, B. (1998, March 23). The Nostalgia Boom: Why the old is new again. *BusinessWeek*, pp. 58–64.
Oswald, M. (2019). Jobs, free trade, and a conspiracy: Trump's use of producerism. In H. Paul, U. Prutsch, & J. Gebhardt (Eds.), *The comeback of populism* (pp. 109–125). Winter.
Oswald, M. (2020). Der Populismus in den USA. In C. Lammert, M. Siewert, & B. Vormann (Eds.), *Hand-buch Politik USA* (pp. 55–72). Springer.
Oswald, M., & Broda, E. (2020). From 2016 to 2020: It's the economy, still. In M. Oswald (Ed.), *Mobilization, representation and responsiveness in the American democracy* (pp. 157–174). Palgrave Macmillan.
Pappas, T. S. (2019). *Populism and liberal democracy: A comparative and theoretical analysis*. Oxford University Press.
Pettigrew, T. F. (2016). In pursuit of three theories: Authoritarianism, relative deprivation, and intergroup contact. *Annual Review of Psychology, 67*, 1–21.
Peugny, C. (2019). The decline in middle-skilled employment in 12 European countries: New evidence for job polarization. *Research and Politics*, (January-March), 1–7.
Pew. (2007, October 4). *World publics welcome global trade—But not immigration, the Pew Global attitudes project*. http://assets.pewresearch.org/wp-content/uploads/sites/2/2007/10/Pew-Global-Attitudes-Report-October-4-2007-REVISED-UPDATED-5-27-14.pdf.
Pew. (2016). *Large majority of Trump supporters say life is worse today than it was 50 years ago for people like them*. http://www.pewresearch.org/fact-tank/2016/10/20/6-charts-that-show-where-clinton-and-trump-supporters-differ/.
Piketty, T. (2018). *Brahmin left vs Merchant Right: Rising inequality & the changing structure of political conflict (Evidence from France, Britain and the US 1948–2017)*,

(WID—World Working paper series, 2018/7). http://piketty.pse.ens.fr/files/Piketty2018.pdf.

Polletta F., & Callahan J. (2017). Deep stories, nostalgia narratives, and fake news: Storytelling in the Trump era. *American Journal of Cultural Sociology, 5*(4), 392–408.

Pourtova, H. (2013). Nostalgia and lost identity. *Journal of Analytical Psychology, 58*(1), 34–51.

Rachman, S. J. (2013). *Anxiety* (3rd ed.). Psychology Press.

Rho, R. (2019, May 23). I duri e destri del profondo Nord il tesoretto è nei piccoli Comuni. *La Republicca*, p. 5.

Rico, G., Guinjoan, M., & Anduiza, E. (2017). The emotional underpinnings of populism: How anger and fear affect populist attitudes. *Swiss Political Science Review, 23*(4), 444–461.

Rodríguez-Pose, A. (2018). The revenge of the places that don't matter (and what to do about it). *Cambridge Journal of Regions, Economy and Society, 11*(1), 189–209.

Salmela, M., & von Scheve, C. (2017). Emotional roots of right-wing political populism. *Social Science Information, 56*(4), 567–595.

Salomo, K. (2019). The residential context as source of deprivation: Impacts on the local political culture. Evidence from the East German state Thuringia. *Political Geography, 69*(March), 103–117.

Schwander, H., & P. Manow (2017). *It's not the economy, stupid! Explaining the electoral success of the German right-wing populist AfD* (Comparative and International Studies (CIS) Working paper no. 94), ETH Zurich/University of Zurich Center. https://ethz.ch/content/dam/ethz/special-interest/gess/cis/cis-dam/CIS_DAM_2017/WP94_A4.pdf.

Singer, P. (1983). *The expanding circle: Ethics and sociobiology*. Oxford University Press.

Smith, A., & M. Anderson (2017, October). *Automation in everyday live*. Pew Research Center. https://www.pewinternet.org/wp-content/uploads/sites/9/2017/10/PI_2017.10.04_Automation_FINAL.pdf.

Smith, C. A., & Lazarus, R. S. (1990). Emotion and adaptation. In L. A. Pervin (Ed.), *Handbook of personality: Theory and research* (pp. 609–637). Guilford.

Smith, H. J., Pettigrew, T. F., Pippin, G. M., & Bialosiewicz, S. (2012). Relative deprivation: A theoretical and meta-analytic review. *Personality and Social Psychology Review, 16*(3), 203–232.

Solomon, T. (2013). Resonances of neoconservatism. *Cooperation and Conflict, 48*(1), 100–121.

Sprong, S. et al. (2019). "Our country needs a strong leader right now": Economic inequality enhances the wish for a strong leader. *Psychological Science*, early view.

Steenvoorden, E., & Harteveld, E. (2018). The appeal of nostalgia: The influence of societal pessimism on support for populist radical right parties. *West European Politics, 41*(1), 28–52.

Stockemer, D. (2017). The success of radical right-wing parties in Western European regions—New challenging findings. *Journal of Contemporary European Studies, 25*(1), 41–56.

Thomassen, L. (2005). Antagonism, hegemony and ideology after heterogeneity. *Journal of Political Ideologies, 10*(3), 289–309.

Tversky, A., & Kahneman, D. (1981). The framing of decisions and the psychology of choice. *Science, New Series, 211*(4481), 453–458.

Valdez, S., & Eger, M. A. (2018). *From radical right to neo-nationalist: Danish party politics, 1973–2011, CARR.* https://www.radicalrightanalysis.com/wp-content/uploads/2018/11/Valdez_Eger_2018_CARR.pdf.

van Tilburg, W., Sedikides, C., Wildschut, T., & Vingerhoets, J. (2019). How nostalgia infuses life with meaning: From social connectedness to self-continuity. *European Journal of Social Psychology, 49*(3), 521–532.

Virdee, S., & McGeever, B. (2018). Racism, crisis, Brexit. *Ethnic and Racial Studies, 41*(10), 1802–1819.

Vlandas, T., & Halikiopoulou, D. (2019). Does unemployment matter? *Economic Insecurity, Labour Market Policies and the Far-Right Vote in Europe, European Political Science, 18,* 421–438.

Wike, R., & Stokes, B. (2018). *In advanced and emerging economies alike, worries about job automation: Many fear robots, computers will eliminate jobs, increase inequality.* Pew Research Center. https://www.pewresearch.org/global/wp-content/uploads/sites/2/2018/09/Pew-Research-Center_In-Advanced-and-Emerging-Economies-Alike-Worries-about-Job-Automation_2018-09-13.pdf.

Wildschut, T., Bruder, M., Robertson, S., van Tilburg, W. A. P., & Sedikides, C. (2014). Collective nostalgia: A group-level emotion that confers unique benefits on the group. *Journal of Personality and Social Psychology, 107*(5), 844–863.

Wilkinson, W. (2018, June). *The density divide: Urbanization, polarization, and populist backlash* (Niskanen Center Research Paper). https://www.niskanencenter.org/wp-content/uploads/old_uploads/2019/06/Wilkinson-Density-Divide-Final.pdf.

Wilson, J. L. (1999). „REMEMBER WHEN…" A Consideration of the concept of Nostalgia. *ETC: A Review of General Semantics, 56*(3), 269–304.

Wodak, R., & Pelinka, A. (Eds.). (2002). *The Haider Phenomenon in Austria.* Transaction Publishers.

Wuthnow, R. (2018). *The left behind: Decline and rage in rural America.* Princeton University Press.

Yang, G. (2003). China's Zhiqing generation: Nostalgia, identity, and cultural resistance in the 1990s. *Modern China, 29*(3), 267–296.

Ylä-Anttila, T. (2017). Familiarity as a tool of populism: Political appropriation of shared experiences and the case of Suvivirsi. *Acta Sociologica, 60*(4), 342–357.

Zürn, M., & de Wilde, P. (2016). Cosmopolitanism and communitarianism as political ideologies. *Journal of Political Ideologies, 21*(3), 260–301.

CHAPTER 8

From Specific Worries to Generalized Anger: The Emotional Dynamics of Right-Wing Political Populism

Christoph Giang Nguyen, Mikko Salmela, and Christian von Scheve

INTRODUCTION

The success of right-wing populist (RRP) parties in Europe and across the globe has spurred research in a range of social science disciplines. This research aims at understanding a broad spectrum of questions related to the success of right-wing populist parties, such as: Who is the populist right? What is their agenda? What are their strategies? Who votes populist? And why? Among the different conceptual and theoretical approaches to addressing these questions, the role of emotions has recently attracted increasing attention. This is certainly because emotions are said to be an essential element of populist discourse, but also because emotions have become increasingly important in the analysis of political phenomena more generally. Regarding populism,

---

C. G. Nguyen (✉)
Chair of German Politics, Freie Universität Berlin, Berlin, Germany
e-mail: christoph.nguyen@fu-berlin.de

M. Salmela
Faculty of Social Sciences, University of Helsinki, Helsinki, Finland
e-mail: mikko.salmela@helsinki.fi

C. von Scheve
Institute of Sociology, Freie Universität Berlin, Berlin, Germany
e-mail: christian.von.scheve@fu-berlin.de

M. Salmela
Center for Subjectivity Research at the University of Copenhagen, Copenhagen, Denmark

© The Author(s), under exclusive license to Springer Nature Switzerland AG 2022
M. Oswald (ed.), *The Palgrave Handbook of Populism*,
https://doi.org/10.1007/978-3-030-80803-7_8

and in particular right-wing populism, two strands of research are especially noteworthy.

First, scholars have started to investigate the association between emotions and right-wing populism from a 'demand' side and looked at the emotions of the electorate as predictors of support for populist movements and right-wing populist parties (e.g., Cramer, 2016; Hochschild, 2016; Rico et al., 2017). This research is based on long-standing empirical insights into the motivating forces of feelings and emotions and their relationship with cognition and political decision-making. Some have argued that there exists a more or less direct relationship between certain emotions and populist electoral outcomes, for example, through processes of frame resonance (e.g., Bonikowski, 2017). In particular, emotions such as anger, fear, resentment, shame, and pride are supposed to be dominant in certain parts of the electorate and that these emotions tend to motivate populist support (e.g., Betz, 2002). Others have suggested that it is much less these (and other) emotions in general that predict right-wing populist support, but rather emotions that have specific targets, in particular events and circumstances perceived as threats to one's well-being (e.g., Marx, 2020; Rico et al., 2017). Not anger, fear, or resentment in general are likely motivators of right-wing support, but the specific intentional directedness of these (and other) emotions. In this perspective, the targets of emotions closely correspond to salient political cleavages, in particular, those addressed by right-wing populists. This includes economic downturn, immigration, crime, and welfare.

Second, research has investigated the 'supply' side of right-wing populism, which typically includes political strategies, arguments, discourse, and rhetoric. Populism, from this vantage point, is also often defined as a 'political style.' Although emotions are essential ingredients of politics as such, populism is supposed to be characterized by a political style that is highly 'emotionalized,' specifically geared toward eliciting emotions among the electorate, and in that capacity is also suspected to stand in opposition to the exchange of facts and arguments. To further define the populist political style with regard to emotions, scholars have investigated speeches, interviews, party manifestos, and campaigns and uncovered a broad range of linguistic and visual devices that express, represent, and elicit emotions (e.g., Breeze, 2019; Matthes & Schmuck, 2017; Wirz, 2018; Wodak, 2015). Populist parties use these strategies with the goal of systematically altering, even if only in the short run, the emotions of the electorate in a way that is conducive to political mobilization, soliciting support and votes.

Looking at these two perspectives, it is evident that the distinction is mainly an analytical one. Emotions that stimulate right-wing populist support might be prevalent in a population for individual (e.g., personality, gender, age), structural (e.g., occupation, status, income), and cultural (e.g., lifestyles, cultural consumptions) reasons. Likewise, exposure to populist discourse might generate these emotions or amplify/attenuate existing ones. Although there is ample research on emotions from demand- and supply-side perspective, no existing studies have yet systematically looked at the role of general emotions vs. emotions aimed at specific targets nor looked into the dynamic nature of emotions and right-wing support. The present chapter fills this void. Based on existing theories and research on emotions and right-wing populist support, we investigate whether emotions generally and emotions with specific targets predict right-wing populist support, and whether support for right-wing parties in turn increases the likelihood to experience general emotions as well as emotions with specific targets. Our empirical analysis is motivated by both, existing theory and pragmatic considerations. We focus on two emotions that have been shown to be associated with political mobilization very generally, and with right-wing support more specifically, namely, anger and fear. For these emotions, longitudinal data are available that allow for the testing of our hypotheses of the dynamic nature of emotions and right-wing support. Regarding specific targets, we look at worries, understood as specific emotional orientations, about prominent political issues and cleavages in right-wing politics and discourse: immigration, crime, employment, and the economy, contrasting them with worries less commonly associated with right-wing populism.

Emotions and Right-Wing Political Populism

Emotions as Predictors of Right-Wing Populist Support

In this section, we review existing research on those emotions that are presumed to motivate support for radical right-wing populism and also discuss some of these emotions as intergroup emotions. Existing research has identified two main clusters of negative emotions behind the rise of right-wing populist parties and movements: feelings of fear associated with insecurity, powerlessness, and déclassement on the one hand, and anger, resentment, indignation, and hate, on the other.

Feelings of fear, insecurity, and powerlessness can be understood as closely tied to social structural and cultural changes in Western societies, such as modernization, globalization, and economic deregulation, that have increased economic precariousness, thus creating opportunities for fears of losing social status and established living standards and of becoming part of a stigmatized group, such as the unemployed. So far, low- or medium-skilled blue-collar, predominantly male workers whose traditional jobs in industries, construction, transportation, and utilities were on the decline for a long time suffered most from these structural changes. However, the same fears can also affect skilled middle-class employees who can anticipate being the next in line. Indeed, threats of precarization or déclassement seem to be more important politically than actual déclassement, for the electorate of the populist right does not only consist of those most negatively affected by globalization and individualization, such as the long-term unemployed, those on welfare benefits

(Eatwell, 2003; Mudde, 2007) and more generally those with lower educational and class backgrounds (Rooduijn, 2018). Instead, the voters of the new right-wing parties "can be characterized as the second-to-last fifth of postmodern society, a stratum which is rather secure but objectively can still lose something" as Minkenberg (2000, p. 187) has observed.

Along with economic precariousness, fear and insecurity in contemporary market societies encompass existential, cultural, physical, and environmental forms of uncertainty (e.g., Bauman, 2001; Flecker et al., 2007; Furedi, 2007; Kinnvall, 2013). 'Islamic' terrorism or cultural invasion are further sources of fear that motivate support for right-wing populist parties advocating cultural protectionism and restrictions on immigration and decisions on refugee status (e.g., Kinnvall, 2013; Mols & Jetten, 2016) Also, feelings of fear and injustice about old age in light of the dismantling of the welfare system are salient. These fears often go hand in hand with an ideology of welfare chauvinism that requires that "in times of scarce resources there would have to be a guarantee that immigrants were not to profit at the expense of the majority population of the social welfare state" (Flecker et al., 2007, p. 57).

Economic changes and increasing strains on labor with their implications for status and living standards are also sources of anger and resentment in contemporary societies (Cramer, 2016; Flecker et al., 2007; Hochschild, 2016; Rackow et al., 2012). With individualized careers and risks, employees become more and more "entrepreneurs of the self" (Foucault, 2008) who compete with each other about various resources and recognition. Accordingly, those who are perceived to avoid work or live off the work of others, are held responsible for creating conditions of increased competition and become targets of anger, resentment, indignation, and hate. Such people include politicians and top managers on high and secure income, welfare recipients and refugees "looked after by the state," and the long-term unemployed who "avoid work," but also at groups perceived to be different from 'us'—ethnic, cultural, political, and sexual minorities—and therefore threats to security, national identity, traditional institutions, gender roles, etc. (see e.g., Brubaker, 2017; Inglehart & Norris, 2019; Wodak, 2015). The predicament of immigrants is especially grave, for if they are employed, they are accused of 'stealing' jobs, whereas if they stay out of the labor force, they are resented for avoiding work or abusing welfare state benefits. With this kind of double bind, right-wing populists can present themselves and their clientele as victims in either case.

Most studies that capitalize on negative emotions as motives for supporting right-wing populist parties or movements discuss these emotions in a rather general manner, without going into detail regarding specific emotions and their interrelations (e.g., Berezin, 2009; Betz, 1994). However, some theorists have suggested ways of connecting the two types of negative emotions behind right-wing populist support, fear- and anger-type, into an overarching mechanism (Nussbaum, 2018; Salmela & von Scheve, 2017, 2018). The connection operates through attributions of responsibility or blame for various worries, insecurities, and fears. If one blames oneself for insecurities at work or in other, increasingly competitive areas of social life, one tends to feel actual or anticipated shame about these insecurities in addition to or instead of fear. Self-blame is supported by the neoliberal view that individuals are responsible for their success and exchange value in both labor market and social life, whatever conditions. If shame is further repressed, as it often is due to its painfulness and negative implications on the self, it is capable of transforming into anger, resentment, or hate through the emotional mechanism of ressentiment (Salmela & von Scheve, 2017, 2018). However, fears and insecurities are also capable of transforming directly into anger through another mechanism, namely, blaming others for those insecurities. Thus, Martha Nussbaum (2018) argues that fear impairs our capacity of deliberative thinking, especially on complex problems and their causes, thereby urging us to pin blame on others and to conduct witch-hunts on those scapegoats. Fear also feeds anger's focus on payback, since vulnerable people think that getting back at wrongdoers is a way of re-establishing lost control and dignity.

In all forms of anger, both direct and transformed, experiencing and expressing anger together with others is an important way of reinforcing this emotion and its action tendencies. The collectivization of anger requires its interpretation as group-based, that is, it being based on the concerns of a group rather than on merely personal concerns. Intergroup emotions have been suggested to be particularly relevant in contexts involving conflict, competition, social comparison, or cleavages regarding culture and identity (e.g., Halperin et al., 2011). They seem to be most frequently aimed at outgroups that are perceived as threats, for example, anger and resentment regarding immigrants, homosexuals, or religious minorities. But intergroup emotions are likewise directed at the ingroup, for instance, in cases of pride and love. In this sense, right-wing populist parties and movements often engage in strategies of making religious or nationalist identities salient in a particular context and/or of discursively attributing emotions to their supporters. Claims such as "We as the German people feel offended by certain religious practices of the Muslim population" are a case at hand that combines both the making salient of a group identity and the attribution of a corresponding emotion to the ingroup.

Emotions and the populist political style

Understanding the importance of emotions for the success of populist parties can also be investigated from a supply-side perspective, that is by looking at various behaviors of populist parties and actors and their associations with emotions. This strategy emphasizes political actors' practices of articulating and representing emotions in discourse (by linguistic and non-linguistic means) as well as communications that are specifically geared toward eliciting emotions in the electorate. Analytically, this perspective is rooted in conceptions of political populism emphasizing discourse, communication, and political style over beliefs and ideologies. Understanding populism from this vantage point prioritizes what populist politicians *do* and *say* over what they think and believe. Needless to say, both are intimately related, but the ways in which political beliefs and ideologies are communicated and performed certainly makes a difference in how they are received and interpreted and how they resonate with an audience.

The existing literature sometimes distinguishes between works that focus on 'discourse' and those that capitalize on 'style.' The discourse perspective on populism is historically tied to the Essex school of discourse analysis and closely linked to the works of Ernesto Laclau (2005). Discourse in this tradition is not limited to the production of text, but encompasses the entire spectrum of the social construction of meaning that is constitutive for society (Laclau, 1980; Stavrakakis, 2004). Importantly, discourse is not somehow 'added' to politics and society, but is the very essence of both, it is constitutive of political subjects, processes, and polities. Populism from this discourse-centered view is more about the forms than the contents of politics, and the characteristic form of populism, according to Laclau (2005), is the pitting of the people against some "power bloc," where both remain "empty signifiers," "symbolic vessels filled with particular content depending on the specifics of the political context within which they are invoked and the cultural toolbox at work" (Aslanidis, 2016, p. 98). Populism in this view amounts to an "anti-status quo discourse that simplifies the political space by symbolically dividing society between 'the people' (as the 'underdogs') and its 'other'" (Panizza, 2005, p. 3). Although the discourse approach to populism is sometimes read as an overarching theory of the political, it has informed countless empirical studies that often combine political theory with insights and methods from linguistics and communication sciences (Aalberg et al., 2017; de Vreese et al., 2018). These empirical studies focus on elements of populism that are also extensively accounted for in ideological definitions of populism, such as references to 'the people,' attacks on a 'corrupt elite' and the discursive construction of various outgroups and minorities (de Vreese et al., 2018, p. 427).

Taking issue with the conceptual extension of the notion of 'discourse' (as an 'all or nothing' concept) and the overlapping of the discourse approach with ideology- and strategy-centered understandings of populism, Benjamin Moffit (2016) suggests conceiving of populism primarily as a political *style*. The concept of style much more than discourse refers to the *performative* aspects of politics. As Moffit and Tormey (2014) argue, it captures "the repertoires of performance that are used to create political relations" (p. 387). The key aim of this approach thus is to establish how "performative repertoires of populist leaders and their followers interact, and how this affects their relationship" (Moffit & Tormey, 2014, p. 388), using conceptual tools mostly stemming from dramaturgical approaches to politics, for instance, performativity, actors, audiences, stages, scripts, etc. (Moffit & Tormey, 2014, p. 390).

With respect to emotions, both approaches consistently emphasize, theoretically and empirically, elevated levels of (in particular negative) emotionality in populist discourse and style as compared to traditional politics. Politicians very generally not only articulate ideas, goals, and strategies to attain these goals, but also circumscribe and promote ways to feel about political issues and cleavages. Ruth Breeze (2019) notes that "politicians who can embody and express feelings that resonate with large sectors of the electorate, or who know how to carry voters with them on an affective level, are often highly successful" compared to those who do not have these capabilities (p. 27). Rhetorically, the populist style is supposed to be characterized by an increased appeal to pathos rather than to facts, and it is supposed to include above-average levels of dramatization, colloquial language, and 'bad manners,' all of which contribute to emotional arousal (see Ekström et al., 2018).

More specific analyses of emotions in populist politics revolve around the prototypical ideological and discursive elements of populism, in particular references to the people, the elite, and various outgroups. Two emotions feature particularly prominently in populist discourse, specifically when it comes to pitting 'the people' against corrupt elites and outgroups and minorities: anger and fear (see Breeze, 2019; Schmuck & Hameleers, 2020). A central element of anger in populist discourse is blame attribution. Populist messages are characterized by blaming elites and minorities for various wrongs and undesirable developments in society. By creating the impression that elites and minorities are actively implicated in bringing about these wrongs, populist discourse attributes responsibility to these groups and relieves 'the people' from responsibility. Identifying agents that are held responsible for one's mischief and suffering is intimately related to anger and resentment directed towards groups that are held responsible (e.g., Hameleers et al., 2017, p. 871; Wirz, 2018). Among other things, this is because anger requires the impression of some form of agency and controllability on the side of the blamed parties (Rico et al., 2017, p. 448).

Fear, on the other hand, is typically related to perceived threat or danger that involves some level of uncertainty. As with anger, populist messages referring to fear typically include assertions that some valued good is at stake, such as economic welfare, cultural integrity, or safety. In fear appeals, however, there is only a limited potential for controlling the threat and the outcome typically remains uncertain. Populist messages have been shown to appeal to fear by constructing various threats to 'the people,' in particular those related to salient political cleavages, such as immigration, economic downturn, security, or culture. Existing research has in fact shown that populist communications characteristically rely on a range of fear appeals related to these threats. Jörg Matthes and Desirée Schmuck (2017), for example, have demonstrated that populist advertising strengthens intergroup anxiety. Frank Mols and Jolanda Jetten (2016) have shown that populist leaders are apt at discursively creating threats and thereby evoke fear. Looking at 40 international elections. Alessandro Nai (2018) shows that populist campaigns contain significantly more fear appeals compared to non-populist campaigns. Likewise, Breeze (2019) in an analysis of UKIP and Labor press releases in early 2017 shows that fear messages are more prominent in UKIP compared to Labor discourse. Finally, Ruth Wodak (2015) has devoted a book-length analysis to populist discourse and its potential to create fear.

Emotions and Right-Wing Populism: A Dynamic Relationship

Based on the research reviewed so far, it seems obvious that emotions are associated with right-wing populism in two analytically distinct ways. First, and from a demand-side perspective, emotions that are prevalent in an electorate for reasons other than political discourse and campaigning—in particular reasons related to social status and inequality—render citizens receptive to populist ideologies and messages and make them likely to engage with and support them. Second, and from a supply-side perspective, populist discourse is specifically geared toward tapping into these emotions, that is to acknowledge, amplify, attenuate, or change them, and toward eliciting other, not necessarily already present emotions in the electorate. Existing research suggests two candidate emotions that are particularly relevant from both perspectives, anger and fear. These emotions are likely to play a role in general terms as well as regarding specific objects or domains of emotions, mostly those that are salient in populist discourse. One can therefore assume that citizens who experience anger and fear more frequently than others are more likely to vote for right-wing populist parties. Regarding specific objects or domains of these negative emotions, it seems likely that domains in which the self (and self-blame) is particularly present (e.g., immigration, crime, employment, health) are more relevant predictors of right-wing populist support than issues that are less focused on the self (e.g., climate, the environment, the economy). Looking at the effects of populist discourse, we would equally assume that it generally increases the experience of anger and fear since populist discourse is known to exacerbate concerns and threats and to attribute blame to outgroups. With regard to specific domains or objects, we would assume that populist discourse increases negative emotions in those domains that are particularly salient within discourse, such as immigration and crime.

Method and Data

To investigate the assumptions outlined above, we use data from a representative survey of the German population, the Socio-Economic Panel Study (SOEP; Giesselmann et al., 2019). Aside from a broad spectrum of sociodemographic indicators and voting behavior, the SOEP also includes questions pertaining to the frequency of the experience of fear and anger as well as items assessing a range of specific worries, which we interpret as domain-specific negative emotions.

Analytical Strategy

We have argued that the relationship between specific worries, generalized negative emotions (in particular anger and fear) and right-wing populist support is likely going to be dynamic. To estimate these complex relationships, we require a model that can estimate the sequential order of voters' worries, emotions, and their support for political parties simultaneously. We do this by employing an autoregressive, cross-lagged panel (CLP) model with respondent-level random intercepts (RI). CLP models use structural equation modeling to simultaneously estimate the relationship between two or more variables over time, considering both the overtime dynamics within each variable, and the relationship between them (see Fig. 8.1).

The traditional CLP model, however, may exhibit bias in cross-lagged regression models if the stability of the measured constructs is trait-like and time invariant (Hamaker et al., 2015). Given strong evidence that emotional predispositions, propensity to worry, and support for right-wing populist parties are, at least in part, based on stable personality traits, this assumption is likely violated here. To address this issue, all models also include a random intercept, calculating the within-person mean for each respondent's level of anger, fear, and populist support. This approach introduces the logic of multilevel modeling into the structural equation framework and allows for a more explicit modeling of the variance at both the within-person and the between-person level. Moreover, this approach assumes temporal invariance of cross-lagged and autoregressive paths over time, and therefore follows the logic of a change score or within-effects pooled model, automatically controlling for unobserved, invariant respondent traits. An additional benefit

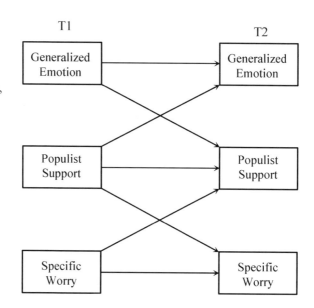

Fig. 8.1 Simplified cross-lagged, autoregressive model between generalized emotions, specific worries, and support for (right-wing) populist parties (*Note* Simplified generalized model of generalized emotion, populist support, and specific worries in a cross-lagged, autoregressive panel setting)

of this technique is the added ease of interpreting the model results. Coefficients now represent the within-person, carry-over effect, where a cross-lagged parameter now indicates "the degree by which deviations from an individual's expected score [on a given variable] can be predicted from preceding deviations from ones expected score [of a different variable], also accounting for individual-differences and wave-to-wave group differences" (Hamaker et al., 2015).

In simpler terms: The cross-lagged coefficients can tell us how becoming more worried about a specific issue at T1 increases a respondent's support for RRP parties at T2, while controlling for their general propensity to be worried about this issue, their general support for RRP parties, and the direct effect of an increase in populist party support at time T1. The same logic applies to the relationship between generalized emotions anger, and fear and RRP party support. Moreover, these models also control for the direct relationship between generalized emotions and specific worries.

Data and Measures

Opting for the SOEP as our main data source is motivated by the broad range of relevant indicators included in the SOEP and by the German political context. Germany had long avoided the emergence of a (nationally) successful right-wing populist party. This changed, with the emergence of the Alternative for Germany (AfD). Although initially founded in 2013 to protest against bailouts in the Eurozone, increasing radicalization following a party split in 2014, and a close link to anti-immigration protests in 2015, have seen them gaining increasing public prominence and electoral support. They were the third strongest party in the 2018 national election and will likely remain a fixture of an increasingly fragmented German political party system. Despite its early technocratic and Eurosceptic roots, the AfD has therefore become a firmly entrenched right-wing populist party in the German party system.

Support for the AfD thus serves as our measure of *right-wing populist support*. Specifically, support is measured through the combination of two variables: Feelings of party affiliation and the strength of that affiliation. The SOEP asks respondents if they feel close to a specific party, and if so, how strong this feeling of closeness is on a Likert Scale ranging between 1 and 5. The dependent variables are built through a combination of those two variables, where 0 indicates no feelings of affiliation and 5 indicates a very strong sense of affiliation.[1] To measure *generalized emotions*, we rely on the SOEP's measure of generalized anger and fear. Specifically, the SOEP asks respondents how frequently they experience anger and fear, ranging from 1 (very rarely) to 5 (very often). To measure specific worries, we rely on a battery of items

---

[1] To check the robustness of these models, we also replicated these models for center-right CDU, the social democratic SPD, the Green party, and the market-liberal FDP. None of these parties show comparable relationships.

that ask respondents to rate how concerned they are over specific topics, with possible answers ranging between 1(not at all) and 3 (very much). We differentiate between issue areas that are commonly associated with the AfD such as crime, immigration, their own or general economic conditions, 'neutral' areas such as health, as well as anti-AfD areas, such as environmental protection or the fight against xenophobia. To facilitate this comparison of effect sizes, all variables have been rescaled to range between 0 and 1.

The RI-CLP automatically control for time-invariant respondent characteristics such as education, gender, or age. Nevertheless, since the SOEP is collected annually, including controls for changes in respondents' socioeconomic conditions could be important. However, including additional controls not only reduces model fit considerably, it also does not change the main results. All models therefore only use respondents' generalized emotions, specific worries, and support for the AfD.

Since the AfD was only founded in 2013, items measuring attitudes toward the AfD only become informative in the last five available waves, covering the years between 2014 and 2018. However, even given this relatively constricted timeframe, the extensive coverage of the SOEP allows us to measure the relationship between affect and populism among 14,887 unique respondents.

Results

Table 8.1 summarizes results of eight CLP models predicting AfD support from anger, fear, and specific worries. Coefficient estimates indicate the autoregressive paths to AfD support and from AfD support, respectively. Empty cells indicate that no significant relationships were found.

Table 8.1 CLP model regressing AFD support on specific worries and fear and anger

Specific Worry	Determinants of AfD Support			Effects of AfD support			Sum. Stat	
	Worry	Anger	Fear	Worry	Anger	Fear	RMSEA	P
Immigration	0.013 ***	0.005 *	–	0.114 ***	0.033 **	–	0.033	0
Crime	0.011 ***	0.006 **	–	0.133 ***	0.039 **	–	0.031	0
Own Econ	0.009 ***	0.005 *	–	0.074 ***	0.041 ***	–	0.03	0
General Econ	0.01 ***	0.006 **	–	0.1 ***	0.042 ***	0.024 *	0.03	0
Health	–	0.006 **	–	–	0.044 ***	0.023 *	0.031	0
Environment	−0.009 ***	0.006 **	–	−0.101 ***	0.047 ***	0.025 *	0.031	0
Climate	−0.006 **	0.006 **	–	−0.078 ***	0.042 ***	0.026 *	0.03	0
Xenophobia	–	0.006 **	–	−0.032 *	0.043 ***	0.026 *	0.031	0

* p<0.05, ** p<0.01, *** p<0.001

Looking at the determinants of AfD support shows that worries about immigration, crime, one's own economic condition, and the general economy lead to subsequent increases in support for the AfD, even when anger and fear are taken into account. As expected, worries about the environment and the climate have negative effects on AfD support while health and xenophobia show no meaningful association. Generalized anger increases support for the AfD, even when controlled for any specific worry, whereas generalized fear does not predict AfD support.

Looking at the effects of AfD support, these relationships appear to be recursive. Becoming more supportive of the AfD is associated with subsequent increases in worries about immigration, crime, one's own economic condition, and the general economy as well as with increases in generalized anger. Becoming more supportive of the AfD is also associated with less worries about the environment, the climate, and xenophobia. Notably, across the different models, the consequences of AfD support for worries and emotions are considerably larger than their role in mobilizing support. Generalized fear does not appear to play a role, neither as a driver nor a consequence of AfD support.

The results in Table 8.1 indicate four key findings: First, there is a clear and recursive relationship between generalized anger and support for the AfD. Individuals who become more angry also become more supportive of the AfD, even when time-invariant respondent characteristics are taken into account. In other words, generalized anger does not only drive support for the AfD, it is also driven by it.

Second, there is a clear relationship between specific worries in areas commonly associated with the AfD, such as crime and immigration, but also more general concerns about both general and personal economic conditions. In all cases, becoming more worried about these issues leads to increased support for the AfD, and this increase is substantially larger than the effects of generalized anger. Conversely, worries over xenophobia, the climate, and the environment, in which the AfD traditionally has taken a very skeptical and dismissive stance, are associated with reduced support for the AfD.

Third, the AfD does little to reduce both anger or worries about specific policy areas, and instead appears to amplify them. Becoming more supportive of the AfD also leads to increased concerns over immigration, crime, and economic conditions, and also increases overall generalized anger. More importantly, this effect is considerably larger (six–ten times the coefficient estimate) than the relationship running from worries and anger to AfD support, suggesting a much more pronounced effect from AfD support to worries and anger than the other way around.

Finally, the relationship between generalized fear and support for the AfD appears to be an artifact of not controlling for more specific concerns. While both right-wing populist party communications in general, and AfD communications in particular, have been associated with a more 'fearful' style, this does not seem to correspond to subsequent increases in generalized fear once we control for more specific worries.

DISCUSSION AND CONCLUSION

In this chapter, we have investigated the dynamic relationship between emotions and populist right-wing support, based on two theoretical perspectives. On the one hand, we have discussed theories that explore how *generalized* negative emotions, such as anger or fear, drive support for right-wing populist parties. On the other hand, we have identified theories that focus on more specific, *targeted* negative emotions, such as worries or blame. We have discussed both of these perspectives from a demand and supply perspective, emphasizing the dynamic relationship between generalized negative emotions, specific worries, and populist right-wing support. In consequence, we have investigated whether generalized fear and anger as well as worries in a number of policy domains motivate support for a populist right-wing party and whether support for such a party, in turn, changes these worries and emotions.

To test these theories empirically, we have used structural equation modeling and panel data from Germany to explore the temporal relationship between generalized negative emotions, specifically targeted worries, and support for a right-wing populist party, namely, the AfD. Using this data, we have shown that taking an explicitly temporal perspective is an important step to reconciling, and expanding, the existing literature on emotions and populist right-wing support. While we do replicate the finding that generalized emotions, particularly anger, increase subsequent support for right-wing populist parties, this effect is comparably smaller than the effects of populist right-wing support on ensuing negative emotions. In other words, it is not so much generalized anger (let alone fear) that drives voters to support the AfD, but rather that voters express more anger once they have become supportive of the AfD. The findings for specific worries in domains commonly associated with populist right-wing parties, such as immigration or crime, are similarly complex. While specific worries do significantly increase AfD support, this support subsequently also increases these worries. In other words, populist right-wing parties do not just benefit from previously existing specific worries, they also nourish and bolster these worries, probably through their specific style and discourse, creating a feedback loop of negative emotionality.

In general, then, taking an explicitly temporal perspective on the relationship between specific and generalized negative emotions and populist right-wing party support demonstrates the complex role that these parties play in the emotional lives of their supporters. Particularly the mechanisms that lead to the 'translation' of specific worries into more generalized anger should be explored in greater depth.

Literature

Aalberg, T., Esser, F., Reinemann, C., Stromback, J., & De Vreese, C. (Eds.). (2017). *Populist political communication in Europe*. Routledge.

Aslanidis, P. (2016). Is populism an ideology? A refutation and a new perspective. *Political Studies, 64*(1S), 88–104. https://doi.org/10.1111/1467-9248.12224.

Bauman, Z. (2001). *The individualized society*. Polity Press.

Berezin, M. (2009). *Illiberal politics in neoliberal times*. Cambridge University Press.

Betz, H. G. (1994). *Radical right-wing populism in Western Europe*. Macmillan.

Betz, H.-G. (2002). Conditions favouring the success and failure of radical right-wing populist parties in contemporary democracies. In Y. Mény & Y. Surel (Eds.), *Democracies and the populist challenge* (pp. 197–213). Palgrave.

Bonikowski, B. (2017). Ethno-nationalist populism and the mobilization of collective resentment. *British Journal of Sociology, 68*(1), 181–213.

Breeze, R. (2019). Emotion in politics: Affective-discursive practices in UKIP and Labour. *Discourse & Society, 30*(1), 24–43. https://doi.org/10.1177/0957926518801074.

Brubaker, R. (2017). Why populism? *Theoretical sociology, 46*, 357–385.

Cramer, K. (2016). *The politics of resentment*. University of Chicago Press.

de Vreese, C. H., Esser, F., Aalberg, T., Reinemann, C., & Stanyer, J. (2018). Populism as an expression of political communication content and style: A new perspective. *The International Journal of Press/politics, 23*(4), 423–438. https://doi.org/10.1177/1940161218790035.

Eatwell, R. (2003). Ten theories of extreme right. In P. H. Merkl & L. Weinberg (Eds.), *Right-wing extremism in the twenty-first century* (pp. 47–73). Frank Cass.

Ekström, M., Patrona, M., & Thornborrow, J. (2018). Right-wing populism and the dynamics of style: A discourse-analytic perspective on mediated political performances. *Palgrave Communications, 4*(1), 1–11. https://doi.org/10.1057/s41599-018-0132-6.

Flecker, J., Hentges, G., & Balazs, G. (2007). Potentials of political subjectivity and the various approaches to the extreme right: Findings of the qualitative research. In J. Flecker (Ed.), *Changing working life and the appeal of the extreme right* (pp. 35–62). Ashgate.

Foucault, M. (2008). *The birth of biopolitics: Lectures at the collège de France 1978–79* (Trans. G. Burchell). New York: Palgrave Macmillan.

Furedi, F. (2007). *Invitation to terror*. Continuum.

Giesselmann, M., Bohmann, S., Goebel, J., Krause, P., Liebau, E., Richter, D., Schacht, D., Schröder, C., Schupp, J., & Liebig, S. (2019). The individual in context (s): Research potentials of the Socio-Economic Panel Study (SOEP) in sociology. *European Sociological Review, 35*(5), 738–755. https://doi.org/10.1093/esr/jcz029.

Halperin, E., Sharvit, K., & Gross, J. J. (2011). Emotion and emotion regulation in intergroup conflict: An appraisal-based framework. In D. Bar-Tal (Ed.), *Frontiers of social psychology. Intergroup conflicts and their resolution: A social psychological perspective* (pp. 83–103). Psychology Press.

Hamaker, E. L., Kuiper, R. M., & Grasman, R. P. P. (2015). A critique of the cross-lagged panel model. *Psychological Methods, 20*(1), 102–116. https://doi.org/10.1037/a0038889.

Hameleers, M., Bos, L., & de Vreese, C. H. (2017). "They did it": The effects of emotionalized blame attribution in populist communication. *Communication Research, 44*(6), 870–900. https://doi.org/10.1177/0093650216644026.

Hochschild, A. R. (2016). *Strangers in their own land. Anger and mourning on the American right*. New Press.

Inglehart, R., & Norris, P. (2019). *Cultural backlash: Trump, Brexit, and authoritarian populism*. Cambridge University Press.

Kinnvall, C. (2013). Trauma and the politics of fear: Europe at the crossroads. In N. Demertzis (Ed.), *Emotions in politics* (pp. 143–166). Palgrave Macmillan.

Laclau, E. (1980). Populist rupture and discourse. *Screen Education, 34*(99), 87–93.

Laclau, E. (2005). *On populist reason*. Verso.

Marx, P. (2020). Anti-elite politics and emotional reactions to socio-economic problems: Experimental evidence on "pocketbook anger" from France, Germany, and the United States. *British Journal of Sociology*, 608–624.

Matthes, J., & Schmuck, D. (2017). The effects of anti-immigrant right-wing populist ads on implicit and explicit attitudes: A moderated mediation model. *Communication Research, 44*(4), 556–581. https://doi.org/10.1177/0093650215577859.

Minkenberg, M. (2000). Renewal of the radical right: Between modernity and anti-modernity. *Government and Opposition, 35*, 170–188.

Moffitt, B. (2016). *The global rise of populism: Performance, political style, and representation*. Stanford University Press. https://doi.org/10.2307/j.ctvqsdsd8.

Moffitt, B., & Tormey, S. (2014). Rethinking populism: Politics, mediatisation and political style. *Political Studies, 62*(2), 381–397. https://doi.org/10.1111/1467-9248.12032.

Mols, F., & Jetten, J. (2016). Explaining the appeal of populist right-wing parties in times of economic prosperity. *Political Psychology, 37*(2), 275–292. https://doi.org/10.1111/pops.12258.

Mudde, C. (2007). *Populist radical right parties in Europe*. Cambridge University Press.

Nai, A. (2018). Fear and loathing in populist campaigns? Comparing the communication style of populists and non-populists in elections worldwide. *Journal of Political Marketing, 1–32*. https://doi.org/10.1080/15377857.2018.1491439.

Nussbaum, M. (2018). *Monarchy of fear*. Oxford University Press.

Panizza, F. (2005). Introduction: Populism and the mirror of democracy. In F. Panizza (Ed.), *Populism and the mirror of democracy* (pp. 1–31). Verso.

Rackow, K., Schupp, J., & von Scheve, C. (2012). Angst und Ärger. Zur Relevanz emotionaler Dimensionen sozialer Ungleichheit. *Zeitschrift für Soziologie, 41*(5), 391–409.

Rico, G., Guinjoan, M., & Anduiza, E. (2017). The emotional underpinnings of populism: How anger and fear affect populist attitudes. *Swiss Political Science Review, 23*(4), 444–461. https://doi.org/10.1111/spsr.12261.

Rooduijn, M. (2018). What unites the voter bases of populist parties? Comparing the electorates of 15 populist parties. *European Political Science Review, 10*(3), 351–368. https://doi.org/10.1017/S1755773917000145.

Salmela, M., & von Scheve, C. (2017). Emotional roots of right-wing political populism. *Social Science Information, 56*(4), 567–595.

Salmela, M., & von Scheve, C. (2018). Emotional dynamics of right- and left-wing political populism. *Humanity and Society, 42*(4), 434–454.

Schmuck, D., & Hameleers, M. (2020). Closer to the people: A comparative content analysis of populist communication on social networking sites in pre-and post-election periods. *Information, Communication & Society, 23*(10), 1531–1548. https://doi.org/10.1080/1369118X.2019.1588909.

Stavrakakis, Y. (2004). Antinomies of formalism: Laclau's theory of populism and the lessons from religious populism in Greece. *Journal of Political Ideologies, 9*(3), 253–267. https://doi.org/10.1080/1356931042000263519.

Wirz, D. (2018). Persuasion through emotion? An experimental test of the emotion-eliciting nature of populist communication. *International Journal of Communication, 12*, 1114–1138. https://doi.org/10.5167/uzh-149959.

Wodak, R. (2015). *The politics of fear: What right-wing populist discourses mean*. Sage.

Part IV

Authoritarian Populism & Fascism

CHAPTER 9

Fascism and Populism

Carlos de la Torre

POPULISTS OR FASCISTS?

The elections of Donald Trump in 2016 and Jair Bolsonaro in 2019 in Brazil, their belligerent use of the presidency to transform democratic rivals into enemies, their praise for right-wing para-military groups, Bolsonaro's nostalgia for dictatorship, Trump's attempt to stay in power using nondemocratic means have brought back the question of fascism and its relationship with populism. For months, Donald Trump falsely claimed electoral fraud and urged his supporters to 'stop the steal.' On January 6, 2021, right-wing militias and activists stormed the U.S. Capitol to stop the certification of Joe Biden as the new president. Some of the insurgents were postfascist activists, but how to make sense of Trump? Was he a proto-fascist or a right-wing populist? What are the boundaries between fascism and populism? Similarly, how to classify European right-wing parties like the French National Rally, the Italian League, and others? Are they populist, nativist and xenophobic, or postfascist? Could right-wing xenophobic populism mute into postfascism?

ARGENTINEAN PERONISM AND THE FIRST DEBATES ON FASCISM AND POPULISM

The United Officers' Group (GOU), a pro-axis, nationalist, Catholic, anti-Communist, and anti-liberal lodge of military officers gave a coup in Argentina

---

C. de la Torre (✉)
Center for Latin American Studies, University of Florida, Gainesville, FL, USA
e-mail: delatorre.carlos@latam.ufl.edu

in 1943. At that time, Argentina was a hub of nationalist, extreme right-wing Catholic and fascist thinking and activism (Finchelstein, 2014). In an internal memo, the GOU explained its pro-Axis alliance: "Hitler's fight, in times of peace and in times of war, will have to guide us from now on" (Bolton, 2014, 16). The goal of the military junta was to Christianize the country making Catholic education mandatory. They made political parties illegal, repressed the organizations of the left, and intervened in the universities by dismissing large numbers of professors.

General Juan Perón emerged as the most intriguing figure of this military government. First, he was Undersecretary in the Ministry of War, then became Minister of War, Secretary of Labor, and vice president. As Secretary of Labor, he established ties with union leaders while repressing Communists, Socialist, and Anarchists. He met labor demands "settling specific conflicts via collective bargaining agreements—supervised by the secretariat—, extended the retirement system, paid vacations, and accident insurance [...]. The Statue of the Peon extended these policies to the rural sector" (Romero, 2002, 93–94). Of Sardinian descent, Perón lived in Italy,

> closely studied Italian Fascism, and joined the mass rallies where Mussolini spoke to the crowds from the balcony of the Palazzo Venezia, a technique he was to master as a feature of his own regime. He regarded Italians and Argentines as similar and saw how a variant of this national-social synthesis could be applied to his country. (Bolton, 2014, 14)

General Perón never hid his admiration for the Duce. When a journalist "told Perón of Mussolini's death and said, 'We will have to erect a monument for him one day', Perón replied, 'One monument? Only one? Please say you mean one on every street corner!" (Bolton, 2014, 14). Perón knew that after its defeat in the war, fascism had run its course. He said fascism was "an unrepeatable phenomenon, a classic style to define a precise and determined epoch" (Finchelstein, 2017, 12). Even though Perón was not a fascist, "fascism played an important role in the ideological genesis of Peronist populism" (Finchelstein, 2014, 65).

It should come as no surprise that the relationship between fascism and Peronism was a prominent intellectual and political topic for Argentinean scholars. Gino Germani (1978) devoted his academic career to explore the similarities and differences between these varieties of authoritarianism. He argued that Italian fascism and Peronism were charismatic movements based on pathological and irrational reactions to stress provoked by rapid social change. Yet they differed because they were products of distinct social structures and had dissimilar class compositions. Whereas the social base of fascism were the downwardly mobile middle classes, the base of Peronism was the new working class. Different from the middle-class supporters of fascism that only attained psychological pseudo gratification in the form of national, ethnic, and racial pride, workers under Perón obtained material, political and symbolic benefits. Germani viewed followers of charismatic movements as irrational, formless, and unstable masses, and used binary oppositions such as rational–irrational, and normal and pathological.

Ernesto Laclau (1977) developed an alternative interpretation of the relationships between fascism and Peronism. He argued that in any capitalist society there are two main contradictions. The first has to do with the antagonistic struggles between capital and labor for the appropriation and distribution of surplus value. The second works at the level of a social formation and are the popular democratic confrontations between the power bloc and the underdog. Class and popular democratic demands could be articulated under socialism, fascism, or Perón's Bonapartism. Socialism is the outcome of the articulation of anti-capitalist demands with popular democratic interpellations. Fascism and populism contained the people/power bloc contradiction within the confines of the capitalist system. The first was the product of a dual crises: "a crisis of the dominant sectors who were incapable of neutralizing by traditional methods the Jacobin potential of popular democratic interpellations; [and] a crisis of the working class which was incapable of articulating them in socialist political discourse" (Laclau, 1977, 135). Differently from fascism that had a precise ideology based on racism and corporatism and used widespread repression, under Perón there was a coexistence of different and often contradictory ideologies such as "populism and clerical anti-liberalism, populism and Nazism, populism and trade-unionist reformism, populism and democratic anti-imperialism, and finally populism and socialism" (Laclau, 1977, 197–198).

The historian Federico Finchelstein (2014, 2017) argues that whereas fascists disdained elections and rely on dictatorial plebiscitarian acclamation, for populist the vote is the only legitimate tool to get to power. Perón was elected in 1946 in clean democratic elections. Similarly, Getúlio Vargas in Brazil, who had created a fascist-inspired corporatist Estado Novo from 1934 to 1945, came back to power in the presidential elections of 1950s as a populist. Whereas fascists abolished all the institutions of democracy and used violence to eradicate internal and external enemies, populism combined a democratic commitment to elections, which also means the selective respect to rights of association and information, with the autocratic idea that the leader is the embodiment of the people.

Finchelstein's provocative argument works for some historical experiences where former fascists became populist by embracing free elections. Yet not all populists had fascist origins. In what follows, the nature of fascism and post-fascism are explained by comparing them with populism.

Fascism

Early approaches to fascism linked it to the irrational response of masses in a state of anomie. It was considered a movement of the angry petty bourgeoise that took place in societies like Germany or Italy that did not attain successful processes of political modernization. Marxists argued that fascism was the product of an acute economic crisis of capitalism, it was a violent reactionary and anti-communist alliance between monopoly capital and its social base made up of the petty bourgeoisie. Modernization theory and Marxism were structuralist theories that took the point of view of the external observer and ignored "fascist own beliefs" (Mann, 2004, 21). They were based on binary oppositions that relegated emotions to the irrational, and on a teleology that there is only one rational path to modernity. However, they were right in linking fascism to structural transformations of capitalism and to class formation.

As a reaction to approaches from above, historians George L. Mosse, Zeev Sternhell, and Emilio Gentile studied fascism from within, "taking into account its participants, its ideas, and its self-representations" (Traverso, 2019, 100). It is worth quoting at length historian Enzo Traversos' summary of their approach,

> According to these three historians, fascism was simultaneously a revolution, and an ideology, a *Weltanschauung*, and a culture. As a revolution, it wished to build a new society. As an ideology, it reformulated nationalism as a rejection of Marxism that served as an alternative to conservatism as well as to liberalism. As a *Weltanschauung*, it inscribed its political project within a philosophy that saw history as a realm of building a "New Man". And as a culture, fascism tried to transform the collective imagination, change people's way of life, and eliminate differences between the private and the public spheres fusing them into a single national community (delimited along ethnic or racial lines) [...]. It was a simultaneously antiliberal and anti-Marxist "spiritualist" and "communitarian revolution". (Traverso, 2019, 101)

Roger Griffin built on fascist self-interpretations to construct a minimum definition of generic fascism as an ideal type. He developed "a succinct, one-sentence definition which could be empirically tested against potential documents of fascist thinking and policy" (Griffin, 2020, 69). He defined fascism as "a genus of political ideology whose mythic core in its various permutations is a palingenetic form of populist ultranationalism" (Griffin, 2008, 88–89). The ultranation is an imagined community that "like a living organism, can decline and 'die', or regenerate itself and return to enough strength culturally and politically to realize renewed greatness inspired by past glories" (Griffin, 2020, 83). Palingenesis is the myth of rebirth from decadence "to be realized by removing obstacles to or 'enemies'" (Griffin, 2020, 83). By populism, Griffin means that fascist aimed to create a movement with "a significant mass following at all levels of society" (Griffin, 2020, 172). Fascism is a populist form of ultranationalism that "seeks to mobilize and unleash the dormant power of 'the people' to cleanse itself from the forces of decadence and regenerate itself in a new era of greatness" (Griffin, 2020, 92).

By focusing on culture and ideology, scholars integrate the instrumental reasons and the emotions that explain popular support. Yet culturalists and ideational approaches have four problems. First, it is not convincing to paint fascists as revolutionaries because differently from Communist revolutions that altered forms of property and relations of production, fascist revolutions "integrated the old ruling classes into their system of power" (Traverso, 2019, 119). Second, as Kevin Passmore (2014, 14) writes, "a major problem with the above theories is that they presume an undifferentiated and ultimately passive mass, integrated into fascism by ritual repetition of ideas and/or by technologies of rule." Third, it is unclear how successfully fascist projects created a New Man. David Reisman argued that "totalitarian control was an unreachable idea" and often "people bow their heads in mock mental obeisance but refuse to internalize the system" (Baehr, 2010, 47; 49). Fourth, these interpretations do not put fascist violence at the center of their explanations.

Populism

Whereas fascists abolished all the institutions of liberal democracy, established violent forms of dictatorship to eliminate internal enemies, and to colonize populations regarded as 'inferior,' populists abide by some of the democratic rules of the game such as election, and hence selectively preserve democratic institutions and rights to information and association. Like fascism, populism continues to be a contested concept. It is defined as a series of moral ideas about politics, a strategy, and a style to get to power and to govern, or a political logic (de la Torre, 2019, 23–64). Scholars diverge on how they construct their concepts as ideal types or as minimal definitions. Historians and interpretative social scientists acknowledge that the complexity of populism cannot be reduced to one main attribute or to a generic and universal definition. Hence, they use accumulative concepts of populism or ideal types that list a series of attributes. For instance, the political theorists Jean Cohen (2019, 13–14) lists ten criteria to identify a movement, leader, or party as more or less populist:

1. Appeal to 'the people' and 'popular sovereignty'—empty signifiers deployed to unify heterogeneous demands and grievances.
2. Pars pro toto logic that extracts the 'authentic people' from the rest of the population via a logic of equivalences by which a set of demands are constructed into a substantive particular identity that stands for the whole.
3. Discourse that pits the people against elites—the political-economic, cultural 'establishment' cast as usurpers who corrupt, ignore, or distort the 'authentic' people's will.
4. Construction of a frontier of antagonism along the lines of a Schmittian friend/enemy conception of the political that identifies alien others who violate the people's values and whom elites unfairly coddle.

5. Unification, typically through strong identification with a leader (or, more rarely, a unified leadership group) claiming to embody the authentic people's will and voice, incarnating their unity and identity.
6. Focus on the symbolic and authorization dimensions of political representation.
7. Performative style of leadership that mimics the habitus (dress, speech, manners) of the authentic people.
8. Dramatic and rhetorical forms of argumentation linking talk about making the nation great again to discourses about the restoration of honor, centrality, and political influence to the authentic people.
9. Focus on alleged crises, national decline, and an orientation to the extraordinary dimensions of politics.
10. Dependence on a host ideology for content and moral substance.

Positivist-oriented scholars sustain that cumulative concepts do not allow for the accumulation of knowledge. They argue that enumerating a series of attributes to define populism results in conceptual stretching that "lump[s] together under the same conceptual roof dissimilar political parties" (Pappas, 2019, 29). They are uneasy with gradations and, hence, opt to define populism in contrast with what it is not. The goal of positivists is to produce a generic definition of populism that can travel and explain experiences in different historical times and places. Their first task is to designate the field of populism. Kurt Weyland (2001) argues that the domain of populism is politics understood as strategic struggles over power. Takis Pappas (2019, 33–35) locates it in the domain of democratic politics; he defines populism as 'democratic illiberalism.' Cas Mudde and Cristóbal Rovira Kaltwasser (2012) argue that its domain is morality, and that populism is a form of Manichaean politics. While for Weyland and Pappas, the role of the leader is crucial, Mudde and Rovira Kaltwasser do not define the leader as central and broaden the populist camp to attitudes, movements, and parties.

Despite controversies about its genus, there is a consensus on what populists do, especially when they get to office. They construct politics as the antagonistic struggle between two camps transforming democratic rivals into existential enemies that need to be contained. Populist appeal to a section of the population considered to represent the people as a whole. A leader is constructed as the embodiment of the promises of change and renewal. Once in office populists followed similar playbooks that are based on the polarization of citizens, and the radicalization of politics as struggles between friends and enemies. They entered into wars with the private media restricting the freedom of information, supervised the activities of organizations of civil society restricting the rights of association, and attempted to control the system of justice to use it to punish critics (de la Torre, 2019).

COMPARING FASCISM AND POPULISM

To differentiate fascists from populists I focus on the historicity of these movements, how they imagined their enemies, how followers were mobilized using charisma, parties, and by their symbolic imagination of politics.

Historicity

Scholars of fascism emphasize the historicity of these phenomena linking it to the combination of the Great Depression, the effects of the Great War, anti-Communism, and the crises of democracy in the 1920s and 1930s. Fascist movements, as the historian Geoff Elley (2013) wrote, were the product of a particular conjuncture. (1) The dislocations, radicalization, normalization of the use of violence, and the banalization of death after World War I (1914–1918). (2) A crisis of political representation and popular consent of democracy. Fascist "combined radical authoritarianism, militarized activism, and the drive for a coercive state, professing a radical nationalist, imperialist, and racial creed, shaped by violent antipathy against liberals, democrats and socialists" (Elley, 2013, 208). (3) Fascist used unrestrained political violence to kill enemies, a practice that was 'shockingly new.' Hence its emergence was the product of a particular and historically specific crisis. As such, even though there are profound disagreements of what fascism is, there is a consensus that it was historically specific, and that whatever came after its military defeat in 1945 was not the same.

In populist studies, there is no such consensus to limit it to a particular time period. Some Latin American scholars argued that populism refers exclusively to the politics of first political incorporation, cultural empowerment, and nationalist economic redistribution of governments of the 1930s and 1940s to the 1970s. Most scholars in Latin America and other world regions, however, do not confine populism to a particular historical period, nor to a particular type of crisis. Different crises of political incorporation resulted in distinct types of populism. When populism emerged with the first incorporation of the excluded against oligarchic privileges, it was more inclusionary. After populism targeted political parties in partially democratized societies when in power, it often led to processes of democratic erosion (de la Torre, 2019).

Enemies

The most frightened particularity of fascism was the use and glorification of violence to get rid of enemies. Populists, as Perón said, were 'herbivorous lions' in so far as they use violent tropes against enemies but remained at the rhetorical level (Finchelstein, 2020, 100). Both isms were anti-pluralists, presenting the contradiction between the people and the power bloc as antagonistic but differed in how violence was used. Sociologist Michael Mann

(2004, 16) writes that paramilitarism "was a key value and the key organizational form of fascism." It was a form of bottom-up political violence that appealed to young and macho constituencies specially in institutions of secondary and higher education, and in the armed forces (Mann, 2004, 26). If men were idealized as virile agents of national regeneration, women were assigned "the task of producing the future citizens, soldiers, and mothers of the race" (Passmore, 2014, 127).

Carl Schmitt—the Nazi intellectual and critic of liberal parliamentarism—put violence at the center of his conception of politics. His existentialist notion of the political as the conflict between friend and enemy always imply the possibility of death, as such the "essential task of politics is not to 'hide' but to develop conflict" (Traverso, 2016, 199). For fascists, war was "the supreme moment of life, exalting battle as a kind of fulfillment for man and for the triumph of strength, speed, and courage" (Traverso, 2003, 94).

Linkages

Charisma is a central linkage in populism and fascism. The power of fascist and populist leaders was embodied "in a single, sacred, irreplaceable body, neither dynastic nor institutional, but precisely charismatic; a body identified with gestures, expressions, a voice; the mystical object around which the crowd can assemble and commune" (Traverso, 2016, 97).

Fascist and populist created parties to give followers "the illusion of being actors, not simple spectators of politics" (Traverso, 2019, 105). When fascism emerged in Italy and Germany or populism in Latin America most political parties were made up of notables that only reached to the public during election times. Populist parties were not paramilitary organizations that systematically used violence to silence internal enemies. Fascist created the militia party that "operated in political struggles with warlike methods and considered political adversaries as 'internal enemies' that must be defeated and destroyed" (Gentile, 2008, 292). Paramilitarism socialized militants into a brotherhood, a comradeship of a "segregated, hardened elite, beyond conventional standards of behavior" (Mann, 2004, 29).

Fascism "was a political religion, with its own set of beliefs and dogmas. As a political religion, it intended to define the meaning and the goal of existence, creating a new political cult centered on the sacralization of the fascist state and on the myth of the Duce, with a tight sequence of collective rituals to celebrate the big events of its 'sacred history'" (Gentile, 2008, 298). Like fascists, some populists in Latin America created political theologies. Perón and Hugo Chávez portrayed themselves as carriers of the unfinished missions of exemplary nationalist figures. Perón claimed that he was leading Argentina's national rebirth to complete General San Martín's unfinished project. Chávez became the carrier of Bolívar's project of national and continental liberation. He was constructed as a redeemer and as the synthesis of the figures of Christ and Bolívar (Lindholm & Zúquete, 2010).

When in power, fascist dissolved leftist and other parties, got rid of the free media, and autonomous organizations of civil society. Under fascism, the private sphere was almost swallowed by the state. There was no room for free and autonomous thinking individuals, nor for autonomous subcommunities. Fascists identified "truth with a transcendental myth rooted in the collective unconscious and then realized by and through the leader" (Finchelstein, 2020, 27). Fascists believed that "elections distorted true representation" (Finchelstein, 2020, 82), and "expressed their citizenship directly by participating in ceremonies of mass assent" (Paxton, 2005, 78–79). Populism incorporated the democratic principle that the only form of legitimacy lies in the vote, with the view of democracy as the participation in ceremonies, demonstrations, and other mass rituals that create a sense of community, belonging, and identity.

Like fascists, populists construct the people as a homogenous body with one will and interest, which is that of the leader only. A diverse population with distinct interests, demands, and proposals is homogenized into a single unitary body. Those who do not agree with the leader are expelled from the people and the nation. Even disloyal fellow travelers could become enemies. Yet as said before, these isms differed in the type of violence used to deal with enemies.

Political Imaginaries

Claude Lefort contrasted the images of the people in monarchies, democratic, and totalitarian regimes. In monarchies the King, like God, had two bodies and the two were inseparable. The king's body was mortal and time bound, as well as immortal and eternal. Once the immortal body of the king and the body of the politic were decapitated during the democratic revolutions of the eighteenth century, the space occupied by the religious political body of the king was opened up. "Power appears as an empty place and those who exercise it as merely mortals who occupy it only temporarily or who could install themselves in it only by force or cunning" (Lefort, 1986, 303). In a democracy, the will of the majority is not the same as the will of the people as a whole. The people of today are not necessarily the people of tomorrow, as the power of today is not the power of tomorrow. Under democracy, the image of the people 'remains indeterminate' and cannot be embodied in an individual like a King or a leader regardless of how popular she is.

The uncertainty of democracy, where power belongs to the people in the abstract but not to a concrete individual who at most could occupy it only temporarily, could lead to its destruction. According to Lefort, the revolutions of the eighteenth century also generated "from the outset the principle that would threaten the emptiness of that space: popular sovereignty in the sense of a subject incarnated in a group, however extensive, a stratum however poor, and an institution or a person, however popular" (Arato, 2012, 23). Totalitarianism, thus, "is an attempt to reincarnate society in the figure of a leader or a party which would annul the social division and would realize the fantasy of people-as-one, in which there is no legitimate opposition, where all factual opposition is conceived of as coming from the outside, the enemy" (Flyn, 2013, 31). Symbolically, this is done by abandoning the democratic imagination of the people as "heterogeneous, multiple, and in conflict" and living in a society where power does not belong to any individual (Lefort, 1986, 297). Under totalitarianism, there are no internal divisions within the people. The divide is between the people—imagined as having one identity and one will—and its external enemies, which need to be eliminated in order to maintain the healthy body of the people.

Benjamin Moffitt (2016, 64) writes that populism is an attempt "to re-embody the body politic, to suture the head back on the corpse. And provide unity in the name of the people through the leader." It aims to get rid of the uncertainties of democratic politics by naming a leader as the embodiment of the people and nation. Yet this attempt is different from fascism, which abolished democracy altogether. The vote for populists is the only legitimate tool to get to power, therefore democratic uncertainty is not fully abolished. The populist imaginary thus lies between democracy and fascist and Communist totalitarianism. Unlike totalitarianism, power under populism was not embodied permanently in the proletariat, the nation, the party, or the Führer. The political theorist Isidoro Cheresky (2015) argued that power in populism is semi-embodied because populists claim legitimacy through winning elections that they could conceivably lose and thus be bound by electoral results.

Even though their legitimacy was grounded in winning elections, populists might have a hard time accepting that they could lose popular elections. If the people are imagined always to be right, and thus having one unified voice and will, it is unconceivable that they could vote for those constructed as the enemies of the people. Trump, for example, repeatedly denounced that his 2020 reelection was stolen and refused to believe the result of electoral authorities' investigation which found no evidence of such a claim. In order to win elections Juan Perón, Hugo Chávez, or Viktor Orbán skewed the electoral playing field. As incumbents, they had extraordinary advantages such as using gerrymandering, changing electoral rules and laws, using the state media, selectively silencing the privately owned media, harassing the opposition, controlling electoral tribunal boards and all instances of appeal, and using public funds to influence the election. When these presidents won elections, the voting moments were relatively clean, but the electoral processes blatantly favored incumbents.

Postfascism and Right-wing Populisms

After Trump's election, the term fascism made a comeback not only in sectors of 'the resistance' but among academic circles. Whereas Douglas Kellner (2016, 20) wrote, "certainly Trump is not Hitler, and his followers are not fascist," Jason Stanley (2018) entitled his book, *How Fascism Works*. He focused on the fascist tactics to achieve power such as the use of a mythic past, propaganda, anti-intellectualism, unreality, hierarchy, victimhood, law and order, sexual anxiety, appeals to the heartland, and a dismantling of public welfare and unity (Stanley, 2018, xiv–xv). While acknowledging that the reader could find the arguments of his book exaggerated, Stanley was more afraid about that possible normalization of fascism. He argued that there is a risk that the words and actions of Trump would not provoke outrage any longer and would appear to be normal. The historian Timothy Snyder wrote a short book with twenty lessons from the twentieth century to resist tyranny. He wrote that the danger that Americans face is to move "from a naïve and flawed sort of democratic republic to a confused and cynical sort of fascism" (Snyder, 2017, 124). Whereas Kellner and Snyder are careful to use fascism to refer to a particular historical phenomenon, Stanley groups all forms of tyranny under the notion of fascism, loosing hence the analytical value of this category and confusing right-wing populist with fascist dictatorial politics.

Identitarian movements emerged in France in 2012 and have sprung all over Europe and in the United States. Their maxim is 'everything is political,' their militancy is a way of life with "the goal of retaking territory and reconquering minds and souls" (Zúquete, 2018, 38; 42). Influenced by New Right thinkers, these young militants have declared that they are in war. In a book published in 2012, New Right ideologues Alain de Benoist and Charles Champetier wrote that "the world is a pluriversum, 'the West pretense to make the world into its own image' by imposing its model on all others in the name of progress is an existential threat to all cultures, obstructing their own unique path, has been happening for a long time in Europe" (Zúquete, 2018, 10). Echoing these existentialists angst, the group Génération Identitaire produced a video in 2012 declaring war. "We have stopped believing that Abddul is our brother, the planet our village and humanity our family. We have discovered that we have roots and ancestors –and thus a future. Our only inheritance is our blood, our soil, and our identity" (Zúquete, 2018, 27).

Following New Right thinkers, Identitarians see themselves as defenders of the people conceived with racial and cultural categories, especially ordinary citizens left behind by the political establishment of the ruling elite. These groups share the view that the "new class war of the twenty first century, is, and will be, between the people (still territorialized, still attached to traditions) and the globalist (and therefore rootless) elites, as a cosmopolitan hyperclass at the center of a cosmocracy" (Zúquete, 2018, 126). Identitarian groups have endorsed right-wing populist parties. Casa Pound supported Mateo Salvini and the Lega, and the French Bloc Identitaire championed Marine Le Pen even though their favorite politician is her niece Marión Maréchal-Le Pen.

Even though some activists and ideologues accept the term identitarian, the most common name in the United States is alternative right or simple alt-right. These groups' origins are "the men-rights and male-supremacy movements that have proliferated in the last few years among young men, particularly in online imageboard communities such as 4chan and 8chan" (Martinez

Hosang & Lowndes, 2019, 121). The alt-right became well-known after Steve Bannon, an admirer of right-wing European populists, became the editor of the Breitbart, saying that it will be "the platform for the alt-right" (Wolff, 2018, 138). Donald Trump during his first presidential campaign retweeted alt-right messages and images of their pet Pepe the Frog (Green, 2017, 148).

Hillary Clinton forcibly denounced the Alt-Right in these terms:

> This is not conservatism as we have known it. This is not Republicanism as we have known it. These are race-baiting ideas, anti-Muslim and anti-immigrant ideas, anti-woman—all key tenets making up an emerging racist ideology known as the 'alt-right' […]. The de facto merger between Breitbart and the Trump campaign represents a landmark achievement for the alt-right. A fringe element has effectively taken over the Republican Party. (Green, 2017, 213)

Her words were prophetic as an array of alt-right militants, right-wing militias, and believers of conspiracy theories such as QAnon became Trump's devotees, while their leader never condemned these extremists. Despite calls for unity, the alt-right is divided in terms of tactics and on race. Some, like Richard Spencer, advocate for a separate racial state to preserve the white race. Others, like Steve Bannon, argues that exclusion and economic oppression are not "the result of institutional racism in the United States but rather of 'globalism' and illegal immigration, hence inviting African American and US Hispanics to be part of his nationalist coalition" (Martinez & Lowndes 2019, 107). The shocking failed coup attempt in the United States and the threats of right-wing militia violence finally forced the police and the system of justice to take seriously the dangers of white supremacy organizations. In his inaugural address to the nation, President Biden proclaimed, "political extremism, white supremacy and domestic terrorism are dangers that we must confront, and we will defeat" (Manjoo, 2021).

Conclusion

This chapter illustrates that fascism was confined to a historical time period, and that after its military defeat in 1945 it muted into something else, postfascism. Despite similarities, populism and fascism differ in their use of violence, and their acceptance of elections to get to power legitimately. Yet the specter of fascism returned with Trump's election and after his Brazilian admirer Jair Bolsonaro became president in 2019. I agree with scholars who argue that these presidents are not fascists, at least yet. Bolsonaro's base of support are the military, angry sectors of the middle class that resented the rule and corruption of the leftist Workers' Party, Christian fundamentalists and right-wing Catholics who are opposed to women and LGTBQ rights, as well as to 'gender ideology.' Not only does he have nostalgia for dictatorship, but he has also led demonstrations calling for military intervention. In May 2020, some of his followers "who name themselves the *Three hundred of Brazil* (alluding to the 300 Spartan Hoplites against the army of Xerxes, 480 BC) met in front of the Federal Supreme Court. They wore white masks and hoods, held burning torches, and demanded the closing of democratic institutions" (Prutsch, 2020, 140). Trump's election energized right-wing extremist groups. Richard Spencer, for example, closed a meeting of the National Policy Institute in 2016 shouting "Hail Trump! Hail our people! Hail victory," which was met "by Nazi salutes from some of the people in the audience" (Zúquete, 2018, 304).

When right-wing xenophobic populists construct the people and its enemies with racial categories of superiority and inferiority, and contamination, as Finchelstein argues, there is a danger that it can mutate to fascism. Strong democratic institutions, the organized resistance of social movements, and the independent media have protected democracy in Brazil and the United States. Yet Bolsonaro and Trump have led processes of democratic erosion, normalizing racism, anti-feminism, and homophobia. Even if these right-wing populists do not transform themselves into a new variant of postfacism, the institutions of democracy, the organizations of civil society, and of the public sphere would need time to recuperate from their autocratic rule.

LITERATURE

Arato, A. (2012). Lefort, the philosopher of 1989. *Constellations, 19*(1), 23–29.
Baehr, P. (2010). *Hanna arendt, totalitarianism, and the social sciences*. Stanford: Stanford University Press.
Bolton, K. (2014). *Perón and peronism*. Black House Publishing.
Cheresky, I. (2015). *El Nuevo Rostro de la Democracia*. Fondo de Cultura Económica.
Cohen, J. L. (2019). Populism and the politics of resentment. *Jus Cogens, 1*, 5–39
de la Torre, C. (2019). *Populisms a quick immersion*. Tibidabo Publishing.
Elley, G. (2013). *Nazism as Fascism*. Routledge.
Finchelstein, F. (2014). *The ideological origins of the civil war. Fascism, populism, dictatorship in twenty century Argentina*. Oxford University Press.
Finchelstein, F. (2017). *From Fascism to populism in history*. California University Press.
Finchelstein, F. (2020). *A brief history of Fascist lies*. California University Press.
Flyn, B. (2013). Lefort as Phenomenologist of the political. In M. Plot (Eds.), *Claude Lefort thinker of the political* (pp. 23–34). Palgrave Macmillan.
Gentile, E. (2008). Fascism and the Italian road to totalitarianism. *Constellations, 15*(3), 291–302.
Germani, G. (1978). *Authoritarianism, Fascism, and national populism*. Transaction Books.
Green, J. (2017). *Devil's Bargain. Steve Bannon, Donald Trump, and the storming of the presidency*. Penguin Press.
Griffin, R. (2008). *A Fascist century: Essays by Roger Griffin*. Palgrave
Griffin, R. (2020). *Fascism a quick immersion*. Tibidabo Publishing.
Kelnner, D. (2016). *American nightmare: Donald Trump, media spectacle, and authoritarian populism*. Sense Publishers.
Laclau, E. (1977). *Politics and ideology in Marxist theory*. Verso.

Lefort, C. (1986). *The political forms of modern society*. MIT Press.
Lindholm, C., & Zúquete, J. P. (2010). *The struggle for the world: Liberation movements for the 21st century*. Stanford University Press.
Manjoo, F. (2021). Finally, a president acknowledges white supremacists. *New York Times*. https://www.nytimes.com/2021/01/22/opinion/biden-white-supremacy.html?action=click&module=Opinion&pgtype=Homepage.
Mann, M. (2004). *Fascists*. Cambridge University Press.
Martinez, H. D., & Lowndes, J. (2019). *Producers, parasites, patriots: Race and the new right-wing poltics of precarity*. Minnesota University Press.
Moffitt, B. (2016). *The global rise of populism: Performance*. Stanford University Press.
Mudde, C., & Kaltwasser, C. R. (2012). *Populism in Europe and the Americas*. Cambridge University Press.
Pappas, T. (2019). *Populism and liberal democracy: A comparative and theoretical analysis*. Oxford University Press.
Passmore, K. (2014). *Fascism a very short introduction*. Oxford University Press.
Paxton, R. (2005). *The anatomy of Fascism*. Vintage Books.
Prutsch, U. (2020). The populist twins: Donald Trump and Jair Bolsonaro. In N. Zadoff, S. Schüller-Sprinngorum, M. Zadoff & H. Paul (Eds.), *Four years after ethnonationalism, antisemitism, and racism in Trump's America* (pp. 123–146). Universitätsverlag.
Romero, L. A. (2002). *A history of Argentina*. Pennsylvania State University Press.
Snyder, T. (2017). *On tyranny: Twenty lessons from the twentieth century*. New York: Tim Duggan Books.
Stanley, J. (2018). *How Fascism works*. Random House.
Traverso, E. (2003). *The origins of Nazi violence*. The New Press.
Traverso, E. (2016). *Fire and blood. The European Civil War 1914–1945*. Verso.
Traverso, E. (2019). *The new faces of Fascism*. Verso.
Weyland, K. (2001). Clarifying a contested concept. *Comparative Politics, 34*(1), 1–22.
Wolff, M. (2018). *Fire and fury: Inside the Trump White House*. Henry Holt and Company.
Zúquete, P. (2018). *The Identitarians. The movement against globalism and Islam in Europe*. Notre Dame University Press.

CHAPTER 10

Populism and Authoritarianism

Gabriella Gricius

INTRODUCTION

Can populism be democratic at its core? Can an authoritarian populist leader still bring about progressive policies? With the advent of leaders like Donald Trump, Viktor Orbán, and Rodrigo Duterte to democratic countries like the United States, Hungary and the Philippines, these questions and the study of authoritarian populism have become ever more prescient. However, defining populism presents its own series of problems, taking into account the many normative judgments and conceptual blur that surround the term (de la Torre, 2000; Mudde, 2007; Zeemann, 2019). Many describe it as a double-edged sword rather than calling it purely negative or positive for democracies (Levitsky & Loxton, 2012; Mudde & Kaltwasser, 2012). Scholars generally concentrate on three drivers of the reemergence of populism: (1) increased outbreaks of terrorism, (2) the fear of mass immigration, and (3) the austere response of governments to the 2008 financial crisis (Bugaric, 2019; Crewe & Sanders, 2020).

Authoritarian populism faces less of the conceptual blur problem that surrounds populism, while it simultaneously is becoming more prevalent among the world's democracies. This chapter focuses on three distinct cases: (1) Hungary, (2) The Philippines, and (3) The United States in an aim to better understand the relationship between authoritarianism and populism and

G. Gricius (✉)
The North American and Arctic Defense and Security Network, Colorado State University, Fort Collins, CO, USA
e-mail: ggricius@colostate.edu

© The Author(s), under exclusive license to Springer Nature Switzerland AG 2022
M. Oswald (ed.), *The Palgrave Handbook of Populism*, https://doi.org/10.1007/978-3-030-80803-7_10

to see whether any progressive policies have arisen from authoritarian populist leadership. In theory, populism supports democracy and could help underrepresented voices be heard. However, in practice, authoritarian populism tends to suppress the more positive aspects of populism while stressing the negative ones.

Populism

Perhaps one of the most commonly used terms in politics is *populism*. Populism has been used to refer to political parties both on the extreme left- and right-wing spectrums. The term is used simultaneously to describe both the positive aspect of direct democracy and the negative side of nativism. Literature focusing on populism suffers from a 'conceptual blur' (Zeemann, 2019, p. 28). However, for the purposes of this article, I will define populism following Cas Mudde's understanding as a thin-centered ideology (e.g., Mudde, 2004, p. 543; 2007, p. 23). This definition focuses primarily on the distinction between 'the corrupt elite' and 'the pure people' and holds them as empty signifiers in order to allow a certain flexibility for populist parties and leaders to construct exact meanings of the elite and people (de la Torre, 2000; Laclau, 1977). Hence, many different varieties of populism emerge, some right-wing and others left-wing in nature.

Scholars widely focus on three main drivers of the reemergence of populism, namely, the fear and perception of mass immigration, the response of governments to the 2008 global financial crisis and increased outbreaks of terrorism (Bugaric, 2019; Crewe & Sanders, 2020). Rather than invest in the public, many governments chose austerity as a measure against the financial crisis, which in turn led to unemployment and a decrease in living standards. This response led many local communities to feel as though they were being left behind. The perception of mass immigration increased the fear in these communities that their government cared more about 'outsiders' than the actual people leading to a stronger propensity to vote for populists.

Populism: A Double-Edged Sword

This success of populist movements naturally inclines scholars to make normative claims about populism. While populism is referred to as mainly negative in today's media, populism is more a double-edged sword. Steven Levitsky and James Loxton (2012, p. 161) refer to populism as both a friend and foe to democracy, explaining that it can act as a corrective to existing democratic regimes but may also pose a direct threat to these same regimes. For example, in some cases, populism can increase the political participation of marginalized groups by giving voice to these groups. Further, populism can increase democratic accountability and invigorate political participation (Mudde & Kaltwasser, 2012, p. 21).

Populism can also have a negative impact on democracy. For example, populism can disregard a 'checks and balances' system already inherent in a functioning democracy. Populism can also lead to politics becoming more moral, make compromise difficult, and lead to norm derogation (Mudde & Kaltwasser, 2012, p. 21; Oswald & Robertson, 2019). However, populism can be both negative and positive. For example, Levitsky and Loxton (2012, p. 161) claim that populism in Latin America is inclusionary in that it allows the mobilization of marginalized groups but is rarely democratizing.

Authoritarian Populism

While there is much debate on the normative implications of populism, authoritarian populism does not have as much of a normative dissonance. Timbro's Authoritarian Populism Index (2019) defines authoritarian populism as an analytical category that can describe both right-wing and left-wing populism with a wide variety of ideologies containing three characteristics: (a) People vs. the Elite, (b) majority rule without speedbumps, and (c) a state with stronger muscles (Timbro, 2019).

These three defining characteristics leave much open to interpretation and are reminiscent of Mudde's thin-centered ideologies. Pippa Norris (2019, pp. 983) goes further, claiming that these movements: "a) advocate conformity with conventional moral norms and traditions within a group, expressing intolerance of out-groups perceived to threaten accepted group norms, b) expect deference and loyalty to the group and its leaders, being intolerant of dissent, and c) seek to strengthen collective security against perceived group threats." Norris and Timbro all seek to remain vague enough on a definition of authoritarian populism to maintain a normative distance and leave an analytical category that can encompass right-wing and left-wing authoritarian populist parties.

In keeping with Mudde's thin-centered definition, this chapter will similarly remain against adding any distinct ideologies to a definition of authoritarian populism. Hence, for the purposes of this chapter, authoritarian populism will be defined as a thin-centered branch of populism whose leaders actively pursue authoritarian policies in office. Furthermore, this chapter will utilize Norris's definition of authoritarian populism in describing the kinds of moral and groupthink choices of these movements.

METHODOLOGY

It is impossible to present a completely comprehensive global overview of authoritarian populist parties and leaders while also delving into the detail and context necessary to understand each case. Therefore, this chapter focuses on three geographically significant cases in which both leaders and parties can be characterized as authoritarian populist, attained executive office in at least minimally democratic countries, and have been in power for at least two years, following the examples set by both Tony Blair's Institute for Global Change, the Timbro Authoritarian Populism Index and Freedom House's Freedom in the World study. Choosing countries that were considered at least minimally democratic when the respective leader came into office according to Freedom House (i.e., Free or Partly Free) left off many other instances of populism, particularly in South & Latin America, Africa, and the Middle East, which have arisen in authoritarian or semi-authoritarian settings. The selection used in the chapter below was further restricted by focusing solely on three successful populist leaders in three different geographic regions that have acted on their authoritarian characteristics publicly: Viktor Orbán in Hungary, Rodrigo Duterte in the Philippines, and Donald Trump in the United States.

To examine these three cases, I will begin by briefly discussing the roots of each leader, analyzing the how and why of their rise from obscurity into power, and move toward examining how the public responded to each gaining power. Then, I will further delve into what makes that particular leader an authoritarian populist according to the definition provided above, how their leadership fits within this category, and how a party formed around them. Last, I will look at their successes, and if any progressive policies or democratic results came about from their leadership by looking at the Varieties of Democracy Index (V-DEM), and IDEA's Democracy Indices.

Victor Orbán: Hungary

Victor Orbán's tenure as Hungarian Prime Minister (1998–2002; 2010–present) is widely viewed as populist authoritarian (Benkova, 2019; Buckley & Byrne, 2018; Kreko & Enyedi, 2018; Toomey, 2018). In 1993, Orbán became the president of Fidesz—taking the party toward a more nationalist and conservative platform. Five years later, Orbán became Hungary's youngest prime minister. In response to a political loss in 2002, Orbán reportedly said he had been 'too honest' in his campaigning and resolved to change tactics (Buckley & Byrne, 2018). Furthermore, Orbán and Fidesz repeatedly tried to undermine the legitimacy of the elections after the fact. Orbán stated "the nation cannot be in opposition, only the government can be opposition against its own people" (Beauchamp, 2018, p. 6; Halmai, 2019, p. 300).

After Hungary became the first European country to need a bailout from the International Monetary Fund in the 2008 financial crisis, the Fidesz Party, and Orbán won the next Hungarian election in 2010 with a landslide. In complete opposition to his attempt to undermine election results in 2002, Orbán claimed that Fidesz's success was a "revolution of the voting booths"—illustrating that his support for the rule of law is dependent on his own success or failure rather than the tenants of rule of law (Halmai, 2019, p. 300). Since then, Orbán and Fidesz have systematically overhauled Hungarian politics toward authoritarian illiberalism while also revising Hungary's history in order to reflect Orbán's current political needs (Scanish & Eisen, 2019, p. 299; Toomey, 2018). For example, in the wake of Orbán's victory in 2010, he made it more difficult to initiate a referendum for the opposition. While previous legislation required 25% of voters, new legislation required at least 50% of the vote, and otherwise—the referendum would be counted as invalid (Halmai, 2019, p. 300). Moreover, Orbán has gerrymandered districts in Hungary (Beauchamp, 2018, p. 7).

Because Orbán and his allied parties won a two-thirds parliamentary majority, they were also able to pass major institutional changes and Hungary experienced "a notable decrease in democratic values, limitations to the freedom of media, and the abolition of the checks-and-balances system, from the Constitutional Court throughout the judiciary system" (Benkova, 2019, p. 1; Norwegian Helsinki Committee, 2013). Due to their parliamentary majority, Fidesz and Orbán were able to replace staff within the Prosecutor-General's Office, the Electoral Commission, state media, and the Constitutional Court (Beauchamp, 2018; Benkova, 2019). Moreover, Fidesz party leaders have been able to avoid any corruption charges despite reports of endemic corruption (Kreko & Enyedi, 2018). In 2011, Fidesz and Orbán additionally adopted and passed a new constitution without consulting the opposition. The Venice Commission, an expert body at the Council of Europe, claimed that the new Hungarian Constitution did not include a statement claiming that the court is independent and separate (Benkova, 2019). According to a new law, all media outlets were also required to register with the Media Council which is entitled to issue fines against 'fake news' (Norwegian Helsinki Committee, 2013). Marius Dragomir, noted Hungarian journalist and academic, also claimed that by 2017, 90% of all media in Hungary was owned either by the state or a Fidesz alley (Beauchamp, 2018, p. 7).

In 2018, Fidesz won its third supermajority victory with 133 seats out of 199 (Rankin, 2018). While some believed that Orbán would step back from his authoritarian populist policies due to pressure building from Brussels, they were sorely mistaken. In April 2018, the government shut down Magyar Nemzet and HetiValasz, two well-known anti-Fidesz media outlets in Hungary. In May 2018, the Basic Law of Hungary passed, making migration significantly more difficult for immigrants. Moreover, amendments passed in May 2018 made it more difficult for citizens to protest these changes (Benkova, 2019). In June 2018, Hungary passed a 'Stop Soros' package of laws, which criminalized support to asylum and residence applications alongside other laws against illegal migration. Orbán and Fidesz have also been successful in forcing Central European University and Open Society Foundations out of Hungary, two organizations supported by George Soros (Benkova, 2019).

Unlike many populist authoritarian leaders, Orbán does not aim to be the sole representation of Hungary. His goal is to polarize the electorate while retaining the support using nondemocratic methods (Kreko & Enyedi, 2018, p. 8). For example, Orbán is best known for his refusal to take the mandated 'quota' of asylum seekers within the European Union. In response, he built razor-wire fences to keep out migrants and made irregular crossing of the borders a criminal offense punishable with up to eight years of imprisonment (Benkova, 2019, p. 2). Orbán uses anti-immigrant sentiments for political gain (for a more detailed discussion of Orbán's populist rhetoric see Halmai, 2018). Put bluntly by Peter Kreko and Zsolt Enyedi (2018, p. 13): "the central Fidesz claim was that Brussels and Soros were scheming to flood Europe with Muslim migrants and that a Fidesz loss would mean the doom of white, Christian Hungary."

Orbán also contrasts himself strongly with Soros. Orbán and Fidesz work in tandem to accuse Soros of wanting to flood the entire continent with migrants—using him as an external threat to mobilize its electorate (Kreko & Enyedi, 2018, p. 12). Orbán has handed out citizenship to one million ethnic Hungarians in neighboring countries since 2010 with the Citizenship Law in 2011, ninety-five percent of which consistently vote for Fidesz in Hungarian elections (The Economist, 2019; Toomey, 2018).

Despite Orbán's continued electoral success, he has neither adopted any progressive policies nor adapted toward a more democratic model of governance. According to both the Varieties of Democracy Index (V-DEM) and IDEA's Global State of Democracy Indices, Hungary has fallen significantly in different measurements of democracy. In V-DEM's measurement of Electoral Democracy Index, Hungary has fallen from 0.769 in 2010 to 0.536 in 2018, while in IDEA's measurement of Representative Government, Hungary has fallen from 0.71 in 2010 to 0.61 in 2018. In 2010, Hungary was rated at 0.649 with respect to V-DEM's Liberal Democracy Index and fell to 0.441 in 2018. In every measurement in both tools, Hungary has fallen significantly (Table 10.1).

In sum, Viktor Orbán's populist ascent to power has been a major catalyst behind Hungary's democratic backsliding since 2010. Using anti-immigrant rhetoric to polarize the electorate while also passing major institutional changes which have made Hungary significantly less democratic, Orban has been successful in maintaining power and continuing to assault the remaining democratic institutions.

Rodrigo Duterte: The Philippines

While relatively unknown internationally, Rodrigo Duterte had a 'Dirty Harry' reputation in the Philippines and had been active in politics for 22 years (Bello, 2016). In 2016, he won the presidential election in the Philippines and has been in power since then. His reputation came primarily from his alleged association with the Davao Death Squad, which targeted criminals and drug dealers, and his deadly orders against criminals, which lead to the death of over 1,400 people (Kine, 2017; Valiquette & Su, 2018). This alleged association matched his discourse, where he often used curse words such as "putang ina," [son of a bitch] and "bakla" [gay] to describe elites (Bello, 2016). Despite his long political history, his accession to the presidency was that of an outsider.

Table 10.1 Hungary V-DEM scores and IDEA indices

Country		Electoral Democracy Index	Liberal Democracy Index	Participatory Democracy Index	Deliberative Democracy Index	Egalitarian Democracy Index
Hungary V-DEM Scores	2008	0.822	0.736	0.606	0.606	0.682
	2009	0.823	0.724	0.6	0.591	0.701
	2010	0.769	0.649	0.558	0.528	0.653
	2011	0.746	0.603	0.511	0.503	0.643
	2012	0.734	0.604	0.51	0.52	0.601
	2013	0.71	0.566	0.484	0.472	0.557
	2014	0.697	0.573	0.458	0.472	0.56
	2015	0.642	0.526	0.434	0.445	0.526
	2016	0.659	0.517	0.446	0.419	0.555
	2017	0.616	0.49	0.395	0.413	0.503
	2018	0.536	0.441	0.323	0.318	0.398
	2010–2018 chg	−0.233	−0.208	−0.235	−0.21	−0.255
Hungary IDEA Global State of Democracy Indices		Representative Government	Fundamental Rights	Checks on Government	Impartial Administration	Civil Society Participation
	2008	0.78	0.77	0.73	0.66	0.62
	2009	0.78	0.77	0.74	0.67	0.62
	2010	0.71	0.72	0.65	0.60	0.56
	2011	0.71	0.72	0.64	0.59	0.54
	2012	0.71	0.71	0.62	0.59	0.54
	2013	0.73	0.70	0.60	0.59	0.48
	2014	0.70	0.70	0.60	0.58	0.44
	2015	0.69	0.69	0.58	0.58	0.49
	2016	0.70	0.70	0.58	0.58	0.46
	2017	0.66	0.70	0.57	0.59	0.46
	2018	0.61	0.66	0.54	0.54	0.46
	2010–2018 chg	−0.1	−0.06	−0.11	−0.06	−0.2

This meant that Duterte was familiar with the tactics of a traditional politician and was able to utilize unorthodox tactics to achieve power and support. According to Juego (2017, p. 133), he can be characterized as a "veteran local political boss who has mastered the language and skills of effective power politics at the local level."

In the Philippines, there are a number of factors that predispose the country towards populist politics. The two most prominent are rising economic inequality and political inequality. The rising economic inequality in the Philippines meant that many marginalized communities found no voice in traditional political parties and therefore sought other politicians, which they felt better understood their needs (Mendoza & Jaminola, 2020). Moreover, inequality in the Philippines materialized through rapid urbanization. Challenges brought by urbanization include the threat of increased crime, illegal drugs, and economic uncertainty. For example, from 2012 to 2014, the Philippines saw an increase of 300% in serious crime. The autonomous region in Mindanao in particular was known for its high levels of crime, murder, kidnapping, and international conflict (Valiquette & Su, 2018).

As a latecomer to the presidential race, Duterte focused on using a narrative of crisis, attempting to show that the Philippines was in a dangerous situation due to rising crime and illegal drugs (Curato, 2016, p. 98). Duterte's message of focusing on crime and drugs came across as genuine given his track record of transforming Davao City from a "relatively conflict-ridden backwater town into a sprawling urban metropolis" (Arugay, 2017, p. 284). According to Royo Maxwell (2019), support for Duterte was driven by three key factors: (1) positive attitudes toward the police/law, (2) perceived seriousness of the national drug/crime problem, and (3) the respondents' region of residence. He promised to violently crackdown on crime and illegal drugs and move the center of power away from Manila-based elites. His support came from a variety of demographics including local citizens, labor migrants, the middle class, the urban poor as well as expats who lived abroad—known collectively as "Duter-tards" (Arugay, 2017; Juego, 2017). Moreover, this wide cross-section of society was the most engaged on Facebook and Twitter. This gave him a significant online presence, particularly important in the Philippines, where 56% of the population is active on social media (Curato, 2017). In 2017, his approval rating was at 82% despite around 4,000–7,000 casualties from the drug war (Kine, 2017; Royo Maxwell, 2019, p. 208). However, domestically, it appears that many Philippine citizens remained sympathetic toward his policies (Royo Maxwell, 2019, p. 215).

Duterte's leadership is inherently authoritarian populist (Arugay, 2017; Curato, 2016, 2017; Royo Maxwell, 2019). In the Philippines, the populist dichotomy is between virtuous citizens ('the people') and hardened criminals ('the dangerous other'). This is often described as penal populism, a political style that builds of societal fear and demands for punitive policies (Curato, 2016, p. 94). Both during his campaign and when he took office, Duterte used a dystopian narrative to feed these fears and answered them with a simple yet urgent solution. Duterte promised to eradicate the drug problem using any means at his disposal. He justified these harsh measures by stating that the Philippines was "infested with illegal narcotics and that addiction [was] running rampant in too many neighborhoods causing crime, disruption and a lowered quality of life" (Royo Maxwell, 2019, p. 208).

In order to achieve this, Duterte uses rough language as well as misogynistic remarks. This machismo is essential to his performance, the cult of personality and narrative as an authoritarian populist, who is the only leader who can save the Philippines using authoritarian tactics (Curato, 2016, p. 95). This attitude and promise to deliver order effectively are part of what makes him so popular. The scorched earth policy against crime that followed his election, criticized by many human rights advocates, has also continued the growth of his popularity in the Philippines. Typical of autocratic regimes, he has also used legalism as a political disciplinary tool and aggressive social media operations to silence dissent (Juego, 2017, p. 140). These authoritarian actions as well as Duterte's tendency toward collective security and groupthink all make his leadership authoritarian populist.

In contrast to other authoritarian populist leaders, Duterte's government focused on reforming the public finance sector, passing the Tax Reforms for Acceleration and Inclusion Act (TRAIN) in 2017 and proposing the Philippine Development Plan (PDP) 2017–2022 (Juego, 2017; Mendoza & Jaminola, 2020). The PDP aims to reduce poverty from 21 to 13% by 2022 while TRAIN aims to lower personal income taxes for the lower and middle class. While the intentions of TRAIN seem to be progressive, its economic and social consequences have not been. Economists estimate that TRAIN exacerbated poverty by 0.26% in many sectors and also worsened inequality. Interestingly, however, overall it is estimated that Philippine poverty decreased by 6.6% from 2015 to 2018. These results suggest that while TRAIN had progressive intent, its lasting impact is yet to be seen (Punongbayan, 2019).

Beyond progressive policies, many Philippine voters see Duterte as an opportunity to regain democratic agency. In the Philippines where elections are often defined by voter buying and intimidation, Duterte has broadened the space for political action (Curato, 2016, p. 102–104). This is reflected in IDEA's Indices, where Civil Society Participation has increased from 0.67 in 2016 to 0.69 in 2018. However, other measures in IDEA's Indices such as Fundamental Rights (2016: 0.62; 2018: 0.60) and Checks on Government (2016: 0.61; 2018: 0.58) have slightly decreased. More dramatic are results according to the V-DEM index. The Philippines has decreased in many democratic indicators. Notably, the Philippine's Liberal Democracy's Index decreased from 0.413 in 2016 to 0.324 in 2018 (Table 10.2).

In sum, Rodrigo Duterte's authoritarian populist leadership, while certainly contributing to a worsening human rights situation in the Philippines, does not appear to have as drastic an impact on Filipino democratic standards as, for example, in Hungary. Using penal populist rhetoric that creates a 'dangerous other' in rising crime and illegal drug usage rates, Duterte uses every

Table 10.2 Philippines V-DEM scores and IDEA indices

Country		Electoral Democracy Index	Liberal Democracy Index	Participatory Democracy Index	Deliberative Democracy Index	Egalitarian Democracy Index
Philippines V-DEM Scores	2014	0.558	0.443	0.373	0.524	0.29
	2015	0.606	0.462	0.415	0.543	0.334
	2016	0.566	0.413	0.382	0.422	0.281
	2017	0.511	0.362	0.344	0.39	0.263
	2018	0.525	0.324	0.34	0.389	0.23
	2016–2018 chg	−0.04	−0.089	−0.042	−0.033	−0.051
Philippines IDEA Global State of Democracy Indices		Representative Government	Fundamental Rights	Checks on Government	Impartial Administration	Civil Society Participation
	2014	0.60	0.63	0.66	0.48	0.74
	2015	0.59	0.64	0.67	0.48	0.79
	2016	0.60	0.62	0.61	0.46	0.67
	2017	0.59	0.60	0.59	0.43	0.70
	2018	0.59	0.60	0.58	0.41	0.69
	2016–2018 chg	−0.01	−0.02	−0.03	−0.05	+0.02

method at his disposal, including a deadly police policy to overcome complex problems within the Philippines and political legalism to silent dissent. Despite these authoritarian tendencies, Duterte's government appears to be, on the surface, attempting to pass progressive economic policies and working within the existing form of democratic governance.

Donald Trump: The United States

For scholars and commentators, Donald Trump represents an existential threat to democracy while, for many others, he is the bulwark against massive social and economic change. Like many other authoritarian populist leaders, Trump has no real political background (Whiteley et. al., 2020, p. 88). Trump's rise to prominence for the presidency was unexpected. During the presidential election, he ridiculed his rivals and expressed patently false opinions about immigrants, as well as Democratic rival Hillary Clinton (Whiteley et. al., 2020, p. 87). Despite this and many other confounding factors, Trump won the electoral college vote in the 2016 US presidential election, although losing the popular vote by more than two percent. It was not merely Trump's popularity that contributed to his rise. Growing inequality in the United States, the outsourcing of skilled and unskilled manufacturing jobs, the unaffordability of healthcare and higher education, and continued economic trauma from the Great Recession all added to Americans growing distrust of mainstream parties. In short, parties and political institutions were unable to respond adequately to rapid political and economic change when many working Americans felt poorer and less secure than earlier generations (McKay, 2020; Whiteley et. al., 2020).

Despite Trump's lack of political experience, many voters chose to support him for the presidency, not only due to economic hardship, but rather as a result of the pull of cultural conservatism and as a backlash against rapid cultural change. Trump promised to "Make America Great Again"—meaning that America would go back to the way it used to be. These voters were united by issues such as antipathy toward Muslims, immigrants, atheists, sexual minorities and support for 'Americanism' (McKay, 2020, p. 110; Norris & Inglehart, 2017). In fact, it was Trump's lack of political establishment past that made him even more attractive to many voters angry at the political establishment (Kellner, 2016). Trump's common refrain of 'Drain the Swamp' was particularly appealing to these voters (Whiteley et. al., 2020, p. 90). Furthermore, when Trump openly expressed racism and xenophobia, it gave credence to many Americans who felt that they had become "strangers in their own land" (Norris & Inglehart, 2016, p. 452).

Trump's leadership is characterized by authoritarian populist tendencies (Arditi, 2019; Haverda & Halley, 2019; McKay, 2020; Norris, 2017; Norris & Inglehart, 2016). Trump's rhetoric is angry, nativist, and invokes fearmongering (Norris, 2017, p. 10). Norris and Inglehart (2016, p. 5) specifically point to "racial resentment, intolerance of multiculturalism, nationalistic isolationism, nostalgia for past glories, mistrust of outsiders, traditional misogyny and sexism, the appeal of forceful strong- man leadership, attack-dog politics, and racial and anti-Muslim animosity" as main points that invoke an us vs. them sentiment. These characteristics dismiss America's traditional liberal democratic leadership role in the world while undermining democratic ideals within America (i.e., the role of the media, the independence of the courts, and the integrity of elections) (Norris, 2017). Rhetorically, Trump uses three devices to support his authoritarian populist approach: (a) the lone wolf device supporting anti-statism, (b) the glorification of action device, and (c) the exactitude of error device represented by xenophobic, ethnonationalist hyperbole (Haverda & Halley, 2019, p. 215). Trump also uses scapegoats, everything from Wall Street bankers to the feared mass of migrants (Kellner, 2016). Many of these rhetorical devices match with Norris's definition of the authoritarian populist in terms of advocating conformity in conjunction with moral norms (i.e., traditional American values), expressing a lack of tolerance for out-groups (i.e., Trump's anti-migrant and outsider stance), and seeking to strengthen collective security (i.e., Anti-migrant and Muslim policies).

However, Trump's rhetoric is not the only authoritarian tendency he possesses. He ignores America's core democratic values and institutions—favoring military power, lessening the importance of international development aid, ignoring traditional allies, expressing hostility toward international trade and climate agreements, criticizing global governance while favoring other strongman rulers (Norris, 2017). Domestically, Trump has also used state funds to support large corporations and his own family—using his position to line his and his family's pockets. According to David Arditi (2019, p. 664), this tendency can be characterized as a grifter economy. Trump has also overtly spent federal money in Republican states, while taking away money from Democratic strongholds and given tax cuts only to demographic groups that supported him (Arditi, 2019). His actions further cement his stance as an authoritarian populist, where he explicitly invokes groupthink against out-groups and rewards as well as expects loyalty from his supporters.

Despite Trump's authoritarian populist leadership, the United States has continued to act as a liberal republic. The constitutional characteristics such as separation of powers, judicial review, federalism, hyper-pluralism, and consistent as well as constant elections all act as guards against demagogues such as Trump (Singh, 2017, p. 35). This has also meant that progressive policies, which both Republicans and Democrats have sought, have been enacted during Trump's presidency. One of the most recent policies has been a large suite of tax cuts. While many of these taxes benefit high earners, multiple large companies have used these tax cuts as a reason to raise salaries for employees. Moreover, Trump has been successful in a number of other policies that have included rolling back regulations to allegedly open up the market and appointing many judges that have Republican leanings (Graham, 2018) (Table 10.3).

10 POPULISM AND AUTHORITARIANISM

Table 10.3 USA V-DEM scores and IDEA indices

Country		Electoral Democracy Index	Liberal Democracy Index	Participatory Democracy Index	Deliberative Democracy Index	Egalitarian Democracy Index
USA V-DEM Scores	2014	0.927	0.868	0.657	0.877	0.764
	2015	0.898	0.838	0.653	0.816	0.725
	2016	0.887	0.822	0.615	0.762	0.676
	2017	0.822	0.727	0.582	0.563	0.667
	2018	0.834	0.741	0.575	0.601	0.629
	2016–2018 chg	−0.053	−0.081	−0.04	−0.161	−0.047
USA IDEA Global State of Democracy Indices		Representative Government	Fundamental Rights	Checks on Government	Impartial Administration	Civil Society Participation
	2014	0.87	0.84	0.83	0.83	0.92
	2015	0.86	0.83	0.82	0.83	0.92
	2016	0.76	0.82	0.82	0.78	0.89
	2017	0.79	0.80	0.74	0.73	0.87
	2018	0.76	0.79	0.77	0.73	0.84
	2016–2018 chg	0.0	−0.03	−0.05	−0.05	−0.05

Trump's authoritarian populist policies have impacted America's democratic values. In all of V-DEM Index's measurements, America's scores have slightly decreased, for example, in the Liberal Democracy Index (2016: 0.822; 2018: 0.741) and the Electoral Democracy Index (2016: 0.887; 2018: 0.834). In IDEA's Indices, the picture is similarly bleak. The only measurement in which America has not decreased is Representative Government where America's score remains the same at 0.76 in both 2016 and 2018. While most scores have decreased, however, the degree is quite low—representing that while Trump has a negative impact on democracy, Trump's election was not as catastrophic as many believed. America's robust democratic institutions may have played an important mitigating factor. The United States is a well-equipped democracy with over 200 years of profession and duration. One populist leader may not be enough to erode such a long tradition of democratic norms and institutions. Using rhetoric that invokes groupthink in immigration and contributes to the idea of a cultural crisis, Trump uses authoritarian policies to strengthen his own position in power. Despite these authoritarian tendencies, the American government has been able to pass policies, some of which are considered progressive (i.e., tax cuts). In short, while Trump has encouraged a shift in mainstream political thinking toward more moral groupthink, the system itself remains mostly unchanged.

Discussion

At least in theory, populism supports popular sovereignty and majority rule—both key parts of democracy. According to Mudde and Kaltwasser (2012, p. 17), one would then expect populists to play positive roles in democracies, particularly by giving voice to the 'silent majority' and mobilizing political participation. Despite this, as the examples of Hungary, the Philippines and the United States show, this is not always the case. When authoritarian populists come to power, authoritarian urges and policies cancel out many of the potential positive aspects of populism. Instead, the negative aspects of populism, namely, the moralization of politics, a contravening of the checks and balances system, and a tendency to favor the wants of the majority rather than the minority become more accentuated.

In the three cases, these negative aspects of populism are, therefore, more prevalent than the positive aspects. Within the V-DEM and Idea Indices data sets, there are only two cases in which the data did not illustrate a downward trend in measuring democracy: (1) No change in the Representative Democracy measurement in the United States from 2016 to 2018, and (2) +0.02 increase in Civil Society Participation in the Philippines from 2016 to 2018. Following theories that focus on populism's positive aspects, it was expected that more case studies would have at the very least a positive trend in Civil Society Participation. However, this was not the case. Mudde and Kaltwasser (2012, p. 24) theorized that populists in government in unconsolidated democracies might favor the more negative aspects of populism because "populism leads to polarization and consequently defense measures from the government, which will threaten the development of liberal democratic institutions and protections." This difference in unconsolidated vs consolidated democracies explains some of the differences between the United States' experience with Donald Trump in opposition to the experiences of Hungary and the Philippines. While the United States has a strong checks and balances system, Hungary's Third Republic, and the Philippine's postcolonial government are not nearly as consolidated.

While populism is a double-edged sword for many democracies, when authoritarian characteristics enter the picture—things become problematic. More than anything else, this illustrates that the relationship between authoritarianism and populism is questionable as authoritarianism brings out populism's worst qualities—turning it into a dangerous one-sided sword that takes aim at democratic norms. With authoritarian leaders like Orban, Trump, and Duterte, populism cannot truly be democratic at its core. Instead, authoritarian populism retains superficial characteristics of democracy, while shrewdly implementing more authoritarian policies over time—threatening the democracy and democratic norms under which it exists. In short, progressive policies—to the extent that they do exist—exist only insofar as they benefit authoritarian populist leaders' own aims and goals. In these cases, it is the type of democratic system that likely plays an important role. While consolidated democracies like the United States may have the institutions and norms to protect against a leader's authoritarian impulses, unconsolidated democracies such as Hungary and in the Philippines may not. Future research may look closer at the relationship between authoritarian populism and consolidated & unconsolidated democracies. Further, once these leaders leave office, it may be interesting to explore their long-term impacts on democratic norms and institutions to have a better measurement of their actual impact.

LITERATURE

Arditi, D. (2019). Digital demagogue: Authoritarian capitalism in the age of Trump and Twitter. *New Political Science, 41*(4), 664–674.

Arugay, A. (2017). The Philippines in 2016: The electoral earthquake and its aftershocks. *Southeast Asian Affairs, 2017*, 277–296.

Beauchamp, Z. (2018, September 13). *It happened there: How democracy died in Hungary*. Vox. https://www.vox.com/policy-and-politics/2018/9/13/17823488/hungary-democracy-authoritarianism-trump.

Bello, W. (2016). *Chronicling an electoral insurgency: "Dutertismo" captures the Philippines*. Transitional Institute.

Benkova, L. (2019). *Hungary-Orban's project towards "illiberal democracy" [Fokus]*. Austria Institut für Europa- und Sicherheitspolitik.

Buckley, N., & Byrne, A. (2018, January 25). The rise and rise of Viktor Orban. *Financial Times*. https://www.ft.com/content/dda50a3e-0095-11e8-9650-9c0ad2d7c5b5.

Bugaric, B. (2019). The two faces of populism: Between authoritarian and democratic populism. *German Law Journal, 20*, 390–400.
Crewe, I., & Sanders, D. (Eds.). (2020). *Authoritarian populism and liberal democracy*. Palgrave Macmillan.
Curato, N. (2016). Politics of anxiety, politics of hope: Penal populism and Duterte's rise to power. *Journal of Current Southeast Asian Affairs, 35*(3), 91–109. https://doi.org/10.1177/186810341603500305.
Curato, N. (2017). Flirting with authoritarian fantasies? Rodrigo Duterte and the new terms of Philippine populism. *Journal of Contemporary Asia, 47*(1), 142–153. https://doi.org/10.1080/00472336.2016.1239751.
de la Torre, C. (2000). *Populist seduction in Latin America: The Ecuadorian experience*. Ohio University Press.
Graham, D. (2018, January 18). Trump's quietly growing list of victories. *The Atlantic*. https://www.theatlantic.com/politics/archive/2018/01/what-trump-has-accomplished/550760/.
Halmai, G. (2019). Populism, authoritarianism and constitutionalism. *German Law Journal, 20*, 296–313.
Halmai, G. (2018). Is there such a thing as "populist constitutionalism"? The case of Hungary. *Fudan Journal of the Humanities and Social Sciences, 11*, 323–339.
Haverda, T., & Halley, J. A. (2019). Trump's 2016 presidential campaign and Adorno's psychological technique: Content analyses of authoritarian populism. *TripleC, 17*(2), 202–220.
Juego, B. (2017). Duterte-led authoritarian populism and its liberal-democratic roots. *Asia Maior, 18*, 129–165.
Kellner, D. (2016). *American nightmare: Donald Trump, media spectacle, and authoritarian populism*. Sense Publishers.
Kine, P. (2017). Philippine President Rodrigo Duterte's "war on drugs." *Harvard International Review, 38*(3), 25–27.
Kreko, P., & Enyedi, Z. (2018). Explaining Eastern Europe: Orban's laboratory of illiberalism. *Journal of Democracy, 29*(3), 39–51.
Laclau, E. (1977). *Politics and ideology in Marxist theory*. Verso.
Levitsky, S., & Loxton, J. (2012). Populism and competitive authoritarianism: The case of Fujimori's Peru. In *Populism in Europe and the Americas: Threat or corrective for democracy* (pp. 160–181). Cambridge University Press.
McKay, D. (2020). Facilitating Donald Trump: Populism, the Republican Party and media manipulation. In *Authoritarian populism and liberal democracy* (pp. 107–122). Palgrave MacMillan.
Mendoza, R., & Jaminola, L. (2020). Is duterte a populist? Rhetoric vs. reality. *CIRSD Horizons* (Winter) (15), 1–17.
Mudde, C. (2004). The populist Zeitgeist. *Government and Opposition, 39*(4), 542–563.
Mudde, C. (2007). *Populist radical right parties in Europe*. Cambridge University Press.
Mudde, C., & Kaltwasser, C. R. (2012). Populism and (liberal) democracy: A framework for analysis. In *Populism in Europe and the Americas: Threat or corrective to democracy* (pp. 1–26). Cambridge University Press.
Norris, P. (2017). *Is Western democracy backsliding?* (No. RWP17-012; Faculty Research Working Paper Series). Harvard Kennedy School.

Norris, P. (2019). Varieties of populist parties. *Philosophy and Social Criticism, 45*(9–10), 981–1012.

Norris, P., & Inglehart, R. (2016). *Trump, Brexit, and the rise of populism: Economic have-nots and cultural backlash. Roundtable on Rage against the Machine: Populist Politics in the U.S., Europe and Latin America* (pp. 1–44).

Norris, P., & Inglehart, R. (2017). Trump and the populist authoritarian parties: The silent revolution in reverse. *Reflections, 15*(2), 443–454.

Norwegian Helsinki Committee. (2013). *Democracy and Human Rights at stake in Hungary: The Viktor Orban Government's drive for centralisation of power* (No. 1–2013).

Oswald, M., & Robertson, J. (2019). A constitutional crisis, norm derogation and the broader impact of partisan polarization in contemporary American politics. In *Mobilization, representation, and responsiveness in the American democracy* (pp. 3–36). Palgrave Macmillian.

Punongbayan, J. (2019, April 25). *[ANALYSIS] How the TRAIN law worsened poverty, inequality*. Rappler. https://www.rappler.com/thought-leaders/228952-how-tax-reform-law-worsened-poverty-inequality-philippines.

Rankin, J. (2018, April 8). Hungary election: Viktor Orbán declares victory—As it happened. *The Guardian*. https://www.theguardian.com/world/live/2018/apr/08/hungary-election-victor-orban-expected-to-win-third-term-live-updates.

Royo Maxwell, S. (2019). Perceived threat of crime, authoritarianism, and the rise of a populist president in the Philippines. *International Journal of Comparative and Applied Criminal Justice, 43*(3), 207–218.

Scanish, M., & Eisen, N. (2019, November 25). *History in the (un)making: Historical revisionism in Viktor Orban's Hungary*. Brooking. https://www.brookings.edu/blog/order-from-chaos/2019/11/25/history-in-the-unmaking-historical-revisionism-in-viktor-orbans-hungary/.

Singh, R. (2017). "I, the people": A deflationary interpretation of populism, Trump and the United States constitution. *Economy and Society, 46*(1), 20–42.

Timbo Authoritarian Populism Index 2019. (2019). Timbro.

The Economist. (2019, August 29). *How Viktor Orban hollowed out Hungary's democracy*. https://www.economist.com/briefing/2019/08/29/how-viktor-orban-hollowed-out-hungarys-democracy..

Toomey, M. (2018). History, nationalism and democracy: Myth and narrative in Viktor Orban's "illiberal Hungary." *New Perspectives, 25*(1), 1–23.

Valiquette, R. T., & Su, Y. (2018, December 13). *The rise of Duterte and Bolsonaro: Creeping authoritarianism and criminal populism*. New Mandala. https://www.newmandala.org/the-rise-of-duterte-and-bolsonaro-creeping-authoritarianism-and-criminal-populism/.

Whiteley, P., Clarke, H. D., & Stewart, M. (2020). Populism plus: Voting for Donald Trump and Hillary Clinton in the 2016 US Presidential election. In *Authoritarian populism and liberal democracy* (pp. 87–105). Palgrave MacMillian.

Zeemann, J. (2019). *Populism beyond the nation. In Populism and world politics: Exploring inter- and transnational dimensions* (pp. 25–53). Palgrave Macmillan.

CHAPTER 11

Authoritarian Populism and Collective Memory Manipulation

Rafał Riedel

Introduction

Since there is little literature focusing on the crossroads of populism and memory studies, and literally no works integrating authoritarian populism and memory manipulation, the present study attempts to develop an original framework to fill this research gap. In the last decades, memory studies as well as studies about populist politics, policies and politicians mushroomed both in quality and quantity. Rarely they are analyzed in conjuncture (Norris & Inglehart, 2019) and the practice of everyday politics shows they coexist, correlate and intertwine. Therefore, the objective of this chapter is to develop a new analytical framework to account for the web of connections between authoritarian populism and collective memory manipulations. By doing so, this paper introduces the problem of memory discourses and their application as political instruments. Public remembrance (and oblivion) is as much about recollecting the past as it is about shaping the present and the future of political communities.

Consequently, a number of interesting and legitimate questions emerge at the crossroads of two strands of the academic literature, namely authoritarian populism and memory politics: What is so specific about authoritarian populism that correlates with collective memory manipulations? How to differentiate between regular memory (re)construction and its manipulation? What

R. Riedel (✉)
Department of Political and Administrative Systems, University of Opole, Opole, Poland
e-mail: riedelr@wp.pl

are the mechanisms of remembrance and oblivion playing a role in authoritarian and populist politics? What prospect is there for engaging in memory production and re-production by politicians? What lessons can we draw from analyzing the intertwining relations of authoritarianism and populism on the one side and memory manipulations on the other? Therefore, the overarching goal of this article is to develop and expand the conceptual resources that construct the area of research dedicated to memory manipulations in authoritarian populist politics. Connecting political science to the substantially historical discourse builds a truly interdisciplinary platform, which allows to see the sources, mechanisms and consequences of memory manipulations from various perspectives. This enhances populism studies by incorporating new elements and points of view.

The article proceeds as follows: First, a short overview of the historicity of populism is presented in order to show that the authoritarian version of populism is an outcome of a specific historical process. The next section presents how populism is generally defined in political science and it narrows down the concept of authoritarian populism. Populism, both as a political practice and as the object of scholarly investigation, raises important and challenging questions about its relation to democracy. Radical populism discredits the existing order and the historical trajectories that led towards it. Populist actors offer some new, highly subjective and alternative topographies of collective memory. Thus, the following section addresses the hotly debated concept of collective memory. Then it delivers the author's understanding of memory manipulations and some explanation when a standard memory (re)production or (re)creation takes the form of manipulation. It is followed by some discussion on the key issues connected with the analyzed topic, like the problem of 'historical justice', healing historical wounds and memory politics. It is illustrated with examples from the European integration process (at the foundations of which there lies the unique collective experience of a grand catastrophe brought by WWII) and the post-communist part of Europe. Central and Eastern Europe offer a specially interesting field for memory studies research due to its specific history as well as due to the authoritarian politics in which it is often trapped (Bugaric, 2019). In the conclusion the author connects the two flows of thought: authoritarian populism and collective memory manipulations building a coherent framework. The article suggests that the overarching authoritarian component in populist memory manipulations lies in the undemocratic nature of the 'we-they' relations, the prioritization of the people's will (over other standards of democracy) as well as in the antagonizing prescriptions that authoritarian populists suggest. As a result, the collective memory can be manipulated in such a way that it serves the interests, the vision and the ideology of those in power.

HISTORICITY OF POPULISM

Populism cannot be fully understood outside of the historical continuum since it is not a trans-historical phenomenon. The current form of populism is an outcome of a specific historical process. It emerged as a form of authoritarian democracy, which could accommodate the sentiment for the totalitarian version of politics with the post-war hegemony of democratic representation. Framing populism historically helps us understand why its return to Europe actualizes this continent's past xenophobic and anti-democratic characteristics. Modern populists are surprisingly open to its pre-democratic foundations. At best they are ambivalent about democracy, and at worst they want to destroy it (Finchelstein, 2014).

The etymology of the term goes back to the ancient Rome where *populares* were the politicians looking for public support. Modern populism accordingly has existed as early as the nineteenth century (agrarian populism in USA in the form of *People's Party* or Russian *narodnichestvo*). One of the first analytical works on populism appeared in 1928 in 'The American Economic Review' where John D. Black published his article on 'The McNary-Haugen Movement'. He discussed political and economic aspects of the relations between the agricultural sector and commerce and industry. This field of analysis correlates very well with the populist ideology from the agrarian revolt in the US in the 1890s and the accompanying concept of the two nations: the nation of the producers (the exploited) and the nation of the well-to-do elites. This distinction gave birth to the political cleavage present in populist politics until today, that is the confrontational relation between the authentic people and the parasitical elite.

Pre-modern forms of populism were used to describe nineteenth century European (predominantly in Russia and France) and American phenomena. They targeted at a more equalitarian role for the masses in the context of the predominantly elitist politics (in Tsarist, Napoleonic or even early American versions). However, the more liberal democracy was established, the more populism evolved towards increasingly regressive standpoints. In late 1980s the term 'neo-populism' made its debut, focusing on Latin America (Dix, 1985), where neoliberal politicians, implementing austerity measures, continued to mobilize surprising levels of popular support while formulating rhetoric and pursuing both free-market and also leftist policies reminiscent of a more classic Latin American populism (Jansen, 2011).

However, as Lawrence Goodwyn claims in his influential work *The Populist Moment*, populism was never simply a protest. At its origins, it was a struggle on behalf of popular government, especially when democracy appeared threatened by corporate gigantism as well as an increasingly powerful and alien state (from the very beginning populism focused on matters vital for political economy). Over the course of history populism presented a variety of political possibilities and experiences on the left (*Peronism*) and on the right (*Chiracquism*). Despite from political positioning, the historical perspective allows one to identify some central themes of populism. Populists identify themselves with the very *heartland* of the imagined political community, which they want to serve. They support an idea of political antagonists as enemies who are potentially traitors to the nation. They share some understanding of the leader as charismatic embodiment of the voice and desires of the nation as a whole. The populists opt for the strong executive and the discursive (often also practical) dismissal of the legislative and judicial branches of authority. They also present an extremely sacralizing understanding of the political and a political theology that considers the people as being formed by those who follow a unique vertical leadership. Populism is very often accompanied by a radical nationalism and an emphasis on the popular culture (as opposed to other forms of culture that do not represent a 'national thought'), which resonates very well with the anti-elitist rhetoric of populists (Riedel, 2018). Populists share an attachment to the vertical forms of democracy (that nonetheless rejects in practice dictatorial forms of government) (Finchelstein, 2014, p. 468).

POPULISM AND ITS AUTHORITARIAN MALFORMATIONS

The existing literature on populism has been plagued by conceptual confusion, deficiency and disagreement. Even more in the case of its authoritarian malformations. Populism as analytical category remains notoriously difficult to define and the term refers to ideologies, movements, political tactic or experience, style, frames and many others. At the same time the utility of populism is precisely in its embrace of a range of diverse and sometimes contradictory political beliefs. A quick overview of the scholarly literature allows us to see populism as ideology, movement, specific political culture, a moralistic imagination of politics, socio-technique, as a syndrome, logic, as demagoguery, electioneering, as a style, as a post-fascist contestation of democracy (maybe neo-fascist), as a symbol, symptom or pathology of democracy, as a way of political expression, as a mode of persuasion, or simply as a mode of political practice.

In general, understanding populism is a set of ideas or argumentation that is catchy and attractive based on emotional and irrational grounds, longing for simple solutions to complicated problems and directly connected to the will of the majority. It very often manifests itself in simplistic equalizing democracy with unlimited will of the majority (tyranny of majority thesis). Populists claim that the majority is by democratic logic 'right' and must be respected. A populist politician gladly uses negative society's mood of discontent and claims to be the spokesman of the unsatisfied (Riedel, 2017). Despite a rich interdisciplinary discourse, students of populism still disagree not only how to explain it but more fundamentally—about what its main features are. As a result, we seem to be witnessing a conceptual cacophony. For Jansen (2011, p. 82) a political project is populist when it is a sustained, large-scale political project that mobilizes ordinary marginalized social sectors into publicly visible and contentious political action, while articulating an anti-elite, nationalistic rhetoric that valorizes ordinary people. Because of that, it is difficult to imagine democratic politics without populism. The domination of predominantly anti-populist logic—consciously or unconsciously, intentionally or unintentionally—may reduce politics to an administrative enterprise with over proportionate input from experts and technocrats (depoliticized democracy, post-democracy, post-politics) (Stavrakakis, 2014).

The most recognized and cited contemporary researcher of populism, Cas Mudde, defines it as a thin-centered[1] ideology that focuses on the antagonism between people and elites against the backdrop of popular sovereignty. Such conceptualization has become the dominant position in the literature. It considers society to be ultimately divided into two homogenous and antagonistic groups 'the pure people' and 'the corrupt elite' (Mudde, 2004, p. 543) and politics is supposed to be an expression of the general will of 'the pure people'. This positions populism in opposition to elitism and pluralism. In populist politics there are less spaces left for minorities and they are often presented as traitors to the real will of the nation or even marionettes of foreign powers. For Jan-Werner Mueller, populism is a particular moralistic imagination of politics, a way of perceiving the political world which places in opposition a morally pure and fully unified people against small minorities, elites in particular (who are placed outside of the authentic people) (Mueller, 2015, p. 83). The populists claim that only they can properly represent the proper people (the proper people extracted from the people). The moralist component of this definition highly depends on distinguishing the moral from the immoral. And the criteria for this is often manipulated by the populist politicians. In the face of a passive political culture, in which very few citizens take an active role in politics, the extracted people may sum up to an actual minority. Populist politicians, acting in the name of the people, may in fact oppress the majority under the moralizing flag of radical democracy.[2]

From that point of view, populism—both as a political practice and as the object of scholarly investigation—raises important and challenging questions about its relation to democracy (Zoltan, 2020). Some, usually from liberal positions, are increasingly worried about illiberal forces gaining power (Halmai, 2019). They sometimes equal populism with xenophobia or plain nationalism. Although, one needs to remember, that populism is not always nationalist. However, there is one feature that is integral to both populist politics and ethno-centric nationalism, it is the assumption about the 'essential people' as constituting a monolithic unit that has an authentic and homogeneous will of its own. On the other side there are others who are concerned with the rise of what they see as 'liberal technocracy' (or outright oligarchy). From these two opposing camps populism can be or desruptive for democracy or its corrective mechanism or indeed its essence (Mueller, 2015).

For Ernesto Laclau populism is the ultimate agent of democratization. Somehow going to the roots of the agrarian populists, this school of thought defines populism as a structural element of systemic calls for equality and against domination—it leads to political emancipation (Laclau, 1977). The benefit of populist politics is that it gives voice to the excluded or marginalized sections of the society as well as it puts issues on the agenda that have normally be ignored by the political establishment. For some populism constitutes a democratizing response to a widespread authoritarian populism; however, authoritarian populism represents undemocratic limitations to democracy as such or at least in its liberal (or pluralist) version. Populism happened to make democracy less pluralistic in political rights and more inclusive in the realm of social rights (Riedel, 2017). Populist democracy tends to be more nationalistic and less cosmopolitan. Populism is also in conflict with democracy with its totalizing view of a society. In more contemporary reincarnations it is a fusion of nationalism (with its notion of the unified people) and authoritarianism (with its lack of tolerance for any alternative discourses).

It is quite a paradoxical statement taking into account that the core of populism is democratic (but not liberal). Such a historical approach allows to see even fascism as emergent from democracy; however, questioning it in the end. At the same time neglecting the diverse historical meanings of populism often leads to broadest definitions, understanding populism as a movement or ideology defending popular sovereignty and opposing the people to the elites. For Margaret Canovan (2005) populism is a legitimate member of the democratic club, but Pierre Rosanvallon (2006) regards it as a perversion of the ideals and procedures of democracy. For Rosanvallon populism is counter-democratic as it degrades democracy in a pathological way. He proposes a definition of populism as a form of political expression in which the democratic project allows itself to be absorbed and fully vampirized by counter-democracy. Such a definition correlates very well with the framing ideas of analysis on populism. It is attentive to populisms' symbolic dimension, its imagination and projections (Canovan 2005, Rossanvallon, 2006).

Populism is an undemocratic response to the undemocratic tendencies of technocracy and globalization, the distrust generated by the *permissive consensus* type of politics so much present in the post-war Europe. It is also a response, symptom and consequence of the lack of true citizens' participation. It is important to remember that populism is not a simple external response to elites (or establishment) but rather a criticism and contestation of democracy from within. Populists often claim that this criticism is a radicalization of democracy by returning the power to the people. Already in the first conceptions of populism as an ideology, it was portrayed as a threat to the rule of law and democracy (Allcock, 1971). Populism is accused of corroding democratic institutions and predominantly the democratic spirit—the belief in democracy. It is supposed to undermine the checks and balances system (like the constitutional court), paving the way to some form of authoritarianism.

Populism seeks to build a political system devoid of the *rule of law*, and therefore it is a pervasive phenomenon. It itself is chauvinistic and fundamentalist aiming at dismantling checks and balances (as not representative, unelected bodies). Populists do not respect the fragile equilibrium between the non-majoritarian institutions and the power of the people. If necessary, they will question the constitutional order (explicitly or implicitly), challenge the international treaties and obligations by various forms of mobilization or pseudo-representation (e.g. plebiscite) (Kaltwasser, 2014). Populism is not just anti-elitist; it is anti-pluralists—and here lies its profoundly undemocratic character (Mueller, 2015). Populist actors promise protection against the insecurities of pluralism. The 'united people' rhetoric offers some kind of harmony of interest. It goes hand in hand with the overestimation, idealization and romanticizing of one's own nation and is accompanied with stereotyping and stigmatizing enemies of the nation—other nations, international organizations, capitalists or minorities. Populist politicians are exploiting persistent patterns of prejudice (Riedel, 2018). The regular problems of everyday life are supposedly related to the presence of foreigners or minorities or other forms of aliens. This results in questioning the universal norms, and amplifying authoritarian tendencies at the cost of democratic pluralism. The tradition of *authoritarian personality* studies of Erich Fromm, Theodor Adorno and the followers teaches us that nationalism strongly correlates with ethnocentrism, xenophobia, racism, anti-Semitism, militarism and authoritarianism (Weiss, 2003). This can be explained by the populist assumption about the homogeneous people, the heartland. Intolerant, anti-pluralist visions of democracy reveal authoritarian syndrome of populism. Populism is therefore a biting critique of the democratic limitations, and it rejects all barriers on the expression of majoritarian will, most notably the independence of key institutions (the guardians of democracy). Populists make politics more polarizing, and by perceiving representative politics as corrupt and divorced from ordinary people, they share the vision of exclusivist nation (Jasiewicz, 2008).

Anti-democratic populism may be to a large extend explained on the basis of latent insecurity developing as a result of the democratic rules of institutionalized conflict, struggle of interest and power shifts (Keane, 1994, Weiss, 2003). The transformation from non-democracy to democracy is a particularly fragile period in which the enthusiasm for democracy building may dry-out very soon in the face of the social and economic unrest. Populist, nationalistic and authoritarian attitudes can be interpreted as a sentiment reaction to the 'shock of modernization' (Riedel, 2019).

Authoritarian populism offers its own, subjective and usually new and alternative topography of memory. The populist diagnostic frame defines the current problem and the enemy. It outsources from the past events—more or less distant history. The 'we-group' is defined in a new way. The same with the 'they-group'. And as a consequence, the new relations between the new 'we' and the new 'they'. Most often the relation is based on antagonism and the populist actor promises radical change which will bring about historical justice. Isaiah Berlin claimed that populism could maintain only in societies standing at the edge of modernization (Berlin, 1968). This would explain the wide spread of populism in the post-transition ex-communist states. But it is also important to remember that populism has never ceased to exist both in the West and in the East. Everywhere populism discredits the existing order (leaders, party system, values, etc.) and promotes alternative one, and therefore populism is an extremally interesting and vitally important concept in studying collective memory. And vice versa, connecting the memory studies with the rich scholarly discourse on populism cross-fertilizes both fields, at the same time offering some new fruitful areas for scientific exploration.

Collective Memory Manipulations: Sources, Mechanisms, Consequences

The concept of collective memory is hotly debated in many disciplines and from many points of view. Various definitions of memory remain extremely vague and connecting adjectives (supposedly making it more precise) with the main concept does not help much: historical memory, collective memory, public memory, social memory, and so on (Allen, 2016; Ogino, 2015; Olik, 2007). However, in order to conceptualize memory manipulations, it is necessary to narrow down the meaning of memory and collective memory.

Some scholars (Sik, 2015) claim that memory is an attribute of an individual (a property of individual mind). However, individual memory is not closed as it is constructed through interactions with others. Individual memory is influenced by the collective representation of the past.[3] We can talk about socially framed individual memories and about collective commemorative representations and mnemonic traces (Olik, 2007, 20). Collective memory is something uncertain and difficult to comprehend. It also changes with time, because those who compose the group change and the framing changes. Collective memory is essentially a reconstruction of the past and very close to collective representation, or collective conscience. At the same time, collective memory is different from history. Undoubtedly, history influences the creation of collective memory but collective memory holds only a part of the past that is still alive in the conscience of the group. In this sense rituals of commemoration are held to reproduce the past in the presence to resurrect mythological origins in the presence (Ogino, 2015). Memory is a total sum of ideas related to the past that at a certain moment crystallizes in a society which lays the foundation of a 'shared interpretation' of history. As such memory—the main structural component in giving society a sense of its own identity—is what makes it possible for a society to inscribe itself into a prolonged time period, into a tradition (Ferretti, 2003, 40). Societies change but the collective memory consciousness endures unchanged across time and generations as old phases remain intact when new ones are superimposed upon them. Therefore, memory battles are much more intense in relation to more contemporary history and memories. Some images, however, remain stable (Zhang & Schwartz, 1997).

Scholars of various disciplines focus on diversified aspects of historical investigations. Some collect and document historical facts, others are much more interested in their interpretations and critical deliberations. Sociologists, political scientists, social psychologists and others focus on how an individual or a group remembers the past as well as what meanings are attached to the historical events, figures, phenomena and processes. Also, on what collective memory tells us about the present society, what does it mean for its members, how do they see themselves (and how they are seen from outside) through the prism of the collective memory, and what kind of consequence stem from this? It is an important constitutive element of the community and its identity. Because history does not merely reproduce facts, it also (re)constructs their meanings and frames them within a cultural, inter-subjectively shared tradition. Collective memory in political culture can be understood as an on-going process of negotiation through time (Olik & Levy, 1997).

The question is when such a natural process of memory reproduction and renegotiation turns into manipulation. To manipulate, by dictionary definitions, means to influence skillfully, especially in an unfair manner. Manipulation as a psychological term refers to a social influence aiming at changing the perception, knowledge, opinion, attitude and finally behavior of others (individuals or social groups). Memory manipulations—as understood by social scientists (it needs to be remembered that it also has its psychological, psychiatric and neurological dimension)—can be defined as an influence organized by societal actors (individuals, institutions, groups) advancing the interests of the manipulator by instrumentalizing history and memory. This means such a (re)creation of collective memory which serves the interests, visions and ideologies of the manipulating actor(s). It contains the very rich *repertoire*, including: selective presentation of historical facts, lying (including lying by omission), denial, (self-) victimization, over-subjective interpretations, rationalization, minimization, projecting the blame, the guilt, exploiting negative memory and negative heritage, public remembrance, memorial management, memory entrepreneurship, nostalgia industries, dark tourism, reconciliation politics, constructing historical justice narrative, moralizing discourses, missionary politics, memory abuse, memory disorder. The instruments and techniques available for memory manipulations remain equally rich and contain, among others: publications, speeches, conferences, media discourse, grants for specific projects, movies, school education and many others aspects of cultural policy.

In (populist) politics, memory manipulation most often refers to bringing historical justice by contemporary means, and it correlates very strongly with identity politics ('we' versus 'they'). The notion of 'historical injustice' used both in international relations and domestic politics raises controversies. Some will claim that it stands for a new and noble type of politics based on high moral standards. Whereas others will criticize that such retrospective politics comes at the cost of present and future-oriented politics (Beverage, 2015). Focusing on the past very often compensates the shortcomings of contemporary politics (the lack of constructive future projects). It draws the attention of the general public out of the real problems of today and leads to misinterpretations of current situations. On the other side the legitimate questions in this context are: Can we fix history? Can we bring more justice by contemporary means (economic, legal, etc.) to historical injustices? Such dilemmas are geared into reconciliation politics (or its neglect). They live at the cross-roads of what we remember from the past and what we can observe today. Our present-day allies—what role did they play in the past? If the past is more dividing than uniting—is it time for reconciliation? Do we need to agree on a common vision of the past? Public remembrance is as much about recollecting the past as it is about shaping the present and the future. The interplay between recollection and future-building is founded on the belief that future peace, stability and prosperity depend on 'coming to terms' with an uneasy past (Rigney, 2012, 251). Historical books focus on the series of conflicts, wars and tensions. They stubbornly ignore the periods of peace, stability and cooperation. The image of the past is overloaded with the confrontation versus collaboration, war versus peace, change versus continuity. Recollecting the past (like writing historical books) is equally about remembering as it is about forgetting. Healing the historical wounds cannot happen at the cost of troublesome past remembrance but it is also impossible when focusing predominantly or exclusively on violence, injustice and other dark parts of history. Achieving the proper balance between remembrance (understood as acknowledging the past) and oblivion (neglecting or marginalizing some other parts of the past) is a moral hazard and generates many difficulties of political nature.

In this context the European integration experience is a very illustrative one. As it is written by Stefan Auer:

> From the outset, the European project has been informed by historical experience in a peculiar way: the constitutive other for the future Europe has been Europe's own past. While nations usually celebrate glorious events in their own history, what was meant to bring Europeans together was the unique experience of the catastrophe: World War II and the Holocaust. (Auer, 2010, p. 1175)

Even negative memory, like war experience, becomes subject to preservation (Ogino, 2015). The politics of memory in united Europe have been devoted to overcome past divisions on the basis of a better mutual understanding of various national perspectives (*acquis historique communitaire*). However, the underlying assumption that all conflicts about history could ultimately be resolved is a misconceived, naïve and deeply apolitical idea (Auer, 2010).

The Financial crisis (2008–2014) has affected memory in societies but it was also affected by the memories of many people and social groups. On one side the remembrance of the 1929–1930s. The Great Depression had an impact on the development of the contemporary Great Recession and some reactions to it. Keeping in mind the ineffectiveness of measures undertaken in 1930s, in line with protectionist and isolationist policies, at the break of the first and second decade of twenty-first century, the response to the economic problems was not mercantilist logic but common market logic that drove the counter-crisis actions. Integrationist answers were applied in the form of non-conventional European Central Bank policies, EU Commission stimulus packages, European Stability Mechanism, among others.

Apart from attacking the supranational elites, there are domestic political actors who are interested in antagonization with their neighbors and other nations. The populist construction of the other (the enemy) exploits the fact that there are (at least) as many histories as nations in Europe. A historical fact has a commonly shared meaning for the members of the specific society or certain social group. Politicians actively set up institutions that will allow the society or some of its groups to keep its memories. Public remembrance and memorial management allow to keep some parts of history alive and some of them become forgotten (negative heritage also has political consequences). Memory politics becomes then an element of identity politics—it tries to answer the question what the unifying narrative for the community is. Various methods, instruments and techniques can be employed in such an undertaking, including memory entrepreneurship (e.g. reconstruction groups, etc.), nostalgia industries (e.g. *Heimat Reisen*), dark tourism, self-victimization (the so called *Olympics of suffering*), memory abuse (Autry, 2017). Very often such practices take the form of missionary politics. A moral community is invested with a mission of salvation against conspiratorial enemies. It seeks to provide the alienated mass of underprivileged citizens with an identity and a sense of belonging (Scalon, 2000), which is the essence of populism.

Populist politicians instrumentalize history and memory for the purpose of the past as a justification for today's legitimacy. Not Weberian tradition of legitimacy but a logic according to which 'our past achievements (merit) legitimize our right to govern' (Luyckx & Janssens, 2020; Weber 1922). The dominant narrative of the past acts as a legitimation of the existing institutions, practices and even individuals. Therefore, memory needs to be renegotiated, recreated and sometimes re-manipulated.

In radical versions, such practices of memory manipulation may lead towards 'memory disorder', as it was coined by Maria Ferretti (2003) in relation to Russians' radical changes in their perceptions and attitudes towards the past (pre-Stalinist, Stalinist, post-Stalinist periods). Memory disorder refers to situations in which attitudes towards the past undergo radical revision. Very often they correlate with manipulating idealized visions of the past ('golden-age-ism'). How illusive and untrue the imagined 'golden age' may be is conveyed by the glorification of the 'golden age' of the socialist era in large fractions of the post-communist societies.

CONCLUDING ... TOWARDS THE ANALYTICAL FRAMEWORK

Authoritarian populism (as an analytical concept) can act as a justified approach to memory and identity studies. Therefore, the conclusion lends itself to connecting the two flows of thought, authoritarian populism and collective memory manipulation, into a coherent framework.

The essence of the authoritarian version of populism is that it plays with the holy triangle of populism, that is: first—the exclusive definition of a 'we-group', second—the confrontational attitude towards the 'they-group' (very flexibly and manipulatively understood), and third—the supposedly homogeneous 'will' that is only properly represented by the populist politician. The authoritarian component in this populist framework stems from the relations between the three above-mentioned elements. The superiority of the 'we-group' over the interest of the 'they-group' (understood as the corrupt elite of insiders or threatening outsiders, e.g. migrants, refugees, foreign capital, alien culture, supranational institutions, etc.). The will of the 'pure people', the heartland, as the utter source of legitimacy may ignore any other standards of liberal democracy, even when in conflict with constitutional constraints.

The most significant characteristics of authoritarian populism are the following: Populists offer a radical version of democracy postulating returning the power to the people. It would not be that bad if it was not for the fact that it is meant to be done at the cost of other important democratic standards like *the rule of law*. Populism, in its authoritarian version, does not respect the fragile balance between the power of the people and the role of non-majoritarian institutions. It criticizes and contests democracy from within. It endangers the rule of law by undermining the checks and balances system. Populism is anti-pluralist, monotheistic, intolerant and anti-liberal. The illusive harmony of interest of the 'united people' legitimizes the radicalization of politics.

Authoritarian populists use many forms of memory manipulation methods and techniques; therefore they offer their own, subjective and usually new and alternative topography of memory. The populist diagnostic frame defines the current problem—who is the 'we' and who is 'they' (the enemy). It connects to the past events (and their memories)—more or less distant history. However, not only the 'we-group' and the 'they-group' are defined in a new way. As a consequence, populist actors construct new relations between the new 'we' and the new 'they'. Most often the relation is based on antagonism and the populist promises radical change which will bring about 'historical justice'. That is already offered in the prescriptive frames delivered by authoritarian populists. The distinction between diagnosing frames and prescriptive frames of authoritarian populism are shown in Table 11.1.

Memory manipulations in relation to the 'we-group' refer to the position it held in the past. If the collective memory holds that the past was glorious (e.g. British empire), the populist narrative will try to convince people that this was lost due to the unfair or unjust actions. Regaining it signifies historical justice. If the collective memory keeps the remembrance of the past, or its fragment, as rather infamous (e.g. Nazi Germany), the memory manipulation may employ denial or rejection (it is not us the Germans, it is the Fascists), rationalization (the *Zeitgeist* was anti-Semitic) or other methods of

Table 11.1 Authoritarian populists' framing of memory

	Diagnosing frames	*Prescriptive frames*
"WE-group"	(Self-)victimization Self-perception of being: – marginalized – exploited – treated unfairly	"Radical change is needed" "No-more (post/neo)colonial exploitation" "We will take what we deserve"
"THEY-group"	External enemy—aggressor, dominator Internal enemy—traitor Corrupt elite (political, economic, intellectual)	"Time for *historical justice*" "They will pay us back" "They will get what they deserve"
The homogenous "WILL"	So far ignored Misunderstood Misused Only we (the populists) understand it, only we can articulate and represent the common will	Missionary politics Moral legitimations Right people doing the right thing Time to do it our way (nativism)

exploiting negative memory and negative heritage. Very often the diagnosis of the 'we-group' situation is that in the more or less distant history it was marginalized, exploited and treated unfairly (e.g. Poland). In such a situation, memory manipulations may aim at self-(over)victimization (nostalgia industry, *Heimatreisen*), projecting any blame or guilt—for good reason or not—outside of the 'we-group' (even in cases of some documented historical guilt—minimization, denial or rejection will be expected).

As a consequence, the prescriptive frame of authoritarian populism will postulate a radical change—even at the cost of democracy standards. The historical trajectories led 'us' to this situation, and from that moment on 'we' will act in order to take what we deserve. The rhetoric of 'no more (post) colonialism', 'no more exploitation' will be present in these locations and situations in which the diagnosing frame was rather pessimistic about the past (e.g. Hungary and the *Trianon trauma*). On the other side, wherever the diagnosis of the past was more optimistic ('golden age' story), the populist narrative will promise getting back the position we deserve or we can afford (e.g. Brexiteers' discourse) (Healy & Tumarkin, 2011).

Memory manipulations in relation to the 'they-group' are very diversified and depend on earlier definitions of the 'we-group'. If 'they' are defined domestically—the corrupt elite (e.g. the post-communists), memory manipulations focus on moralizing discourses and exploit negative memories. If, however, the 'they-group' is sought outside in the international community, the prescriptive frame will emphasize the oppressor or aggressor role of this alien force. The simple mechanism of defining 'us' in relation to the dominant or endangering 'they' brings a mobilization effect. And playing with fears is mastered by authoritarian populists (e.g. anti-Western discourse in Russia), including the real and imagined fears outsourced from the past.

The prescriptive frame in relation to the 'they-group' is again highly dependent on the earlier definitions of the 'we-group' as well as on earlier diagnostic frames of the 'they-group'. If 'they' were understood in domestic terms—for example, as the non-patriotic part of the society or even the traitors, then authoritarian populists will seek to neutralize them, bring justice (e.g. 'pay us back' rhetoric), make them responsible or even some forms of physical violence—depending on the level of radicality. At the same time, if 'they' are defined as an external actor, the prescription will depend on the previously defined problem. Accordingly, politics of memory may include reconciliation or its rejection (or both, as it is in the case of contemporary Ukrainian–Polish relations), blame-trading, stereotypes building, projecting negative heritage and many others.

In the case of the third constitutive component of populism, that is the 'homogenous will of the people', the employed frames vary in relation to how the 'we-group' was defined. Usually, however, the populist diagnostic frame focuses on the fact that the preferences, needs, interests and finally the will of the people are not understood very well and therefore cannot be articulated and represented by any other actors but the populist politician. The historical interpretations of how this 'will' was treated previously will also follow this line of argumentation: 'so far ignored', 'marginalized', 'misused'.

As a consequence, the prescriptive frame in relation to the 'will' of the people will exploit moralizing language. The 'will of the people is the highest form of legitimizing populist actors' actions. 'Right people are doing the right thing' type of rhetoric is the essence of the missionary politics. Once in power, the populist promise that now it is time to do it 'our way' and whoever opposes it is defined as the enemy (see the diagnosing 'they' frame). And here, the vicious cycle (or rather triangle) of authoritarian populism starts again in the (re)definitions of 'we' and our 'will' and 'them'. The diagnosing and prescriptive frames are manipulatively employed in the (re)constructions of memory serving the interests of authoritarian populists.

The overarching authoritarian component in populist memory manipulations lies in the undemocratic nature of 'we-they' relations, the prioritization of the people's will (over other standards of democracy) as well as in the antagonizing prescriptions that authoritarian populists suggest. The collective memory will be manipulated in such a way that it serves the interest, the vision and the ideology of those in power. The contemporary 'we' will be glorified as a consequence of the historical trajectory logic. 'They' were enemies in the past and still are. Only 'we' can truly and effectively represent you and your 'will'. 'We' are historically legitimized. Any opposition to realizing this homogenous 'will' must be broken, even at the cost of democratic standards (civic rights, rule of law, *checks and balance* institutions). That is because no *non-elected* body can be a barrier in the process of satisfying the will of the people. No legal system (national or supranational), no authority can stop 'us' (the populist politicians) from consuming the electoral results. Manipulating memory is thus justified by the simplistic definition of democracy equalizing it with the will of majority. Reproduced collective memory is geared towards populist politics, postulating the 'historical justice' of those in power.

Acknowledgements This research was possible thanks to the support provided by Katholischer Akademischer Ausländer-Dienst (KAAD).

Notes

1. 'Thin' due to the fact that its particular ideas are of limited scope, complexity and ambition, it is not a complete ideology in opposition to full ideologies, like: nationalism, socialism or liberalism. Michael Freeden explained a thin-centered ideology that is arbitrary in serving itself from wider ideational contexts, it flexibly removes or replaces some concepts, it lacks internal integrity and coherence.
2. The very core components of populism are highly flexible: the definition of the people, the imagined 'other' as well as the general and unified will. This triangle may take various shapes depending from the context. It also affects many important questions of democracy theory—the relation between the authorities and the governed, the legitimacy and representation question, as well as many other related issues on modes of decision-making, redistribution mechanisms, relations with the international community and so on.
3. In this sense, one may claim that there is no such thing as an individual memory.

Literature

Allcock, J. B. (1971). "Populism": A brief biography. *Sociology, 5*(3), 371–387.
Allen, M. (2016). The poverty of memory: For political economy in memory studies. *Memory Studies, 9*(4), 371–375.
Auer, S. (2010). 'New Europe': Between cosmopolitan dreams and nationalist nightmares. *JCMS, 48*(5), 1163–1184.
Autry, R. (2017). *Desegregating the past: The public life of United States and South Africa*. Oxford University Press.
Berlin, I. (1968). To define populism. *Government and Opposition, 3*(2), 137–179.
Bevernage, B. (2015). The past is evil/evil is past: On retrospective politics, philosophy of history, and temporal Manichaeism. *History and Theory, 54*, 333–352.
Black, D. J. (1928). The McNary-Haugen movement. *The American Economic Review, 18*(3), 405–427.
Bugaric, B. (2019). Central Europe's descent into autocracy: A constitutional analysis of authoritarian populism. *International Journal of Constitutional Law, 17*(2), 597–616.
Canovan, M. (2005). *The People*. Polity Press.
Dix, H. R. (1985). Populism: Authoritarian and democratic. *Latin American Research Review, 20*(2), 29–52.
Ferretti, M. (2003). Memory disorder. Russia and Stalinism. *Russian Politics and Law, 41*(6), 38–82.

Finchelstein, F. (2014). Returning populism to history. *Constelations*, *21*(4), 465–482.
Halmai, G. (2019). *Populism, authoritarianism and constitutionalism*. German Law Journal, *20*, 296–313.
Healy, C., & Tumarkin, M. (2011). Social memory and historical justice. *Journal of Social History*, *44*(4), 1007–1019.
Jansen, S. R. (2011). Populist mobilisation: A new theoretical approach to populism. *Sociological Theory*, *29*(2), 75–96.
Jasiewicz, K. (2008). The new populism in Poland. The usual suspects? *Problems of Post-Communism*, *55*(3), 7–25.
Kaltwasser, C. R. (2014). The responses of populism to Dahl's democratic dilemmas. *Political Studies*, *62*, 470–487.
Keane, J. (1994). Nations, nationalism and citizens in Europe. *International Social Science Journal*, *4*, 169–184.
Laclau, E. (1977). *Politics and ideology in Marxist theory*. New Left Books.
Luyckx, J., & Janssens, M. (2020). Ideology and (de)legitimation: The Belgian public debate on corporate restructuring during the Great recession. *Organization*, *27*(1), 110–139.
Mudde, C. (2004). The populist Zeitgeist. *Government and Opposition*, *39*(4), 542–543.
Mueller, J.-W. (2015). Parsing populism. Who is and who is not a populist these days? *Juncture*, *22*(2), 80–89.
Ogino, M. (2015). Sociology of collective memory. In *International encyklopedia of the social and behavioral sciences* (2nd ed., vol. 4). Elsevier.
Olik, J. (2007). *The politics of regret*. Routledge.
Olik, J., & Levy, D. (1997). Collective memory and cultural constraint: Holocaust myth and rationality in German politics. *American Sociological Review*, *62*, 921–936.
Norris, P., & Inglehart, R. (2019). *Cultural backlash: Trump, Brexit, and authoritarian populism*. Cambridge.
Riedel, R. (2017). Populism and its democratic, non-democratic and anti-democratic potential. *Polish Sociological Review*, *3*(199), 287–298.
Riedel, R. (2018). Nativism versus nationalism and populism—Bridging the gap. *Central European Papers*, *6*(2), 18–28.
Riedel, R. (2019). Populism is the only game in town. Poland's illiberal turn as an authoritarian threat. *Sicherheit und Frieden* (Security and Peace), *37*, 24–28.
Rigney, A. (2012). Reconciliation and remembering: (How) does it work? *Memory Studies*, *5*(3), 251–258.
Rosanallon, P. (2006). *Democracy past and future*. Columbia University Press.
Scalon, T. (2000). *What we owe to each other*. Belknap Press.
Sik, D. (2015). Memory transmission and political socialization in post-socialist Hungary. *The Sociological Review*, *63*, 53–71.
Stavrakakis, Y. (2014). The return of the "people": Populism and anti-populism in he shadow of the European crisis. *Constelations an International Journal of Critical and Democratic Theory*, *21*, (2), 505–528.
Weber, M. (1922). Die drei reinen Typen der legitimen Herrschaft. *Preussische Jahrbücher*, *187*, 1–2.
Weiss, H. (2003). A cross-national comparison of nationalism in Austria, the Czech and Slovak Republics, Hungary and Poland. *Political Psychology*, *24*(2), 377–401.

Zhang, T., & Schwartz, B. (1997). Confucius and the cultural revolution: A study in collective memory. *International Journal of Politics, Culture and Society, 11*(2), 189–212.

Zoltan, A. (2020). Re-feudalizing democracy: An approach to authoritarian populism taken from institutional economics. *Journal of Institutional Economics, 16*, 105–118.

CHAPTER 12

The (Almost) Forgotten Elitist Sources of Right-Wing Populism Kaltenbrunner, Höcke and the Distaste for the Masses

Phillip Becher

Elitist "Critiques" of Right-Wing Populism

"The elites are not the problem; at this moment in time, the people are the problem" (Der Bundespräsident, 2016).[1] When then-President Joachim Gauck uttered these words during an interview broadcast on German national television in 2016, in the wake of the results of the Brexit referendum, they were widely regarded as an appropriate and critical remark on the resurgence of nationalist tendencies in Europe, expressing themselves inter alia in the electoral rise of far-right political parties and movements. However, by siding with the elites and identifying the people as 'the problem', the former German head of state not only seemed to confirm the key narrative of right-wing populists, since the *AfD* and similar political parties are now successfully campaigning in many Western countries as the allegedly only true people's opposition against 'the establishment'" (see e.g. Höcke, 2018, p. 185). With his words, Gauck also unwillingly disclosed his own affinity with right-wing political traditions of thought and adopted a strong tendency within liberal (and occasionally within left-wing) critiques of right-wing populism in contemporary journalism and science. The latter often express elitist positions themselves (Jann, 2018, pp. 187–189), seeking to identify subaltern social classes, with their alleged mass attraction to the far-right, as a new "reactionary subject" (Brumlik, 2017) and referring to them as "the mob" ("*Pöbel*") or "pack" (Mielke, 2015).[2] Such harsh remarks help right-wing populists in establishing their pose as

---

P. Becher (✉)
Faculty of Arts and Humanities, University of Siegen, Siegen, Germany
e-mail: becher@phil.uni-siegen.de

© The Author(s), under exclusive license to Springer Nature Switzerland AG 2022
M. Oswald (ed.), *The Palgrave Handbook of Populism*,
https://doi.org/10.1007/978-3-030-80803-7_12

the new and true friends of "the people" (Höcke, 2018, p. 219), just as the "democratic" attire of right-wing populism is taken at face value even by serious scholars (Zúquete, 2015).

Elitist Thought from Historical to New Right

Historian David D. Roberts (1979, p. 308) has pointed out that traditional fascism earned its place in the political family of the right by adopting the anti-democratic and (embourgeoisied) aristocratic stances that advanced conservative ideologists had interwoven at the *fin de siècle*. Canonical thinkers of elite sociology such as Vilfredo Pareto, Gaetano Mosca and Robert Michels proved highly influential for the ideological formation of fascism (see Gregor, 1969, pp. 39–53 for an affirmative but nonetheless informative account). These ingredients offered the programmatic foundation of fascist ideology, whereas its demagogic aspects were derived from other sources.[3] While canonical elite sociology does have a certain diagnostic capability (Jann, 2007, pp. 186–230)—once this is unearthed below the surface of its manifest ideological content—its primary political aims and recommendations with regard to political structures are clear: Elite sociologists defend a pyramidal social order, which they regard as the most effective way of structuring a society ridden with social antagonisms and thus averting democratic claims.

It seems as though the intellectual masterminds of the contemporary far-right have abandoned the "tunnel of fascism" (Tarchi, 1982), leaving explicit nostalgia for the historical fascist regimes mainly to the lunatic fringes, as Armin Mohler (1973, p. 172) himself once put it. What is more, the relationship between traditional fascism and contemporary right-wing populism is much disputed (see Schmidinger, 2011 and de la Torre in this volume). Nevertheless, it is clear that traditional fascism and the new right share an affinity for certain key thinkers—and the latter intellectual movement provides the ideological fabric of right-wing populism (Gessenharter, 2003). When the likes of Pareto, Mosca and Michels gave fascism the "support of the new social sciences" (Sternhell et al., 1995, p. 32), they systematically spelled out what had already been a central part of Nietzsche's critique of culture and his discourse on "decadence" (Carey, 1992, pp. 71–79), as well as Gustave Le Bon's "science fiction" (p. 26), with regard to the relationship between elites and the masses. All of these canonical authors of the right—alongside others such as Julius Evola or José Ortega y Gasset—have become points of reference for the political and intellectual right in recent times. Both the "post-fascist" Italian right (Alleanza Nazionale—Ufficio Internet, 1998) and the German far-right think tank *Institut für Staatspolitik* (Lisson, 2008) make use of this canon. These elitist sources of right-wing populism are, however, largely ignored within current political and academic discussions. Critiques of right-wing populism are usually content with criticising its populism, rather than analyzing its position with the political right.

Almost Forgotten Sources

In order to fill the aforementioned research gap, it is necessary to look at influential ideologists who revived the basic ideas of elitist thought and worked for the programmatic development of an emerging European right-wing populism in the 1970s and 1980s. In what follows, the focus is on one of these key thinkers, Austrian publicist Gerd-Klaus Kaltenbrunner (1939–2011) (see Leggewie, 1987, pp. 178–186; Steber, 2017, pp. 272–286), whose central statements shall be analyzed using the method of ideology critique (Ritsert, 1972) and contextualized with regard to the recent political development of right-wing populism. My critical re-reading of Kaltenbrunner thus traces an almost forgotten intellectual history of current right-wing populism and its echoes in the politics of the contemporary far-right, and provides a transnational perspective, since Kaltenbrunner was and is widely read and received not only in his home country, but also in (West-)Germany. My analysis seeks to stimulate future discussions of the tension emerging from the fact that a political movement poses as the advocate of the "forgotten people" against an alleged "left-wing elite," while an intellectual scene in the background of this movement expresses its distaste for the masses.

Kaltenbrunner's elitist utterings and their contents were favorably reviewed and echoed in the journal of the West-German employers' association (Zürn, 1984, p. 441), which indicates the taste of the upper social strata for this view of society. Kaltenbrunner's words also found their way into the political education of Austria's right-wing populist *Freedom Party* (Kaltenbrunner, 1994—content-wise identical with Kaltenbrunner, 1979, 1982a). Kaltenbrunner's texts have recently been made available again by the publishing policy of the aforementioned *Institut für Staatspolitik* (Kaltenbrunner, 2015, 2017).

Kaltenbrunner's "Education for the Case of Emergency"

Marxist social scientist Reinhard Opitz was clear in his verdict on Kaltenbrunner. Opitz (1985, p. 283) not only viewed Kaltenbrunner as a prime example for the merging of neo-conservatism and the new right, he also suggested that Kaltenbrunner was "a prominent fascist in our midst" (Opitz, 1999, p. 625).[4] Despite Kaltenbrunner's (1973)—feeble—efforts to posthumously distance Vilfredo Pareto as one of the fathers of elite sociology from fascism, Opitz' harsh judgment becomes plausible when reading Kaltenbrunner's seminal essay on elites entitled *Elite—Erziehung für den Ernstfall*. It was first published as a book in 1984, has since been re-printed periodically (most recently in 2017) and is circulated within right-wing groups. With this essay, Opitz (1985, p. 283) argues, Kaltenbrunner changes the rationale of elitism in contemporary conservative thought from a pluralist justification to a "vitalist social-Darwinist" one, deemed fit for imperialism in the era of missiles. However, Kaltenbrunner's summary of basic assumptions of elite sociology and mass psychology, combined with a proposal for a right-wing program for a reconstruction of state and society proves valuable for the far-right in a world after the Cold War, as can be seen later in this paper. Within the political works of his oeuvre, the elite essay marks the beginning of the late period in Kaltenbrunner's work, after his quasi-liberal stance in the 1960s, and after his specific stake in the German-speaking contribution to neo-conservatism in the 1970s (see Elm, 1984, pp. 259–274).[5] Kaltenbrunner (1985, p. 271) himself claimed to belong to the tendency of traditionalism.

This self-categorization establishes a link between him and Italian spiritual racist Julius Evola.[6] Evola was the doyen of traditionalism, whose classification as a fascist thinker is disputed by conservative authors (see e.g. Gregor, 2005, pp. 191–221), but whose position within the fascist universe—he sought actively to further "fascistize'"—cannot be denied (Becher, 2020, pp. 493–498). After World War II, Evola declared that his "principles are only those that before the French Revolution every well-born person considered healthy and normal" (cited in accordance with Furlong, 2011, p. 1). In a similar manner, his fellow traditionalist Kaltenbrunner (2017, p. 8) claims that the word "elite," in line with the "dominating Zeitgeist" of the 1980s, has (in his view falsely) acquired a pejorative connotation, referring to "characteristics that once were circumscribed with words like 'noble', 'select', 'elegant' or 'formidable'." Conversely, Kaltenbrunner paints elite structures as a common phenomenon, crucial for the operation of any given society (pp. 8, 32–33 and 57). This, in turn, renders quasi-pathological almost any objection to elitism. Accordingly, Kaltenbrunner argues that egalitarians, the Marxists among them identified as main protagonists, are driven by their own will to power, simply hidden behind their agitation against inequality, and thus are "wanna-be-elites" (p. 10—see similarly pp. 21–23). They furthermore display "sheer lust for destruction, hatred for form, authority, hierarchy, education, bonding and beauty; the death wish and the resentment of the incapable, especially those incapable of reverence, love and joy" (p. 11). It is not class struggle, he argues, but the Paretian elite circulation that is the driving force of history (p. 57). Differences and inequalities among people, in Kaltenbrunner's thinking, serve as a rationale to proclaim the legitimacy of elites (pp. 9–10). In well-established conservative manner, Kaltenbrunner represents these differences as ineluctable "natural" realities with reference to allegedly indisputable findings of biology, psychology and anthropology (pp. 49–50). Furthermore, Kaltenbrunner argues, elites are necessary because an industrial society cannot survive without them as creative minorities that work in the public interest; hence, "[e]lites [...] belong to the most important capital of a nation" (p. 14). Consequently, the fostering and education of elites should be one of the state's main tasks (p. 13).

Although, in this essay, Kaltenbrunner never explicitly denounces democracy as such and even asserts a principal compatibility of his ideas with democracy as practiced in his time (pp. 34–36), we are well-advised to question what shall remain of democratic ideals and practices once his proposals are implemented: "[in] case of emergency it does not come down to whether democracies are sufficiently democratic, but whether they can fall back on capable, competent and stirring minorities." (p. 58) More bluntly, Kaltenbrunner points out that an "[i]ndustrial society plus democratic constitution does not equal a state that is up to the case of emergency" (p. 15). The "case of emergency," a keyword that reminds the reader of the political thought of Carl Schmitt, is the crucial moment for which elites are to be educated, according to Kaltenbrunner (p. 15). What exactly this case refers to is never defined by Kaltenbrunner and thus remains an empty signifier and a gateway for arbitrariness on part of present or prospective elites. Moreover, Kaltenbrunner (p. 37) evokes the no less nebulous problem of an alleged "ungovernability" in order to show how the crises of Western countries suggest the need of fierce elites (pp. 59–64). Another related phrase Kaltenbrunner coined elsewhere caught the eye of Opitz (1985, p. 287). In an interview, originally published in 1984 in the journal *Mut*, Kaltenbrunner recycled classical anti-bourgeois poses of fascism[7] and elaborated: "[W]orld history is simply not animated by merchants, traders and councilors of commerce, but by fighters, by soldiers, by partisans, in short: by elites that are strong in faith and prepared for the ordeal." (Kaltenbrunner, 1985, p. 271) This is another clear nod to Evola and his "primacy of the warrior's ethic over that of the merchant" (Campi, 1995, p. 121).

According to Kaltenbrunner, one of the reasons Western societies have allegedly become almost "ungovernable" is the power of the political and economic organizations of the working class. The trade unions, with their leaders painted as a counter-elite, are either capable of halting the country and overruling even a majority government (Kaltenbrunner, 2017, p. 48), or they are already in charge of the country, as Kaltenbrunner points out with a nod to Great Britain in the mid-1980s, tapping into a key topos of Thatcherite Toryism (Hall, 1979) that portrayed union bosses as having quasi-dictatorial power (Kaltenbrunner, 2017, p. 42). In this context, Kaltenbrunner delivers a pseudo-empirical inversion of real power relations (p. 43) when he points out the (since then drastically diminished) high percentage of unionists in the mid-1980s among members of the German Bundestag and claims that this allows "at least certain conclusions with regard to the real composition of the West-German power elite." His concerns about parliament, however, are hypocritical, since Kaltenbrunner recommends introducing a "senate-like body" alongside parliament for the decision-making process. This body ought to be composed of experts independent from "the fluctuating fashions and the passions of the mass" (p. 55), thus partly cutting off parliamentary decisions from universal suffrage. In this instance, he quotes Friedrich August von Hayek[8] as inspiration for this model. This is one of the modes that pave the way for a "super-elite" ("*Über-Elite*"), expected to prevail against veto groups, with their particularistic interests and to defend the state against the rise of such interest groups (pp. 43–46).

Björn Höcke: Elitist Content in Populist Shape

One of the most eye-catching and prominent German right-wing populist politicians is Björn Höcke (b. 1972), leader of the Thuringian state association of the *AfD*, whose importance at federal level is enhanced by the uproar his public remarks frequently provoke in the media. Höcke has not only gained notoriety for his demand of a turnaround in commemorative culture with regard to German history (Manucci, 2020, p. 87), he is also closely connected with one of the leading right-wing intellectuals in contemporary Germany, Götz Kubitschek (2019) and his network around the *Institut für Staatspolitik*. Widely viewed as a prototype of a right-wing populist, his 2018 book *Nie zweimal in denselben Fluss*, when read critically in terms of its ideological content, gives ample evidence of a blatant elitism and an anti-democratic stance. The publication, comprising interviews that right-wing artist and writer Sebastian Hennig conducted with Höcke, offers insights into Höcke's political creed in his own words. It allows the reader to watch him unfold right-wing elitist conceptions of state and society of a Kaltenbrunnerian type, although Höcke does not explicitly acknowledge a direct influence of Kaltenbrunner on the formation of his political ideas in this book. However, at the 20th Winter Academy of the *Institut für Staatspolitik* that took place in early 2020, Höcke referred explicitly to Kaltenbrunner's essay on elites and voiced the following recommendation: "Read, read and again read." (cited in accordance with Institut für Staatspolitik, 2020).

Höcke (2018, p. 74) poses as a renegade and free-thinker claiming to "never have been a 'disciple' of anyone," although his book is replete with references to politicians and thinkers of a "big-tent" right, even if Kaltenbrunner as a direct point of reference is absent from the interview. Thus, the reader encounters classical heroes of elite sociology such as Pareto and Michels (p. 227). Furthermore, Höcke's recurring mention of Niccolò Machiavelli and his instructions for successful statesmanship (pp. 153, 225–226 and 286) are indicative of Höcke's propensity for elitist political thought, but it would be erroneous to label the Florentine philosopher as right-wing. The way Höcke evokes Machiavelli's authority owes not so much to the interpretation of Machiavelli as republican *and* a proponent of a progressive bourgeois absolutism (see Kofler, 1971, pp. 191–203), but to the distinctive elitist and vulgar-machiavellist (Gramsci, 1949, p. 9) reading of him. The latter was highly prominent in the European right between the wars, especially within the German Conservative Revolution, Nazism (Freyer, 1938) and Italian fascism (Mussolini, 1924; Prezzolini, 1928).

The elitist base of his political understanding as developed in Höcke's book is highly reminiscent of Kaltenbrunner, who—with or without being explicitly quoted—thus functions as implicit source for current right-wing populism in Höcke's variant: Kaltenbrunner himself simply combined traditional elitist and anti-democratic ideas and applied them to the world of the early 1980s, when his essay was originally written. The enduring interest in Kaltenbrunner's essay indicates an ongoing ideological need for such theorizations in the political camp of the far-right. Höcke's book indicates that he has taken up this historical repertoire and now applies it to the world of the late 2010s and early 2020s. In his most influential work on the *Oligarchical Tendencies of Modern Democracy*, Robert Michels (1968, p. 355) describes the ostensibly eternal circulation of elites with recourse to the following Italian saying: "There is a new conductor, but the music is just the same." Although this is—to say the least—a not sufficiently complex analysis of society, it indeed rings true as concerns of the historical sequence of the ideologues Kaltenbrunner and Höcke, with their respective roles as timely mouthpieces, orchestrating elitist resonances. And yet, while faithfulness to the same basic tune is undeniable, some changes and variations are likewise apparent.

Höcke's populism is one with reservations. While he (2018, p. 133) prefers the term "close to the people" (*"volksverbunden"*) as opposed to "völkisch," he nevertheless expresses a deep-rooted mistrust toward the masses, whose advocate he elsewhere proclaims to be:

> When the populists now speak in the name of the people and position themselves against the establishment, the following problems occur: We as people are already highly fragmented and basically do not put forth a unitary popular will anymore, but rather a dissonant cacophony. In addition, the rising mood of protest outside of the polling booth can become laden with irrationality and become counterproductive [...]. A responsible politician should, despite all proximity to the citizens, not make himself dependent on the swinging moods of the people, all the more so because they might have been manipulated. Even with a reinstated inner union he has to have a sense of the 'volonté generale' and, if need be, make the right decision *against* current public sensibilities and *for* the people[9] – thus not high-handedly and autocratically, but in the sense of serving the people. This distinguishes a statesman from a pure populist, who is always in danger of plummeting ochlocratically. (pp. 235–236—emphasis in the original)

Höcke's usage of the word *ochlocracy* is of special interest because he submits the term to a specific re-signification. He asserts that German party democracy, whose development furthered the descent of political elites (p. 154), has degenerated first into an oligarchy and then to an ochlocracy, which he translates as "rule of the bad" (p. 227). This merely formal qualification says nothing much about the meaning of the term. Although Höcke (p. 225) refers to Polybios' classical differentiation of types of constitutions, he does not engage with this theory. In Polybios' view, democracy finds its negative equivalent in ochlocracy—the Latin term for "mob rule." Scoring a theoretical hat-trick in which party democracy spawns oligarchy (Polybios' negative foil for the—in his view—positively connoted aristocracy), which in turn mysteriously transforms itself into an ochlocracy; Höcke glosses over the specific contempt for the masses that is inscribed in the latter term. He thus signifies "ochlocracy" in a demagogic-manipulative way and combines it with an agitation against the ruling elites, which are marked as globalist, decaying and alien to the concerns of the people and the needs of the nation (see e.g. pp. 219 and 271). *AfD* honorary chairman Alexander Gauland (2019, pp. 16–19) paints a similar picture.

Still, what defines the dominant thread of Höcke's book is a programmatic pro-elitist stance, given that to represent the people's opposition to the now ruling elites is merely a temporary concern to Höcke (2018, p. 232). His case, simply put, is that the currently ruling elite has failed to fulfill the expectations of the political right (see e.g. pp. 154 and 285) and has inhibited the formation of a new elite deemed fit for the Kaltenbrunnerian task (p. 286). Interestingly, he refers to the currently ruling elite as a "political class"—a concept imbued with resentment and rhetoric, with limited analytical value when compared to other concepts of class (Fülberth, 1996). Once the "political class" has been ousted, with the desired help from functioning parts of the old elite in the state apparatuses, which Höcke views as healthy and uncorrupted (Höcke, 2018, pp. 225, 232–233 and 287), and once the "head of the rotting fish" (p. 226), to use Höcke's proverb, has been changed, he proposes a not-so-people-friendly governmental course. Evoking, in bright colors, a national mentality which transfers the energies of popular protest into the construction of "a renewed order" (p. 213), Höcke charges the *AfD* with the task of "refin[ing]" popular protest, integrating it into a "rational and party-political program and strategy" (p. 234). What is more, Höcke refers to Oswald Spengler and his notion that "a people […] is always also what one makes of it" (p. 285) and leaves no doubt that within this context "one" refers to the political leadership. These remarks are reminiscent of the words Benito Mussolini uttered shortly before the March on Rome in 1922, which reveal the aforementioned dependence of fascist thought on elite sociological topoi: "[T]he task of fascism is to make of it [the mass] an organic whole with the Nation in order to have it tomorrow, when the Nation needs the masses, much as the artist needs raw material in order to forge his masterpieces." (cited in accordance with Falasca-Zamponi, 2000, p. 21).

Kaltenbrunner's fierce elites reappear in a different guise in Höcke's book, where he posits the need for a "disciplinarian" and a "demanding and encouraging political elite that re-awakes our people's spirit" (Höcke, 2018, p. 286). Despite allusions to people's sovereignty (p. 277), Höcke subscribes to the primacy of state sovereignty in Carl Schmitt's sense, which becomes particularly clear when he dreams of a state free from the "grasp of societal-particularistic forces" (p. 274), equipped to face the ominous case of emergency as invoked by Höcke, Kaltenbrunner and others in a shared Schmittian tradition.

Conclusion and Prospects

Although the current *AfD* is a right-wing populist, not a classical fascist party, the "tunnel of fascism" seems to have more than one entrance: The vibrant themes of elite sociology and mass psychology combined with Kaltenbrunnerian political proposals within Höcke's argument underline the party's function as a door opener for neo-fascist forces. Themes of this repertoire (without having to be explicitly bound to Kaltenbrunner himself as a source) also receive their echoes outside of party politics and can expect wide resonance. Conservative commentator and best-selling author Douglas Murray, for instance, calls out globalist and technocratic elites for turning their backs on the nation (Fritsch, 2020, p. 34). At the same time, Murray identifies sinister and partly pathological (post-) Marxist agitators as the current driving forces behind social unrest and the "deranged" masses, thus displaying classical themes of elite sociology and mass psychology (Murray, 2019). The far-right has never stopped being anti-democratic. The combination of elitist content and populist shape defines the core of contemporary right-wing populism.

Acknowledgements The author owes his deepest thanks to Katrin Becker for the kindest support imaginable in the preparation of this paper.

Notes

1. All translations of citations of originally non-English sources in the course of this article are the author's, except where stated otherwise.
2. See Wendt (2017) for a critique of this position.
3. See Lenk (1971) for this differentiation between program and demagoguery.
4. See Kaltenbrunner (1980) as an example for a publication in an Italian journal with neo-fascist ties.
5. See however Kofler (1984, pp. 47–50) as a critique of what the author conceives to be Kaltenbrunner's liberal-conservative anthropology in the mid-1970s.
6. See Kaltenbrunner (1982b, pp. 405–413) for his in-depth take on Evola.
7. These poses were, however, only expressions of bourgeois ideology themselves (see Silva, 1975, p. 208).
8. Lucid cases of fierce elitism in liberal political thought were delivered by Hayek's decidedly more conservative fellow liberal Wilhelm Röpke, see e.g. Röpke (1965, pp. 149–150).
9. The original quote reads "*für* das Volk." The German preposition "für," which is italicized in Höcke's book, does not only mean "in favor of," but, in certain contexts, can also denote "instead of," thus signaling an act of replacing one thing for another. In line with this second denotation, Höcke would here be arguing for a disempowerment of the people. The ambiguity in his German wording seems to be no mere coincidence with regard to his basic line of argument.

Literature

Alleanza Nazionale—Ufficio Internet. (1998). Catalogo completo dei libri presenti nella "bibliodestra". Accessed on 28th June 2020 at https://web.archive.org/web/19980120040818fw_/http://alleanza-nazionale.it/politica/bibliodestra_libri.html.
Becher, P. (2020). *Faschismusforschung von rechts. A. James Gregor und die ideozentrische Deutung des italienischen Faschismus*. PapyRossa-Verlag.
Brumlik, M. (2017). Vom Proletariat zum Pöbel. *Blätter Für Deutsche Und Internationale Politik, 62*(1), 56–62.
Campi, A. (1995). What is Italy's national alliance? *Telos, 105*, 112–132.
Carey, J. (1992). *The intellectuals and the masses: Pride and prejudice among the literary intelligentsia, 1880–1939*. Faber and Faber.
Der Bundespräsident. (2016). ARD-Interview "Bericht aus Berlin". Accessed on 28th June 2020 at http://www.bundespraesident.de/SharedDocs/Reden/DE/Joachim-Gauck/Interviews/2016/160619-Bericht-aus-Berlin-Interview.html.
Elm, L. (1984). Der "neue" Konservatismus. Das Desaster von gestern als Leitbild für morgen. In idem (Ed.), *Leitbilder des deutschen Konservatismus* (pp. 227–274). Pahl-Rugenstein Verlag.
Falasca-Zamponi, S. (2000). *Fascist spectacle. The aesthetics of power in Mussolini's Italy*. University of California Press.
Freyer, H. (1938). *Machiavelli*. Bibliographisches Institut.
Fritsch, A. (2020). "Die Grünen sind ein merkwürdiger Kult". Bestseller-Autor im Gespräch. *Tichys Einblick, 5*(1), 32–34.
Fülberth, G. (1996). Herrschende oder "politische" Klasse? *Marxistische Blätter, 34*(1), 30–33.
Furlong, P. (2011). *Social and political thought of Julius Evola*. Routledge.
Gauland, A. (2019). Populismus und Demokratie. *Sezession, 17*(88), 14–20.
Gessenharter, W. (2003). Rechtspopulismus und Neue Rechte in Deutschland. Abgrenzung und Berührungspunkte. In H.-P. Burmeister (Ed.), *Ursachen und Folgen des Rechtspopulismus in Europa* (pp. 113–122). Evangelische Akademie Loccum.
Gramsci, A. (1949). *Note sul Machiavelli sulla politica e sullo stato moderno [1932-1934]*. Einaudi.
Gregor, A. J. (1969). *The ideology of Fascism. The rationale of totalitarianism*. The Free Press/Collier-Macmillan.
Gregor, A. J. (2005). *Mussolini's intellectuals. Fascist social and political thought*. Princeton University Press.
Hall, S. (1979). The great moving right show. *Marxism Today, 23*(1), 14–20.
Höcke, B. (2018). *Nie zweimal in denselben Fluss. Björn Höcke im Gespräch mit Sebastian Hennig* (2nd ed.). Manuscriptum Verlagsbuchhandlung.
Institut für Staatspolitik. (2020). Das war die 20. Winterakademie des IfS. Accessed on 28th June 2020 at https://staatspolitik.de/das-war-die-20-winterakademie-des-ifs.
Jann, O. (2007). *Zur Genealogie des politisch inszenierten Marktdiktats. Wissenspolitologischer Forschungsansatz und Realanalyse*. Tectum.
Jann, O. (2018). Der demokratische Griff nach der Notbremse. Entfremdungsdiskurse und kulturelle Hegemoniekämpfe. In W. Thaa & C. Volk (Eds.), *Formwandel der Demokratie* (pp. 175–195). Nomos.
Kaltenbrunner, G.-K. (1973). Autorenporträt Vilfredo Pareto. *Criticón, 3*(18), 152–154.

Kaltenbrunner, G.-K. (1979). Vorwort des Herausgebers. In idem (Ed.), *Rechtfertigung der Elite. Wider die Anmaßung der Prominenz* (pp. 7–14). Verlag Herder.

Kaltenbrunner, G.-K. (1980). Profeti conservatori. Kierkegaard – Donoso Cortés – Bachofen. *Intervento, 9*(44–45), 113–119.

Kaltenbrunner, G.-K. (1982a). Eliten zur Wahl [1979]. In idem (Ed.), *Was anders werden muss. Stichworte für eine politische Alternative* (pp. 160–167). Verlag Herder.

Kaltenbrunner, G-K. (1982b). *Europa. Seine geistigen Quellen in Porträts aus zwei Jahrtausenden. Band II*. Glock und Lutz.

Kaltenbrunner, G.-K. (1985). "Europäische Eidgenossenschaft". Ein MUT-Gespräch mit Gerd-Klaus Kaltenbrunner [1984]. In idem (Ed.), *Wege der Weltbewahrung. Sieben konservative Gedankengänge* (pp. 259–273). Mut-Verlag.

Kaltenbrunner, G.-K. (1994). Eliten zur Wahl [1979]. In L. Höbelt, A. Mölzer, & B. Sob (Ed.), *Freiheit und Verantwortung. Jahrbuch für politische Erneuerung 1994* (pp. 180–183). Freiheitliches Bildungswerk.

Kaltenbrunner, G.-K. (2015). *Rekonstruktion des Konservatismus [1972]*. Verlag Antaios.

Kaltenbrunner, G.-K. (2017). *Elite. Erziehung für den Ernstfall [1984]* (4th ed.). Verlag Antaios.

Kofler, L. (1971). *Zur Geschichte der bürgerlichen Gesellschaft. Versuch einer verstehenden Deutung der Neuzeit* [1948] (4th ed.). Hermann Luchterhand Verlag.

Kofler, K. (1984). *Der Konservatismus*. VSA-Verlag.

Kubitschek, G. (2019). Dieter Stein las Björn Höcke. *Sezession*. Accessed on 28th June 2020 at https://sezession.de/60376/dieter-stein-las-bjoern-hoecke.

Leggewie, C. (1987). *Der Geist steht rechts. Ausflüge in die Denkfabriken der Wende* (2nd ed.). Rotbuch Verlag.

Lenk, K. (1971). *Volk und Staat. Strukturwandel politischer Ideologie im 19. und 20. Jahrhundert*. Verlag W. Kohlhammer.

Lisson, F. (2008). Vom Wesen der Massen. *Sezession, 6*(24), 14–17.

Manucci, L. (2020). *Populism and collective memory. Comparing Fascist legacies in Western Europe*. Routledge.

Michels, R. (1968). *Political parties. A sociological study of the oligarchical tendencies of modern democracy* [1912]. The Free Press.

Mielke, G. (2015). Jetzige Pegida-AfD zu sehr ‚Pack'-Partei. *SWR Landesschau Aktuell Rheinland-Pfalz*. Accessed on 28th June 2020 at ¦https://web.archive.org/web/20151118161000/http://www.swr.de/landesschau-aktuell/rp/interview-mit-manizer-politikwissenschaftler-gerd-mielke-afd-ist-speerspitze-der-pegida-subkultur/-/id=1682/did=16440736/nid=1682/1f3r3i9/index.html.

Mohler, A. (1973). Der faschistische Stil. In G.-K. Kaltenbrunner (Ed.), *Konservatismus international* (pp. 172–198). Seewald Verlag.

Murray, D. (2019). *The madness of crowds. gender, race, identity*. Bloomsbury Continuum.

Mussolini, B. (1924, November 24). Prelude to Machiavelli. *The living age* (pp. 420–423).

Opitz, R. (1985). Zur Ableitung der Elitekonzeption der "Neuen Rechten" am Beispiel Gerd-Klaus Kaltenbrunners. In *Intelligenz, Intellektuelle & Arbeiterbewegung in Westeuropa. Materialien einer Konferenz des IMSF, 16./17. März 1985* (pp. 283–287). Institut für Marxistische Studien und Forschungen.

Opitz, R. (1999). Juden raus – Türken raus – Demokratie raus. Zur Geschichte und Aktualität reaktionärer und faschistischer Strategien [1984]. In idem (Ed.), *Liberalismus – Faschismus – Integration. Edition in drei Bänden. Band II* (pp. 616–632). BdWi-Verlag.

Prezzolini, G. (1928). *Nicolo Machiavelli. The Florentine.* Brentano's Publishers.

Ritsert, J. (1972). *Inhaltsanalyse und Ideologiekritik. Ein Versuch über kritische Sozialforschung.* Athenäum-Verlag.

Roberts, D. D. (1979). *The syndicalist tradition and Italian Fascism.* Manchester University Press.

Röpke, W. (1965). Jenseits von Angebot und Nachfrage [1958] [excerpt]. In idem (Ed.), *Fronten der Freiheit. Wirtschaft – Internationale Ordnung – Politik* (pp. 117–163). Seewald Verlag.

Schmidinger, T. (2011). Rechtsextremismus und autoritärer Etatismus. Oder warum der neue Rechtsextremismus keine faschistische Herrschaft hervorbringt und trotzdem die Demokratie aushöhlt. In C. Dietrich & M. Schüßler (Eds.), *Jenseits der Epoche. Zur Aktualität faschistischer Bewegungen in Europa* (pp. 48–60). Unrast.

Silva, U. (1975). *Kunst und Ideologie des Faschismus.* S. Fischer Verlag.

Steber, M. (2017). *Die Hüter der Begriffe. Politische Sprachen des Konservativen in Großbritannien und der Bundesrepublik Deutschland, 1945–1980.* Walter de Gruyter.

Sternhell, Z., Sznajder, M., & Asheri, M. (1995). *The birth of fascist ideology. From cultural rebellion to political revolution* [1989] (3rd ed.). Princeton University Press.

Tarchi, M. (1982). Dalla politica al "politico". Il problema di una nuova antropologia. In *Al di là della destra e della sinistra. Atti del Convegno "Costanti ed evoluzioni di un patrimonio culturale"* (pp. 7–29). Libreria Editrice Europa.

Wendt, H. (2017). Proleten, Pöbel, Professoren. Micha Brumlik sucht das reaktionäre Subjekt. *Marxistische Blätter, 55*(3), 10–13.

Zúquete, J. P. (2015). "Free the people". The search for "true democracy". In Western Europe's far-right political culture. In C. de la Torre (Ed.), *The promise and perils of populism* (pp. 231–264). University Press of Kentucky.

Zürn, P. (1984). Auch Eliten sind nicht machbar. *Der Arbeitgeber, 36*(11), 441–442.

Part V

Economic Populism, Inequality & Crises

CHAPTER 13

Populism and the Economics of Antitrust

Aurelien Portuese

THE INTERCONNECTEDNESS OF ECONOMIC AND POLITICAL POPULISMS

Dani Rodrik outlines a distinction between "economic populism" and "political populism". Economic populism, he argues (Rodrik, 2018, p. 196), despises institutional and regulatory restraints on economic policy as narrowing excessively available policy options in the pursuit of the common interest—the "general will" in Rousseauist language (Fleschi, 2004, p. 142; Gidron & Bonikowski, 2014, p. 6; Williams, 2010). This economic populism, however, disliked by economists "for good reason" (Rodrik, 2018, p. 196), is two-fold. The first dimension of economic populism pertains to the attempt to scrap desirable restraints imposed on power-holders to prevent them from pursuing "short-sighted policies" given the high discount rates of politicians (Rodrik, 2018, p. 197). As an illustration, the regulatory constraints underpinning the independence of monetary policies represent a desirable barrier to the prevention of economic populism.

On the contrary, the other dimension of economic populism pertains to the attempt to scrap undesirable restraints entrenched by special-interest groups generating benefits for their members but harm to the entire society (Rodrik, 2018, p. 197). As an illustration, the drawbacks brought about by the very independent monetary policies carried out since the 1980s focusing excessively

---

A. Portuese (✉)
The Schumpeter Project on Competition Policy, Information Technology and Innovation Foundation, Washington, DC, USA
e-mail: aportuese@itif.org

on low inflation are evidence of the excessively delegated rules which harm society. Equally, trade agreement rules captured by special interest groups stifle global welfare inasmuch as institutionalized arbitration mechanisms may only benefit disenfranchised economies in expense of the same global welfare (Cottier, 2018; Rodrik, 2018, p. 198). Economic populism thereby becomes advisable whenever a contextual analysis of rising political populism pairs with excessive and lasting policy autonomy (Rodrik, 2018, pp. 198–199).

Therefore, economic populism is not necessarily bad, Rodrik argues, because the latter set of constraints that economic populism wishes to wave "may in fact be the only way to forestall its much more dangerous cousin, political populism" (Rodrik, 2018, p. 199). Although delineations between economic populism and political populism can undoubtedly be drawn, economic populism may not forestall political populism but rather may foretell the advent of its "dangerous cousin", political populism.

First, economic populism inevitably conduces to political populism (a). Second, political populism is itself the prerequisite to economic populism (b). Therefore, this mutual reinforcing relationship between the two legs upon which populism rests—economic and political variances—is both historically and prospectively confirmed. As a consequence, tackling the economic seeds of political populism appears both necessary and preceding any effective attempt to tackle political populism.

From Political Demagoguery to Economic Policy

The populist style is engrained with demagogic rhetoric made of diatribes against the political establishment—be they politicians, institutions, agencies, political parties. The designation of the political establishment as the cause of all the problems endured by the "plain people" constitutes an essential feature of this political demagoguery (Eatwell & Goodwin, 2018, pp. 44–47). The "true", "pure" or "real" people designated by the discourses of populist leaders represent the voiceless, the silent majority of citizens who feel as though they are unheard, marginalized and powerless under the current political and economic system (Jagers & Walgrave, 2007). This rhetoric targets not only the political elite but also the "global elite" as the threats to the welfare and well-being of the "real people" (Elchardus & Spruyt, 2016, p. 114; Hawkins, 2009, p. 3; Mudde, 2007, p. 23). Populists capitalize on these divides in society through exaggerations and popular anxieties (Hofstadter, 1962). Thus, by designating the global elite as being responsible for the current political and economic lost system of liberal democracies, the populist leaders are able to vilipend the defective political system and the flawed economic policies enforced by this consensual establishment. Against mainstream ideas conveyed by the global establishment, national populists are able to construe a reactionary nostalgia (see Betz & Oswald in this volume).

Against the so-called all-embracing "oligarchy" composed of political and economic elites (Fleschi, 2004, p. 142), populist leaders draw a direct link between the corrupt, self-interested political elite and the economic choices this elite perpetuates against the powerless masses. Removing the political elite thus becomes the prerequisite to foresee changes in economic policies. On the other hand, a more popular economic policy aimed at protecting the "plain people" can only come to the fore thanks to the "new" populist leaders propelled to power because they are charismatic demagogues (Eatwell & Goodwin, 2018, pp. 61–62; Laclau, 1977).

Embodying a "thin ideology" (Stanley, 2008), populism is essentially made of demagogic discourses (Bonikowski, 2016; Elchardus & Spruyt, 2016). The rhetoric of populism is designed to address the difficulties faced by the hard working-class deprived of any consideration by the elite. Right-wing populists stress that these economic difficulties come from globalized threats such as immigration. Left-wing populists lampoon the globalized *laissez-faire* (free trade and free markets). But, as rightly pointed out by Roger Eatwell and Matthew Goodwin (2018, p. 47), "both left-wing and right-wing populists promise to give a voice to ordinary people and curb powerful elites who threaten their interests [...] But [...] it is not always easy to attach neat labels to 'right-wing' populists, who increasingly share concerns about socio-economic inequalities, but in particular how they apply to whites". Unquestionably, the socio-economic resentment of being left behind strongly fuel both right-wing and left-wing populisms so that such distinction, as well as the distinction between economic and political populisms, are not satisfactory (Akkerman et al., 2013). Rather, an inextricable tie can be found between both left-wing and right-wing populisms as well as between economic and political populisms.

From Economic Populism to Political Authoritarianism

Left-wing populism shares with right-wing populism a tendency to erect protectionist barriers (if not attaining autarchy [Pappas, 2016]) which is grounded in xenophobia and nationalism (right-wing populism) or conducive to xenophobic and nationalistic resentments (left-wing populism). Also, political populism (as illustrated by white supremacism, Islamophobia, anti-semitism, anti-elitist, anti-foreigners, anti-intellectuals) can only be addressed through the correction of (sometimes perceived) economic injustices (Magni, 2017; Rodrik, 2017, p. 14). The redistribution of (political and economic) power and wealth shall come from some categories of individuals (e.g. big corporations, wealthy classes...who are the "oligarchs"; e.g. assets of Muslims, Jews, foreigners...who are insufficiently nationalistic) to the "real people"— the "white" in West or the native people in other parts of the world. One can wonder how such tax-and-transfer economic policy (if not upfront seizing) of economic properties from some minorities to the majority of the people can take place without violence and complains legitimately voiced by these minorities. The violation of minorities' rights through violent and authoritarian means appears inevitable (Norris, 2019; Pappas, 2016). Pinochet's regime provides a powerful illustration of the fact that the apparently economically liberal policies required authoritarian means, thereby paving the way for the inevitable political illiberalism (or populism) of this ill-fated regime. Thus, economic populism can only be achieved through a "new" institutional and political system wherein violence and authoritarianism are effectively enforced in order to thwart minorities' rights, to shun the free press and to dodge the deliberative democratic process (Altemeyer, 1996).

Flourishing in a new *Zeitgeist* (Mudde, 2004), across-the-globe populisms are fundamentally illiberal—against parliamentarian democracy as well as against free markets and free trade, against an independent judiciary as well as against free press, free competition and free enterprise, against open-mindedness and cultural diversity and against economic globalization and free innovation (Krastev, 2007; Pappas, 2012). Populism favors nostalgia over innovation, nationalism over regionalism or globalism, referenda over elections, *Realpolitik* over cooperation...—in short, populism scorns the rule of law and prefers discretionary politics.

In conclusion, populism can be defined as a state of illiberal democracy whereby both political liberalism and economic liberalism are eschewed, albeit with variances in degrees and priorities, and whereby charismatically demagogic rulers invoke democratic support via the general will.

Economic Anthropology of Populism

Disenfranchisement and Injustice

The "little guy" feels that the big and powerful have gained from the economic development not on the basis of their merits, not because of their virtues, but rather because of this closely-knit group which self-protects their own interests at the expense of the voiceless majority (Kazin, 1995, p. 1; Magni, 2017; Rodrik, 2017). This group to blame has got a name: the elite (Geahigan, 1985; Hayward, 1996; Iakhnis et al., 2018; Smith, 1981, 1982). As there cannot be populism without a foe, the elite constitutes the necessary and "basic antagonism" (Judis, 2016, p. 15) needed for populists who perceive it as a powerful group of conspirators doing the people harm.

Populism can only flourish in times of economic crisis—thereby evidencing the economic roots of any populism (Eichengreen, 2018, p. x; Judis, 2016). These economic crises weigh heavily on households which cannot make ends meet and who undeniably start thinking that redistributive justice from the wealthy to the middle-popular classes is ineffective and yet imperative (Akkerman et al., 2013). Middle-income classes believe that populist leaders are the only democratic candidates able to address their concerns by tackling the wealthy and big corporations (Lowndes, 2017). Middle-income citizens feel disenfranchised by the market economy which has not delivered on the promises formulated by the political elite. Be it in Europe or in the US, or in any Western democracies, the market economy, it is believed, has failed to ensure what Amartya Sen would describe as "capabilities" (Pettit, 2001; Robeyns, 2011; Sen, 1985, 1992, 1999): powerless and voiceless, the hard-working middle class has not yet reaped off the expected benefits of global capitalism (Peters, 2017).

As populism thrives upon the "broken promises of democracy", it can be argued that economic populism thrives upon the broken promises of capitalism. Laypeople feel disenfranchised due to their inability to compete with low-income developing countries which represent some "social dumping" and threaten their standards of living. Evidenced by numerous polls, this shared feeling constitutes the crux of the mobilizing power upon which populism prospers (Akkerman et al., 2013; Woertz, 2017). Unsurprisingly, this economic disenfranchisement pertains to the very essence of justice—the situation faced, or likely to be faced, by hard-working middle-class individuals is perceived as unjust (Gidron & Bonikowski, 2014). This injustice lays upon a remarkably simple, yet fundamental, principle of the market economy—competition based on merits. This perceived lack of meritorious competition is double-edged: it rests upon the unfair competition brought about by both external and internal forces.

On the external drivers of unfair competition, foreign workers are considered not to be competing on the basis of their merits but through a regulatory race to the bottom, and thus, an unfair competition on social and environmental standards (Lamp, 2018; Paul, 1994, 2015)—so-called "social dumping" (Elmslie & Milberg, 1996, p. 51; Rodrik, 2018, pp. 13–16). Gains from trade are hypothetically redistributed in order to compensate the losers—*i.e.* those unable to cope up with capital intensive technology, innovation-driven business models and cost-savings business strategies (Lamp, 2018; Shaffer, 2019). However, this hypothetical compensation does effectively never occur in a sovereign States-dominated global community wherein no such tax-and-transfer has ever been designed overall, let alone be enforced by the authority of law (Paul, 2015; Rodrik, 2018, pp. 10–12). Cottier (2018, p. 8) argues that the "surge of populism can only be explained by fatal omissions in past domestic and international policy, and it would be expected that these omissions will be proactively addressed by the new bilateralism", as opposed to the mainstream multilateralism prevalent until now. The unfair competition that "social dumping" constitutes provides for voters the chief rationale to resort to populist answers—a stringent reality particularly within the European Union (Alber & Standing, 2000; Bernaciak, 2012; Eurofound, 2016; Mosley, 1995).

On the internal drivers of unfair competition, wealthy individuals and big corporations are increasingly perceived as taking the lion's shares of the national economy, of fully benefitting from the global economy, without reasonable treble gains being passed onto lower income classes and onto small businesses. The populist backlash essentially results from the sense of economic injustice as illustrated by the famous 1892 Omaha Platform with which the US People's Party (*"The Populists"*) stated:

> We charge that the controlling influences dominating both these parties have permitted the existing dreadful conditions to develop without serious effort to prevent or restrain them. Neither do they now promise us any substantial reform. They have agreed together to ignore, in the coming campaign, every issue but one. They propose to drown the outcries of a plundered people with the uproar of a sham battle over the tariff, so that capitalists, corporations, national banks, rings, trusts, watered stock, the demonetization of silver and the oppressions of the usurers may all be lost sight of. They propose to sacrifice our homes, lives, and children on the altar of mammon; to destroy the multitude in order to secure corruption funds from the millionaires.

From the second half of the nineteenth century populism to the New Deal's form of "neo-Populism", America has experienced decades of tradition of economic populism which has vividly been revived by Donald Trump as a campaigner and as a President (Inglehart & Norris, 2016). By 2016, with Trump's election, "America was thus ripe for a populist insurrection. Growth had slowed. Inequality has risen. Globalization and automation heightened insecurity for workers lacking vocational training, trade union funds, or an extensive insurance state on which to fall back. A financial crisis undermined faith in the competence and integrity of decision makers" (Eichengreen, 2018, p. 117).

More generally, in all Western democracies, the sentiment of disenfranchisement due to economic injustice caused by the big and powerful (corporations and individuals) is constitutive of the main divides exploited by the populists: small versus big, us versus others (Gidron & Bonikowski, 2014).

Small v Big, Us v Others

In this quest for a greater decentralization of economic and political power as well as for a more forceful redistributive justice system, the defense of small firms appears to be the best way to fulfill the needs of the laypeople against those of the detached powerful CEOs and other corporate globalists.

Indeed, economic populism has consistently thrived upon the opposition between small shops versus big corporations, between local boutiques versus globalized firms. Economic populism is currently being revived upon these premises. One of the most vocal campaigners of the 1890 US elections, the year of the passing of the Sherman Act, Mrs. Mary Elizabeth Lease of Kansas is reputed to have said:

> Wall Street owns the country. It is no longer a government of the people, by the people and for the people, but a government of Wall Street, by Wall Street and for Wall Street. The great common people of this country are slaves, and monopoly is the master (…) The parties lie to us and the political speakers misled us (…) The common people are robbed to enrich their master (…) There are thirty men in the United States whose aggregate wealth is over one of one-half billion dollars. There are half a million looking for work (…) We

want money, land and transportation. We want the abolition of National Banks, and we want the power to make loans direct to the government (...) The people are at bay, let the bloodhounds of money who have dogged us thus far beware. (quoted in Hicks, 1961, p. 160)

Historically, economic populism championed the anti-bigness sentiment under the veil of protecting small boutiques and farmers in disenfranchised local, rural areas. The thrust of US populism can be recapped, since the birth of the populist party in late nineteenth century, in the words of Ignatius L. Donnelly who wrote the preamble of the St Louis and Omaha Platforms which created the populist party. Indeed, he targeted the so-called plutocrats whose "colossal fortunes, unprecedented in the history of the world, while their possessors despite the republic and endanger the liberty" at the expense of farmers and workers whose "fruits of the toil of millions were boldly stolen" (quoted in Hicks, 1961, p. 405). The essential idea was that of powerful individuals and corporations to be dismantled for the laypeople to make their ends meet. Against big corporate powers, the populist proposals were not so much about breaking up companies but rather the nationalization of the corporations' assets (with a clear emphasis on railroads companies' assets): "the land, including all the natural resources of wealth, is the heritage of all the people and should not be monopolized for speculative purposes, and alien ownership of land should be prohibited" (St Louis Platform, February 1892).

Today, populisms vilipend bigness from all fronts. In the US, Trump has ironically claimed that "politicians, the big donors and the special interests have bled this country dry and stripped our middle class and stripped our companies of its jobs and its wealth" (Trump, 2016); the British populist party the UKIP stated that "UKIP is not in the pockets of big businesses and we will make them pay their way" (UKIP, 2017); and the French Front National argued that "the big ones get everything and its always less for the little people and the middle classes" due to the "globalist and multiculturalist ideology" (Ivaldi & Mazzoleni, 2019). The "producerist" features of populist movements exemplify the virtues of small businesses and ordinary entrepreneurs as opposed to the vices of big businesses (Ivaldi & Mazzoleni, 2019, p. 22).

Economic Anthropology of Antitrust

Populist Roots of Antitrust

"Be afraid of economic 'bigness'. Be very afraid" argues Tim Wu (2018a) as a leading figure of the resurgence of populist antitrust made possible by today's big tech companies (Khan, 2016, 2017, 2018, 2019a, 2019b; Khan & Chopra, 2020; Khan & Vaheesan, 2017). This populist tradition of antitrust originates from mid-nineteenth century America's industrialization which spurred innovation and triggered what was considered as "cut-throat competition" for farmers and small shops: the advent of railroads and refrigerated wagons were disruptive innovations which enabled transportation costs to tumble, thus allowing for price competition with geographical areas once insulated to emerge. Products and services were delivered to rural areas where farmers started to experience unmatchable competition. The innovation, capital investments and corporate power required for the establishment of a network of railroads and of pipelines for the booming oil industry started to dwarf the trivial economic power of dispersed farmers. Farmers felt the need to gather, to consolidate their powers—both economically and politically. Thus, they formed Alliances in different states, with different names, with different priorities, even gathering workers from urban areas with the Knights of Labor.

These grassroots' movements have quickly identified the corporate power of big firms as the source of their troubles: these big corporations grew exponentially, either by internal or by external growth, and abused their corporate power to outcompete farmers with low prices and greater quantity. Thereby, contrary to shared beliefs, the agrarian revolt—the Farmer Movement—which predated the call for aggressive antitrust policy—the Trust Movement—has not emerged out of a lack of competition from the big companies (or trusts), but rather, these movements emerged out of excessive competition—the so-called "cut-throat competition".

Be that as it may, the Trust Movement flowing out of the Farmers Movement had to have both a political embodiment and a legislative materialization. The political reality of the Trust Movement came to the fore with the "People's Party" (also designated as "The Populists"): this political party based on populists premises (anti-elite, anti-bigness, anti-free market, anti-representative democracy) had an influential role in the popular demand for introducing federal antitrust laws. The trust movement had already achieved to have twelve US States to pass State antitrust laws (Wu, 2018a). Due to the jurisdictional limits inherent to States laws especially when the matter was to break up the Rockefeller's Standard Oil Trust located in multiple States, the populists' representatives claimed that only federal antitrust laws could be of any effect to clamp down the powerful big trusts.

The Populist Revolt has been "defused by freight rate regulation, interest rate regulation, and changes to the gold standard, limited reforms that went some way towards addressing the complaints of farmers and others, together with political reforms such as the referendum processes and direct election of senators advocated by the Populist Party" (Eichengreen, 2018, p. 145). Not less importantly, this Populist Revolt was defused by antitrust regulation: the Sherman Act of 1890. Self-motivated by personal political revenge, Senator John Sherman introduced a Bill at the Senate entitled "A bill to protect trade and commerce against unlawful restraints and monopolies". The practice of antitrust enforcement has moved away from populism (anti-bigness and legally formalistic assessments) towards a more economic approach to antitrust with the advent of the Chicago School of antitrust in the 60s in the US and in the 90s in Europe (Kovacic, 2003).

Antitrust Cycles

Similar to business cycles, antitrust enforcement has experienced "cycles" under which more economically rational antitrust enforcement has gained and lost importance at different periods (Wright et al., 2019). Interpreted as an adequate vehicle to foster economic efficiency through the consumer welfare standard, antitrust policies have gained more economic expertise at the expense of political partisanship and economically unsound legal formalism. Decades of improvement in designing and enforcing antitrust policies have enabled both US antitrust laws and EU competition laws to export their regimes successfully all over the world, for the benefit of the competitiveness of the world economy (Crane, 2018; Kovacic, 2003).

However, the rise of big tech companies and its populist reactions against globalization have benefitted those who advocate for a return to the early years of the Sherman Act (Khan, 2016, 2018, 2019a, 2019b; Wu, 2018b). Economic experts have been excessively heard, legal standards and presumptions have been excessively discarded, and most importantly, markets have excessively concentrated at the expense of the laypeople and of the small shops the new antitrust populists argue (Khan, 2019a, 2019b; Wu, 2018a, 2018b). The focus should therefore no longer be on the evidence of the consumer harm in order to allege an anticompetitive conduct, but instead the focus should be on how legitimate the claims of smaller rivals are and how much can we ensure economic decentralization of power through breakups and blocked mergers (Wright & Portuese, 2020). The economic insights learnt for many years need to be discarded as inapplicable to today's concentrated economy, antitrust populists argue (Wright & Portuese, 2020). This powerful line of advocacy casting away economic experts lies at the heart of economic populism more generally. Some scholars legitimately foresee the coming fall the current populist cycle of antitrust (Crane, 2018; Wright et al., 2019).

TACKLING ANTITRUST POPULISM

Tackling antitrust populism will be achieved by proposing as alternative a robust antitrust policy (Portuese, 2020). Such robust antitrust policy will be situated within the classical liberal framework which is deemed to be the least detrimental system given the informational costs and knowledge problem inherent to antitrust enforcement. Thus, a robust antitrust policy would take seriously the information problem and would ensure that the burden of proof of evidencing the need for regulatory interventionism remains to the plaintiffs (Portuese, 2020).

Anti-experts and the Holistic View

As a premise for tackling antitrust populism, there is a need to rehabilitate the value of experts in antitrust. But these experts are the prime targets of populists

(Portuese, 2020; Schrepel, 2019, p. 61). Populists are aware of the fact that experts are massively scorned by the laymen (Cheng & Hsiaw, 2017). Indeed, people are said to have had "enough of experts". The anti-expert stance of populism dates back to the famously named nineteenth century US political party "Know-Nothing Party" to Brexiteers' famous quote (Michael Gove said *"I think the people in this country have had enough of experts"*, Wallace, 2019) through Trump's former head of the transition team Myron Ebell who once claimed that "the people of America have rejected the expertariat, and I think with good reason because I think the expertariat have been wrong about one thing after another, including climate policy" (quoted Lamberts, 2017). Such "tyranny of experts" (Lieberman, 1970) has been regularly stigmatized as being one of the causes of social problems.

This anti-experts/anti-elite comeback from a rationally designed regulatory framework towards a politically laden antitrust enforcement is currently being praised on both sides of the Atlantic from people with very different backgrounds—from European Ministers to US scholars (Schrepel, 2019; Vaheesan, 2014; Wright & Portuese, 2020). The rationale underpinning populist antitrust to embrace this holistic perspective lies upon the demise of the weight of economic analysis in general (ING, 2017; Romer, 2020), and in antitrust enforcement in particular after a rise of antitrust economics, the populist backlash advocate for a return to antitrust politics, thanks to the weakening of the antitrust agencies' independence (Giles, 2019; Portuese, 2020; Wallace, 2019). Having departed from the governmental grips in order to acquire a hardly fought independence, antitrust agencies may be subject, according to antitrust populists, to experience the same drawbacks which justified the rise of their independence some decades ago (Schrepel, 2019). Epitomized by the "death of expertise" (Nichols, 2017) in favor of the reign of (party-)politics, this new cycle in antitrust enforcement is nothing other than a return to the governmental grips on antitrust agencies—and onto any regulatory agencies sooner or later since the holistic view of populists cannot admit lack of political control. Richard Hofstadter (1966, p. 34) once wrote that "in the original American populistic dream, the omnicompetence of the common man was fundamental and indispensable. It was believed that he could, without much special preparation, pursue the professions and run the government". Today, the laypeople's perceived omnicompetence entitle themselves to shape antitrust enforcement without further need of experts, for the benefits of a strongly felt popular re-empowerment but highly, probably for the harm of the consumers. Indeed, a hostile antitrust enforcement fraught to political considerations would irremediably neglect the consumer welfare—*i.e.* the standard of reasoning in competition policies (Schrepel, 2019). The appeal for populism appears to make acceptable those economic losses for the sake of perceived political gains of re-empowerment (Gidron & Bonikowski, 2014).

Antitrust experts (mostly, economists) are discarded by populists because of their low esteem among laypeople because they gained an "outsized influence" in antitrust matters (Vaheesan, 2014, p. 400). This anti-expert view justifies the holistic perspective taken by antitrust populists: antitrust agencies need to be in full control of elected politicians otherwise there would be a "democratic deficit" in antitrust enforcement (Crane, 2008; Khan, 2019b, p. 778). This tenet presupposes that antitrust agencies would lose their hard-fought independences from party-politics (Crane, 2008). Indeed, populism is essentially holistic in the sense that populists want the rulers to be in full control of economic and political leeway in order to fully represent the "real people". No counter-power, checks and controls are necessary otherwise these are perceived as devised in order to protect some (elitist) interests against the popular interests. Indeed, "in addition to being antielitist, populists are always antipluralist: populist claim that they, and only they, represent the people (...) The core claim of populism is thus a moralized form of antipluralism (...) There can be no populism, in other words, without someone speaking in the name of the people as a whole". Rosenblum (2008, pp. 25–59) interestingly recaps this idea of holism as fitting the description of any populisms: "Partisans of holism confront both the political pluralism that is the universal circumstance of parties and the actuality of parties. Their party is a means to erase or repress the rest". Antipartisans, populists would suffer no internal restraints made of separation of powers, regulatory independences', judicial reviews, institutionalized opposition groups, labor unions, and a free press.

How can holism be of relevance to antitrust populism? The holistic apprehension of populists antitrust entails that the existential delegation of powers handed over to autonomous regulatory agencies appears to be both immoral and inefficient—immoral because the will of the people must be represented by elected populist politicians who are the only one bestowed with popular confidence, and inefficient because the unnecessary delegation of powers multiplies the number of actors, the deliberative process, and thereby the length of time needed for decisions to be adopted (Khan, 2019b, p. 778). Consequently, the whole rationale for antitrust agencies to be insulated from party politics appears to become meaningless for antitrust populists.

Indeed, the holistic perspective to antitrust enforcement derails the excess of "technocracy antitrust" (Crane, 2008)—bureaucrats turned enforcers with unaccountable delegation of powers—against "populist antitrust"—democratically elected politicians turned enforcers with direct popular accountability (Khan, 2019b). This blunt opposition appears to be entrenched between an unaccountable technocratic antitrust enforcement made of experts and rational decision-making process with a fully accountable popular antitrust enforcement made of elected politicians receptive of the people's changing priorities and needs (Crane, 2018). Tackling antitrust populism therefore also means defending antitrust agencies' independences and the role of experts in these agencies—party-politics and political agenda must be kept at bay from the functioning of antitrust agencies (Crane, 2018).

Anti-unfair Competitiveness—The Industrialist Perspective

Antitrust populism epitomizes a fight against bigness and against experts. It also rests upon a much more legitimate, because economically substantiated, claim that global competition has become unfair. Global competition takes place, it is argued, on unfair premises: trade agreements have been inadequately designed in order to tackle issues of "social dumping" of regulatory standards and unfair competition through State-sponsored enterprises or excessive State aids (Meyer, 2019; Shaffer, 2019). Meyer (2019, pp. 36–37) aptly recaps the history of trade agreements on laypeople by saying that the

> theory of 'trickle down trade liberalization' did not bear fruit. The liberalized international trading system persistently punished certain individuals and communities, and the government never stepped in with assistance adequate to the challenge. Instead, domestic economic policies in many developed countries, including the United States, failed to deal with economic inequality. In response, voters in developed countries world-wide began to take international trade liberalization and the institutions that support it hostage: negotiate trade agreements that create a more equitable, sustainable international economic system or we will vote to tear the entire house down. The Trump trade wars and Britain's hurtle toward an immediate and likely highly damaging exit from the European Union are the most visible examples of this crisis, but the strength of far-right parties across Europe testify to the breadth of the sentiment.

Unfair competition out of trade agreements spurs radical popular reactions to which only populists can answer with matching radicalism (Peters, 2017). Thus, the current fate of the globalized economy with a regulatory race to the bottom for the living standards of individuals has fueled, and is likely to continue fueling, economic populism in developed countries (Paul, 1994, 2015; Peters, 2017; Shaffer, 2019). For, there cannot be sound antitrust enforcement and a healthy world competition if countries open trade on unfair competition basis. Fair competition does not necessarily imply income equality: Rodrik rightly points out that "people understand that unequal abilities, effort, or moral deservingness imply that a fair distribution in society would also be unequal" (Rodrik, 2018). Unfair competition is unbearable because unmeritorious rivalry takes place between unashamed cheaters. This needs to be fixed unless populism will continue to prosper. But, the current ill-fated complementarity between antitrust rules and trade rules is partly due to the neglect by the WTO to competition rules since 2004 of the Working Group on the Interaction between Trade and Competition Policy (WGTCP) created in 1996. The WTO indeed has announced that:

> In July 2004 the General Council of the WTO decided that the interaction between trade and competition policy (in addition to investment, and transparency in government procurement) would no longer form part of the Work Programme set out in the Doha Ministerial Declaration and therefore that no

work towards negotiations on any of these issues will take place within the WTO during the Doha Round. (WTO, 2020)

What have we done since 2004 to substitute this blatant vacuum and to better address the issues of unfair competition at the trade level with respect to domestic antitrust rules? Not much, and quite nothing (Paul, 2015; Shaffer, 2019). Peoples can be willing to engage in international competition but only on the basis of "fair trade": regulatory dumping provides for unfair competition and spurs populism (Rodrik, 2019). We need a bold multilateral reform agenda in order to make world antitrust and world trade agreements functioning in symbiosis so that both competition can be maximized and free trade can be further liberalized. The absence of an ambitious world antitrust policy, let alone, agency, can only contribute to both deterrence in embracing free trade and difficulties in keeping at bay populism. In that regard, the bilateral initiative between the EU and China to work on ensuring competition on the merits between the two markets is laudable. Indeed, the Memorandum of Understanding on "a dialogue in the area of the State aid control regime and the Fair Competition Review System" signed on April 9, 2019 is a step in the right direction in absence of multilateral initiatives (DG Comp, 2019). Antitrust populism is no answer domestically in any event but can continue to thrive in the future also because of the legitimate needs to better integrate fair market access provisions into free trade agreements.

LITERATURE

Akkerman, A., Mudde, C., & Zaslove, A. (2013). How populist are the people? Measuring populist atittudes in voters. *Comparative Political Studies, 47*(9), 1324–1353.

Alber, J., & Standing, C. (2000). Social dumping, catch-up or convergence? Europe in a comparative global context. *Journal of European Social Policy, 10*(2), 99–119.

Altemeyer, B. (1996). *The authoritarian specter*. Harvard University Press.

Bernaciak, M. (2012). *Social dumping: Political catchphrase or a threat of labour standards?* (Working Paper 2012/06), Brussels, ETUI.

Bonikowski, B. (2016). Three lessons of contemporary populism in Europe and the United States. *The Brown Journal of World Affairs, 23* (Fall/Winter), 9–24.

Cheng, I-H., & Hsiaw, A. (2017). *Distrust in experts and the origins of disagreement* (Tuck School of Business Working Paper No. 2864563).

Cottier, T. (2018). *Trade policy in the age of populism: Why the new bilateralism will not work* (Brexit: The International Legal Implications, Paper No. 12—February 2018). Centre for International Governance Innovation.

Crane, D. (2008). Technocracy and antitrust. *Texas Law Review, 86*, 1174–1177.

Crane, D. (2018). Antitrust's unconventional politics. *Virginia Law Review Online, 104*, 118–135.

DG Comp. (2019). *Memorandum of understanding on a dialogue in the area of the state aid control regime and the fair competition review system*. Signed in Brussels on the 9th of April 2019. Accessible at: https://ec.europa.eu/competition/international/bilateral/mou_china_2019.pdf.

Eatwell, R., & Goodwin, M. (2018). *National populism*. Pelican Books.
Eichengreen, B. (2018). *The populist temptation*. Oxford University Press.
Elachardus, M., & Spruyt, B. (2016). Populism, persistent republicanism and declinism: An empirical analysis of populism as a thin ideology. *Government and Opposition, 51*(1), 111–133.
Elmslie, B., & Milberg, W. (1996). Free trade and social dumping: Lessons from the regulation of us interstate commerce. *Challenge, 39*(3) (May–June), 46–52.
Eurofound. (2016). *Social dumping*. Accessible at: https://www.eurofound.europa.eu/observatories/eurwork/industrial-relations-dictionary/social-dumping.
Fleschi, C. (2004). *Fascism, populism and the French Fifth Republic: In the shadow of democracy*. Palgrave.
Geahigan, G. (1985). The elitist-populist controversy: A response to Ralph Smith. *Studies in Art Education, 26*(3), 178–180.
Gidron, N., & Bonikowski, B. (2014). *Varieties of populism: Literature review and research agenda* (Weatherhead Center Working Paper Series, 13–0004).
Giles, C. (2019, November 3). Economists among 'least trusted professionals' in UK. *Financial Times*.
Hawkins, K. A. (2009). Is Chavez populist? Measuring populist discourse in comparative perspective. *Comparative Political Studies, 42*(8), 1040–1067.
Hayward, J. (1996). *Elitism, populism, and European politics*. Clarendon Press.
Hicks, J. D. (1961). *The populist revolt*. University of Nebraska Press.
Hofstadter, R. (1962). *Anti-intellectualism in American Life*. Vintage Books.
Hofstadter, R. (1966). *Anti-intellectualism in American Life*. New York, NY: Vintage Books.
Iakhnis, E., Rathbun, B., Reifler, J., & Scotto, T. J. (2018). Populist referendum: Was 'Brexit' an expression of nativist and anti-elitist sentiment? *Research & Politics, 5*(2), 1–7.
ING. (2017). *ING-economics network survey of the public's understanding of economics*. Accessible at: https://www.economicsnetwork.ac.uk/sites/default/files/Ashley/IN-EN%20Survey%20Report%20May%202017.pdf.
Inglehart, R. F., & Norris, P. (2016). *Trump, Brexit, and the rise of populism: Economic have-nots and cultural backlash* (Harvard Kennedy School Faculty Research Working Paper Series. RWP16–026).
Ivaldi, G., & Mazzoleni, O. (2019). Economic populism and producerism: European right-wing populist parties in a transatlantic perspective. *Populism, 2*(1), 1–28.
Jagers, J., & Walgrave, S. (2007). Populism as political communication style: An empirical study of political parties' discourse in Belgium. *European Journal of Political Research, 46*(3), 319–345.
Judis, J. B. (2016). *The populist explosion: How the great recession transformed American and European politics*. Columbia Global Reports.
Kazin, M. (1995). *The populist persuasion: An American history*. Cornell University Press.
Khan, L. (2016). Amazon's antitrust paradox. *Yale Law Journal, 126*, 710.
Khan, L. (2017). The ideological roots of America's market power. *Yale Law Journal Forum, 127*, 960.
Khan, L. (2018). The new brandeis movement: America's antimonopoly debate. *Journal of European Competition Law & Practice, 9*(3), 131–132.
Khan, L. (2019a). The separation of platforms and commerce. *Columbia Law Review, 119*(4), 973–1098.

Khan, L. (2019b). Comment on Daniel A. Crane: A premature postmortem on the Chicago school of antitrust. *Business History Review, 93*, 777–779.

Khan, L., & Chopra, R. (2020). The case for 'unfair methods of competition' rulemaking. The *University of Chicago Law Review, 87*, 357–379.

Khan, L., & Vaheesan, S. (2017). Market power and inequality: The antitrust counterrevolution and its discontents. *Harvard Law & Policy Review, 11*, 235.

Kovacic, W. E. (2003). The modern evolution of U.S. competition policy enforcement norms. *Antitrust Law Journal, 71*(2), 378.

Krastev, I. (2007, September 18). The populist moment. *Eurozine.*

Laclau, E. (1977). *Politics and ideology in Marxist Theory; capitalism—fascism—populism*. Verso.

Lamberts, R. (2017, May 12). Distrust of experts happen when we forget they are human beings. *The Conversation.*

Lamp, N. (2018, December 3). How should we think about the winners and losers from globalization? Three narratives and their implicatons for the redesign of international economic agreements (*Queen's University Legal Research Paper, No. 2018-102*).

Lieberman, J. K. (1970). *The tyranny of the experts: How professionals are closing the Open society*. Walker.

Lowndes, J. (2017). *Populism in the United States*. In C. R. Kaltwasser, P. Taggart, P. O. Espejo, & P. Ostiguy (Eds.), *The Oxford handbook of populism* (pp. 232–247). Oxford University Press.

Magni, G. (2017). It's the emotions, Stupid! Anger about the economic crisis, low political efficacy, and support for populist parties. *Electoral Studies, 50*, 91–102. https://www.sciencedirect.com/science/article/abs/pii/S026137941730080X.

Meyer, T. (2019). The law and politics of socially inclusive trade. *University of Illinois Law Review, 2019*, 32–47.

Mosley, H. (1995). The 'social dumping' threat of European integration: A critique. In B. Unger & F. van Waarden (Eds.), *Convergence or diversity? Internationalization and economic policy response* (pp. 182–199). Avebury.

Mudde, C. (2004). The populist zeitgeist. *Government and Opposition, 39*(4), 542–563.

Mudde, C. (2007). *Populist radical right parties in Europe*. Cambridge University Press.

Nichols, T. (2017). *The death of expertise: The campaign against the established knowledge and why it matters*. Oxford University Press.

Norris, P. (2019). Varieties of populist parties. *Philosophy and Social Criticism, 45*(9–10), 981–1012.

Pappas, T. S. (2012). *Populism emergent: A framework for analyzing its contexts, mechanics, and outcomes* (Working Paper. Robert Schuman Centre for Advanced Studies). European University Institute.

Pappas, T. S. (2016). Modern populism: Research advances, conceptual and methodological pitfalls, and the minimal definition. In W. R. Thompson (Ed.), *Oxford Research Encyclopedia of Politics*. Oxford University Press. Date of access 15 April 2020. https://oxfordre.com/politics/view/10.1093/acrefore/9780190228637.001.0001/acrefore-9780190228637-e-17.

Paul, J. R. (1994). Free trade, regulatory competition and the autonomous Market Fallacy. *Columbia Journal of European Law, 1*(1), 29–62.

Paul, J. R. (2015). The cost of free trade. *The Brown Journal of World Affairs, 22*(1), 191–209.

Pettit, P. (2001). Capability and freedom: A defense of Sen. *Economics and Philosophy, 17*, 1–20.

Peters, M. A. (2017). The end of the neoliberal globalization and the rise of authoritarian populism. *Educational Philosophy and Theory, 50*(4), 323–325.

Portuese, A. (2020). Beyond antitrust populism: Robust Antitrust. *Journal of Economic Affairs, 40*(2), 237–258.

Robeyns, I. (2011). The capability approach. *The Stanford encyclopedia of philosophy*, Eward N. Zalta (Ed.). https://plato.stanford.edu/cgi-bin/encyclopedia/archinfo.cgi?entry=capability-approach.

Rodrik, D. (2017). Populism and the Economics of Globalization. *NBER Working Paper 23559*, June 2017. https://www.nber.org/papers/w23559.

Rodrik, D. (2018). Is populism necessarily bad economics? *AEA Papers and Proceedings, 108*, 196–199.

Rodrik, D. (2019). Globalization's Wrong Turn. And How It Hurt America. *Foreign Affairs, 98*(4), July/August 2019. https://drodrik.scholar.harvard.edu/files/dani-rodrik/files/globalizations_wrong_turn.pdf.

Romer, P. (2020, March/April) The dismal kingdom. Do economists have too much power? *Foreign Affairs*.

Rosenblum, N. L. (2008). *On the side of the angels: An appreciation of parties and partisanship*. Princeton University Press.

Schrepel, T. (2019). Antitrust without romance. *NYU Journal of Law & Liberty, 13*, 326.

Sen, A. (1985). *Commodities and capabilities*. North-Holland.

Sen, A. (1992). *Inequality reexamined*. Sage and Harvard University Press

Sen, A. (1999). *Development as freedom*. Knopf.

Shaffer, G. (2019). Retooling trade agreements for social inclusion. *University of Illinois Law Review, 2019*, 1–44.

Smith, R. A. (1981). Elitism versus populism: A question of quality. *Art Education, 34*(4), 5–6.

Smith, R. A. (1982). Elitism versus populism: The continuing debate. *The Journal of Aesthetic Education, 16*(1), 5–10.

Stanley, B. (2008). The thin ideology of populism. *Journal of Political Ideologies, 13*(1), 95–110.

Trump, D. (2016). *Remarks at the Central Florida Fairgrounds in Orlando*. Florida, November 2, 2016. https://www.presidency.ucsb.edu/documents/remarks-the-central-florida-fairgrounds-orlando-florida.

UKIP. (2017). *Britain Together*. Manifesto, UKIP. http://ucrel.lancs.ac.uk/wmatrix/ukmanifestos2017/text/UKIP.txt.

Vaheesan, S. (2014). The evolving populisms of antitrust. *Nebraska Law Review, 93*, 371–428.

Wallace, T. (2019, November 22). Voters really have had enough of experts: Trust in economists has slumped since referendum. *The Telegraph*.

Williams, D. J. (2010). Political ontology and institutional design in Montesquieu and Rousseau. *American Journal of Political Science, 54*(2), 525–542.

Woertz, E. (2017). Populism in Europe: From symptom to alternative? (Ed.) *CIDOB Report* #1, 2017;

Wright, J. D., Dorsey, E., Klick, J., & Rybnicek, J. M. (2019). Requiem for a paradox: The dubious rise and inevitable fall of Hipster antitrust. *Arizona State Law Journal, 51*(1), 293–369.

Wright, J. D., & Portuese, A. (2020). Antitrust populism: Towards a taxonomy. *Stanford Journal of Law, Business & Finance, 13*, 131–181.

WTO. (2020). *Interaction between trade and competition policy.* Accessible at: https://www.wto.org/english/tratop_e/comp_e/comp_e.htm.

Wu, T. (2018a, November 10). Be afraid of economic 'Bigness'. Be very afraid. *The New York Times.*

Wu, T. (2018b). *The curse of bigness: Antitrust in the new gilded age.* Columbia Global Reports.

CHAPTER 14

The Red Herring of Economic Populism

Paris Aslanidis

INTRODUCTION

Despite its enormous popularity in many other fields of social scientific inquiry, the concept of populism remained largely ignored by Western economists until the end of the Cold War. This only changed, when star academic economists Jeffrey Sachs and Rüdiger Dornbusch popularized the theory of economic populism (henceforth TEP) as an explanatory framework for the macroeconomic failures of Latin American governments. Since then, the direct link between populism and overly expansionist, fiscally disastrous economic policies has continued to animate the thought of economists, policymakers and pundits. Combining macroeconomic analysis with a moral injunction against fiscal profligacy, the schematic model of the populist cycle remains TEP's most enduring contribution. That purported cycle goes through the sequentially climactic phases of excessive deficit spending, short-term growth, market bottlenecks, shortages and hyperinflation which is followed by a deterioration in the balance of payments and an inability to service debt obligations, closing with the overthrow of the government and the restoration of economic orthodoxy, usually under IMF supervision.

Ironically, at the same time that populism was becoming a household name among economists, political experts were moving in the opposite direction.

P. Aslanidis (✉)
MacMillan Center for International & Area Studies and Department of Political Science, Yale University, New Haven, CT, USA
e-mail: paris.aslanidis@yale.edu

Comparative analysis was showing that the fiscal policy of ruling populists—in Latin America and elsewhere—was extremely variegated. Given that erratic behavior, no empirical association between populism and specific patterns of economic policy could be reasonably defended, according to many political scientists.

Those two fields of social science have since followed diverging paths. Political scientists remain firm in barring economic dimensions from their definitions of populism, while economists keep shrugging their shoulders at that challenge. TEP's popularity has outgrown its origins as a distinctly Latin American species of macroeconomic failure and now encompasses even mildly expansionist policies by governments around the world (e.g. Benczes, 2014; de Bolle, 2016; Kahn, 2015; Lothian, 2017; Pamuk, 2018; Velasco, 2017).

Part of the responsibility for the abiding misconception that populism is tied to specific economic inputs and outputs lies with scholars of political science. Their widespread skepticism for 'economic populism' has not so far been coupled with a serious attempt to directly engage with TEP so as to challenge its shaky internal logic and flawed empirical predictions. My contribution in this handbook aims to close that lacuna. The chapter begins with an historical review to reveal the unacknowledged roots of TEP in the work of Latin American structuralist economists in the 1970s. It then turns to emphasize that TEP fails to satisfy even a rudimentary need for operationalizability and falsifiability, betraying a deliberately vague analytical framework that operates in the absence of a control group. Those limitations are highlighted with a cursory empirical survey. The chapter closes with a discussion of the ideological and normative factors that condition TEP's enduring and unwarranted popularity.

TEP Overview

Prevailing views on economic populism are fundamentally inspired by two seminal research papers published in 1989 for the U.S. National Bureau of Economic Research (NBER) Working Paper Series: *Macroeconomic Populism in Latin America* by Rüdiger Dornbusch and Sebastian Edwards; and *Social Conflict and Populist Policies in Latin America* by Jeffrey Sachs. Their simultaneous discovery of economic populism was not a matter of coincidence. As the Cold War drew to a close, and as President Ronald Reagan had just concluded his second term, self-assured champions of supply-side economics were enjoying an increasingly hegemonic status. At the same time, Latin America was languishing in its lost decade and was unable to recover from the contagious effects of the 1982 Mexican crisis, forcing American strategists to assess Latin American sovereign debt as a grave risk for economic stability and key foreign policy objectives. A series of disorderly defaults would cripple an over-exposed U.S. commercial banking system, necessitating federal bailouts that were incompatible with Reaganite economic doctrine.[1] Worse still, the ensuing sociopolitical upheaval would facilitate Soviet infiltration in

Latin America. As the region's indebtedness and economic laggardness had become a serious liability for American interests, academic and institutional economists were encouraged and given financial support to urgently identify and remedy the policy malaise that hampered the adjustment to fiscal orthodoxy of those nations.

As part of that agenda, the NBER papers by Sachs, Dornbusch and Edwards (henceforth SD&E), were applauded for suggesting a fresh perspective on the cyclical complications of the region's economic systems. The elusive culprit was discovered and termed economic populism. Sachs (1989) argued that Latin America's endemic and extreme income inequality induces social pressure for redistributive policies, instigating a particular type of policy failure—the populist policy cycle—identifiable by 'overly expansionary macroeconomic policies which lead to high inflation and severe balance of payments crises' (p. 5). The crisis comes in an escalating series of stages: demand-driven expansion fosters short-term euphoria after which the economy eventually enters the collapsing phase of the cycle and real wages drop, ultimately defeating the purpose of the endeavor. The end of the populist cycle produces a swing of the pendulum from populism to economic orthodoxy before eventually pivoting back to economic populism. Sachs's theory thus offered both an intuitive description of the problem and a blueprint for its solution: now that the illness had finally been diagnosed, experts should devise policies to arrest its disastrous circular motion, thereby unlocking the true potential of the local economies.

The argument by Dornbusch and Edwards (1989) was essentially identical. They defined 'macroeconomic populism' as 'an approach to economics that emphasizes growth and income distribution and deemphasizes the risks of inflation and deficit finance, external constraints and the reaction of economic agents to aggressive non-market policies' (p. 1).[2] Their engaging theory was equipped with a detailed periodization of populist economics into four distinct stages that begin with exuberance but end in tragedy. In Stage I, demand-driven expansion produces wage growth and controllable inflationary pressures; in Stage II, the first bottlenecks appear and inflation increases substantially; in Stage III, the crisis reaches its peak, with shortages and hyperinflation crippling economic activity, capital flight draining precious reserves and real wages dropping dramatically, necessitating the implementation of too little, too late stabilization programs, which prove ineffective; in Stage IV, a new political regime takes over to adopt orthodox programs of fiscal consolidation to help the economy recover. The sociopolitical backlash against economic orthodoxy eventually reboots the cycle of macroeconomic populism.

OLD WINE IN OLD BOTTLES

Upon its introduction, TEP was enthusiastically embraced by academics and policymakers who appreciated its geometric elegance, its appealing and climactic nature, and its potential to entice both lay and scholarly audiences. Nevertheless, its intuition was hardly novel. The cognitive constructs of economic populism, the populist cycle and the populist pendulum had originally been invented by Latin American *structuralist* economists in the 1970s.

The concept of populism was introduced into Latin American political sociology in the 1960s as an umbrella term for *peronismo* in Argentina and *varguismo* in Brazil (di Tella, 1965; Germani, 1962). These immensely consequential movements of the 1930s and 1940s had been too eclectic to allow straightforward categorization into the existing ideological camps of the West at the time. 'Populism' was thus recruited to fill the gap, inaugurating a welter of literature.

The classification of Peron and Vargas as populists—along with dozens of other Latin American leaders—caught the attention of local economists, who began to freely engage with the concept. During much of the 1970s, expert opinion in the region was mainly split between the ascending camp of the monetarists, who favored restricting the money supply and blamed inflation on loose fiscal policy, and the structuralist economists, who doubted that their inelastic economies were amenable to free-market recipes and therefore favored heterodox means instead (Baer, 1967). It was this latter school of thought that eventually came up with the notion of 'economic populism'.

A theory of economic populism was first suggested by Argentina's Marcelo Diamand (1972),[3] an idiosyncratic economist and entrepreneur who argued that his country's economic problems were rooted in the asymmetric productivity of agriculture and industry under the regime of Import Substitution Industrialization (ISI).[4] Diamand urged the Argentinian government to adopt a pragmatic, non-ideological national approach to tackle the co-occurrence of high unemployment and hyperinflation that had first emerged when ISI policies began to lose steam in the early 1950s. Expressing a general distrust for academically oriented policymakers, he felt that both monetarists and Keynesians lacked the proper analytical tools to deal with Latin American socioeconomic idiosyncrasies due to their monolithic academic training and propensity for intellectual turf wars that rendered them victims of ideological tunnel vision.

Diamand first used the term populism when Juan Peron returned to power in 1973 at which time he described the prevailing governing culture in Latin America as one of 'semi-organized thought, based on an inconsistent mixture of structuralist and Keynesian ideas, which also exhibits a perceptible influence of Marxism' (Diamand, 1973, p. 422).[5] Central tenets of that thought were national economic independence, a more equal distribution of income and greater state control of economic activity. Borrowing from the sociological vocabulary, he formed a highly consequential axiomatic resolution 'for want of a better name' (Diamand 1973, p. 422) and declared that those ideas shall be called 'national-populism or simply populism'.

Diamand supplied a comprehensive formulation of his populism-orthodoxy pendulum four years later. The populist cycle, which rests on one end of the pendulum, begins.

> with an increase in real wages, an upturn of economic activity, a generalized euphoria in the industrial and commercial sector, a certain worsening of the situation of agriculture and a discriminatory policy against foreign capital. What ensues is disorder, a crisis of authority, an overflow of syndicalism, and a bitter struggle for the distribution of income between different social sectors. The consequences are inflation, a general fall in productivity, the deterioration of the budget, shortages, and a balance of payments crisis. Finally, populism falls victim to economic and social chaos, loses the support of society, and is removed from power. (Diamand, 1977, pp. 385–386)

The populist cycle as elaborated by SD&E in 1989 can be found almost word for word in the quote above. The crucial difference is that for structuralists like Diamand, the Scylla of populism was as crushing as the Charybdis of economic orthodoxy: 'the economic cycle produced by the infeasibility of orthodox policies', Diamand (1978, p. 37) claimed, 'overlaps with a political cycle hallmarked by pendular swings between orthodoxy and populism'. One should therefore strive to avoid the populist extreme without veering all the way into orthodoxy, because the orthodox cycle exhibits its own stages of decline: it 'usually begins with stabilizing plans that, in most cases, involve a devaluation, an increase in agricultural income, a deliberate effort to attract foreign capital, a fall in real wages and a recession, of greater or lesser depth' (Diamand, 1977, p. 386). Orthodox economists will casually explain away the recession and fall in real wages as 'nothing more than temporary damages that correspond to an inevitable period of sacrifice, necessary to restore order and sanitize the economy' (Diamand, 1977, p. 386). As with the populist cycle, orthodox policies register certain initial successes before economic conditions deteriorate:

> the inflation rate decreases, financial capital flows from abroad and the economy is reactivated. But efforts to lower state expenditures and induce greater industrial efficiency do not prosper. Also, due to multiple pressures, the government is forced to give in, allowing wages to increase. The experience of the past indicates that at some point in the process there always comes a crisis of confidence. The flow of foreign capital is reversed. Financial loans that had entered the country begin to flee. There is a strong pressure on foreign exchange reserves, a crisis in the exchange market and a strong devaluation. Real wages fall, demand decreases and the recessive process begins a new. (Diamand, 1977, pp. 386–387)

To answer for their policy failures, both populism and liberal orthodoxy end up shifting the blame to special interests tied to the other camp. The proper policy should aim at stopping the pendular movement by means of rational, pragmatic, middle-of-the-road actions.

TEP's roots in Diamand's pendulum should have become evident to the reader. Yet, a question remains: how could a non-academic with no significant reputation or the necessary professional networks outside Latin America influence some of the brightest minds in American economic academia? The answer lies in the popularization of Diamand's brainchild by one of Argentina's top structuralist economists and policymakers, Aldo Ferrer.

Ferrer, who later served as Argentina's Minister of Economy, was a leading left-wing proponent of national development and his take on economic populism was introduced in *Crisis y Alternativas de la Política Económica Argentina* (1977). In a chapter titled, 'The Vicious Cycle of Liberalism-Populism,' he echoed Diamand by placing populism and (economic) liberalism at the two extremes of a pendulum with swings that sequentially granted the two forces equally disastrous governmental tenures: the first characterized by the irresponsible promotion of short-term consumption and the latter by recession, unemployment and depressed wages. For Ferrer (1977), the incessant swing of the pendulum prevented authorities from instilling a coherent economic order to foster sustained development and a healthy redistributive framework. Committed to the twin principle of balanced budgets and full employment, Ferrer promoted the idea of Argentinization via an economically nationalist and centrist program that prioritized independent development to achieve growth, savings, and a sustainable expansion of both employment and wages.

Ferrer's book stirred a heated debate between structuralists and market liberals in the pages of the major economic journal of the nation, the *Desarrollo Económico* (see e.g. de Pablo, 1977; Ferrer, 1978).[6] The loose and severely undertheorized use of populism quickly came under fire. A review by Zapiola and Leguizamon (1978, p. 293) complained that:

> when the author refers to the vicious cycle, he speaks of populism and liberalism. When he deals with history, he talks about Peronism and liberalism. There is no definition of populism in the book, nor an explanation of this identification between populism and Peronism, so that ... we will dispense with this debatable and much discussed concept and we will focus on what Ferrer proposes, which is a theory of Peronism.

Lavagna (1978), in another review, exposed the superficial classification of various currents of thought into liberalism and populism. Reality defied Ferrer's impressionistic theory: populists did not invariably enact populism and such was the case with liberals and liberalism. Even if one half-heartedly acquiesces to Ferrer's classificatory whims, Lavagna added, it soon becomes obvious that the narrative of alternation cannot stand: populism did not always follow on the heels of liberalism and vice versa.

Two years later, Foxley and Whitehead (1980) vigorously questioned the 'mechanical connection between loosely labelled "populism" and economic instability'. Peronism 'governed for a decade (1945–1955),' Foxley and

Whitehead (1980, p. 827) pointed out, 'with less instability than that country has since experienced under successive governments mostly committed to excluding the Peronists from power;' and, generally, Peron's populism 'was not so different from the populism achieved by the governing party in Mexico which has demonstrated success, by Latin American standards, in managing a basically private-enterprise economy and minimizing economic instability'.

Thus, TEP had been a well-known theory before SD&E repackaged it for mainstream economists. The original Latin American version had been promptly and convincingly criticized for its lack of conceptual consistency and its failure to withstand empirical scrutiny. Nevertheless, TEP's early critics, cogent as they may have been, failed to commit the populist pendulum to the dustbin of academic history. Ferrer felt confident enough to haughtily dismiss his critics. Conceding that perhaps some irregular intervals existed between the various swings of his pendulum, he advised academics not to waste time squabbling over the conceptual nitty–gritty of the whole affair. As he put it, some concepts are very much like giraffes: very difficult to define but easily recognizable as soon as one stumbles upon them (Ferrer, 1979).

TEP's Northward Migration

Gradually, the Latin-American-born theory of economic populism found a new home in U.S. academic circles where SD&E appropriated it as their own. However, something crucial was lost along the way. The original theory suggested a two-pronged attack against both liberal orthodoxy and populism. In its North American mutation, TEP attenuated or altogether omitted to mention the first prong, while the one against populism became the dominant pillar of the new narrative. Half of the geometry in Diamand's populism-orthodoxy pendulum and Ferrer's cycle of liberalism-populism was discarded, and the remainder was repackaged and sold in the United States by SD&E as the populist cycle and the populist pendulum. Instead of arguing against two equally harmful extremes, TEP now assumed a Manichaean good versus evil form, invoking a pendulum that swings between a positive and a negative extreme.

The geographical and temporal distance that separated Diamand and Ferrer in Argentina from Sachs and Dornbusch in New England was covered by numerous Latin American economists educated in the U.S. who formed the conveyor belt for TEP's northward migration. That began as early as 1979 when the U.S. Department of State commissioned the Brookings Institution with organizing a panel to debate the causes of hyperinflation and balance-of-payments crises in Latin America. The conference proceedings were published in a 517-page volume in 1981. Fifteen economists debated the same problem from every angle, yet only two contributors of Latin American descent, Carlos F. Diaz-Alejandro and Alejandro Foxley, used the concept of populism in their analyses. None of the other authors mentioned the word 'populism' even once.

Foxley (1981) explicitly cited Diamand's work as his intellectual influence. Yet, contrary to Diamand, he acknowledged some merit in both the structuralist and monetarist types of stabilization policies, directing his criticism solely against those 'populist regimes' which apply 'extended price controls, while at the same time expanding wages, government expenditures, and money supply' (Foxley, 1981, p. 195). In his contribution, Diaz-Alejandro (1981) employed the same theme, explaining the economic outcomes of populist administration in a series of stages which, again, bear a striking resemblance to SD&E's subsequent formulation.

Economic populism, nevertheless, did not immediately catch on. References to the concept remained sporadic during most of the 1980s. TEP only won general acclaim after SD&E mobilized it in their NBER papers and drew on the combined forces of their global academic authority and the political momentum to popularize it. TEP became a widely recognizable industry standard that most analysts today adopt uncritically. Its inception can now be traced back to Sachs's and Dornbusch's interactions—through academic collaboration or as hired economic consultants—with various Latin American economists and policymakers who by that time had already been exposed to the concept of economic populism and its pendular form for almost two decades.[7]

A Fresh Look at TEP's Analytical Flaws

TEP is at heart a causal-taxonomic schema that purports to identify a distinct type of economic policy of governing officials which it then associates with specific—and dire—politico-economic outcomes. The construct of economic populism seems to refer to an economically qualified type of populism, a species of the genus populism that stands out for its specifically macroeconomic characteristics. However, the choice of genus begs a crucial question: even if a recurring pattern of failed macroeconomic policies based on careless deficit spending has been identified, what is particularly *populistic* in economic populism?

Unfortunately, TEP leaves the defining characteristics of the overarching populist genus unspecified. We are not told what constitutes populism at the basic level before its status can be further refined as economic. The conceptual glue that brings together economic populism, political populism, right-wing populism, progressive populism, media populism and so on under the same genetic type is absent. As the early critics pointed out, the modifier fails to justify its association with the concept's subject. The crucial decision to name the phenomenon economic populism and not, for instance, economic nationalism or economic protectionism or, simply, excessive deficit spending is left unaccounted for. The only genus-producing impression is the term's empirical association with policies once enacted by leaders (e.g. Peron, Vargas, Garcia, etc.) who had already been identified and widely referred to as populists by various academics and commentators. In other words, the economic qualification is justified on the deterministic assumption that populist politicians cannot help but implement a form of economic populism once in power.

SD&E can, in turn, invoke Ferrer's giraffe to dismiss critics of TEP's problematic conceptual structure. However, their conceptual misgivings are coupled with a flawed analytical framework for empirical analysis. The operationalization of (macro)economic populism is deliberately vague and its case selection follows a cherry-picking logic with no control group to validate findings.

In terms of operationalization, TEP posits that populist economic policy is characterized by 'overly expansionist macroeconomic policies' (Sachs, 1989, p. 5) and 'a redistribution of income, typically by large real wage increases' (Dornbusch & Edwards, 1989, p. 6). How overly expansionist should the measures be and how large an increase should real wages register to allow inclusion of a particular case into the set? The availability of statistical data would lead one to expect recourse to a measurable economic metric, e.g. deficit spending per annum exceeding a certain threshold as a percentage of GDP, or a measure of wage appreciation compared to national inflation or to some stable point of reference. However, nothing like that is suggested by TEP scholars. The need for precision in selecting and operationalizing indicators of the purported phenomenon is brushed aside. Instead, the theory relies empirically on a bold and comprehensive—yet, still tacit—claim. To determine whether expansionist economic policy is governed by a populist rather than a generic demand-driving logic, we need to wait for the proper outcomes. If triple-digit hyperinflation and sovereign debt default ensue, leading to regime change and an orthodox stabilization program, then we can safely call it macroeconomic populism. If the cycle does not close, then the pendulum fails to swing all the way, and macroeconomic populism does not materialize. Thus, the theory exhibits no real predictive capacity: it only works when it works.

The circular logic described betrays the trappings of a perfectly unfalsifiable model that has hardwired the outcome of its theoretical premises into its definition. Instead of suggesting a set of measurable indicators to allow the testing of its causal claim, the positive outcome of the hypothesis is taken for granted and the outcome itself is transposed as an indicator. A proper test for the theory would have mobilized a large dataset of populist governments to juxtapose their economic policies with fiscal outcomes and to assess whether the latter correlate with the purported populist cycle and its deterioration into runaway inflation, bankruptcy and so on. TEP theorists did nothing of the sort. They simply elevated their hypothesis into a foregone conclusion and then went on to perform their case selection on the dependent variable, cherry-picking cases of known failed economies under populist administration and comfortably vindicating their theory. Hence, Sachs (1989) analyzed Argentina under Peron (1946–1949), Chile under Allende (1971–1973), Brazil under Sarney (1985–1988) and Peru under Garcia (1985–1988) while Dornbusch and Edwards (1989) limited their analysis to the Chilean and Peruvian cases.[8]

As with the backlash against Ferrer in the late 1970s, some analysts expressed uneasiness with the methodology of the NBER papers. Faucher (1991), for instance, criticized the crude semantic shift that transformed populism into a distinct type of economic policy, arguing that the actual policies of populist politicians were too erratic to allow deriving any sort of pattern. Relying on contemporary empirical examples from Argentina and Peru, he concluded that pragmatic considerations and the need to achieve favorable political objectives shaped the populist decision-making calculus. An increasingly populist political rhetoric could straightforwardly be combined with the implementation of anti-popular, orthodox adjustment programs.

Criticism also came from within. Perhaps unexpectedly for its editors, strong reservations were echoed by several contributors in *The Macroeconomics of Populism in Latin America* (Dornbusch & Edwards, 1991), a volume that was supposed to verify TEP on a wide empirical scale. Bazdresch and Levy (1991, p. 224) complained that the distinction between populists and non-populists 'cannot be made ex post on the basis of which regimes succeeded and which did not'. That would lead to, as Rabello de Castro and Ronci (1991, p. 152) explained in the same book, 'the extreme of labeling every failed growth policy or distributive action as populist'. In a subsequent section, Drake (1991) cited several cases of bait-and-switch populism, where political outsiders won power on a platform of radical economic redistribution only to enforce strict orthodoxy once in power. Moreover, Drake (1991) questioned the classificatory principles that registered cases such as Allende (Chile) and Sarney (Brazil) with the populist camp, arguing that they represented socialism and conservatism, respectively, rather than populism, an argument repeated by several other authors in the volume. While the majority of empirical contributions in Dornbusch and Edwards (1991) disputed core aspects of the editors' TEP framework in one way or the other, Dornbusch and Edwards avoided confronting their critics.

Drake's observation that populist leaders all too frequently adopted orthodox economic policies was confirmed by several political scientists in the 1990s. Capitalism's triumph over socialism and the significance of free-market ideology for political strategy did not escape the attention of Latin American politicians, even the populists among them, who showed extraordinary skill in navigating the uncharted waters of the new international status quo. Political actors widely recognized as exhibiting a typically populist outlook began embracing a laissez-faire discourse. As Roberts (1995) and Weyland (1996) among others have repeatedly shown, leaders such as Menem in Argentina, Fujimori in Peru and Collor de Mello in Brazil won the popular vote in 1989 and 1990 campaigning with the typical populist playbook. However, once in power, they ruthlessly implemented orthodox economic programs, shock treatments that followed the guidelines of the Washington consensus and enjoyed the enthusiastic endorsement of international financial institutions. Those 'neoliberal populists' undermined TEP's basic planks, leading most scholars to altogether disassociate populism from economic policy and to criticize theories of economic populism as too reductionist and economistic to be of any value in analyzing the populist phenomenon (de la Torre & Arnson, 2013; Hawkins, 2010; Knight, 1998).

Menem, Fujimori and Collor were not mere exceptions to a rule and their significance lies mostly in the irony of their co-occurrence with the triumph of TEP. Their example was followed by several others who similarly embraced fiscal orthodoxy alongside their populist rhetoric and strategy (Murillo, 2000; Stokes, 2001) and one needs only to look outside Latin America to discover scores of other cases at odds with TEP. The 'unexpected affinities' (Weyland, 1996) between populism and neoliberalism have notoriously been observed in Western Europe during the late 1980s and especially the 1990s when populist parties swore by fiscally conservative agendas, leading political scientists to speak of a winning formula for the populist right that included eradicating economically interventionist policies (Kitschelt & McGann, 1995).[9] Important cases of pro-market, right-wing populism in Canada, Australia and Turkey (Aytaç & Öniş, 2014; Snow & Moffitt, 2012) add to the battery of empirical refutations of TEP at the most fundamental level.

Spotting black swans—i.e. populist politicians with extreme pro-market fiscal outlooks—is the shortest route to refute the standard economic populism thesis. Yet, there is also a vast grey zone that allows a more nuanced perspective. That zone is populated by populist politicians too numerous to catalogue here who do not side with free markets, privatizations and deregulation but are also against excessive fiscal expansion and nationalizations. The seminal *Foreign Affairs* article by Castañeda (2006) offers a straightforward and catalytic example. Castañeda (2006, p. 29) divided the Latin American left into the right sort, 'modern, open-minded, reformist, and internationalist' former communists; and the wrong 'nationalist, strident, and close-minded' sort, 'born of the great tradition of Latin American populism'. Chavez in Venezuela, Kirchner in Argentina, Morales in Bolivia, Humala in Peru and Correa in Ecuador comprised the latter group. However, despite the preference of those leaders for demand-driven growth, their national economies have not only survived the assumed economic onslaught, but, in most cases, have performed surprisingly well. Bolivia, Ecuador, Peru and even Argentina registered healthy rates of growth under populist rule in the past couple of decades, despite the onset of the Great Recession.

In a later revisitation of the topic, Edwards (2010), obviously cognizant of those embarrassing empirical discrepancies, attempts to deflect criticism by means of a semantic shift, rebranding leaders such as the Kirchners, Chavez, Morales, Correa, Ortega and Lugo, as neopopulists rather than populists. 'In a way', Edwards claims, 'these neopopulists seem to understand the need for maintaining overall fiscal prudence and reasonably low inflation':

it is still too early to know if these populist politicians will be willing or able to maintain fiscal caution during a major downturn such as those generated by the global crash of 2008. In fact, at the time of this writing, in mid-2009, there is already some indication that Argentina and Venezuela have slipped into the old practices of traditional populism. Whether these countries will go through the populist cycle discussed above, a cycle that invariably ends with frustration, is still to be seen. (Edwards, 2010, p. 171)

TEP's circular logic is in full swing in the passage, epitomizing the attempt to salvage its non-falsifiability by conflating necessary conditions, causes and outcomes. Are we dealing with traditional populists or neopopulists, whatever the latter means? Real-life indicators are not sufficient to form a verdict. To surmise what they are suffering from, we need to wait and see if the patients are officially pronounced dead.

The ostensibly obvious exception is Venezuela, even though a *reductio ad Venezuelanum* cannot save TEP. It was December 1998 when Hugo Chavez won his first election, but by all indications the populist cycle has not yet been brought to a close. His chosen heir, Nicolas Maduro, continues to service Venezuela's debt obligations, even at the cost of undermining the regime's prized social welfare programs. Therefore, despite the otherwise terrible state of the Venezuelan economy, a swing of the pendulum toward inevitable regime change and an orthodox program of fiscal consolidation has failed to materialize. TEP is silent on how many weeks, months or years it takes for a full rotation of the populist cycle, yet a gyration that lasts more than twenty years is too slow to be of any meaning. An orthodox economic program will eventually be taken up by one of Venezuela's subsequent leaders, as happens invariably in almost every state in the world. But will that be adequate to claim that TEP has been vindicated? It is difficult to take the theory's analytical value seriously if it cannot find validation in the thoroughly accommodating context of the Venezuelan debacle.

Edwards' distinction between real populists and neopopulists reveals another problematic aspect, this time with regard to TEP's chosen unit of analysis. If we strictly follow the theory, we will be forced to exclude from our set every political force that operates in the opposition. Economic populism cannot be assessed at the programmatic level during or prior to an electoral campaign. Rather, it is a product of macroeconomic policy decisions implemented by governing institutions, meaning that economic populists can only reside in presidential palaces. To meet the criteria of inclusion, a politician must rise to power, form a government, implement fiscal policy, enmesh the economy into the cogs of the dreaded populist cycle, and then only when the cycle makes a complete rotation can we classify our case as an economic populist. Yet, this unacknowledged logical implication goes against our most basic understanding of the populist phenomenon as something emerging at the political margins prior to building adequate momentum to challenge the establishment.

The Ideological Nature of TEP's Political Economy

Economists may opt to overlook TEP's conceptual and methodological discrepancies; however, they cannot but recognize the inadequately sophisticated core of TEP's political economy argument. The theory seems to suggest a *post-hoc ergo propter hoc* premise that exaggerates the impact of aggregate demand stimulation over other domestic causal factors of economic failure—especially in the developing world—such as inelastic labor markets, natural resource dependency, oversized agricultural sectors, natural disasters, public health emergencies, guerilla insurgencies and so on. Most importantly, TEP grossly overlooks exogenous factors such as global growth patterns, interest rate fluctuations, recessions in trade partners' economies, commodity price swings, military conflict, trade wars, international sanctions and other external constraints of the real world.[10] Having turned a blind eye to the interplay between domestic and international economic factors, TEP simplistically treats national economies as closed systems uniquely conditioned by the type of fiscal policy pursued by governing officials. We are, therefore, forced to consider that perhaps ideological, rather than analytical, considerations lay behind TEP's lopsided economic perspective.

TEP scholars could have allowed their theory to remain falsifiable by setting a threshold for overly expansionist policy or large wage increases to be tested through measurable indicators that allow an objective verdict on whether the populist cycle materializes when thresholds are violated. That would, however, expose numerous false positives, thereby attenuating the thrust of TEP's sweeping normative declaration: beware of giving power to the populists because they always end up destroying your national economy. Dornbusch and Edwards (1989, p. 1) explicitly invited appraisal of their paper as 'a warning that populist policies do ultimately fail; and when they fail it is always at a frightening cost to the very groups who were supposed to be favored'.

Dornbusch was frank about that conceptual and ideological sleight of hand. In an interview given during the heydays of TEP, the German-born MIT professor disclosed something he never conceded in his academic writings: 'We say that macroeconomic populism always fails', Dornbusch acknowledged, 'because we only count the failures and we do not count the successes. President Reagan was a populist and he got his way. He left the account in the hands of President Bush and maybe he will leave it to a Democrat' (de la Torre, 1990, p. 815).

Reagan was, however, never mentioned as an economic populist in the voluminous work of SD&E, something that would have opened the floodgates for hundreds of cases of successful excessive deficit spending policies, from FDR's New Deal to post-war Japan, to the economic miracles of South Korea and China and Trump's trillion-dollar deficits, thus undermining the theory's shock value. Implicating politicians and governments of the developed world would also endanger TEP's popularity among mainstream academics and institutional stakeholders. Instead, through its exclusive application to maverick politicians in economically precarious peripheral nations, TEP becomes a cross-partisan rallying cry against the common foe of populism, thereby papering over the fundamental disagreements between monetarists and Keynesians on matters of fiscal and monetary policy.

Conclusion: The Sad Fate of Weaponized Concepts

Populists claim to represent the people in a struggle to curb the power of unaccountable elites and to restore sovereignty to the vast majority. There is no reason to a priori attach a specific economic agenda to that premise. Both restrictive and expansionist policies—and everything in-between—can (and have) been framed by populists as serving the cause of the 'have-nots' while hurting the interests of the 1 percent. Populists' actual policy decisions will rely on momentum, political opportunity, the local structure of the economy, the international setting and all those other factors that political agents typically take into account when planning their strategy.

By ignoring the obvious, the TEP thesis betrays normative considerations. Since populism broke out of its historical specificity in the mid-1950s to become a universal concept applicable to all sorts of empirical instances, its students have repeatedly succumbed to the temptation of weaponizing the word to turn it against their ideological opponents (Allcock, 1971; Kazin, 1998; Novick, 1988). In many ways, populism has become a political Rorschach blot: anyone is free to see in it whatever they desire, from the very essence of progressivism to outright fascism. TEP serves a useful role by adding a negative economic dimension to an already negative political one, thereby investing populism with a deterministic aura that boosts the drama of the anti-populist argument. TEP's narrative becomes intuitive and seductive by borrowing familiar symbols of mathematical regularity and geometrical finesse from the hard sciences. Spinning the story in the form of cycles and pendula provides a semblance of scientific rigor that lends further credence to the underlying theory. A theory of such elegance is easily sold to the public, allowing journalists to add an academic veneer to their op-eds and authorizing politicians to mobilize economic science against their ideological foes. Empirical counterarguments may be thrown up against TEP in earnest but dissenting voices will find it hard to rise above the clamor of the ticking pendulum and the revolving circle.

Notes

1. In August 1982, loans to the region by the top nine U.S. banks amounted to 180 percent of their primary capital (Devlin, 1989).
2. Their paper was subsequently published in the *Journal of Development Economics* (Dornbusch & Edwards, 1990).
3. Bresser Pereira (1991) claims that Argentinian engineer and economist Adolfo Canitrot was the first to employ 'economic populism' in its contemporary

meaning. Canitrot (1975) introduced a protean theory of stages for the rise and demise of economic populism.
4. ISI was a type of protectionist economic policy expounded by structuralist economists and traditionally associated with state-driven industrialization in Latin America and South East Asia.
5. Original in Spanish. All translations by the author.
6. Perhaps the fiercest liberal critic was Juan Carlos de Pablo, Dornbusch's co-author in Dornbusch & de Pablo (1987), an NBER paper where the MIT economist first employs the concept of the populist cycle.
7. Sachs consulted the Bolivian government in drafting Supreme Decree 21,060 (August 1985) that introduced a number of pro-market reforms for the first time. Dornbusch worked as a World Bank consultant for Peru and advised policymakers (some of them his former students) in several other countries of the region.
8. All these episodes had already been widely associated with populism in political science work.
9. The trend continues today in the same region, even if somewhat attenuated (Afonso & Rennwald, 2018).
10. For criticism on this point see See Diaz-Alejandro (1984) and Foxley & Whitehead (1980).

Literature

Afonso, A., & Rennwald, L. (2018). The changing welfare state agenda of populist radical right parties in Europe. In P. Manow, B. Palier & H. Schwander (Eds.), *Welfare democracies and party politics: Explaining electoral dynamics in times of changing welfare capitalism* (pp. 171–196). Oxford University Press.

Allcock, J. B. (1971). "Populism": A brief biography. *Sociology, 5*(3), 371–387.

Aytaç, S. E., & Öniş, Z. (2014). Varieties of populism in a changing global context: The divergent paths of Erdoğan and Kirchnerismo. *Comparative Politics, 47*(1), 41–59.

Baer, W. (1967). The inflation controversy in Latin America: A survey. *Latin American Research Review, 2*(2), 3–25.

Bazdresch, C., & Levy, S. (1991). Populism and economic policy in Mexico, 1970–1982. In R. Dornbusch & S. Edwards (Eds.), *The macroeconomics of populism in Latin America* (pp. 223–262). The University of Chicago Press.

Benczes, I. (Ed.). (2014). *Deficit and debt in transition: The political economy of public finances in Central and Eastern Europe*. Central European University Press.

Bresser Pereira, L. C. (1991). Populism and economic policy in Brazil. *Journal of Interamerican Studies and World Affairs, 33*(2), 1–21.

Canitrot, A. (1975). La experiencia populista de redistribución de ingresos. *Desarrollo Económico, 15*(59), 331–351.

Castañeda, J. G. (2006). Latin America's left turn. *Foreign Affairs, 85*(3), 28–43.

de Bolle, M. (2016). More lessons from Brazil's boom-bust: The "populist paradigm" revisited. Retrieved May 21, 2020, from Peterson Institute for International Economics website: https://www.piie.com/blogs/realtime-economic-issues-watch/more-lessons-brazils-boom-bust-populist-paradigm-revisited.

de la Torre, C., & Arnson, C. J. (2013). Introduction: The evolution of Latin American populism and the debates over its meaning. In C. de la Torre & C. J. Arnson (Eds.), *Latin American populism in the twenty-first century* (pp. 1–35). Woodrow Wilson Center Press.

de la Torre, R. (1990). Conversación con Rudiger Dornbusch: Un economista pragmático. *El Trimestre Económico, 57*(227(3)), 805–820.

de Pablo, J. C. (1977). Aldo Ferrer y la política económica en la Argentina de posguerra. *Desarrollo Económico, 17*(67), 511–520.

Devlin, R. (1989). *Debt and crisis in Latin America: The supply side of the story.* Princeton University Press.

Di Tella, T. S. (1965). Populism and reform in Latin America. In C. Veliz (Ed.), *Obstacles to change in Latin America* (pp. 47–74). Oxford University Press.

Diamand, M. (1972). La estructura productiva desequilibrada argentina y el tipo de cambio. *Desarrollo Económico, 12*(45), 25–47.

Diamand, M. (1973). *Doctrinas económicas, desarrollo e independencia.* Paidos.

Diamand, M. (1977). El péndulo argentino: ¿empate político o fracasos económicos? In J. C. et al. & Agulla (Ed.), *Pensar la República* (pp. 385–409). Fundacion Pinero Pacheco.

Diamand, M. (1978). Towards a change in the economic paradigm through the experience of developing countries. *Journal of Development Economics, 5*(1), 19–53.

Diaz-Alejandro, C. F. (1981). Southern cone stabilization plans. In W. R. Cline & S. Weintraub (Eds.), *Economic stabilization in developing countries* (pp. 119–147). The Brookings Institution.

Diaz-Alejandro, C. F. (1984). Latin American debt: I don't think we are in Kansas anymore. *Brookings Papers on Economic Activity, 1984*(2), 335–403.

Dornbusch, R., & de Pablo, J. C. (1987). *Argentina: Debt and macroeconomic instability* (NBER Working Paper No. 2378.).

Dornbusch, R., & Edwards, S. (1989). *Macroeconomic populism in Latin America* (NBER Working Paper No. 2986), Cambridge.

Dornbusch, R., & Edwards, S. (1990). Macroeconomic populism. *Journal of Development Economics, 32*(2), 247–277.

Dornbusch, R., & Edwards, S. (Eds.). (1991). *The macroeconomics of populism in Latin America.* University of Chicago Press.

Drake, P. W. (1991). Comment. In R. Dornbusch & S. Edwards (Eds.), *The macroeconomics of populism in Latin America* (pp. 35–40). The University of Chicago Press.

Edwards, S. (2010). *Left behind: Latin America and the false promise of populism.* The University of Chicago Press.

Faucher, P. (1991). *The improbable stabilization and inconceivable popular market capitalism: Argentina, Brazil, Mexico and Peru.* Paper presented at the Conference of the International Political Science Association, Buenos Aires, July 22–26.

Ferrer, A. (1977). *Crisis y Alternativas de la Política Económica Argentina.* Buenos Aires: Fondo de Cultura Económica.

Ferrer, A. (1978). Crisis y alternativas de la política económica argentina. Una Respuesta. *Desarrollo Económico, 17*(68), 647–653.

Ferrer, A. (1979). Crisis y alternativas de la política económica argentina. Respuestas a Comentaristas. *Desarrollo Económico, 19*(73), 125–135.

Foxley, A. (1981). Stabilization policies and their effects on employment and income distribution: A Latin American perspective. In W. R. Cline & S. Weintraub

(Eds.), *Economic stabilization in developing countries* (pp. 191–233). The Brookings Institution.
Foxley, A., & Whitehead, L. (1980). Economic stabilization in Latin America: Political dimensions—Editor's introduction. *World Development, 8*(11), 823–832.
Germani, G. (1962). *Política y sociedad en una época de transición.* Paidos.
Hawkins, K. A. (2010). *Venezuela's Chavismo and populism in comparative perspective.* Cambridge University Press.
Kahn, R. (2015, December). *Addressing economic populism in Europe: Global economics monthly.* Retrieved from https://www.cfr.org/sites/default/files/pdf/2015/12/December2015GEM.pdf.
Kazin, M. (1998). *The populist persuasion: An American history* (Revised). Cornell University Press.
Kitschelt, H., & McGann, A. J. (1995). *The radical right in Western Europe: A comparative analysis.* Michigan University Press.
Knight, A. (1998). Populism and neo-populism in Latin America, especially Mexico. *Journal of Latin American Studies, 30*(2), 223–248.
Lavagna, R. (1978). Aldo Ferrer y la política económica en la Argentina de posguerra (II). *Desarrollo Económico, 17*(68), 654–664.
Lothian, T. (2017). *Law and the wealth of nations: Finance, prosperity, and democracy.* Columbia University Press.
Murillo, M. V. (2000). From populism To neoliberalism: Labor unions and market reforms in Latin America. *World Politics, 52*(2), 135–168.
Novick, P. (1988). *That noble dream: The "objectivity question" and the American historical profession.* Cambridge University Press.
Pamuk, S. (2018). *Uneven centuries: Economic development of Turkey since 1820.* Princeton University Press.
Rabello de Castro, P., & Ronci, M. (1991). Sixty years of populism in Brazil. In R. Dornbusch & S. Edwards (Eds.), *The macroeconomics of populism in Latin America* (pp. 151–173). The University of Chicago Press.
Roberts, K. M. (1995). Neoliberalism and the transformation of populism in Latin America: The Peruvian case. *World Politics, 48*(1), 82–116.
Sachs, J. D. (1989). *Social conflict and populist policies in Latin America* (NBER Working Paper No. 2897).
Snow, D., & Moffitt, B. (2012). Straddling the divide: Mainstream populism and conservatism in Howard's Australia and Harper's Canada. *Commonwealth & Comparative Politics, 50*(3), 271–292.
Stokes, S. C. (2001). *Mandates and democracy: Neoliberalism by surprise in Latin America.* Cambridge University Press.
Velasco, A. (2017). How economic populism works. Retrieved May 21, 2020, from Project Syndicate website: https://www.project-syndicate.org/commentary/economic-populism-temporary-success-by-andres-velasco-2017-02.
Weyland, K. (1996). Neopopulism and neoliberalism in Latin America: Unexpected affinities. *Studies in Comparative International Development, 31*(3), 3–31.
Zapiola, M. G., & Leguizamón, C. M. (1978). Aldo Ferrer y la politica económica en la Argentina de posguerra (III). *Desarrollo Económicò, 18*(70), 291–302.

CHAPTER 15

Populist Mobilization in the United States: Adding Political Economy to Cultural Explanations

Christian Lammert and Boris Vormann

Introduction

Populism is looming large on the agenda of the social sciences. In most cases the literature deals with related phenomena in the context of liberal and representative democracies, often defining populism as an anti-pluralist "exclusionary form of identity politics" (Müller, 2016: 3) or as an authoritarian "cultural backlash" (Norris & Inglehart, 2019). In this chapter, we try to shift the focus away from populist actors, parties and governments and address instead the political, economic and social contexts in which populism can become successful in mobilizing electoral majorities in the first place. We are less interested in a normative discussion of populism nor do we explore the type of programs populists might pursue once in office (see Lammert, 2020; Vormann & Weinman, 2020 for such analyses). Rather, we focus on the contexts and scenarios in which populists thrive and to which they vow to offer political and economic alternatives.

In brief, we see populism as the result of specific political and economic developments that dovetail with dynamics of cultural backlash and white resentment. It produces crisis tendencies of its own once populist leaders take office, but is itself not the root cause of democracy's ailment in the West.

C. Lammert (✉)
Chair of Politics, JFKI, Free University of Berlin, Berlin, Germany
e-mail: christian.lammert@fu-berlin.de

B. Vormann
Bard College Berlin, Berlin, Germany
e-mail: b.vormann@berlin.bard.edu

We contend that the recent success of populism across so many different country contexts needs to be viewed as a global phenomenon which has produced specific effects in particular institutional and historical contexts. For this chapter, our main focus lies on these developments in the United States.

Culture vs. Economy: A False Dichotomy

The recent rise in populism around the world often seems to be triggered by disparate, sometimes even local issues. From a more general perspective, however, these populist uprisings often share common features: feelings of disenfranchisement among parts of the electorate, of being left out of global economic booms and of discomfort at seeing familiar social orders upended. Even if context matters, we do think that global comparative analyses (e.g. Blyth & Hopkin, 2020) are very helpful in understanding the factors facilitating what are ultimately similar national agendas.

In public discourses on populism, particularly when such phenomena gained momentum in the mid-2010s, two dominant positions evolved. The one side argued by highlighting cultural factors to explain the successful mobilization of populists, while the other side emphasized the importance of economic factors. Are Trump's presidency, the Brexit and the rise of right-wing populist parties in continental Europe the consequence of a deepening rift in values between social conservatives and social liberals, whereby conservatives start to support xenophobic, ethno-nationalist and authoritarian politicians? Or is the success of populist mobilization more a sign of voters' economic anxiety and insecurity, fueled by events such as the financial crisis of 2008, the politics of austerity and globalization?

We think that both positions cannot be neatly separated but are closely linked to each other. In fact, they are two sides of the same medal. More recently, cultural explanations seem to have gained dominance. Particularly in the context of social protests in reaction to the police killing of George Floyd, it became clear once more how much race remains a crucial issue in US politics. But racism has a long history in the U.S., dating back to its very founding. Given that it has been such an enduring feature of US society, to which extent can it help us explain why Trump was voted into office? While race should by no means be rejected as a factor in the rise of populism, of course, we need to develop an understanding at what moments in time it becomes a decisive factor. As we contend, we should see race not only as a category of identity, but also of political and economic discrimination so as to reconcile cultural and politico-economic explanations for populist mobilization.

These modifications notwithstanding, of course, cultural arguments do raise important points, some of which also go beyond the question of race. As segments within younger post-World War II generations became richer, better educated and more secure, influential parts of the population adopted post-materialist values that emphasize secularism, personal autonomy and diversity at the expense of religion, traditional family structures and conformity. As a result, older generations might have become alienated. A similar argument has been made with regard to processes of urbanization, a process of spatial sorting that divides societies in terms of not only economic fortunes, but also of cultural values. This process creates on the one side thriving enclaves within multicultural, high-density metropolitan areas that are integrated in global networks of exchange and circulation where socially liberal values predominate. On the other, the deepening urban–rural divide disconnects populations from the main state infrastructure. This geographical separation is reflected also in the fact that regions are increasingly uniform in terms of social conservatism and aversion to diversity. Of course, the disconnect equally applies, if not even more so, to disenfranchised minority populations. But it seems as though perceived entitlements and relative decline are pertinent factors for electoral mobilization, particularly among the white majority population.

The cultural argument can only go so far in explaining the rise of populism, however. Numerous studies reveal a clear connection between economic shocks and the political support for populists. Research by economist David Autor (Autor et. al., 2017), for instance, clearly shows that votes for Trump in the 2016 presidential election were strongly correlated with the magnitude of adverse China trade shocks. All else being equal, the greater the loss of jobs due to rising imports from China, the higher the support for Trump in that election. Such findings clearly cannot simply be rejected out of hand. But it seems more difficult to link it immediately to a story of culture *tout court*.

Even if the cultural and economic arguments in the debate seem to be in tension at first glance, both come together in a specific form. Because cultural trends—such as post-materialism and urbanization described above—are of long-term nature, they do not fully account for the timing of the populist backlash. In more recent work, even proponents of the cultural argument do not dismiss the relevance of economic developments entirely. Pippa Norris and Ronald Inglehart (2019), for example, argue that medium-term economic conditions and the growth of social diversity accelerated the cultural backlash. In their empirical analysis they show, that economic factors did play a role in support of populist parties.

Economic and cultural arguments really only seem in tension if we ignore the political dimension of what is at stake. In the remainder of our discussion, we foreground long-term political factors and how they are intricately linked to economic developments to provide a hotbed for (the cultural dimensions) of white revanchism. We think that such a more complex understanding of the political economy of racism, which we can only sketch here, helps us better articulate critiques of American illiberalism not simply as an irrational outbreak, but as a context-specific development embedded in power relations and existing institutional settings.

Political Factors in U.S. Populist Mobilization

The juxtaposition of economic and cultural-identitarian explanations is misleading, because it tends to obfuscate political problems at the root of populist mobilization. In the United States, the rise in authoritarian populism has gone hand in hand with a number of processes. We foreground three to then show how they interact with economic and cultural developments: First, the decline of trust in government and political institutions more broadly, second, the decline in government's responsiveness to the expressed policy preferences of the middle class and lower income groups, and third the rise of political polarization.

Trust

The decline of trust in the U.S. government dates back to the mid-1960s (Lammert & Vormann, 2020; PEW, 2017). Five decades ago, close to 75% of the U.S. population trusted the federal government; that number has dropped to below 25%. More generally speaking, Americans have low regard for elected officials. When asked about candidates running for office in the last several elections, only about half (47%) would assess the candidates overall as "good," with just 7% saying they were "very good." About as many (52%) express a negative view. Roughly six in ten Americans report that if they contacted their member of the U.S. House of Representatives with a problem, it would either not be very likely (40%), or not likely at all (21%) that they would get help addressing it. Just 7% indicate their representative would be very likely to help, while 30% say this would be somewhat likely (Pew, 2018).

The United States has fallen in global rankings over the past decade, from 18th place in the 2008 Democracy Index to 25th in 2018 (Economist Intelligence Unit, 2019). This primarily reflects a deterioration in the category "functioning of government," as political polarization has become more pronounced and public confidence in institutions has weakened. Declining trust in political institutions was the main reason why *The Economist* downgraded the United States to the level of a flawed democracy in 2016—for the first time in the history of the index. The 2016 report, for its part, mentions several reasons for this decline in popular confidence, which started with the Vietnam War, continued with the Watergate scandal and persisted until the Iraq War and the financial crisis, only to be aggravated by repeated government shutdowns in the 2010s (Economist Intelligence Unit, 2019).

Responsiveness

The decline of trust, difficult to explain from a cultural-identitarian vantage point alone, might also be described as the result of a broader public perception that democratic politics and processes are no longer working in the people's interest—or at least not responding to their preferences. Political scientists Benjamin Page and Martin Gilens have found that middle-class Americans or lower income groups have little or no influence over U.S. public policy and that "when large majorities of Americans favor policy changes—when 70 to 80% want change—they get it less than half the time" (Page & Gilens, 2017). According to Page and Gilens government is just listening to the interests of the super-rich, the top 1% in the income distribution. Because of this, the authors pose the important question whether US-democracy should not be labeled as an oligarchy instead.

Two separate factors are at play here (Lammert & Vormann, 2018): (a) Special interests and powerful campaign donors influence policy and (b) technocratic agencies without direct political accountability are able to formulate policy decisions without taking citizens' desires into account:

> a. Political spending in elections is growing more concentrated among the wealthiest few. In 2012, almost half of all the money spent in federal elections came from just one-tenth of one-tenth of 1% of Americans (Bonica et. al., 2013). The share of contributions from the top 0.01% of the voting population grew to 40% in 2016—up from just 16% in the 1980s (Edsall, 2018).
> b. Furthermore, the dominance of corporations and business interests exists not only in election spending but also in lobbying of elected officials and decision-makers. In their book, *The Unheavenly Chorus: Unequal Political Voice and the Broken Promise of American Democracy*, Schlozman et al. (2013) found that organizations representing business interests accounted for 72% of all lobbying expenditures, while labor organizations made up just 1%. In response to the concentrated power of wealth in the political sphere, political mechanisms have the propensity to concentrate benefits among the wealthy but disperse the costs of policies onto the population as a whole—particularly marginalized communities—contributing to the decline of trust in government.

Polarization

With trust and responsiveness on the decline, politics in the United States have also become more polarized. In the past, a common complaint about America's democracy had been that the policy positions of major candidates were almost indistinguishable, suggesting that political parties lacked any firm principles (APSA, 1950). But that has drastically changed over time. In 2006, researchers observed that a "growing body of empirical research shows that the parties in government, particularly those in Congress, are each growing more homogeneous in their policy positions, while the differences between the two parties' stands on major policy issues are expanding" (Layman et al., 2006).

In 2013, the same organization that criticized US-parties for lacking a clear political and ideological profile, defined the rising polarization of political parties in the United States as a threat to the democratic process (Mansbridge & Martin, 2013). Growing partisan polarization in Congress results in part in a legislative gridlock (Mann & Ornstein, 2016). Bipartisan agreement on larger reform proposals have become unthinkable. Those shifts and the legislative gridlock in Washington D.C. have resulted in today's hyperpartisan political and societal divide government, creating a fertile ground for populist mobilization. The Republican Party's questioning of the election outcomes 2020 is just the most recent, but also the most extreme form that these divisions have taken so far.

Here, it is true that political and cultural arguments overlap the most. They are indeed complementary. What a political perspective foregrounds, in addition to things discussed so far, are the institutional factors that have given rise to such polarization, including the importance of party strategies to influence the political game by affecting voting rights, districts and campaign finance. These strategies are the cumulative result of political calculations from within the institutional working of US democracy. The causal relationship to white resentment, which culturally often seems to run from identity to effect, is reversed from such a political point of view: revanchism is a political tool in a concrete institutional setting.

Economic Factors in U.S. Populist Mobilization

In the United States, emergency policy following the financial crisis and the collapse of the banking sector of 2008 measures led to the formation of powerful grassroots movements such as the tea party movement on the right and the widespread Occupy movement, mainly on the left. For many US citizens, the ad hoc measures taken to stabilize the economy only were seen as benefitting a select few, while ordinary people had to bear the costs, proving to them that the system was stacked against them. Against the longer standing backdrop of political factors, this and the gloomy prospects of structural transformations are the straw that broke the camel's back, and prepared the ground for populist mobilization.

Paradoxically, if we take a first look at polling data, economic hardship appears to be only weakly related to support for authoritarian populists. According to exit polls from the 2016 U.S. presidential election, Hillary Clinton defeated Donald Trump by 13 points among those earning less than $30,000 a year, and Trump's lead was strongest among those earning between $50,000 and $99,999 (CNN, 2018). It therefore doesn't seem quite clear, at least at first sight, to what extent economic inequality might explain the rise of populist politics. The decisive point here is to understand how identity categories intersect with class politics.

Deep Inequalities

Crucially, those in the slightly higher income brackets tend to be lower middle-class *white* populations, fearing the loss of their living standards. This fear is not entirely unfounded. Income inequality in the United States is extremely high in comparison to other advanced industrialized economies, and it has increased massively since the 1970s (Lammert, 2018; World Bank, 2018). While incomes for American families in the bottom two-thirds of the income distribution more than doubled between 1947 and 1979, in terms of real dollars, they have remained flat since then—even while average productivity has nearly doubled (Page & Gilens, 2017). At the same time, the share of pretax income going to the richest Americans matches the previous peak of inequality at the end of the 1920s (Piketty, 2014). Raw state-level data show a positive association between the basic measure of income inequality, the Gini coefficient, and Donald Trump's lead in the 2016 election (Darvas & Efsathio, 2016).

Given the importance of beliefs and perceptions in the literature that relies on individual-level data (Lammert & Vormann, 2020), the support for right-wing populism might be better explained by the extent to which voters *perceive* the economic system as unfair, rather than studying broader aggregate measures of economic health or income dispersion, such as the Gini coefficient. Popular accounts, such as Luigi Zingales' celebrated 2012 book, *A Capitalism for the People*, suggest that ideas of meritocracy and economic mobility associated with America's social and economic model have weakened in recent decades, with policies and institutions increasingly favoring cronyism and rent-seeking, resulting in a sense that the system is being rigged by and for a corrupt elite (Zingales, 2012).

Gloomy Prospects: White Privilege Compromised

Add to this volatile mix the structural changes on the labor markets which have further deepened the perceived and real grievances in larger parts of the US society. More and more jobs are vulnerable to outsourcing and automation, particularly those that require lower qualifications. The jobs of white middle-classes of the post-World War II economic boom are at risk of being displaced—or have long been offshored or automatized.

The politics of resentment emerging from this context have a strong gender dimension and not all of these structural changes are easily captured in unemployment statistics. As Nicholas Eberstadt has shown, the male population in the US is leaving the labor force in record numbers (Eberstadt, 2016). Today, the work rate of men between the age of 25 and 54 is only slightly lower than it was in 1940, at a time when the United States still was recovering from the Great Depression. The phenomenon of declining male labor participation sets the United States apart from other advanced industrialized economies. And even the economic recovery that we have seen under the Obama and the

Trump administration has not significantly changed that pattern. Additionally, the economic impact of COVID-19 has had an enormous impact already, but its long-term consequences on populist mobilization remain to be seen.

The labor market crisis of American men is compounded by factors that are, again, not strictly economic. Anne Case and Sir Angus Deaton found that since the 1990s, "middle-aged non-Hispanic whites in the U.S. with a high school diploma or less have experienced increasing midlife mortality." (Case & Deaton, 2020). The factors include a rise in "deaths of despair"—deaths by drugs, alcohol, and suicide—as well as a stalling of decline in mortality from heart disease and cancer. Case and Deaton suggest that the increases in these deaths are accompanied by a measurable deterioration in economic and social well-being for these populations.

Furthermore, current trends in educational achievement in the United States hint at the possibility that, in coming decades, the poor labor market performance of men might perpetuate itself. While men have historically dominated high-paid professions, resulting in a gender pay gap noticeable across all advanced economies, according to researchers David Autor and Melanie Wasserman, "[o]ver the last three decades, the labor market trajectory of males in the U.S. has turned downward along four dimensions: skills acquisition; employment rates; occupational stature; and real wage levels." (Autor & Wassermann, 2013).

The resulting loss of relative status among formerly privileged white men is leading some to turn to divisive populist politics to vent their anger and frustration. From this perspective, the labor market crisis in the United States also has psychological impacts that are contributing to populism. This is where we see a strong connection with existing cultural arguments. In U.S. culture, work remains a critical means of maintaining social relationships and a sense of dignity, while the absence of work generates despair. Arthur C. Brooks coined this as a "dignity deficit"—a potent resource ripe for unscrupulous political candidates to translate into popularized anger (Brooks, 2017). Donald Trump was very successful in mobilizing these angry voters through a politics of fear and resentment (Vormann & Weinman, 2020).

Conclusion

Seeking to avoid easy binaries, we argued that there are deeper economic, social and political factors that we have to take into account in order to understand why populist parties and actors can successfully mobilize sufficient parts of the electorate. In most of the cases, the success of populist parties and movements point to deeper structural problems within democracies that are harnessed by populist demagogues through strategies of resentment and racism. These deeper problems have developed over decades and are primarily the result of specific public policies (Vormann & Lammert, 2019). In turn, the 2008 financial crisis has brought this situation to a boiling point and prepared the ground for a politics of fear.

The economic conditions of historically marginalized groups such as women and people of color might have improved in recent decades. But there is still a long way to go, even if white male resentment sometimes distracts public discourses from this fact. In 2016, women working full time in the United States typically were still paid just 80% of what men earned; the wage gap for women of color has been even more pronounced (Blau & Kahn, 2016). But even if true emancipation seems far from achieved, the United States will continue to face a significant challenge if the gradual closing of the existing gaps goes hand in hand with an absolute decline of educational and labor market outcomes for white men, a majority of whom seems easily drawn to politicians who stoke their sense of resentment.

Literature

APSA. (1950). Toward a more responsible two-party system: A report of the committee on political parties of the American Political Science Association. *American Political Science Review, 44*, 1–99.

Autor, D., Dorn, D., Hanson, G., & Majlesi, K. (2017). A note on the effect of rising trade exposure on the 2016 presidential election. Appendix to Dorn, D., Hanson, G., & Majlesi, K. (2016). *Importing political polarization? The electoral consequences of rising trade exposure (No. w22637)*. National Bureau of Economic Research.

Autor, D., & M. Wasserman. (2013). Wayward sons: The emerging gender gap in labor markets and education. Third Way, available at http://economics.mit.edu/files/8754.

Barber, M., & N. McCarty. (2013). Causes and consequences of polarization. In J. Mansbridge & C. J. Martin. (Eds.), *Negotiating agreement in politics*, American Political Science Association. Available at https://scholar.harvard.edu/files/dtingley/files/negotiating_agreement_in_politics.pdf.

Blau, F. D., & L. M. Kahn. (2016). *The gender wage gap: Extent, trends, and explanations* (Discussion Paper 965). IZA Institute of Labor Economics, available at http://ftp.iza.org/dp9656.pdf.

Blyth, M., & J. Hopkin. 2020. Global Trumpism: Understanding anti-system politics in western democracies. In B. Vormann & M. Weinman (Eds.), *The emergence of illiberalism: Understanding a global phenomenon* (pp. 101–123).

Bonica, A., et. al. (2013), Why hasn't democracy slowed rising inequality? *Journal of Economic Perspectives, 27*(3), 103–124. Available at https://legacy.voteview.com/pdf/jep_BMPR.pdf.

Brooks, A. C. (2017). The dignity deficit. *Foreign Affairs*, March–April, available at https://www.foreignaffairs.com/articles/united-states/2017-02-13/dignity-deficit.

Case, A., & Deaton, S. A. (2020). *Deaths of despair and the future of capitalism*. Princeton University Press.

CNN Politics. (2018). Exit Polls. Available at http://www.cnn.com/election/results/exit-polls, Last accessed May 2018.

Darvas, Z., & K. Efstathio. (2016). Income inequality boosted Trump vote. *Bruegel*. Available at http://bruegel.org/2016/11/income-inequality-boosted-trump-vote/.

Dionne, E. J., Jr., Ornstein, N.-J., & Mann, T. E. (2017). *One nation after Trump: A guide for the perplexed, the disillusioned, the desperate, and the not-yet deported.* St. Martin's Press.

Eberstadt, N. (2016). *Men without work: America's invisible crisis.* Templeton Press.

Economist Intelligence Unit. (2019). *Democracy index 2018: Me too? Political participation, protest and democracy.* Retrieved from http://www.eiu.com/.

Edsall, T. B. (2018, October 7). How did the democrats become favorites of the rich? *The New York Times.* Accessed February 04, 2018. Available at https://www.nytimes.com/2015/10/07/opinion/how-did-the-democrats-become-favorites-of-the-rich.html.

Lammert, C. (2018). Einkommens- und Wohlstandsungleichheit und der Zustand der Demokratie in den USA. In W. Gellner & M. Oswald (Eds.), *Die gespaltenen Staaten von Amerika* (pp. 209–222). Springer Verlag.

Lammert, C. (2020). The crisis of democracy: The United States in perspective. In B. Vormann & M. Weinman (Eds.), *The emergence of illiberalism: Understanding a global phenomenon* (pp. 124–139).

Lammert, C., & Vormann, B. (2018). The heavenly chorus sings with a strong upper-class accent. In P. Horst, P. Adorf, & F. Decker (Eds.), *Die USA - eine scheiternde Demokratie?* (pp. 235–252). Campus Verlag.

Lammert, C., & Vormann, B. (2020). When inequalities matter most: The crisis of democracy as a crisis of trust. In T. Michael (Ed.), *Mobilization, representation, and responsiveness in the American democracy* (pp. 139–156). Palgrave Macmillan.

Layman, G. C., Carsey, T. M., & Horowitz, J. M. (2006). Party polarization in American politics: Characteristics, causes, and consequences. *Annual Review of Political Science, 9*, 83–110.

Lee, F. E. (2009). *Beyond ideology: Politics, principles, and partisanship in the U.S. senate.* University of Chicago.

Levy, P. (1952). *Toward a more responsible two-party system.* A Report of the Committee on Political Parties of the American Political Science Association.

Lindsey, B., & Teles, S. (2017). *The captured economy: How the powerful enrich themselves, slow down growth, and increase Inequality.* Oxford University Press.

Mann, T. E., & Ornstein, N. J. (2016). *It's even worse than it looks: How the American constitutional system collided with the new politics of extremism.* Basic Books.

Müller, J. W. (2016). *What is populism?* University of Pennsylvania Press.

Norris, P., & Inglehart, R. (2019). *Cultural backlash: Trump, Brexit, and authoritarian populism.* Cambridge University Press.

Page, B. I. & M. Gilens (2017). *Democracy in America? What has gone wrong and what we can do about it.* University of Chicago Press.

Pew (2017). *Public trust in government: 1958–2017.* Retrieved from http://www.people-press.org/2017/05/03/public-trust-in-government-1958-2017/.

Pew (2018). *The public, the political system and American democracy.* Pew. Retrieved from https://www.people-press.org/2018/04/26/the-public-the-political-system-and-american-democracy/.

Piketty, T. (2014). *Capital in the twenty-first century* (p. 2014). Harvard University Press.

Schlozman, K. L., Verba, S., & Brady, H. E. (2013). *The unheavenly chorus.* Princeton University Press.

Vormann, B., & Lammert, C. (2019). *Democracy in crisis.* Pennsylvania University Press.

Vormann, B. & M. Weinman (2020). From a politics of no alternative to a politics of fear: The Emergence of illiberalism and its variants. In Boris Vormann & Michael Weinman (Eds.). *The emergence of illiberalism: Understanding a global phenomenon* (pp. 3–26).

World Bank. (2018). All the ginis dataset, available at https://data.worldbank.org/data-catalog/all-the-ginis. Last accessed May 2018.

Zingales, L. (2012). *A capitalism for the people: Recapturing the lost genius of American prosperity*. Basic books.

Part VI

Populism & Gender

CHAPTER 16

Right-Wing Populism and Gender

Gabriele Dietze

Introduction

The political platforms of European right-wing populist parties attach great importance to statements about womanhood, family, sexuality, and the category of gender. Nevertheless, research on right-wing populism (RWP in the following) and gender is narrow. The subject is almost absent in the growing body of established canonized theoretical work on RWP. Occupation with gender-questions concentrates on a few select fields. Voting behavior plays a central role—here, the so-called gender gap is mainly addressed, i.e., the fact that significantly fewer women vote right-wing populist parties (Spierings & Zaslove, 2015). And the gender gap raises the question of whether right-wing populist parties are 'men's parties' (Erzeel & Rashkova, 2017; Mudde & Kaltwasser, 2015).

The men's-parties-verdict does not hold up in the long run. Western European RWP parties are increasingly led by women (Meret et al., 2016). These party leaders are no decorative accessories, but influential and power-conscious personalities who offer nation-specific brands of 'feminization' of right-wing politics: Pia Kjærsgaard 1996–2011, in Denmark, who presented herself as a prudent housewife; Siv Jensen since 2006 in Norway, who performs as a single independent professional politician; Marine Le Pen since 2011 in France, who took up the dynastic inheritance of her father Jean Marie Le Pen, but staged herself as a self-confident working mother (Geva, 2020); and Alice Weidel,

G. Dietze (✉)
Institut für Europäische Ethnologie, Humboldt University, Berlin, Germany
e-mail: gabriele.dietze@rz.hu-berlin.de

© The Author(s), under exclusive license to Springer Nature Switzerland AG 2022
M. Oswald (ed.), *The Palgrave Handbook of Populism*,
https://doi.org/10.1007/978-3-030-80803-7_16

who has been one of the two top candidates for the German AfD since 2017 and lives in a same-sex relationship with children. This seeming contradiction between progressive life-arrangements of female RWP leaders and backward party politics concerning gender relations is a kind of 'calculated ambivalence' (Reisigl, 2020) suggesting modernity by downplaying the real programmatic shortcomings for women.

Not only leading women have carved out an important place in RWP parties, but female rank and file join their notorious anti-immigration hostility, described by the term 'femonationalism' (Farris, 2017). The AfD (Alternative for Germany), for example, organizes 'women's marches' against allegedly sexually aggressive foreigners. RWP appeals furthermore to an alleged female protective instinct directed to her/the family. Swedish scholars speak in this regard of 'care racism' (Sager & Mulinari, 2018). Umit Erel writes about RWP in the UK and states that family ideals are understood as 'care for the nation's future. Care is then articulated for racist activism' (Erel, 2018, p. 157). Akwugo Emejulu observes right-wing US Tea Party women gathering around the concept 'concerned motherhood' (Emejulu, 2011, p. 140). These allusions to care and motherhood are all the more interesting because modern Feminism is also concerned with care, but with entirely different motives: On the one hand, there is a discussion of a necessary new feminist ethics of care (Parton, 2003). And on the other hand, debates on Neoliberalism's effort to shrink the welfare-state and leave unpaid domestic care for children and the elderly to women.

It is striking that RWP's family and women's politics use 'feminist' frames. But if that happens, the frames are emptied of their gender justice seeking content and transformed via 'frame-co-optation' (Cullen, 2020) into a 'pro-women against-feminists' stand. Anti-feminism is essential, and women in the RWP like to position themselves as a paradoxical anti-modern avant-garde. Following Zygmunt Bauman, they indulge in a 'retrotopian' (Bauman, 2019) affect (selling the past as future). RWP rejects Feminism as a 'modern' normative enterprise designed to abolish traditional womanhood and its advantages of full-time motherhood and stay-at-home-privilege. I call this sentiment 'emancipation fatigue' (Dietze, 2020). The all-encompassing RWP Anti-feminism has drawn a considerable body of research (Lang & Peters, 2018; Maihofer & Schutzbach, 2015; Saresma, 2018).

The populist obsession with gender and sexuality is hard to overlook. Populist actors conjure up the heteronormative nuclear family as the only model of social organization, attack reproductive rights, question sex education, criticize a so-called 'gender ideology,' reject same-sex marriage and adoption rights for gay couples, seek to re-install biologically understood binary gender differences und lead crusades against LGBTQI-Activism (Swan, 2018). Although this fixation on traditional family and gender-values has become an omnipresent feature in the right-wing discourse, established RWP-research has rarely addressed this aspect. Nor have RWP gender-discourses been considered as important for the attractiveness of populism.

One attributes the success of right-wing populism usually to nationalistic, economic, or culturalist reasons (Brubaker, 2017; Gidron & Hall, 2017; Norris & Inglehart, 2019). If you look into handbooks that canonize the knowledge of subjects, you will find, for instance, in *The Routledge Handbook of Global Populism* (de la Torre, 2018), not a single article on gender and RWP. The *Oxford Handbook of Populism's* entry on gender argues that there is only a 'weak relationship' between populism and gender (Abi-Hassan, 2017, p. 441). The three-volume handbook *Populism and the Crisis of Democracy* has one gender-related contribution, which centers on gender(ed) nationalism and migration (Hadj-Abdou, 2019). Only the *Oxford Handbook of the Radical Right* offers an article treating the subject Gender and RWP as a legitimate object of knowledge but restrains itself mostly to considerations on voting behavior and questions of political representation (Coffé, 2018).

As unpleasantly scarce as the topic is in the official scientific/academic landscape, the more pleasing is emergent research that places gender at the center of RWP investigation. Particularly fruitful for such an approach is the combination of gender studies and critical social or cultural or media studies. These transdisciplinary efforts command a sophisticated toolbox to look into the relatively new phenomenon. Two perspectives have proved to be fruitful: First, an advanced understanding of gender. The latter must be seen as a social construction, as a cultural practice, as an axis of inequality, and as a link to the division of labor in the context of neoliberal globalization, poverty, and structural racism. Secondly, one has to take into account that RWP does use gender not only as an issue itself, but it uses gender as a 'convenient proxy' (Apperly, 2018) to build alliances, to popularize worldviews and to instill fear and discord. In short gender-talk works as well as a meta-language for political maneuvering and for negotiating different conditions of inequality and power in the context of current struggles over hegemony and resources forged by Neoliberalism.

INTERSECTIONALITIES

A gender perspective on RWP has the theoretical advantage that gender studies usually work with Kimberley Crenshaw's concept (Crenshaw, 2017) of intersectionality (Lutz et al., 2016). Thus, one has to employ a multifactorial analysis. Intersectionality means that other categories of social stratification—race, ethnicity, class, sexuality, geopolitics, religion, and ability—have to be taken into account. Intersectionality is by no means just a theoretical model or a method of investigation, but a mandate for political coalition-building (see Chapter 17 Julia Roth in this volume). Intersectional feminists provide platforms against right-wing populism in the US (Gökarıksel & Smith, 2017) and Latin America (Bidaseca & Loi, 2017; Roth, 2019), as well as in Germany, represented in the campaign *#ausnahmslos* (without exception), with which intersectional feminists opposed the racist interpretations of sexual violence as innate only in Muslim migrants.

Of particular importance for the question at hand are the intersections of gender with class, location, and geopolitical position. The neoliberal revolution is a central backdrop of current right-wing populism. Related critical gender-sensitive research (Fraser, 2016) is, therefore, of great importance for any consideration of right-wing populism and gender. Neoliberalism means the economization and commodification of many areas of life. What is more, is the erosion of the welfare state. The shift from solidarity to individual responsibility, for instance, engenders the referral back to the family as the agency of care, i.e., mostly to women. The Corona Crisis (Donner, 2020) made this highly visible. And the redistribution of social wealth has an immense impact on the gender order. Gender issues are furthermore structurally connected to globalization and the effects of Neoliberalism in questions of pay and breadwinning as well as in the international division of labor (Wichterich, 2000) and the 'Global Chain of Care' (Hochschild, 2015).

Equally important as the intersection of gender, class, and geopolitics is the intersection of gender with race and ethnicity. The Right-wing 'obsession with gender' is most closely linked to the exclusion of racialized others, conceived as dangerous for the white national body. The narrative of migrants as a sexual threat, as it was brought forward by the 'cultural panic' surrounding the harassments at New Year's Eve 2015/2016 in Cologne, Germany, is exemplary. Additionally, US president Donald Trump's slur of the 'Mexican rapist intruder' provides striking examples and has triggered a variety of RWP-responses, for instance, the slogan 'rapefugees not welcome.' Such sexualized populist strategies of othering result in a unique variation when it comes to Women of Color, expressed in the intricate combination of sexism and racism.

The most recent example was the discriminatory reaction of the US-American president Donald Trump to the nomination of Kamala Harris, a woman of African-Indian descent for vice president in 2020 (A. Butler, 2020). Trump called Harris 'nasty' and 'disrespectful'—a racist dog whistle that especially black women should not behave 'uppity'. Furthermore, Trump claimed that Harris was not born in the United States, which would disqualify her for the destined office. In fact, Harris was born in Oakland, California. This 'birtherism', which was also used against President Obama, is a conglomeration of exclusion mechanisms. It stigmatizes the targeted person as a 'foreigner,' not belonging to the nation, but also as an intruder and impostor.

Birtherism corresponds to the European immigration struggles about either 'blood-right'—*ius sanguinis* citizenship by parental nationality—or land right—*ius solis*, citizenship by birthplace—at which point the populist right champions *ius sanguinis*. According to this, a legitimate citizen would only be the one whose ancestors have lived for generations in the respective country and looked like the autochthonous population. In this respect, birtherism is closely linked to the white fear of being 'outnumbered' by the fertility of non-autochthonous 'invaders' (Fixmer-Oraiz, 2019). Right-wing actors launch selective pro-natalism campaigns (Schultz, 2015), targeting particularly white women to procreate. Feminists, especially activists in pro-choice campaigns, are regarded as enemies and 'baby-killers' called 'feminazis.' Recent transnational efforts to abolish or limit reproductive rights are closely related to this narrative (Gökarıksel et al., 2017).

Research Report[1]

General Literature

Although a research-field 'right-wing populism and gender' is only beginning to emerge, we can draw on several pioneer publications: the special issue 'Gender and the Populist Radical Right Politics' of the journal *Patterns of Prejudice* (Spierings et al., 2015) and anthologies on Europe such as *Gender and Far-Right Politics in Europe* (Bitzan et al., 2017), *The Triumph of Women: The Female Face of the Far-Right in Europe* (Gutsche, 2018)[2] and *Right-Wing Populism and Gender: European Perspectives and Beyond* (Dietze & Roth, 2020). The journal *Sings* launched a special issue 'Gender and the Rise of the Global Right' (Graff et al., 2019). Besides, particular issues of gender-theoretical journals have lately been published on specific topics of gender and right-wing populism.[3] Historical feminist research has been dealing with women in the extreme right since early on, e.g., with women from the far-right in the KluKluxKlan (Blee, 2008) or in a global perspective (Bacchetta & Power, 2013), as well as in extremist and neofascist parties (Amesberger & Halbmayr, 2002; Birsl, 2013; Bitzan, 2017). Research on contemporary Gender and RWP has originated many studies of particular national contexts.[4] And quite a lot of comparative studies of different countries on the subject have appeared.[5]

Special Subjects

Related fields such as 'anti-genderism' are not only significant issues for RWP (Brandini-Aissis & Ogando, 2018; Hark & Villa, 2015) this intricate kind of Anti-Feminism and Misogynie are broader phenomenon (Gunnarson-Payne, 2019; Kuhar & Paternotte, 2017). Anti-genderism immerses in religious (Case, 2019) and anti-feminist discourses (Lang & Peters, 2018), which reach far into those sectors of the middle class that are slipping more and more to the right (Zick et al., 2019). Fights against a so-called 'gender ideology' are often related to worries over 'endangered masculinity' (Erzeel & Rashkova, 2017; Kimmel, 2017; Norocel, 2010; Strick, 2020a). Referring to the example of Donald Trump, Simon Schleusener gives special attention to patriarchal gender relations and capitalist socialization and subjectification (Schleusener, 2020).

A central dimension for the analysis of gender and the right-wing populist complex is the examination of affects, emotions, and sexuality (Rico et al., 2017; Strick, 2020b; Wodak, 2015). The fields of gender, family, and sexual politics are densely loaded with emotions—fears, passions, impulses to protect—which right-wing populist actors trigger and transfer into affective patterns. Patterns such as 'concern'—think of the many 'concerned citizens' (*besorgte Bürger*, in German) and 'concerned mothers' in RWP propaganda. Particularly anger understood as male virtue gets cultivated as legitimate 'political feeling.' Tapping into and creating affect is an effective means of RWP political communication (Salmela & von Scheve, 2017). Eszter Kováts illustrates how an affective strategy work in the Hungarian context, where feelings of hatred toward allegedly dangerous foreigners and feminists are kindled and supported by an illiberal populist government (Kováts, 2020).

Another important topic in the RWP obsession with gender is sexual politics. Sexuality has to be contained in the safe space of the heteronormative family. RWP attacks early sex education in French, and German campaigns, such as *manif pour tous* or *Demo für Alle* (Moeser, 2020; Schmincke, 2020). Simultaneously one can observe a kind of 'strategic progressivism' in sexual matters in Europe and the United States. Scholars speak of 'sexual nationalism' (Mepschen & Duyvendak, 2012) or 'sexual exceptionalism' (Bracke, 2011; Dietze, 2019; Puar, 2011). These positions project sexism onto racialized others constructed as intruders and sexual threats to native women and the occidental culture. In this way, domestic sexual violence is made invisible and shifted/transferred onto immigrant 'orientals.'

A similar structure is at work in the US, conjuring up the phantasm of black or immigrant rapists as a way to deflect attention away from white systemic sexism. It is, therefore, no coincidence that the successful #MeToo campaign was founded by African American women. The organizers panned the Twitter platform as a forum for young black women who wanted to share experiences of racism at the workplace and found out that sexual harassment is one of the most pressing problems. White and other women picked up on this and forged #MeToo into a powerful weapon to hold white (and other) sexually aggressive men to account. The RWP position is, as always in sexual politics, still split. When it comes to criticizing hegemonic patriarchy's sexual misconduct, RWP sees only an excess of political correctness (Lukose, 2018). When it comes to Muslim sexual harassment, German and Austrian right-wingers launched a kind of right-wing #MeToo with the campaign #120dezibel (Jäger et al., 2019), urging women to defend themselves against attacks from strangers with a noisy pocket alarm.

Promoting seemingly contradictory positions and getting away with them is substantial for RWP. Martin Reisigl calls these strategies 'calculated ambivalences' (Reisigl, 2020). It allows right-wing populist actors to communicate positively with either faithful sexually conservative followers or with a more modern constituency. The German AfD, for instance, allows openly gay activists into the party, as long as they endorse (non-queer) homosexuality and take a stand against gender-ambivalence and confirm to desire one clear-cut gender (men, in the case of the AfD's gay group) (Wielowiejski, 2020). When it comes to Western women, they can be presented as already 'fully emancipated' and as having achieved sexual self-determination. The political platforms of RWP, however, promote full-time motherhood. Political engagement of women fares as an extension of their gender-role. The Hungarian right-wing populist Victor Orbàn supported the election of Ursula von der Leyen as president of the European Commission on the grounds of her being a mother of seven. Looking from this angle, equality politics and gender mainstreaming thus appear as not only unnecessary but also as harmful: firstly, it condemns women to an eternal victim position. Secondly, it undermines the agency of 'autochthonous' women to choose between occupation beyond the house or stay-at-home-housewifery.

Gender as Meta-Language

Right-wing populists not only raise questions of gender because they touch deep inner beliefs, but also because it is a tool to forge alliances or to draw borders. A study by the Friedrich Ebert Foundation on European anti-gender mobilization in 2015 is accordingly titled 'Gender as Symbolic Glue' (Kovàts & Poim, 2015). Leila Hadi-Abdou speaks of the RWP employment of gender as a 'boundary-making strategy' (Hadj-Abdou, 2019). Hungary's illiberal government employs post-colonial wording when it perceives gender mainstreaming as introduced by the EU as 'Western imperialism' aimed at destroying the cultural identity of a small country. Pope Francis, who coined the term 'gender ideology,' speaks of ideological colonization. Poland chooses a language of contamination when denouncing gender as 'Ebola from Brussels' (Korolczuk & Graff, 2018). Judith Butler recently described the right-wing obsession with gender in psychoanalytical terms as a replacement, condensation, and abbreviation of cultural anxiety (J. Butler, 2020). All these deployments make the notion of gender into an 'ideological matrix' (Engeli, 2019, p. 231), a suitable tool for scandalizing, internal exclusion, and external border-drawing.

The category gender is furthermore instrumental for RWP meta-politics in an epistemological sense. Because the usage of gender challenges the very existence of two sexes understood as immutable natural fact—regardless of any tendencies to a more flexible and fluid understanding of incorporated sex-identity in recent decades. Populists do not tire invoking the allegedly inescapable 'biological' difference of the sexes. They see both sexes as antagonistic and complementary. This conviction naturalizes heteronormative couplings and reifies any difference of power between men and women. As deconstructive Feminism has claimed, assuming two (and only two) sexes as binary and hierarchically arranged is essential for order per se. The right-wing struggle against gender is thus a struggle against the dissolution of 'natural' orders, indeed a challenge of order in general (Sauer, 2017). Order, or more precisely, law and order, is the air RWP breezes. In this respect, the sexes cannot be socially constructed. They would then be malleable and lose their function to describe and guarantee hierarchical orders, particularly masculine domination (Bourdieu, 2001).

Outlook

Intersectional Feminisms such as 'NiUnaMenos' in Argentina, the International Women's Strike of March 8, or the Women's Marches in the US provide a powerful counterforce to the right-wing populist trend. Their insistence on alliances with groups representing different forms of discrimination goes against the core of RWP's self-conception in general and RWP women's politics in particular. The populist idea of 'people as one' cannot cater to feminist justice claims because they must be enforced against the perdurability of patriarchal power. As 'special interests,' they will destroy the needed unity. In contrast, intersectional feminists forge alliances on an idea of the 'people as many' (Emejulu, 2011). They perform an inclusive form of solidarity as opposed to the exclusive notion that is grounded in the imaginary of the national supremacy predominating the RWP. Queer-intersectional Feminism is so to speak a natural and radical adversary of RWP.

Notes

1. The research report draws on the introduction of the anthology. *Right-Wing Populism and Gender: European Perspectives and Beyond* (Dietze & Roth, 2020). The text is revised, and updated with new references. I thank Julia Roth for inspiration and cooperation.
2. Publication of the 'Friedrich Ebert Stiftung'. Available online http://library.fes.de/pdf-files/dialog/14636.pdf. Accessed 16.08.2020.
3. *Women's Studies International Forum* (May–June 2018, vol. 68, on 'Feminisms in Times of Anti-Genderism, Racism and Austerity'); *Feministische Studien* (November 2018, vol. 36, no. 2, on the normalization of neo-reactionary policies); *Femina Politica* (2018, vol. 27, no. 1, 'Angriff auf die Demokratie' assault on democracy); *Politics and Governance* (2018, vol 6, no. 3, the Feminist project under threat in Europe); *West European Politics* (2017, vol. 40, no. 4, Gender and the radical right in comparative perspective).
4. See for example from the Netherlands: (de Lange & Mügge, 2015; Verloo, 2018); Scandinavia: (Akkerman & Hagelund, 2007; Keskinen, 2018; Norocel, 2013; Saresma, 2018; Siim & Mokre, 2013); Italy: (Donà, 2020; Farris, 2017); France: (N. Mayer, 2015; Moeser, 2020; Morgan, 2017; Scrinzi, 2017); Germany: (Dietze, 2018; Jägeret al., 2019; Lang & Fritzsche, 2018), Slovenia (Pajnik et al., 2016); Austria: (Goetz, 2018; S. Mayer et al., 2015; Sauer, 2017); Poland: (Grzebalska & Pető, 2018; Korolczuk & Graff, 2018); Hungary: (Kovàts & Poim, 2015), UK (Emejulu, 2017; Erel, 2018), Finland.
5. Comparison of: North–South (Moghadam & Kaftan, 2019); all Western Europe (Akkerman, 2015), Denmark, Norway and Austria (Meret & Siim, 2013), Italy, France (Scrinzi, 2014), Finland Spain (Kantola & Lombardo, 2019).

Literature

Abi-Hassan, S. (2017). Populism and gender. In C. R. Kaltwasser, P. A. Taggart, P. O. Espejo, & P. Ostiguy (Eds.), *The Oxford handbook of populism* (pp. 426–444). Oxford University Press.

Akkerman, T. (2015). Gender and the radical right in Western Europe: A comparative analysis of policy agendas. *Patterns of Prejudice, 49*(1–2), 37–60.

Akkerman, T., & Hagelund, A. (2007). 'Women and children first!': Anti-immigration parties and gender in Norway and the Netherlands. *Patterns of Prejudice, 41*(2), 197–214.

Amesberger, H., & Halbmayr, B. (Eds.). (2002). *Rechtsextreme Parteien, eine mögliche Heimat für Frauen?*. Leske+ Budrich.

Apperly, E. (2018). Why Europe's far-right is targeting gender studies. *The Atlantic*. Retrieved from https://www.theatlantic.com/international/archive/2019/06/europe-far-right-target-gender-studies/591208/.

Bacchetta, P., & Power, M. (2013). *Right-wing women: From conservatives to extremists around the world*. Routledge.

Bauman, Z. (2019). *Retrotopia*. Premier Parallèle.

Bidaseca, K., & Loi, Y. (2017). 8M: Ni una Menos: Paro Internacional de Mujeres. In *8M: Ni una Menos: Vivos nos Queremos* (pp. 9–14). Milena Caserola.

Birsl, U. (2013). *Rechtsextremismus: Weiblich*. Springer-Verlag.

Bitzan, R. (2017). Research on gender and the far-right in Germany since 1990: Developments, findings, and future prospects. In M. Köttig, R. Bitzan, & A. Petö (Eds.), *Gender and far-right politics in Europe* (pp. 65–79). Palgrave.

Bitzan, R., Köttig, M., & Petö, A. (2017). *Gender and far-right politics in Europe*. Palgrave.

Blee, K. M. (2008). *Women of the Klan: Racism and gender in the 1920s*. University of California Press.

Bourdieu, P. (2001). *Masculine domination*: Stanford University Press.

Bracke, S. (2011). Subjects of debate: Secular and sexual exceptionalism and Muslim women in the Netherlands. *Feminist Review, 98*(1), 28–46.

Brandini-Aissis, M., & Ogando, A. C. (2018). Gender ideology and the Brazilian elections. Retrieved from http://www.publicseminar.org/2018/11/gender-ideology-and-the-brazilian-elections/.

Brubaker, R. (2017). Between nationalism and civilizationism: The European populist moment in comparative perspective. *Ethnic and Racial Studies, 40*(8), 1191–1226.

Butler, A. (2020). Kamala Harris is already facing sexist and racist attacks—And they'll only get worse. *NBC*. Retrieved from https://www.nbcnews.com/think/opinion/kamala-harris-already-facing-sexist-racist-attacks-it-ll-only-ncna1236620.

Butler, J. (2020). *Gender whose fantasy?* Paper presented at the 10th anniversary of the Fachgesellschaft Geschlechterstudien, TU Berlin.

Case, M. A. (2019). Trans Formations in the Vatican's war on "gender ideology". *Signs: Journal of Women in Culture and Society, 44*(3), 639–664.

Coffé, H. (2018). Gender and the radical right. In J. Rydgren (Ed.), *The Oxford handbook of the radical right* (pp. 200–211). Oxford University Press.

Crenshaw, K. W. (2017). *On intersectionality: Essential writings*. The New Press.

Cullen, P. (2020). From neglect to threat: Feminist responses to right wing populism in the European Union. *European Politics and Society*, 1–18.

de la Torre, C. (2018). *Routledge handbook of global populism*: Routledge.

de Lange, S. L., & Mügge, L. M. (2015). Gender and right-wing populism in the low countries: Ideological variations across parties and time. *Patterns of prejudice, 49*(1–2), 61–80.

Dietze, G. (2018). Rechtspopulismus und Geschlecht. Paradox Und Leitmotiv. *Femina Politica, 27*(1), 34–47.

Dietze, G. (2019). *Sexueller Exzeptionalismus. Überlegenheitsnarrative in Immigrationsabwehr und Rechtspopulismus.* Transcript.

Dietze, G. (2020). Why are Women attracted to right-wing populism? Sexual exceptionalism, emancipation fatigue, new maternalism. In G. Dietze & J. Roth (Eds.), *Right-wing populism and gender in Europe and beyond* (pp. 147–165). Transcript.

Dietze, G., & Roth, J. (Eds.). (2020). *Right-wing populism and gender in Europe and beyond.* Transcript.

Donà, A. (2020). The populist Italian Lega from ethno-regionalism to radical right-wing nationalism: Backsliding gender-equality policies with a little help from the anti-gender movement. *European Journal of Politics and Gender, 3*(1), 161–163.

Donner, F. (2020). How women are getting squeezed by the pandemic. *New York Times.* Retrieved from https://www.nytimes.com/2020/05/20/us/women-economy-jobs-coronavirus-gender.html.

Emejulu, A. (2011). Can "the people" be feminists? Analyzing the fate of feminist justice claims in populist grassroots movements in the United States. *Interface: Special Issue on Feminism, Women's Movements and Women in Movements, 3*(2), 123–151.

Emejulu, A. (2017). Feminism for the 99%: Towards a populist feminism? Can feminism for the 99% succeed as a new kind of populism? *Soundings: A Journal of Politics and Culture, 66,* 63–67.

Engeli, I. (2019). Gender and sexuality research in the age of populism: Lessons for political science. *European Political Science,* 1–10.

Erel, U. (2018). *Saving and reproducing the nation: Struggles around right-wing politics of social reproduction, gender and race in austerity Europe.* Paper presented at the Women's Studies International Forum.

Erzeel, S., & Rashkova, E. R. (2017). Still men's parties? Gender and the radical right in comparative perspective. *West European Politics, 40*(4), 812–820.

Farris, S. R. (2017). *In the name of women's rights: The rise of femonationalism.* Duke University Press.

Fixmer-Oraiz, N. (2019). *Homeland maternity.* Illinois University Press.

Fraser, N. (2016). Progressive Neoliberalism versus reactionary populism: A choice that feminists should refuse. *NORA-Nordic Journal of Feminist and Gender Research, 24*(4), 281–284.

Geva, D. (2020). Daughter, mother, captain: Marine Le Pen, gender, and populism in the French National Front. *Social Politics: International Studies in Gender, State & Society, 27*(1), 1–26.

Gidron, N., & Hall P. A. (2017). The politics of social status: Economic and cultural roots of the populist right. *The British Journal of Sociology, 68*(1), 57–84.

Goetz, J. (2018). "Aber wir haben die wahren Natur der Geschlechter erkannt". Geschlechterpolitiken, Antifeminismus und Homofeindlichkeiten im Denken der "Identitären". In J. M. Sedlacek, A. Winkler, & J. Goetz (Eds.), *Untergangster des Abendlandes: Ideologie und Rezeption der rechtsextremen "Identitären"* (pp. 253–284). Marta Press.

Gökarıksel, B., & Smith, S. (2017). Intersectional Feminism beyond US flag hijab and pussy hats in Trump's America. *Gender, Place & Culture, 24*(5), 628–644.
Graff, A., Kapur, R., & Walters, S. D. (2019). Gender and the rise of the global right. *Signs: Journal of Women in Culture and Society, 44*(1), 541–560.
Grzebalska, W., & Pető, A. (2018). The gendered modus operandi of the illiberal transformation in Hungary and Poland. *Women's Studies International Forum, 68*, 164–172.
Gunnarson-Payne, J. (2019). Challenging "gender-ideology" (Anti)gender politics in Europe's populist moment. *The New Pretender,* (10, February), 1–10.
Gutsche, E. (Ed.). (2018). *Triumph of women: The female face of the populist and far-right in Europe.* Friedrich Ebert Stiftung.
Hadj-Abdou, L. (2019). 'Gender (ed) nationalism' of the populist radical right: An extreme typicality. In G. Fitzi, J. Mackert, & B. S. Turner (Eds.), *Populism and the crisis of democracy* (Vol. 3 Migration, Gender and Religion, pp. 94–111).
Hark, S., & Villa, P.-I. (Eds.). (2015). *Anti-Genderismus. Sexualität und Geschlecht als Schauplätze aktueller politischer Auseinandersetzungen.* Transcript.
Hochschild, A. R. (2015). Global care chains and emotional surplus value. In D. Engster & T. Metz (Eds.), *Justice, politics, and the family* (pp. 249–261). Routledge.
Jäger, M., Kroppenberg, M., Nothardt, B., & Wamper, R. (2019). *#120Dezibel: Frauenrechte oder Antifeminismus? Populistische Diskursstrategien der extremen Rechten und Anschlussstellen im politischen Mainstream.* Retrieved from https://nbn-resolving.org/urn:nbn:de:0168-ssoar-68584-6.
Kantola, J., & Lombardo, E. (2019). Populism and feminist politics: The cases of Finland and Spain. *European Journal of Political Research, 58*(4), 1108–1128.
Keskinen, S. (2018). *The 'crisis' of white hegemony, neonationalist femininities and antiracist Feminism.* Paper presented at the Women's Studies International Forum.
Kimmel, M. (2017). *Angry white men: American masculinity at the end of an era.* Hachette.
Korolczuk, E., & Graff, A. (2018). Gender as "ebola from Brussels": The anticolonial frame and the rise of illiberal populism. *Signs: Journal of Women in Culture and Society, 43*(4), 797–821.
Kováts, E. (2020). Post-Socialist conditions and the Orbán government's gender politics between 2010–2019 in Hungary. In G. Dietze & J. Roth (Eds.), *Right-wing populism and gender: European perspectives and beyond* (pp. 75–99). Transcript.
Kovàts, E., & Poim, M. (Eds.). (2015). *Gender as symbolic Clue: The position and role of conservative and far-right parties in the anti-gender mobilizations in Europe.* Friedrich Ebert Stiftung.
Kuhar, R., & Paternotte, D. (2017). *Anti-gender campaigns in Europe: Mobilizing against equality.* Rowman & Littlefield.
Lang, J., & Fritzsche, C. (2018). Backlash, neoreaktionäre Politiken oder Antifeminismus. Forschende Perspektiven auf aktuelle Debatten um Geschlecht. *Feministische studien,* (2), 335–346.
Lang, J., & Peters, U. (2018). *Antifeminismus in Bewegung: Aktuelle Debatten um Geschlecht und sexuelle Vielfalt.* Marta Press.
Lukose, R. (2018). Decolonizing Feminism in the #MeToo era. *The Cambridge Journal of Anthropology, 36*(2), 34–52.
Lutz, H., Vivar, M. T. H., & Supik, L. (2016). *Framing intersectionality: Debates on a multi-faceted concept in gender studies.* Routledge.

Maihofer, A., & Schutzbach, F. (2015). Vom Anti-Feminismus zum Anti-Genderismus. Eine zeitdiagnostische Betrachtung am Beispiel Schweiz. In S. Hark & I.-P. Villa (Eds.), *(Anti-) Genderismus. Sexualität und Geschlecht als Schauplätze aktueller politischer Auseinandersetzungen* (pp. 201–218).

Mayer, N. (2015). The closing of the radical right gender gap in France? *French Politics, 13*(4), 391–414.

Mayer, S., Sori, I., & Sauer, B. (2015). Gendering 'the people': Heteronormativity and 'ethno-Masochism' in populist imaginary. In M. Ranieri (Ed.), *Populism, media, and education. Challenging discrimination in contemporary digital societies* (pp. 84–104). Routledge.

Mepschen, P., & Duyvendak, J. W. (2012). European sexual nationalisms: The culturalization of citizenship and the sexual politics of belonging and exclusion. *Perspectives on Europe, 42*(1), 70–76.

Meret, S., & Siim, B. (2013). Gender, populism and politics of belonging: Discourses of right-wing populist parties in Denmark, Norway and Austria. In B. Siim & M. Mokre (Eds.), *Negotiating gender and diversity in an emergent european public sphere* (pp. 78–96). London: Palgrave.

Meret, S., Siim, B., & Pingaud, E. (2016). Men's parties with women leaders: A comparative study of the right-wing populist leaders Pia Kjærsgaard, Marine Le Pen and Siv Jensen. In G. Lazarides & G. Campani (Eds.), *Understanding the populist shift* (pp. 122–149). Routledge.

Moeser, C. (2020). Sexual Politics as a tool to 'undemonize' right-wing siscourses in France. In G. Dietze & J. Roth (Eds.), *Right-Wing populism and gender: European perspectives and beyond* (pp. 117–133). Transcript.

Moghadam, V. M., & Kaftan, G. (2019). *Right-wing populisms north and south: Varieties and gender dynamics.* Paper presented at the Women's Studies International Forum.

Morgan, K. J. (2017). Gender, right-wing populism, and immigrant integration policies in France, 1989–2012. *West European Politics, 40*(4), 887–906.

Mudde, C., & Kaltwasser, C. R. (2015). Vox populi or vox masculini? Populism and gender in Northern Europe and South America. *Patterns of Prejudice, 49*(1–2), 16–36.

Norocel, O. C. (2010). Constructing radical right populist resistance: Metaphors of heterosexist masculinities and the family question in Sweden. *Norma, 5*(2), 170–183.

Norocel, O. C. (2013). "Give us back Sweden!": A feminist reading of the (re) interpretations of the folkhem conceptual metaphor in Swedish radical right populist discourse. *NORA-Nordic Journal of Feminist and Gender Research, 21*(1), 4–20.

Norris, P., & Inglehart, R. (2019). *Cultural backlash: Trump, brexit, and authoritarian populism.* Cambridge University Press.

Pajnik, M., Kuhar, R., & Šori, I. (2016). Populism in the Slovenian context: Between ethno-nationalism and re-traditionalisation. In *The rise of the far-right in Europe* (pp. 137–160). Springer.

Parton, N. (2003). Rethinking professional practice: The contributions of social constructionism and the feminist 'ethics of care'. *British Journal of Social Work, 33*(1), 1–16.

Puar, J. (2011). Abu Ghraib and US sexual exceptionalism. *Works and Days, 29*(115–142).

Reisigl, M. (2020). Mit zweierlei Maß gemessen–Kalkulierte Ambivalenz in rechtspopulistischen Repräsentationen von Geschlechterverhältnissen. *Zeitschrift für Literatur und Linguistik, 50*(203–229).

Rico, G., Guinjoan, M., & Anduiza, E. (2017). The emotional underpinnings of populism: How anger and fear affect populist attitudes. *Swiss Political Science Review, 23*(4), 444–461.

Roth, J. (2019). *Can feminism trump populism? Right-wing trends and intersectional contestations in the Americas*. WVT/Bilingual Press.

Sager, M., & Mulinari, D. (2018). Safety for whom? Exploring femonationalism and care-racism in Sweden. *Women's Studies International Forum, 68*, 149–156.

Salmela, M., & von Scheve, C. (2017). Emotional roots of right-wing political populism. *Social Science Information, 56*(4), 567–595.

Saresma, T. (2018). Gender populism: Three cases of Finns party actors' traditionalist anti-feminism. *Nykykulttuurin tutkimuskeskuksen julkaisuja*(122), 177–199.

Sauer, B. (2017). Gesellschaftstheoretische Überlegungen zum europäischen Rechtspopulismus. Zum Erklärungspotenzial der Kategorie Geschlecht. *PVS Politische vierteljahresschrift, 58*(1), 3–22.

Schleusener, S. (2020). 'You're Fired!' retrotopian desire an right wing class politics. In G. Dietze & J. Roth (Eds.), *Right-wing populism and gender. European perspectives and beyond* (pp. 167–185). Transcript.

Schmincke, I. (2020). Sexual politics from the right. Attacks on gender, sexuality and Sex-Education. In G. Dietze & J. Roth (Eds.), *Right-wing populism and gender: European perspectives and beyond* (pp. 59–73). Transcript.

Schultz, S. (2015). Reproducing the nation: The new German population policy and the concept of demographization. *Distinktion: Scandinavian Journal of Social Theory, 16*(3), 337–361.

Scrinzi, F. (2014). *Gendering activism in populist radical right parties. A comparative study of women's and men's participation in the Northern League (Italy) and The National Front (France)*. In-Progress preliminary analysis report.

Scrinzi, F. (2017). Gender and women in the Front National discourse and policy: From 'mothers of the nation' to 'working mothers'? *New Formations, 91*(91), 87–101.

Siim, B., & Mokre, M. (2013). *Negotiating gender and diversity in an emergent European public sphere*. Palgrave Macmillan.

Spierings, N., & Zaslove, A. (2015). Gendering the vote for populist radical-right parties. *Patterns of Prejudice, 49*(1–2), 135–162.

Spierings, N., Zaslove, A., Mügge, L. M., & de Lange, S. L. (2015). Gender and populist radical-right politics. *An Introduction: Patterns of Prejudice, 49*(1–2), 3–15.

Strick, S. (2020a). The 'alternative right': Masculinities and ordinary affects. In G. Dietze & J. Roth (Eds.), *Right-wing populism and gender in Europe and beyond* (pp. 207–230). Transcript.

Strick, S. (2020b). Right-wing world-building: Affect and sexuality in the 'alternative right'. In H. Paul (Ed.), *The comeback of populism: Transatlantic perspectives, ed. Heike Paul, Ursula Prutsch, and Jürgen Gebhardt (Heidelberg: Winter Verlag, 2019)* (pp. 157–182). Winter Verlag.

Swan, W. (2018). Building allies: Resisting oligarchy, populism, authoritarianism, and economic nationalism. In W. Swan (Ed.), *The Routledge Handbook of LGBTQIA Administration and Policy* (pp. 393–397). Routledge.

Verloo, M. (2018). Gender knowledge, and opposition to the feminist project: Extreme-right populist parties in the Netherlands. *Politics and Governance*, 6(3), 20–30.

Wichterich, C. (2000). *The globalized woman: Reports from a future of inequality.* Spinifex Press.

Wielowiejski, P. (2020). Identarian gays and threatening queers, or: How the far-right constructs new chains of equivalnece. In G. Dietze & J. Roth (Eds.), *Right-wing populism and gender: European perspectives and beyond* (pp. 135–145). Transcript.

Wodak, R. (2015). *The politics of fear: What right-wing populist discourses mean.* Sage.

Zick, A., Küpper, B., & Berghan, W. (2019). *Verlorene Mitte—Feindselige Zustände. Rechtsextreme Einstellungen in Deutschland 2018/19.* Dietz.

CHAPTER 17

'The Gendered Politics of Right-Wing Populism and Instersectional Feminist Contestations'

Julia Roth

INTRODUCTION

In October 2018, the Hungarian parliament issued a decree that cancelled accreditation and funding for gender studies programs at the two universities in the country that offer them. Prime Minister Victor Orban justified this move with the government's standpoint 'that people are born either male or female.' (Kent & Tapfumaneyi, 2018).

When the newly elected Brazilian president, Jair Bolsonaro, visited US president Donald Trump on March 19, 2019, he emphasized their common struggle as being against 'political correctness,' 'fake news,' and 'the gender ideology' (Goldberg, 2019).

In his speech at the convention of the German extremist right-wing party Alternative für Deutschland (AfD) in 2015, the chairman of the party's parliamentary group in the federal state of Thuringia, Björn Höcke, claimed that 'we have to re-discover our manhood. Because only if we rediscover our manhood, will we be manly. And only of we are manly we will be well-fortified, and we have to become well-fortified, dear friends!'.[1]

During the recent rise in right-wing populism, the gender(ed) politics of right-wing populist actors are articulated in very different ways. Nevertheless, while the field of research in right-wing populism is now quite established and is expanding very quickly, the function of gender in and for populism remains little studied (Sahar Abi-Hassan, 2017, p. 248). Consequently, this

J. Roth (✉)
American Studies, Bielefeld University, Bielefeld, Germany
e-mail: julia.roth@uni-bielefeld.de

article will in the following first refer to the logics of populism and subsequently elaborate on and make a claim for the relevance of a systematic gender perspective for research on right-wing populism in order to take into account the full range of the workings of gender as a foundational criterion in right-wing discourse. Then, the author will argue for the notion of a 'right-wing populist complex' for addressing the manifold dimensions and actors that add to right-wing populist discourses. Further, the author will carve out five prototypical or exemplary patterns of en-gendering in right-wing discourse; finally, the author will reflect on the potential of feminist movements as a platform and counter-discourse to exclusionary notions of the social.

Gender and the 'Right-Wing Populist Complex'

Since, as a 'thin-centered ideology' (Canovan, 1982; Mudde, 2004), populism necessarily is attached to—and sometimes is even assimilated into—other ideologies, it can take many shapes and relate to other concepts, forming context-specific interpretive frames in order to promote the respective political projects. Given the central role of gender for most recent populist discourse, a 'feminist theory of populism'—or a critical feminist theory of populism—is required. This is all the more relevant, since the most prominent controversy to the right-wing contestations to women's and gender rights have been intersectional feminist movements such as the Women's March and Not My President in the US; *Marielle Presente* and *#EleNão* in Brazil, the Black Protest in Poland, and *NiUnaMenos* in Argentina and Mexico. These movements also refer to the people as marginalized and claim to represent the people against a homogenous exclusive understanding as well.

Since different modes of political objectives and utterances have, by now, been assembled under the umbrella term 'right-wing populism,' it seems productive to expand and elaborate on the concept and relate right-wing populism not only to parties, movements, or organizations, but also to media discourses, narratives, and forms of action. It is therefore prolific to speak of a 'right-wing populist complex' (see Dietze & Roth, 2020a). This notion of a 'complex' makes it possible to include religious fundamentalisms and formations of Catholicism as well as certain fractions of mainstream feminism (also called 'femonationalism,' see Farris, 2012, 2017) that partake in the stigmatization of male Muslim migrants and refugees as a sexual threat to 'autochthonous' women (Hark & Villa, 2017). This 'complex' further englobes parts of the liberal bourgeois camp that have shifted to the right (Zick et. al., 2019) via their polemics against 'genderism' or and an alleged 'censorship.'

The notion of a right-wing populist 'complex' also provides a frame through which to connect different narratives relating gender to various fields of inquiry and to not only focus on actors or formations of the right-wing populist complex, but also on the intersections of gender with other categories of social stratification such as race, ethnicity, class, and religion. This way, gender issues are structurally connected to globalization and the effects of gendered neoliberal transformations and encompass the question of the gendered division of labor as well as—and as connected to—the international division of labor. A further important field of study consists in the ways in which right-wing agents orchestrate the current shift to the right by the evocation of feelings and affects (see Wodak, 2015) as related to gender, race, class, and sexuality.

While gender ideologies have always been important for right-wing actors, 'only recently has a gender-based strategy moved to the forefront of [...] right-wing populist actors' (Sauer, 2017, p. 1, translation JR), as Birgit Sauer emphasizes in her pioneering 2017 article. Sauer points to the ways in which gender provides ample metaphoric material, since gender is a category that usually evokes emotional responses as part of 'neoliberal affective governmentality' (Sauer, 2020, p. 31, cf. Sauer & Penz, 2017). Gender tackles everyday experiences that everyone can relate to because everyone is gendered in a certain way. Sauer ascribes to gender a crucial role for the 'joining of a national-populist project of ethnic or national homogeneity and exclusionary citizenship in the biopolitical arrangements' (Sauer & Penz, 2017, p. 14, translation JR) of the new right. In right-wing populist discourse, such arrangements are related to a long tradition of nativist notions centering on the ('autochtonous') female body as guarantor for the maintenance of the nation (Yuval-Davis, 1997).[2] In her critical study on anti-gender politics of right-wing parties, Juliane Lang interpreted these 'gendered and sexual normatives' of right-wing discourse as attempts of a reproduction of the national (*völkisch*) order (Lang, 2013, p. 97), and she thus pushed for a combination of right-wing extremism and gender research (ibid., p. 178; see also Dietze & Roth, 2020a; Sauer, 2020).[3]

Examining the 'communicative patterns' or 'schemes' that can currently be observed in radical right and right-wing populist discourse sheds light onto how these practices and politics are intrinsically 'gendered.' In relation to the right-wing populist logic, different patterns of gendering serve different functions.

RIGHT-WING POPULIST PATTERNS OF GENDERING

If we read populism first and foremost as a logic (e.g., Müller, 2016, p. 129) and focus on the functions of gender within these logics, the following five patterns of gendering can be observed (see Roth, 2021):

1. Pattern I: Gender as 'Affective Bridge' in (Mass) Media.
2. Pattern II: Appropriating Women's Politics for Femonationalist Arrangements
3. Pattern III: Against 'Gender Ideology' and Affirmative Action
4. Pattern IV: Reverse Anti-Colonialism in Radical Religious and Femoglobal Alliances

Table 17.1 Right-wing populist patterns of gendering

Communicative pattern	Gendering	Antagonistic populist logic
'Fake News' and/or 'Affective Truths'	**Gender as 'affective bridge' in (Mass) media** Gendering of Scandals Gendering of ('ethnic') Others	Emotional appeal Simplicity of argument Facts vs. (Gender) Ideology
'Normal' people vs. politically correct gender police	**Appropriating women's politics and femonationalist alliances**	(Re-)naturalization of binary roles, heteronormative order
'Genderism' as existential threat	**Against 'gender ideology' and affirmative action** (White) (Re) Masculinization	'Genderism' and immigrants as scapegoats for all wrongs
Gender as 'Ideological Colonization'	**Reverse anti-colonialism** In Radical Religious and Femoglobal Alliances	Reverse anti-colonialism (Self-Victimization) 'Natural' order vs. 'chaotic,' menacing gender diversity
Ethno-Sexism and Intersectionality from Above	**Gendering of social inequalities** **Gendering of fear** 'Ethno-Sexism' and 'Exclusive Intersectionality'	Sexual exceptionalism Self-Aggrandizement (superior vs. Inferior sexual regimes) Modernization + Retraditionalization

5. Pattern IV: Gendering of Social Inequalities, Gendering of Fear (Table 17.1).

Pattern I: Gender as 'Affective Bridge' in (Mass) Media

Proceeding from the observation that populism and mass media share a variety of similar logics and systemic affinities, mass media—and, increasingly, social media—play a crucial role for current right-wing populist creations of echo chambers or 'bubbles' which are crucial for their racist and anti-immigrant mobilizations. As a 'communicative scheme' (Stegemann, 2017, p. 22; see also Reisigel, 2012) or 'communicative pattern' (Costa, 2018), right-wing populism gains from its entanglements with the workings of mass media. Current right-wing populists offer a new, or revived, exclusionary narrative, pretending to be saying 'what everyone was thinking,' and 'shunning the politically correct.' Despite their outright opposition to and defamation of classical journalism and media as part of the hostile 'elite', (mass and social) media play a fundamental role for right-wing populist discourse. Even though they depend on media and take advantage of the shared logics of populism and media regarding attention economies and emotionality (see Diehl, 2017), such populist actors usually condemn 'the media' as the enemy. Since (commercial) media depend on large audiences, populist actors help them gain viewers through their continuous disregard for taboo, the production of scandal as well as through the affective appeal and simplicity of their arguments (ibid.). Expressed in paradoxical patterns ranging from sexist and misogynist remarks for causing scandals, to an opposition to 'gender ideology' against feminists and gender studies and 'sexual exceptionalism' against immigrants, 'gender' is increasingly interpolated by numerous right-wing populist actors in order to affectively bridge these contradictions. Gender and sexuality provide a useful meta language for that matter, because gender already relies on a naturalized binary hierarchy and evokes affective responses. Moreover, populists make use of the logic of 'sex sells' that is also omni-present in (mass) media.

Pattern II: Appropriating Women's Politics for Femonationalist Alliances

Numerous right-wing populist actors transfer the political hierarchy to the gender hierarchy through the defense of a particular hegemonic masculinism. Simultaneously, however, right-wing populist parties present themselves as defenders of women's rights (particularly White women) while they advocate anti-emancipatory positions. Furthermore, while men still dominate in most populist parties, the number of women is increasing and women are also becoming more and more prominent in leadership positions (see the study by Gutsche, 2018). Often, these women are among the strongest supporters of anti-feminist and anti-genderist politics while supporting their parties' politics to limit immigration or affirmative action programs and emphasize a distinct cultural identity. A common argument among these groups is that gender equality has already been achieved, and the different roles taken are the result of individual choices and values, while feminism discriminates against men (and is thus 'anti-equality'). Religiously motivated conservative women in many places justify their support with their interest in the well-being and protection of children, family and the nation, as well as, often, 'Pro-life' (anti-abortion) politics. White/'autochtonous' women can feel advantaged through their 'femonationalist' (see Farris, 2012, 2017) alliances with White men against immigrants or other minorities. Claiming to be in the possession of a more advanced gender regime enables the participating women to see themselves as fully emancipated and not effected by structural discrimination. When political differences and racial and class hierarchies are transferred to gender hierarchy, the binary becomes legible and affectively accessible.[4]

Pattern III: Against 'Gender Ideology' and Affirmative Action

Through the opposition to gender politics and left-wing agendas ('identity politics'), right-wing populists have managed to unite and create alliances among a number of actors, including religious groups from Christian churches, fundamentalist Muslims and Jews to far right parties and conservatives (Grzebalska et al., 2018, p. 34). Many right-wing actors have increasingly constructed 'gender ideology,' 'the gender craze,'[5] or 'genderism' as one of the central internal threats to children, families, and thus, as an existential threat to (the reproduction of) the nation. Meanwhile, immigrants are projected as being a menace to national citizens, particularly to 'autochtonous' women (imagined as mothers, educators, and care givers). Through this discursive pattern, actors of the right-wing populist complex push through restrictions such as the exclusion of LBGTQI persons from public offices or the army and restrict resources for these groups and their access to health care, oppose access to free and safe abortion, delete questions about gender identity from census surveys, and reverse the recognition of same-sex couples, or campaign against inclusionary educational materials. Following the logic of the right-wing populist complex, affirmative action programs and gender rights activists are imagined as unjustly advantaging minorities (mostly immigrants, People of Color, women), who enjoy privileges that are denied to the 'real' people (see Hochschild, 2016). Analogue narratives had been circulated as early as the 1990s in conservative Catholic and conservative intellectual circles (see Case, 2019). More recently, this paradigm is also projected onto the global scale as a globally spread menace.

Pattern IV: Reverse Anti-Colonialism in Radical Religious and Femoglobal Alliances

The term 'gender ideology' was coined by the Vatican in the 1990s, when a strategy that came to be known as gender mainstreaming entered politics as a means of progressive efforts to make gender equality a central focus of UN documents and policies (see Case, 2019, p. 640).[6] Gender was attacked for the dismantling of traditional family values. Pope Francis introduced the notion of 'gender ideology' as 'ideological colonization' to condemn governments and NGOs from the EU and the US or other multinational or supranational institutions that tie grants for the education of the poor to gender equality measures or educational materials on sexual diversity. The thusly constructed narrative of a common enemy provides a new language, a sort of 'Reverse Anti-Colonialism' (Roth, 2020), presenting conservative and religious groups as a minority under attack which finds 'resonance with the allegedly colonised, from the global South to Eastern Europe.' (Case, 2019, p. 650; Korolczuk & Graff, 2018). A similar pattern can also be observed among (predominantly White male) internet activists around the so-called Alt-Right, who see 'gender' as an oppressive regime and themselves not as aggressors, but as victims in a condition of permanent threat. In Latin America, anti-gender campaigns have gained momentum against the backdrop of the rise of Pentecostal and Neo-Pentecostal religious groups and the simultaneous weakening of progressive presidencies. Gender thus provides a crucial arena within the populist logics as an 'enemy within' and simultaneously as an 'outside' global threat to the community and its (supposedly shared) moral values (the populist *volonté générale*). Gender can constantly be re-signified and create different enemies through the 'moral panic' (Rubin, 1984) caused by sexual politics.

Pattern V: Gendering of Inequalities, Gendering of Fear

Following right-wing populists' imaginaries, the transgression of naturalized gender and ethnic/national borders threatens the community's alleged homogeneity. The exclusion of the transgressor of this community and the suspension of marginalized groups such as immigrants can be justified through the strategic use of gender and ethnicity for processes of Othering dynamics (Roth, 2020). Right-wing groups use gender equality to justify their racist rhetoric and policies by characterizing Muslim or non-White/non-'belonging' males as dangerous to Western societies. Through the 'ethno-sexist' (Dietze, 2016b) narrative of the immigrant or Muslim sexual perpetrator, purportedly oppressed and silenced masculinities can imagine themselves once again as 'protectors' (of White women).

INTERSECTIONAL FEMINIST CONTESTATIONS

Gender and anti-sexism build a platform for a contestation to the contestation by the right-wing actors to women's and LGBTQI rights. The contemporary scenario of feminist movements in the context of right-wing populist politics demonstrate how feminism/gender functions as a platform for resistance and counter-narratives to the described right-wing populist tendencies and what possible effects they (can) have. Both the campaigns and elections of Donald Trump in the US (2016/2017) and Jair Bolsonaro in Brazil (2018) were accompanied by massive social protests led by feminists, mostly feminists of color with an intersectional agenda. Also, in places like Poland, the political turn to the extreme right was met with huge feminist demonstrations for women's, gender and reproductive rights and against the restriction of the right to abortion. And the Black Lives Matter protests against racist violence have spread from the US, were they originated in 2014 to manifold locations on a global scale and launched a new debate on racist structures. Claiming to represent the 'people' for which right-wing populist actors pretend to speak, these groups form strategic alliances and unite marginalized and excluded bodies and voices in the streets, hand in hand with those in solidarity and in favor of pluralistic and inclusive societies. The activists of the Women's March, *#NiUnaMenos*, *#NiUnaMas* and *Marielle Presente!*, the *Black Lives Matter* movements and others place the populist myth of separateness, pureness and linearity under severe scrutiny. They practice a form of 'embodied intersectionality' (Mirza, 2013) to confront and stop the right-wing trend by building a strategic imagined (counter-) community. The current feminist movements address multidimensional and intersectional axes of oppression and relate them to the structural inequalities like patriarchy, neoliberal capitalism and colonial legacies that reproduce them. All of the recent movements contest, protest and resist this violence. They oppose the resulting persistent and revived inequalities, many of them claiming a new form of the political and a new language. By bringing together diverse and manifold precarious bodies and bodies in solidarity in the streets and in networks to oppose racist and sexist right-wing attacks, these movements contest and resist the right-wing populist ethno-sexism in order to create a new sense of 'the people' as interdependent, beyond the exclusionary logics of right-wing populism, and thus, of public space and democracy/sociability (Butler, 2015). Current feminist protestors unite different bodies that are precarious, invisibilized, and politically voiceless through masculinist, nativist White supremacist discourse in the public space, making their presences a 'claim' (ibid.). By evoking a long legacy of colonial-racist and patriarchal oppression, many of the protesters uncover the structures that make unchecked White male public speaking possible to begin with. The new feminist movements emerge in the context of White heteronormative masculinism represented by actors of the right-wing populist complex in many places that currently seek to oppose the pluralization of societies and life forms.

Outlook

Right-wing populist discourses have recently increasingly focused on gender topics and gender as an arena, platform, a mega language. Gender and sexuality are used as an affective bridge to address, negotiate and challenge certain (populist) aims in the struggle over cultural hegemony. Gender serves right-wig populist actors in many places to catapult issues such as demography, anti-immigration, national belonging and citizenship, (re)distribution etc. into the public arena. This happens in the current phase of late neoliberal capitalism in which diverse populations globally are to a growing extent affected by so-called 'precarization,' which becomes operative through the overall sell-out of the active remnants of social democracy, while promoting ideologies of individual responsibility and self-entrepreneurship (see Butler, 2015).

Simultaneously, an increase in 'intersectional' feminist contestations to the right-wing contestations can be observed on a global scale, serving as a sociopolitical force against the recent right-wing conservative and populist trend and the neoliberal de-solidarization of broad parts of societies all over the world.

In the context of the current crises of democracies and neoliberalism with regard to aspects of its discursive functioning and logics, an intersectional gender perspective can provide decisive new insights to the research and theorizing on right-wing populism that are otherwise invisible. By transferring economic and global inequalities and hierarchies to the—established binary—gender hierarchy, right-wing discourse naturalizes these hierarchies and thus attaches them to received (gendered and racialized) narratives, imaginaries and effects of belonging. A critical gender lens is therefore not only crucial but necessary in order to adequately describe the related phenomena. An intersectional gender lens can help to better analyze, describe and criticize current right-wing populist tendencies and the related racist, sexist, and homophobic politics. Such an approach can help to bring the multiple positioned workings of feminisms and the corresponding alliances into view and widen the scope toward thinking through new analytical categories and spatialities based on solidarity and connectedness. Furthermore, a respective intersectional, relational gender approach can offer points of entry for new conceptualizations and theoretical frameworks for the current struggles over hegemony in which the actors of the right-wing populist complex emerge and in which they operate.

Notes

1. Björn Höcke, original (AfD party convention, November 2015, translation by the author): "Wir müssen unsere Männlichkeit wieder entdecken. Denn nur wenn wir unsere Männlichkeit wiederentdecken, werden wir mannhaft. Und nur wenn wir mannhaft werden, werden wir wehrhaft, und wir müssen wehrhaft werden, liebe Freunde!".
2. Manuela Boatcă analyses the role of gender for the establishing and maintenance of global inequalities as a condition of possibility for capitalism and the related structures that enabled to 'transfer the cost of reproduction of wage-workers from capitalist enterprise or state to the household.' She describes the respective subordination and exclusion of women via naturalized social categories as 'gendering as defining-into-nature' (2015, p. 73).
3. See Efremowa (2019) for the historical continuities of right-wing nationalist politics and gender in Germany from the Wilhelmine empire to the Pegida program.
4. Birgit Sauer (2020) has thus described right-wing populist rhetorics as White 'masculinist identity politics,' a pattern that we can also see in the discourses of Alt.Right male activists online and offline (see Strick, 2020).
5. "Genderwahn" in German.
6. Without using the term 'gender' yet, the Ratzinger Report of 1980, following the Beijing Conference on Women, had already put together all of the elements of what conservative opponents would come to call the 'ideology of gender' (see Case, 2019, p. 640).

Literature

Abi-Hassan, S. (2017). Populism and gender. In C. Rovira Kaltwasser, P. Taggart, P. Ochoa Espejo & P. Ostiguy (Eds.), *The Oxford handbook on populism* (pp. 2–22). Oxford University Press.

Boatcă, M. (2015). *Global inequalities beyond Occidentalism*. Ashgate.

Butler, J. (2015). *Notes toward a performative theory of assembly*. Harvard University Press.

Canovan, M. (1982). Two strategies for the study of populism. *Political Studies, 30*(4), 544–552.

Canovan, M. (2002). Taking politics to the people: Populism as the ideology of democracy. In I. Mény & I. Surel (Eds.), *Democracies and the populist challenge*. Palgrave Macmillan.

Case, M. A. (2019). Transformations in the vatican's war on 'gender ideology.' *Signs: Journal of Women in Culture and Society, 44*(3), 639–664.

Costa, S. (2018, October 19). Im brasilianischen Wahlkampf ist Verleumdung Programm. *Süddeutsche Zeitung*. Retrieved from https://www.sueddeutsche.de/politik/brasilien-wahlkampf-bolsonaro-1.4173643.

Diehl, P. (2017). *Why do right-wing populists find so much appeal in mass media?* The Dahrendorf Forum. Retrieved from https://www.dahrendorf-forum.eu/why-do-right-wing-populists-find-so-much-appeal-in-mass-media/.

Dietze, G. (2016). Ethnosexismus: Sex-Mob-Narrative um die Kölner Sylvesternacht. *Movements. Journal for Critical Migration and Border Regime Studies*, 2(1), 177–185.

Dietze, G., & Roth, J. (2020a). Right-Wing populism and gender: A preliminary cartography of an emergent field of research. In *Right-Wing populism and gender: European perspectives and beyond* (pp. 7–21). Transcript.

Dietze, G., & Roth, J. (Eds.). (2020b). *Right-Wing populism and gender: european perspectives and beyond*. Transcript.

Efremowa, A. (2019). *'Gender und Nation'. Ein diskursanalytischer Vergleich der argumentativen Logiker zwischen dem wilhelminischen Antifeminismus und Anti-Gender-Diskurs der AfD*. Universität Bielefeld (Dissertation). (Unpublished)

Farris, S. R. (2012). Femonationalism and the 'regular' army of labor called migrant women. *History of the Present: A Journal of Critical History*, 2(2), 184–199.

Farris, S. R. (2017). *In the name of women's rights: The rise of Femonationalism*. Duke University Press.

Goldberg, M. (2019, January 18). The heartbreak of the 2019 women's March. *The New York Times*. Retrieved from https://www.nytimes.com/2019/01/18/opinion/womens-march-antisemitism.html.

Grzebalska, W., Kováts, E., & Petö, A. (2018). Gender as symbolic glue: How 'gender' became an umbrella term for the rejection of the (neo)liberal order.' *Luxemburg Magazine*, 32–37. Retrieved from https://www.zeitschrift-luxemburg.de/lux/wp-content/uploads/2018/09/LUX_Breaking_Feminism_E-Paper.pdf.

Gutsche, E. (Ed.). (2018). *Triumph of the women? The female face of the populist & far right in Europe*. Friedrich-Ebert-Stiftung.

Hark, S., & Villa, P. I. (Eds.). (2017). *Unterscheiden und Herrschen. Ein Essay zu den Ambivalenten Verflechtungen von Rassismus, Sexismus und Feminismus in der Gegenwart*. Transcript.

Hochschild, A. R. (2016). *Strangers in their own land: Anger and mourning on the American right*. The New Press.

Kent, L., & Tapfumaneyi, S. (2018). Hungary's PM bans gender study at colleges saying 'people are born either male or female'. *CNN*. Retrieved from https://edition.cnn.com/2018/10/19/europe/hungary-bans-gender-study-at-colleges-trnd/index.html.

Korolczuk, E., & Graff, A. (2018). Gender as 'ebola from brussels': The anticolonial frame and the rise of illiberal populism. *Signs: Journal of Women in Culture and Society*, 43(4), 797–821.

Lang, J. (2013). Frauenbilder in der NPD zwischen Modernisierung und traditionellen Vorstellungen: Positionen zu Feminismus, Emanzipation und Gender Mainstreaming. In Amadeu-Antonio-Stiftung & Heike Radvan (Eds.), *Gender und Rechtsextremismusprävention* (pp. 89–104).

Mirza, H. (2013). 'A second skin': Embodied intersectionality, transnationalism and narratives of identity and belonging among muslim women in Britain. *Women's Studies International Forum*, 36(January-February), 5–15.

Mudde, C. (2004). The Populist Zeitgeist. *Government and Opposition, 39*, 542–563.
Mudde, C., & Rovira, C. (2017). *Populism: A very short introduction*. Oxford University Press.
Müller, J. W. (2016). *What Is populism?* Penguin.
Reisigl, M. (2012). Zur Kommunikativen Dimension des Rechtspopulismus. In Sir Peter Ustinov Institut (Ed.), *Populismus. Herausforderung oder Gefahr für die Demokratie?* (pp. 141–162). New Academic Press.
Roth, J. (2021). *Can feminism trump populism? Right-wing trends and intersectional contestations in the Americas*. WVT/Bilingual Press.
Roth, J. (2020). Intersectionality Strikes Back: Right-Wing patterns of en-gendering and feminist contestations in the Americas. In G. Dietze & J. Roth (Eds.), *Right-Wing populism and gender: European perspectives and beyond* (pp. 257–273). Transcript.
Rubin, G. (1984). Thinking sex: Notes for a radical theory of the politics of sexuality. In C. S. Vance (Ed.), *Pleasure and danger: Exploring female sexuality* (pp. 267–293). Pandora.
Sauer, B. (2017). Gesellschaftstheoretische Überlegungen zum europäischen Rechtspopulismus. Zum Erklärungspotenzial der Kategorie Geschlecht. *Politische Vierteljahresschrift, 58*(1), 3–22.
Sauer, B., & Penz, O. (2017). Affective governmentality: A feminist perspective. In C. Hudson, M. Rönnblom, & K. Teghtsoonian (Eds.), *Gender, governance and feminist analysis* (pp. 39–58). Routledge.
Sauer, B. (2020). Authoritarian Right-Wing populism as masculinist identity politics: The role of affects. In G. Dietze & J. Roth (Eds.), *Right-Wing populism and gender: European perspectives and beyond* (pp. 25–43). Transcript.
Stegemann, B. (2017). *Das Gespenst des Populismus. Ein Essay zur politischen Dramaturgie*. Theater der Zeit.
Strick, S. (2020). The Alternative right, masculinities, and ordinary affect. In *Right-Wing populism and gender: European perspectives and beyond* (pp. 233–259). Transcript.
Wodak, R. (2015). *The politics of fear: What Right-Wing populist discourses mean*. Sage.
Yuval-Davis, N. (1997). *Gender and nation*. Sage.
Zick, A., Küpper, B., & Berghan, W. (2019). *Verlorene Mitte—Feindselige Zustände. Rechtsextreme Einstellungen in Deutschland 2018/19*. Dietz.

CHAPTER 18

Popular Sovereignty and (Non)recognition in Venezuela: On the Coming into Political Being of 'el *Pueblo*'

Sara C. Motta and Ybiskay Gonzalez Torres

INTRODUCTION

One of the most current and prominent examples of the discussion of populism in Latin America is articulated in relation to the case of *Chavismo* in Venezuela. Populism scholars have almost exclusively studied the figure of Hugo Chávez and the *Chavista* government or *Chavista* populism. Less is said about the '*Chavista pueblo*' or the movements to which these people belong, and when they are mentioned is to negate and elide their political rationality and being otherwise.

Accordingly, this chapter aims to contribute to the study of populism by building on the decolonial notion that sees social/political struggles as epistemic/ontological struggles, and by considering the ways in which trauma and political (non) being and (non) recognition are articulated in people's self-identification and constitution as *Chavistas*. In doing so, we seek to decenter the exclusive focus on the populist leader as the central figure of populism and give more concrete shape to how to conceptualize 'el pueblo' as a subject emerging out of ontological and epistemological struggles, which is crucial to ensure that the 'el pueblo' are not reduced to datum nor conceptualized as merely an object of the populist leader. Moreover, as we take 'el pueblo's'

S. C. Motta (✉) · Y. Gonzalez Torres
College of Human and Social Futures, Newcastle Business School (Politics and Policy), University of Newcastle, Newcastle, NSW, Australia
e-mail: sara.c.motta@newcastle.edu.au

Y. Gonzalez Torres
e-mail: ybiskay.gonzaleztorres@newcastle.edu.au

struggles for political recognition seriously, we break with the conceptual lenses that reproduce a representation of 'el pueblo' as non-beings and unreasoning. To do so, the chapter engages critically with the argument that the constitution of a popular struggle begins and culminates in the representative function of a unifying signifier, as Laclauian research on populism usually endorses (Kim, 2019; Stavrakakis et al., 2016). Rather, the chapter pays attention to what decolonial feminist scholars identify as the fundamental barrier to the very constitution of popular social struggles and political subjectivities: the epistemological and ontological stratification of social and political existence (Motta, 2011a). This stratification is premised on the negation of (political) being and non-recognition of the damné. Therefore, conceptualizations of the struggles and political subject-hood of those participating in what are argued to be populist movements *without* showing the violence of negation that tends to normalize this order of (non)being, reproduces the elision and negation of their claims, knowledges and diverse forms of political being.

Our argument is made in three parts. First, we offer a critique of the concept of populism by tracing the complex ways that it elides the political being of the popular *othered*. Then, we develop our decolonial feminist framework and methods to examine the narratives articulated by supporters of *Chavismo* in Venezuela through interviews carried out between May and July 2016. In the third part, we develop an analysis of these narratives which focuses on three themes: trauma/non-being as the ontological starting point of popular political subjectivity and how the emergence of the popular subject is necessarily misrecognized as violent by the hegemonic White subject of modernity and liberal sovereignty; a process of 'reconocimiento'/recognition of (political) being; and non-being/no reconocimiento with a focus on how logics of non-recognition continue to exist within popular political subjectivity. The chapter concludes by foregrounding the ethical, epistemological and political responsibility to engage with el pueblo and popular political subjectivity and being through: the deconstruction of any and all conceptual lenses which reproduce their/our non-being and unreason, including that of populism; and by an affirmative engagement with and through decolonial feminisms and the other multiple philosophies and theoretical-political languages of the damné.

Critique of Populism and Its Others

The term 'populism' is a highly contested concept. However, despite its lack of settled definition, most scholars and prominent political figures warn about the dangers of populism and urge liberal regimes to fight against it. Populism is represented as a disease, or as Benjamin Arditi (2007) describes it, a 'drunk uncle' that no one wants at the party, for its disruptive capacity to point toward elite failures in forging democratic governance. As, María Pía Lara (2018, p. 37) argues populism is a 'combat concept' because in its semantics lies the possible death or cure of democracy. Accordingly, not only does populism as a combat concept enable the avoidance of facing unsolved questions of sovereignty, power and political (non)being in democracy, but it also prevents us from distinguishing between liberatory progressive popular movements and movements that (re)produce and intensify oppressions and exclusions of/as the popular.

Amidst this clamor, some scholars claim that we need to remove the word 'populist' from political analysis. For instance, Barry Cannon (2018) argues that populism is conceptually loose; not only does it include many movements and parties, and leaders who have little in common, but the label 'populist' tends to marginalize political movements that challenge the political status quo, regardless of their ideological positions or programmatic proposals. Similarly, Sara C. Motta (2011b) argues that the concept of populism has many problems because it has been used to explain different phenomena while simplifying political analysis to a narrow modern/colonial conceptualization of political agency. To Motta, the concept of populism fosters a political analysis that is incapable of capturing a dynamic historic process because it focuses on liberal democratic normative assumptions and political normality in which modern elites are posited as the moral guides of liberal democracy. Such a normative framework assumes that mass mobilizations oppose party participation, and masses lack rationality and the ability to determine their political futures. Motta notes that while ignoring the dynamics of state/society relationships and the distribution of power in society, the concept of populism masks the complexity of politics and power, in particular the popular logics and/as materiality of those excluded and elided from political reason and subjectivity in liberal sovereignty and state theory (Motta, 2011b, p. 44). Both Cannon and Motta conclude that the concept of populism privileges an analysis that devalues the political agency of the popular classes by acting as a label that marginalizes political movements that challenge the political status quo. Instead of focusing on acts of representation as populist studies usually endorse, we ask: who are the protagonists of these movements, what are their forms of political being and knowing, and how do they emerge as political subjects and constitute an 'other' politics?

We build on academic analyses dealing with such questions that are rooted in decolonial studies (Ciccariello-Maher, 2010; McKean, 2016). As George Ciccariello-Maher (2010) argues when poor and racialized people appear publicly claiming access to (political) being and belonging, such appearance is considered an act of violence. However, it is this 'public appearance of colonized and racialized non-beings which creates the necessary groundwork for their entry into being' (Ciccariello-Maher, 2010, p. 1). In other words, the inscription of violence onto and about racialized popular class subjects adds another dimension to our understanding of the structuration of power relations. This makes conceptually visible the space and subjectivity of Whiteness, in which populist conceptualizations of political struggle are represented and contained. In this way, Ciccariello-Maher, quoting McKean (2016), particularly criticizes Laclau's concept of populism as a concept that 'naturalizes the racial dimensions of hegemonic identity' (Ciccariello-Maher, 2019, p. 511).

Ciccariello-Maher argues, that in Laclau's framework, 'a prioritisation of equivalence over difference creates a process of internal homogenization and outward closure toward all that is too different and incommensurable' (Ciccariello-Maher, 2019, p. 510). This is due to the central role Laclau gives to the universal and hegemony in his theory of populism. In this framework, the universal refers to an internal system of signification constituted through differentiation from an illegible outside as a hegemonic expansion. Moreover, in such a hegemonic expansion, the concept of the empty signifier provides a means by which anyone can identify with the people. However, as McKean notes, 'some subjects are constituted with a racial identity that prevents their unmediated identification with the people as a whole' (2016, p. 799). Consequently, according to McKean, Laclau's account of populism 'left marginalised identities as outside politics and unrepresentable' (2016, p. 799), and therefore reproduces this negation of the political being of the raced and feminised other(ed).

However, Ciccariello-Maher does not explore the internal occlusion of difference that decolonial feminists introduce (Anzaldúa, 1987; Lugones, 2010; Motta, 2017, 2018) with their specific focus on the intricacies of the internalization of the oppressor's logics into the colonized other and the banishment of all that is considered feminized and racialized: the embodied, affective, spiritual and cultural from political reason and (political) being. This brings scholarly attention to an exploration of popular political reason and being which focuses on the emergence of other logics and embodiments of reason that are a core part of the appearance of raced and feminized subjects as political subjects at all.

We add therefore to Ciccariello-Maher' s critiques of populism the problematique of the (non)being of the feminized and racialized (political) subject as central to the development of an affirmative critique of populism's occlusion and elision of ontological and epistemological logics and rationalities of popular politics otherwise.

Decolonial Feminisms Framework

Situating our affirmative critique within the traditions of decoloniality, and in particular decolonial feminisms, implies an engagement that begins from recognition of the non-being of the damné, of the colonized, and racialized and feminized more broadly, that is the constitutive underside of modern reason and sovereignty/the state. Decoloniality as emergent from Latin America demonstrates how the construction of the modern subject of knowing and the state apparatus of rule of which it is apart was always constructed in relation to its other. Capitalist modernity has always been capitalist coloniality (Lugones, 2010; Motta, 2018; Vázquez, 2012).

This other is represented as the illiberal savage of unreason, to be tamed, named, constrained, and mastered (Motta, 2017). Such a representation and/as material practice is premised in the hierarchical dualisms that are the mark of modernity between culture/nature, secular/spirit, masculine/feminine, mind/body, reason/nature, white/black, citizen/savage (Maldonado-Torres, 2007; Motta, 2016). The former of these binaries is seen as the mark of Enlightenment and modernity, and becomes embodied in the knowing-subject of coloniality: the White, masculine, bourgeois subject of mastery; vis-a-vis its other, the raced and feminized non-subject of tradition, irrationality and underdevelopment (to be mastered) (Motta, 2017).

This violent bordering practice out of which modern sovereignty, the state and the political come into being involves the active denial through annihilation and/or assimilation of other ways of being, knowing and creating the world (Anzaldúa, 1987; Lugones, 2010; Motta, 2018). It involves mastery of nature and colonized subjects and communities, and a logic of non-being and containment which slices across the body politic in which there is a hierarchy between subject-citizens and non-subject less-than-human communities, bodies and lands. Systemic and systematized onto-epistemological violence is the experience of the damné and the weave through which subjugation and non-being are (re)produced (Motta, 2018). As Gloria Anzaldúa (2002, p. 541) describes:

> This system and its hierarchies impact people's lives in concrete and devasting ways and justify a sliding scale of human worth used to keep humankind divided. It condones the mind theft, spirit murder, exploitation and genocide de los otros.

Perhaps the most corrosive aspect of coloniality is the internalization within the damné that they/we are indeed less than human, and unworthy of care, recognition, and love, and lacking in rational capabilities and capacities, and reason. As Ciccariello-Maher (2010, p. 3) paraphrasing Fanon describes '[this] lack of reciprocity leads the slave—in a gesture of internalized self-hatred—to turn toward the master.' This can result in a practice in which the other looks for recognition through assimilation and (dis)embodies further the exile from self; other and cosmos constitutive of capitalist coloniality.

However, as decolonial feminists have demonstrated to stop in our conceptualization and analysis at the internalization of non-being would reproduce the myths of coloniality to assume that 'global capitalist colonial system is in every way successful in its destruction of people's, knowledges, relations and economies' (Lugones, 2010). Rather we must remember:

> For 300 years she was invisible, she was not heard. Many times she wished to speak, to act, to protest, to challenge [...] She hid her feelings; she hid her truths; she concealed her fire [...] but she kept stoking her inner flame [...] a light shone through her veil of silence [...] the spirit of the fire spurs her to

fight for her own skin and piece of ground to stand on, a ground from which to view the world —a perspective, a home ground where she can plumb the rich ancestral roots into her own ample mestiza heart. (Anzaldúa, 1987, p. 45)

Indeed, for the dignity and possibilities of self-liberation and healing of the epistemological and ontological wounds of the gendered and racialized subjects of the colonial difference 'challenging the old self's orthodoxy is never enough; you must submit a sketch of an alternative self' (Anzaldúa, 2002, p. 559) and, paraphrasing Fanon, recognize your humanity through recognition of yourself as a subject (of reason) (Motta, 2018, p. 189).

Such a process of affirmative decolonizing critique is by necessity constituted through a stepping inwards to the embodied experiences of the contradictions of living between 'los intersticios' in the borderlands of non-being in which trauma is systemic and systematic, and the wisdoms that result (Motta, 2018). Liberatory decolonizing critique as praxis cannot be enacted as Lorde (2015) argues 'with the master's tools.' Rather as Anzaldúa continues 'What I want is...the freedom to carve and chisel my own face, to staunch the bleeding with aches, to fashion my own gods out of my entrails. And if going home is denied me then I will have to stand and claim my space, with my own lumber, my own bricks and mortar' (1987, p. 22).

The freedom to create ourselves as political beings breaks the coordinates and containments of knowing-being, reason/rationality and political subjectivity of capitalist coloniality that universalizes the White masculinized subject of knowing and politics as the main protagonist of politics and knowledge. Such freedom to carve and chisel our own political faces is necessarily experienced and misrecognized as violent within the coordinates of Whiteness as it shatters the illusions of peace, prosperity, liberty, reason, and progress exposing the unreason and unfreedom in which this system is rooted (Fanon quoted by Ciccariello-Maher, 2010, pp. 4–5).

A decolonial feminist framework therefore brings our analytic and epistemological attention to some core themes that can direct an engagement and enmeshment within popular reason and political being as it is emergent in *Chavismo*. These include beginning from the experience of (non)being; embodying a coming to political being through processes and practices of self-recognition; and navigating the perils and the potential (re)traumatization of non-recognition at the point of appearance on the political stage as popular reason and political subjectivity.

Narrative Analysis

Non-being (Trauma) as the Ontological Starting Point of Popular Political Subjectivity

Populist theorists divert our attention from 'the other' by emphasizing the process of populism either as a logic of articulation (Laclau, 2006) or as an ideology (Mudde, 2004). Frequently, analysis of populism focuses on the leader as *the* political actor, rather than exploring the way in which the populist frontier between people and elite emerges and what this implies for the framing of this dynamic as populist at all. This section reveals how such a political frontier carries the embodied memory of earlier traumas and ongoing traumas of non-being, typical of racialized and feminized subaltern communities excluded from political being and reason.

Venezuelan historical legacies of exclusion of indigenous, black and mestizos can be seen in the process of nation-building (Coronil, 1997) and in the process of neoliberalization of the state in which the communities living the popular sectors were positioned 'outside' civil society (Uribe & Lander, 1995). As Alice, a woman in her 40s from the Andes Region in Venezuela, who supports the Bolivarian Revolution, and teacher at the Bolivarian University, argues:

> In the past, [...] we had a neoliberal state that was undercutting public goods and services. The *Caracazo* had already happened, but they [the state] continued with the process of privatizing services without consulting the people. They did not ask and did it under the legitimating guise of what they called 'civil society'. [...] And this civil society was promoted with events, with books about civil society. [...] they [civil society] were [represented as] a small group, an elite, not the people. That was not democracy.

Such exclusion of the popular sectors from civil society and citizenship had been reinforced and reproduced in privately owned media texts prior to the election of Chavez to government. But, when the private media aligned with the opposition in 2001, they began to systematically represent the popular sectors allied with *Chavismo* as a mob, horde, rabble, lumpen, whereas, those subjects supposedly making up civil society were represented as acceptable, reasonable, and respectable (Duno Gottberg, 2004, p. 118). Indeed, the Opposition in the media exalted how it was only they who did not follow, nor need to follow, a leader. They did this as a mean to differentiate themselves from *Chavistas* who they claimed blindly followed Chávez and, in this way, the Opposition established their 'rational autonomy'; as can be seen in the following text:

> The best opposition [...] is based in democratic culture [...] [the best opposition] does not need a leader to function, and does not allow any old decision to become perversely collective [...] little by little [this best opposition] turns its back on the 'revolution' which does not provide for a serene daily life nor material well-being. (Caula, 2000)

According to this text, while the term 'serene' denotes their wish to stop the 'violence' allegedly introduced by *Chavismo*, 'material well-being' denotes the framework against which popular subjectivities and reason are considered irrational and unable to act according to the capitalist 'mode of civilization.' In other words, the popular subjectivity's 'incapacity' to reproduce modernity and their lack of connections with the North/West, makes them irrational, and thus pre-political or politically impotent. Once the popular sectors allied with *Chavismo* have been represented as irrational, the next step is to imply that they are uneducated and naïve (politically) and are thus open to being paid and manipulated by a populist leader. This editorial from the newspaper El Nacional, dated the 14 October 2002 and entitled the 'Government's Response' making reference to the Opposition's demands for a change of government due to political instability, is an example of this:

> The response of the President and his entourage to the concerns of Venezuelan society about the grave crisis we are experiencing [...] consisted of bringing the usual lumpen in from the interior of the country once again, bussing them in with their morsel of bread and bottle of rum.

The Coordinadora Democrática CD, a former civil organization that grouped members of the Opposition a few months after the attempted coup in April 2002, in its founding documents also represents civil society as those with political agency in civil society and strongly related to groups of business. For instance, the CD defines its idea of the reconstruction of Venezuela needed after the fall of the Chávez government as:

> [a process] to recover cohesion as Venezuelans who inhabit a single Republic and a single Nation; and to re-institutionalize the Venezuelan state, civil and democratic, committed to justice and strengthening citizenship [...] [A] national reconstruction is needed where we all feel represented, composed of all the forces committed to democracy and open to dialogue with all sectors. (Coordinadora Democrática, 2002)

In such an understanding of consensus and democratic representation, the popular sectors pay a high price. They become silenced because the only subjects invited to 'dialogue' are those sectors recognized as productive taking into account their participation in the market, either as owners or organized labor, as can be seen in the following text:

> through mechanisms of dialogue and consultation, the active participation of the productive sectors—business, trade unions, other economic sectors—in the definition of public policies is one of the pillars of this program of reconciliation and reconstruction. (Coordinadora Democrática, 2003, p. 15)

In this representation of dialogue and democracy, those in the productive sector are synonymous with those included in the formal economy. However, the majority of Venezuelans were and still are in the informal economy. By 2003, an estimated 49%, or 4.3 million of the economically active population, was employed in the informal sector (Buxton, 2005), whereas in 2019 the ILO estimates that 33.8%, or 9.6 million people are own-account workers in vulnerable situation (ILOStat, 2020), most of them living in informal shantytowns settlements, outside of the borders that define civilization and modernity. Therefore, popular subjectivities are not only considered as pre-political, politically irrational, and non-productive but also as a potential danger to reconciliation, reconstruction, and political stability. This leads us to a dimension in which the people from the popular sectors are denied their own (political) being because their represented identity can only serve as a canvas for the differentiation from the White/civilized. Under this hegemonic author(ial)ity, popular sectors' visibility is barbaric (as opposed to civilized) and thus, considered the main cause of the problems facing the nation, state, and polity.

The popular sectors experience of this ongoing representation (as discourse and materiality) of non-being is traumatic. They are inscribed with the terms of non-thinking, irrational, unfeeling, as Alice says in her interview:

> For them [the political elite], we were not human beings affected by the situation [of neoliberalism]; it was as if [for them] the poor do not think, do not understand. But people think; we evaluate what we want and do not want; whether we are on the left or right of the political spectrum whatever, the point is that we are a thinking people. In Latin America, we think and feel, and more when we suffer the consequences of situations like this [neoliberalism].

In confronting an imposed system of white supremacy premised on their own non-being, popular subjects' new visibility during the Chavez governments becomes the 'invader' of spaces previously reserved for select elite White minorities. This visibility is necessarily within this context read as a violent act because it defies the hegemonic representation of a unified nation and an understanding of democracy inscribed in a tradition of modern identity that promises progress. An earlier example of this interpretation was how the events of the *Caracazo*[1] were represented. For those in the popular sectors, the Caracazo was the eruption of the *pueblo*, having an active and dignified meaning-being, but for the political elite, it carried a horrific meaning. As Coronil and Skurski demonstrate in their citation of Gonzalo Barrios, president and founder of the Action Democratic party in March 1989, the Caracazo was 'the horror, the primitive, the uncontrollable, from a civilised point of view' (1991, p. 321). In reference to this event, Gonzalo Barrrios concluded his speech by telling the story of a British General who sent a missionary to convince an African chief of the benefits of British occupation. But the chief rejected the offer, and the missionary, on reporting the news, suggested that the chief was right. 'The General,' said Gonzalo Barrios, 'naturally paid no attention to the missionary and gave orders to blast the natives with gunfire (*plomo cerrado*)' (1991, p. 321). We can see in this quote the violent myths embedded in the discourses of modern nation and democracy, reproducing a discourse of division between the elite/colonizer and the *pueblo*, as well as a prescription for the *pueblo*: the *pueblo* must be controlled and has to control itself. In other words, within this discourse of division, such a prescription is an everyday relationship of subordination, hidden in the monolithic representation of elite/*pueblo*.

In short, the dehumanizing division and frontier between citizen subject and non-subject lumpen is a starting point of understanding popular political subjectivity that dominant frameworks of populism studies elide, and which raise questions about the uses and misuses of populism to engage meaningfully with the political being and reason of the *pueblo*. To illustrate this elision with greater depth we move to the processes and nature of reconocimiento/recognition of (political) being within and potentially overflowing of *Chavismo*.

Process of 'Reconocimiento'/Recognition of (Political) Being

It would be predictable to begin a discussion of reconocimiento/recognition of (political) being from within decoloniality or decolonial readings of populism with a focus on key moments of rupture in the political history of the *pueblo*. Without negating the historical, political, and existential significance of such events, in particular the *Caracazo* in the context of the *pueblo* and popular reason in contemporary Venezuela, a feminist decolonial lens begins from another place/moment. Our focus becomes as much, if not more, on the intercizes of how the bordering practices of (non)being and (non)reconocimiento are (re)produced and transgressed in the everyday intimacies of modern sovereignty and subjectivity. Here, as Thelma, a black woman in her 60s supporter of Chávez, illustrates in her memory of occupying the classroom at the Catholic University in Caracas in the 2000s; the borders and containments of coloniality against the raced and feminized non-subject are rearticulated and contested with dignity and voice in the (in)visibilized spaces of reason and citizenship, including that of the classroom:

> In fact, one day a teacher indirectly told me, he did not know that I was in his class and pointing there [towards the hill of Antímano, a popular area of Caracas] said that people from there were 'marginal'. And I told him I am not outside of anything, if I do not have money to buy the news, I will see it on TV in the evenings; and I am not uninformed of anything, and if the newspaper is old, for me it is new because I am going to read it. And if I were on the margin/sidelines I would not have been here, because you are talking about all of us [living there] as people not paying for services, not being literate. But, here at the University, I was asked for the electricity bill to demonstrate my address. Instead, it is those who actually live without concern for what is happening in their environment, their country, their community, who can be considered as on the sidelines and margins. In this way, I am not outside of anything, therefore, I am not marginal even because you say so.

Thelma re-articulates marginality in/as this moment of reconocimiento of her political being. She voices with dignity and wisdom how marginality is not reducible to a reproduction of the dominant and violent fantasies of the oppressors, in which those on the margins are (mis)represented as illegal, irrational and at a distance from civilized reason on the hills of the popular barrios. In fact, she voices how to be of the margins is to be aware and concerned about your surroundings, your country and your community. Thus, this misrepresentation is to negate the very knowing-being of those 'on those hills' and reproduce a relationship of non-recognition and dehumanization.

Identifying her oppressors and re-signifying dominant violent discourses in this way, Thelma demonstrates, as Ciccariello-Maher (2010, p. 4) argues, paraphrasing Franz Fanon that, in the face of such ontological blockage, full humanity can only emerge through the effort to impose one's existence (as 'subjective certainty') onto another (thereby converting it into 'objective fact'). In this 'quest of absoluteness,' the resistance of the other yields *desire*, what Fanon calls 'the first milestone on the road that leads to the dignity of the spirit.' This dignity of the spirit which Thelma recounts, embodies a turn away from the 'master's logics' toward a process of 'making oneself known' (Ciccariello-Maher, 2010, p. 5) as an autonomous (black) popular political subject.

A feminist decolonial lens therefore turns our attention to the intimacies of non-reconocimiento and the ways in which coloniality and its violent borders and bordering practices are not merely external but impact the internal (non)being of the damné. Accordingly, a focus on reconocimiento of political being of 'el *pueblo*' involves a turn toward the processes of reconocimiento understood as an internal existential and epistemological relationality of the *pueblo* itself. Alice, a teacher at the Bolivarian University,[2] describes this as including but not reducible to constitutional and institutional processes and practices of change:

> With the Constitution we established something of great power, we opened spaces for the power 'el pueblo'. What does this mean? Well, it is that el pueblo becomes actor and author in its own right. How to create a citizen/citizenship? This is a collective answer. It is not for me to answer. It is emergent through [collective] practice.

Here, the political process of coming together and self-recognition as a people is deeply pedagogical as it involves the unlearning of the oppressor's logics that they [el *pueblo*] have nothing to offer to the constitution and theorization of the political and citizenship. Central to this is the practice of collective organization, reflection and analysis by and for the *pueblo* about what political citizenship might involve. This is not, as suggested by Alice, a model imposed from above (even as it is instituted oft times by the state) but rather a practice emergent from the power and creativity of the *pueblo* in its diversity from below. This is equally an (un)learning of the dominant repertoires of citizenship, reason and expertise of modernity/coloniality and a learning/re-membering of the embodied wisdoms and creativity of the *pueblo* in its becoming.

Such pedagogical and epistemological praxis of reconocimiento of political being of el *pueblo* necessarily ruptures the containments and logics of modern reason and the knowing-subject of coloniality (Lugones, 2010; Motta, 2017, 2018). It involves an epistemological privileging of the wisdoms of the embodied experience of non-being and the struggle for active processes of agency of survival, resilience, solidarity, and resistance. It cannot stop or be held by the disembodied abstractions of enlightenment mastery and knowing of, for and about 'el *pueblo*' as object to be tamed, misnamed, and maimed. Instead, it overflows these borders and moves into spaces of 'diálogos de saberes' and encountering the creativity of/as the deep wisdoms. Roberto, a man in his 30s and ex worker in the Ministry of Culture in the 2010s, touches this with his reflections about the emergence of, and possibilities *and* tensions in creating the conditions for the nurturing of the political subjectivity as self-reconocimiento of el *pueblo*:

> The political subject is emerging. There are many young people, but I look with worry at the spaces where they are trained/developed politically because I believe that the spaces which will enable significant political growth such as cooperatives are not there. These types of spaces would enable the youth to connect to creative experiences that can sustain other tools/methods. I think these are the types of spaces we need, that can generate knowledge dialogues and exchanges.

Roberto articulates the tensions between the process of constitution of political reconocimiento of the *pueblo* from above as/through state institutionality, and its relationship with the emergence of political reconocimiento of the *pueblo* from a prefigurative, pedagogical co-constitutive process from below as multiple becoming (in form and content). It is to these tensions between reconocimiento/no-reconocimiento del pueblo in its internal construction of political subjectivity and popular reason, that we now turn.

Non-being/Non-reconocimiento

Decolonial freedom of the racialized and feminized other involves a process of self-recognition as an autonomous political subject of political reason. The constitution of political being and recognition of el pueblo is beset both internally and externally (as we have demonstrated in section one through the Opposition's violent misrecognition) with the ongoing realities and newly emergent forces of non-recognition.

Internal to Chavismo as Roberto illustrates, the process of institutionalization of el pueblo into the state has imbricated with a dynamic which reproduces non-recognition. Such state/sovereign subjectivity has tended to reimpose a logic of (non)recognition on the political subjectivity of el pueblo. Roberto explains:

> In the example of a craftsperson, if you ask them why they continue with their craft even if it doesn't generate enough income, they will answer you, that 'their grandfather taught them'; thus, we can see there is a subjectivity emergent here, but when you look at the institutions this isn't here. And this process happens not only with craftspeople but for example in the agricultural sector and we are not taking this into consideration. It is primordial that we understand this subjectivity when policies are designed. Understand that the object produced also extends to a subjectivity.

Roberto talks as a participant in 'el proceso' and as a member of el pueblo. He illustrates the embodied and heartfelt tensions of this internal dynamic between recognition/non-recognition. He notes how from el pueblo their forms of doing and creating/producing are deeply tied to forms of knowledge and (political) subjectivity but that this is not recognized in the actions of the institutions and the design of state policies. He goes on to suggest that in order that there be a politics and policymaking integral to el pueblo they must begin from and engage with such political subjectivity. This involves engagement with the imminent knowledges and ways of being of popular subjects in relation to their labor both formal (as illustrated by Roberto) and the invisibilized labors of social reproduction, which ensure the reproduction of the life of the pueblo and are often feminized (Motta, 2014; Motta & Seppälä, 2016). Such embodied and dialogical engagement would involve moving past the logic of Sovereignty and the Modern State toward other modes of constituting governance; a process of reconocimiento and coming into political being that is emergent within the contradictions of Chavismo.

We illustrate such internal tensions between recognition/non-recognition within the dynamics of popular politics to demonstrate how the nuanced and popular-led conceptualization of el pueblo as knowing-being political subject that we are suggesting is not a call to reproduce monolithic renditions of el pueblo. We do not seek to reify a pure and authentic popular political being as a constituted ontology without concrete historical genealogies and struggles of political emergence. This would be to construct a mirror image of the negation of el pueblo's political being, which much of populism studies reproduce. Rather our critique of populism as conceptual and theoretical framing is emergent from el pueblo and the contradictory and complex struggles to nurture a political being otherwise.

Conclusion

In conclusion, we have developed a critique of the current contours and containments of populism studies for either its elision of the possibility of autonomous popular political being and reason, or for its containment of that potential being into a language of representation and homogeneity in which this being remains outside representation. We have undertaken this task through foregrounding a decolonial feminist lens which engages with how trauma and political (non) being and (non) recognition constitute the point of emergence of el pueblo's self-identification and constitution as *Chavistas, and how this articulation is a distinct moment of visibility of black feminised being and reason.*

Our steps involved firstly deconstructive critique of the elisions, silences, and violence of populism studies as regards its (non)relationship with el pueblo. We then moved to an affirmative critique that engaged with narratives of Chavistas and the Opposition to bring to thought the practices of (non)being articulated by elites and the Opposition toward those represented as outside, so called civil society in Venezuela both, before and after Chávez's election to president. We then analyzed the process of becoming (political)being and reconocimiento demonstrating how this requires turning towards an internal existential and epistemological relationality of the *pueblo* itself. However, this process exhibits tensions between an understanding of *el pueblo* as an object to be tamed and the possibilities in creating the conditions for the self-reconocimiento of *el pueblo*. We ended on these tensions of non-being/no reconocimiento with a focus on how logics of non-recognition continue to exist within Chavismo itself. As Ciccariello-Maher describes:

> the slave [will] be freed from this two-sided blockage of the dialectic, enforcing recognition (externally) onto the master while developing (internally) a degree of autonomy and self-confidence. (Ciccariello-Maher, 2010, p. 3)

As the quote above suggests, decolonial freedom of the racialized and feminized other involves a process of self-recognition (external and internal) as an autonomous political subject of political reason. However, *el pueblos*' process of self-reconocimiento is facing the logics of non-recognition from elite groups reproducing a historic violent negation of their political being and reason while also facing containment from the logic of Sovereignty and the Modern State which crisscrosses Chavismo. The task for populism studies is to develop *with* el pueblo languages, logics and practices that support the process of self-reconocimiento and black feminised freedom.

Notes

1. The *Caracazo* was a spontaneous popular protest, sparked just after the structural adjustment program by Carlos Andres Perez in 1989, and which was strongly repressed by the state for five days.
2. A university created by presidential decree N° 2.517 under the Chávez government in Caracas in 2003.

Literature

Anzaldúa, G. (1987). *Borderlands - La Frontera: The New Mestiza*. Aunt Lute Books.
Anzaldúa, G. (2002). Now let us shift ... The path of conocimiento ... inner work, public acts. In A. Keating & G. Anzaldúa (Eds.), *This bridge called my back: Writings by radical women of color* (pp. 540–578). Routledge.
Arditi, B. (2007). *Politics on the edges of liberalism: Difference, populism, revolution, agitation*. Edinburgh University Press.
Buxton, J. (2005). Venezuela's contemporary political crisis in historical context. *Bulletin of Latin American Research, 24*(3), 328–347.
Cannon, B. (2018). Must we talk about populism? Interrogating populism's conceptual utility in a context of crisis. *New Political Science, 40*(3), 477–496.
Caula, S. (2000, December 9). Cultura democrática. El Universal.
Ciccariello-Maher, G. (2010). Jumpstarting the decolonial engine: Symbolic violence from Fanon to Chavez. *Theory & Event, 13*(1).
Ciccariello-Maher, G. (2019). Populism, universalism, and democracy in Latin America. In L. Jenco, M. Idris, & M. Thomas (Eds.), *The Oxford handbook of comparative political theory* (pp. 504–524). Oxford University Press.
Coordinadora Democrática. (2002). *Resumen Bases para un Acuerdo Democrático de Reconstrucción Nacional: 05 de Julio*. http://www.urru.org/papers/resumen_bases_acuerdo_reconstruccion.htm
Coordinadora Democrática. (2003). Propuesta de Consensos para Políticas Públicas. In C. C. P. d. l. C. Democrática (Ed.), *Coordinadora Democrática* (pp. 61). Coordinadora Democrática.
Coronil, F. (1997). *The magical state: Nature, money, and modernity in Venezuela*. University of Chicago Press.
Coronil, F., & Skurski, J. (1991). Dismembering and remembering the nation: The semantics of political violence in Venezuela. *Comparative Studies in Society and History, 33*(2), 288–337.
Duno Gottberg, L. (2004). Mob outrages: Reflections on the media construction of the masses in Venezuela (April 2000–January 2003). *Journal of Latin American Cultural Studies, 13*(1), 115–135.
ILOStat. (2020). *International labour organization statistics*. Available from ILO Retrieved 30/06/2020, from ILO https://ilostat.ilo.org/data/country-profiles/
Kim, S. (2019). Radical democracy and left populism after the squares: 'Social movement' (Ukraine), Podemos (Spain), and the question of organization. *Contemporary Political Theory, 5*, 1–22.
Laclau, E. (2006). Why constructing a people is the main task of radical politics. *Critical Inquiry, 32*, 646–680.
Lara, M. P. (2018). A conceptual analysis of the term 'populism.' *Thesis Eleven, 149*(1), 31–47.
Lorde, A. (2015). The master's tools will never dismantle the master's house. In C. Moraga & G. Anzaldúa (Eds.), *This bridge called my back, writings by radical women of color* (4th ed., pp. 94–101). State University of New York (SUNY) Press.
Lugones, M. (2010). Toward a decolonial feminism. *Hypatia, 25*(4), 742–759.
Maldonado-Torres, N. (2007). On the coloniality of being. *Cultural Studies, 21*(2–3), 240–270.
McKean, B. L. (2016). Toward an inclusive populism? On the role of race and difference in Laclau's politics. *Political Theory, 44*(6), 797–820.

Motta, S. (2011). Notes towards prefigurative epistemologies. In S. Motta & A. G. Nilsen (Eds.), *Social movements in the global south: Dispossession, development and resistance* (pp. 178–199). Palgrave Macmillan UK.

Motta, S. (2011). Populism's Achilles' heel: Popular democracy beyond the liberal state and the market economy in Venezuela. *Latin American Perspectives, 38*(1), 28–46.

Motta, S. (2014). Latin America: Reinventing revolutions, an "other" politics in practice and theory. In R. Stahler-Sholk, H. E. Vanden, & M. Becker (Eds.), *Rethinking Latin American social movements: Radical action from below* (pp. 21–42). Rowman & Littlefield Publishers.

Motta, S. (2016). Decolonising critique: From prophetic negation to prefigurative affirmation. In A. C. Dinerstein (Ed.), *Social sciences for an other politics: Women theorizing without parachutes* (pp. 33–48). Palgrave.

Motta, S. (2017). Latin America as political science's other. *Social Identities, 23*(6), 701–717.

Motta, S. (2018). *Liminal subjects: Weaving (our) liberations*. Rowman & Littlefield International, Limited.

Motta, S., & Seppälä, T. (2016). Feminized resistances. *Journal of Resistance Studies, 2*(2), 5–32.

Mudde, C. (2004). The populist zeitgeist. *Government and Opposition, 39*(4), 541–563.

Stavrakakis, Y., Kioupkiolis, A., Katsambekis, G., Nikisianis, N., & Siomos, T. (2016). Contemporary left-wing populism in Latin America: Leadership, horizontalism, and postdemocracy in Chávez's Venezuela. *Latin American Politics and Society, 58*(3), 51–76.

Uribe, G., & Lander, E. (1995). Acción social, efectividad simbólica y nuevos ámbitos de lo político. In E. Lander (Ed.), *Neoliberalismo, sociedad civil y democracia. ensayos sobre América Latina* (pp. 15–58).

Vázquez, R. (2012). Towards a decolonial critique of modernity. Buen Vivir, relationality and the task of listening. *Capital, Poverty, Development, Denktraditionen Im Dialog: Studien Zur Befreiung Und Interkulturalität, 33*, 241–252.

> Part VII

New Populisms and Cleavages

CHAPTER 19

Environmental Populism

Aron Buzogány and Christoph Mohamad-Klotzbach

INTRODUCTION

Before the Corona pandemic captured global attention, both public discourse and political science debates throughout the West were dominated by two crises: the crisis of liberal democracy and the environmental crisis (Forchtner, 2019a, 2019b). On the one hand, the rise of populism has reinforced discussion about manifold contestations of the Western liberal model of representative democracy and free-market capitalism. On the other hand, public perception of the salience of environmental crisis has reached a new peak following the difficulties to address these problems in international negotiations, accumulating extreme weather events and the worldwide diffusion of climate protest by groups like Fridays for Future or Extinction Rebellion. While populism and climate change discourses have their own distinct ideological roots, in this contribution we focus on the overlap between them.

Conceptually, populism and environmentalism—the larger political discourse in which climate issues are usually discussed—both have rather vague boundaries. Populism can be regarded as a communication style (Jagers

---

A. Buzogány (✉)
InFER - Institute of Forest, Environmental, and Natural Resource Policy, University of Natural Resources and Life Sciences (BOKU), Vienna, Austria
e-mail: aron.buzogany@boku.ac.at

C. Mohamad-Klotzbach
Comparative Politics and German Government, University of Wuerzburg, Würzburg, Germany
e-mail: ch.mohamad@uni-wuerzburg.de

© The Author(s), under exclusive license to Springer Nature Switzerland AG 2022
M. Oswald (ed.), *The Palgrave Handbook of Populism*,
https://doi.org/10.1007/978-3-030-80803-7_19

& Walgrave, 2007), a strategy (Weyland, 2001) or a cultural phenomenon (Aslanidis, 2020) but the most often used definition is the ideational one by Mudde (2004) who considers populism as a 'thin ideology'. Mudde argues that populism can be associated with different host ideologies, such as liberalism, socialism, conservatism—and ecologism (Mudde, 2004, p. 544). At its turn, environmentalism—understood as an anthropocentric view on human-nature relations—is also often regarded to be 'thin'. However, while environmentalism puts forward reformist propositions, is status-quo oriented and can accompany different mainstream political ideologies, it is rarely seen as an ideology (Dobson, 2007). In contrast, ecologism, environmentalism's more radical eco-centric twin which calls for thorough transformation of state, market and society, is often seen to be an ideology in its own right (Dobson, 2007; Heywood, 2017). While environmentalism is at odds with populisms' anti-elitism and anti-institutionalism, ecologism shares some features with populism's critique of the establishment, the elites and the global reach of the market. Where they disagree is the role of democracy: Ecologism usually subscribes to radical versions of democracy, while populism is oriented towards a strong leader.

The current interest in environmental populism stems from populist right-wing parties, movements and leaders around the world challenging the narrative of climate change and transitions towards sustainability by arguing that these go against the interest of 'the real people'. Right-wing populists often deny or are at least sceptical about the existence of anthropogenic climate change (like Trump in the United States) or put economic issues before environmental ones (like Bolsonaro in Brazil). In ideological terms, right-wing populists oppose values such as civil rights, pacifism, feminism or environmentalism that are associated with the 'liberal script' (Börzel & Zürn, 2021) because they challenge some of their core beliefs.

While populism is currently discussed in its radical-right wing variant and environmentalism is usually seen to be aligned with left or left of centre parties, there are both historical and contemporary exceptions and there is also an important overlap between right-wing ecology and populist identity politics in different world regions (Forchtner, 2019a, 2019b; François, 2016; Olsen, 1999). Studies discussing the relationship between populism and environmentalism historically argue that populism was often a left-wing strategy (Meyer, 2008). Also some activists of the new climate movement, such as Fridays for Future, and scholars echoing theorists such as Chantal Mouffe (2020) regard pro-environmental populism as a potential force to counter anti-environmental populism or as an opportunity to broaden democracy (Beeson, 2019; Bosworth, 2020; Davies, 2020; Zulianello & Ceccobelli, 2020). Inclusive forms of environmental populism turn exclusionary populism on its head and show how the 'real people' around the world are affected by environmental degradation while globalized elites reap profits by using carbon-intensive technologies.

These examples should help us formulating a comprehensive definition of environmental populism. We regard populism as a discourse which is used by parties, movements or individuals employing anti-elite and anti-establishment elements and claim direct connections with voters. Populists also assume society to be characterized by a Manichean division between 'the pure people' and 'the corrupt elite'. We can define environmental populism as comprising two aspects: (a) populist's usage of discourse concerning the environment; (b) populist discourses by groups or individuals concerned with the environment. Our focus will be on the communicative perspective on populism as discussed in branches of political science, sociology or studies of (environmental) communication. We incorporate both supply- and demand-side views on populism (Eatwell, 2003; Golder, 2016) and look at the role of knowledge producers (such as parties, social movements, think tanks, NGOs) as well as individuals who support or disagree with these positions.

In the sections that follow, we highlight some of these complexities of environmental populism by first providing an overview of the emergence and the different varieties of environmental populism (2). We show that different types of populisms can go together with specific discourses of environmental populism concerning worldviews, policies, or the role of science. The third section discusses explanations put forward to understand environmental populism, focusing on the materialist, idealist and strategic accounts (3). In section four we discuss evidence concerning the policy effects of populists on environmental and climate policies (4). Finally, the concluding part points to some open questions and hints to further research (5).

VARIETIES

In this section, we first discuss the genealogy of movements associated— sometimes rather loosely—with environmental populism. This will be followed by mapping different branches of contemporary populism regarding their discourses related to the environment. Conflicts related to human-nature relations, such as natural resource use, have been historically important factors for the emergence of modern populism. One of the most important still resounding lineages comes from agrarian populism. For Roger Eatwell and Matthew Goodwin (2018), the Russian *narodniks*, an intellectual movement championing the case of peasantry in nineteenth century Russia can be seen as the first modern populist movement. Margaret Canovan (1981) provides a classic distinction between agrarian and political populism. Her typology differentiates three forms of agrarian populism. Intellectual agrarian populism, like the *narodniks*, is a progressive movement to the benefit of peasantry and in support of land reforms. Farmer's movement's populism, in late nineteenth-century North America and in Germany has championed state subsidies for agriculture. The third form of agrarian populism, small-holding peasants' movements, blended ideas about voluntary cooperation between peasants, support of family property and values and an antagonism to urban elites into specific forms of agrarian socialism. Examples include the US People's Party during the nineteenth century (Giesen, 2019) as well as parties and movements in Eastern and Central European countries following World War I (Brock, 1977). Current research has started paying increased attention to the re-emergence of rural populism across the world in the early twenty-first century (Brass, 2000; De Lange & Rooduijn, 2015; Mamonova & Franquesa, 2020; Strijker et al., 2015).

A second trace of environmental populism can be found in the history of the environmental movement. In *Ecopopulism*, one of the classic texts on the history of the US environmental movement, Andrew Szasz (1994) describes how the Not-in-my-Backyard (NIMBY) discourse of the anti-hazardous toxics movement became a radical environmental populist feature that was adopted by large parts of the movement. Also John M. Meyer (2008) identifies paternalism and populism as the US environmental movement's two central discourses. While the paternalist line regards environmentalism to be the avant-garde, the populist discourse is more concerned with conflicts between the local people and 'far-away' elites. More broadly, populist environmentalism 'represents a relatively independent movement of dissent, by ordinary people working at the local level, from the dominant ideologies of modernisation, development and growth' (Garavan, 2007), and has been discussed in the context of place-based local activism that blends discourses of belongingness, nationalism and health (Park, 2013). Such place-related conflicts remain important and recurring issues in contemporary environmentalism and are put into a global perspective by the global climate justice movement (Bosworth, 2019).

Some of the historical lineages of environmental populism are still present in contemporary political discourses even if their direct influence has often diminished. In order to provide an overview of the literature on environment-related stances of contemporary populists, we map different varieties of populism related to the thicker host-ideologies, such as liberalism, conservatism or socialism. Conceptually, we differentiate here between three kinds of populisms—*radical right-wing, market liberal* and *left-wing*. While the literature on populist 'varieties' includes also other subtypes, these often lack specific positions on environmental issues (Rovira Kaltwasser et al., 2017; Verbeek et al., 2017; Zulianello, 2020). Environment and climate related issues are not high on the agenda of populist parties of any feather. While most researchers regard migration to be at the core of (right-wing) populist parties' policy agendas, there is re-emerging interest in 'secondary' policy positions, such as socio-economic issues, when determining the 'winning formula' behind their successes (Ivaldi & Mazzoleni, 2019; Otjes et al., 2018). At least for populist radical right and populist market liberal parties, environmental and climate policies are rather distant 'tertiary' issues that often emerge due to counter-mobilizations to environmentalist and ecologist forces. Table 19.1 characterizes the three populist subtypes according to their general worldview

Table 19.1 Three kinds of populism and their relationship concerning environmental policies

	Populist radical right-wing	*Populist market liberal*	*Populist left-wing*
Ontology	National vs rootless cosmopolitans	Individualism	Egalitarianism
	Discontent against ruling elite	Free market	Anti-capitalism
	Nativism, protectionism	Meritocracy	Concern about distributional effects of climate policies
	Cultural homogenity	Running states as business	participatory democracy
	Traditionalism	Against big government	Sceptical of potential greenwashing
	Justice for ordinary people		
	People as (imagined) nation		
Epistemology	Climate sceptics	business goes first	Science believer
	Science is driven by international elites		Holistic political ecology
Global Cooperation	Intergovernmental commitments against national interest		Concern about distributional effects of climate policies advocated by international institutions
	Protectionism		
Examples	AfD, PiS, Sweden Democrats	Forza Italia	Podemos
		Trump	Five Stars Movement
			Syriza

Source Buzogány et al., 2021 and Buzogány & Mohamad-Klotzbach, 2021

related to nature (ontology), their views on science (epistemology), and their relation to global cooperation concerning climate and environmental issues.

Populist radical right (PRR) parties define 'the people' in nativist terms and are usually xenophobic, nationalist and often racist. PRR parties' relation to nature is predetermined by their opposition to ruling elites and the Manichean 'us vs. them' dichotomy. This perspective is addressed in historically informed work on the intimate ties between nationalism and nature (Conversi, 2020; Forchtner, 2019c; Forchtner & Kølvraa, 2015; Forchtner et al., 2018; Lawton, 2019; Lubarda, 2021; Olsen, 1999). Early studies include work on 'ecofascism' (Biehl & Staudenmaier, 1995), and trace Nazi ideology's conceptualization of nature to Romanticism and nineteenth-century German nature mysticism (Uekötter, 2006, 2007). However, far-right ecological thought is not limited to fascism but includes much wider conservative and national-populist currents as well (Lubarda, 2021). Located mostly within the humanities, this scholarship shows that far-right parties are supportive of 'green patriotism' and environmental conservation when this concerns the protection of their homelands (Forchtner, 2019b). Nature protection related discourses have often emerged parallel to nation-building processes in the eighteenth–nineteenth century, showing a strong relationship between the people and the landscapes, they inhabit. Forests, watercourses, mountains or animals have often become mythical symbols of national belongingness and are often still very present in far-right thought. In Germany, such historical lineages include Romanticism, nationalism, Malthusianism, eugenics or the heritage of early twentieth-century reformist movements. In France, a common point of reference for far-right identitarian ecology is the Nouvelle Droite's theory of ethnopluralism which suggests that different races should be kept separate in their natural habitat (François & Nonjon, 2021). Other recurring elements are the critique of monotheism and of Enlightenment, a cult of Neopaganism and of pre-modern agrarianism together with the propagation of localism (or 'bioregionalism') (François & Nonjon, 2021). Often, this coincides with inheritances from agrarian populism and a rural voter base which is usually still the largest electoral reservoir for these parties.

Concerning climate change policies, Stella Schaller and Alexander Carius (2019) show that PRR parties justify and communicate climate policy using four frames of argumentation: economic damage, homeland and nature, national sovereignty and scientific dissent. For instance, the AfD in Germany often complains about the destruction of the 'traditional' landscape or the threat to local bird populations by wind farms (Schaller & Carius, 2019: 14 ff.). PiS' in Poland uses a cultural narrative against decarbonization which threatens values of popular lifestyles (Huber et al., 2021; Żuk & Szulecki, 2020). At the same time, the Sweden Democrats propagate advanced climate policies despite their denial of man-made climate change (Schaller & Carius, 2019: 20). Also the Austrian FPÖ is readily acknowledging climate change to be a problem and has been regarded to be supportive of renewable energy (Ćetković & Hagemann, 2020). These differences show the difficulties to find a common denominator of PRR parties' climate and environment-related positions. While nature protection has an important historical heritage on the radical right wing (Forchtner, 2019c) this does often go together with opposition to climate policies which are usually opposed because of their internationalist cross-boundary character. At the same time, these positions are slowly eroding due to populist radical right-wing parties' need to rejuvenate and attract younger voters (Ruser & Machin, 2019).

Concerning the epistemological dimension, a growing body of work focuses on climate change denialism in populist platforms and among right-wing extremists (Yan et al., 2021). PRR parties often embrace climate denialism or scepticism in parallel to anti-elitism and a critique of international cooperation (Hess & Renner, 2019). Many PRR parties do not only deny anthropogenic climate change but their discourse includes evidence, process and response scepticism (Rahmstorf, 2004). However, even if 'climate skepticism' or the denial of man-made climate change is undisputedly the most common position within the entire 'far-right' spectrum, there are also ambivalent and even some affirmative positions (Forchtner, 2019a: 2).

Regarding the international dimension, far-right populists usually reject international agreements under the pretext of defending national sovereignty (Huber et al., 2021). This is often combined with the scepticism of the science global treaties are based on. Along these lines, PRR parties claim that these treaties are too expensive, socially unjust, ecologically harmful and ineffective (Schaller & Carius, 2019). At the same time, scepticism of international climate policies does not automatically turn PRR parties against alternative energy sources. For instance, Marine Le Pen launched the *Nouvelle Ecologie* movement in opposition to international climate policy-making, but continued supporting renewable energy policies in order to make France less dependent on imported energy sources (Wagener & Machin, 2019).

Populist market liberals differ from PRR mainly insofar as they put economic reasoning first. They usually regard popular sovereignty to be threatened by state interventions under the disguise of climate and energy policies. At the same time, populist market liberals usually are free marketers and open to multilateralism and regional integration when it encourages trade liberalization. Market liberal populists usually subscribe to an individualistic worldview which sets them apart from PRR actors collectivism. Consequently, they support the needs of the 'people' and of popular sovereignty, which is seen in danger through 'economically unreasonable' policies and climate policy measures. Climate action is often regarded as an attempt to take away jobs from those who deserve them and to impose new taxes. Typical for this 'economic damage' frame is the argument that climate protection measures, such as the promotion of non-competitive renewable energies, will harm the economy by driving up energy prices and destroying industrial branches (Arning & Ziefle, 2020; Raymond, 2020). Therefore, populist market liberal's preferred policies are *climate policy nationalism* or *climate policy conservativism* (Vihma et al., 2020). Where populist market liberals are similar to PRR is the critique of the mainstream consensus on 'political correctness' regarding climate change. This overlap comes also from the perceived necessity to counter-mobilize against ideological antagonists, such as green parties or the climate movement which calls for fundamental policy change (Lockwood, 2018; Selk et al., 2019).

Regarding the epistemological dimension, literature shows that knowledge production related to climate scepticism by contrarian think tanks is often linked to market liberal interests (Almiron et al., 2020; Cann & Raymond, 2018; Plehwe, 2014). Most of this work concerns the US, where particularly the Heartland Institute has become infamous for sowing the seeds of scepticism (Ruser, 2018). Some inroads were made also in other parts of the world, but the success of these 'merchants of doubt' (Oreskes & Conway, 2011) has remained limited to some European neoliberal think tanks, such as the European Institute for Climate and Energy (EIKE) in Germany, the Austrian Economic Center or the French Institut Économique Molinari (Almiron et al., 2020; Busch & Judick, 2021; Haupt, 2020).

With regard to the international dimension, the emphasis of populist market liberals is often on national sovereignty even though the same actors also support economic globalization. It is more that the support of the global South and the financial implications this might have is the reason for why these actors oppose global climate action. Paralleling the criticism of statism voiced at the national level, international organizations are ridiculed for being bureaucratic and ineffective.

Finally, *left-wing populism* combines core populist attributes, such as people-centrism, anti-elitism and popular sovereignty, with a class-based understanding of social conflicts. This results in emphasizing economic exploitation and calling for a strong interventionist state (Huber et al., 2021). In general, left-wing populist parties tend to be strongly pro-environmental and pro-climate. Particularly Southern European inclusionary populist movement-parties, such as *Podemos* in Spain or the Italian *Movimento Cinque Stelle (Five Star Movement)*, hold strong pro-environmental positions and combine them with a populist rhetoric. While one of the 'stars' in the Five Star Movement's name stands for the environment, Syriza in Greece has made climate change and renewables to two of the four pillars of its 2019 election manifesto (Huber et al., 2021). Additionally, we can find left wing-populisms also in Latin America, e.g. in Bolivia combining discourses of environmental justice and indigenous rights.

An important conflict that emerges between different goals of left-wing populists concerns the prioritization of ecological goals in contrast to social ones. Distributional effects of climate and environmental policies are of central concern as they often affect core constituencies of left-wing-parties. The emerging conflicts are typical of globalized capitalisms mode of production (Mitchell, 2009), and of the energy metabolism Western societies' 'imperial mode of living' relies on (Brand & Wissen, 2021). Punctual reforms related to 'greening' global capitalism are not seen to lead to any meaningful results and the most important question socio–ecological transformation raise is how to step behind capitalism and its reliance on economic growth (Kallis, 2019). While the degrowth movement and environmental justice movement represent these ideas most clearly, their influence on populist left parties remains weakly institutionalized despite undeniably existing sympathies. One exception is Podemos in Spain, which propagates new forms of community-based solidarity economics and relies on the heritage of the anti-austerity Indignados movement (Neyra, 2019).

Relating to the epistemological dimension, left-wing populists propagate reliance on science and hold holistic views of environmental problems seen in a global perspective. At the same time, this perspective often remains critical of the way *how* science is produced and propagates inclusive, participatory modes of knowledge production not limited to scientists but involving local knowledge. According to Mattia Zulianello and Diego Ceccobelli (2020) this reliance on *vox populi* instead of a technocratic *vox scientifica* is what sets Greta Thunberg's transformative discourse apart of the left populist discourses. At the same time, left-wing populists and Thunberg share the emphasis on 'monism, moralisation, a Manichean vision of the world, a critique of key features of the metapolitical status quo' (Zulianello & Ceccobelli, 2020, p. 623).

Concerning the international dimension, populist left-wing actors usually support international agreements if they allow for the protection of the weak— but become protectionist when it comes to trade because of the fear of labour displacement (Rone, 2018). At the same time, they are critical of the global political and economic establishment and call for democratizing and opening up international organizations to include the voices the Global South and of social movements (Huber et al., 2021).

In summary, this overview of three archetypes of populism shows that their way of addressing environmental concerns is highly different. None of the populism denies the importance of sustainability per se. Environment is a powerful valence issue: no one is openly against 'a better environment' (Cox & Béland, 2013). But we can identify important structural differences that go back to ideological dissimilarities and their path-dependencies as well to the societal embedding of these actors. The next section provides an overview of explanations related to environmental populism.

EXPLANATIONS

After having sketched the different varieties of environmental populism, we turn to explanations given for framing environmental and climate issues by populist actors. We differentiate between three main explanations: interest-based, ideology-based and strategic-political ones, and focus both on party positions (supply side) and positions of individuals (demand side).

The first family of explanations that links populism and the climate change underlines the importance of economic *interests*. This structuralist and materialist approach focuses on economic challenges related to climate change and the sustainability transitions that are taking place (Lockwood, 2018). These processes lead to substantial and often painful structural changes in core industrial sectors which were often the backbones of the old industrial model of economic development. Obvious examples for such sectors include the coal industry but also other fields like automobile industry or agriculture, which all face difficulties and market pressure due to neo-liberal globalization and structural changes due to changes in consumption patterns (Haas, 2020; Knuth,

2019; Reusswig et al., 2020; Żuk & Szulecki, 2020). Consumption patterns and previously accepted lifestyles become less excepted and more expensive. Organic food, electric cars, energy-efficient housing and renewable energy comes with a price that households with lower incomes cannot afford. This means that green technologies and environmentally conscientious behaviour can reinforce existing social inequalities. The *gilets jaunes* protests by the economically and geographically marginalized against increased fuel prizes introduced to finance energy transition in France illustrate the importance of grievances related to social justice for those feeling 'left-behind'. Another interpretation of the same development underlines the interests of incumbent fossil industrial sector and their allies in state administrations supporting the 'carbon lock-in' (Unruh, 2000), or interpret populist parties' opposition to sustainability transitions as the defence of the 'imperial lifestyle' they hope to keep or achieve (Eversberg, 2018).

The second family of explanations is *ideology-based*. Ideational explanations relate to (right-wing) populisms anti-elite, socially conservative and nationalist values and their aversion to globalism, liberalism and the loss of national sovereignty (Lockwood, 2018). According to this perspective, the backlash against liberal-democratic values stems from populist actor's ideological aversion to climate protection measures. Ideology-based accounts explain populist parties' opposition to energy transitions as a conflict between 'detached urban elites' and 'ordinary rural citizens' (Eichenauer et al., 2018, p. 645; Fraune & Knodt, 2018; Selk et al., 2019). At the same time, environmental concerns and climate change policies are paradigmatic cases of internationalization carried out by distant elites holding globalist ideologies. International agreements, such as UN climate negotiations are often used by populist actors to show how the cosmopolitan establishment betrays national interests. Ruling elites undermine sovereignty and propagate postmaterialist values that collide with national interests. Additionally, if policies propagated by these elites refer to distributive justice in favour of the Global South and future generations, this can further strengthen fears of losses.

A third account underlines the role of *strategic considerations*. Delegation of decision-making powers to unaccountable bureaucrats, scientists and environmentalists is a perfect scapegoat but populist's reactions are neither purely interest-based nor only ideological. From a strategic perspective on populism (Weyland, 2001), they can be seen as cynical reactions designed to maximize support, either through attracting new voters or by reacting to the increasing success of competitor parties, such as green parties. Supporting this view, Tarek Abou-Chadi (2016) study of party manifestos in sixteen Western European countries from 1980 to 2011 shows that green party successes prompt other parties to lessen their environmental ambitions and formulate clear opposition to them. At the same time, strategic consideration might also lead to changes in position held by populist parties, for instance as they become more open to climate change issues in order to accommodate younger voters (Ruser & Machin, 2019; Wagener & Machin, 2019). Perhaps unsurprisingly,

Lars E. Berker and Jan Pollex (2021) show in a subnational comparison of party competition in the German Bundesländer, that especially the Green Party aligns with the *Fridays for Future* movement, while the AfD position themselves in clear contrast to the ideas of the movement.

Some of these supply-side arguments are echoed also at the demand side. Survey research shows economic factors, such as GDP per capita and unemployment to be important predictors of climate change concern, suggesting the relevance of the interests-based first account (Duijndam & van Beukering, 2020). Martin Dolezal and Swen Hutter (2012: 69–71) show that concerning the structure of the demand space in the 2000s in Europe, environmental politics is either connected to economic preferences (UK, Germany and Switzerland) or is more related to aspects of cultural liberalism as in France, Austria and the Netherlands. Others find support for ideology explanations and argue that populist voters feel their view on climate change to be unrepresented and, thus, oppose climate and environmental policies due to their anti-elitist stances (Huber, 2020). Similarly, Riley E. Dunlap, Aaron M. McCright and Jerrod H. Yarosh (2016) suggest that in the US right-wing voters oppose climate policy because of their support for the free market.

Other studies show that the rise of right-wing populist parties and post-truth politics influences how people think about climate and environment, leading to more polarization within the public (Batel & Devine-Wright, 2015, 2018; Kammermann & Dermont, 2018). While such findings are well-established in the US context, recent studies show a growing relevance of climate related ideological polarization also in Western Europe but not in Central and Eastern Europe, where these policies salience remains lower (McCright et al., 2016). At the same time, other studies show education to mediate pro-climate changes beliefs but does not change the effects of right-wing ideology (Czarnek et al., 2021).

Effects

While the previous sections mainly concerned populist's discourses related to environment and climate, the policy effects of these forces are at the centre of attention here. Donald Trump's presidency, marked by the US's abandonment of the Paris Treaty or Jair Bolsonaro's policies regarding climate change have shown clearly that populists in power do often have a negative policy effect. According to Antto Vihma et al. (2020, 23–24) different types of climate populists propagate different policy responses. While *climate denialists*, represented strongly in the US, see no need for policy action, *climate policy nationalists* recognize the need for policy responses, but fear that this will result in comparative benefits for other countries (most prominently for China). *Climate policy conservatives* do not deny the need for climate policies, but they doubt the efficacy of proposed policy instruments and strongly believe in market forces that drive innovation and problem solution.

Empirical evidence partly supports the negative effect of populists on policy outcomes. Christian Kroll and Vera Zipperer (2020) show that countries' performance on the 17 Sustainable Development Goals (SDGs) is related to electoral support for populist parties, even if their argument is that progress on SDGs will be a force against populism. Looking at populists in government office, Jahn (2021) reports increasing green-house gas emissions. Other studies focus more on the output dimension and analyse the policies propagated by populist parties. For instance, studies by Stefan Ćetković and Christian Hagemann (2020) and Aron Buzogány and Stefan Cetkovic (2021) show that populists have a negative effect on climate policy efforts both on the national and the European level. However, the emerging picture is more complex than outcome-oriented studies would suggest. This results from the fact that still few populist parties assume government duties and if they do levelling their issue-ownership remains low. Rising polarization and fragmentation in the European Parliament has also facilitated more ambitious decision-making. Case studies of the Nordic countries, the Netherlands and Austria show that energy and climate policy efforts do not always weaken when populists are strong but their electoral success indirectly contributes to policy improvements because of the polarization of the political arena that strengthens the government influence of smaller progressive parties (Ćetković & Hagemann, 2020). Pointing into a similar direction Huber et al. (2021) find substantial differences in climate change policy discourses, positions and actions across and within different populist parties and suggest that these are explained by left-right cleavages of host-ideology but not populism per se. At the same time, they find government participation to have a dampening effect on policies. Both the Austrian FPÖ, which rejected the Paris Agreement, and the Polish PiS have become more supportive of renewable energy policies than their previous discourse would have allowed to expect. In sum, these Europe-focused studies show rather mixed effects of populist parties on climate policies and not support the view that they would lead to a gridlock (Huber et al., 2021).

Stepping beyond European examples there is a strong track of research that focuses on the environmental politics of left-wing governments in Latin America where extractivism, resource exploitation, and the petro-state plays a key role. Studies on Ecuador show how the left-wing populist President Rafael Correa first announced the Yasuní-ITT initiative, which banned oil exploitation in the Yasuní National Park based on external funding, but due to the oil price volatility the initiative had been stopped after a few years (Kingsbury et al., 2019: 530). Additionally, the government' attacked anti-oil environmentalist and indigenous critics as external threats' (Lyall & Valdivia, 2019, p. 354).

Focusing on Bolivia, Diego Andreucci (2018) shows how the left-wing populist president Evo Morales gained power by aligning with the economic and ecological interests of the indigenous people. However, as a president he embraced the resource extraction policies he was critical of and attacked those environmentalists who stood against his 'Process of Change'. In a similar way, Adam Bledsoe (2019) shows extractivism and environmental racism to be part of both progressive and conservative administrations in Brazil. His analysis of the environmental conflicts in the Bay of Aratu show that governing parties from the populist left (Working Party) to the centre-right (Brazilian Democratic Movement) pursue these policies.

Examples from the United States give further insights on different aspects of the relationship between environmentalism and populism. Sarah Knuth (2019) focuses on the left-populist green-collar movement of environmentalists, organized labour, and community justice organizers which started to grow in the 2000s. Especially during the Obama administration, the movement advocated investments into renewable energy industries and job-creation for different social groups. One key result was the very idea of a 'Green New Deal', which was pushed forward by left-wing democrats such as Alexandria Ocasio-Cortez (Friedman, 2019). In another study, Erik Kojola (2019) focuses on the connection between right-wing extractive populism and their voters and argues that 'class, race, and gender dynamics of place-based identities and moral economies tied to mining are a key part of the micropolitics of right-wing populism'. (Kojola, 2019: 377). This micropolitical embedding explains the long-term support of pro-industry policies of market-liberal populists among those who are negatively affected by the reduction of social and environmental protection (Kojola, 2019: 378).

These studies show that both left-wing and right-wing populist governments use environmental issues to mobilize their supporters. But in the long run, it seems that the interests of both state-led or private companies and other veto players will have higher chances to win the battle against the environmental supporters. This is especially true when populist actors are prone to extractivist policies instead of investing in renewable energy industries and new resource efficient technologies. In that sense, the so-called 'resource curse' is becoming a curse for the environment as well.

OUTLOOK

Environmental issues—especially when connected to the climate change-debate—are becoming increasingly salient on the national and the subnational levels in both democratic and authoritarian regimes. They are related to existing political institutions and the political order in general, including economic issues, aspects of social inequality and minority rights. And they will be a key issue to deal with for populist parties and movements to mobilize their supporters in elections. Some of the policies proposed to counter populism—such as more deliberation and responsiveness or the reduction of different sorts of inequalities—can have positive outcomes also for the environment (Bang & Marsh, 2018). But the ongoing partisan polarization on climate change and the public backlash against environmental policies (as exemplified by protests against *Energiewende* in Germany or the *gilets jaunes* movement in France) shows that climate policies need to be based on broad public support and to take into account concerns of the vulnerable and the marginalized (Dryzek et al., 2019).

This chapter has shown that research on environmental populism is growing exponentially over the last few years and is being addressed from different disciplinary perspectives reaching from contemporary history, history of ideas, sociology, comparative politics, geography to environmental studies. At the same time, our overview also shows that this research is still strongly Eurocentric and mostly related to cases where populist governments are in power. Methodologically, there is joyful coexistence of both quantitative and qualitative approaches in the field. Both approaches help us to understand the relationship between environmentalism and populism, and the dynamics and path dependencies in political decision-making by populist actors. We also find that the majority of studies focuses on right-wing populist parties or governments, while only a small minority being interested in left-wing actors or market-liberal actors. This distinction could be used for further research in understanding similarities and differences between populist's strategies, arguments, and policies. In the future, it would be thus useful to expand the research on other regions and use cross-area comparisons to gain a more profound understanding the drivers of decision-making by populist concerning environmental and climate issues.

Literature

Abou-Chadi, T. (2016). Niche party success and mainstream party policy shifts—How green and radical right parties differ in their impact. *British Journal of Political Science, 46*(02), 417–436. https://doi.org/10.1017/S0007123414000155

Almiron, N., Boykoff, M., Narberhaus, M., & Heras, F. (2020). Dominant counter-frames in influential climate contrarian European think tanks. *Climatic Change, 162*(4), 2003–2020.

Andreucci, D. (2018). Populism, hegemony, and the politics of natural resource extraction in Evo Morales's Bolivia. *Antipode, 50*(4), 825–845.

Arning, K., & Ziefle, M. (2020). Defenders of diesel: Anti-decarbonisation efforts and the pro-diesel protest movement in Germany. *Energy Research & Social Science, 63*, 101410.

Aslanidis, P. (2020). Major directions in populism studies: Is there room for culture? *Partecipazione e Conflitto, 13*(1), 59–82.

Bang, H., & Marsh, D. (2018). Populism: A major threat to democracy? *Policy Studies, 39*(3), 352–363.

Batel, S., & Devine-Wright, P. (2015). Towards a better understanding of people's responses to renewable energy technologies: Insights from social representations theory. *Public Understanding of Science, 24*(3), 311–325.

Batel, S., & Devine-Wright, P. (2018). Populism, identities and responses to energy infrastructures at different scales in the United Kingdom: A post-Brexit reflection. *Energy Research & Social Science, 43*, 41–47.

Beeson, M. (2019). *Environmental populism: The politics of survival in the anthropocene*. Springer.

Berker, L. E., & Pollex, J. (2021). Friend or foe?—Comparing party reactions to Fridays for Future in a party system polarised between AfD and Green Party. *Zeitschrift Für Vergleichende Politikwissenschaft.* https://doi.org/10.1007/s12286-021-00476-7

Biehl, J., & Staudenmaier, P. (1995). *Ecofascism: Lessons from the German experience.* AK Press Edinburgh.

Bledsoe, A. (2019). Afro-Brazilian resistance to extractivism in the Bay of Aratu. *Annals of the American Association of Geographers, 109*(2), 492–501. https://doi.org/10.1080/24694452.2018.1506694

Börzel, T., & Zürn, M. (2021). Contestations of the liberal international order: From liberal multilateralism to postnational liberalism. *International Organization, 75*(2). https://doi.org/10.1017/S0020818320000570

Bosworth, K. (2019). The people know best: Situating the counterexpertise of populist pipeline opposition movements. *Annals of the American Association of Geographers, 109*(2), 581–592.

Bosworth, K. (2020). The people's climate march: Environmental populism as political genre. *Political Geography, 83,* 102281. https://doi.org/10.1016/j.polgeo.2020.102281

Brand, U., & Wissen, M. (2021). *The imperial mode of living: Everyday life and the ecological crisis of capitalism.* Verso Books.

Brass, T. (2000). *Peasants, populism, and postmodernism: The return of the agrarian myth.* Psychology Press.

Brock, P. (1977). *Polish revolutionary populism: A study in agrarian socialist thought from the 1830s to the 1850s.* University of Toronto Press.

Busch, T., & Judick, L. (2021). Climate change—That is not real! A comparative analysis of climate-sceptic think tanks in the USA and Germany. *Climatic Change, 164*(1), 1–23.

Buzogány, A., & Ćetković, S. (2021). Fractionalized but ambitious? Voting on energy and climate policy in the European Parliament. *Journal of European Public Policy, 28*(7), 1038–1056. https://doi.org/10.1080/13501763.2021.1918220

Buzogány, A., & Mohamad-Klotzbach, C. (2021). Populism and nature—the nature of populism: New perspectives on the relationship between populism, climate change, and nature protection. *Zeitschrift für Vergleichende Politikwissenschaft (ZfVP)* (forthcoming).

Buzogány, A., Gora, M., & Costa, O. (2021). Contesting the EU's External Democratization Agenda: An analytical framework and application to populist parties in power. *Cambridge Review of International Affairs* (forthcoming).

Cann, H. W., & Raymond, L. (2018). Does climate denialism still matter? The prevalence of alternative frames in opposition to climate policy. *Environmental Politics, 27*(3), 433–454.

Canovan, M. (1981). *Populism.* Houghton Mifflin Harcourt P.

Ćetković, S., & Hagemann, C. (2020). Changing climate for populists? Examining the influence of radical-right political parties on low-carbon energy transitions in Western Europe. *Energy Research & Social Science, 66,* 101571.

Conversi, D. (2020). The ultimate challenge: Nationalism and climate change. *Nationalities Papers, 48*(4), 625–636. https://doi.org/10.1017/nps.2020.18

Cox, R. H., & Béland, D. (2013). Valence, policy ideas, and the rise of sustainability. *Governance, 26*(2), 307–328. https://doi.org/10.1111/gove.12003

Czarnek, G., Kossowska, M., & Szwed, P. (2021). Right-wing ideology reduces the effects of education on climate change beliefs in more developed countries. *Nature Climate Change*, *11*(1), 9–13.

Davies, W. (2020). Green populism? Action and mortality in the anthropocene. *Environmental Values*, *29*(6), 647–668.

De Lange, S. L., & Rooduijn, M. (2015). Contemporary populism, the agrarian and the rural in Central Eastern and Western Europe. In *Rural protest groups and populist political parties* (pp. 321–344). Wageningen Academic Publishers.

Dobson, A. (2007). *Green political thought*. Routledge.

Dolezal, M., & Hutter, S. (2012). Participation and party choice: comparing the demand side of the new cleavage across arenas. In H. Kriesi, E. Grande, M. Dolezal, M. Helbling, D. Hoeglinger, S. Hutter & B. Wüest, *Political conflict in Western Europe* (pp. 67–95). Cambridge: Cambridge University Press.

Dryzek, J. S., Bächtiger, A., Chambers, S., Cohen, J., Druckman, J. N., Felicetti, A., Fishkin, J. S., Farrell, D. M., Fung, A., & Gutmann, A. (2019). The crisis of democracy and the science of deliberation. *Science*, *363*(6432), 1144–1146.

Duijndam, S., & van Beukering, P. (2020). Understanding public concern about climate change in Europe, 2008–2017: The influence of economic factors and right-wing populism. *Climate Policy*, 1–15.

Dunlap, R. E., McCright, A. M., & Yarosh, J. H. (2016). The political divide on climate change: Partisan polarization widens in the US. *Environment: Science and Policy for Sustainable Development*, *58*(5), 4–23.

Eatwell, R. (2003). Ten theories of the extreme right.

Eatwell, R., & Goodwin, M. (2018). *National populism: The revolt against liberal democracy*. Penguin UK.

Eichenauer, E., Reusswig, F., Meyer-Ohlendorf, L., & Lass, W. (2018). Bürgerinitiativen gegen Windkraftanlagen und der Aufschwung rechtspopulistischer Bewegungen. In *Bausteine der Energiewende* (pp. 633–651). Springer.

Eversberg, D. (2018). Innerimperiale Kämpfe: Drei Thesen zum Verhältnis zwischen autoritärem Nationalismus und imperialer Lebensweise. *PROKLA. Zeitschrift Für Kritische Sozialwissenschaft*, *48*(190), 43–54.

Forchtner, B. (2019). Climate change and the far right. *Wiley Interdisciplinary Reviews: Climate Change*, *10*(5), e604. https://doi.org/10.1002/wcc.604

Forchtner, B. (2019b). *The far right and the environment: Politics, discourse and communication*. Routledge.

Forchtner, B. (2019). Nation, nature, purity: Extreme-right biodiversity in Germany. *Patterns of Prejudice*, *53*(3), 285–301. https://doi.org/10.1080/0031322X.2019.1592303

Forchtner, B., & Kølvraa, C. (2015). The nature of nationalism: Populist radical right parties on countryside and climate. *Nature and Culture*, *10*(2), 199–224.

Forchtner, B., Kroneder, A., & Wetzel, D. (2018). Being skeptical? Exploring far-right climate-change communication in Germany. *Environmental Communication*, *12*(5), 589–604.

François, S. (2016). L'extrême droite française et l'écologie. Retour sur une polémique. *Revue Francaise d'Histoire des Idees Politiques* (2), 187–208.

François, S., & Nonjon, A. (2021). "Identitarian Ecology" The far right's reinterpretation of environmental concerns. *Illiberalism Studies*. https://www.illiberalism.org/identitarian-ecology-rights-reinterpretation-environmental-concerns/

Fraune, C., & Knodt, M. (2018). Sustainable energy transformations in an age of populism, post-truth politics, and local resistance. *Energy Research & Social Science, 43*, 1–7.

Friedman, L. (2019, February 21). What is the Green New Deal? A climate proposal, explained. *The New York Times*. https://www.nytimes.com/2019/02/21/climate/green-new-deal-questions-answers.html Accessed 1 March 2021.

Garavan, M. (2007). Resisting the costs of 'development': Local environmental activism in Ireland. *Environmental Politics, 16*(5), 844–863. https://doi.org/10.1080/09644010701634224

Giesen, D. (2019). Agrarian populism in the 19th century: Four sources of partial success. *American Journal of Economics and Sociology, 78*(3), 649–674. https://doi.org/10.1111/ajes.12282

Golder, M. (2016). Far right parties in Europe. *Annual Review of Political Science, 19*, 477–497.

Haas, T. (2020). Die Lausitz im Strukturwandel: Coal phase-out in the area of conflict between authoritarian populism and progressive renewal. *PROKLA. Zeitschrift Für Kritische Sozialwissenschaft, 50*(198), 151–169.

Haupt, S. (2020). Zitierkartelle und Lobbyisten Vergleichende Perspektiven auf die Klimawandelleugner. *Forschungsjournal Soziale Bewegungen, 33*(1), 170–184.

Hess, D. J., & Renner, M. (2019). Conservative political parties and energy transitions in Europe: Opposition to climate mitigation policies. *Renewable and Sustainable Energy Reviews, 104*, 419–428. https://doi.org/10.1016/j.rser.2019.01.019

Heywood, A. (2017). *Political ideologies: An introduction*. Macmillan International Higher Education.

Huber, R. A. (2020). The role of populist attitudes in explaining climate change skepticism and support for environmental protection. *Environmental Politics, 29*(6), 959–982. https://doi.org/10.1080/09644016.2019.1708186

Huber, R. A., Maltby, T., Szulecki, K., & Ćetkovic, S. (2021). Is populism a challenge to European energy and climate policy? Empirical evidence across varieties of populism. *Journal of European Public Policy* (forthcoming). https://doi.org/10.13140/RG.2.2.24124.77441

Ivaldi, G., & Mazzoleni, O. (2019). Economic populism and producerism: European right-wing populist parties in a transatlantic perspective. *Populism, 2*(1), 1–28.

Jagers, J., & Walgrave, S. (2007). Populism as political communication style. *European Journal of Political Research, 46*(3), 319–345.

Jahn, D. (2021). Populist parties in government and greenhouse gas emissions: Deepening social division in the European Union. *Journal of European Public Policy* (forthcoming).

Kallis, G. (2019). Socialism without growth. *Capitalism Nature Socialism, 30*(2), 189–206.

Kammermann, L., & Dermont, C. (2018). How beliefs of the political elite and citizens on climate change influence support for Swiss energy transition policy. *Energy Research & Social Science, 43*, 48–60.

Kingsbury, D. V., Kramarz, T., & Jacques, K. (2019). Populism or petrostate?: The aterlives of Ecuador's Yasuni-ITT initiative. *Society & Natural Resources, 32*(5), 530–547.

Knuth, S. (2019). Whatever happened to green collar jobs? Populism and clean energy transition. *Annals of the American Association of Geographers, 109*(2), 634–643.

Kojola, E. (2019). Bringing back the mines and a way of life: Populism and the politics of extraction. *Annals of the American Association of Geographers, 109*(2), 371–381.

Kroll, C., & Zipperer, V. (2020). Sustainable development and populism. *Ecological Economics, 176*, 106723. https://doi.org/10.1016/j.ecolecon.2020.106723

Lawton, G. (2019). The rise of real eco-fascism. *New Scientist, 243*(3243), 24. https://doi.org/10.1016/S0262-4079(19)31529-5

Lockwood, M. (2018). Right-wing populism and the climate change agenda: Exploring the linkages. *Environmental Politics, 27*(4), 712–732.

Lubarda, B. (2021). Beyond ecofascism? Far-right ecologism (FRE) as a framework for future inquiries. *Environmental Values* (forthcoming).

Lyall, A., & Valdivia, G. (2019). The speculative petro-state: Volatile oil prices and resource populism in Ecuador. *Annals of the American Association of Geographers, 109*(2), 349–360.

Mamonova, N., & Franquesa, J. (2020). Populism, neoliberalism and agrarian movements in Europe. Understanding rural support for right-wing politics and looking for progressive solutions. *Sociologia Ruralis, 60*(4), 710–731.

McCright, A. M., Dunlap, R. E., & Marquart-Pyatt, S. T. (2016). Political ideology and views about climate change in the European Union. *Environmental Politics, 25*(2), 338–358.

Meyer, J. M. (2008). Populism, paternalism and the state of environmentalism in the US. *Environmental Politics, 17*(2), 219–236. https://doi.org/10.1080/09644010801936149

Mitchell, T. (2009). Carbon democracy. *Economy and Society, 38*(3), 399–432.

Mouffe, C. (2020). Why a populist left should rally around a green democratic transformation. *Opendemocracy.* https://www.opendemocracy.net/en/rethinking-populism/left-populist-strategy-post-covid-19/

Mudde, C. (2004). The populist zeitgeist. *Government and Opposition, 39*(4), 541–563. https://doi.org/10.1111/j.1477-7053.2004.00135.x

Neyra, R. (2019). Constructing the people: Left populism and degrowth movements. *The European Legacy, 24*(5), 563–569. https://doi.org/10.1080/10848770.2018.1550896

Olsen, J. (1999). *Nature and nationalism: Rrigth-wing ecology and the politics of identity in contemporary Germany.* Macmillan.

Oreskes, N., & Conway, E. M. (2011). *Merchants of doubt: How a handful of scientists obscured the truth on issues from tobacco smoke to global warming.* Bloomsbury Publishing USA.

Otjes, S., Ivaldi, G., Jupskås, A. R., & Mazzoleni, O. (2018). It's not economic interventionism, stupid! Reassessing the political economy of radical right-wing populist parties. *Swiss Political Science Review, 24*(3), 270–290.

Park, M. (2013). The trouble with eco-politics of localism: Too close to the far right? Debates on ecology and globalization. *Interface: A Journal on Social Movements, 5*(2).

Plehwe, D. (2014). Think tank networks and the knowledge–interest nexus: The case of climate change. *Critical Policy Studies, 8*(1), 101–115. https://doi.org/10.1080/19460171.2014.883859

Rahmstorf, S. (2004). *The climate sceptics.* http://www.pik-potsdam.de/~stefan/Publications/Other/rahmstorf_climate_sceptics_2004.pdf

Raymond, L. (2020). Carbon pricing and economic populism: The case of Ontario. *Climate Policy, 20*(9), 1127–1140. https://doi.org/10.1080/14693062.2020.1782824

Reusswig, F., Lass, W., & Bock, S. (2020). Abschied vom NIMBY: Transformationen des Energiewende-Protests und populistischer Diskurs. *Forschungsjournal Soziale Bewegungen, 33*(1), 140–160. https://doi.org/10.1515/fjsb-2020-0012

Rone, J. (2018). Contested international agreements, contested national politics: How the radical left and the radical right opposed TTIP in four European countries. *London Review of International Law, 6*(2), 233–253.

Rovira Kaltwasser, C., Taggart, P. A., Espejo, P. O., & Ostiguy, P. (2017). *The Oxford handbook of populism*. Oxford: Oxford University Press.

Ruser, A. (2018). *Climate politics and the impact of think tanks: Scientific expertise in Germany and the US*. Springer.

Ruser, A., & Machin, A. (2019). Nationalising the climate: Is the European far right turning green?. *Green European Journal*. https://www.greeneuropeanjournal.eu/nationalising-the-climate-is-the-european-far-right-turning-green/

Schaller, S., & Carius, A. (2019). *Convenient truths*. Adelphi Research.

Selk, V., Kemmerzell, J., & Radtke, J. (2019). In der Demokratiefalle? Probleme der Energiewende zwischen Expertokratie, partizipativer Governance und populistischer Reaktion. In *Energiewende in Zeiten des Populismus* (pp. 31–66). Springer.

Strijker, D., Voerman, G., & Terluin, I. (2015). *Rural protest groups and populist political parties*. Wageningen Academic Publishers.

Szasz, A. (1994). *Ecopopulism: Toxic waste and the movement for environmental justice*. University of Minnesota Press.

Uekötter, F. (2006). *The green and the brown: A history of conservation in Nazi Germany*. Cambridge University Press.

Uekötter, F. (2007). Green Nazis? Reassessing the environmental history of Nazi Germany. *German Studies Review*, 267–287.

Unruh, G. C. (2000). Understanding carbon lock-in. *Energy Policy, 28*(12), 817–830.

Verbeek, B., Zaslove, A., Rovira Kaltwasser, C., Taggart, P., Ochoa Espejo, P., & Ostiguy, P. (2017). *The Oxford handbook of populism*.

Vihma, A., Reischl, G., Andersen, A. N., & Berglund, S. (2020). Climate change and populism: Comparing the populist parties' climate policies in Denmark, Finland and Sweden. In *FIIA reports*. Finnish Institute of International Affairs.

Wagener, O., & Machin, A. (2019). The nature of green populism? *Green European Journal*. https://www.greeneuropeanjournal.eu/nationalising-the-climate-is-the-european-far-right-turning-green/

Weyland, K. (2001). Clarifying a contested concept: Populism in the study of Latin American politics. *Comparative Politics*, 1–22.

Yan, P., Schroeder, R., & Stier, S. (2021). Is there a link between climate change scepticism and populism? An analysis of web tracking and survey data from Europe and the US. *Information, Communication & Society*, 1–40. https://doi.org/10.1080/1369118X.2020.1864005

Żuk, P., & Szulecki, K. (2020). Unpacking the right-populist threat to climate action: Poland's pro-governmental media on energy transition and climate change. *Energy Research & Social Science, 66*, 101485. https://doi.org/10.1016/j.erss.2020.101485

Zulianello, M. (2020). Varieties of populist parties and party systems in Europe: From state-of-the-art to the application of a novel classification scheme to 66 parties in 33 countries. *Government and Opposition, 55*(2), 327–347.

Zulianello, M., & Ceccobelli, D. (2020). Don't call it climate populism: On Greta Thunberg's technocratic ecocentrism. *The Political Quarterly, 91*(3), 623–631. https://doi.org/10.1111/1467-923X.12858

CHAPTER 20

Medical Populism

Gideon Lasco

INTRODUCTION

The COVID-19 pandemic continues to rage all over the world; a health crisis lies front and center in the everyday lives of billions. While a viral infection is at the core of the pandemic, it has become clear that the responses of individual political actors are just as crucial in understanding nations' responses to the crisis, and ultimately, in making sense of why some have fared better than others.

Even before COVID-19, medical issues—from vaccine scandals to contagion scares—have been labile tropes of politicization, reflecting and reinforcing the moral panics around these issues—from fin-de-siècle cholera epidemics being blamed on Chinese migrants, to the Ebola scare in 2014 being used as pretext by United States President Donald Trump to demand that the US "immediately stop all flights from EBOLA infected countries or the plague will start and spread inside our 'borders'" (realdonaldtrump, 2014). The fact that race can be cast in terms of "hygiene" speaks of how seamlessly concerns about the individual body can be conflated with xenophobic concerns about the body politic. More incisively, scholars have noted that "historically, populist leaders may have benefited when health of their populations deteriorates" (Gugushvili et al., 2020).

G. Lasco (✉)
Department of Anthropology, University of the Philippines, Quezon City, Philippines
e-mail: pdlasco@up.edu.ph

Development Studies Program, Ateneo de Manila University, Quezon City, Philippines

© The Author(s), under exclusive license to Springer Nature Switzerland AG 2022
M. Oswald (ed.), *The Palgrave Handbook of Populism*,
https://doi.org/10.1007/978-3-030-80803-7_20

Relevantly for the contemporary period, long before the world's attention to vaccines for COVID-19 led to "vaccine nationalism," politicians have used vaccines as populist tropes—either to appeal to conspiracy-minded constituencies (as with the far-right parties in Italy) or to burnish their governance credentials (as with the proponents of the dengue vaccine—the first of its kind—in the Philippines). The immediacy of communication made possible by virtual platforms like Twitter and YouTube has made political discourse around these health issues more immediate and more visceral, and while the political efficacy of politicians' response to health crises is questionable, it is clear that they have real-life consequences to people. Trump's endorsements of hydroxychloroquine, for instance, led to people being poisoned from ingesting the said drug, while his downplaying of the pandemic arguably led to more deaths in the US—after which he left office having presided over the most devastating medical calamity in American history.

This chapter discusses medical populism as a framework that can be used to characterize and interrogate the ways in which the COVID-19 pandemic and other health crises have been politicized and responded to by political actors all over the world. Building on the populism literature in general and from conceptions of populism as a style in particular (Jagers & Walgrave, 2007; Moffitt, 2016), I define medical populism as *a political style that simplifies and spectacularizes health crises while forging divisions between the "people" and infectious or dangerous "others."* Central to medical populism are dramatic performances of political actors as well as invocations of knowledge claims to dramatize and simplify complex medical issues, as this chapter intends to discuss.

POPULISM AND HEALTH CRISES

Despite its overuse in public discourse and academic scholarship, the concept of populism has retained analytic usefulness, as the introduction and various chapters of this book evince. Particularly productive has been the consensus of populism not as having a fixed set of contents—but as a familiar repertoire of styles or performances (Brubaker, 2017; Moffitt, 2016). Prominent in these repertoires are the forging of divisions between the "people" and the "establishment" or "others," hewing closely to most definitions of populism. Of late, there has been a lot of reflection as to how technologies like social media have magnified the capacity of populists (Postill, 2018).

As far as health crises are concerned, analyses that consider individual political actors using the lens of populism have mostly been fairly recent. Problematizing the nebulous nature of "moral panics" and the need to recognize the role of individuals in reinforcing them, Gideon Lasco and Nicole Curato (2019, p. 1) noted:

> Moral panics set the scene for two possible responses: (1) a technocratic response which seeks to soothe public outcry by letting experts and institutions

of accountability take over and (2) a populist response which further spectacularises the crisis and pits 'the people' against the failed and untrustworthy establishment.

Conceptualizing the second response, the authors introduced medical populism as "a political style that constructs antagonistic relations between 'the people' whose lives have been put at risk by the 'unscrupulous establishment'," arguing that while any issue can be used a populist trope, medical concerns and health emergencies are particular vulnerable to politicization, given how they tap into people's fears of disease and death while also demanding urgent responses. Subsequent works in the past two years have made use of, and refined, this framework (Lasco & Larson, 2020; Lasco, 2020a; Lasco, 2020b), while other social scientists have also engaged with its elements (Speed & Mannion, 2020; Żuk & Żuk, 2019), articulating its instantiations in various parts of the world.

Four interrelated elements comprise the framework of medical populism, each of which is discussed in the following sections. Take note that some of these elements may not necessarily be manifest in a leader's political style. Of "downplaying," for instance—a form of simplification discussed below—Brett Meyer (2020, p. 4) notes that "contrary to popular perceptions, only a minority of populist leaders, five of the 17 currently in power, have downplayed the crisis." (See also Brubaker, 2020). Nonetheless, the framework captures the *repertoire* of styles that characterize the leadership of medical populists.

SIMPLIFICATION

Politicians—*especially those currently in power*—simplify crises by either downplaying, even denying—or offering simplistic solutions. In the words of Rogers Brubaker (2017, p. 367), populism "performatively devalues complexity through rhetorical practices of simplicity, directness, and seeming self-evidence, often accompanied by an explicit anti-intellectualism or epistemological populism." This is particularly salient in health crises which rest on a complex body of knowledge—i.e., biomedicine—that is not always epistemologically accessible, and is thereby vulnerable to such anti-intellectual, anti-establishment attacks, as when politicians rail against a "medical-pharmaceutical complex," on top of a general milieu of distrust toward experts and scientific knowledge (Mede & Schäfer, 2020).

One dramatic example of simplification is **denying the existence of a crisis or its central feature altogether**, as when South African President Thabo Mbeki denied that HIV causes AIDS, arguing instead that it is poverty, malnutrition, and ill health that leads to weakened immune systems (Lasco & Curato, 2019). The COVID-19 pandemic has seen echoes of such denialism in the responses of Brazilian President Jair Bolsonaro, who likened COVID-19 to "just a little cold," and Trump, who compared it to the seasonal flu (Lasco, 2020b).

A less dramatic example of simplification involves **downplaying the crisis**, pledging that it will go away soon; that it can be addressed within a promised time frame (e.g., Philippine President Rodrigo Duterte's 2016 campaign promise to eliminate drugs in his country within three to six months of his election); or casting doubt on the epidemiological figures by claiming a figure of their own. We saw the third in Bangladesh in 2019, when some politicians disputed the high number of dengue fever cases being reported by newspapers. Under COVID-19, various global leaders have also resorted to making numerical claims—often presenting lower numbers of deaths or cases—to downplay the magnitude of the pandemic in their respective countries.

Another form of simplification is **making easy diagnoses to complex problems, and accordingly offering easy solutions**. Southeast Asia's drug wars have been in part based on the idea, promoted by leaders like Duterte and Thai Prime Minister Thaksin Shinawatra, that killing people who use drugs will solve criminality (Lasco, 2020a). Vaccine scandals around the world have been based on simplistic claims about vaccines causing various forms of harm, from abortion to autism (Lasco & Larson, 2020).

In the COVID-19 pandemic, numerous examples abound of world leaders touting easy solutions to the pandemic, often going against the advice of their own public health officials. These solutions have ranged from prayer to potions, but what they have in common is how they tap into ideas that resonate with the people: In Tanzania, for instance, President John Magufuli's claim that "Corona in our country has been removed by the powers of God" appeals to the religiosity of his constituents (Odula, 2020); while in Madagascar, President Andry Rajoelina's much-touted herbal tonic—marketed both as prevention and remedy—taps into the cultural affinity with such cures, as articulated by his own officials in the following terms: "It's in our culture as Malagasy people to use decoctions like this" (Ioussouf, 2020).

One final example of simplification is the **invocation of false dichotomies**; that is, pitting two ideas against each other as if they are mutually exclusive. In the ongoing Philippine drug war, politicians have often asked their audience to choose between the "human rights of the criminals" versus the "human rights of their victims," as if one cannot respect both. Under COVID-19, we have seen leaders pitting strict public health measures against reopening the economy, as if supporting one can only come at the expense of the other.

SPECTACULARIZATION

The second element of medical populism is spectacularization—the performance of crises and dramatization of government responses. As Lasco and Curato, referencing Benjamin Moffitt (2016), note, "While a technocratic response to moral panics promotes measured responses that emphasise certainty and stability, facts, not fear, medical populists draw power from spectacular and dramatized portrayals of the crisis" (2019). We must add that in the case of people already in power, the dramatization may not be of the crisis itself but from how they are responding to it.

In the first instance, the performance of crisis involves **dramatizing the deadly and virulent nature of the disease or medical(ized) emergency in question**. In the Philippines, one example was seen during the dengue vaccine scandal, where a public attorney took to parading parents with pictures of their children who allegedly died after receiving the vaccine. The same public attorney organized dramatic autopsies of children, again in pursuit of the claim that it was the vaccine that killed them. Such actions doubtless heighten people's perceptions of the scandal, tapping into their "deepest atavistic fears of suffering and death" (Heath, 2006, p. 146).

Another way to make a spectacle out of a crisis is by **making epidemiological claims that paint a larger magnitude of the problem**. In both the Philippines and Indonesia, leaders invoked figures of "millions of drug addicts" to reinforce moral panics around drug use and justify draconian anti-drug campaigns (Lasco, 2020a). In the COVID-19 pandemic, opposition leaders have cited higher-than-reported numbers to support their case that the government's response is inadequate.

As for the dramatization of government's responses to the crisis, we see this accomplished in the form of **rhetoric and imagery of war and mass mobilization**. In Honduras in 2019, for instance, the President announced a *"mega-operativo"* (mega-operation) to combat dengue in what he called *"Dia D"* (D-Day). Beyond the mundane use of "war" on diseases (e.g., "War on COVID-19"), we have seen more colorful allusions, as when the Trump administration called its vaccine program "Operation Warp Speed" and when Russia called its vaccine "Sputnik V." Beyond such militaristic rhetoric, various countries, from Peru to South Africa, have mobilized soldiers and even tanks to dramatize their responses as part of quarantines and "strict lockdowns." Elsewhere, mass mobilization accomplished a similar effect, as when Indian Prime Minister Narendra Modi enacted a "Janata curfew" on March 22, 2020 involving more than a billion people.

Meanwhile, and to illustrate how simplification and spectacularization can in fact go hand in hand, we also see the **spectacle of downplaying** and denial as part of medical populism. Examples include Belarusian President Alexander Lukashenko dramatically playing ice hockey in late March 2020, dismissing the world's reaction as "frenzy and psychosis," declaring that it "is better to die standing on your feet than to live on your knees;" and Trump theatrically removing his mask outside the White House after having been hospitalized for COVID-19 in October 2020.

Forging of Divisions

The third element is the forging of divisions, which is at the heart of even the most minimalist formulations of populism. As Giorgos Katsambekis and Yannis Stavrakakis (2020, p. 4) put it in their survey of the COVID-19 pandemic, populism is "a kind of politics that champions 'the people' and their sovereignty while antagonizing unresponsive political 'elites' or a multi-faceted 'establishment'." In the case of health crises, the "establishment" can take the form of medical and pharmaceutical institutions, global bodies, and foreign countries (e.g., "the West"); at the same time, the division can also be "horizontal" (Lasco & Curato, 2019) and include "dangerous others" such as migrants and foreigners that are cast as vectors of disease.

Within this element, divisions can either be vertical or horizontal, building on pre-existing cultural, political, and religious fault lines. **Vertical divisions pit the public against entities that are perceived to be powerful**—for instance, a superpower like China or a global institution like the World Health Organization (WHO). When politicians in Nigeria called for a boycott of the polio vaccine in the early 2000s, they tapped into the country's powerful Christian elite's resentment toward Muslims, as well as a milieu of anti-colonial sentiments. As Gideon Lasco and Heidi J. Larson (2020, p. 4) explained, the boycott was partly

> rooted in the divergent colonial and post-colonial experiences of the predominantly-Muslim North (where the vaccine boycott took place) and the Christian south (which held political power at the time of the boycott). The fact that the communities where polio was endemic also happened to be predominantly Muslim allowed leaders to say that Muslims were particularly targeted by the vaccine.

Similar sentiments can be seen during the COVID-19 pandemic, as when Ayatollah Ali Khamenei of Iran declared: "The import of American and British vaccines to the country is banned [...] If their Pfizer manufacturer can produce a vaccine, then why do they want to give it to us? They should use it themselves so they don't experience so many fatalities. Same with the U.K." (Hagdoost, 2021); and when Trump railed against the WHO, blaming it for the pandemic (Lasco, 2020b).

On the other hand, **divisions can also be horizontal, in which the public is pitted against dangerous or infectious "others" often belonging to a marginalized or minoritized group**. This was seen during the SARS outbreak of 2003, as well as the beginning of the COVID-19 pandemic, when Asians were perceived to be the dangerous "others" and stigmatized. Religious and political divisions can also be invoked by leaders, blaming journalists, activists, and critics for the crisis.

To reiterate an earlier point, these divisions do not happen from scratch, but rather, build on pre-existing notions, prejudice, conflict, and perceptions about an institution or group of people. Thus, Venezuelan President Nicolas Maduro could claim that COVID-19 is actually a biological weapon against China (Wyss, 2020), while Republicans in America could claim that the weapon is *by* China, citing "common sense" (Pengelly, 2020). Such divisions, however, can diminish in prominence as new information and political developments emerge.

INVOCATION OF KNOWLEDGE CLAIMS

Finally, medical populists do not just communicate health crises to their constituents; they conceptualize them in ways that either run contrary to public health discourse—or share elements with it—by making knowledge claims. These knowledge claims can include any aspect of the crises. Common examples include the origin or etymology of epidemics (e.g., "It came from a laboratory in China!"), the epidemiology of a certain condition, the efficacy and safety of treatments and cures, the nature of certain diseases, and the susceptibility of a place or group of people.

On one hand, this invocation can involve **fake news and even conspiracy theories** that typically feature malign intent on the part of powerful elites to harm the people: a common theme in vaccination scandals that forge vertical divisions. Inherently divisive and spectacular, conspiracy theories in the context of health crises often involve powerful elites using disease and treatment alike to control populations and reap immense profits—while tapping into the pre-existing mistrust of elites held by many (Romer & Jamieson, 2020). More commonly, knowledge claims are also invoked when politicians endorse certain drugs and treatments.

While these claims are often tied to the rise of the "post-truth age," they can also involve the **selective use of scientific discourse**. Strategically, they may "politicize expertise in order to gain legitimacy and use narratives of expert-driven governance to establish a direct link with voters" in what Lenka Buštíková and Pavol Baboš call "technocratic populism" (2020, p. 497). Moreover, the language of science and medicine can figure in promised cures, as when politicians speak of pharmaceutical drugs (e.g., chloroquine, ivermectin) as treatment. More subtly, political actors are quick to invoke scientific knowledge when it fits their simplistic or dramatic accounts—but are just as quick to shun the nuances involved. For instance, in the Philippines, leaders decided to require face shields, citing "scientific evidence"—but did not distinguish between outdoor and indoor spaces, leading to "one-size-fits-all" policies (Lasco, 2021).

Regardless of their epistemological provenance, knowledge claims are central to medical populism, and challenging such claims that are inimical to public health is an essential mandate that will require better science communication and a longer-term project of "rebuilding a culture of trust" (Parmet & Paul, 2020).

CONCLUSION

In this chapter we surveyed the elements of medical populism, making use of the COVID-19 pandemic and other recent health crises as illustrative examples. Regardless of the medical and political consequences of leaders' actions, they validate Cas Mudde's (2020) observation that there is "not one single 'populist response' to the coronavirus pandemic." Moreover, despite evidence suggesting that populist policies are detrimental to public health (Gugushvili et al., 2020), populist-led governments may not necessarily be associated with failed pandemic responses as measured by epidemiological outcomes or by these governments' opposition to public health guidance or science-based policies (Meyer, 2020).

Which brings us back to the dichotomy suggested by Lasco and Curato (2019): that between the populist and technocratic styles. What exactly constitutes a "technocratic response" deserves further scholarship, and so do possible typologies to further characterize responses to health crises. The elements of the medical populist style, however, are not mutually exclusive with other responses. Simplification, for instance, can raise public understanding of complex issues, while spectacle—if viewed as ritual—can help give people a sense of confidence and reassurance amid uncertainty. Of course, vertical divisions can involve rightful critiques of the political or medical elites' corruption or incompetence, leading to accountability. As Katsambekis and Stavrakakis (2020, p. 8) note, the "populist actors to represent and unify social grievances against the political elites held responsible—if, of course, such credible actors do emerge. And this might actually be a good thing for democracy, as long as such populist projects are articulated with an inclusive and pluralistic vision of society."

Meanwhile, just as mixed as medical populists' success in dealing with health crises is their political success in the aftermath of such crises. Trump's spectacular defeat in the 2020 US elections may signal a repudiation of his medical populism, but many of his peers around the world seem to have emerged—thus far—unscathed, with the likes of Bolsonaro and Duterte still popular in their respective countries, and with approval ratings even higher than some of their technocratic counterparts. As the COVID-19 pandemic has also illustrated, populist performances during health crises can help set the stage for authoritarian measures, allowing political actors to gain more power—or maintain it (Thompson & Ip, 2020; Vieten, 2020).

Clearly, the world will continue to contend with medical populism—regardless of its medical or political efficacies—for years and decades to come.

Literature

Brubaker, R. (2017). Why populism? *Theory and Society, 46*(5), 357–385.
Brubaker, R. (2020). Paradoxes of populism during the pandemic. *Thesis Eleven*, 0725513620970804.
Buštíková, L., & Baboš, P. (2020). Best in COVID: Populists in the time of pandemic. *Politics and Governance, 8*(4), 496–508.
Gugushvili, A., Koltai, J., Stuckler, D., & McKee, M. (2020). Votes, populism, and pandemics. *International Journal of Public Health, 65*(6), 721–722.
Hagdoost, Y. (2021, January 8). Iran bans U.S., U.K. COVID-19 vaccines in feud with West. *Bloomberg*. https://www.bloomberg.com/news/articles/2021-01-08/khamenei-bans-u-s-u-k-covid-19-vaccines-amid-feud-with-west
Heath, I. (2006). Combating disease mongering: Daunting but nonetheless essential. *PLoS Med, 3*(4), e146.
Ioussouf, R. (2020, August 13). Madagascar president's herbal tonic fails to halt Covid-19 spike. *BBC*. https://www.bbc.com/news/world-africa-53756752
Jagers, J., & Walgrave, S. (2007). Populism as political communication style: An empirical study of political parties' discourse in Belgium. *European Journal of Political Research, 46*(3), 319–345.
Katsampekis, G., & Stavrakakis, Y. (Eds.). (2020). *Populism and the pandemic: A collaborative report*. Populismus.
Lasco, G. (2020a). Drugs and drug wars as populist tropes in Asia: Illustrative examples and implications for drug policy. *International Journal of Drug Policy, 77*, 102668.
Lasco, G. (2020). Medical populism and the COVID-19 pandemic. *Global Public Health, 15*(10), 1417–1429.
Lasco, G. (2021, January 29). Face shield nation. *Philippine Daily Inquirer*.
Lasco, G., & Curato, N. (2019). Medical populism. *Social Science & Medicine, 221*, 1–8.
Lasco, G., & Larson, H. J. (2020). Medical populism and immunisation programmes: Illustrative examples and consequences for public health. *Global Public Health, 15*(3), 334–344.
Mede, N. G., & Schäfer, M. S. (2020). Science-related populism: Conceptualizing populist demands toward science. *Public Understanding of Science, 29*(5), 473–491.
Meyer, B. (2020). *Pandemic populism: An analysis of populist leaders' responses to COVID-19*. Tony Blair Institute for Global Change. https://institute.global/policy/pandemic-populism-analysis-populist-leaders-responses-covid-19
Moffitt, B. (2016). *The global rise of populism: Performance, political style, and representation*. Stanford University Press.
Mudde, C. (2020, March 27). Will the coronavirus 'kill populism'? Don't count on it. *The Guardian*. https://www.theguardian.com/commentisfree/2020/mar/27/coronavirus-populism-trump-politics-response
Odula, T. (2020, June 9). God has 'removed' coronavirus, Tanzania's president claims. *AP*. https://apnews.com/article/fcaaa816cd9ba159c840b5366107da50
Parmet, W. E., & Paul, J. (2020). COVID-19: The first posttruth pandemic. *American Journal of Public Health, 110*(7), 945–946.
Pengelly, M. (2020, April 11). Republican who floated virus conspiracy says 'common sense has been my guide'. *The Guardian*. https://www.theguardian.com/us-news/2020/apr/11/republican-tom-cotton-coronavirus-china

Postill, J. (2018). Populism and social media: A global perspective. *Media, Culture & Society, 40*(5), 754–765.

realdonaldtrump. (2014, August 2). The U.S. must immediately stop all flights from EBOLA infected countries or the plague will start and spread inside our "borders." Act fast! [Twitter post]. https://www.thetrumparchive.com/?results=1&searchbox=%22immediately+stop+all+flights%22

Romer, D., & Jamieson, K. H. (2020). Conspiracy theories as barriers to controlling the spread of COVID-19 in the US. *Social Science & Medicine, 263*, 113356.

Speed, E., & Mannion, R. (2020). Populism and health policy: Three international case studies of right-wing populist policy frames. *Sociology of Health & Illness, 42*(8), 1967–1981.

Thomson, S., & Ip, E. C. (2020). COVID-19 emergency measures and the impending authoritarian pandemic. *Journal of Law and the Biosciences*, lsaa064. https://doi.org/10.1093/jlb/lsaa064

Vieten, U. M. (2020). The "new normal" and "pandemic populism": The COVID-19 crisis and anti-hygienic mobilisation of the far-right. *Social Sciences, 9*(9), 165.

Wyss, J. (2020, February 28). As coronavirus lands in Latin America, Venezuela's Maduro amps up conspiracy theories. *Miami Herald*. https://www.miamiherald.com/news/nation-world/world/americas/venezuela/article240728261.html#storylink=cpy

Żuk, P., & Żuk, P. (2019). Right-wing populism in Poland and anti-vaccine myths on YouTube: Political and cultural threats to public health. *Global Public Health, 15*(6), 790–804.

CHAPTER 21

Global Populism

Daniel F. Wajner

Introduction

This chapter seeks to further our understanding of the populist phenomenon by surveying state-of-the-art research on the global dimension of populism. Since the second half of the 2010s, political analysts have expressed increasing concern that an era of *global populism* has dawned (De la Torre, 2018; Grzymala-Busse, 2017; Hadiz & Chryssogelos, 2017; Moffitt, 2016; Stengel et al., 2019). Britain's 2016 Brexit referendum, the election of Donald Trump's, multiple populist movements and the rise of populist leaders around the world bear witness to these claims.

The very idea of "global populism," however, remains puzzling. What is truly "global" about the current populist momentum? Moreover, in what way are these global political trends "populist"? These two sides of the same coin appear too vaguely defined and raise several questions about the very existence of a cross-border populist phenomenon and its idiosyncratic nature. This is certainly not surprising, because scholars of comparative politics and political theory, who have dominated populist theorizing, have traditionally approached populism as a domestic category of political analysis, thus devoting little systematic attention to international drivers, patterns, and impact. Consequently, the notions of "peoples" and "elites," the two core

D. F. Wajner (✉)
Department of International Relations and The European Forum, Hebrew University of Jerusalem, Jerusalem, Israel
e-mail: daniel.wajner@mail.huji.ac.il

analytical categories of populism, have remained local, although world politics has become increasingly transnational.

In recent years, the scientific quest to elucidate the international features of populism has evolved and diversified. International Relations (IR) scholars have delved into the phenomenon, attempting to provide relevant responses to many outstanding questions concerning the implications of the current populist wave for the present and future of world politics. These scholars have made significant progress in discussing the global dimensions of contemporary populist leadership in various regions by developing initial theoretical links and accumulating rich empirical evidence (e.g., Boucher & Thies, 2019; Chryssogelos, 2017; Destradi & Plageman, 2019; Drezner, 2017; Krebs, 2021; Löfflman, 2019; Söderbaum et al., 2021; Verbeek & Zaslove, 2017; Voeten, 2020; Wajner, 2019; Wojczewski, 2020; Zeemann, 2019). In the search for similarities and differences, new theoretical and empirical gaps have emerged, highlighting aspects overlooked by previous works that addressed the foreign dimension of populism (see Holsti & Rosenau, 1996; Hughes, 1975; Liang, 2006; Mead, 2011).

This chapter explores the expanding academic output on global populism, analyzing the scientific progress achieved according to three different categories: *sources*, *patterns*, and *effects*. To this end, the author proceeds as follows. The first section is devoted to explanations of populism's appearance on the world stage and how it became a global phenomenon. The second section discusses research evidence regarding the implementation of populist patterns "abroad": how populist performances are "staged" on the international scene. The third section delves into the literature evaluating the potential impact of populism on the international system; particularly, how populist trends may affect transnational, regional, and global spheres. Finally, the concluding remarks discuss the extent to which scientific progress has been made, while suggesting topics and methodologies that may improve the study of global populism in the future. Thus, the chapter draws critical lessons for emerging academic engagement with the transnational dimensions of populism, as well as relevant policy implications for international cooperation, regional integration, and global governance.

The Populist Rise to the Global Arena

The simultaneous emergence of populist movements and leaders across the globe is not a new phenomenon. The Global South has experienced continuous waves of populism, specifically those that occurred in Latin America and Eastern Europe. It can therefore be argued that the main novelty of today's "global" populist phenomena is, in fact, that it is now widespread in most Western democracies of the Global North. However, populist movements and leaders have also proliferated sporadically in North America, Western Europe, and other areas of the "North" (e.g., Hawkins et al., 2018; Mudde & Rovira-Kaltwasser, 2012; Weyland & Madrid, 2019). What is so special, then, about this era of global populism?

The first explanation for the growing interest in this previously unidentified phenomenon argues that while populist leaders appeared at regular intervals all over the world, their attempts to attain power were less successful in the past. Only in Latin America did waves of populists ascend to government in a wide range of countries, socioeconomic contexts, and ideological variations (see Conniff, 1999; Ellner, 2012; Filc, 2015; Levitsky & Loxton, 2013; Panizza, 2005; Roberts, 1995). The novelty of current Global Populism lies, therefore, not in the simultaneous emergence of populist forces in the political arena but rather in their growing assumption of governmental functions, including the management of foreign policy, regional integration, and national security. The empirical proliferation of illiberal democratic regimes and their consequent hijacking of the global political agenda explains why populism has, for the first time, attracted the attention of IR scholars as a relevant category of political analysis.

Hence, with the aim of filling the existing lacunae, in recent years IR scholars have published multiple studies mapping the emergence of populist leaderships on the international stage and comparing the common drivers in their processes of power accumulation. Benjamin Moffitt's pioneering book (2016), as well as the volumes edited by Carlos De la Torre (2018), Frank Stengel, David MacDonald, and Dick Nabers (2019), and Daniel Stockemer (2019), have collated the knowledge scattered across regions, developing initial theoretical links between populism and global politics. The literature was also enriched by the work of Bertjan Verbeek and Andrej Zaslove (2017), the special issues coordinated by Vedi Hadiz and Angelos Chryssogelos (2017) and Amy Skonieczny and Amentahru Wahlrab (2019), and the reports of the "Global Populisms" cluster at Stanford University led by Anna Grzymala-Busse (e.g., Grzymala-Busse et al., 2020 Fukuyama et al., 2020). IR scholars have likewise contributed in-depth case studies and comparative analyses of populists in foreign policymaking roles, with special focus on the United States (Boucher & Thies, 2019; Löfflman, 2019; Nabers & Stengel, 2019), Western and Eastern Europe (Diodato & Niglia, 2018; Grzymala-Busse, 2017, 2019; Verbeek & Zazlove, 2015), Southeast Asia (Arugay, 2018; Plagemann & Destradi, 2018; Wojczewski, 2020), the Middle East (Altinors, 2021; Kaliber & Kaliber, 2019; Özpek & Yaşar, 2018; Priego, 2018), and Latin America (Wajner, 2019, 2021a; Wehner & Thies, 2021).

A second explanation for the academic exploration of Global Populism is the increasing "internationalization" of populists themselves: the fact that populist governments not (only) simultaneously act in international spheres but also depend on global, or at least transnational, legitimation sources is also novel. Indeed, both populist discourse and attitudes are strongly linked to debates about the absorption of migrants and "others" more broadly, the extent of globalization and regional integration, and reactions to external threats (see Bonikowski & Gidron, 2016, pp. 1596–1599, Boucher & Thies, 2019, pp. 719–720; Casullo, 2019, pp. 55–59; Inglehart & Norris, 2016, pp. 7–8; Özdamar & Ceydilek, 2020, pp. 2–13; Rico et al., 2017, pp. 376–377; Verbeek & Zazlove, 2015, pp. 531–539). As Chryssogelos (2018, p. 11) asserts, the very conditions of regionalization and globalization make it almost impossible to untangle the internal/external dimensions of populism. More specifically, the socioeconomic impact of border porousness is considered the "touchstone" of the recent rise of populist tendencies in Europe and the United States (Chryssogelos, 2017, p. 4). The singling out of foreign elites as responsible for crises has traditionally occurred in areas with a long-standing history of populism, such as Latin America (Grigera, 2017; Sagarzazu & Thies, 2019; Wajner & Roniger, 2019) or in European countries such as Greece or Italy (McDonnell & Werner, 2020; Rooduijn & Akkerman, 2017; Stavrakakis & Katsambekis, 2014).

Furthermore, not only have populist "claims" gradually become transnational but so too its core "empty signifiers" (see Laclau, 2005), which transcend national boundaries through the incorporation of regional and global imaginations. Contemporary populist governments must "go out" to (re)legitimize the source of their own political power (Wajner, 2021b). The current global scenario requires that populists expand the notions of "people" and "elites," seeking overseas the esteem they do not receive at home. Therefore, populist governments seek self-legitimation from other "peoples" that face similar cross-border challenges resulting from a de-territorialized world, such as migration, trade, environment, or terrorism, proposing similar responses to them. The transformation of the state via delegation, supranationalization, and technocratization demands the discursive recreation of "elites" and "others" beyond the national level (Chryssogelos, 2017, pp. 2–6; De Cleen et al., 2020, pp. 146–154; Destradi & Plagemann, 2019, p. 7; Moffitt, 2017, pp. 410–413; Verbeek & Zaslove, 2017, pp. 6–8; Zeemann, 2019, pp. 44–46). By internationalizing problems, populists in power can also deflect domestic social demands, claiming that effective policy responses presuppose actions in the global arena. The demarcation of the "self" from the "other" projects onto the global scene and connects the populists more deeply with their followers, justifying policies and better responding to frustrations (see Albertazzi & McDonnell, 2007, p. 3; Grzymala-Busse et al., 2020, pp. 6–7; Hadiz & Chryssogelos, 2017, pp. 399–402; Wojczewski, 2020, pp. 396–400).

The Patterns of Global Populism

In parallel to the study of populism's global drivers, in recent years a vast amount of literature has focused on behavioral mechanisms within the international dimension of populism, i.e., how populist leaders interact with other foreign actors and audiences once they have risen to power. IR scholars have tackled this question from various perspectives, delving into the planning and implementation of foreign policy, the formulation of national security, the use of diplomatic channels, the role of regional integration, and the backlash against transnational bureaucracies, among other aspects. As a result, several academic debates have emerged.

A first discussion concerns the role of ideology in how populist governments shape their foreign and security policies. The populist narrative regarding the restoration of a just and glorious past of popular sovereignty initially led scholars to identify populists with dogmatic policies vis-à-vis the international system, primarily of a nationalist, protectionist, and isolationist character (see Hughes, 1975; Liang, 2006; Mead, 2011). Nevertheless, recent studies of *populist foreign policies* have exposed a more complex picture, questioning the allegedly significant influence of populist dogmatism on foreign policy issues (Chryssogelos, 2017, 2018; Verbeek & Zaslove, 2017). The work of Sandra Destradi and Johannes Plagemann (2019) has been especially influential in this sense, arguing that various "thick" and "host" ideologies tacked onto populism can be equally influential in molding foreign policy (in this vein see also Stockemer, 2019, p. 124). Similar to other types of policymaking, rulers" functional and contextual constraints often affect their definition of national interest. For that reason, when comparing its different waves, it is difficult to single out a unified "populist foreign policy" phenomenon (Wajner, 2019, 2021a). Indeed, the growing literature strengthens the conclusion that decision-making processes under populist governments are highly unpredictable (see Biegon, 2019; Boucher & Thies, 2019, p. 713; Löfflmann, 2019, pp. 127–128; Drezner, 2017, p. 28; Krebs, 2021).

Likewise, scholars debate the diplomatic style of populist governments in contrast to non-populist governments. Such studies highlight the personalization of diplomatic ties under populist governments, the centralization of decision-making processes, and the emphasis on public diplomacy (Destradi & Plageman, 2019, pp. 14–16; Wajner, 2019, pp. 214–216; Wojczewski, 2020, pp. 404–406). Although these preferences are certainly not limited to populism, today's populist governments seem to be recreating and exploiting existing trends. Indeed, several scholars discern the quintessence of populist appeal as the ability to connect with multiple audiences through affective styles, emphatic narratives, and symbolic esthetics (see Arugay, 2018; Drezner, 2017; Moffitt, 2016; Skonieczny, 2018; Stockemer, 2019). With the aim of performing authentically in diplomatic contacts, populists give carte blanche to their feelings using "bad manners" that include local slang, mannerisms, and insults (Moffitt, 2016, p. 44). Daniel Drezner skillfully analyzes the diplomatic style of these "angry populists." By acting like "ordinary people" who are guided by "common-sense" in their diplomatic relations, populists strengthen their portrayal as "genuine" leaders, aware that such a deviation from political correctness resonates positively across multiple audiences (Drezner, 2017, pp. 30–39).

Moreover, studies demonstrate that, with the support of public relations and propaganda tools, populist leaders attempt to (re)create the affective relationship of sacrifice, martyrdom, and heroism with regional and global publics. The cult of the leader and conspiracy theories reach a climax in times of drama or scandal, catalyzing the sense of constant crisis and persecution along with the belief that victory is on the horizon, and thus consolidating the mutual liaison with transnational followers (see Albertazzi & McDonnell, 2007, pp. 3–5; Biegon, 2019, pp. 522–521; Casullo, 2019, pp. 58–59; Hadiz & Chryssogelos, 2017, pp. 407–408; Inglehart & Norris, 2016, p. 5; Senkman & Roniger, 2019). Naturally, since the transnational category of "people" is harder to characterize than its domestic parallel, the populist "performer" encounters a major challenge in constructing a narrative (Moffitt, 2017, pp. 415–477). In this regard, media communications play a crucial role. Globalization processes enable greater interconnection due to faster real-time interaction and direct transnational activism (Grzymala-Busse et al., 2020, pp. 9–11; Verbeek & Zaslove, 2017, pp. 12–14). Through the use of digital platforms such as Facebook and Twitter, populists boost transnational bonds of political identification and mobilization, allowing "media populists" to bypass intermediaries (Boucher & Thies, 2019, pp. 713–714; Moffitt, 2016, pp. 74–81).

Another interesting debate among IR scholars' concerns populist behavior vis-à-vis regional and global cooperation schemes. The most recent works contradict the previous stance, according to which populist opposition to cosmopolitan sentiments and international bureaucracies was linked to isolationism (Inglehart & Norris, 2016, pp. 5–7; see also Betz, 1994; Mead, 2011; Liang, 2006). IR scholars certainly stress the populist reaffirmation of the people's "control" over global governance by dividing global public goods more "fairly"; yet this does not essentially result in opposition to all integration processes, only those influenced by political opponents (Chryssogelos, 2017, p. 14; 2018, p. 9; Destradi & Plagemann, 2019, pp. 2–4; Verbeek & Zaslove, 2017, pp. 7–8; Biegon, 2019, p. 530). The call for popular sovereignty is clearly at odds with the "liberal script" of regional integration, but it does not necessarily oppose alternative or competing regionalist "scripts" (Söderbaum et al., 2021, pp. 1–2; see also Borriello & Brack, 2019, pp. 834–836; Börzel & Zürn, 2020, pp. 7–9). Indeed, populists in the Global South, especially in Latin America and Eastern Europe, have devoted significant efforts to new and renewed cooperation schemes in an effort to enhance transnational solidarities and "peripheral" support (Wajner, 2021b). Populists have also championed the creation of ad-hoc institutional "clubs" that show "strong" populists performing as "primus inter pares" (Drezner, 2017, pp. 28–35; Moffit, 2016, pp. 7–8; Wojczewski, 2020, pp. 17–18), in a symbolic form of "a la carte" international cooperation (Söderbaum et al., 2021, pp. 10–13).

Particularly prominent here is the populist ideational projection of a permanent struggle between "the people" and "the elites" onto regional and global spheres. When these "empty signifiers" transcend national boundaries to incorporate new transnational imaginations, populists attain external corroboration for the "true" archetype that they promote (Chryssogelos, 2017, p. 2; Moffitt, 2017, pp. 410–412; Zeemann, 2019, pp. 44–46). Since popular and national interests do not always overlap, the contradictions between these two categories are particularly manifest (see also Chryssogelos, 2018, p. 8; De Cleen & Stavrakakis, 2017, pp. 308–310; Miller, 2019; Wojczewski, 2020, p. 406–409). By invoking the existence of a "fully unified people" that goes beyond national labels, various ethno-national and religious diasporas have succeeded in bypassing the need for a shared geographic space and mediating institutions (see Destradi & Plagemann, 2019, p. 6; McDonnell & Werner, 2020, pp. 197–230). Moreover, the separation of "the nation" from "the people" facilitates the development of global populist solidarities between like-minded "peoples" (Zeemann, 2019, pp. 28–40). In a sense, the populist empowerment of these transnational networks in support of mass festival mobilization constitutes an extrapolation of traditional populist patronage techniques to the international scene (Wajner, 2019, p. 215).

IR scholars have also addressed the flipside of projecting "the people" onto the international scene: the backlash against transnational "elites." In addition to the local alienation of foreign populations and the marginalization of the traditional "deep state" in foreign and security policies, populists gradually focus their discursive attacks on technocrats in all kinds of transnational authorities: international organizations, regional organizations, multinational companies, non-governmental international organizations (see Zürn, 2018, pp. 9–13, 62–79). Erik Voeten's work (2020) stands out in this regard, offering a comprehensive exploration of the populist adverse reaction to international courts that "fail to reflect the vox populi." Populist governments implement blaming tactics, targeting "corrupted" technocrats that "go too far" in defending minority rights against the majority's will. This accords with the undermining of multilateral regimes in issue-areas that are, almost by definition, transnational, such as trade, security, immigration, environment, health, human rights, international aid, and academic exchanges (Biegon, 2019, pp. 529–530; Boucher & Thies, 2019, pp. 712–720; Chryssogelos, 2018, pp. 4–11; Destradi & Plagemann, 2019, pp. 14–16; Drezner, 2017, pp. 26–33; Jenne & Mudde, 2012, pp. 147–155; Nabers & Stengel, 2019, pp. 123–124; Ozpek & Yasar, 2018, pp. 206–210; Skonieczny, 2018, pp. 62–69; Verbeek & Zaslove, 2017, pp. 12–17; Wojczewski, 2020, pp. 402–404).

Similar discursive patterns are apparent in the populist offensive against the "conspiring" and "distorting" international media (Chryssogelos, 2017, pp. 1–4; Plagemann & Destradi, 2018, pp. 286–289; Löfflmann, 2019, pp. 115–117; Moffitt, 2016, pp. 41–45; Sagarzazu & Thies, 2019, p. 205) and against academics who employ anti-science rhetoric (Szabados, 2019). Populists try to delegitimize the global "swamp," claiming that it is unrepresentative yet wields power and that it is responsible for crises yet unaccountable (on the legitimacy/authority link in global governance, see Zürn, 2018; Tallberg & Zürn, 2019). The resulting antagonism toward these "distrustful" elites not only contributes to diverting criticism of domestic governmental failures but also reaffirms the self-legitimation of the "peoples" as "pure" victims and the populist leaders as their sole "protectors" (Wajner, 2021b), as evidenced by the populist performance amid the COVID-19 pandemic (see Stavrakakis & Katsambekis, 2020).

THE POPULIST IMPACT ON THE INTERNATIONAL SYSTEM

IR scholars have also explored the theorization of populism by studying its possible effects. Although the time frame does not yet allow a longitudinal assessment of how the global rise of populist governments will affect world politics in the long term, some works have highlighted clearly identifiable changes and proposed expected future trends.

Many scholars apply structuralist approaches when assessing the global impact of populism. The rise of populist leaderships has revived recurring debates about the future of the international order, fueled by the accusation that populist regimes are eroding its underlying liberal principles and practices: the *liberal international order* (LIO) (see Ikenberry, 2018; Jahn, 2018; Stokes, 2018). The special issue of *International Organization* edited by David Lake, Lisa Martin, and Thomas Risse (2021) provides an especially prominent contribution to discussions on this topic, clarifying what is essentially "liberal," "international," and "orderly" about the LIO and addressing the central challenges it has historically faced from both internal (i.e., populism) and external forces.

Populism is certainly not the only illiberal trend involved in undermining the LIO, and other "adversaries," from both within and without, are attacking it "from different fronts" (see Adler-Nissen & Zarakol, 2021; Cooley & Nexon, 2020; Patman, 2019; Posner, 2017). Nevertheless, populist trends are considered the most dangerous, or at least the most urgent, and are viewed as increasing the likelihood that other threats to the LIO may intensify and succeed (see Fukuyama, 2017). In a similar vein, the Berlin-based SCRIPTS Cluster of Excellence co-chaired by Tanja Börzel and Michael Zürn is currently promoting the study of different contestations to the *liberal script*, including the populist "alternative" (see Börzel & Zürn, 2020). Indeed, grounded primarily in "a tale of two worlds" vision, contemporary populists have led calls for an alternative world order (see Kacowicz & Wajner, 2021), thus catalyzing the possibility that the self-fulfilling prophecy of increasingly bifurcated regions will come to pass.

Other IR scholars have focused on "meso" levels, such as the possible consequences of how populist regimes deal with international security issues. There is a consensus that the aforementioned populist style of policymaking is making the international scene much more unpredictable (Destradi & Plagemann, 2019, pp. 1–2; Stengel et al., 2019, pp. 366–368). As Ronald Krebs (2021, pp. 10–12, 21) asserts, the rise of anti-pluralist trends is undermining the state's ability to consistently design and execute a grand strategy, sustain it over time, and reap its productive benefits, consequently leading to a "fractured world." Populists seem more likely to fuel international crises by using threats, diversionary maneuvers, and rally-round-the flag tactics (Drezner,

2017, pp. 33–39). They also display a greater readiness to interfere in foreign matters using sophisticated tactics in order to gain influence and exacerbate tensions (Grzymala-Busse et al., 2020, p. 9; Nye, 2018).

Furthermore, opponents can easily (mis-)read the populist narrative regarding a declining hegemonic position, the respect conferred on authoritarian rulers, and their unilateral search for "better deals" on security as a display of revisionist attitudes. This erratic behavior, combined with the populist tendency to antagonize rival transnational elites and securitize the presence of vulnerable foreign groups, hints at an international order that is increasingly prone to violence, radicalization, and polarization (see Biegon, 2019, pp. 531–533; Löfflmann, 2019, pp. 120–129; Miller, 2019; Wojczewski, 2020, pp. 18–21). Conversely, existing evidence about how populist governments tackle conflicts highlights a willingness among populists to "pay" the audience costs by delaying military action and seeking rapprochement, thus de-escalating conflicts and facilitating a "way out" (see Arugay, 2018, p. 6; Biegon, 2019, p. 532; Destradi & Plagemann, 2019, pp. 7–8; Drezner, 2017, p. 35).

In addition, several authors have turned their attention to the role of populism in the changing dynamics of global governance and regional integration (see Destradi & Plagemann, 2019, pp. 4–5, 10–11; Söderbaum et al., 2021). On the one hand, populist hegemony in regional spheres may induce a setback for the increasingly "internationalized" state (see Chryssogelos, 2018; Steger, 2019). On the other hand, the populist wave may lead to a different type of globalist and regionalist process, based on a kind of *"populist international"* (De la Torre, 2017; McDonnell & Werner, 2020) or *"illiberal international"* (Grzymala-Busse, 2019). Certainly, amid the (still) ongoing crises surrounding the "return of sovereignty" in the implementation of "Brexit," it is too early to draw conclusions regarding the populist implications for the future of European integration (see e.g., Borriello & Brack, 2019; Markovitz, 2019; Patman, 2019, pp. 296–297; Tallberg & Zürn, 2019, p. 600). Moreover, the fact that populist Euroscepticism reveals several faces, with different drivers (Roch, 2021, pp. 7–11; Stengel, 2019, pp. 6–7), makes the evaluation of its concrete impact even more challenging. Yet we can learn from the Latin American experience, in which the populist wave of the last two decades caused a substantive change in the regional integration model, diminishing the image of regional organizations as "stepping stones" toward the global stage and transforming them into "stumbling blocks" (Wajner & Roniger, 2019, pp. 465–467; Haftel et al., 2020).

Similar debates regarding the transnational effects of populism have discussed socioeconomic standpoints, in particular because the fervor to "win" and put the people "first" largely concerns cross-border subjects such as trade and immigration (Biegon, 2019; Cohen, 2019; Skonieczny, 2018; Verbeek & Zaslove, 2017). Since populism feeds on the socioeconomic grievances of globalization, it could catalyze greater global disparities through the implementation of nationalist and protectionist economic policies (see Rodrik,

2018; Skonieczny, 2018, pp. 341–349). Different varieties of populism can affect the global business environment and, accordingly, the strategies of large corporations (Devinney & Hartwell, 2020). The gap between the social performance of populist governments and their promises can have direct consequences not only for local social cohesion (von Gustedt & Gratius, 2019) but also for global social-welfare policy systems (Milner, 2019). For instance, growing anti-elitist and nativist attitudes may lead to a reduction in foreign aid spending levels (Heinrich et al., 2021). Moreover, the populist revival can expose the beginning of a fundamental global crisis at the social foundations of the state system and its consequent inability to manage economic crises (Chacko & Jayasuriya, 2017, p. 126). Indeed, the COVID-19 pandemic has highlighted how dangerous a lack of international coordination can be for the prevention, administration, and resolution of international crises, and the "populist deniers" have intensified the problem rather than finding a solution to it. As Kurt Weyland once noted at the 2018 LASA conference in Barcelona, "Things may be bad, but populists make them worse."

Last but not least, some research has delved into the normative erosion caused by populist backlashes and the appropriate international response (see Grzymala-Busse et al., 2020, pp. 5–15; Hawkins, 2016, pp. 253–257; Rovira-Kaltwasser & Taggart, 2016, pp. 205–210; Wiesehomeier et al., 2020). It remains unclear whether the populist "revolution" is mostly discursive, purely "for show," or can have a more substantial impact on the principles of what we call *world society*. The traditional debate regarding whether populists are authoritarian threats or democratic correctives (see Koch, 2020; Mudde & Rovira-Kaltwasser, 2012; Panizza & Miorelli, 2009; Stengel, 2019; Zúquete, 2018) is transferred here to the global scene. Indeed, on the local level, as populist governments progressively encounter more socioeconomic crises and, consequently, also legitimacy crises, they increasingly strengthen illiberal elements in order to avoid losing power, with direct implications for formal institutions, representative democracies, and political freedoms (see De la Torre, 2018, 41; Grzymala-Busse et al., 2020; Finchelstein, 2019; Levitsky & Ziblatt, 2018; Mounk, 2018; Müller, 2017; Pappas, 2019). Likewise, such a consolidation of anti-pluralistic tendencies and public attitudes could also occur at the global level (Krebs, 2021, pp. 5–9; Löfflmann, 2019, pp. 124–130). Moreover, populists seem to demonstrate a gradual trend of foreign policy radicalization: the longer they are in power, the more they must "go abroad" to divert crises or explain what is happening at home (Wajner, 2021b). Therefore, even if populists ultimately lose power, they may leave behind a different type of (transnational?) political culture that will prove difficult to change in the short term.

Global Populism: Quo Vadis?

This chapter has explored the emerging academic discussions concerning the transnational dimensions of populism by scrutinizing the scientific progress achieved and contributing to a better understanding of current populist phenomena. To this end, three main categories were analyzed: sources, patterns, and effects.

Such an exploration reveals that over the last four years a richer picture has emerged, in particular regarding the first two categories. IR scholars have developed substantial theoretical insights concerning the "transnational" sources of this simultaneous rise of populism all over the globe. They have also gathered vast empirical evidence on the behavioral patterns of populist governments in their international interactions. Meanwhile, investigation of the third category is moving more slowly, although it has increased exponentially in the past two years, addressing the policy implications of populism for multiple issue-areas of regional and global dimensions. In all three categories, however, numerous topics require further explanation.

Regarding the drivers of global populism, IR scholars can contribute to a deeper understanding of the *diffusion* of populism on the international scene, particularly by incorporating Constructivist and English School perspectives, which appear to be most appropriate for addressing this type of macro-legitimation strategy based on ideational elements. Likewise, IR scholars can provide new analytical tools to analyze the variables explaining the conditions in which populist leaders and movements are more successful in attaining power. IR theorizing on populism could return to the shadows if it does not offer convincing answers to certain, as yet unanswered, key questions in this regard: Is global populism really transnational, international, regional, or "glocal"? Do the drivers of global populism differ depending on cultural, social, or economic particularities?

As for the patterns of global populism, IR scholars should increase efforts to demonstrate whether populists design, plan, and implement foreign policy in a substantially different way. The main question remains unresolved: Do "global populism" and "populist foreign policy" exist as autonomous categories of political analysis? More specifically, are diplomatic, media, or performative trends better exploited by populist governments than by their non-populist counterparts? This is not only a theoretical but also an empirical challenge, which must be addressed via in-depth case studies and comparative analyzes, as time now enables us to explore a variety of geographical, historical, and ideological variance. To this end, it is crucial to incorporate quantitative methods that will systematically distinguish different behaviors among populists toward international organizations and bureaucracies, as well as content analysis tools to compare the foreign policy discourse of populist governments with that of non-populist ones.

Last but not least, it seems evident that the events of recent years are leaving a mark on the global arena. However, it remains difficult to assess the scope and scale of this mark, and it is even more challenging to predict what the future holds for the current international order. IR scholars must make significant efforts to develop academic and policy-oriented knowledge about the possible implications of populism for specific issue-areas in which the main gaps are still evident, including the international human rights system and the global governance of "soft" political issues, while delving deeper into the impact on regional integration, security, and trade.

In this sense, scientific progress in the study of global populism greatly depends upon whether populism will reveal itself to be an ephemeral or a long-lasting phenomenon. Similar to current debates regarding the impact of COVID-19 on international politics, global populism could be a transitory and painful occurrence that will quickly be "resolved" with the discovery of a vaccine, or, alternatively, it may be a lasting anomaly that "is here to stay," forcing us to learn to live with it and minimize its consequences. In any case, as stated earlier, the populist "viral load" may remain long after populists leave power. It is worth remembering that populism was often pronounced "dead" in Eastern Europe and Latin America during the years of totalitarian regimes and authoritarian dictatorships, respectively, but it soon returned in different "mutations." The main pending question is, therefore, how to prevent, manage, and ultimately mitigate populist trends in other countries and populist effects on the international scene? IR research can also contribute to formulating "antibodies" in the face of this difficult yet imperative challenge that characterizes contemporary global politics.

Literature

Adler-Nissen, R., & Zarakol, A. (2021). Struggles for recognition: The liberal international order and the merger of its discontents. *International Organization, 75*(2), 611–634.

Albertazzi, D., & McDonnell, D. (Eds.). (2007). *Twenty-first century populism: The spectre of Western European democracy*. Palgrave-Macmillan.

Altinors, G. (2021). The justice and development party in Turkey: Populism, personalism, organization (book review). *Mediterranean Politics, 26*(1), 139–140.

Arugay, A. A. (2018, October). When populist perform foreign policy: Duterte and the Asia-Pacific region order. *SWP Working Papers 4*(1). https://www.swp-berlin.org/fileadmin/contents/products/projekt_papiere/Arugay_BCAS_Philippines.pdf

Betz, H. G. (1994). *Radical right-wing populism in Western Europe*. Springer.

Biegon, R. (2019). A populist grand strategy? Trump and the framing of American decline. *International Relations, 33*(4), 517–539.

Bonikowski, B., & Gidron, N. (2016). The populist style in American politics: Presidential campaign discourse, 1952–1996. *Social Forces, 94*(4), 1593–1621.

Borriello, A., & Brack, N. (2019). I want my sovereignty back! *Journal of European Integration, 41*(7), 833–853.

Börzel, T. A., & Zürn, M. (2020). *Contestations of the Liberal Script: A research program*. SCRIPTS Working Paper Series No. 1, https://www.scripts-berlin.eu/publications/working-paper-series/Working-Paper-No-1-2020/index.html.

Boucher, J. C., & Thies, C. G. (2019). "I am a tariff man": The power of populist foreign policy rhetoric under President Trump. *The Journal of Politics, 81*(2), 712–722.

Casullo, M. E. (2019). How to become a leader: Identifying global repertoires for populist leadership. In *Populism and world politics* (pp. 55–72). Palgrave-Macmillan.

Chacko, P., & Jayasuriya, K. (2017). Trump, the authoritarian populist revolt and the future of the rules-based order in Asia. *Australian Journal of International Affairs, 71*(2), 121–127.

Chryssogelos, A. (2017). Populism in foreign policy. In Cameron G. Thies (Ed.), *The Oxford Encyclopedia of Foreign Policy Analysis.*

Chryssogelos, A. (2018). State transformation and populism: From the internationalized to the neo-sovereign state?, *Politics, 40*(1), 22–37.

Cohen, J. L. (2019). Populism and the politics of resentment. *Jus Cogens, 1*(1), 5–39.

Conniff, M. (Ed.). (1999). *Populism in Latin America.* University of Alabama Press.

Cooley, A., & Nexon, D. (2020). *Exit from hegemony: The unraveling of the American global order.* Oxford University Press.

De Cleen, B., & Stavrakakis, Y. (2017). Distinctions and articulations: A discourse theoretical framework for the study of populism and nationalism. *Javnost-the Public, 24*(4), 301–319.

De Cleen, B., Moffitt, B., Panayotu, P., & Stavrakakis, Y. (2020). The potentials and difficulties of transnational populism: The case of the democracy in Europe movement 2025 (DiEM25). *Political Studies, 68*(1), 146–166.

De la Torre, C. (2017). A populist International?: ALBA's democratic and autocratic promotion. *SAIS Review of International Affairs, 37*(1), 83–93.

De la Torre, C. (Ed.) (2018). *Routledge handbook of global populism.* Routledge.

Destradi, S., & Plagemann, J. (2019). Populism and international relations: (Un)predictability, personalisation, and the reinforcement of existing trends in world politics. *Review of International Studies, 45*(5), 711–730.

Devinney, T. M., & Hartwell, C. A. (2020). Varieties of populism. *Global Strategy Journal, 10*(1), 32–66.

Diodato, E, & Niglia, F. (2018). *Berlusconi 'the diplomat': Populism and foreign policy in Italy.* Springer.

Drezner, D. W. (2017). The angry populist as foreign policy leader: Real change or just hot air. *Fletcher f. World Aff., 41,* 23.

Ellner, S. (2012). The distinguishing features of Latin America's new left in power: The Chávez, Morales, and Correa governments. *Latin American Perspectives, 39*(1), 96–114.

Filc, D. (2015). Latin American inclusive and European exclusionary populism: Colonialism as an explanation. *Journal of Political Ideologies, 20*(3), 263–283.

Finchelstein, F. (2019). *From fascism to populism in history.* University of California Press.

Fukuyama, F. (2017). *What is populism?.* Tempus-Corporate.

Grigera, J. (2017). Populism in Latin America: Old and new populisms in Argentina and Brazil. *International Political Science Review, 38*(4), 441–455.

Grzymala-Busse, A. (2017). Global populisms and their impact. *Slavic Review, 76*(S1), S3–S8.

Grzymala-Busse, A. (2019). Conclusion: The global forces of populism. *Polity, 51*(4), 718–723.

Grzymala-Busse, A., Fukuyama, F., Kuo, D., & McFaul, M. (2020). *Global populisms and their challenges.* Global Populisms Cluster. Stanford University, https://stanford.app.box.com/s/0afiu4963qjy4gicahz2ji5x27tednaf

Hadiz, V. R., & Chryssogelos, A. (2017). Populism in world politics: A comparative cross-regional perspective. *International Political Science Review, 38*(4), 399–411.

Haftel, Y. Z., Wajner, D. F., & Eran, D. (2020). The short and long (er) of it: The effect of hard times on regional institutionalization. *International Studies Quarterly*, 64(4), 808–820.

Hawkins, K. A. (2016). Responding to radical populism: Chavismo in Venezuela. *Democratization*, 23(2), 242–262.

Hawkins, K. A., Carlin, R. E., Littvay, L., & Rovira-Kaltwasser, K. (2018). *The ideational approach to populism: Concept, theory, and analysis*. Taylor&Francis.

Heinrich, T., Kobayashi, Y., & Lawson, E. (2021). "Populism and foreign aid." European Journal of International Relations, forthcoming.

Holsti, O., & Rosenau, J. (1996). Liberals, populists, libertarians, and conservatives: The link between domestic and international affairs. *International Political Science Review*, 17(1), 29–54.

Hughes, T. (1975). Liberals, populists, and foreign policy. *Foreign Policy*, 20, 98–137.

Ikenberry, G. J. (2018). The end of liberal international order? *International Affairs*, 94(1), 7–23.

Inglehart, R. F., & Norris, P. (2016). *Trump, Brexit, and the rise of populism: Economic have-nots and cultural backlash*. Harvard Papers.

Jahn, B. (2018). Liberal internationalism: Historical trajectory and current prospects. *International Affairs*, 94(1), 43–61.

Jenne, E. K., & Mudde, C. (2012). Hungary's Illiberal turn: Can outsiders Help? *Journal of Democracy*, 23(3), 147–155.

Kacowicz, A. M., & Wajner, D. F. (2021). Alternative world orders in an age of globalization: Latin American scenarios and responses. In A. Acharya, & D. Tussie (Eds.), *Latin America in global international relations* (pp. 11–30). Routledge.

Kaliber, A., & Kaliber, E. (2019). From de-Europeanisation to anti-Western populism: Turkish foreign policy in flux. *The International Spectator*, 54(4), 1–16.

Koch, C. M. (2020). Varieties of populism and the challenges to Global Constitutionalism: Dangers, promises and implications. *Global Constitutionalism*, 1–39.

Krebs, R. R. (2021). Pluralism, populism, and the impossibility of grand strategy. In *The Oxford Handbook of Grand Strategy* (Forthcoming).

Laclau, E. (2005). *On populist reason*. Verso.

Lake, D. A., Martin, L. L., & Risse, T., (2021). Challenges to the Liberal International Order: Reflections on International Organization. *International Organization*, 75(2), 225–257.

Levitsky, S., & Loxton, J. (2013). Populism and competitive authoritarianism in the Andes. *Democratization*, 20(1), 107–136.

Levitsky, S., & Ziblatt, D. (2018) *How democracies die*. Broadway Books.

Liang, CS. (2006) *Europe for the Europeans: The foreign and security policy of the populist radical right*. Routledge.

Löfflmann, G. (2019). America first and the populist impact on US foreign policy. *Survival*, 61(6), 115–138.

Markowitz, S. (2019). Populism curtailed? Globalization and the debate over genetically modified organisms in the European Union. *Populism*, 2(2), 157–183.

McDonnell, D., & Werner, A. (2020). *International populism: The radical right in the European Parliament*. Oxford University Press.

Mead, W. R. (2011). The tea party and American foreign policy: What populism means for globalism. *Foreign Affairs*, 90(2), 28–44.

Miller, B. (2019). Populism, nationalism and the international order. Paper presented at the *EISA-PEC Conference*, Sofia.

Milner, H. V. (2019). Globalisation, populism and the decline of the welfare state. *Survival, 61*(2), 91–96.
Moffitt, B. (2016). *The global rise of populism: Performance, political style, and representation*. Stanford University Press.
Moffitt, B. (2017). Transnational populism? Representative claims, media and the difficulty of constructing a transnational 'people.' *Javnost-the Public, 24*(4), 409–425.
Mounk, Y. (2018). *The people vs. democracy: Why our freedom is in danger and how to save it*. Harvard University Press.
Mudde, C., & Rovira-Kaltwasser, C. (2012). *Populism in Europe and the Americas: Threat or corrective for democracy?* Cambridge University Press.
Müller, J. W. (2017). *What is populism?* Penguin UK.
Nabers, D., & Stengel, F. A. (2019). Sedimented practices and American identity in Donald J. Trump's Election Campaign. In *Populism and world politics* (103–135). Palgrave-Macmillan.
Nye, J. (2018). How sharp power threatens soft power. *Foreign Affairs, 24*.
Özpek, B. B., & Tanriverdi Yaşar, N. (2018). Populism and foreign policy in Turkey under the AKP rule. *Turkish Studies, 19*(2), 198–216.
Özdamar, Ö., & Ceydilek, E. (2020). European populist radical right leaders' foreign policy beliefs: An operational code analysis. *European Journal of International Relations, 26*(1), 137–148.
Panizza, F. (2005). *Populism and the mirror of democracy*. Verso.
Panizza, F., & Miorelli, R. (2009). Populism and democracy in Latin America. *Ethics & International Affairs, 23*(1), 39–47.
Pappas, T. S. (2019). *Populism and liberal democracy: A comparative and theoretical analysis*. Oxford University Press.
Patman, R. G., et al. (2019). The liberal international order and its populist adversaries in Russia, UK and USA. In F. Stengel (Ed.), *Populism and world politics* (pp. 277–303). Palgrave-Macmillan.
Plagemann, J., & Destradi, S. (2018). Populism and foreign policy: The case of India. *Foreign Policy Analysis, 15*(2), 283–301.
Posner, E. A. (2017). Liberal internationalism and the populist backlash. *Ariz. St. LJ, 49*, 795–819.
Priego, A. (2018). El populismo islámico: una respuesta no occidental a la globalización. *Revista CIDOB d'Afers Internacionals, 119*, 161–184.
Rico, G., Guinjoan, M., & Anduiza, E. (2017). The emotional underpinnings of populism: How anger and fear affect populist attitudes. *Swiss Political Science Review, 23*(4), 444–461.
Roberts, K. M. (1995). Neoliberalism and the transformation of populism in Latin America: The Peruvian case. *World Politics, 48*(1), 82–116.
Roch, J. (2021) "Friends or foes? Europe and 'the people' in the representations of populist parties." *Politics, 41*(2), 224–239.
Rodrik, D. (2018). Populism and the economics of globalization. *Journal of International Business Policy, 1*(1–2), 12–33.
Rooduijn, M., & Akkerman, T. (2017). Flank attacks: Populism and left-right radicalism in Western Europe. *Party Politics, 23*(3), 193–204.
Rovira-Kaltwasser, C. R., & Taggart, P. (2016). Dealing with populists in government: A framework for analysis. *Democratization, 23*(2), 201–220.
Sagarzazu, I., & Thies, C. (2019). The foreign policy rhetoric of populism: Chávez, oil and anti-imperialism. *Political Science Quarterly, 72*(1), 205–214.

Senkman, L., & Roniger, L. (2019). *América Latina tras bambalinas: Teorías conspirativas, usos y abusos*. Latin American Research Commons.

Skonieczny, A. (2018). Emotions and political narratives: Populism, Trump and trade. *Politics and Governance, 6*(4), 62–72.

Skonieczny, A., &.and Wahlrab, A. (2019). Introduction to the special issue on exploring global gopulisms, *Populism* 2(2), 105–109.

Söderbaum, F., Spandler, K., & Pacciardi, A. (2021). Contestations of the liberal international order: A populist script of regional cooperation. In *Elements in International Relations*. Cambridge University Press.

Stavrakakis, Y., & Katsambekis, G. (2014). Left-wing populism in the European periphery: The case of SYRIZA. *Journal of Political Ideologies, 19*(2), 119–142.

Stavrakakis, Y., & Katsambekis, G. (2020). *Populism and the pandemic: A collaborative report*. Populismus.

Steger, M. B. (2019). Mapping atiglobalist populism: Bringing ideology Bxack In. *Populism, 2*(2), 110–136.

Stengel, F. A., MacDonald, D. B., & Nabers, D. (2019). *Populism and world politics: Exploring Inter-and transnational dimensions*. Palgrave-Macmillan.

Stengel, F. A. (2019). Forget populism! *Global Discourse, 9*(2), 445–451.

Stockemer, D. (Ed.) (2019). *Populism around the world*. Springer.

Stokes, D. (2018). Trump, American hegemony and the future of the liberal international order. *International Affairs, 94*(1), 133–150.

Szabados, K. (2019). Can we win the war on science? Understanding the link between political populism and anti-science politics. *Populism, 2*(2), 207–236.

Tallberg, J., & Zürn, M. (2019). The legitimacy and legitimation of international organizations: Introduction and framework. *The Review of International Organizations, 14,* 581–606.

Verbeek, B., & Zazlove, A. (2015). The impact of populist radical right parties on foreign policy: The Northern League as a junior coalition partner in the Berlusconi Governments. *European Political Science Review, 7*(4), 525–546.

Verbeek, B., & Zazlove, A. (2017) Populism and foreign policy. In Rovira-Kaltwasser, C, Taggart, P.A., Espejo, P.O. & Ostiguy (Eds.),*The Oxford handbook of populism* (pp. 384–405).

Voeten, E. (2020). Populism and backlashes against international courts. *Perspectives on Politics, 18*(2), 407–422.

von Gustedt, A. Á., & Gratius, S. (2019). Populism and social cohesion in Latin America: Two sides of the same coin?. *Fundacion Alternativas* (n.d.), https://www.fundacionalternativas.org/public/storage/opex_documentos_archivos/e34077c8b9a83c19b673faf9578600c5.pdf.

Wajner, D. F. (2019). Making (Latin) America great again: Lessons from populist foreign policies in the Americas. In F. Stengel, D. B. MacDonald, & D. Nabers (Eds.), *Populism and world politics* (pp. 195–225). Palgrave-Macmillan.

Wajner, D. F. (2021a). Exploring the foreign policies of populist governments: (Latin) America first. *Journal of International Relations and Development, 24*(3), 651–680.

Wajner, D.F. (2021b). The populist way out: Why contemporary populist leaders seek transnational legitimation. Paper presented at the 2021 Annual Summit of the International Studies Association, Las Vegas (online).

Wajner, D. F., & Roniger, L. (2019). Transnational identity politics in the Americas: Chavismo's regional legitimation strategies. *Latin American Research Review, 54*(2), 458–475.

Wehner, L. E., & Thies, C. G. (2021). The nexus of populism and foreign policy: The case of Latin America. *International Relation-s, 35*(2), 320–340.

Weyland, K., & Madrid, R. L. (Eds.). (2019). *When democracy Trumps populism: European and Latin American lessons for the United States.* Cambridge University Press.

Wiesehomeier, N., Hawkins, K., & Chryssogelos A. (2021). *The ideational approach to populism: Consequences and mitigation.* Cambridge University Press (forthcoming).

Wojczewski, T. (2020). Populism, Hindu nationalism, and foreign policy in India: the politics of representing 'the people'. *International Studies Review, 22*(3), 396–422.

Zeemann, J. (2019). Populism beyond the nation. In *Populism and world politics* (pp. 25–53). Palgrave-Macmillan.

Zúquete, J. P. (2018). From left to right and beyond: The defense of populism. In *Routledge handbook of global populism* (pp. 416–434). Routledge.

Zürn, M. (2018). *A theory of global governance: Authority, legitimacy, and contestation.* Oxford University Press.

CHAPTER 22

Populism and the Cosmopolitan–Communitarian Divide

Frank Decker

THE LIPSET–ROKKAN THESIS REVISITED

When Seymour Martin Lipset and Stein Rokkan (1967) devised their famous thesis of 'frozen' cleavages more than fifty years ago, they could not have foreseen just how rapidly the subsequent development of political party systems in Western democracies was going to put their theory to the test. Beginning in the 1970s and accelerating in the following decades, the transformation of party systems was, on the one hand, evident in the decline in support suffered by the mainstream parties of the political left and right. At the same time, new—ecological, right-wing populist and regionalist—parties began to appear on the political stage, many of which would go on to become permanent actors in their respective party systems.

While the revival of regionalist sentiments stood in direct contrast to Lipset and Rokkan's presumption—shaped by modernization theory—that territorial conflicts in industrial societies would see a demise at the hands of 'functional' conflicts, scholars interpreted ecological and right-wing populist parties as the consequence of new cleavages. These complemented and ran diagonal to the existing religious-confessional and class cleavages that, according to Lipset and Rokkan, bore the primary responsibility for the formation of party systems in the nineteenth and twentieth centuries.

F. Decker (✉)
Institut für Politische Wissenschaft und Soziologie, Rheinische Friedrich-Wilhelms-Universität Bonn, Bonn, Germany
e-mail: frank.decker@uni-bonn.de

Similar to the historical cleavages whose genealogy was illustrated in Lipset and Rokkan's essay in a fascinating manner, these new cleavages evolved in a chronological, albeit more condensed, succession. While most Green parties emerged in the 1970s and early 1980s, right-wing populist actors arrived on the political stage over a more extended timeframe between the middle of the 1980s and the 2010s—with the Alternative for Germany as the most notable latecomer. The Danish and Norwegian representatives had, for their part, already pioneered right-wing populist ideas in the 1970s (Betz, 1994).

Electoral results reveal a substantial increase in support for right-wing populists in the 2010s. This has coincided with an even higher combined contraction in vote shares for Christian conservative and social democratic parties, with the latter suffering comparatively higher losses as defections are not just limited to their own ideological camp—to the Greens and left-wing parties—but also extend to right-wing populist actors. At least on the surface puzzling, it is this particular phenomenon that has inspired some political party and democracy scholars to attribute the rise of right-wing populism to a supposedly new cleavage which is claimed to have emerged over the past decade and can be traced back to the consequences of an accelerated globalization. Conceptually, it is purported to be based on the antagonism between cosmopolitanism and communitarianism.

According to Wolfgang Merkel,[1] this conflict can be reduced to the question whether (and to what extent) the borders of nation states ought to be opened or (remain) closed. The border question refers to "the full range of goods, services, capital, the labor force, refugees, human rights or the cessation of national competencies to supranational regimes in favor of transnational policies" (Merkel, 2017, 9, translated by the author). It therefore has an economic and cultural dimension. While cosmopolitans combine liberal positions on economic and socio-cultural questions, communitarians couple the desire for economic safety central to the welfare state with the political yearning for self-determination present in culturally defined communities. The central divide is formed by the respective interpretation of the nation. Based on a universalist understanding of human rights, cosmopolitans aspire to open the nation internally to foreign and global influences while overcoming national borders externally through intergovernmental or—even more ideally—supranational cooperation. Globalization is, in principal, seen in a positive light. Communitarians, on the other hand, retain a particularistic understanding of culture and political allegiances. They take a skeptical view of globalization and expect national political actors to shield their citizens against its supposedly negative consequences (De Wilde et al., 2019).

Does the Cosmopolitism–Communitarianism Divide Constitute a New Cleavage?

As plausible as this juxtaposition may appear at first glance, there are some doubts as to whether it constitutes a genuinely new cleavage that provides an additional explanatory contribution going beyond existing cleavage theories to understand recent changes in party systems.

The first objection rests on the sociological underpinnings of the distinction between cosmopolitanism and communitarianism. Merkel himself acknowledges that economic interests fail to offer a sufficient explanation. According to him, it is primarily human capital—that is to say educational and cultural capital—which shapes cosmopolitan attitudes. In that respect, it is at its core a cultural cleavage whose increasing importance reflects the transition from an industrial society to today's knowledge society. While economic capital constituted the primary dividing line between the working class and bourgeoisie in the industrial society, the social stratification of today's knowledge society is, above all, dependent on cultural capital that has taken a place alongside (not necessarily in place of) income. Sociologist Andreas Reckwitz (2020) succinctly described the effects of this contemporary structural change on life and the workplace in his book 'Society of Singularities.'

The second objection relates to the observation that economic and cultural divides overlap within the cosmopolitanism–communitarianism conflict. This hardly represents a new revelation and is instead a rather well-established consensus in the field of cleavage theory. The phenomenon of intersecting cleavages was visible in the era of the traditional conflicts, particularly concerning the relationship between religious-confessional and economic class allegiances. Regular church-going members of the working class tended to support Christian-democratic or conservative parties rather than their social democratic counterparts well into the 1960s in most European countries. This only changed as a result of broader secularization trends and the accompanying growth in importance of the economic over the religious cleavage. The affinity of today's social democratic and left-leaning voters for right-wing populist actors was also already captured by the formula of 'working-class authoritarianism' that Lipset (1960, 97 ff.) shaped in the 1950s.

The latter relates to another important—third—point. One of Lipset and Rokkan's central conclusions was the finding that societal conflicts do not engender the formation of parties and ideological camps by themselves— instead they need to be politically mobilized at the hands of existing elites. This also applies to their preservation. Once elites enter a relationship with a certain part of the electorate, this relationship requires constant renewals and care. The 'representation gap'[2] identified by Merkel and other voices in the field of right-wing populism research offers no theoretical added value either. Its central claim of established parties increasingly moving away from the policy preferences of their potential clients is, first of all, trivial. Furthermore, this suggests an estrangement that is the result of a culturally detached and aloof elite which—originating in the ascendant middle class—supposedly shares a common cosmopolitan outlook even if some parts of it occasionally propagate communitarian positions out of electoral considerations (Merkel, 2017, 16).

This leads to a fourth and final argument that is linked to the concept of the supposedly new cleavage. Intended as ideal types, they constitute a grotesque exaggeration, if not even a caricature of opposites that in reality is little more than fiction as the public always strives for both: individual self-expression *and* social integration. Just as 'cosmopolitans' appreciate and seek out social moorings[3] while often adopting restrictive positions when cultural diversification affects their immediate environment, most 'communitarians' possess a positive attitude toward cultural diversity and immigration as long as they retain the feeling of being in control over these processes and, therefore, their own surroundings (Meyer, 2018, 14). These terms are instead located on different levels. The actual dividing line does not run between cosmopolitans and communitarians but rather within both groups—between the liberal advocates of global competition and representatives of a value-based, global humanism on one side and between an identitarian and socially liberal communitarianism on the other.

Cleavages and the Left–Right-Distinction

A summary of these objections illustrates that the contrast between cosmopolitanism and communitarianism fails to expand on the 'new' cleavage model of the 1990s that has since gained widespread acceptance within the field of political party research. Building on the functional dimension of Lipset and Rokkan's design, it distinguishes between a socio-economic (distribution-related) and cultural (value-related) cleavage. When assessing cleavages, this simplified scheme differentiates itself from the classical model by, first of all, relying less on the relationship between parties and particular social groups while placing more emphasis on the fundamental ideological policy positions the parties represent. With the interests and values of citizens in post-industrial societies having become more detached from the rigid features of social structures, these positions are reflected within the electorate primarily on the basis of attitudes and beliefs. Moreover, the religious-confessional cleavage has been replaced by a general cultural one in which libertarian stances such as tolerance, a non-conformist mindset and multiculturalism are confronted by authoritarian attitudes such as an affinity for order, the protection and preservation of conventional lifestyles and national pride.

Any criticism of this juxtaposition also starts by addressing the conceptual and terminological choices. Authoritarian positions mark an extreme variant of the previously mentioned positions; a more general and less pejorative designation of 'conservative' is preferable. Even more problematic is the common use of the term 'libertarian' for the opposite camp as it also denotes a radical form of market liberalism that is primarily associated with the economic cleavage. Using the more general label of liberal positions appears more appropriate.

A second objection is directly tied to this. The manner in which this scheme is depicted in virtually all contemporary political science textbooks suggests a left–right divide related exclusively to the economic cleavage as its cultural counterpart is either completely separate or diagonal to it (see e.g., Kitschelt & Hellemans, 1990). This is not just questionable in the sense that the new cleavage scheme precisely intends to be rooted in the ideological positioning of political actors. It also contradicts the intuitions of political science that have come to naturally apply the blanket term 'left-liberal' to culturally liberal attitudes while labeling conservative or authoritarian positions as 'right-wing populist'.

Differing interpretations of equality stand at the center of the left–right divide. "The theme that recurs in all the variations is the distinction between a horizontal or egalitarian perception of society and a vertical or inegalitarian perception of society" (Bobbio, 1996, 58). This distinction can be found on both the economic and the cultural axis of conflict. Economic questions revolve around the theme of material equality. In principal, the right interprets the results of the free market to be fair while the left seeks to mitigate inequality by redistributing wealth to the less fortunate through government programs. Battles concerning equal rights define the cultural axis. While the left advocates for the eradication of the disadvantages certain social groups and minorities continue to endure, the right considers some forms of inequality as justifiable, pointing to natural differences between the genders, ethnic groups or sexual identities.

Graphically combining the cleavage model with the left–right distinction can be achieved through pairing both the horizontal economic and vertical cultural conflict axis before rotating them counter-clockwise by 45°. The free quadrants can then be used to mark the positions parties occupy in a given party system along the economic and cultural axes (Decker, 2018, 55). The fact that individual parties may inhabit different ideological positions along the respective spectrums is precisely the strength of this two-fold scheme. After all, combining left-leaning values on cultural matters with right-of-center economic preferences is a characteristic of many liberal parties. The opposite is true for the right-wing populists that are positioned at the extreme right pole on the cultural axis (Fig. 22.1). While their economic and social platforms promoted free market policies during their early years, many parties of the populist right have since become some of the most ardent defenders of the welfare state (Fenger, 2018).

THE MISCONCEPTION OF INGLHART'S POSTMATERIALISM

The supposed inability of accurately capturing the politics of values within the left–right frame is a misunderstanding that can be traced back to the work of American social scientist Ronald Inglehart (1977). His theory on a 'post-materialist' shift in values, developed in the early 1970s, operationalized material and immaterial values in such a manner that the former only concurred with right-of-center and the latter with left-of-center positions.[4] Inglehart himself did not hide his own sympathies for a leftist postmaterialism. By the time the parties of the New Right emerged in the 1980s, it had

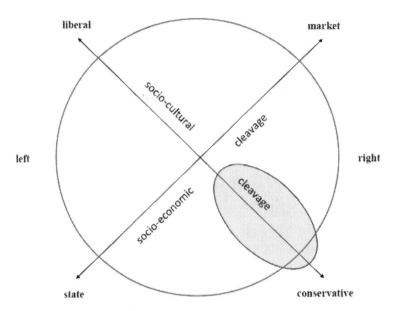

Fig. 22.1 Placement of right-wing populism within the conflict line model of contemporary party systems (*Own illustration* The big circle marks the sphere of constitutionality)

become apparent that Inglehart's classification made little sense. After all, their agenda was just as much shaped by value-related topics as that of the New Left of the 1970s, to which they represented something of an immediate reaction. The New Right was therefore also a part of the 'post-materialist' segment of the political spectrum—only that it held completely opposite (conservative or authoritarian) positions (Flanagan, 1987, 1308).

If this interpretation is correct, the emergence of Green parties has just as little to do with a 'new' cleavage as the rise of right-wing populism does. Instead, they are the result of changes in the relevance of political issues which has shifted priorities both within and between the distribution and value-related spheres.[5] At the same time, the contexts of these conflicts have expanded both in terms of space and time. While debates related to redistribution were largely limited to the social policy domain of nation-states until the 1960s (dependent on the position in the work force), they subsequently began to incorporate the underprivileged position of the Third World along with the detrimental impact on future generations as part of the ecological crisis. This has presented the social democrats of the mainstream left with a particular challenge as they have had to balance conflicting interests resulting from a variety of contexts of equality—between national and international obligations, domestic and foreign workers as well as today's and future generations.

Past and present domestic debates in Europe's democracies—relating to an intensification of European integration, the preservation of the welfare state, meeting climate change objectives and, not least, migration and refugee policies—indicate an aggravation of these conflicts. Clashes within many left-of-center and far-left parties, where a minority openly calls into question the pro-migration positions espoused by the leadership and large parts of the parties' rank-and-file, demonstrate just how blurred the front lines have become. On the surface, such demands for more restrictive immigration policies appear to have been borrowed from the populist right. A closer look illustrates, however, that an insistence on protecting the domestic labor market and welfare state from being overwhelmed by migratory movements can also be rooted in leftist thought—as long as it, for example, goes hand in hand with acknowledging international obligations such as combating the causes of displacement and ensuring the accommodation of refugees close to their countries of origin (Betts & Collier, 2017).

How Can the Rise of Populism Be Explained?

If this conclusion is correct, then populism should not necessarily be interpreted as solely or primarily rooted in cultural conflicts—instead it is an economic phenomenon as well (Manow, 2018). A closer look at the political map of Europe supports such an assertion. It illustrates an expansion of right-wing populist parties in western and northern Europe while their left-wing counterparts are more dominant in the south. The former region is composed of highly competitive and open economies in conjunction with extensive welfare states and a large population share of migrants and minorities. In these countries, value-related conflicts concerning the cultural allegiance of migrants are fused with distribution-related clashes about wages and government programs that primarily affect the lower third or quarter of the population and parts of the middle-class anxious about their own social and economic decline. This is exacerbated by the pressures placed on the welfare state by globalization—whose losers it is supposed to protect (Rodrick, 2018).

The exact interplay between the economic and cultural cleavages remains a controversial topic among the scholars of right-wing populism. Philip Manow's (2018, 16) assertion that cultural conflicts merely serve to 'charge' economic problems in order to subsequently exploit them politically, falls short on two counts. The cultural cleavage is, first of all, composed of different disputes and sub-conflicts with few possessing the same importance pertaining to redistribution policies as the topic of migration holds. Legal equality for homosexuals, for example, does not take away anything from anybody else. Value-related conflicts, moreover, carry a significant relevance of their own beyond the question of redistribution—with their importance corresponding to the scope of cultural discrepancies between immigrants and their new host societies (Miller, 2016).

Mainstream and former 'catch-all' parties have been the biggest losers of the transformation of party systems. As they take up a centrist and partially indistinguishable position on both axes, they are harmed by polarization while the ideologically more radical representatives, located toward the edges of the respective poles—market liberals and far-left socialists on the economic, the Greens and far-right populists on the cultural axis—profit.

Opinions differ as to how to best address this dilemma. Within the center-right camp, recent debates have revolved around refugee policies as some call for a more restrictive turn to shore up their 'open flank' in relation to upstart populist challengers while others fear relinquishing liberal positions will result in an exodus of moderate voters. Social democrats are similarly divided as one camp wants to push back against the leftist-liberal positions on cultural issues while, at the same time, preferring a more left-wing stance on welfare and economic policies. Alternatively, appeals are made to continue this balancing act as policies and strategies are drawn up that resolve to bring together parts of the center-left's electorate whose ideological preferences appear to be growing ever further apart.

Regardless of the future positioning of center-right and center-left parties, they will find it difficult to regain significant shares of voters from their new competitors in an increasingly broad and fragmented party system. This problem is exacerbated by electoral results that force the two camps to work together against their will. As a result, dissatisfied voters may only be further encouraged to cast their vote for parties at the ideological fringes—including those of the populist right. In light of this challenging environment, curbing the populist revolt and preventing a further escalation of economic and cultural conflicts through decent governance would already constitute an achievement.

Notes

1. British publicist David Goodhart (2017, 19 ff.) similarly argues for a distinction between the 'somewhere' and the 'anywhere'.
2. Within the German context, see e.g., Patzelt (2017).
3. As Michael Hartmann (2016) has shown in his research on elites, this even applies to the most affluent groups within the cosmopolitan jet set. Most German CEOs of foreign companies, for example, spend their time in Austria and Switzerland rather than the US or Asia—in other words, they remain within their own, familiar cultural and linguistic environment.
4. Struggles against rising prices and the maintenance of order are cited as examples for materialism while the protection of free speech and political participation are considered to be indicators for post-materialism.
5. Despite being values-based, environmental protection is primarily part of the socio-economic conflict axis as it requires varying degrees of state intervention in the free market.

Literature

Betts, A., & Collier, P. (2017). *Refuge: Reforming a broken refugee system*.
Betz, H.-G. (1994). *Radical right-wing populism in Western Europe*.
Bobbio, N. (1996). *Left and right: The significance of a political distinction*.

Decker, F. (2018). Parteiendemokratie im Wandel, 2. Aufl., Baden-Baden.
De Wilde, P. et al. (Eds.). (2019). *The struggle over borders: Cosmopolitanism and communitarianism*.
Fenger, M. (2018). The social policy agendas of populist radical right parties in comparative perspective. *Journal of International and Comparative Social Policy*, 34(3), 188–209.
Flanagan, S. C. (1987). Values in industrial societies. *American Political Science Review*, 81, 1303–1319.
Goodhart, D. (2017). *The road to somewhere: The populist revolt and the future of politics*.
Hartmann, M. (2016). *Die globale Wirtschaftselite. Eine Legende*.
Inglehart, R. (1977). *The silent revolution: Changing values and political styles among Western Publics*.
Kitschelt, H., & Hellemans, S. (1990). The left-right semantics and the new politics cleavage. *Comparative Political Studies*, 23, 210–238.
Lipset, S. M. (1960). *Political man: The social bases of politics*.
Lipset, S. M., & Rokkan, S. (Eds.). (1967). *Party systems and voter alignments* (p. 1967). Cross-National Perspectives.
Manow, P. (2018). *Die Politische Ökonomie des Populismus*.
Merkel, W. (2017). Kosmopolitismus versus Kommunitarismus. Ein neuer Konflikt in der Demokratie. In P. Harfst, I. Kubbe, & T. Poguntke (Eds.), *Parties, Governments and Elites* (pp. 9–23).
Meyer, T. (2018). Heimat, Nation – Sozialdemokratie? *Die Neue Gesellschaft / Frankfurter Hefte*, 65(11), 39–42.
Miller, D. (2016). *Strangers in our midst: The political philosophy of immigration*.
Patzelt, Werner J. (2017), Der 18. Deutsche Bundestag und die Repräsentationslücke. Eine kritische Bilanz. *Zeitschrift für Staats- und Europawissenschaften*, 16(2/3), 245–285.
Reckwitz, A. (2020). *The society of singularities*.
Rodrik, D. (2018). Populism and the political economy of globalization. *Journal of International Business Policy*, 1(1), 12–33.

CHAPTER 23

Populism and the Recasting of the Ideological Landscape of Liberal Democracies

Albena Azmanova

THE RISE OF THE ANTIESTABLISHMENT VOTE

Ideologically unconventional parties and movements that opposed globalization but espoused free market capitalism domestically while also demanding social protection—such as the *Pim Fortuyn List* in the Netherlands, *ATTAC* in France and *Bloco de Esquerda* in Portugal—began mobilizing well before the economic and social crisis that the 2007–2009 financial meltdown triggered. This mobilization began in the 1990s—a decade of solid economic growth and low unemployment (Stiglitz, 2003). By then, however, the social effect of neoliberal globalization began to be felt.

Since the 1980s, center-left and center-right governments had committed to global market integration. They sought to ensure the competitiveness of national economies in the global marketplace via product- and labor market deregulation, as well as by cutting expenditures for public services and social insurance. This coincided with the Information Technology revolution, which, combined with the liberalization of finance, enabled low-cost market entry as well as access to countries with cheap supplies of labor. These policy changes generated a political economy marked by the proliferation of both economic opportunities (for employment and profit) and social risks (of job loss and loss of investment). Overall, this led to the spread of economic and social insecurity—a condition of generalized precarity affecting the material

---

A. Azmanova (✉)
Brussels School International Studies, University of Kent, Brussels, Belgium
e-mail: A.Azmanova@kent.ac.uk

© The Author(s), under exclusive license to Springer Nature Switzerland AG 2022
M. Oswald (ed.), *The Palgrave Handbook of Populism*,
https://doi.org/10.1007/978-3-030-80803-7_23

and/or psychological welfare of people across class, skills- and income levels (Azmanova, 2020).

Precarity is strongly economically stratified. It encompasses a variety of experiences related to the insecurity of livelihoods—from the economic misery of the 'precariat', a group akin to the 'proletariat' (Standing, 2011), to the psychological strain of what Alissa Quart (2018) has called the 'middle precariat'—a professional class encompassing professors, nurses, administrators in middle management, caregivers, and lawyers, all struggling to cope with life in the 'always on' economy. Within the remit of precarity belong also the grievances about poor work–life balance and psychological strain of the highly skilled professionals in the IT industry and the managers of international corporations who are particularly subjected to the ever intensifying pressures of global economic competition. While precarity sharply increased after the global financial crisis of 2008, measures of stress and anxiety continued to be on the rise after the economy recovered in the course of the following decade (Blyth & Lonergan, 2020; Fleming, 2017). At the same time, a series of corruption and mismanagement scandals beset political and economic elites (e.g., the accounting scandal at Enron in 2001 and the 2008 United Kingdom parliamentary expenses scandal), thus undermining trust in the main political and economic institutions of liberal democracies.

The destabilization of the political and socioeconomic environment (despite growth and low unemployment) enabled populist leaders to mobilize unprecedented electoral support by claiming that ruling elites were reaping the benefits of growing prosperity yet leaving society in ruins. In this context, antiestablishment parties and movements began their assent in electoral politics, articulating their rejection of precarity into a policy agenda constituted by four key concerns: physical insecurity, political disorder, cultural estrangement, and employment insecurity—the components of a new 'order-and-security', anti-precarity, agenda (Azmanova, 2004). Such sentiments were generated not only and not necessarily by impoverishment, job loss or damages to collective cultural identities, but to *perceived* and *anticipated* losses of livelihoods and damages to social status, most often attributed to the effect of 'open border' policies. Technocratic elites further lost credibility in the global financial crisis in 2008, triggering an outrage that found expression in both right-wing and left-wing antiestablishment mobilizations (Judis, 2016). The articulation of this substantive policy platform casts doubts on the appropriateness of assigning the term 'populism' to these political entities. Populism is usually described as an antiestablishment stance without a specific content (Laclau, 2005, 15); its distinctive feature is a purely reactive stance to political rule (Judis, 2016; Müller, 2016), an engagement with what Max Weber (1994, 165) called 'negative politics'—hostile confrontation without a coherent programmatic stance and with no credible ambition to govern. Many of the parties described as 'populist' have managed to enter parliaments and governments thereby effectively engaging with political rule. They have done so on a policy platform for accountable and democratic politics (e.g., calls for restraining the power of corporations and the political establishment), revising trade agreements in view of protection of national businesses and curbing immigration (Azmanova, 2018).

However, as these formations appeal for cultural, economic, and social protection, they cannot confidently be positioned along the left–right ideological divide that has structured the landscape of electoral politics throughout the life of liberal democracies. This suggests that a profound alteration of these societies' ideological landscape is under way.

Changes in the Ideological Map of Capitalist Democracies

Ever since the French revolution of 1789 set the left–right vectors of ideological orientation and the rise of class politics in late nineteenth century infused the left–right divide with the capital–labor dynamics of social conflict, the ideological landscape of capitalist democracies has been structured along two axes. A horizontal, economic, axis configured attitudes to state intervention in the domestic economy—in a spectrum between free markets on the right and regulated markets on the left. A vertical axis structured public demand and policy supply regarding culture—with preferences spanning from traditional values on the right to liberal ones on the left. A peculiarity of the twentieth-century political landscape was that ideological preferences combining economic and cultural liberalism, on the one hand, and cultural and economic protectionism, on the other, were marginal. The landscape of electoral politics was dominated by Socialist and Social Democratic parties on the left and Conservative and Christian Democratic parties on the right (Kitschelt, 1997; Laponce, 1981) (Fig. 23.1).

At the very end of the twentieth century analysts registered that disagreements between the big political families regarding economic policy had almost disappeared; subsequently, the main distribution of policy preferences aligned almost completely with the vertical axis opposing liberal to conservative sociocultural positions (Kitschelt, 2004). Ideological cross-class voting (e.g., workers voting for center-right parties) and the rise of 'catch-all' parties in the late twentieth century prompted diagnoses that the left–right electoral divide was disappearing without being replaced by a new overarching paradigm (Mair, 2007; McKnight, 2005; Perrineau, 2002). With the advent of neoliberal globalization, the structural opposition between globalization 'winners' and 'losers' has given shape to a cleavage which has become embedded into existing two-dimensional national political spaces (Kriesi et al., 2006).

The upsurge in unorthodox ('populist') parties and movements at the close of the twentieth century, however, is suggesting the emergence of a novel overarching paradigm. In partisan terms, many of these new formations are expressing a seemingly incongruous set of stances combining cultural liberalism (e.g., regarding gender equality and LGBTQ rights) with anti-Muslim

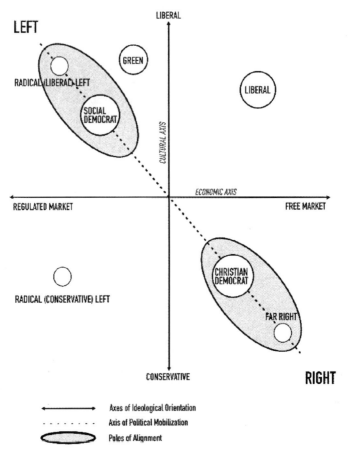

Fig. 23.1 Ideological landscape twentieth century (*Source* Azmanova, 2020)

sentiment, endorsement of free markets domestically, opposition to global trade, and appeals for a social safety net.

The novel dynamics of electoral competition and ideological contestation signal not only a new aggregation of preferences regarding economy and culture (away from the prevalent clustering of free market and cultural traditionalism on the right and the regulated market and cultural liberalism on the left), but a change in the nature of the ideological fault lines of political conflict and cooperation. Thus, in the current context, the economic axis no longer denotes attitudes to state intervention in the economy (supporting either free or regulated markets)—the neoliberal consensus has ended the salience of this issue altogether as center-left parties shifted to the right on economic policy. The free-versus-regulated market policy contention of the late twentieth century has been effectively recast by attitudes toward globalization, forming an axis spanning *market openness* versus *closed domestic markets*. The former dichotomy concerns domestic economic policy, the latter—foreign trade. (Azmanova, 2011, 2020).

The content of the cultural axis of political contestation has also altered. The progressive agenda of civil rights, identity recognition and ecological concerns came to be accepted by most center-right parties in Europe as well as by the moderate wing of the Republican Party in the United States, forming the trans-ideological consensus of 'progressive neoliberalism' (Fraser, 2017). The mainstreaming of identity politics together with the rise of new public concerns about political mismanagement and physical risks (especially following the wave of terrorist attacks) has given rise to a new frame of reference articulating politically salient social concerns along the cultural axis of ideological battles. Attitudes to immigration became a key element in this new framework. Consequently, the liberal-versus-traditionalist cultural divide has been replaced by a cosmopolitanism-versus-nationalism dichotomy, fostered by contrasting judgments on the impact and desirability of open border policies.

This recasting of the ideological landscape has translated into a novel aggregation of public demand and political supply in electoral politics. A new alliance of social forces is being formed around a 'risk' (or 'fear') pole of political mobilization. Here parts of capital and labor align behind policies of economic patriotism, a combination of domestic market liberalization and a closed (protected) economy, as well as cultural sovereigntism, typically voiced in anti-immigrant rhetoric. An opposite pole is forming by parties and their supporters who experience globalization as an advantage in terms of wealth creation and increasingly flexible and versatile lifestyles, as well as those celebrating the capacity of new technologies to mitigate climate change and improve societal wellbeing. The emerging new societal alliances are replacing the old left–right axis of ideological orientation with an opportunity–risk divide, shaped by attitudes to the social effect of globalization (Azmanova, 2004, 2011, 2020) (Fig. 23.2).

The Coronavirus pandemic that beset these societies in the spring of 2020, as well as the efforts to cope with the ensuing economic crisis, has exacerbated both the condition of general social precarity and aggravated existing inequalities. This is likely to consolidate further the nascent radical transformation of the ideological landscape of capitalist liberal democracies, unless a radical policy shift engenders new lines of conflict and cooperation.

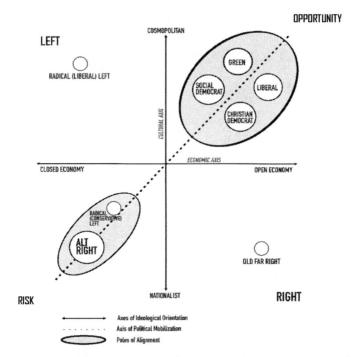

Fig. 23.2 Ideological landscape twenty-first century (*Source* Azmanova, 2020)

Literature

Azmanova, A. (2020). *Capitalism on edge: How fighting precarity can achieve radical change without crisis or Utopia*. Columbia University Press.

Azmanova, A. (2018). The populist catharsis: On the revival of the political. *Philosophy and Social Criticism, 44*(4), 399–411.

Azmanova, A. (2011). After the left-right (dis)continuum: Globalization and the remaking of Europe's ideological geography. *International Political Sociology, 5*(4), 384–407.

Azmanova, A. (2004). The mobilisation of the European left in the early 21st century. *European Journal of Sociology, 45*(2), 273–306.

Blyth, M., and E. Lonergan. (2020). Newcastle upon Tyne: Agenda Publishing.

Fleming, P. (2017). *The death of homo economicus: Work, debt, and the myth of endless accumulation*. Pluto Press.

Fraser, N. (2017, January 28). Against progressive neoliberalism, A new progressive populism. *Dissent*.

Judis, J. (2016). *The populist explosion: How the great recession transformed American and European politics*. Columbia Global Reports.

Kitschelt, H. (2004). *Diversification and reconfiguration of party systems in postindustrial democracies*. Friedrich Ebert Stiftung.

Kitschelt, H. (1997). European party systems: Continuity and change. In M. Rhodes, P. Heywood, & V. Wright (Eds.), *Developments in Western European politics* (pp. 131–150). Macmillan.

Kriesi, H., Grande, E., Lachat, R., Dolezal, M., Bornschier, S., & Frey, T. (2006). Globalization and the transformation of the national political space: Six European countries compared. *European Journal of Political Research, 45*, 921–956.

Laclau, E. (2005). *On populist reason*. Verso.

Laponce, J. (1981). *Left and right—A topography of political perceptions*. University of Toronto Press.

Mair, P. (2007). Left–right orientations. In R. J. Dalton & H.-D. Klingemann (Eds.), *The Oxford handbook of political behaviour* (pp. 206–222). Oxford University Press.

McKnight, D. (2005). *Beyond right and left: New politics and the culture wars*. Allen & Unwin.

Müller, J.-W. (2016). *What is populism?* University of Pennsylvania Press.

Perrineau, P. (2002). Les évolutions de la Ve République: l'affaiblissement de l'antagonisme gauche/droite. *Cahiers Francais, 300*(1), 48–54.

Quart, A. (2018). *Squeezed: Why our families can't afford America*. HarperCollins.

Standing, G. (2011). *The precariat: The new dangerous class*. Bloomsbury Publishing.

Stiglitz, J. E. (2003). *Globalization and its discontents*. New York: Norton.

Weber, M. (1994 [1918]). Parliament and government in Germany under a new political order. In *Max Weber: Political writings*, ed. Peter Lassman & R. Speirs (pp. 130–211). Cambridge University Press.

Part VIII

Populism Discourses

CHAPTER 24

Meaning Matters: The Political Language of Islamic Populism

Inaya Rakhmani and Vedi Hadiz

Introduction

A voluminous literature on the rise of populism has recently developed, largely focused on Latin America, Europe and the USA. Whether discussing the spectacle of American Trumpism (Peck, 2019), support for the Alternative für Deutschland in Germany, or for Brexit in the UK (Norris & Inglehart, 2019), most scholars associate twenty-first century populism with the imperatives and machinations of mass electoral politics. There is general agreement too that populism involves the political mobilization of everyday grievances of 'ordinary people' against 'corrupt elites'—frequently by use of new media technology—linking such grievances to disenchantment with existing institutions of governance (Mudde & Kaltwasser, 2018).

It is useful to situate the emergence of early twenty-first century populisms as a response to a set of shared global challenges, whether within developed or developing democracies and economies. As such we shift the focus to the

---

This article benefitted from some of the ongoing research conducted under Australian Research Council Discovery Project 180100781.

I. Rakhmani
Asia Research Centre, Universitas Indonesia, Kota Depok, Jawa Barat, Indonesia
e-mail: inaya.r@ui.ac.id

V. Hadiz (✉)
Asia Institute, University of Melbourne, Melbourne, VIC, Australia
e-mail: vedi.hadiz@unimelb.edu.au

'Global South' by addressing the structural roots of populism within context-specific cases. We do so because the literature on populism as a whole does not do justice to the diverse, historically shaped phenomenon of populism beyond the advanced capitalist societies and its traditional interest in Latin America.[1]

We suggest that it is also useful to approach early twenty-first-century populisms as a reaction to the adverse effects of neoliberal transformations that have caused matters of identity and difference to take up new meaning and significance. While experienced differently within and between societies, these massive transformations have resulted in rising levels of wealth accompanied by social inequalities, followed by increasing precarity (Kalleberg, 2018; Standing, 2011). In a nutshell, the approach taken here addresses populism—but specifically Islamic populism—as an expression of pervasive anxieties and grievances linked to such circumstances. We take the case of Indonesia and, to better understand a culturally-specific manifestation of populism, compare its dynamics with that of select countries in the Global South—which are less frequently the subject of analysis within the literature on populism. These countries are selected in spite of their distinctive historical experiences because populist mobilizations here have been particularly marked by political languages drawn from religious cultural resources, even when addressing such profane problems as social inequality, marginalization, and abuse of power.

We further argue that the language of religiously-infused populist politics in these cases have been appropriated by dominant or ascendant social coalitions. This is most perceptible during mass mobilizations in the midst of electoral competition, within which mass and social media have been instrumental. We focus on the contradictions between expressions of anxiety and grievances, as well as their appropriation by elites through a political language with which users nevertheless try to make sense of their social world. Our findings are based on long-term research carried out on Indonesia, but also Egypt and Turkey, where Islamic versions of populism have been significant. We draw on comparisons with the Hindutva movement in India as well in order to gain more general insights into the forging of religiously derived languages of populist politics—especially via the media and the processes of electoral politics.[2] Our analysis links political economy and cultural analysis by way of the symbolic dimensions of power and interest examined in what is widely known as the Cultural Political Economy (CPE) project (Jessop, 2004, 2008, 2010). In one of its milestones, Ngai-Ling Sum and Bob Jessop (2013) offer a framework that places culture within political economy, thereby opening avenues to study semiotics not as a means to 'replace, but to deepen, critical political economy' (p. viii). With this in mind, we bring together the concerns of Hadiz and Chryssogelos (2017) and those of Sum and Jessop (2013) in our chapter. Throughout the chapter, we put culture at the center of political economy, thus employing a cultural political economy framework (Sum & Jessop, 2013) to address our empirical findings.

The Forging of Religious Populism

The global emergence of populist politics has been depicted as a crisis of democracy. Paradoxically, democracy and its associated institutions of participation and representation are more widely accepted around the world today than they were a century ago. The crux of the matter lies in the fact that the kind of hypothetical equality promised by the realms of democratic participation and representation have not ensured economic equality. This has not escaped the attention of scholars, some of whom have argued that wealth inequalities translate into unequal ability to influence the political process, which in turn produces distrust of electoral institutions (Lammert & Vormann, 2020).

The premise that there is a link between pervasive economic insecurity and twenty-first century populism is important, though it is surely too complex to postulate in terms of simple linear causality. The ways in which populism displays itself are molded by concrete historical circumstances and by the particular kinds of cultural resources made available to provide meaning to such circumstances. Understanding early twenty-first century populism therefore requires structural analysis of neoliberal capitalism coupled with a historically rich detailing of how cultural references become redefined as they are mobilized in struggles over power and wealth in contemporary societies.

In Islamic populism, the ummah—or community of believers—takes the place of the 'people' in delineating the virtuous masses from the venal elites against whom they are notionally pitted. In its political lexicon, the ummah, which is portrayed as having been socio-economically, culturally, or politically marginalized by nationalist or secular elites, finds equivalence with the deprived 'people' associated with more conventional populisms.

Here, we bring into the analysis the cultural aspects of populism. We do this as they are linked to specific political economies, often overlooked in mainstream, positivist political science. We do so by examining the language of Islamic populism, the way it has been forged by historical circumstances and the cultural resources made available by them. We also address the changing nature of the tools that forge such political language, especially as they involve the mass media, which has been increasingly useful in ensuring the potency of 'popular conviction' (Gramsci, 1971: 377). In short, we treat culture as an immaterial force that is utilized by elites within struggles over power and resources. We posit that such uses of cultural resources are facilitated by anxieties born out of the increasingly blatant reality of socio-economic inequalities and the consequent unequal access to the institutions of governance.

We elaborate our analysis reflectively, based on a qualitative meta-analysis (Flick, 2014)[3] of research carried out between 2013 and 2020. We focus on manifestations of Islamic populism in Indonesia, in comparison with Egypt and Turkey, as well as Hindutva in India, as a way to draw insights from populist projects that redefine shared historical memories through a religious political lexicon. The cultural references they rely on resonate with many because they too were forged by historical conditions that can be traced, most significantly, to a world order dominated by colonial powers in the early twentieth century. We also look at changes in mass media over time to understand how the redefinition of cultural symbols and identities—according to the perceived needs of state or nation-building (or economic development)—have now fed into contemporary populist political language. We furthermore link them to political elites benefiting from a particular production of meaning.

Throughout the 1960s to 1980s, the Egyptian (Abu-Lughod, 2008), Turkish (Öncü, 2005) and Indonesian (Kitley, 2000) states had systematically shaped their respective developmentalist narratives through national state broadcasting (and education) systems. In the 1990s, the global wave of economic liberalization then allowed private media to produce information and entertainment alternatives but only for media capital to be concentrated in a handful of entrepreneurs tied to ruling elites. While the advent and adoption of the internet among intellectuals and activists in early 2000s Egypt (Eaton, 2013), Turkey (Saka, 2020) and Indonesia (Lim, 2003) seemed to promise new forms of autonomous civil society organization, after a while the spaces for digital dissent narrowed due to government censorship (Turkey), containment through controversial laws on social media activism (Egypt and Indonesia) or distortion by a disinformation industry (Kajimoto & Stanley, 2019). These changes show how socio-technological tools have long helped to forge the aforementioned 'popular conviction' (Gramsci, 1971, p. 377), whereby the formation of mainstream discourses, generated through commercial mass— and now social—media closely resembles the process otherwise dubbed the 'manufacturing of consent' (Herman & Chomsky, 1988).

A major point to emphasize is that the mainstreaming of political discourses, including via the media, cannot be understood in separation from struggles over power and material resources. In this regard, comparing the Indian and Indonesian experiences can yield some useful insights. In India, Hindu nationalist organizations played a central role in the fight against Western colonial rule. However (like their Muslim counterparts in Indonesia), their aspirations were not accommodated upon the attainment of independence by new secular ruling elites that had come out of the colonial-era bureaucratic and education systems. The latter were to be organized politically in the Indian case within the Congress Party, led by the Nehru-Gandhi dynasty, which utilized the media as an instrument of its statist-oriented capitalist development project.

In Indonesia, though to a lesser extent, bureaucratic elites were fostered within Soekarno's Indonesian National Party (PNI), even if it was only during the authoritarian New Order that the growing corps of politico-bureaucratic officials were to be harnessed effectively within Soeharto's Functional Party (Golkar; which won a series of heavily rigged elections for three decades). The New Order's stronghold over mass media notably helped subdue Islamic dissent over the perceived marginalization of Islamic social forces. By the 1970s and 1980s, such dissent had become increasingly depicted as contravening the state's modernization project.

Both in India and Indonesia, these state-led media systems were eroded as neoliberal globalization induced privatization. Yet the new and more complex system that emerged, while notionally based on free markets, have never been separated from elite-level contests for political and economic dominance. However, the exponentially growing literature on populism remains inadequate to explain such diverse expressions and modes of transmission, in which the changing mass media industry has played an increasingly central role. Nor does it capture the inherently distinctive content of the populism represented by the Hindu nationalism of India (Gudavarthy, 2019), where Prime Minister Modi has mobilized a mass Twitter following, challenging the monopoly of traditional media (Prince, 2015), or the Islamic populism of Erdogan's Turkey (Elçi & Ezgi, 2019), where media corporations have been largely appropriated by the holders of state power (Corke et al., 2014).

It is no coincidence though that countries like India and Indonesia, widely considered future economic high-flyers, have exhibited the emergence of populisms. Such populisms have, to different degrees, affected the dynamics of competition over power and resources within their respective democratic frameworks. In both countries, much-lauded economic development has been accompanied by starker social inequalities (IMF, 2015), creating fertile environments for populisms. Such economic development, after all, have less redressed inequalities than furthered the political and economic agendas largely associated with contending elite coalitions. The imaginings of internally homogenous religious communities, it should be underlined, have blurred class and other divisions and have been absorbed by elite agendas. Still, the social agents of Hindutva have redefined the terms of national political discourse more profoundly since winning national state power in India in 2014 and incrementally over a period going back to the late 1990s. This is notable compared to the social agents of Indonesian Islamic populism, who have never been close to achieving such a position.

In India, the BJP (Bharatiya Janata Party)-led Hindutva project has been partly directed against bureaucratic and business elites notionally associated with the Nehru-Gandhi dynasty, who are depicted as being Westernized, technocratized and culturally aloof from the travails of the common people. Within this project, 'belonging' to the nation is increasingly being defined according to adherence to Hindu identity and solidarity. Given the history of Partition in 1947 and long enmity with Pakistan, the war that led to the establishment of Bangladesh in 1971, and still ongoing conflict over Kashmir, that identity and solidarity has been strengthened when juxtaposed against India's sizeable Muslim minority. In 2019, the BJP government passed legislation that effectively cast Muslims as second class citizens, displaying that their loyalty to the country was suspect (Slater & Masih, 2019).

Religious cultural references play a big role in defining who gets included and excluded from the Hindutva project and confronting perceived sources of threat. They have featured regularly in mobilizations related to electoral competition. For example, the cow is a sacred religious symbol for Hindus but is sacrificed by Muslims in their own rituals (Brass, 2000). Thus, the BJP has campaigned for the prohibition of cow slaughter, which constitutes an act that brings together diverse Hindus by pitting them against Muslims. The commercial media is an important instrument here in constructing Muslims as a threat to India (Gudavarthy, 2019), as it becomes increasingly reconceived as a Hindu nation. The media monetizes on trending topics on platforms like Twitter, where a debate between devout and meat-eating Hindus resulted in the #BeefBan hashtag, which was subsequently mainstreamed into political debate. There was little discussion though on the effects of beef ban on people working in the beef industry, both Muslims and Hindus (Mangaldas, 2017). Public discussion focused instead on the way Muslims ritualize the death of a cow. Mainstream media thus found equivalence in the failure of secular elites, linked to the formerly dominant Congress Party, to safeguard the nation, and their perceived fixation on liberal, Western jargon of cultural tolerance.

There is a similar discursive pattern in Indonesia, where the relative economic marginality of the majority Muslim population is purportedly maintained by secular nationalist elites (Anderson, 1983).[4] In this narrative, familiar to the activists of a range of Islamic organizations up to the present-day, Muslims pioneered the struggle for national independence but were locked out of power once it was achieved (Federspiel, 2001). Furthermore, the imposition of the state ideology of Pancasila for seven decades, reinforced through mass media and national education (Hefner, 1997; Sen & Hill, 2007), has had the effect of constraining attempts to shape the state in a way that directly benefits the ummah (Formichi, 2012; Hadiz & Teik, 2011).

Democratization after 1998, following the fall of Soeharto's New Order, has not changed these circumstances, despite the alleviation of media censorship and a thriving news sector. This is because the influx of capital into the mass media has benefited private enterprises, which are largely beyond the ambit of Indonesia's historically negligible Islamic bourgeousie, but inextricably linked to political and business interests that go back to the New Order era. The abject failure of Islamic political parties to win national state power despite their own deep involvement in corrupt, money politics-driven inter-oligarchic competition continues (Hadiz, 2017); even as news and information carrying Islamic populist messages proliferate through alternative and fragmented channels within social media.

Such messages, significantly, have been appropriated by nationalist-secular politicians to further their own interests. Among them is failed 2014 and 2019 presidential candidate Prabowo Subianto, a former New Order era general and businessman. The effect was to create for him a Muslim support base, which while failing to take him to the presidency, has nevertheless contributed to the mainstreaming of the lexicon of Islamic populism within Indonesian political contests (Hadiz, 2018a).

It is worth pointing out that we have observed the rejection of some of the cosmopolitan aspirations that used to be the markers of liberal modernity in the countries we scrutinize (see Hadiz, 2016, 2018; Rakhmani, 2016;

Rakhmani & Zakiah, 2020). In fact, political discourses within mass and social media have recently shown more aggressive highlighting of often ethnically and religiously embedded values. This, in turn, has provided the cultural references for illiberal and exclusionary politics (Lim, 2017), while mainstreaming the lexicon of religious forms of populism. When wedded to existing discourses of marginalization, the product is frequently a broader language of politics that go together with the interests of dominant or ascendant social coalitions rather than pose a fundamental threat to them (Hadiz, 2018b).

We propose reflecting on concerns about broader neoliberal transformations that have affected the Global South generally and the Muslim world specifically. Statements of political positions, we suggest, associated with the emergence of Islamic populism, have strengthened tendencies toward defining difference based on markers of identity (Rakhmani, 2019). This is apparent in public orations by clerics and religious organizations, magnified by mass and social media, that often provoke a sense of shared grievances against an ethnic and religious other. Their statements make their way to television news programs and trending topics on social media, benefiting from a media infrastructure dictated by market-driven ratings and algorithms. At the same time the rapid spread of information through mass and social media have recalibrated the strategies of dominant social alliances in their struggles over the institutions of political and economic governance to include the appropriation of these sorts of statements for their own purposes.

It is no coincidence that religious populists, whether in Indonesia, Egypt, Turkey—or India—have relied on the symbolic power of religion to mask actual growing diversity among their adherents, due largely to growing social inequalities tied to neoliberal transformations. In Egypt, the Muslim Brotherhood so successfully positioned itself as the alternative to the Mubarak government during the Arab Spring in 2010–2011 that it came to be the main beneficiary of a short-lived democratization process. This is because it had effectively wielded Islamic-derived ideas of social justice and the like (associated with organization luminaries such as Hasan Al-Bana and Sayid Qutb), in ways that came to dominate political dissent despite the presence of secular opposition groups to the regime. This should be acknowledged even if subsequent events saw the suppression and banning of the Muslim Brotherhood by a resurgent military apparatus bent on safeguarding its own vast economic and political interests (Hadiz, 2016) from the Arab Spring. In Turkey, the AKP had accomplished much the same with a religiously derived political vernacular to distinguish its modernizing project from that of the statist-Kemalist tradition, which had been tainted by the early 2000s through economic mismanagement.

In short, the emphasis on shared religious identity in both Egypt and Turkey has helped to redefine how modern contests over power and resources have taken place in those countries. This is so in Indonesia too though to levels that has yet to match the previous two cases. We flesh out these points in more detail in the next section while explaining the way Islamic populist languages of politics are constructed and activated by the culture industry.

Making, Mediating and Mobilizing

Anderson (2009) has usefully suggested that populism is always culturally specific. In order to be effective, it must draw on available cultural references and make use of symbolism that resonate within specific circumstances (Anderson, 2009, p. 219). Elsewhere, Anderson (1990) had dissected the language of Indonesian politics, associated both with Soekarno's radical nationalist jargon and with early New Order developmentalism. In the first of these, he argued that the Indonesian national language was part of a project to unify a sprawling, diverse, and internally contradictory new nation-state through the use of revolutionary imagery, which promised progress toward modernity. In the second, he analyzed how cultural artifacts, ranging from cartoons to monuments, simultaneously expressed the developmentalist ambitions of the authoritarian New Order (1966–1998) and the new anxieties brought about by social changes unleashed through intensified capitalist development. We understand culture as 'the ensemble of social processes by which meanings are produced, circulated and exchanged' (Thwaites et al., 1994, p. 1). Cultures comprise of 'the often implicit ethical and moral valuesValues, sentiments, commitments, feelings, temporal horizons, attitudes to the environment and judgements that shape everyday life, organizational practices, institutional orders and societal self-understandings' (Sum & Jessop, 2013, p. 8). These are sewn into the very fabric of societies in the 'Global South' Global South increasingly engaged with the broader neoliberalized Neoliberal/neoliberalism capitalist world, albeit in different ways, such as those discussed by Hadiz (2016) and many others (Hutchison, 2007; Jayasuriya, 2018; Robison, 2006; Robison & Goodman, 1996; Rodan, 2018; Rodan et al., 2001).

Rakhmani's work (2016), among others, shows renewed interest among scholars of contemporary Indonesia in how the languages of politics are shaped by, and come to affect, broader dynamics linked to the social contradictions of capitalist development. She observes how morally justifiable consumption habits assist the Muslim middle class to navigate the uncertainties of the neoliberal social world, while simultaneously producing new forms of social segregation through Islamic gated communities and provision of privatized social services directed at the ummah. She underlines how these are tied to the ways in which Islamic symbols are mediated and reproduced by commercial media predominantly owned by conglomerates with ties to established centers of political power for reasons having to do with profitability rather than moral affinity.

Indonesia's Islamic populism has not been as successful as Turkey's, where the AKP (Justice and Development Party), led by Recep Tayyip Erdogan, has dominated politics for two decades. Nor has it been as successful as Islamic populism in Egypt, where its main social agent, the Muslim Brotherhood, briefly claimed control over the state after dominating civil-society opposition to the Mubarak regime. Hadiz (2016) has argued that Indonesian Islamic populism has been much less underpinned by coherent cross-class alliances, and that it continues to be hampered by the absence of a culturally Islamic big bourgeoisie. In fact, many of the gated Muslim communities could be seen as a defensive response—on the part of more affluent members of the ummah—to the dominance of giant ethnic Chinese-owned conglomerates in Indonesia.

Soeharto's New Order had already portrayed the 'Chinese' in Indonesia as monolithically wealthy. Media reporting at the time regularly fortified the commonly held idea that ethnic Chinese economic avarice was responsible for the social inequalities that had intensified with economic growth; ignoring the fact that Soeharto himself was deeply implicated in this political economic patronage system (Schwarz, 1999). The specific narrative propagated by Islamic activists came to find some convergences with this broader narrative, though the emphasis shifted to how foreign capital and businesses associated with state officials, especially during the New Order—largely operated with those that were ethnic-Chinese owned—conspired to ensure the economic subordination of Muslims (Chua, 2008).

A major example of the pitting of the ummah against the ethnic Chinese in Indonesia took place in reporting about the largest religiously-driven mass demonstrations in the country, directed against then Jakarta governor Basuki 'Ahok' Tjahaja Purnama—a Christian of Chinese descent. The demonstrations occurred in December 2016 during campaigning for the gubernatorial election in the following year. The movement it spawned, known as the Action to Defend Islam and mobilized through the hashtag #AksiBelaIslam, aimed to imprison Ahok for blasphemy after an edited video of his speech in a closed official meeting went viral. It was instrumental too in the rise of incumbent Governor Anies Baswedan, who has strong Muslim credentials, as well as current Vice President Ma'ruf Amin, a key figure in the issuing of the Indonesian Ulema Council's (MUI) blasphemy fatwa (edict issued by religious authority) against Ahok. The movement was successful in that Ahok failed to win reelection in 2017—losing to Anies—and ended up serving a jail term for committing blasphemy.

It is notable though that Anies' main sponsor was the Gerindra (Great Indonesia Party; the political vehicle of Prabowo Subianto) and that Ma'ruf's rise to the vice presidency was backed by the PDIP (Indonesian Democratic Party for Struggle), the secular-nationalist vehicle that sponsors President Jokowi. Both their cases show how the mainstreaming of the language of Islamic populism, notionally in the interest of the 'downtrodden' ummah, has actually benefitted established political alliances.

A large part of the problem is the flimsy nature of the class alliances underpinning Indonesian Islamic populism. It has been more problematic in Indonesia to integrate the urban poor into a coherent Islamic populist project, for example. In Turkey, an identifiably Islamic and culturally conservative newer bourgeoisie emerging from the Anatolian cities and towns have been a key element in the cross-class alliance that has kept the AKP in power, nurturing the ambition of surpassing the more established Istanbul-based big bourgeoisie—traditionally linked to the secular Kemalist vehicle, the CHP (Republican People's Party). In the absence of an Islamic bourgeoisie comparable to Turkey's, material resources have not been available to the social agents of Indonesian Islamic populism to drive and sustain the sort of mass charitable, health and welfare activities that can bring the poor together with the rich under the umbrella of a common faith. Notably, the Muslim Brotherhood in Egypt was also supported by a growing business component tolerated by the Mubarak government from the 1990s, and which also made possible large scale charitable and health services that primarily targeted the poor (Clark, 2004). Thus, in Indonesia, Islamic populism has been largely espoused by pious sections of the educated middle class who find ways of inviting the masses of urban poor into their project especially when there has been backing from opportunistic oligarchic elites in times of intense electoral competition (Hadiz, 2018a, b).

While there are cultural specificities in the developments described above, parallels can be found outside the Muslim world. The case of India and its Hindutva project is anchored in the idea that authentic Indians are endangered by nefarious internal and external Muslim forces seeking to derail the country's economic development. But the BJP's populism, like the AKP's in Turkey, is wedded to the further neoliberalization of the Indian economy. This in itself is not unique. As we have pointed out, populism has not been about fundamentally redressing issues of social and economic inequalities as such. It often has more to do with contests over the state's economic and political levers and the mobilization of cultural expressions of discontent for that purpose. In this case, the Hindutva project is partly backed by a domestic bourgeoisie (Jaffrelot et al., 2019) that had been curtailed by the lumbering state-dominated economy arising from Congress' traditional commitment to economic statism, inherited from the Nehru era, as well as by affluent sections of an influential diasporic community (Teltumbde, 2006).

The forging and mobilization of the associated languages of politics have real, material consequences. The Hindu supremacist narrative, for instance, has been followed by violent, anti-Muslim attacks and bombings for decades. Islamic populism has affected the workings of Indonesia's democracy in ways that undermine inclusivity. The language of populism, in fact, can be simultaneously personal and political; leaving groups with Muslim attributes in India and Chinese ones in Indonesia vulnerable to harassment and violence. In the latter country, Shia Muslims, who are a distinct minority, along with Ahmaddiyas, have also been subject to harassment and violence by vigilante groups claiming to safeguard the interests of an implausibly monolithic ummah (Makin, 2017).

Mass and social media, notionally part of the culture industry, have played an important role in shaping imaginings of homogenous political communities based on common adherence to religious faith. Television dramas, for example, have added the allure of Turkey's popular stars to the attractiveness of its modernising economy, made possible by the purported moral rectitude of the AKP's leaders (Al-Ghazzi & Kraidy, 2013). While Turkish television producers do not always have good relationships with the ruling party, the AKP has used the fruits of their labour to promote Turkish authority in the Middle East by appealing to the glories of the Ottoman past. Tapping on to 'national pride', such products of the culture industry (see Öncü, 2005) have helped shape a broad-based solidarity that brings together socio-economically diverse sections of society under the mediated and mobilised banner of religion. This was seen in 2016, when huge crowds gathered in Istanbul to commemorate 563 years since the Ottoman siege of the city in the so-called Conquest Rallies (DW, 2016). This opportunity was used by the AKP to stir up national pride by employing neo-Ottoman narratives (Karakaya, 2018) that exploit nostalgia for a long-gone empire, which, despite its historically multicultural nature, remains a reference point for the identification of Turkishness with Islam.[5]

Similarly cutting across class barriers to gain mass support, the Bollywood and Egyptian culture industry has done much to reproduce collective animosity toward minorities. In India (Kumar HM, 2013), the blockbuster, Hum Aapke Hain Kaun (Who Am I To You), for example, depicts the Muslim middle class by way of their religious rituals; providing an emphasis on difference rather than including them as members of modern Indian society. In Egypt, once considered the Hollywood of the East, the Islamic populist project gained momentum together with the growing production and consumption of film and television in the late twentieth century. In fact, popular culture was placed at the center of the piety movement, thus helping to propagate moral positions that demarcate affiliations based on identity (Tartoussieh, 2007). While the slogan 'Muslim, Christian, we are all Egyptian' was chanted in the protests against Mubarak in 2011, new attacks against minority groups such as the Copts—perceived to be disproportionately wealthy because of protection from the Mubarak regime—soon ensued (Iskaned, 2012).

Not surprisingly, there are parallels in Indonesia too. Here, private television stations produce moralistic television shows that are markedly devoid of meaningful interaction between different religious and ethnic groups. At the same time, they construct a benevolent and morally upright image of affluent Muslims by depicting them as caring toward their less affluent co-religionists (Rakhmani, 2016). Such formulaic representations of the ummah have also made way to the streaming of Azab (Punishment), widely popularized by social media. "Non-Muslims" are portrayed as infidels, and Muslims straying from the righteous path, usually toward hedonism and Western values, are punished for their sins. These mass and social mediations of inclusion–exclusion helps shape a community of believers that defines itself against 'others' while simultaneously disregarding its own internal heterogeneity and contradictions. This is the political language that constitute the cultural resource pool of Islamic populism, and one that is manufactured by the cultural industry and mobilized by contending political elites. They are culturally specific, historically-rooted, but—when properly compared—can provide us deeper and richer understanding about the characteristics of Islamic populism in the Muslim world and beyond.

Conclusion

We have posited that the political language of Islamic populism, while having specific historical and cultural resonance, has had its significance magnified by the availability of media by which individuals come to make sense of their position in their societies and in the world. The culture industry have provided no less than new ways of articulating difference and identity, feeding into a political language that has been reshaped in mobilizations of the ummah to the benefit of contending political elites.

We have suggested that Islamic populism involves the homogenizing of an actually diverse ummah (in terms of members' social and economic circumstances) against notionally uniform non-believer elites. The idea of a community of believers thus blurs class and other distinctions, distracting the project away from the realization of promised economic equality. As a result, the political language of Islamic populism has been much more useful in configuring elite coalitions in their competition over power. Such was the case in mobilizations of the ummah against a perceived infidel leader in Indonesia's capital city Jakarta, the reliving neo-Ottoman narratives in Istanbul Conquest Rallies, or in the brief ascension to power of the Egyptian Muslim Brotherhood in the aftermath of the Arab Spring.

In this chapter, we have intimately linked culture to political economy to explain Islamic populist struggles that are aimed to redefine states and societies—within an increasingly neoliberalized world—while acknowledging that their outcomes have differed across societies. Thus, the AKP has ruled in Turkey since 2002, the Muslim Brotherhood only briefly held state power in Egypt under the presidency of Morsi, while Indonesian Islamic populism has remained relatively more marginal in contests over power.

We also dealt with the complexities of material realities and their social representation (Jones, 2008) by focussing on their links to the practices of political struggle. We brought in examples from non-Muslim majority India to show how such links are not exclusively found in the Muslim world. Taken together, our examples point to how populist politics can be forged by fortifying ambiguous but shared identities based on doxa and dogma. We have also shown that the media, in its various forms, has helped to reshape the shared identities that provide a means through which people navigate through the uncertainties of the neoliberal order. The irony is that these same identities have tended to be appropriated and refitted to reinforce rather than dismantle existing hierarchies of political and economic power.

Notes

1. With that in mind, this chapter extends the proposition made by Hadiz and Chryssogelos (2017) on the need to broaden and deepen research on populism by employing cross-regional perspectives and 'analytical frameworks that can address global and historically diverse manifestations of populism' (p. 400).
2. Semi-structured interviews were carried out by authors in these countries with purposively selected actors including politicians, campaign industry operators, experts, and grassroots activists. The Indian analysis is based on secondary material.
3. Qualitative meta-analysis, or at times mentioned as meta-synthesis, is a secondary analysis of primary data addressing a main research question. The aim of this method is to provide a comprehensive picture to research findings accross distinctively different studies, as well as evaluate the methodological effects in the primary study. The ultimate goal is to discover 'the essential elements and translating the results into an end product that transforms the original results into a new conceptualization' (Schreiber et al., 1997, p. 314).
4. Or those inclined toward pre-Islamic belief systems that used to predominate amongst the traditional *pamong praja* or the bureaucratic strata identified initially with the history of pre-colonial Javanese kingdoms.
5. In fact, Turkish melodrama (*dizi*) too is being broadcast in Indonesia and Egypt; one of the most profound is *Muhteşem Yüzyıl* (Magnificent Century), a tell-tale of King Suleiman, leader of the sixteenth century Ottoman empire (Rakhmani & Zakiah, 2020).

Literature

Abu-Lughod, L. (2008). *Dramas of nationhood: The politics of television in Egypt.* University of Chicago Press.

Al-Ghazzi, O., & Kraidy, M. M. (2013). Neo-Ottoman Cool 2: Turkish nation branding and Arabic-language transnational broadcasting. *International Journal of Communication, 7*, 2341–2360.

Anderson, B. (2009). Afterword. In K. Mizuno & P. Phongpaichit (Eds.), *Populism in Asia* (pp. 217–220). NUS Press.

Anderson, B. R. (1983). Old state, new society: Indonesia's new order in comparative historical perspective. *Journal of Asian Studies, 42*(3), 477–496.

Anderson, B. R. (1990). *Language and power: Exploring political cultures in Indonesia.* Cornell University Press.

Brass, P. R. (2000). Elite groups, symbol manipulation and ethnic identity among the Muslims of South Asia. In J. H. Smith (Ed.), *Nationalism: Critical concepts in political science* (pp. 879–909). Routledge.

Chua, C. (2008). *Chinese big business in Indonesia: The state of capital.* Routledge.

Clark, J. A. (2004). *Islam, charity, and activism: Middle-class networks and social welfare in Egypt, Jordan, and Yemen.* Indiana University Press.

Corke, S., Finkel, A., Kramer, A. J., Robbins, C. A., & Schenkkan, N. (2014). *Democracy in crisis: Corruption, media, and power in Turkey*. Freedom House.
DW. (2011, January 28). *Protests in Egypt continue despite government shut down of Internet*. Retrieved July 2020, from Deutsche Welle: https://www.dw.com/en/protests-in-egypt-continue-despite-government-shut-down-of-internet/a-14801752.
DW. (2015, March 20). *Indian media milks the beef ban*. Retrieved July 2020, from Deutsche Welle: https://www.dw.com/en/indian-media-milks-the-beef-ban/a-18331188.
DW. (2016, May 29). *Erdogan holds mass celebration on Ottoman conquest anniversary*. Retrieved from Deutsche Welle: https://www.dw.com/en/erdogan-holds-mass-celebration-on-ottoman-conquest-anniversary/a-19292255.
Eaton, T. (2013). Internet activism and the Egyptian uprisings: Transforming online dissent into the offline world. *Westminster Papers in Communication and Culture, 9*(2), 3–24.
Elçi, S. E., & Ezgi, A. (2019). Populism in Turkey. In D. Stockemer (Ed.), *Populism around the world: A comparative perspective* (pp. 89–108). Springer.
Federspiel, H. M. (2001). *Islam and ideologi in the emerging Indonesian state: The Persatuan Islam (PERSIS), 1923 to 1957*. Brill.
Flick, U. (2014). *The SAGE handbook of qualitative data analysis*. Sage.
Formichi, C. (2012). *Islam and the making of the nation: Kartosuwiryo and political Islam in twentieth-century Indonesia*. KITLV Press.
Gramsci, A. (1971). *Selections from the Prison notebooks of Antonio Gramsci*. International Publishers.
Gudavarthy, A. (2019). *India after Modi: Populism and the right*. Bloomsbury.
Hadiz, V. R. (2016). *Islamic populism in Indonesia and the Middle East*. Cambridge University Press.
Hadiz, V. R. (2017). Indonesia's year of democratic setbacks: Towards a new phase of deepening illiberalism? *Bulletin of Indonesian Economic Studies, 53*(3), 261–278.
Hadiz, V. (2018a). The 'floating' ummah in the fall of 'Ahok' in Indonesia. In *TRaNS: Trans-Regional and -National Studies of Southeast Asia*, 1–20. https://doi.org/10.1017/trn.2018.16.
Hadiz, V. R. (2018b). Imagine all the people? Mobilising Islamic populism for right-wing politics in Indonesia. *Journal of Contemporary Asia, 48*(4), 1–18.
Hadiz, V. R., & Chryssogelos, A. (2017). Populism in world politics: A comparative cross-regional perspective. *International Political Science Review, 38*(4), 399–411.
Hadiz, V. R., & Teik, K. B. (2011). Approaching Islam and politics from political economy: A comparative study of Indonesia and Malaysia. *The Pacific Review, 24*(4), 463–485.
Hadiz, V., & Rakhmani, I. (2017, December 1). *Marketing morality in Indonesia's democracy*. Retrieved July 2019, from Asian Currents: http://asaa.asn.au/marketing-morality-indonesias-democracy/.
Hefner, R. W. (1997). Print Islam: Mass media and ideological rivalries among Indonesian Muslims. *Indonesia, 64*, 77–103.
Hefner, R. W. (2012). Islamic radicalism in democratizing Indonesia. In S. Akbarzadeh (Ed.), *Routhledge handbook of political Islam* (pp. 105–118). Routledge.
Herman, E. S., & Chomsky, N. (1988). *Manufacturing consent: The political economy of the mass media*. Pantheon Books.
Hutchison, J. (2007). The 'disallowed' political participation of Manila's urban poor. *Democratization, 14*(5), 853–872.

IMF. (2015). *Causes and consequences of income inequality: A global perspective*. International Monetary Fund.

Iskaned, E. (2012). *Sectarian conflict in Egypt: Coptic media, identity and representation*. Routledge.

Jaffrelot, C., Kohli, A., & Murali, K. (2019). *Business and politics in India*. Oxford University Press.

Jayasuriya, K. (2018). Authoritarian statism and the new right in Asia's conservative democracies. *Journal of Contemporary Asia, 48*(3), 2–21.

Jessop, B. (2004). Critical semiotic analysis and cultural political economy. *Critical Discourse Studies, 1*(2), 159–174.

Jessop, B. (2008). A cultural political economy of competitiveness and its implications for higher education. In B. Jessop, N. Fairclough, & R. Wodak (eds), *Education and the knowledge-based economy in Europe* (pp. 13–39). Sense Publishers.

Jessop, B. (2010). Cultural political economy and critical policy studies. *Critical Policy Studies, 3*(3–4), 336–356.

Jones, M. (2008). Recovering a sense of political economy. *Political Geography, 27*(4), 377–399.

Kajimoto, M., & Stanley, S. (2019). *Information disorder in Asia and the Pacific: Overview of misinformation ecosystem in Australia, India, Indonesia, Japan, the Philippines, Singapore, South Korea, Taiwan, and Vietnam*. University of Hong Kong. Journalism & Media Studies Centre.

Kalleberg, A. L. (2018). *Precarious lives: Job insecurity and well-being in rich democracies*. Polity Press.

Karakaya, Y. (2018). The conquest of hearts: The central role of Ottoman nostalgia within contemporary Turkish populism. *American Journal of Cultural Sociology*. https://doi.org/10.1057/s41290-018-0065-y

Kitley, P. (2000). *Television, Nation, and Culture in Indonesia*. Athens: Ohio University Press.

Kumar HM, S. (2013). Constructing the nation's enemy: Hindutva, popular culture and the Muslim 'other' in Bollywood cinema. *Third World Quarterly, 34*(3), 458–469.

Laclau, E. (2005). *On populist reason*. Verso.

Lammert, C., & Vormann, B. (2020). When inequalities matter most: The crisis of democracy as a crisis of trust. In M. T. Oswals (Ed.), *Mobilization, representation, and responsiveness in the American democracy* (pp. 139–156). Palgrave Macmillan.

Lim, M. (2003). From war–net to net–war: The internet and resistance identities in Indonesia. *International Information & Library Review, 35*(2–4), 233–248.

Lim, M. (2017). Freedom to hate: Social media, algorithmic enclaves, and the rise of tribal nationalism in Indonesia. *Critical Asian Studies, 49*(3), 411–427.

Makin, A. (2017). Homogenizing Indonesian Islam: Persecution of the Shia Group in Yogyakarta. *Studia Islamika, 24*(1), 1–32.

Mangaldas, L. (2017, June 5). *India's got beef with beef: What you need to know about the country's controversial 'beef ban'*. Retrieved August 2020, from Forbes: https://www.forbes.com/sites/leezamangaldas/2017/06/05/indias-got-beef-with-beef-what-you-need-to-know-about-the-countrys-controversial-beef-ban/#6ec8a91553c2.

Min, S. S. (2006). 'Eventing' the May 1998 affair: Problematic representations of violence in contemporary Indonesia. In C. A. Coppel (Ed.), *Violent conflicts in Indonesia: Analysis, representation, resolution* (pp. 39–57). Routledge.

Mudde, C., & Kaltwasser, C. R. (2018). Studying populism in comparative perspective: Reflections on the contemporary and future research agenda. *Comparative Political Studies, 51*(13), 1667–1693.

Norris, P., & Inglehart, R. (2019). *Cultural backlash: Trump, Brexit, and authoritarian populism*. Cambridge University Press.

Öncü, A. (2005). Becoming "secular Muslims": Yaşar Nuri Öztiirk as a super-subject on Turkish Television. *Religion, Media, and the Public Sphere, 227*.

Peck, R. (2019). *Fox populism: Branding conservatism as working class* (Vol. 36). Cambridge University Press.

Prince, L. (2015). *Modi effect: Inside Narendra Modi's campaign to transform India*. Hodder & Stoughton.

Rakhmani, I. (2016). *Mainstreaming Islam in Indonesia: Television, identity, and the middle class*. Palgrave Macmillan.

Rakhmani, I. (2019). The personal is political: Gendered morality in Indonesia's halal consumerism. *TRaNS: Trans-Regional and -National Studies of Southeast Asia*, 1–22. https://doi.org/10.1017/trn.2019.2.

Rakhmani, I., & Zakiah, A. (2020). Consuming halal Turkish television in Indonesia: A closer look at the social responses towards Muhtesem Yuzyul. In Y. Kaptan, E. Algan, & B. Aydin (Eds.), *Television in Turkey local production, transnational expansion and political aspirations* (pp. 245–265). Palgrave Macmillan.

Robison, R. (2006). *The neo-liberal revolution: Forging the market state*. Palgrave Macmillan.

Robison, R., & Goodman, D. S. (1996). *The new rich in Asia: Mobile phones, McDonalds and middle-class revolution*. Routledge.

Rodan, G. (2018). *Participation without democracy: Containing conflict in Southeast Asia*. Cornel University Press.

Rodan, G., Hewison, K., & Robison, R. (2001). *The political economy of South-East Asia: Conflict, crises and change*. Oxford University Press.

Saka, E. (2020). *Social media and politics in Turkey: A journey through citizen journalism, political trolling, and fake news*. Rowman & Littlefield.

Schreiber, R., Crooks, D., & Stern, P. N. (1997). Qualitative meta-analysis. In J. M. Morse (Ed.), *Completing a qualitative project: Details and dialogue* (pp. 311–326). Sage.

Schwarz, A. (1999). *A nation in waiting: Indonesia's search for stability*. Allen & Unwin.

Sen, K., & Hill, D. T. (2007). *Media, culture and politics in Indonesia*. Equinox Publishing.

Slater, J., & Masih, N. (2019, December 11). *India passes controversial citizenship law excluding Muslim migrants*. Retrieved June 2020, from The Washington Post: https://www.washingtonpost.com/world/asia_pacific/india-poised-to-pass-controversial-citizenship-law-excluding-muslim-migrants/2019/12/11/ebda6a7e-1b71-11ea-977a-15a6710ed6da_story.html.

Standing, G. (2011). *The precariat: The new dangerous class*. Bloomsbury Academic.

Sum, N.-L., & Jessop, B. (2013). *Towards a culture political economy: Putting culture in its place in political economy*. Edward Elgar.

Tartoussieh, K. (2007). Pious stardom: Cinema and the Islamic revival in Egypt. *The Arab Studies Journal, 15*(1), 30–43.

Teltumbde, A. (2006). Hindu fundamentalist politics in India: The alliance with the American Empire in South Asia. In V. R. Hadiz (Ed.), *Empire and neoliberalism in Asia* (pp. 247–261). Routledge.

The World Bank. (2019). *Aspiring Indonesia: Expanding the middle class*. The World Bank.

Thwaites, T., Davis, L., & Mules, W. (1994). *Tools for Cutural Studies*. Palgrave Macmillan.

CHAPTER 25

Populism, Anti-populism and Post-truth

Antonis Galanopoulos and Yannis Stavrakakis

INTRODUCTION

'Post-truth' has been at the forefront of global public debate(s)—and its *Wikipedia* entry testifies to that—especially within the context of the Trump election in the US and the BREXIT referendum in the UK. 'Post-truth' also figured as the Word of the Year 2016 for the *Oxford Dictionary*. According to Sean Illing's view, which is given a prominent place by *Wikipedia* (2020), post-truth indicates the lack of 'shared objective standards for truth'; or according to the aforementioned *Dictionary*, it involves: 'Relating to or denoting circumstances in which objective facts are less influential in shaping public opinion than appeals to emotion and personal belief' (Oxford University Press, 2017). This is how post-truth is commonly defined—which immediately puts forward the first difficulties and questions emerging at the intersection of knowledge and politics.

Aristotle already knew that social and political affairs—the domain of *Rhetoric*—cannot be resolved by recourse to a type of reasoning that centres merely on scientific objectivity and certainty—they require one to take into account the dynamics of debate, controversy, argument and persuasion. No simplistic false–truth dichotomy can provide a tenable solution here:

> Aristotle is loath to abandon any respectable opinion and deny it outright as containing not a glimmer of truth. He prefers instead to resolve the conflicts

A. Galanopoulos (✉) · Y. Stavrakakis
School of Political Sciences, Aristotle University of Thessaloniki, Thessaloniki, Greece

among respectable opinions by giving a judiciously qualified formulation of the issue, so that at least in some sense and to some degree each side will turn out to have been correct. (Denyer, as cited in Haskins, 2004, p. 5)

Of course, Aristotle is no cultural relativist. Yet, even in a paradoxical way not devoid of tensions, he does understand that one has 'to come to terms with rhetoric as a culturally and contextually specific social institution' (Haskins, 2004, pp. 6, 13) different from logic and dialectics. Why is this necessary, in fact independently of one's epistemological standpoint? Simply because, 'in dealing with certain persons, even if we possessed the most accurate scientific knowledge, we should not find it easy to persuade them by the employment of such knowledge'. For scientific discourse is concerned with instruction, but in the case of such persons' instruction is impossible; our proofs and arguments must rest on generally accepted principles' (*Rhetoric* 1355a12 quoted by Haskins, 2004, pp. 13–14).

Such an epistemological pluralism of sorts is particularly relevant as far as the political sphere is concerned and extends onto a type of pluralism, which is political *stricto* sensu. Since antiquity, we have lived in unequal societies; and yet, all attempts to legitimize oligarchic rule invariably result in the generation of a democratic supplement, precisely to the extent that political stability and legitimization also required the organization of consent, that is to say hegemony. As Jacques Rancière cogently observes, 'there are people who govern because they are the eldest, the highest-born, the richest, or *the most learned*'. And yet this aristocratic 'power of the best' cannot be legitimized 'except via the power of equals': 'There is no service that is carried out, *no knowledge that is imparted*, no authority that is established without the master having, however little, to speak "equal to equal" with the one he commands or instructs'. In a nutshell, '[i]t is this intrication of equality in inequality that the democratic scandal makes manifest in order to make it the basis of public power' (Rancière, 2007, pp. 47–48, emphasis added).

Ignoring this pragmatic line of thought going from Aristotle to Rancière, focusing instead on some sort of *politicized (objectivist) epistemology*, the contemporary debate on 'post-truth' and fake news is often shaped on the basis of a hierarchical division between the knowledgeable and the ignorant, the worthy and the unworthy, those who have a supposedly privileged access to truth and those who are denied such a privilege a priori. Arguably, the BREXIT referendum and the Trump victory have reactivated 'elite anxiety about the consequences of political ignorance', something far from new to the extent that such fears of democracy degenerating into 'rule by the poor, who will use their power to steal from the rich' or into 'rule by the ignorant, who will use their power to do the dumbest things' have been circulating since Plato, the great enemy of democracy (Runciman, 2016). And yet, how certain is it that the emerging educational divide is merely a divide between knowledge and ignorance? What if it indicates 'a clash between one worldview and another'? (Runciman, 2016).

Likewise, this is how Bruno Latour has reflexively summarized the lessons from the 2016 American presidential election, where the presumption of a superior technocratic knowledge seems to have disallowed an effective registering of growing political division and polarization:

> Indeed, our incapacity to foresee has been the main lesson of this cataclysm: how could we have been so wrong? All the polls, all the newspapers, all the commentators, the entire intelligentsia. It is as if we had completely lacked any means of encountering those whom we struggled even to name: the 'uneducated white men', the ones that 'globalization left behind'; some even tried calling them 'deplorables'. There's no question that those people are out there, but we have utterly failed to hear their voices, let alone represent them. (Latour, 2016)

Given the disastrous side-effects of such arrogance, it is surprising that, since then, we seem to encounter more and more arguments that connect 'post-truth' and/or 'fake news' with populism and present both phenomena as mutually reinforcing pathologies of a perceived political normality backed with a reified epistemic superiority. Hugo Rifkind, for instance, columnist and lead writer of *The Times,* has, along these lines, equated fake news with populism and presented both phenomena as a two-headed beast (Rifkind, 2017). Other analysts argue that there is even a causal relation between the two phenomena. For instance, Silvio Waisbord (2018) claims that 'the upsurge of populist politics is symptomatic of the consolidation of post-truth communication as a distinctive feature of contemporary politics' (Waisbord, 2018, p. 2), but as he believes simultaneously that 'it would be wrong to suggest that populism is exclusively or naturally the outcome of post-truth communication' (Waisbord, 2018, p. 14), he eventually terms their relation as one of elective affinity.

In the contemporary political sphere, the establishment, faced with the emergence of a repressed Other, often expressed through obscene and repulsive political forms, seems to be radicalizing its discourse. Mainstream politicians and prominent members of the media and the academic establishment seem to claim a—neutral, allegedly non-political—*epistemic superiority* based on the possession of a (single) truth and on incarnating a *supreme rationality*. This claim implies the condemnation of the irrationalism and the reliance on 'post-truth' by the opponents (populism) often irrespective of their concrete ideological profile (inclusionary vs. exclusionary).

In short, mainstream political forces in the West seem to claim power by right of their exclusive access to truth. In a provocative essay in the *Los Angeles Review of Books*, Emmett Rensin discussed how knowledge asymmetries have become not only the root of political conflicts but the basis of policy itself, arguing that the most important development in US politics of recent years is that American liberalism ceased to perceive politics as an ideological conflict but as a struggle against 'idiots unwilling to recognize liberalism's monopoly on empirical reason' (Rensin, 2017). In this schema, the problem with the opponents of liberalism is supposed to be that they are *objectively* wrong.

In this way mainstream political claims camouflage themselves as epistemic authority and demand a total extra-political acceptance.

This does not mean, yet, that it is impossible to speak about populism in epistemological terms. In fact, Saurette and Gunster (as cited in Ylä-Anttila, 2018, p. 358) coined the term 'epistemological populism', naming by this term a political epistemology that is based on the knowledge of 'the common people', which they possess by virtue of their proximity to everyday life. The true question is whether one can speak about *epistemological populism* in a non-arrogant and non-ignorant way, avoiding banal stereotypes and taking into account the political core of epistemological claims, asymmetries and struggles, especially when they enter or shape the public domain. For example, in order to explore the contesting epistemic authorities at stake, Tuomas Ylä-Anttila (2018, p. 359) has put forward the concept of *counter knowledge*, defining it as the knowledge that challenges establishment knowledge, replacing orthodox knowledge authorities with new ones. Hence, populist forces do not simply oppose knowledge, reason and so on, but they may also question the very foundations of established knowledge or elite knowledge, which impose the supposedly one and only rational policy choice. Recognizing that populist forces can establish their own relation with the production of knowledge, instead of treating them merely as irrational political agents, is a big step towards a better understanding of populism and its relation to post-truth and towards a more rigorous and self-reflexive *politicized epistemology*.

Taking into account the aforementioned connection between populism and post-truth politics—both phenomena understood in pejorative terms—that was established in the Western political and media sphere after the double electoral shock of 2016, we will focus, in this chapter, on how post-truth politics were conceptualized in Greece and how they were incorporated into the dominant populism/anti-populism cleavage that increasingly marks Greek politics. In the final section of the paper, we will move again from the specific to the general and more abstract level, namely to the status of truth itself in politics.

In our argument, we will tackle the following inter-related questions:

- What is the relationship between the debates on 'post-truth', on the one hand, and that on 'populism', on the other?
- How can we, in an effective and rigorous way, politically account for the emerging polarized terrain (populism vs. anti-populism) from the point of view of the *truth wars* it entails?

Post-truth and Anti-populism in Greece

In the analysis of our case, we follow the formal approach to populism developed by Ernesto Laclau (2005) and the general theoretical and methodological background of the so-called 'Essex School' (Howarth et al., 2000; Laclau & Mouffe, 2001). It needs to be stressed that in this chapter, we do not focus on populism per se, but instead we mainly examine mainstream, anti-populist discourse. Our purpose is to highlight the framing of populism by mainstream politicians and other figures, such as pundits and academics. This approach is valuable for populism research, not only because the phenomenon of anti-populism is under-researched, but most importantly because we believe that the kernel of both phenomena is revealed when they are studied together. Besides, the label 'populism' is rarely used as a self-descriptor; most generally it is attributed as a negative designation by a dominant, anti-populist discourse (Demata et al., 2020, p. 11). Therefore, a crucial challenge for contemporary populism research is the incorporation of the study of anti-populism into the canon of populism research (De Cleen et al., 2018; Stavrakakis, 2018). Consequently, in this section of our chapter we study mainstream discourses about populism and we explore how mainstream actors in Greece rushed to include in their anti-populist arsenal the polemical notion of 'post-truth' and/or 'fake news'.[1]

The way in which the Greek financial crisis was managed (post-2010) encouraged division and polarization, since the social dislocations triggered by the implementation of draconian austerity measures have caused a radical restructuring of social identities and the whole party landscape. In tandem, the dominant anti-populist discourse proceeded quickly to employ a polemical notion of 'post-truth'. Indeed, the correlation of populism with post-truth has been systematically promoted in Greece as part of a stereotypical anti-populist and normative discourse that accompanied the implementation of austerity policies in the country. As a result, Greece seems to constitute a fertile ground for illuminating the problems of both populism and post-truth.

In order to provide an adequate framing and legitimization to the strategy of austerity applied in Greece since 2010, the crisis was discursively constructed not only as an economic one but also as indicative of a *moral* and a *cultural* pathology. Within this framework, the implementation of the fiscal programme imposed became increasingly associated with discourses around 'normality'. Greece was portrayed as an exception to the norm, as the dysfunctional party deviating from a given European standard of normality. Therefore, the country needed guidance, discipline and even punishment in order to put its house in order and to be rehabilitated into the family of 'normal' European states. Austerity policies and 'creative destruction' through the troika-imposed structural reforms were simply presented as the necessary steps in this necessary process of transforming Greece into a 'normal' European country (Stavrakakis & Galanopoulos, 2019).

In order to acquire political effectiveness, this discourse about normality has relied on the production and demonization of its Other. Populism emerged as the synecdoche of everything pathological in Greek politics: irresponsibility, demagogy, corruption, destruction, irrationalism. Not only was it to blame for the crisis itself, but it was also what obstructed the implementation of the required rational solutions, namely austerity. Indicatively, regarding the risks of populism, Elias Papaioannou, Professor of Economics at the London Business School, wrote in the daily *Kathimerini* that 'the deepest reason for the failure of the memoranda policies was the diffuse populism that dominated the country' (Papaioannou, 2016), while European Commission Vice-President Valdis Dombrovskis argued that Greece has been forced to suffer tougher austerity than it would have been necessary because of the populist stance of the Greek government in 2015 (Dombrovskis, 2016).

A necessary step, therefore, in achieving 'normality' was the prevalence of responsibility and rationality over populism understood either as the mark of a particular party formation, namely SYRIZA (Coalition of the Radical Left), or as a generalized political spirit or political culture that has been supposedly dominant in Greece at least since 1974, throughout the so-called post-authoritarian period. This discursive scheme can be found not only in political discourses but also in journalistic and academic arguments, creating a mutually reinforcing interdependent triangle.

In another characteristic example, Kyriakos Mitsotakis, currently Prime Minister of Greece, portrayed himself, especially since 2016, when he ascended to the leadership of the New Democracy party, as a tough opponent of populism to which he opposes pragmatism, rationality, truth and responsibility. In an interview with *Newsweek* in December 2016, Mitsotakis argued that there is a clear distinction between populism and realism, one which the world is gradually discovering but which was always present in Greek politics since democracy was re-established (Mitsotakis, 2016a). Speaking in the plenary of the European People's Party, he argued that: 'Greece was the first country to bring a populist government into power. Nevertheless, the pendulum is now shifting in the opposite direction. We will prove that a policy based on truth, rationality and moderation will prevail again' (Mitsotakis, 2017a). Finally, at an Economist conference in Athens he stated that 'New Democracy's task is to lead the country safely in the post-populist era' (Mitsotakis, 2016b). Such formulations continue to mark New Democracy's discourse in power.

It is precisely along these lines that the introduction of the epistemic oppositions between truth and post-truth have reshaped the confrontation between political discourses in Greek public sphere, associating populism with post-truth politics, on the one hand, and anti-populist politics with objective facts, rationality, expert knowledge and technocracy, on the other. The dichotomy 'truth vs. lie/post-truth' became identical to the dichotomy 'modernization vs. populism' that runs through the whole post-authoritarian period in Greece. Here modernization is associated with truth, rationality, responsibility and is perceived as 'the normal', while populism is equated with demagogy, lies, irresponsibility, irrationality and thus is presented as an abnormal, deviant form of politics.

We can observe a very interesting example in another speech by Kyriakos Mitsotakis:

> Power itself in Greece is interwoven with the need to manipulate messages to serve its own political interests. However, the systematic distortion of a series of concepts –the so-called post-truth politics– were introduced in Greece before becoming –as a concept– part of the global vocabulary. We have been at the vanguard in this turn of events. We have perfected the language of populism. We, as New Democracy, have chosen to use the term 'Truth Agreement'. We did it precisely because we wanted to demonstrate, through the employment of the concept of 'truth', how we perceive the political discourse against populism. (Mitsotakis, 2017b)

In fact, already in 2014, former Prime Minister (2012–2015) Antonis Samaras had declared:

> Populism relies mainly on 'sweet lies', on false promises of 'easy solutions' and 'quick fixes', totally unsubstantiated but very 'attractive', leading, of course, to grave disappointments and to social unrest. Extremism relies on hate and unmasked violence, widespread expectations of disaster and nihilist ideologies, leading to the complete breakdown of public order and democratic legitimacy. Populism often feeds the fire of extremism and vice versa. The underlying crisis is their common breading ground and together they generate a vicious cycle, a devastating process, during which social cohesion and democracy usually fall apart. So, what do we do during such crisis to avert those twin evils of populism and extremism? For starters, we fight the lies with the Truth. (Samaras, 2014)

Not surprisingly, we also meet such arguments in the social democratic camp as well. At an event discussing national-populism, Evangelos Venizelos, former leader of PASOK and former vice-president of the Greek government (2012–2015), stated that the basic dimension of national-populism involves an anti-rational view and therefore a new rational front, a new enlightenment, is required (Venizelos, 2017a). Presenting the book *Populism. A short introduction* by Cas Mudde and Cristóbal Kaltwasser, he mentioned that 'My approach is that populism is not an ideology. It is a cognitive and cultural model, which is intersected with holistic character ideologies. In fact, populism is challenging the achievements of modernity' (Venizelos, 2017b).

Truth then appears to be an important link within the equivalential chain of normality and seems to be directly related to responsibility and rationality. Populism, on the other hand, is linked, in this mainstream anti-populist discourse, to irrationality and lies. Accordingly, anti-populism is now framed within stark dichotomies like the one between the rational and the irrational, the normal and the pathological. In *On Populist Reason*, Ernesto Laclau had already connected the pejorative depiction of populism in the academic and political fields with the denigration of the masses and the old discussion concerning mass psychology, arguing that populism is often presented as the simple opposite of political forms dignified with the status of full rationality (Laclau, 2005, p. 19).

Indeed, the denouncement of the *abnormal* populism by the proponents of normality often employs pathological metaphors, castigating the 'disease' of populism—which is seen as a virus-like infection—or its monstrosity, using either zoomorphic metaphors or references to the beast/monster of populism. For example, former Prime Minister Samaras argued in his speech during the proceedings of the European People's Party conference in Madrid in 2015 that populism is not an ideology but a 'disease' connected with extreme parties from both sides of the political spectrum (Samaras, 2015). For her part, Anna Diamantopoulou, former education minister of PASOK, has declared that populism is more than a threat, that the 'monster of populism' must be crushed for good, otherwise it will eventually and terminally poison the healthy prospects of the country (Diamantopoulou, 2016). The medical metaphor of the 'virus' has been used lately in relation to fake news as well, with arguments calling for the *vaccination* of society against the virus of fake news; at any rate, the latest attempts to understand the spread of post-truth and fake news are often based on the use of epidemiological models for the transmission of infectious diseases (see, for example, Kucharski, 2016), providing another connection with populism, which is treated in similar terms.

Truth, Post-truth and Political Representation

The stark anti-populism described above simultaneously affects the depiction of the voter in mainstream discourse. Anti-populism creates an image of voters as, essentially, people guided by their emotions and not by documented, evidence-based positions and rational views. This discourse creates an image of cynical populist politicians, of shameless demagogues, who, by using fraudulent means and utilizing fake news, deceive the people of lower social strata and the uneducated. Thus, voters are presented as prone to deception, victims of their addiction to the sweet venom of populism. Arguably, this depiction of voters as an ignorant mass, guided by emotions, passions, stereotypes and superstitions, ultimately serves the purpose of delegitimizing popular sovereignty in favour of market and technocratic sovereignty.

For example, in an article entitled 'The Last Spasms of Reactive Populism', Aristides Hatzis identified some similarities among those who voted for Donald Trump, in favor of Brexit and supported the 'No' in the Greek referendum. He compares these three different votes on different issues with different stakes and finds that voters in all three cases were characterized by mistrust towards experts and intellectuals, rejection of rational arguments and facts, political ignorance, economic illiteracy and 'the fact that they did not have the tools to interpret the complex world that ultimately scared them'

(Hatzis, 2016). The article ends with the sweeping suggestion that what these voters actually reject is the twenty-first century itself.

Yet, as Benjamin De Cleen has argued, populism is not necessarily demagogic while the equation of populism with post-truth politics and the subsequent critique of post-truth populist politics can lead to a rather problematic delegitimization of 'the people' as led by emotions rather than by well-informed opinions. The idea, he continues, that 'objective facts' should shape public opinion loses sight of the unavoidable emotional and affective elements present in all kinds of politics (De Cleen, 2018, p. 270). Recently, Kurt Sengul (2019) has also concluded that the suggestion of an elective affinity between populism and post-truth communication is contestable.

Indeed, the debate over populism, post-truth politics and fake news on the one hand, and rationality, truth and politics based on facts and knowledge of experts on the other, essentially presupposes the transformation of political confrontation into a supposedly neutral epistemological debate around truth, thereby causing a series of concerns about the very essence of the political. We no longer have a confrontation between different political alternatives, but between what is true and what is false. The policy that allegedly bears the 'quality' of truth presents itself as self-evident, as one that cannot be challenged, whereas all other proposals are reduced to cheap and even conscious lies, with the sole aim of luring the popular vote. Truth dictates a single policy, the rational and responsible one, which, in the case of Greece, will at last make the country a 'normal European country', a proper member of the EU family.

Ultimately, the result of this strategy is not only the elimination of populism from political confrontation and the public sphere but the end of *politics* itself, if politics is indeed regarded as a struggle between alternative political projects. Thus, we are faced with the triumph of the post-political (Mouffe, 2005, p. 7), with the prevalence of meritocratic technocracy, of the responsible rationalist who reveals the one and only truth and can develop the only political project that corresponds to this truth. Whatever falls outside this consensus, whatever challenges even at a very minimal level the dominant doctrine, is immediately rejected as populism or as post-truth and lies. The conflict between radically different political projects is transformed into a conflict between rational, technocratic decisions and absurd, emotional, populist attitudes.

Theoretical and Political Implications

A set of distinct issues, from the more ontological to the more ontic level, are at stake here. For a start, we almost never question the status of 'truth' as the indisputable and taken-for-granted foundation of social life. Yet, is truth the only value upon which a good life can be based? What if our different versions of truth are but distinct social constructions over-determined by our social, class and identity positioning, by the way we collectively structure our desires and seek our enjoyment(s)? What if, in other words, the very nature of social reality and truth is inherently partial and 'mythical'? Some of these questions transcend the scope of this paper, but should, nevertheless be highlighted at this point even if their only purpose would be to energize a future research agenda. In this section, we can only offer a preliminary treatment.

In social life, we cannot seem to escape what Roland Barthes calls *myth*: a special type of discourse that becomes naturalized, represses its contingent and historical articulation and presents itself as an obvious and indisputable certainty, as *truth*. At his point, Barthes' critical stance is of great interest to us (Barthes, 2013). Truth and knowledge production –both mediated by language and discourse– are always over-determined by processes of articulation that very rarely operate in isolation from power relations. This is why Michel Foucault, always alert to the intricacies of the power/knowledge nexus, coins the paradoxical term 'Regimes of Truth', meaning the frameworks that regulate public discourse and distinguish what can be said from what cannot, what *is* from what *is not* given credibility and assigned truth value (Foucault, 1991, p. 73).

What then if, to put it provocatively, every *truth* is a *post-truth*, at least in the political sphere which is at stake in this chapter and where a war of interpretations is inescapable? Is this not what hegemony and political antagonism is about? Is this not what links Aristotle (mentioned in the beginning of this chapter) to Laclau in acknowledging the *Rhetorical Foundations of Society*? (Laclau, 2014). It is only from the point of view of a mythical, unreflexive attachment to (our) 'regime of truth' that post-truth can be so easily delineated and condemned. Yet, this is precisely what puts in doubt the *epistemic* validity of such distributions and highlights, instead, their *political* character.

This does not mean that we are condemned to inhabit a relativist—if not solipsistic—universe. From a Lacanian psychoanalytic point of view, for example, it is possible to subscribe to a radical constructionist understanding of social reality without renouncing the primacy of our encounters with the *real*; only this real is not a representationalist real, it is not identical to our symbolic and imaginary constructions, it is what exceeds this reality, what stimulates our desire to represent it but also reveals the inadequacy of our (always partial) representations.[2] In fact, what seems to be unfolding before our eyes is the collapse of the politico-symbolic preconditions of sharing a common, constructed truth, a 'truth' that has become hegemonic, politically and discursively, establishing a certain consensus. Suddenly the (supposed) One is split into Two. And thus, we encounter a division between two antithetical—equally fantasmatic (underpinned by desire and the quest for enjoyment, for different types of enjoyment)—regimes of truth. As Bruno Latour has cogently put it:

> We thus find ourselves with our countries split in two, each half becoming ever less capable of grasping its own reality, let alone the other side's. The first half —let us call them the globalized— believe that the horizon of emancipation and modernity (often confused with the reign of finance) can still expand to embrace the whole planet. Meanwhile, the second half has decided to retreat to

the Aventine Hill, dreaming of a return to a past world. Thus, two utopias: a utopia of the future confronting a utopia of the past. The opposition between Clinton and Trump illustrated this rather well: both occupied their own bubbles of unrealism. For now, the utopia of the past has won out. But there's little reason to think that the situation would be much better and more sustainable had the utopia of the future triumphed instead. (Latour, 2016)

All major theories of ideology in modernity have assumed an extreme opposition between what is true and what is false along representationalist lines. This assumption was consistent with the drive of Enlightenment modernity to replace all uncertain beliefs with rational representations of the social, to replace the false with the true (Stavrakakis, 1997). The crucial issue here is who is able to judge true from false? Whenever one person—be it the scientist or the party leader—or social group—the intelligentsia, the party or technocracy—has claimed to possess a supreme knowledge mirroring reality—crystallized in ideas such as class consciousness, racial purity or TINA and the like—and giving it the right to impose it on those suffering from 'false consciousness', the result has been disastrous. What dominates here is the fantasy of 'a direct and unmediated access to reality' (Fink, 2007, p. 222). Who can seriously claim today to embody such a power?

Hence the theory of ideology and contemporary political discourse need to abandon such discredited representationalist conceptions of truth and reality; they need to move beyond objectivism and rationalism. The 'myth of reality' as an objective whole can only be an effect of signification and discursive articulation (Lacan, 1993, pp. 199, 249). Moreover, it is an articulation rooted in fantasy (Lacan, 1998, p. 95). What Lacan formulated from his 1955–1956 seminar is today a commonplace in social theory, epistemology and the study of ideology. Within such a framework, 'reality' becomes the ideological representation *par excellence*, a point forcefully made by Slavoj Žižek (1989) in his *Sublime Object of Ideology*, arguably the most important contribution of psychoanalysis to the theory of ideology and discourse analysis in the last two decades: Ideology is not a dreamlike illusion that we build to escape insupportable reality; in its basic dimension it is a fantasy-construction which serves as a support for our 'reality' itself. In vain do we try to break out of the ideological dream by 'opening our eyes and trying to see reality as it is', by throwing away the ideological spectacles (Žižek, 1989, pp. 45, 48).

And *reality-testing*, a recourse to 'objective facts', is, alas, of no use here:

> How then would our poor German, if he were a good anti-Semite, react to this gap between the ideological figure of the Jew (schemer, wire-puller, exploiting our brave men and so on) and the common everyday experience of his good neighbor, Mr Stern? His answer would be to turn this gap, this discrepancy itself, into an argument for anti-Semitism: 'You see how dangerous they are? It is difficult to recognize their real nature. They hide it behind the mask of everyday appearance – and it is exactly this hiding of one's real nature, this duplicity, that is a basic feature of their Jewish nature'. An ideology really succeeds when even

the facts, which at first sight contradict it, start to function as arguments in its favour. (Žižek, 1989, p. 49)

Conclusion

This chapter focused on the correlation between populism and post-truth and the polemical uses of the notion of 'post-truth' within mainstream political discourses in the West. We started by describing the emerging terrain: Brexit and Trump were the inaugural events of the ongoing truth wars. Specific political forces, usually of an elitist and liberal background, claimed an epistemic superiority against their 'irrational' opponents and the 'ignorant' masses that support them. Yet, the issue is not of an epistemic order, because the rationality that is supposedly prioritized is often of an instrumental, political nature. In our post-political era, epistemic authority, the access to the one and only truth, is often understood as the foundation of political authority. This stance is not solely an epistemic issue but a deeply political matter, and this very political essence we attempted to register and restore in this chapter.

Trying to understand more thoroughly the relationship between the debates on post-truth and the ones on populism we moved towards crisis-ridden Greece. On the basis of an analysis of the Greek case, we examined how Greek mainstream anti-populist discourse employed the polemical notion of 'post-truth'. The Greek case helped us to highlight the political claims and narratives involved in this debate. Finally, and on the basis of that case-specific analysis, we tried to challenge the very notion of truth at a broader level, in its rather simplistic, mythical renderings. We argue that we need to discuss the political implications that can be produced by the connection of populism and post-truth, but what is also needed at the same time is to dig even deeper and explore the *political* implications of our constant appeals to truth. In this way, we may not only discover the 'truth in the heart of heresy' but also 'death in the heart of truth', quoting a very intriguing dialogue from the British TV series *Doctor Who*.

Notes

1. In our analysis we approach 'post-truth' and 'fake news' as a label and not as a genre, see Egelhofer and Lecheler (2019).
2. For a more comprehensive elaboration see Stavrakakis (2007, pp. 5–14).

Literature

Barthes, R. (2013). *Mythologies*. Hill & Wang.
De Cleen, B. (2018). Populism, exclusion, post-truth: Some conceptual caveats, comment on 'The rise of post-truth populism in pluralist liberal democracies: Challenges for health policy'. *International Journal of Health Policy and Management*, 7(3), 268–271.

De Cleen, B., Glynos, J., & Mondon, A. (2018). Critical research on populism: Nine rules of engagement. *Organization, 25*(5), 649–661.

Demata, M., Conoscenti, M., & Stavrakakis, Y. (2020). Riding the populist wave: Metaphors of populism and anti-populism in the Daily Mail and the Guardian. *Ipestoria, 5*, 8–35.

Diamantopoulou, A. (2016). *Populism and social democracy's distress*. https://www.socialeurope.eu/populism-social-democracys-distress.

Dombrovskis, V. (2016). *Greece government populism made adjustment worse—EU's Dombrovskis*. https://uk.reuters.com/article/uk-eurozone-greece-dombrovskis-idUKKCN11W1GX.

Egelhofer, J. L., & Lecheler, S. (2019). Fake news as a two-dimensional phenomenon: A framework and research agenda. *Annals of the International Communication Association., 43*(2), 97–116.

Fink, B. (2007). *Fundamentals of psychoanalytic technique*. W. W. Norton.

Foucault, M. (1991). 'Truth and power', interview given to Alessandro Fontana and Pasquale Pasquino. In P. Rabinow (Ed.), *The Foucault reader* (pp. 51–75). Penguin.

Haskins, E. (2004). Endoxa, epistemological optimism, and Aristotle's rhetorical project. *Philosophy & Rhetoric, 37*(1), 1–20.

Hatzis, A. (2016, November 16). The last spasms of reactive populism. *Kathimerini*. http://www.kathimerini.gr/883828/opinion/epikairothta/politikh/oi-teleytaioi-spasmoi--toy-antidrastikoy-laikismoy [in Greek].

Howarth, D., Norval, A. J., & Stavrakakis, Y. (Eds.). (2000). *Discourse theory and political analysis: Identities, hegemonies and social change*. Manchester University Press.

Kucharski, A. (2016). Study epidemiology of fake news. *Nature, 540*(7634), 525.

Lacan, J. (1993). *The seminar of Jacques Lacan. Book III: The psychoses, 1955–56*. Routledge.

Lacan, J. (1998). *The seminar of Jacques Lacan. Book XX: Encore, on feminine sexuality, the limits of love and knowledge, 1972–73*. W. W. Norton.

Laclau, E., & Mouffe, C. (2001). *Hegemony and socialist strategy*. Verso.

Laclau, E. (2005). *On populist reason*. Verso.

Laclau, E. (2014). *The Rhetorical Foundations of Society*. Verso.

Latour, B. (2016, November 17). Two bubbles of unrealism: Learning from the tragedy of Trump. *Los Angeles Review of Books*. https://lareviewofbooks.org/article/two-bubbles-unrealism-learning-tragedy-trump/.

Mitsotakis, K. (2016a, December 12). Greek opposition leader Kyriakos Mitsotakis on why the country is done with populism. *Newsweek*. https://www.newsweek.com/2016/12/23/greece-kyriakos-mitsotakis-interview-opposition-leader-alexis-tsipras-next-530838.html.

Mitsotakis, K. (2016b, June 12). The debt of new democracy is to lead the country to the post-populism era. *To Vima*. https://www.tovima.gr/2016/06/22/politics/mitsotakis-xreos-tis-nd-na-odigisei-ti-xwra-sti-meta-laikismo-epoxi/ [in Greek].

Mitsotakis, K. (2017a, November 14). The experiment of SYRIZA has cost approximately 100 billion. *Kathimerini*. http://www.kathimerini.gr/934560/article/epikairothta/politikh/mhtsotakhs-to-peirama-syriza-exei-kostisei-peripoy-100-dis [in Greek].

Mitsotakis, K. (2017b, February 18). Populism will be defeated by reality and reason. *Iefimerida*. http://www.iefimerida.gr/news/322013/mitsotakis-o-laikismos-tha-ittithei-apo-tin-pragmatikotita-kai-ton-ortho-logo-eikones [in Greek].

Mouffe, C. (2005). *On the political*. Verso.
Oxford University Press. (2017). *Word of the year 2016*. https://languages.oup.com/word-of-the-year/2016/.
Papaioannou, E. (2016, August 14). Populism is the deepest reason for the failure of memoranda policies. *Kathimerini*. http://www.kathimerini.gr/870999/article/epikairothta/politikh/o-laikismos-va8yteros-logos-apotyxias-twn-mnhmoniakwn-politikwn [in Greek].
Rancière, J. (2007). *The hatred of democracy*. Verso.
Rensin, E. (2017, June 18). The blathering superego at the end of history. *Los Angeles Review of Books*. https://lareviewofbooks.org/article/the-blathering-superego-at-the-end-of-history/.
Rifkind, H. (2017, May 9). Populism and fake news are a two-headed beast. *The Times*. https://www.thetimes.co.uk/article/populism-and-fake-news-are-a-two-headed-beast-fv2nnvmk7.
Runciman, D. (2016, October 5). How the education gap is tearing politics apart. *The Guardian*. https://www.theguardian.com/politics/2016/oct/05/trump-brexit-education-gap-tearing-politics-apart.
Samaras, A. (2014, September 16). Speech of Prime Minister Antonis Samaras in the event 'Athens Forum 2014: Democracy under pressure'. https://primeminister.gr/2014/09/16/12930 [in Greek].
Samaras, A. (2015, October 22). Samaras to EPP: Populism is a disease connected with extreme parties. *Proto Thema*. https://www.protothema.gr/politics/article/520483/samaras-sto-elk-o-laikismos-einai-arrostia-pou-sundeetai-me-akraia-kommata/ [in Greek].
Sengul, K. (2019). Populism, democracy, political style and post-truth: Issues for communication research. *Communication Research and Practice.*, 5(1), 88–101.
Stavrakakis, Y. (1997). Ambiguous ideology and the Lacanian twist. *Journal of the Centre for Freudian Analysis and Research, 8 & 9*, 117–130.
Stavrakakis, Y. (2007). *The Lacanian left: Psychoanalysis, theory, politics*. SUNY Press.
Stavrakakis, Y. (2018). Populism, Anti-Populism and Democracy. *Political. Insight, 9*(3), 33–35.
Stavrakakis, Y., & Galanopoulos, A. (2019). Discursive Uses of "abnormality" in the Greek crisis. In K. Power, T. Ali, & E. Lebdušková (Eds.), *Austerity discourses: An inter-disciplinary critical analysis* (pp. 177–195). Routledge.
Venizelos, E. (2017a, February 18). The need for a new rational front against national-populism. *Evenizelos*. https://www.evenizelos.gr/373-sticky-top/5556-2017-02-19-11-39-31.html [in Greek].
Venizelos, E. (2017b, May 26). Populism as a challenge to the achievements of modernity. *Evenizelos*. https://www.evenizelos.gr/speeches/politicalspeeches/412-politicalspeeches2017/5610-2017-05-28-08-30-21.html [in Greek].
Waisbord, S. (2018). The elective affinity between post-truth communication and populist politics. *Communication Research and Practice, 4*(1), 17–34.
Wikipedia. (2020). *Post-truth*. https://en.wikipedia.org/wiki/Post-truth.
Ylä-Anttila, T. (2018). Populist knowledge: 'Post-truth' repertoires of contesting epistemic authorities. *European Journal of Cultural and Political Sociology.*, 5(4), 356–388.
Žižek, S. (1989). *The sublime object of ideology*. Verso.

CHAPTER 26

Experience Narratives and Populist Rhetoric in U.S. House Primaries

Mike Cowburn

INTRODUCTION

In recent years, concern about polarization in Congress has increased attention on the nomination process. Academics and popular media position parties as having lost control, advocating that the openness of the nomination system has resulted in an influx of ideologically extreme outsiders willing to use populist rhetoric against both the institution of Congress and party establishments. This chapter considers how changes in the use of experience narratives and populist rhetoric in U.S. House of Representatives primaries have impacted the quality of general election nominees. I first consider competing definitions of populism to justify the focus on style and rhetoric, then identify the features of populist style in the U.S. Applying this framework to intraparty contests, identified by Frances Lee (2020) as the site of populist threat in the U.S., I argue that populist rhetoric has become more prevalent in recent electoral cycles. I find that competence has become less central in intraparty competitions, where candidates who use populist rhetoric and have no prior electoral experience have increasingly been able to earn the nomination. While significant attention has been paid to Donald Trump's rhetoric, analysis of congressional candidates has been comparatively scarce. Yet, my results indicate a spread of populist rhetoric to nomination contests, with consequences for the dynamics of intraparty competition and the quality of congressional nominees in both parties.

M. Cowburn (✉)
Freie Universität Berlin, Berlin, Germany
e-mail: m.cowburn@fu-berlin.de

© The Author(s), under exclusive license to Springer Nature Switzerland AG 2022
M. Oswald (ed.), *The Palgrave Handbook of Populism*,
https://doi.org/10.1007/978-3-030-80803-7_26

The strong two-party system and open system of candidate nomination in the U.S. mean it is likely that populist threats will come from within rather than outside of the major parties. It is unlikely that candidates who use populist rhetoric will be able to form a viable alternative party with any realistic chance of winning power, particularly at the national level. Consequently, outsiders target the nomination process as a potential route into the legislative branch. In Europe, especially under proportional systems, populist outsiders must form new organizations as nomination processes are tightly guarded by party elites who hold the power of (de)selection. U.S. parties do not have these tools, so candidates who use populist rhetoric are funneled into the major parties.

Defining Populism

When discussing populism, it has become almost mandatory to remark on the difficulty of pinning down the definition, with some scholars even citing the acknowledgment of this difficulty (Panizza, 2005). Many scholars, particularly on the left, reject the term, labeling it, 'a massive misnomer, a journalistic cliché, and political epithet that serves more to stigmatize than to analyze' (Tamás, 2017; see also D'Eramo, 2013). Critics argue that the label is positioned as derogatory and applied to movements as normatively 'bad', or, alternatively, that the term is too broad to be analytically useful. Because populists have diffuse ideological positions and are not identifiable through strategic behavior or structural organization, disparate projects are often grouped under the label (Brubaker, 2017, p. 358), with any identifiable tropes so widespread that they have become clichéd (Lee, 2020, p. 374). Jan-Werner Müller argues that overuse of the term may not only be meaningless but actively harmful, as it 'only plays into the hands of populists while increasing the frustrations and sometimes outright anger of those who actually seek more political participation' (2014, p. 485). The term's persistent contestation does not mean it should be abandoned but rather cautions and challenges us to consider the ways in which populism can be conceived of.

Competing definitions of populism largely agree on its central feature: an opposition between a singular 'people' and an 'elite' who threaten the unified citizenry. Most commonly, tension comes along what Rogers Brubaker (2017) terms a 'vertical dimension', with division between the 'pure people' and a 'corrupt elite' (Mudde, 2004, p. 543). Others emphasize the eradication of internal differences, in particular the creation of 'the people' as a monolithic group (Jagers & Walgrave, 2007, p. 322). Discourse analysts focus on the power of framing, claiming that by labeling the people as unified, populists attempt to bring this group into existence and position their voice—and their voice alone—as capable of representing the people (Moffitt & Tormey, 2014, p. 388). From these points of agreement, definitions diverge, I follow existing typologies in the literature: thin ideology, discourse, strategy, practice, and finally the adopted use in this chapter, populism as rhetoric and style.

The most widespread understanding is of populism as a thin ideology, 'that politics should be an expression of the volonté générale (general will) of the people' (Mudde, 2004, p. 543). Cas Mudde (see also Canovan, 2002) positions populism as a thin ideology against elitism and pluralism. Elitism shares the foundational belief in division between 'the people' and an 'elite' but contends the 'elite' are best placed to rule. Pluralism, in contrast, rejects the group homogeneity in populism and elitism. Nadia Urbinati (1998, p. 110) takes a similar view of populism as ideology, with emphasis on the prioritization of unity over equality putting it at odds with pluralism. The definition of populism as ideology is identified through the promotion of a noble people, the disparagement of an 'elite', and appeals to popular sovereignty (Mudde & Kaltwasser, 2013). Defined as a thin ideology, actors are either populist or not.

Defining populism as ideology has been criticized for being too thin to have any utility, in part due to the ideological diversity of those that are labeled populist. The definition is moreover problematic because populism lacks many of the features of an ideological movement; few politicians or parties adopt the label, no global movements exist, and there are no identifiable thinkers or theorists (Moffitt & Tormey, 2014, p. 383). Though populists position 'the people' against an 'elite', they also frequently define an 'other', often portrayed as undeserving and whose existence is a threat to 'the people'. Brubaker extends the concept of populism beyond vertical division to include a horizontal dimension of 'outsiders', who do not conform to cultural or ethnic requirements to be within 'the people', regardless of citizenship status. Brubaker claims that the 'other' is crucial to populism, which is based on the 'tight discursive interweaving' (2017, p. 363) of these two groups.

Criticism of Mudde also comes on conceptual grounds, with some scholars proposing an alternative definition of populism as discourse (Aslanidis, 2016; Laclau, 1985). Rooted in discourse analysis, this approach focuses on the frequency of populist terminology in texts. Stemming from the work of Ernesto Laclau, who, like Urbinati, sees populism as a contest between equality and unity, arguing that this tension structures political life. Laclau identifies populism through references to 'the people' that manifest an 'equivalential, antagonistic discursive logic' (Stavrakakis, 2004, p. 259). Mario Poblete is more specific, arguing that 'discourse has to establish a contradiction and/or an antinomy rather than a mere difference' (2015, p. 205). Benjamin Moffitt and Simon Tormey criticize this approach for being overly focused on word usage, without regard for stylistic concerns (2014, p. 383). Further, as with ideology, the discursive definition is criticized for being too universal to enable application; if discourses of populism structure politics, then it becomes difficult to separate the two concepts.

A third definition advocates that populism is better understood as strategy. This approach focuses on how elites gain support, arguing that populists do this through direct, unmediated communication with a mass public (Weyland, 2001, p. 14). Hans-Georg Betz (2002) contends that other facets of populism are subsidiary to the strategic role they play for elites to earn power. Kirk Hawkins (2010, p. 39) criticizes this definition for being too narrow and overly focused on material aspects of politics, alleging that politics is more encompassing than the strategic aspects of power alone. Further, the definition focuses on populist organizers, with comparatively little attention on 'the people'.

Literature from sociology conceives of populism as 'a mode of political practice – as populist mobilization' (Jansen, 2011, p. 75) and problematizes the idea of populism as stable—of being present or absent—in actors, and instead positions the term as action. Robert Jansen (2011) argues that this definition is preferable because it is spatially and temporally bound and is therefore usable, for example in comparative studies. Understanding populism as social practice forces us to consider which practices we should deem populist, with Jan Jagers and Stefaan Walgrave (2007) arguing that the crucial action is style, determined through attention to rhetoric. Following this understanding, populism is a style, or 'repertoire' (Brubaker, 2017, p. 373) that can be called upon in and is primarily identified through rhetoric.

There are several notable features of populist rhetoric. As with previous definitions, reference to 'elites' and 'the people' as unified forces in competition is central. Populist rhetoric often frames 'elites' as the institutions of liberal democracy that are 'blocking' the true will of the singular people. In this framework, democratic institutions' loss of legitimacy must be resolved through 'antagonistic re-politicization' (Brubaker, 2017, p. 364) that reestablishes direct control over sites of power that have become overly technocratic. Populist rhetoric rails against the functions of parliaments, 'such as extended deliberation, which populists consider dithering' (Müller, 2014, p. 487), preferring swift action, which legislative bodies are ill-equipped to deliver. Populist rhetoric favors simple solutions and devalues complexity, with extraordinary measures framed as necessary to protect 'the people' from crisis. More generally, populist rhetoric invokes a distrust of complexity and is dismissive of expertise.

Understanding populism as a rhetorical style has several advantages. First, as noted by Terri Bimes and Quinn Mulroy (2004), conceiving of populism as style forces us to think further about how government works. Second, it provides a clearer understanding of populism's targets, often framed as the establishment or via institutions of government. Third, defined rhetorically, populism becomes measurable over time (see Bonikowski & Gidron, 2016), so that we can identify when actors are becoming more populistic. Finally, defining populism as a style means it is 'totally stripped from all pejorative and authoritarian connotations' (Jagers & Walgrave, 2007, p. 323). For these reasons, I use this definition here.

Populism in the United States

Though twenty-first-century populism is a global phenomenon, considering the in-country specificities of U.S. populist rhetoric is important. Populist rhetoric and style have been present since the nation's founding, stretching from agrarian movements during the revolution, to the insurgent presidency of Andrew Jackson, into the anti-trust People's Party, socialist and prohibition movements of the early twentieth century, Father Coughlin's radio addresses, Huey Long, the New Deal labor movement, the New Left in the 1960s, George Wallace, the Christian Right, Ronald Reagan, Ross Perot, through to the Tea Party and progressive left movements in the twenty-first century. Indeed, there is hardly any period of U.S. history untouched by some degree of populist fervor. Conflict between the powerful and the powerless has given 'discord and meaning' to political discussion in the U.S., often involving 'debates about the meaning of Americanism itself' (Kazin, 2017, p. 2). Because America originated as both a political project and a nation, populist rhetoric is necessarily intertwined in shared ideals of 'the people'. Such rhetoric is therefore used to demarcate group membership to indicate who is contributing to the ongoing project, with those outside of the constructed 'people' seen as 'transgressing the nation's founding creed' (Kazin, 2017, p. 2). Adherence to shared ideals further shapes U.S. populism in advocating the will of the common people by upholding existing systems, most notably through a valorization of democracy. U.S. populist rhetoric rarely calls for the dismantling of constitutional structures but is instead optimistic, claiming that anything be achieved when the voices of ordinary Americans are followed.

Because the constitutional order and nation are rarely targeted, U.S. populist rhetoric instead focuses on the actors and institutions responsible for having 'corrupted' the project of America by ignoring the will of 'the people'. A common target is the federal government, or Washington D.C. itself, often the manifestation of a fear of centralized authority (Brewer, 2016). The vast geographic expanse, particularly the physical distance between the nation's capital and much of the agrarian population in the country's early history, was interpreted as a source of difference in early populist rhetoric. As in other countries, 'the people' are positioned as virtuous, in the U.S. this has a clear racial dynamic. Membership of 'the people' has been defined by and restricted to White citizens, with racial disunity being the most frequently invoked horizontal divide in populist rhetoric, often connected to references to rural regions as the 'real' America. The vertical dimension includes a rejection of experts, who 'are often perceived as telling the people what is good for them' (Brewer, 2016, p. 253) and diverting the popular will. Due to its long history, populist rhetoric exists within 'normal' political discourse in the U.S., with evidence that many Americans are comfortable with populist rhetoric (Hawkins et al., 2012), and a willingness to embrace notions of a 'wholesome people in contradistinction to a corrupt, out-of-touch political elite' (Lee, 2020, p. 372). Mark Brewer finds evidence of a receptive audience for populist rhetoric, arguing that this has been activated in the modern era (2016, p. 257). Consequently, current trends of populist rhetoric are best understood as a continuation of the U.S. history of populism rather than a new phenomenon.

Populism in Congressional Primaries

Having considered the question of *what* populism is, I now turn attention to the question of *where* it manifests. The U.S. has a strong two-party system, with third parties unable to gain any meaningful power. At the same time, the U.S. has one of the most open systems of candidate selection in the world, giving party elites limited gatekeeping power. The constitutional arrangement and electoral rules hinder outsider parties while providing opportunities to candidates who use populist rhetoric through 'an incentive structure that tends to divert populist impulses into the mainstream parties' (Lee, 2020, p. 374), meaning the nomination process is often the site of populist rhetoric. Because the U.S. electorate is primed to receive populist rhetoric (Hawkins et al., 2012; Hibbing & Theiss-Morse, 1995) and the system is unable to satisfy these demands from outside of the major parties, populist rhetoric is present in the Democratic and Republican nomination processes. Recent analyses of populist rhetoric have tended to focus on Trump, who was able to capture the Republican presidential nomination due to the openness of system. Yet, populist rhetoric has also become increasingly common in congressional nominations.

Congressional primaries have received greater academic attention in the twenty-first century, following decades of scholarship focused largely on presidential nominations. In recent years, entire volumes have been written about congressional (Boatright, 2013, 2014; Hassell, 2018) or non-presidential (Hirano & Snyder, 2019) primary contests, with specific focus on candidate quality and 'outsider' threat, with evidence of increased numbers of contested races since 2010 indicating a shift in dynamics (see Appendix). Congressional primaries have become sites of struggle for power within the parties, particularly after the influx of Tea Party-supported candidates in the 2010 Republican primaries and a more recent wave of progressive Democrats. Increased attention on primary elections has come at a time when trust in the institution of Congress has reached record lows; only 11% of respondents had a 'great deal' or 'quite a lot' of confidence in Congress in 2019 (Gallup, 2020a).[1] Despite these negative perceptions, voter engagement in the primary process has increased substantially in recent electoral cycles (DeSilver, 2018) after decades of decline until 2006.

The low regard of Congress among voters has given primary candidates an effective way to frame campaigns against the institution using populist rhetoric. Primary candidates now frequently position themselves as outsiders able to bring much needed reform to the ineffective legislative body. Though the tactic of framing Congress as ineffective is not new, it has taken on fresh relevance in recent electoral cycles. Party establishments are also now frequently attacked by candidates using populist rhetoric in primaries, as the parties themselves have also become less favorably viewed (Gallup, 2020b).

Analysis

The following analysis considers changes in the reasons for primary contests, the prior experience of major party nominees, and their connection to growing populist rhetoric. I coded two variables to conduct this analysis; first, whether the dominant narrative in a primary contest was candidates' competence or experience, and second, whether the nominee had previously held elected public office. I hypothesize that the prevalence of competence narratives and rates of nominee experience will decline as populist rhetoric increases over time. Coding was carried out using an original dataset of all contests and nominees between 2006 and 2018.[2] A minimum of two candidates on the ballot were required for a contest to be coded for narrative. All nominees were coded for quality.

Coding for experience narratives was determined based on the answer to the question 'why are you running for Congress?', with information obtained from campaign websites or media interviews. When candidates gave answers such as 'because I would be the best person to represent the district', 'I have the best chance of winning the general election', or 'because of my previous experience in…' contests were coded as competence primaries. All other answers, such as ideological differences, prioritization of different issues, racial, or tactical competitions were coded as non-competence.[3] Where multiple or alternate reasons were given, the highest priority reason was coded, usually determined by position in the answer to motivation for running. If an initial reason was given with further reasons, the initial reason was coded. Primary elections that focused on candidates' competence or experience, especially those concerned with prior experience in public office, were much less likely to feature populist rhetoric. In these data, populist rhetoric most frequently came from candidates who had not previously held office, in primary contests that focused on characteristics other than competence.

Prior experience in public office is central to literature on candidate 'quality' in elections. Though the term quality has normative implications, it is widely used to refer to candidates who have previously held elected office. Some measures weight based on previously held political positions (Goodliffe, 2001, 2007; Squire, 1992) or include values for non-elected roles (Canon, 1990; Krasno & Green, 1988). The most common method, developed by Gary Jacobson (Jacobson & Kernell, 1981; Jacobson, 1989), is a binary measure of whether or not a candidate has previously held elective office. Jacobson's measure is preferred due to the ease of data collection and evidence that 'the simple electoral office dichotomy captures the most important component of candidate quality' (Bond et al., 1997, p. 284). Gary Cox and Jonathan Katz (1996) indicate that the value of prior experience increased between 1946 and 1990, becoming more closely associated with higher party vote share and explaining the increased incumbency advantage. Jacobson (2015) shows the incumbency advantage has declined in recent cycles, with implications for the importance of candidate quality. Nominees were coded for quality using Jacobson's dichotomous method. Since all incumbents are coded as quality, the non-incumbent data are of specific interest. Data for all nominees, non-incumbents, and non-incumbents who earned the nomination via contested primaries are shown separately.

Figure 26.1 indicates that the percentage of contested primaries taking place for competence reasons declined significantly between 2006 and 2018 in both parties. In 2008, more than 40% of primaries were competence-based, by 2018 this figure was below 20% for both parties. In the Republican Party this decline came after 2008, with a big drop in 2010 and a continued downward trend. In the Democratic Party, competence primaries fluctuated between 2006 and 2012 and only declined substantially after 2014.

During this period there was a large increase in the number of contested primaries (see Appendix). These contests increasingly took place for non-competence reasons, such as policy or ideological differences within parties. New groups and candidates who were more comfortable using populist rhetoric to demean both Congress and the formal party apparatus entered the nomination process, both contributing and reacting to a decline in institutional perceptions. Competence primaries often took place between two candidates who had held local office—commonly state legislators or city council members—who would point to their record in office as evidence of their ability to work effectively in government. Other competence primaries took place not between elected officials but between candidates with a wealth

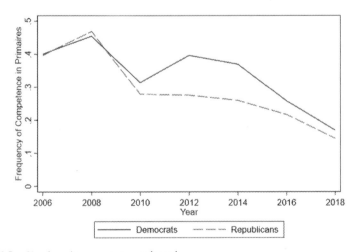

Fig. 26.1 % primaries competence based

of experience in other fields, often business, the military, education, or healthcare. These candidates framed their experience in general terms, stating that their prior success in these fields would effectively translate into government service, rather than emphasizing policy positions stemming from their experience.

Non-competence primaries included different dynamics but most frequently featured candidates with different ideological or policy positions, meaning that these contests were fought over policy rather than valence factors. Candidates tended to have narrower support from groups based on ideological or demographic identity, or due to adherence to specific positions. Sometimes these candidates had similar backgrounds to candidates in competence primaries but framed previous roles in terms of policy outcomes. Generalized competence was replaced by specific areas of expertise. These primaries exhibited a far higher degree of populist rhetoric, with candidates making direct appeals to 'the people' outside of party structures. Candidates were more critical of the institutions of Congress and even the party apparatus as 'elite' institutions. There were ideological links, with candidates on the Democratic left and Republican right more likely to criticize the party establishment as having failed 'the people', meaning populist rhetoric likely has consequences for the problem of polarization in Congress.

Alongside declining rates of competence primaries, a similar downturn in the quality of non-incumbent nominees has occurred. Because competence and prior experience have a less prominent position in primary campaigns, fewer nominees had experience in elective office by 2018. Figure 26.2

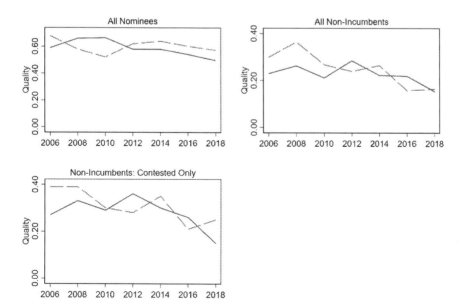

Fig. 26.2 Candidate quality

indicates this pattern across three different groups. The first graph shows the trend across all nominees. This figure is higher because it includes incumbents who are, by definition, quality. The second graph shows quality among all non-incumbents, while the third only includes data from non-incumbent nominees from contested primaries. In the Republican Party, the decline in non-incumbent candidate quality comes after 2008 when competence became less important in primaries. The exception was 2014, which had a higher rate of quality candidates, likely due to the perception that the party would have a strong midterm election. Among Democrats, the trend was flatter, though decline in non-incumbent quality occurred after the high point of 2012, again in line with competence data trends.

Discussion and Conclusion

As numbers of contested primaries have increased and focus has moved away from candidate competency, populist rhetoric has become more prevalent. Meanwhile, the percentage of candidates with prior experience in elective public office has decreased in both parties. Though these data are not conclusive in showing that the reduced focus on competence and simultaneous increase in populist rhetoric are responsible for the decline of candidate quality, there are several reasons to suspect these phenomena may be linked. This section considers changes in intraparty dynamics connected to these trends.

In the past two decades, regulatory changes have expanded the influence of outside groups in congressional primaries and weakened the power of formal party structures, which traditionally promoted experienced candidates unlikely to use populist rhetoric. First, the 2002 *Bipartisan Campaign Reform Act* limited soft money donations to parties, giving groups who could continue to accept soft money a structural advantage, making it easier for outside groups to raise and spend money in primaries and harder for traditional party groups to advertise close to an election. Then, in 2010, the *Citizens United v. Federal Election Commission* Supreme Court decision removed restrictions on corporations, ruling that it was unconstitutional to restrict PACs from using independent money to support a candidate. Consequently, formal party structures required wider networks of donors as large contributors were now limited in the amount of support they could provide. Alan Gerber (1998) shows that changes in campaign finance regulations that level the playing field disproportionately benefit non-incumbents, suggesting that changes in the twenty-first century may have assisted outsider candidates more likely to use populist rhetoric.

Changes in communication technology have enabled outsider candidates to compete in terms of fundraising and organizing (Cohen et al., 2008). The internet has provided opportunities for insurgent groups and candidates to raise money. Additionally, candidates may require less money for organizing or getting out their message online. Frances Lee (2020) argues that because candidates who use populist rhetoric are often trying to challenge the political system, they further benefit from lower financial barriers to entry as these would be exactly the candidates excluded in the previous information environment.

Technological changes have also had profound effects on the media ecology, which some scholars advocate has fostered a populist style of coverage that has further advantaged candidates using similar rhetoric (Brubaker, 2017, p. 370). Jens Rydgren (2005) indicates that a more diffuse media environment broadens the range of political frames that voters are exposed to, making them both more likely to receive populist rhetoric and to situation it in the realm of 'normal' political discourse. Questions of style have come to dominate media coverage, resulting in an increasingly stylized political sphere, where stylistic difference and repertoire have taken on greater resonance (Moffitt & Tormey, 2014, p. 387). As style becomes the dominant focus of political division, it follows that less attention would be given to personal competency in a further devaluing of prior political experience. Cristóbal Rovira Kaltwasser (2014) argues that emphasis on stylist difference is most prevalent when ideological cleavages between establishment parties decline due to policy convergence. Though this trend is not present in an American polity with highly polarized parties, there is evidence that as the parties have moved apart they have become internally ideologically homogenous (McCarty et al., 2006), meaning intraparty contests are likely to be the site of populist rhetoric and stylist differentiation.

Parties' organizational structures have also altered. Structural change has concentrated on the nomination process, with outsider groups gaining influence through an ability to 'screen candidates for party nominations based on loyalty to their agendas' (Bawn et al., 2012, p. 571). Seth Masket (2009) shows that *informal party organizations*[4] now play an important role in nominations. Organizations such as Club for Growth, American for Prosperity or MoveOn now provide support networks to candidates who are comfortable using populist rhetoric within a wider narrative of challenging establishment parties. Cory Manento (2019) shows that candidates with interest group PAC support now win congressional primaries more frequently than in the past. Such candidates have less allegiance to party establishments and may be more inclined to engage in populist rhetoric as a result.

The unpopularity of establishment party forces has enabled outside groups to exert power during the nomination process. Establishment parties globally have struggled to retain voters, leading to the formation of new parties in many countries. In the U.S., for the systemic reasons previously mentioned, dissatisfaction has been funneled into the major parties. The decline in trust has meant that candidates no longer need to position themselves as the most qualified or experienced when attempting to win the nomination, indeed, in some races it may be harmful to have prior political experience, with fears of being labeled an insider. Lee argues that U.S. parties are further vulnerable to internal populist challenges due to representation gaps caused by racial dynamics in the party system, showing that the major parties have become less polarized on race issues at a time of growing 'racial divergence in the electorate' (Lee, 2020, p. 379).

Frustrations with party establishments have spilled over into dissatisfaction with the system at large, fostering a demand for a direct connection between voters and those in power. Brubaker contends that this pressure is a consequence of 'growing technical, economic, and legal complexity and opacity of structures of governance and the growing distance between citizens of the most consequential loci of collective decision making' (2017, p. 370). Not only do U.S. citizens feel that their institutions are working ineffectively, they perceive power to have been taken away from elected bodies and given to bureaucrats in a rise of technocracy. Müller notes rising skepticism about liberalism in liberal democracies, with citizens more likely to take issue with checks and balances, finding 'no need for them at best, and, [that] at worst, they obstruct the expression of the genuine popular will' (Müller, 2014, p. 489). Countervailing forces present in liberalism and democracy have been widely noted both in scholarly literature and popular media, with governments in previously democratic countries such as Hungary and Poland now understood as illiberal democracies.

In the U.S., populist illiberal tendencies have been somewhat restricted by a combination of cultural deference to constitutional order and systemic design. However, as Lee (2020) argues, the challenge of populism in the U.S. will likely concentrate on liberal norms and values rather than on the continued existence of democratic institutions. The presence of populist rhetoric is a continuous feature of U.S. politics, but it is important to demarcate both usage and consequences of the phenomena. The site of populist challenge is within the major parties and is already visible in shifting narratives of House primary campaigns and a decreased importance of prior experience in public office.

Notes

1. This was an increase from the historic low of 7% in 2014, likely because Democrats saw the institution as providing checks on President Trump.
2. 2,489 contests in 49 states were analyzed, Louisiana does not hold congressional primaries.
3. Trends in the distribution of other categories are analyzed elsewhere, see (Cowburn, 2020).
4. Defined as "networks of office holders, interest group leaders, activists, consultants, and assorted others...[who] form alliances and conspire to control nominations and elect people who will be faithful to them while in office" (Masket, 2009, p. 20).

Appendix: Numbers of Contests, Candidates and Votes

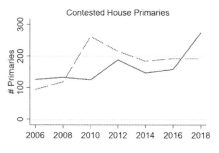
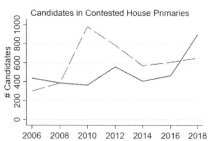
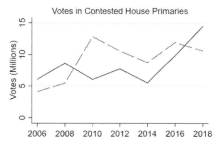

Literature

Aslanidis, P. (2016). Is populism an ideology? A refutation and a new perspective. *Political Studies, 64*(1), 88–104.

Bawn, K., Cohen, M., Karol, D., Masket, S., Noel, H., & Zaller, J. (2012). A theory of political parties: Groups, policy demands and nominations in American politics. *Perspectives on Politics, 10*(03), 571–597.

Betz, H.-G. (2002). Conditions favoring the success and failure of radical right-wing populist parties in contemporary democracies. In Y. Mény & Y. Surel (Eds.), *Democracies and the Populist Challenge* (pp. 197–213). Palgrave Macmillan.

Bimes, T., & Mulroy, Q. (2004). The rise and decline of presidential populism. *Studies in American Political Development, 18*(2), 136–159.

Boatright, R. G. (2013). *Getting primaried: The changing politics of congressional primary challenges*. University of Michigan Press.

Boatright, R. G. (2014). *Congressional primary elections*. Routledge.

Bond, J. R., Fleisher, R., & Talbert, J. C. (1997). Partisan differences in candidate quality in open seat house races, 1976–1994. *Political Research Quarterly, 50*(2), 281–299.

Bonikowski, B., & Gidron, N. (2016). The populist style in American politics: Presidential campaign discourse, 1952–1996. *Social Forces, 94*(4), 1593–1621.

Brewer, M. D. (2016). Populism in American politics. *The Forum, 14*(3), 249–264.

Brubaker, R. (2017). Why populism? *Theory and Society, 46*(5), 357–385.

Canon, D. T. (1990). *Actors, athletes, and astronauts: Political amateurs in the United States Congress*. University of Chicago Press.

Canovan, M. (2002). Taking politics to the people: Populism as the ideology of democracy. In Y. Mény & Y. Surel (Eds.), *Democracies and the populist challenge* (pp. 25–44). Palgrave Macmillan.

Cohen, M., Karol, D., Noel, H., & Zaller, J. (2008). *The party decides: Presidential nominations before and after reform*. University of Chicago Press.

Cowburn, M. (2020). The transformation of the congressional primary. In M. T. Oswald (Ed.), *Mobilization, representation, and responsiveness in the American democracy* (pp. 105–120). Palgrave Macmillan.

Cox, G. W., & Katz, J. N. (1996). Why did the incumbency advantage in U.S. house elections grow? *American Journal of Political Science, 40*(2), 478–497.

D'Eramo, M. (2013). Populism and the new oligarchy. *New Left Review*. https://newleftreview.org/issues/II82/articles/marco-d-eramo-populism-and-the-new-oligarchy.

DeSilver, D. (2018, July 27). Turnout in this year's U.S. House primaries is up, especially on the democratic side. *Pew Research Center*. http://www.pewresearch.org/fact-tank/2018/07/27/turnout-in-this-years-u-s-house-primaries-is-up-especially-on-the-democratic-side/.

Gallup. (2020a). *Confidence in institutions*. Gallup.Com. https://news.gallup.com/poll/1597/Confidence-Institutions.aspx.

Gallup. (2020b). *Party images*. Gallup.Com. https://news.gallup.com/poll/24655/Party-Images.aspx.

Gerber, A. (1998). Estimating the effect of campaign spending on senate election outcomes using instrumental variables. *American Political Science Review, 92*(2), 401–411.

Goodliffe, J. (2001). The effect of war chests on challenger entry in U.S. house elections. *American Journal of Political Science, 45*(4), 830–844.

Goodliffe, J. (2007). Campaign war chests and challenger quality in Senate elections. *Legislative Studies Quarterly, 32*(1), 135–156.

Hassell, H. J. G. (2018). *The party's primary: Control of congressional nominations*. Cambridge University Press.

Hawkins, K. (2010). *Venezuela's chaivsmo and populism in comparative perspective*. Cambridge University Press.

Hawkins, K. A., Riding, S., & Mudde, C. (2012, January). *Measuring populist attitudes*. Working Paper Series on Political Concepts. ECPR Committee on Concepts and Methods, International Political Science Association.

Hibbing, J. R., & Theiss-Morse, E. (1995). *Congress and public enemy: Public attitudes toward American political institutions*. Cambridge University Press.

Hirano, S., & Snyder, J. M. (2019). *Primary elections in the United States*. Cambridge University Press.

Jacobson, G. C. (1989). Strategic politicians and the dynamics of U.S. house elections, 1946–86. *The American Political Science Review, 83*(3), 773–793.

Jacobson, G. C. (2015). It's nothing personal: The decline of the incumbency advantage in US house elections. *The Journal of Politics, 77*(3), 861–873.

Jacobson, G. C., & Kernell, S. (1981). *Strategy and choice in congressional elections*. Yale University Press.

Jagers, J., & Walgrave, S. (2007). Populism as political communication style: An empirical study of political parties' discourse in Belgium. *European Journal of Political Research, 46*(3), 319–345.

Jansen, R. S. (2011). Populist mobilization: A new theoretical approach to populism. *Sociological Theory, 29*(2), 75–96.

Kaltwasser, C. R. (2014). The responses of populism to Dahl's democratic dilemmas. *Political Studies, 62*(3), 470–487.

Kazin, M. (2017). *The populist persuasion: An American history*. Cornell University Press.

Krasno, J. S., & Green, D. P. (1988). Preempting quality challengers in house elections. *The Journal of Politics, 50*(4), 920–936.

Laclau, E. (1985). *Hegemony and socialist strategy: Towards a radical democratic politics*. Verso.

Lee, F. E. (2020). Populism and the American party system: Opportunities and constraints. *Perspectives on Politics, 18*(2), 370–388.

Manento, C. (2019). Party crashers: Interest groups as a latent threat to party networks in congressional primaries. *Party Politics*, 1–12.

Masket, S. E. (2009). *No middle ground: How informal party organizations control nominations and polarize legislatures*. University of Michigan Press.

McCarty, N., Poole, K. T., & Rosenthal, H. (2006). *Polarized America: The dance of ideology and unequal riches*. MIT Press.

Moffitt, B., & Tormey, S. (2014). Rethinking populism: Politics, mediatisation and political style. *Political Studies, 62*(2), 381–397.

Mudde, C. (2004). The populist zeitgeist. *Government and Opposition, 39*(4), 541–563.

Mudde, C., & Kaltwasser, C. R. (2013). Exclusionary vs. inclusionary populism: Comparing contemporary Europe and Latin America. *Government and Opposition, 48*(2), 147–174.

Müller, J.-W. (2014). "The people must be extracted from within the people": Reflections on populism. *Constellations, 21*(4), 483–493.

Panizza, F. (2005). *Populism and the mirror of democracy*. Verso.

Poblete, M. E. (2015). How to assess populist discourse through three current approaches. *Journal of Political Ideologies, 20*(2), 201–218.

Rydgren, J. (2005). Is extreme right-wing populism contagious? Explaining the emergence of a new party family. *European Journal of Political Research, 44*(3), 413–437.

Squire, P. (1992). Challenger quality and voting behavior in U.S. Senate elections. *Legislative Studies Quarterly, 17*(2), 247–263.

Stavrakakis, Y. (2004). Antinomies of formalism: Laclau's theory of populism and the lessons from religious populism in Greece. *Journal of Political Ideologies, 9*(3), 253–267.

Tamás, G. M. (2017). *The mystery of 'populism' finally unveiled*. OpenDemocracy. https://www.opendemocracy.net/en/can-europe-make-it/mystery-of-populism-finally-unveiled/.

Urbinati, N. (1998). Democracy and populism. *Constellations, 5*(1), 110–124.

Weyland, K. (2001). Clarifying a contested concept: Populism in the study of Latin American politics. *Comparative Politics, 34*(1), 1–22.

CHAPTER 27

The Framing of Right-Wing Populism: Intricacies of 'Populist' Narratives, Emotions, and Resonance

Julia Leser and Rebecca Pates

Introduction

After decades of researching populism, many questions still remain unanswered. In addition to the incongruities of defining what populism actually is, there is a lack of understanding of what is causing the global rise of populist parties (Hawkins et al., 2017, 356), in particular in regard to the many regional peculiarities of populist politics. For instance, the question of why the German right-wing populist party *Alternative für Deutschland* (AfD) continues to be more successful in Eastern Germany than in the West remains a puzzle. Prevalent explanations see voters' dissatisfaction with the political and social system as a reason for choosing the nationalist AfD. Depending on the theory, this dissatisfaction is associated with the feeling that progressive globalization leads to a loss of status, power, or economic stability in disenfranchised areas such as the German East (Patzelt, 2018, 887). Although research has shown that it is not necessarily 'the disenfranchised' who vote for the AfD, but rather people with higher and average incomes (e.g., Bergmann et al., 2016), it is still argued that Eastern AfD voters would be afraid of the future, because they are expected to be among the potential losers of Germany's modernization, characterized by economic globalization (Lengfeld, 2017, 227). Others

J. Leser (✉)
Department of European Ethnology, Humboldt University, Berlin, Germany
e-mail: julia.leser@hu-berlin.de

R. Pates
Department of Political Theory, Leipzig University, Leipzig, Germany
e-mail: pates@uni-leipzig.de

© The Author(s), under exclusive license to Springer Nature Switzerland AG 2022
M. Oswald (ed.), *The Palgrave Handbook of Populism*,
https://doi.org/10.1007/978-3-030-80803-7_27

suggest that the widespread dissatisfaction with democratic politics, and thus a greater share of populist sentiments, is the legacy of communism (Minkenberg, 2010; Mudde & Rovira Kaltwasser, 2017, 36), or that the rise of populism in the East is linked to "social disintegration and feelings of a lack of recognition" (Weisskircher, 2020, 7; cf. Kalmar & Shoshan, 2020). A multiplicity of hypotheses persists, yet upon taking a closer look, the electoral success of the AfD varies regionally within Eastern Germany, with more people voting for the AfD in rural areas and particularly in areas close to the Eastern border (Dellenbaugh-Losse et al., 2020).[1] The East is not *the* East. There are significant regional differences in voting behavior, and in addition, there is a lack of empirical evidence for most of the attributes that supposedly make Eastern Germans more prone to vote for populist parties.

The puzzling search for answers concerning the rise of the AfD in Eastern Germany reflects the greater struggle for researchers to come up with explanations for the rise of populist parties on a global level. Recently, there has been a "growing awareness of, and sensitivity to, the complexity but also to the seemingly irreconcilable contradictions inherent in contemporary radical right-wing populism" (Betz, 2020, 3). In order to embrace the complexities that constitute the global and multifaceted phenomenon of populism, we propose a), a shift of scholarly attention to the particularities of framing political issues in populist practice, and b), the facilitation of micropolitical approaches in researching these framing practices and their responses.

In regard to our first proposition, we agree with Michael Herzfeld who suggested that instead of asking "What is populism?," we should be asking "How does populism work?" (Herzfeld, 2019, 122; cf. Wodak, 2015, 2). For the effectiveness of populist politics is apparent, we should rather inquire how populist parties succeed in appealing to (potential) constituencies and mobilizing voters. How populism works has been discussed in terms of how framings and narratives are being used in populist rhetorics (e.g., Mayer et al., 2014; Wodak, 2015, 2019).[2] First, populist framings are commonly identified as promoting a "vision of society as divided into the two antagonistic moral categories of the 'pure' people and the 'corrupt' elites" (Mudde, 2007, 23). This framing promotes the construction of a social divide using a moral distinction, because 'the people' are "viewed not only as sovereign, but also as homogeneous, pure, and virtuous" while "[t]he elite is seen as 'evil'" (Akkerman et al., 2014, 1327; cf. Canovan, 1999). Second, there is a tendency in right-wing populist rhetorics to establishing problematic situations and, in particular, scenarios of crises that seemingly threaten the political imaginary of "the people" (Pelinka, 2018, 622; Wodak, 2015).[3] Third, populist rhetorics can be characterized in regard to offering "preconceived solutions" (Mayer et al., 2014, 253) to these scenarios, often in form of proposing "scapegoats that are blamed for threatening or actually damaging our societies" (Wodak, 2015, 1; cf. Jagers & Walgrave, 2007, 234). As a composition, these framings are seen as "ideational narratives" that seem to elicit "a panoply of emotions" (Betz, 2020, 4). Through these framings, populist parties are thought of as successfully constructing fear (Wodak, 2015), attributing blame (Busby et al., 2019; Hameleers et al., 2018), producing rage and anger toward imagined enemies (Jensen, 2017; Salmela & von Scheve, 2017), and elevating a sense of nostalgia for the "better" past (Gest et al., 2017; Göpffarth, 2020; Kenny, 2017; Steenvoorden & Harteveld, 2018).

Yet how emotions work in populist framings, narratives, and rhetorics to generate appeal remains unclear. Research suggests that latent populist sentiments and xenophobic resentments among the population can be activated by populist rhetorics (e.g., Hawkins et al., 2020). Emotions are thus thought of as providing a breeding ground for populism, and as resources that populist parties are able to mobilize, instrumentalize, and manipulate. But this conception is challenged in empirical research on the role of emotions in populist politics, and it has been shown that a focus on negative emotions tends to overlook the ambivalence and ambiguity of how emotions work in political practice (Busher et al., 2018, 4; Leser & Spissinger, 2020). While populist politics can be characterized by emotional dynamics, we should assume that these dynamics are more complex than manipulation or exploitation of people's sentiments and resentments (Herzfeld, 2019, 134; Mazzarella, 2019, 51). Emotional dynamics are better grasped in their situated nature and as functioning in "mechanisms of circulation, accumulation, expression, and exchange that give them social currency, cultural legibility, and political power" (Ioanide, 2015, 2). Thus, while a focus on populist framings, narratives and the use of emotions might certainly be of benefit for understanding populist parties' success, a closer look into the context and situatedness of populist framing practices and the modalities in which their emotional overtures resonate with (potential) constituencies is needed.

Thus, in regard to our second proposition, micropolitical approaches could improve our understanding of how populist mobilization works in practice and provide insights into why people might be attracted to populist politics, because "to engage in micropolitics is to pay attention to the connections between affective registers of experience and collective identities and practices" (Bennett & Shapiro, 2002, 5). While research on right-wing populism has been dominated by "externalist approaches" and a focus on either demand or supply side (Castelli Gattinara, 2020), we concur with Robert Jansen's (2011, 75–7) suggestion to treat "populism as a mode of political *practice*" and to "focus on actually enacted, spatially and temporally bounded projects of *populist mobilization*." In focusing on particular contexts and situations of populist practices, micropolitical approaches can be used to analyse how practices of framing and mobilization relate to, and connect with, the addressees of populist politics, and how they resonate with potential voters—either in microcontextual approaches that focus on framings, discourses, and narratives mobilized around particular topics (e.g., Herzfeld, 2019; Jensen, 2017), or approaches informed by political anthropology, e.g., ethnography and fieldwork in sites of right-wing populist mobilization (e.g., Göpffarth, 2020; Hochschild, 2016; Leser & Spissinger, 2020).[4]

In this contribution, we thus use a micropolitical approach to analyze how the right-wing populist party AfD framed the "wolf debate" in their campaigning efforts in Eastern Germany in 2019, and how these framings resonated with people in Eastern German rural areas that the AfD sought to address with these framings. This contribution draws on ethnographic data, interviews, and textual data such as official party statements, and offers a situated approach to understanding right-wing populism, providing insights into framing techniques that serve to cause affective resonance with people who, supposedly, feel left behind.

Populist Wolf Politics in Eastern Germany

During the 2019 regional state elections in three Eastern German *Länder*, the AfD succeeded in getting the highest results in their short history. In Saxony, Thuringia and Brandenburg, the party achieved more than 20% and came up second respectively. The timing of their success was "highly symbolic," as the elections "were held exactly three decades after the autumn of 1989, when mass protests in cities such as Berlin and Leipzig erupted in the GDR" (Weisskircher, 2020, 1). During the months preceding the state elections, right-wing populist parties such as the AfD and the (now dissolved) *Blue Party* took up the topic of the returning wolves to German territories as a campaigning subject. Almost extinct for 200 years, wolves had continued to return to Germany from Eastern Europe since the early 2000s.[5] In 2019, most of the wolves had settled in thinly populated areas, predominantly in the Eastern German states. And while sightings have been rare and most wolves remain invisible to human eyes, the topic of the wolves was made present and visible in the AfD campaigns targeted at rural populations.

In the German *Bundestag*, AfD politician Karsten Hilse among others problematized the return of wolves in speeches and petitions, claiming that the wolves would threaten "densely populated and agricultural areas (*Kulturlandschaften*)," particularly in the East, and that "the further spread of wolves should be limited," demanding an "upper limit" for the German wolf population and the permission to shoot wolves,[6] despite the fact that wolves in Germany are listed as a protected species. In his address to the *Bundestag* on February 21, 2019, Hilse stated in concern to the "wolf problem":

> What does the affected rural population say? What does the livestock owner do when the big bad wolf has repeatedly haunted his premises, when he finds his pasturage in the morning with his sheep barely alive, their bellies ripped open, their intestines oozing out, or their hind legs chewed on? He takes action. If a government leaves their people alone with their worries and commits a thousand-fold breaking of laws in regard to refugee and migration politics, then inhibitions are lowered, and people will take things into their own hands.[7]

In their campaigning efforts, and in multiple speeches, statements, campaigning events, and information materials, AfD politicians aimed for constructing a narrative of westward moving wolves into German territories—where they supposedly do not belong—and, as is apparent in Hilse's speech, rhetorically paralleling this emergent, threatening situation with a perceived "invasion" of migrants into Germany. The "culprit" in this narrative is "the government" who is framed as unresponsive to the "real" needs and worries of the affected population, and intentionally letting "those who do not belong" into our country (Pates & Leser, 2021). The solution Hilse proposed in his speech and in petitions was simple: people should have the right to shoot wolves.

While noting that this particular framing of "wolf politics" is undoubtedly populist in character, we further notice the visceral detail of wolves killing sheep in Hilse's speech. The wolf here is portrayed as a killer of whom the rural population in particular *should* be afraid. On local AfD election placards and flyers, pictures of children were used along with captions such as "Children in danger – Wolves advance further," and when we talked to AfD member of the Saxon parliament Ivo Teichmann, he told us,

> In my electoral district, pupils [...] were waiting for the bus and a wolf came by just a few meters away. They were lucky that the wolf wasn't hungry or aggressive. But especially in winter, when they're in peril, you never know how they would react. [...] Just before, the wolf came by a farm, there was an older lady who saw it, too [...] and she was very worried.[8]

Christoffer Kølvraa analyzed the *Danish People's Party's* (DPP) framing of the returning wolves to Denmark and observed in a similar manner that "[t]he effect of such subjunctive discourse was to shift the object of the political debate from the likelihood of being attacked by wolves on the basis of what is known, to the legitimacy of harbouring a fear of wolves on the basis of what might be imagined" (Kølvraa, 2020, 114). Thus, the strategy of the "returning wolves" narrative put forward by right-wing populist rhetorics aims at addressing anti-establishment sentiments by framing "the government" as the culprit, anti-immigration resentments by framing the returning wolves as a "dangerous invasion," and, in addition, nourishing fear of wolves instead of recognizing the scientific evidence.

Telling the story of returning wolves in this manner, the AfD as well as the *Blue Party* organized numerous campaigning events in the Eastern German rural areas, enacting themselves as those who take the local population's worries seriously, as the ones who come and listen. As a member of the Saxon parliament Kirsten Muster said to the agitated audience in one of the *Blue Party's* campaign events in Saxon Lusatia: "You are not included on this matter enough, you are not being heard enough."[9] What the party offered to agitated farmers whose sheep had been killed or who were at least afraid this could happen, is recognition of their worries, not judging them as irrational, and a valorization of their emotional interests—it is a promise of being taking seriously, of not being ashamed of one's own fears and worries, and of being listened to. It is through these promises and emotional overtures that populist rhetorics and performances work best, as Arlie R. Hochschild explained in the case of Trump's success in her ethnographic study of Trump supporters:

> Trump allowed them both to feel like a good moral American and feel superior to those they considered "other" or beneath them. This giddy, validating release produced a kind of "high" that felt good. And of course people wanted to feel good. The desire to hold on to this elation became a matter of *emotional self-interest*. (Hochschild, 2016, 230)

Similarly, the AfD portrays itself as attending to those (e.g., rural populations) deemed left behind and unrecognized by "established" parties. In these framings, however, the "left-behind" are coproduced in performance, and it remains a matter of inquiry how those addressed this way react to these emotional overtures, and how the populist framing of the returning wolves resonates with the affected populations.

THE COMPLEXITIES OF POPULAR RESENTMENTS

In our ethnographic exploration of the wolf issue in Eastern Germany's rural areas, in addition to attending campaigning events on the topic by various, including populist parties, we talked to numerous members of the rural population who were in one way or another affected by the return of wolves: sheep farmers, hunters, local business owners and associates of official wolf protection measures.[10] In accordance with similar research projects (e.g., Frank et al., 2016; Heinzer, 2016; Skogen et al., 2017; von Essen & Allen, 2017), we found a high degree of complexity and ambivalence in standpoints on the wolf issue, as well as "deeper" conflicts underlined by particular sentiments and resentments. We talked to people from pro- and anti-wolf camps, but the majority of people were ambivalent in their opinion, and in most instances, the wolf as such was not the *real* problem. For a hunter we talked to, regulating nature and wildlife populations are an inherently rightful human endeavour; wolves and other "invasive" animals, he argued, "are immigrating to Germany and causing problems." This conception of regulating migrating animal populations coincided with his anti-immigration sentiments: "To let people immigrate into a country increases the population density, and the conflicts in that country."[11] In his view, wolves are object to economic calculation, as is nature, as are the general migration dynamics of wolves and people alike. The wolf issue was an occasion to articulate general anti-immigration sentiments.

We furthermore found strong anti-urban sentiments, as "we [the rural population] are being governed by people living in the cities, because the majority and their sentiments decide the elections, and not us few who live in the countryside."¹² Many extended this feeling of unfair treatment to the voters of Green parties and nature conservation organizations who, after all, would support wolf protection measures rather than care about the needs of farmers protecting their sheep.

Underlying conflicts about "hierarchical social structures and power" (Skogen et al., 2017, 2) are essential in framing the wolf issue. In particular, populist sentiments in the sense of mistrust in government and a feeling of politicians' unresponsiveness to the problems of sheep farmers were prevalent in our explorations. Most sheep farmers in Eastern Germany face or have faced structural issues: Since reunification in 1989, Germany started to import wool, while many businesses in the East perished or transformed into large-scale operations. Small farmers in particular struggle. While they *can* apply for governmental subsidies to install necessary protection measures for their flocks in order to protect their sheep from wolf attacks, that involves complex bureaucratic procedures, and, as one farmer put it, "the farmer is not the kind of guy who sits down and fills in pages and pages of forms in order to get fences subsidized, [...] he didn't study filling-in forms."¹³ For farmers, an associate of a local NABU (*Nature and Biodiversity Conservation Union*) organization explained to us, the wolf issue means "extra work, expenses, and, in the worst case, the death of their animals."¹⁴ In her opinion, the sheep farming business in general was suffering immensely, not because of wolves, but because of the struggle to make profits. In addition, she felt that rural areas and agriculture in general have been neglected political issues for years, and she felt for the farmers, explaining,

> The farmers are lacking a lobby, and I feel that [...] through taking up wolves as an issue, the farmers are getting a voice and getting listened to in the first place, because farmers are sympathetic characters in society, politicians know that. There is a lot of coverage about how bad off farmers are. [...] and to take up that topic, and to get that attention, farmers can use that issue to point out their needs on the political level.¹⁵

Populist sentiments, i.e., the sense that politics is failing the farmers, are framed here as an important driving force, as a potential for making oneself heard. For many of the complicated structural issues affecting farmers in Eastern Germany, political recognition is lacking, and a form of "wolf populism" can be used to garner political attention. However, others problematize the perceived unresponsiveness of "established" politicians to farmers' problems as a force to drive people into the hands of populist parties. One farmer told us that he could understand his colleagues who vote for the AfD, because "it is a protest party, because you are not being heard, [...] but it cannot be the goal that people are so insecure that they vote for the AfD, can it? [...] Out of desperation? [...] It's not just tragic, it's dangerous."¹⁶ While they disqualified the AfD as a valid solution to their problems, these farmers still saw the potential of the populist party in resonating with people's discontent toward the "established" parties:

> Now, here, in the Eastern German *Länder*, the AfD is getting an upsurge, because of their big mouths, even if they don't have to offer any solutions, at least they're talking about the problems that are moving the people. [...] Even if they're, in my opinion, not capable of governing or having good concepts. But they're striking the people's feeling [...] as it was in 1985/1986, [the feeling] that the system is going down the pan, that nothing works anymore.[17]

In this view, voting for the AfD is framed as the last straw, the last means to *do politics*, at least to express one's own feeling of helplessness. Many farmers could relate to this perspective, but they still questioned the AfD's ability to make a change and thus, did not vote for them. Among the farmers we talked to, we met one owner of a large sheep farming business who openly, almost proudly, identified himself as an AfD voter. He explained,

> I vote for the AfD. [...] The big parties, [...] are drifting. [...] And I am doing very well, financially. And I don't have a lack of education either, [...] I have a university degree [...] and I am not afraid. I don't have 'diffuse fears'. I am okay with the wolf being here. [...] But many other people are not. [...] And this is my duty, as we were just talking about Christian responsibility, [...] social responsibility. It is my duty to speak up for these people who are not that strong, who are not that educated, who can't articulate their problems as well.[18]

While he felt the need to emphasize that he is neither deprived nor uneducated to challenge the perceived stigma of AfD voters, he simultaneously enacted the "simple" people who would need someone like him to speak up. During our interview, he continuously emphasized his support for the protection of nature and wildlife, but made it clear that he would not vote for the Green party, because in his eyes, the Greens were "decadent Bolsheviks who are disconnected from real life, [...] it is an urban intellectual upper class who vote for the Greens."[19] Thus, when people legitimize their voting for the AfD as an act of revolt and resistance, we need to look closer into the conception of those they are revolting against: Here, it is those who are construed in opposition to the "real" and the "simple" people, the Greens and those who vote Green, who are supposedly making decisions on "our" way of life but dismissing the issues that really lie in "our" interest. It is a performance of revolt against a felt stigmatization by those conceived "better than us."

Yet populism in the form of platitudes was often challenged by our interlocutors. "There are these platitudes like 'Nobody listens to me!'," said a volunteer at the Contact Office *Wolves in Saxony*, "how often am I hearing this! [...] and then there is no level of trust, and then people aren't talking at all."[20] While mistrust and anger at a political situation can be made productive, a simple reduction into a generalized mistrust "against all enemies" is seen as dangerous by many, because such an attitude would render any political discussion impossible. However, we encountered these populist sentiments "against all" not only in the anti-wolf camp, but among associates of nature protection organizations in the pro-wolf camp, too:

> If some laws are to be implemented, the people have to decide und not those who we voted into office. Because I didn't vote for them! They're not representing my opinion. They're representing their opinion, don't they? All liars, frauds, all of them. Politics, it's bad. [...] Now everybody complains about the AfD. Why are they so strong? I can tell you, because *they* [the government] made them strong. Because *they* are making all these promises and not keeping them.[21]

Skepticism toward "the government," and even a certain "culture of complaint" are not unusual, particularly in the Eastern German states, as ethnographer Juliane Stückrad (2010) has shown. This does not make Eastern Germans more prone to support populist parties in general. On the contrary, we observed many instances in which this form of skepticism extended to the politics of the AfD. During the already mentioned campaign event of the populist *Blue Party*, members of the audience openly questioned the credibility of their claims of "bringing change," and many farmers and hunters we talked to dismissed the AfD campaigns for their lack of offering valid solutions considering the wolf issue. One hunter fell into an agitated rant when the topic of the AfD came up, she said: "They're discussing this topic, but I won't expect them to have read even one scientific article, everything is composed of different stories and I just can't stand it!"[22] Populist parties provide particular narratives around the return of the wolves, offering a different kind of knowledge and emotional framing, and strategically, these are *supposed* to resonate with widespread populist sentiments among particular populations. Yet these overtures are also widely contested. With some people, this strategy of framing the return of wolves as a crisis resonates—but often for other reasons than striking the supposedly fertile grounds of fears and anxieties. Others remain skeptical to these overtures, or are even getting furious about the AfD's obvious strategy, and thus do not accept the epistemological premises of these framings—and in these instances, apparently, the attempted mobilization fails.

Conclusion

> [H]aving acknowledged the affective intensity of the populist symptom, we should avoid dismissing it as either cynically instrumental (a mode of manipulation) or as tactically ornamental (political style as surface distraction). How would our analysis look different if we granted the symptom its own integrity, its own truth? (Mazzarella, 2019, 51)

As Hans-Georg Betz (2020, 25) argues for the case of Eastern Germany, "[t]he experience of deprivation is bound to provoke a panoply of negative emotions, such as anxiety, frustration, anger and resentment," but these resentments do not automatically make voters for populist parties. The dynamics between anti-government resentments and populist overtures in particular are more complex than we might assume. Not the whole "East" of Germany suffers from deprivation and grievances, while some segments of the population do, and in particular instances, people have good reasons to call out political misrecognition of structural dilemmas. But it seems imperative to further understand the complexities of populist dynamics and the driving forces to gain political recognition of structural struggles. As Erica von Essen and Michael Allen (2017, 146) point out, "[u]nderstanding complexity and ambivalence may point to […] more flexible and productive policy responses that take seriously without valorizing reactionary movements."

As William Mazzarella puts it in the quote above, we should question the analytical benefit of suspending populist agents as mere seducers or exploiters of popular resentments. Indeed, populist parties attempt to appease to the rural population in Eastern Germany by framing the returning wolves as harbingers of crises, providing a narrative with clear-cut culprits and victims. And indeed, populist sentiments are widespread among these addressees. But sometimes these sentiments are enacted where we would not expect them, and the other way around, and often for reasons that go beyond the framings of populist parties. We should attend to these complexities and attune our analyses to the ambivalences in populist (non-)mobilization. Micropolitical approaches on populist framings can further our understanding of the local and topical particularities of populist sentiments and the shape that these take in regard to struggling with problems of the social, political, and even the seemingly *natural* worlds—in particular concerning cleavages in voting behavior (West/East, urban/rural) and our attempts to find explanations. Further, micropolitical approaches can deepen our understanding of how populist politics relate to and resonate with people's sentiments toward particular issues, and most importantly, how such politics do not relate and not resonate. Focusing on "resonant encounters" (Mazzarella, 2017, 136) we can grasp the dynamics between political parties and their (potential) constituencies, instead of analyzing both as separate entities. Exploring the lived realities of different people in different places, such approaches can shed light on the myriad of problems people are facing, on political agents offering solutions to these problems, and on the societal complexities that challenge democracies today.

Notes

1. The observation of a clear urban/rural divide in votes for the AfD is not only true for Eastern Germany, but the rural population shows a higher affinity for the AfD across the country. Similar trends can be observed in France

with regard to support for the Front National, in Great Britain with regard to support for Brexit or in the USA with regard to Trump supporters.
2. Populist rhetorics is understood as "an anti-elite, nationalist rhetoric that valorizes ordinary people" and is comprised of "collections of symbolic actions, styles of expression, public statements (spoken or written), definitions of the situation, and ways of elaborating ideas that broadly invoke or reinforce a populist *principle*, which reciprocally legitimates and animates political action" (Jansen, 2011, 83–84).
3. For the right-wing populist party *Freiheitliche Partei Österreichs* (FPÖ), Wodak (2019, 204) has identified, for example, a "threat scenario consisting of an imagined 'invasion' by so-called 'illegal migrants'," implying that people would be "claiming to be refugees but are in fact travelling to rich European countries to live off welfare and benefits, and thereby endanger the prosperity of those countries."
4. For an overview of anthropological research on populism, see Mazzarella (2019).
5. In 2018/2019, the Federal Documentation and Counselling Centre on the Topic of Wolves counted 145 wolf territories in Germany, including 105 wolf packs, 29 couples, and 11 lone wolves; see https://www.dbb-wolf.de/Wolfsvorkommen/territorien/status-und-reproduktion?Bundesland=&Jahr=2018 (Accessed on June 23, 2020).
6. Drucksache 19/594, German *Bundestag*, January 31, 2018.
7. K. Hilse, 'Wolfsmanagement und -monitoring', *Deutscher Bundestag: Parlamentsfernsehen*. [Video file] (21 February 2019), URL: www.bundestag.de/mediathek?videoid=7328919#url=L21lZGlhdGhla292ZXJsYXk/dmlkZW9pZD03MzI4OTE5JnZpZGVvaWQ9NzMyODkxOSZ2aWRlb2lkPTczMjg5MTk=&mod=mediathek [Accessed 24 November 2019], cited in Pates and Leser (2021); translation by the authors.
8. Interview with AfD politician I. Teichmann, 2019; all interview quotes have been translated by the authors.
9. K. Muster, *Blue Party* campaign event on the topic of wolves, Wittichenau (Saxony), January 23, 2019.
10. We are grateful to Pauline Betche and Anna Bentzien for letting us use their interviews in addition to our own material.
11. Interview with a hunter, Saxony, 2019.
12. Interview with a member of the farmers' association, Brandenburg, 2019.
13. Interview with a farmer/hunter, Mecklenburg-West Pomerania, 2019.
14. Interview with a NABU associate, Mecklenburg-West Pomerania, 2019.
15. Interview with a NABU associate, Mecklenburg-West Pomerania, 2019.
16. Interview with a farmer, Mecklenburg-West Pomerania, 2019.
17. Interview with a member of the farmers' association, Brandenburg, 2019.
18. Interview with a sheep farming business owner, Mecklenburg-West Pomerania, 2019.
19. Interview with a sheep farming business owner, Mecklenburg-West Pomerania, 2019.
20. Interview with a volunteer at the Contact Office *Wolves in Saxony*, 2019.
21. Interview with associate NABU, Saxony, 2019.
22. Interview with a hunter, Mecklenburg-West Pomerania, 2019.

Literature

Akkerman, A., Mudde, C., & Zaslove, A. (2014). How populist are the people? Measuring populist attitudes in voters. *Comparative Political Studies, 47*(9), 1324–1353.

Arzheimer, K., & Berning, C. C. (2019). How the Alternative for Germany (AfD) and their voters veered to the radical right, 2013–2017. *Electoral Studies, 60*, 102–140.

Bennett, J., & Shapiro, M. J. (2002). Introduction. In J. Bennett & M. J. Shapiro (Eds.), *The politics of moralizing* (pp. 1–10). Routledge.

Bergmann, K., Diermeier, M., & Niehues, J. (2016). *Parteipräferenz und Einkommen. Die AfD – eine Partei der Besserverdiener? IW-Kurzbericht 19*. Institut der Deutschen Wirtschaft Köln.

Betz, H.-G. (2020). The emotional underpinnings of radical right populist mobilization: Explaining the protracted success of radical right-wing populist parties. CARR Research Insight 2020.2. London, UK: Centre for Analysis of the Radical Right.

Busby, E. C., Gubler, J. R., & Hawkins, K. A. (2019). Framing and blame attribution in populist rhetoric. *The Journal of Politics, 81*(2), 616–630.

Busher, J., Giurlando, P., & Sullivan, G. B. (2018). Introduction: The emotional dynamics of backlash politics beyond anger, hate, fear, pride, and loss. *Humanity & Society, 42*(4), 399–409.

Canovan, M. (1999). Trust the people! Populism and the two faces of democracy. *Political Studies, 47*, 2–16.

Castelli Gattinara, P. (2020). The study of the far right and its three E's: Why scholarship must go beyond Eurocentrism, Electoralism and Externalism. *French Politics, 18*, 314–333.

Dellenbaugh-Losse, M., Homeyer, J., Leser, J., & Pates, R. (2020). Toxische Orte? Faktoren der regionalen Anfälligkeit für völkischen Nationalismus. In L. Berg & J. Üblacker (Eds.), *Rechtes Denken, Rechte Räume? Demokratiefeindliche Entwicklungen und ihre räumlichen Kontexte* (pp. 47–82). Transcript.

Frank, E., Heinzer, N., & Tschofen, B. (2016). *Wolfsmanagement als kultureller Prozess* (Working Paper zum Symposium). "WOLFSMANAGEMENT: WISSEN_SCHAF(F)T_PRAXIS". SNF-Projekt "Wölfe: Wissen und Praxis", ISEK – Institut für Sozialanthropologie und Empirische Kulturwissenschaft, Universität Zürich.

Gest, J., Reny, T., & Mayer, J. (2017). Roots of the radical right: Nostalgic deprivation in the United States and Britain. *Comparative Political Studies, 51*(13), 1694–1719.

Göpffarth, J. (2020). Activating the socialist past for a nativist future: Far-right intellectuals and the prefigurative power of multidirectional nostalgia in Dresden. *Social Movement Studies*, 1–18.

Hameleers, M., Bos, L., & de Vreese, C. (2018). Framing blame: Toward a better understanding of the effects of populist communication on populist party preferences. *Journal of Elections, Public Opinion and Parties, 28*(3), 380–398.

Hansen, M. A., & Olsen, J. (2019). Flesh of the same flesh: A study of voters for the Alternative for Germany (AfD) in the 2017 federal election. *German Politics, 28*(1), 1–19.

Hawkins, K. A., Read, M., & Pauwels, T. (2017). Populism and its causes. In C. Rovira Kaltwasser, P. A. Taggart, P. Ochoa Espejo, & P. Ostiguy (Eds.), *The Oxford handbook of populism* (1st ed., pp. 341–364). Oxford University Press.

Hawkins, K. A., Rovira Kaltwasser, C., & Andreadis, I. (2020). The activation of populist attitudes. *Government and Opposition, 55*(2), 283–307.

Heinzer, N. (2016). Der Wolf M64 im Lötschental. Ethnographische Schlaglichter aus einem Wolfsdurchzugsgebiet. *Schweizer Volkskunde, 106*(3), 62–66.

Herzfeld, M. (2019). How populism works. In B. Kapferer & D. Theodossopoulos (Eds.), *Democracy's paradox: Populism and its contemporary crisis* (pp. 122–138). Berghahn.

Hochschild, A. R. (2016). *Strangers in their own land: Anger and mourning on the American right.* The New Press.

Ioanide, P. (2015). *The emotional politics of racism: How feelings trump facts in an era of colorblindness.* Stanford University Press.

Jagers, J., & Walgrave, S. (2007). Populism as political communication style: An empirical study of political parties' discourse in Belgium. *European Journal of Political Research, 46*(3), 319–345.

Jansen, R. S. (2011). Populist mobilization: A new theoretical approach to populism. *Sociological Theory, 29*(2), 75–96.

Jensen, U. (2017). *Zornpolitik.* Suhrkamp.

Kalmar, I., & Shoshan, N. (2020). Islamophobia in Germany, East/West: An introduction. *Journal of Contemporary European Studies, 28*(1), 1–14.

Kenny, M. (2017). Back to the populist future? Understanding nostalgia in contemporary ideological discourse. *Journal of Political Ideologies, 22*(3), 256–273.

Kølvraa, C. (2020). Wolves in sheep's clothing? The Danish far right and 'wild nature'. In B. Forchtner (Ed.), *The far right and the environment: Politics, discourse and communication* (pp. 107–120). Routledge.

Lengfeld, H. (2017). Die „Alternative für Deutschland": Eine Partei für Modernisierungsverlierer? *Kölner Zeitschrift Für Soziologie, 38*, 379–399.

Leser, J., & Spissinger, F. (2020). The functionality of affects: Conceptualising far-right populist politics beyond negative emotions. *Global Discourse, 10*(2), 325–342.

Mayer, S., Ajanovic, E., & Sauer, B. (2014). Intersections and inconsistencies: Framing gender in right-wing populist discourses in Austria. *NORA—Nordic Journal of Feminist and Gender Research, 22*(4), 250–266.

Mazzarella, W. (2017). *The mana of mass society.* The University of Chicago Press.

Mazzarella, W. (2019). The anthropology of populism: Beyond the liberal settlement. *Annual Review of Anthropology, 48*(1), 45–60.

Minkenberg, M. (Ed.). (2010). *Historical legacies and the radical right in post-Cold War Central and Eastern Europe.* ibidem-Verlag.

Mudde, C. (2007). *Populist radical right parties in Europe.* Cambridge University Press.

Mudde, C., & Rovira Kaltwasser, C. (2017). *Populism: A very short introduction.* Oxford University Press.

Pates, R., & Leser, J. (2021). *The Wolves are coming back: On the politics of fear in Eastern Germany.* Manchester University Press.

Patzelt, W. J. (2018). Mängel in der Responsivität oder Störungen in der Kommunikation? Deutschlands Repräsentationslücke und die AfD. *Zeitschrift für Parlamentsfragen, 49*(4), 885–895.

Pelinka, A. (2018). Identity politics, populism and the far right. In R. Wodak & B. Forchtner (Eds.), *The Routledge handbook of language and politics* (pp. 618–629). Routledge.

Salmela, M., & von Scheve, C. (2017). Emotional roots of right-wing political populism. *Social Science Information, 56*(4), 567–595.

Skogen, K., Krange, O., & Figari, H. (2017). *Wolf conflicts: A sociological study*. Berghahn Books.

Steenvoorden, E., & Harteveld, E. (2018). The appeal of nostalgia: The influence of societal pessimism on support for populist radical right parties. *West European Politics, 41*(1), 28–52.

Stückrad, J. (2010). *"Ich schimpfe nicht, ich sage nur die Wahrheit": Eine Ethnographie des Unmuts am Beispiel der Bewohner des Elbe-Elster-Kreises, Brandenburg*. Ludwig.

von Essen, E., & Allen, M. (2017). A reluctant right-wing social movement: On the 'good sense' of Swedish hunters. *Journal of Rural Studies, 50*, 139–147.

Weisskircher, M. (2020). The strength of far-right AfD in Eastern Germany: The East-West divide and the multiple causes behind 'populism.' *The Political Quarterly*, 1–7.

Wodak, R. (2019). Entering the "post-shame era": The rise of illiberal democracy, populism and neo-authoritarianism in Europe. *Global Discourse, 9*(1), 195–213.

Wodak, R. (2015). *The politics of fear: What right-wing populist discourses mean*. Sage.

CHAPTER 28

Populism and Collective Memory

Luca Manucci

INTRODUCTION

History and memory are crucially different, and the way in which a society decides to remember its past has concrete, long-lasting consequences. Political actors and institutions compete to organize collective memories and memorialize the past because it allows them to select which aspects to pass on, forget, or silence.[1] The outcome of this—often conflictual—process reflects how a country decides to remember and commemorate its own past thus forming a representation of its present. Collective memories have three main effects for the study of populism in a given society, country, or political system: first, collective memories determine which ideas of power are acceptable; second, they shape the national collective identity; third, they define the realm of what can be said in the public debate.

This means that different collective memories create favorable conditions for some political ideologies and unfavorable conditions for others. In particular, in this chapter I analyze the links between collective memories of an authoritarian past and the social acceptability of the populist ideology. The argument is that in countries with collective memories that strongly stigmatize the authoritarian past, populism is less likely to be socially acceptable, while in countries that silence, deny, or refuse to acknowledge the authoritarian past, populism is more likely to thrive (Manucci, 2020).

L. Manucci (✉)
Institute of Social Sciences, University of Lisbon, Lisbon, Portugal
e-mail: luca.manucci@ics.ulisboa.pt

© The Author(s), under exclusive license to Springer Nature Switzerland AG 2022
M. Oswald (ed.), *The Palgrave Handbook of Populism*,
https://doi.org/10.1007/978-3-030-80803-7_28

The way in which a society remembers and memorializes its past has profound implications. Individual behaviors, values and voting preferences can be linked to past events and how those events have been framed, narrated and included into a collective myth that often relies on invented traditions (Hobsbawm, 1983). Therefore it is not surprising to observe that politicians use mythologized understandings of the past to mobilize memory as an instrument of politics and identity in the present, manipulating collective memories for ideological purposes (Ricoeur, 2004; Verovšek, 2016). The struggle over an official, national memory of the past is so important because it determines the social acceptability and electoral success of different ideas of power, including populism.

Despite the fact that populism has been studied from a multitude of perspectives, disciplines and approaches, this chapter insists on the importance of an aspect too often overlooked: collective memories. Why are collective memories relevant for the study of populism? They are relevant because 'what and how societies remember and forget largely determines their future options. Myths and memories define the scope and nature of action, reorder reality and legitimate power holders' (Barahona de Brito & Sznajder, 2010, p. 500). The legitimacy of populist actors, in other words, is determined, among other things, by collective memories.

In order to understand contemporary populism, its success or failure, its acceptability or rejection, it is essential to study collective memories of the authoritarian past because the process of memory-building shapes collective identities, determining who we are, and who we are not (Berger, 2002). In particular, collective memories of traumatic pasts usually frame elected elites, immigrants, or various out-groups as morally corrupt enemies of the nation (Levitsky & Ziblatt, 2018; Zubrzycki & Woźny, 2020). The way in which we decide to remember our past forms a collective identity that resonates with a populist construction of 'the people' and its enemies.

This is relevant because populism divides society along the lines of those who belong to a community, a more or less broad understanding of 'the people' based on cultural, moral or economic elements, and those who are excluded from it and therefore are its enemies, a specific elite or some alien group according to the type of populist discourse articulated. This implies that defining a 'people' requires first to construct 'powerful myths that draw on a collective memory of an imagined past in order to define who belongs to "the people"' (Bull, 2016, p. 217).

The relationship between collective memories and political power is far from being just a debate for political theorists, since it can manifest itself in disruptive confrontations. For example, heated debates cyclically arise about the name of streets and squares or the presence of statues that remind us of a history that we no longer want to celebrate. The death of George Floyd, a black man killed by the police in Minneapolis, Minnesota, prompted a new wave of Confederate memorial removals across the United States. In a rapid escalation, the statue of seventeenth-century slave trader Edward Colton was hauled to the ground and into Bristol harbor, and Belgium started a critical reflection about the statues commemorating King Leopold II, responsible for the death of 10 million people in Congo.

Statues represent a narrow and rather superficial aspect of the memorialization of the past, but they are powerful symbols because they are the plastic manifestation of collective memories once they crystallize and become tangible.[2] Removing a statue of Cecil Rhodes, who paved the way for apartheid in South Africa, does not automatically mean that justice is restored and the process of coming to terms with the colonial past is concluded. In fact, collective memories are neither permanent nor immutable: they are the result of continuous negotiations and conflicts.[3] The past, or rather the collective memory we elaborate about that past, provides the guidelines for the rejection or acceptance of certain beliefs (e.g. racism), ideas (e.g. nationalism), but also political actors and discourses, including populist ones. For this reason 'any conception of politics that ignores the power that myths or memories play in moulding identities and structures of power is destined to fail' (Bell, 2008, p. 162).

To explore the impact of collective memories on the acceptability of populism, the chapter is structured as follows. In the next section, I define collective memories and the ways in which they can illuminate the success or failure of contemporary populism. I explain that the study of populism should be connected to the literature on democratization and authoritarian legacies, arguing that this connection introduces often-neglected cultural and historical factors. The following section presents empirical cases for the study of populism through the lenses of collective memories, with examples from Europe and Latin America, showing how the formation of different collective memories of the authoritarian past can concretely affect the levels of social acceptability for populist discourses. I conclude by discussing directions for future research and proposing to consider also memories concerning not only authoritarianism but also colonialism and civil wars and their impact on contemporary populism.

Authoritarian Past and Populism

Collective memories can shape political scenarios for centuries, and in many different ways. In Germany, for example, the same places that witnessed violent attacks on Jews during the Black Death plague in 1349 showed more anti-Semitic attitudes five hundred years later: their inhabitants engaged in more anti-Semitic violence in the 1920s and were more likely to vote for the Nazi Party before 1930 (Voigtländer & Voth, 2012). Wodak and Forchtner (2014) focus on the memories of the victory of a Christian coalition over Ottoman forces besieging Vienna in 1683 and how this event still provides a reservoir for anti-Turkish sentiments. In particular, they show how the right-wing populist Freedom Party of Austria (*Freiheitliche Partei Österreichs*—FPÖ) used a comic book for its political propaganda by constructing

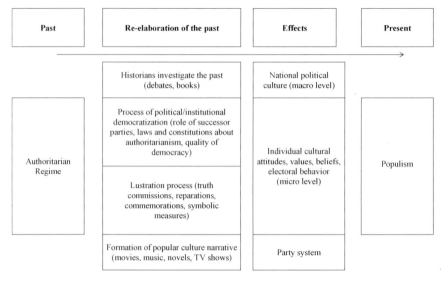

Fig. 28.1 How the authoritarian past shapes the populist present

a populist worldview where the underdog FPÖ is with 'the people' while opposing Muslim migrants and the 'Social-Democratic establishment'.

In this chapter, however, I focus on the links between populism and a specific type of collective memories: those built around an authoritarian past. This choice is due to two main reasons: first, authoritarian regimes and populist actors share a set of illiberal elements, and second, the literature on authoritarian legacies and democratization offers many points of contact for the study of populism. Concretely, to link the collective memories of an authoritarian past to the success or failure of populism, the analysis should follow these two steps. First, it is necessary to examine how new democratic regimes that faced an authoritarian experience decide to incorporate that past into national history (Aguilar & Humlebaek, 2002, p. 121), in other words which collective memories of the authoritarian past are formed. At this point, it is possible to evaluate to what extent these collective memories constitute an advantage or a disadvantage for populist actors and discourses. The next sections disentangle these two steps and provide a detailed account of the reasons behind this approach (Fig. 28.1).

Authoritarian Past

As already mentioned above, I focus on the memory of authoritarian regimes because they share a number of illiberal elements with contemporary populism. Whether one follows a discursive approach (Laclau, 2005; Mouffe, 2005), an ideational definition (Hawkins & Rovira Kaltwasser, 2017; Mudde, 2004) or understands populism as a type of mobilization (Jansen, 2011), it is possible to connect the study of populism to the literature on collective memories because of populism's inherently illiberal nature.[4] While it is possible that populist actors embrace, at a discursive level, liberal values such as free speech, gender equality and minorities' protection, populism remains essentially illiberal for three reasons. First, populists consider political opponents as enemies rather than legitimate adversaries, accusing them to betray the interests of the common people (Jansen, 2011). Second, in a majoritarian understanding of democracy they consider the 'will of the people' as corresponding to any opinion expressed by a majority, with disregard for minority rights and checks and balances (Pinelli, 2011). Third, at the institutional level populist actors almost invariably attack the press and hinder the independence of the judiciary system, claiming of doing so to return the power to 'the people' against corrupt elites (Krämer, 2018; Prendergast, 2019).

Populism shares several illiberal elements of past authoritarian regimes independently from its ideological, religious or social features. For example, in Latin America neoliberal and conservative populists (Carlos Menem in Argentina, Alberto Fujimori in Peru, Fernando Collor de Mello in Brazil), as well as left-wing populists (such as Hugo Chavez of Venezuela, Evo Morales of Bolivia and Rafael Correa of Ecuador) have damaged liberal democracy and established competitive authoritarianism that controls the media and undermines the opposition.[5] Moreover, comparing three populist leaders such as Recep Tayyip Erdoğan, Hugo Chávez and Rafael Correa, it emerges that left, right or religious populism operates through similar mechanisms: an anti-establishment image, a plebiscitary understanding of democracy and a Manichean worldview (Selçuk, 2016). Finally, populist actors in power usually undermine liberal democracy and establish some form of illiberal, authoritarian rule: recent examples include Hungary, India, Turkey, Brazil and the Philippines.

For these reasons, populism is often considered to be a threat for liberal democracy (Rovira Kaltwasser, 2012) and is labeled as proto-totalitarian (Abts & Rummens, 2007; Urbinati, 1998): once it becomes part of the political landscape, it makes that system irreconcilable with liberal democracy. One can therefore expect that in countries stigmatizing and rejecting the authoritarian past, populism will be unsuccessful in elections and socially not acceptable as a discourse. On the other hand, populism will thrive in countries that did not come to terms with their past, and where therefore the authoritarian past enjoys a certain degree of legitimacy or, at least, the absence of a social and political stigma. Given the characteristic of authoritarian regimes, the literature investigating the effects of authoritarian legacies mostly focused on penalizing effects on electoral performances of radical and extreme political parties (Golder, 2003). These studies are mostly about Europe and its fascist past, and observe the presence of a series of constraints showing that the stigmatization of populist ideas is stronger when those ideas are proposed in combination with a radical or extreme ideology (Caramani & Manucci, 2019). As Jan-Werner Müller (2016) argues, after World War II, European political systems were built on a distrust of popular sovereignty fueled by the experience of fascism.

Collective memories can help explain the presence, success and social acceptability of populism when used in combination with other supply- and demand-side variables. While political opportunity structures are a well-established field of research, and the mediatization of politics is emerging as an increasingly important one (Stanyer et al., 2017), cultural opportunity structures should be considered when analyzing the social acceptability of populist messages. Economic performance, levels of corruption, credibility of populist actors and other short-term factors interact with cultural, long-term opportunity structures and together affect the success and acceptability of populism across countries. The next section illustrates how, from an empirical point of view, different collective memories of an authoritarian past can create more or less favorable conditions for populism's social acceptability.

Authoritarian Legacies

When the authoritarian past is analyzed in relationship with contemporary politics, the focus is normally on the effects of authoritarian legacies on individuals rather than on the impact of collective memories on societies. The argument proposed here is that authoritarian legacies and the study of collective memories of the authoritarian past are not mutually exclusive: to the contrary, they are complementary approaches that can illuminate different aspects of contemporary populism, including its electoral performance and its social acceptability.

The literature on authoritarian legacies is burgeoning despite little consensus on how to conceptualize them (Wittenberg, 2015), and especially how to empirically measure them and establishing their effects (Simpser et al., 2018). Several studies focus on Eastern Europe, its communist or pre-communist legacies and their impact on patterns of electoral behavior, state-society relations, quality of democracy and attitudes toward democracy (Grzymała-Busse, 2002; Neundorf, 2010; Pop-Eleches & Tucker, 2020). Other studies focus on Latin American and South European countries, concluding that past authoritarian regimes and their legacies have influenced, and continue to influence, democratic practice. In particular, 'authoritarian legacies stand a better chance of being eliminated if democratic reforms and democrats themselves seek to contribute to a public sphere that engages in collective debates over memories' (Hite & Cesarini, 2004, p. 17). The impact of authoritarian legacies on the democratization process, party systems and quality of democracy should focus on the presence of populist actors and discourses, their electoral performance and social acceptability.

Linked to the study of authoritarian legacies, although often implicitly, is the literature on transitional justice. It focuses on truth commissions, trials, purges, compensations and amnesties as a way of dealing with authoritarian legacies, as well as museums, street name changes and forensic work (Barahona de Brito & Sznajder, 2010). The connection between collective memory, transitional justice and democratization has become the focus of much scholar attention: first concerning countries from the third wave of democratization (de Brito et al., 2001), and since the fall of the Berlin Wall also on Central and East Europe (David, 2015; Nalepa, 2010).

Recent studies on democratization and authoritarian legacies, show that parties' ideological stances are judged by their policy implications but also assessed according to whether they are opposed to the ideology of the previous regime (Dinas, 2017). Moreover, the ideology of the previous regime can affect public opinion and party competition after the democratic transition (Dinas & Northmore-Ball, 2020). Scholars should stress more explicitly the links between populism and the literature on transitional justice and democratization, to determine the effects of lustration mechanisms, successor parties and democratization process on the performance of populist actors and social acceptability of populist discourses. The next section illustrates how to do so by providing concrete examples.

Empirical Applications

This section presents an overview of empirical cases showing how fascist, communist and military regimes produce long-lasting legacies that can throw some light on the electoral performance of populist actors and the social acceptability of populist discourses. The focus is on Europe and Latin America both for reasons of space and because it is possible to observe the impact of authoritarian legacies only when a democratization process took place. For example, in post-soviet countries (the only exception being the Baltic States) the status of democracy, pluralism, and civil society is at best ambiguous (March, 2017). Other interesting cases would have deserved more attention. For example, Japan struggles to come to terms with Second World War history (Seaton, 2007) and it is often depicted as a country suffering from collective amnesia and depicting itself as a victim (Berger, 2012). Mongolia approved a law that grants compensation for the victims of Stalinist political repression, but never established a truth commission and chose not to pursue the perpetrators of violence, indicating a general repression of public memory (Kaplonski, 2008).[6]

A burgeoning literature examines populism in Europe, but its links to the legacies of both fascism and communism have rarely been the object of systematic and comparative analyses.[7] Germany, in particular, has been considered for a long time immune to right-wing populism and radical right parties because it came to terms with its Nazi past (a process called *Vergangenheitsbewältigung*).[8] While a culture of contrition prevented a resurgent far right in Germany, Austria nourished a culture of victimization that proved to be favorable for the rise of right-wing populism (Art, 2006). Assuming the guilt for the atrocities of the Nazi regimes reduced the opportunity structures for the far right as well as right-wing populist actors, at least until the recent success of Alternative for Germany (Arzheimer, 2019). In Italy, a country that never came to terms with its fascist and colonial past (Focardi, 2013), the post-fascist party National Alliance became part of the first Berlusconi's government in the 1990s, and two members of the family Mussolini ran for a seat in the European Parliament elections of 2019.

Three Southern European countries belonging to the third wave of democratization—Greece, Portugal and Spain—have been compared in terms of party system and electoral behavior (Gunther, 2005), authoritarian legacies (Barahona de Brito & Sznajder, 2010) and democratization processes (Cavallaro & Kornetis, 2019).[9] Moreover, the bias against a right-wing ideology due to the authoritarian past, may explain why the right-wing parties of Greece, Portugal and Spain have been constantly treated by their electorates as the most right-wing in Europe, despite these parties holding relatively moderate right-wing positions according to their manifestos (Dinas, 2017). Recently, the performance of populist far-right parties in Portugal and Spain has been examined by taking into consideration the levels of stigma attached to the authoritarian regimes of Francisco Franco and António de Oliveira Salazar (Mendes & Dennison, 2020; Manucci, 2020).

This type of research constitutes an excellent example of how the impact of collective memories of the authoritarian past can influence the presence and success of populism in contemporary politics. Spain, similarly to what happened in Chile with the regime of Augusto Pinochet, went through a *ruptura pactada*, which allowed the regime of Francisco Franco to negotiate its departure.[10] Consequently, 'letting bygones be bygones' became a foundation for democratic consolidation and a politics of forgetting created and solidified the country's democratic institutions (Aguilar, 2008; Encarnación, 2014). This seemed to form a strong stigma against populist radical right parties (Alonso & Rovira Kaltwasser, 2015), at least until 2019 when Vox became the third most voted for party in Spain. Similarly, in Portugal the carnation revolution that ended almost half a century of authoritarian rule enjoyed a large consensus, and this created mechanisms that closed the window of opportunity for the radical right (Pinto, 2006), although there is higher agreement regarding 'authoritarian legacies' compared to 'transitional legacies' (Raimundo & Generoso de Almeida, 2019).[11] Also in Greece all political forces recognized the dictatorship era (1967–1974) as a major setback but, contrary to Portugal, the country experienced populism since the early 1980s when PASOK established its long hegemony, a feature of the Greek political system that was reactivated after the economic crisis of 2008. The socio-economic crisis became a crisis of representation (Halikiopoulou & Vasilopoulou, 2018), and populist parties could be found both in power and in opposition, and across the ideological spectrum (Stavrakakis & Katsambekis, 2019).

Communist legacies in East Europe are well studied, in particular their effects on electoral behavior and values (Pop-Eleches & Tucker, 2011) and their impact on party systems and competition (Grzymała-Busse, 2006). Shortly after the fall of the Berlin Wall, George Schöpflin (1993) correctly predicted that post-communist legacies would haunt the region even after the democratic systems and rule of law were instituted. Indeed, those legacies have an impact on the success of radical right parties in Eastern Europe (Bustikova & Kitschelt, 2009) and countries in Central and Eastern Europe continue to experience informal legacies and to be divided between the 'winners' of the transition and reform processes and the losers (Seleny, 2007). In Poland, the right-wing populist party Law and Justice (Prawo i Sprawiedliwość—PiS) originated from the anti-communist Solidarity trade union, and it continues to fight the influence of the Communist era security apparatus in Polish society (Pankowski, 2010). As early as 2006–2007 a three-party populist coalition attempted to break with the liberal-democratic model of post-communist transition, arguing that radical action was necessary in order to remove from power a network of politicians, business people and media figures associated with the communist regime (Stanley, 2016).[12] In a similar way, Hungary successfully transitioned from communism to liberal democracy, only to experience an autocratic evolution a few years later (Pappas, 2014). The populist radical right party of Viktor Orbán, Fidesz, carried out a systematic devaluation of 1989 as a revolution, insisting on the interwar period—when Hungary was ruled by right-wing autocrat (and ally of Hitler) Miklós Horthy—as a foundational myth for the country (Palonen, 2018).[13]

Other former communist countries reckoned with their past more or less successfully. In Romania, Bulgaria and Slovakia communism is the most relevant legacy in explaining what makes the citizens of these countries endorse democracy, regret communism or turn to populism. The poor performance of governments and their lack of accountability led to populism because the 'populist syndrome' is caused by residual authoritarianism. In particular, 'considering minorities a threat, agreeing with the government bypassing parliament and approving communism retrospectively turn out to be predictors' for a populist vote (Mungiu-Pippidi & Mindruta, 2002, p. 209).

Former Yugoslavia, where communist legacies are intertwined with military conflicts and ethnic nationalism, received less attention but its transition to democracy and the formation of populist movements has not been completely neglected. In the late 1980s populism began to bloom as a reaction to the crisis and then disintegration of the Yugoslav federation, originating the so-called anti-bureaucratic revolution of 1988–1989 (Mikucka-Wójtowicz, 2019). In Serbia and Croatia, the current 'wave of populism' stems from the unfulfilled expectations of democracy. In Serbia, a country that hardly came to terms with its past, a politician who used to praise war criminal Ratko Mladić and his greater Serbian ideology such as Aleksandar Vučić has been elected Prime Minister in 2014 and then President in 2017. In Slovenia the process of state formation brought about both ethno-nationalist and ethno-religious populism, with the construction of new enemies and groups of 'others' (Pajnik et al., 2016).

Latin America is another region that would particularly benefit a comparative analysis of authoritarian legacies, since most countries in the last decades experienced military dictatorships and populist governments. In Brazil, because of the dark legacy of the 1964–1985 military regime, politicians have been reluctant to define themselves as right wing (Power & Zucco, 2009), a phenomenon nicknamed *direita envergonhada* (ashamed right) referring to political conservatives who do not wish to identify themselves as such. Things changed in the last decade, when the pervasive 'culture of amnesia' gave place to a more active 'politics of memory' (Schneider, 2011). However, this 'turn to memory' did not enhance the country's democratic credentials but rather allowed president Bolsonaro to foster a vision of the dictatorship as a 'democratic revolution' (Ryan, 2016), to the point of ordering the country's armed forces to commemorate the 55th anniversary of the 1964 military coup.

In Argentina, the legacy of the military dictatorship also known as National Reorganization Process (1976–1983) has always been very relevant, and the fact that it was preceded by decades of Peronism adds a further layer of memories to deal with, to the point that one could argue that Argentine fascism shaped the country's political culture (Finchelstein, 2014). Despite a very active discussion about the country's authoritarian past, with human rights organizations and left-wing parties pressing for justice, the lack of a real closure represents a political-cultural impediment to more profound democratization (Muller et al., 2016).

The military dictatorship of Augusto Pinochet (1973–1990) left profound marks on the political culture and democratization process of a Chile. As a result, the country remains haunted by divided memories (Wilde, 1999) and the party system is deeply influenced by the cleavage between those who supported authoritarian rule and those who opposed it (Torcal & Mainwaring, 2003). After one year of intense protests often repressed by the police, a national plebiscite to change the constitution adopted under the military dictatorship of Augusto Pinochet was held in 2020, starting a process of institutional distancing from the legacies of Pinochet's dictatorship.[14]

Conclusions

Authoritarian legacies and collective memories are relevant for the comprehension of populism because they form a blueprint for the legitimacy or stigmatization of populist actors and discourses. With the passage from an authoritarian regime to democracy, engaging in a collective process of *Vergangenheitsbewältigung* creates varying degrees of legitimacy for political discourses promoting illiberal ideas of power, as well as a certain ideological bias in reaction to the ideology of the past authoritarian regime. In other cases, the authoritarian past can be used as mythological material for the creation of a society that rejects pluralism, rule of law and minority rights.

Populism can instrumentally manipulate the past to justify new lines of conflict between those that belong to an imagined community and those who are excluded from it. As we have seen, this can happen in two ways. First, when a country does not come to terms with its past and the collective memory of the authoritarian regime fails to produce a stigma of that idea of power. Second, when a past authoritarian regime is strongly condemned and this produces an ideological shift that rejects the past and legitimizes populist actors opposing the past regime. In both cases, countries that experienced an authoritarian past and then transitioned to liberal democracy are more likely to legitimize populist ideas of power that reject liberal principles. This, in turn, can produce a further vulnerability of democracy and lead toward a return of authoritarian tendencies, whether or not procedural democratic principles are respected.

The constant re-negotiation of the meanings to attribute to the past, as the chapter has shown, is an always-changing conflictual process. For example, in 2014 Dilma Roussef's government launched a truth commission that published an exhaustive report of dictatorship abuses, and in 2019, Jair Bolsonaro became president of Brazil promoting, among other things, a positive image of the military government while downplaying the human rights abuses it perpetrated. Every generational or political cohort can influence the way in which collective memories evolve: textbooks, official celebrations, museums, symbolic gestures, reparations, truth commissions, books, movies, to name just a few, are tools that contribute to this process.

While this chapter focused on authoritarian regimes, it is important to mention that other types of collective memories. For example, colonialism, slavery and wars interact with other aspects of a country's past and contribute to shape its collective identity and political culture. Colonialism played an important role in producing mostly inclusive populism in Latin America and exclusionary populism in Europe. In particular, its "hierarchic and exclusionary traits will continue to influence the conceptualization of the people, and the effect of this influence on populist movements depends on the position of such movements vis-à-vis the colonial relationship" (Filc, 2015, p. 269).

The wounds left by systemic racism are still visible in the United States, where monuments and memorials dedicated to the Confederate States of America, a government that fought for the perpetuation and expansion of slavery, are the object of much controversy. It is interesting to note that even the confederate general Robert Lee opposed building public memorials to the rebellion, arguing they would keep open the war's many wounds. Political attitudes, electoral behavior and public opinion, including racial antagonism and ideological conservatism (Valentino & Sears, 2005) and self-identification with the Republican party (Acharya et al., 2016) are still largely affected by the legacies of the civil war. The election of Donald Trump in 2016—preceded by the Charleston church shooting in 2015 and followed by the

Unite the Right rally in Charlottesville in 2017—, the protests against confederate monuments and the requests of the Black Lives Matter movement, all resonate with long-lasting historic legacies and collective memories.

Future research should investigate also subnational and international levels of collective memories. For example, as the German case shows, the country developed two different memories of the Nazi past and the Holocaust since the West and the East fell under the influence of the Allies and the Soviet Union respectively, and this is reflected in the success of populist parties like AfD and Die Linke in the East compared to the West. In a similar way, Belgium shows how two regions with different historical legacies such as Flanders and Wallonia manifest different reactions of mainstream parties and the media that, in turn, produce very different levels of success for populist radical right parties (de Jonge, 2020). Collective memories also have an international dimension, as Aleida Assmann suggests when talking about the role of the Holocaust universal reference and global icon forming a transnational memory (Assmann, 2010).

Furthermore, future research should investigate the links between lustration mechanisms and authoritarian legacies to determine what kind of reparations, commissions and symbolic gestures allow countries to come to terms with their past and stigmatize authoritarian tendencies. In particular, how the process of *Vergangenheitsbewältigung* translates in terms of opportunity structures for populist actors at the institutional level and in terms of patterns of democratic consolidation. Moreover, it is essential to study how collective memories affect cultural attitudes and electoral behavior at the individual level through surveys that explore, in a direct way, the links between individual memory, evaluation of the past authoritarian regime, ideological self-placement and the presence of populist attitudes.

Finally, it is important to understand how communities form and negotiate collective memories, for how long these memories have an impact on political culture and individual values, when and under which circumstances they start fading. While a correct process of socialization can prevent the fading of collective memories, a natural generational change combined with the advent of new critical junctures might change the approach toward official narratives of the past. Over time, societies perceive the 'remote' past as less and less relevant for the present, and this mechanism is crucial to understand contemporary democracies as well as populist tendencies.

Notes

1. Maurice Halbwachs, who died in the Nazi concentration camp of Buchenwald and was one of the first scholars to explore the collective dimension of memory, argued that collective memory is always mediated through complex mechanisms of conscious manipulation by elites and unconscious absorption by members of society (1925). However, it would be misleading to ignore also a bottom-up dimension of memory-building, in which social movements can bring certain

issues into the limelight, putting pressure on the elites and contributing to shape the country's collective memory.
2. A community collectively remembers and ritualizes its past through commemorations and holidays, names of public streets and squares, statues, textbooks and symbolic actions, but also elements of popular culture such as movies and TV shows. Several studies, for example, show that the media influence and shape collective perceptions of the past, see e.g. (Kligler-Vilenchik et al., 2014; Neiger et al., 2011).
3. Several factors can trigger an evolution or a metamorphosis in collective memories: e.g. the emergence of social movements, debates among historians, international controversies and trials.
4. Moffitt (2020) argues that populism can be considered as inherently illiberal only following an ideational approach. However, in the following paragraphs I show how populism is an illiberal phenomenon regardless of its definition.
5. This inevitably eroded horizontal accountability in Latin American countries governed by populist politicians (Ruth, 2018).
6. Moreover, one could observe how in Turkey, collective memory of the Armenian genocide and past wrongs against several minorities (including Kurdish and Alevi), are still far from the mainstream (Kaya, 2017).
7. A growing literature observes how Europe built its politics of memory (Fogu & Kansteiner, 2006; Judt, 1992; Müller, 2002), and came to terms with its authoritarian past (Borejsza & Ziemer, 2006). Rousso (1990) focused on the memory of the Nazi occupation in France, speaking of a "Vichy Syndrome" because of the reluctance to come to terms with the past. However, in memory studies the connection to populism is often missing. Single country studies make a connection between the fascist past and populism (Betz, 1988; Kitschelt & McGann, 1995) but in a non-systematic way.
8. This does not mean that the German process of coming to terms with the past was easy or completely spontaneous. In fact, Germany started it only in the 1950s and under pressure from the Allies. Moreover, Eastern Germany followed a very different script since it fell under the Soviet influence and therefore developed a radically different collective memory of the Holocaust and the Nazi past. In particular, the East defined itself in heroic terms for having defeated Nazism (Herf, 1997).
9. Interestingly, during the protests against austerity measures imposed by the European institutions during the Great recession, in all three countries the social protests established a parallel between the lack of democracy during the authoritarian past and the impositions of the Troika (Fishman, 2019; Kornetis, 2019; Lobo et al., 2016, p. 164).
10. Interestingly, Aleida Assmann (2014) argues that what has developed over the years between Spain and Argentina is a case of transnational memory-alliance relating to the respective traumatic legacies. Moreover, she claims that the introduction of Argentinian terminology and symbols (e.g. *desaparecido*) served as an external trigger for Spanish memories to re-emerge in the social debates.
11. In 2019, the far right party Chega obtained a seat in the parliament, thus ending Portuguese 'exceptionalism'.
12. PiS won the elections again in 2015 fueling anti-establishment and anti-communist sentiments and representing a backlash against the liberal turn of the post-Soviet world and the revolt against the elites that after 1989 reached a 'liberal consensus' considered as illegitimate.

13. Poland and Hungary have populist parties not only in power, but also in opposition: the Kukiz'15 movement in Poland, led by punk rock musician turned politician Paweł Kukiz, and the radical and nationalist Jobbick in Hungary.
14. The authoritarian past re-emerged also in May 2020 when Pinochet's great-niece, Macarena Santelices, became Chile women's minister, and she had to resign because before her nomination she had praised the 'good side' of a dictatorship in which over 300 women were raped under torture.

Literature

Abts, K., & Rummens, S. (2007). Populism versus democracy. *Political Studies, 55*(2), 405–424.

Acharya, A., Blackwell, M., & Sen, M. (2016). The political legacy of American Slavery. *The Journal of Politics, 78*(3), 621–641.

Aguilar, P. (2008). Transitional or post-transitional justice? Recent developments in the Spanish case. *South European Society and Politics, 13*(4), 417–433.

Aguilar, P., & Humlebaek, C. (2002). Collective memory and national identity in the Spanish democracy. *History & Memory, 14*(1/2), 121.

Alonso, S., & Rovira Kaltwasser, C. (2015). Spain: No country for the populist radical right? *South European Society and Politics, 20*(1), 21–45.

Art, D. (2006). *The politics of the Nazi past in Germany and Austria*. Cambridge University Press.

Arzheimer, K. (2019). "Don't Mention the War!" how populist right-wing radicalism became (almost) normal in Germany. *Journal of Common Market Studies, 57*, 90–102.

Assmann, A. (2010). The Holocaust—A global memory? Extensions and limits of a new memory community. In A. Assmann & S. Conrad (Eds.), *Memory in a global age* (pp. 97–117). Palgrave Macmillan.

Assmann, A. (2014). Transnational memories. *European Review, 22*(4), 546–556.

Barahona de Brito, A., & Sznajder, M. (2010). The politics of the past: The Southern Cone and Southern Europe in comparative perspective. *South European Society and Politics, 15*(3), 487–505.

Bell, D. (2008). Agonistic democracy and the politics of memory. *Constellations, 15*(1), 148–166.

Berger, T. (2002). The power of memory and memories of power: The cultural parameters of German policy-making since 1945. In J. W. Müller (Ed.), *Memory and power in Post-War Europe: Studies in the presence of the past* (pp. 76–99). Cambridge University Press.

Berger, T. (2012). *War, guilt, and world politics after World War II*. Cambridge University Press.

Betz, H.-G. (1988). *New politics of the right: Neo-Populist parties and movements in established democracies*. St Martin's press.

Borejsza, J. W., & Ziemer, K. (Eds.). (2006). *Totalitarian and authoritarian regimes in Europe: Legacies and lessons from the twentieth century*. Berghahn Books.

Bull, A. C. (2016). The role of memory in populist discourse: The case of the Italian Second Republic. *Patterns of Prejudice, 50*(3), 213–231.

Bustikova, L., & Kitschelt, H. (2009). The radical right in post-communist Europe: Comparative perspectives on legacies and party competition. *Communist and Post-Communist Studies*, *42*(4), 459–483.

Caramani, D., & Manucci, L. (2019). National past and populism: The re-elaboration of fascism and its impact on right-wing populism in Western Europe. *West European Politics*, *42*(6), 1159–1187.

Cavallaro, M. E., & Kornetis, K. (Eds.). (2019). *Rethinking democratisation in Spain, Greece and Portugal*. Palgrave Macmillan.

David, R. (2015). Transitional justice and changing memories of the past in Central Europe. *Government and Opposition*, *50*(1), 24–44.

de Brito, A. B., González-Enríquez, C., & Aguilar Fernández, P. (Eds.). (2001). *The politics of memory: Transitional justice in democratizing societies*. Oxford University Press.

de Jonge, L. (2020). The curious case of Belgium: Why is there no right-wing populism in Wallonia? *Government and Opposition*. https://doi.org/10.1017/gov.2020.8

Dinas, E. (2017). Political socialisation and regime change: How the right Ceased to be wrong in post-1974 Greece. *Political Studies*, *65*(4), 1000–1020.

Dinas, E., & Northmore-Ball, K. (2020). The ideological shadow of authoritarianism. *Comparative Political Studies*, *53*(12), 1957–1991. https://doi.org/10.1177/0010414019852699

Encarnación, O. (2014). *Democracy without Justice in Spain: The politics of forgetting*. University of Pennsylvania Press.

Filc, D. (2015). Latin American inclusive and European exclusionary populism: Colonialism as an explanation. *Journal of Political Ideologies*, *20*(3), 263–283.

Finchelstein, F. (2014). *The ideological origins of the Dirty War: Fascism, populism, and dictatorship in twentieth century Argentina*. Oxford University Press.

Fishman, R. M. (2019). How National histories shaped the politics of crisis: South European Contrasts. In M. E. Cavallaro & K. Kornetis (Eds.), *Rethinking democratisation in Spain, Greece and Portugal* (pp. 229–247). Palgrave Macmillan.

Focardi, F. (2013). *Il Cattivo Tedesco e il Bravo Italiano: La Rimozione delle Colpe della Seconda Guerra Mondiale*. Laterza.

Fogu, C., & Kansteiner, W. (2006). The politics of memory and the poetics of history. In R. N. Lebow, W. Kansteiner, & C. Fogu (Eds.), *The politics of memory in Postwar Europe* (pp. 284–310). Duke University Press.

Golder, M. (2003). Explaining variation in the success of extreme right parties in Western Europe. *Comparative Political Studies*, *36*(4), 432–466.

Grzymała-Busse, A. (2002). *Redeeming the communist past: The regeneration of communist parties in East Central Europe*. Cambridge University Press.

Grzymała-Busse, A. (2006). Authoritarian determinants of democratic party competition: The communist successor parties in East Central Europe. *Party Politics*, *12*(3), 415–437.

Gunther, R. (2005). Parties and electoral behavior in Southern Europe. *Comparative Politics*, *37*(3), 253–275.

Halbwachs, M. (1925). *Les cadres sociaux de la mémoire*. F. Alcan.

Halikiopoulou, D., & Vasilopoulou, S. (2018). Breaching the social contract: Crises of democratic representation and patterns of extreme right party support. *Government and Opposition*, *53*(1), 26–50.

Hawkins, K., & Rovira Kaltwasser, C. (2017). The ideational approach to populism. *Latin American Research Review, 52*(4), 513–528.

Herf, J. (1997). *Divided memory: The Nazi past in the two Germanys*. Harvard University Press.

Hite, K., & Cesarini, P. (Eds.). (2004). *Authoritarian legacies and democracy in Latin America and Southern Europe*. University of Notre Dame Press.

Hobsbawm, E. (1983). Introduction: Inventing traditions. In E. Hobsbawm & T. Ranger (Eds.), *The invention of tradition* (pp. 1–14). Cambridge University Press.

Jansen, R. S. (2011). Populist mobilization: A new theoretical approach to populism. *Sociological Theory, 29*(2), 75–96.

Judt, T. (1992). The past is another country: Myth and memory. *Daedalus, 121*(4), 83–118.

Kaplonski, C. (2008). Neither truth nor reconciliation: Political violence and the singularity of memory in post-socialist Mongolia. *Totalitarian Movements and Political Religions, 9*(2–3), 371–388.

Kaya, A. (2017). Turkish Vergangenheitsbewältigung: The Unbearable Burden of the Past. In M. Gabowitsch (Ed.), *Replicating Atonement* (pp. 99–127). Palgrave Macmillan.

Kitschelt, H., & McGann, J. A. (1995). *The radical right in Western Europe: A comparative analysis*. University of Michigan Press.

Kligler-Vilenchik, N., Tsfati, Y., & Meyers, O. (2014). Setting the collective memory agenda: Examining mainstream media influence on individuals' perceptions of the past. *Memory Studies, 7*(4), 484–499.

Kornetis, K. (2019). Public memory of the transitions in Spain and Greece: Toward a change of script? In M. E. Cavallaro & K. Kornetis (Eds.), *Rethinking democratisation in Spain, Greece and Portugal* (pp. 71–87). Palgrave Macmillan.

Krämer, B. (2018). Populism, media, and the form of society. *Communication Theory, 28*(4), 444–465.

Laclau, E. (2005). *On populist reason*. Verso.

Levitsky, S., & Ziblatt, D. (2018). *How democracies Die*. Crown.

Lobo, M. C., Pinto, A. C., & Magalhães, P. (2016). Portuguese democratisation 40 years on: Its meaning and enduring legacies. *South European Society and Politics, 21*(2), 163–180.

Manucci, L. (2020). *Populism and collective memory: Comparing fascist legacies in Western Europe*. Routledge.

Manucci, L. (2020). The shadow of the authoritarian past in the Iberian Peninsula: Failures and success of radical right populist parties. *Relações Internacionais*, Special Issue: 45–59.

March, L. (2017). Populism in the Post-Soviet States. In C. Rovira Kaltwasser, P. Taggart, P. Ochoa Espejo, & P. Ostiguy (Eds.), *The Oxford handbook of populism* (pp. 214–231). Oxford University Press.

Mendes, M., & Dennison, J. (2020). Explaining the emergence of the radical right in Spain and Portugal: Salience, stigma and supply. *West European Politics, 44*(4), 752–775. https://doi.org/10.1080/01402382.2020.1777504

Mikucka-Wójtowicz, D. (2019). The Chameleon nature of populist parties: How recurring populism is luring 'the people' of Serbia and Croatia. *Europe-Asia Studies, 71*(3), 450–479.

Moffitt, B. (2020). *Populism*. Polity.

Mouffe, C. (2005). *On the political*. Routledge.

Mudde, C. (2004). The populist Zeitgeist. *Government and Opposition, 39*(4), 542–563.

Muller, F., Bermejo, F., & Hirst, W. (2016). Argentines' collective memories of the military Junta of 1976: Differences and similarities across generations and ideology. *Memory, 24*(7), 990–1006.

Müller, J. W. (Ed.). (2002). *Memory and power in post-war Europe: Studies in the presence of the past*. Cambridge University Press.

Müller, J. W. (2016). *What is populism?* University of Pennsylvania Press.

Mungiu-Pippidi, A., & Mindruta, D. (2002). Was Huntington right? Testing cultural legacies and the civilization border. *International Politics, 39*(2), 193–213.

Nalepa, M. (2010). *Skeletons in the closet: Transitional justice in Post-Communist Europe*. Cambridge University Press.

Neiger, M., Meyers, O., & Zandberg, E. (Eds.). (2011). *On media memory: Collective memory in a new media age*. Palgrave Macmillan.

Neundorf, A. (2010). Democracy in transition: A micro perspective on system change in post-socialist societies. *The Journal of Politics, 72*(4), 1096–1108.

Pajnik, M., Kuhar, R., & Šori, I. (2016). Populism in the Slovenian context: Between ethno-nationalism and re-traditionalisation. In G. Lazaridis, G. Campani, & A. Benveniste (Eds.), *The rise of the far right in Europe* (pp. 137–160). Palgrave Macmillan.

Palonen, E. (2018). Performing the nation: The Janus-faced populist foundations of illiberalism in Hungary. *Journal of Contemporary European Studies, 26*(3), 308–321.

Pankowski, R. (2010). *The Populist Radical Right in Poland*. Routledge.

Pappas, T. (2014). Populist democracies: Post-Authoritarian Greece and Post-Communist Hungary. *Government and Opposition, 49*(1), 1–23.

Pinelli, C. (2011). The populist challenge to constitutional democracy. *European Constitutional Law Review, 7*(1), 5–16.

Pinto, A. C. (2006). Authoritartian legacies, transitional justice and state crisis in Portugal's democratization. *Democratization, 13*(2), 173–204.

Pop-Eleches, G., & Tucker, J. (2011). Communism's shadow: Postcommunist legacies, values, and behavior. *Comparative Politics, 43*(4), 379–399.

Pop-Eleches, G., & Tucker, J. (2020). Communist legacies and left-authoritarianism. Comparative Political Studies, 53(12), 1861–1889.

Power, T., & Zucco, C. (2009). Estimating ideology of Brazilian legislative parties, 1990–2005: A research communication. *Latin American Research Review, 44*(1), 219–246.

Prendergast, D. (2019). The judicial role in protecting democracy from populism. *German Law Journal, 20*(2), 245–262.

Raimundo, F., & Generoso de Almeida, C. (2019). The legacy of the Portuguese transition to democracy: April-Warriors versus November-Warriors. In M. E. Cavallaro & K. Kornetis (Eds.), *Rethinking Democratisation in Spain, Greece and Portugal* (pp. 45–70). Palgrave Macmillan.

Ricoeur, P. (2004). *Memory, history, forgetting*. University of Chicago Press.

Rousso, H. (1990). *Le Syndrome de Vichy de 1944 à nos Jours*. Seuil.

Rovira Kaltwasser, C. (2012). The ambivalence of populism: Threat and corrective for democracy. *Democratization, 19*(2), 184–208.

Ruth, S. (2018). Populism and the erosion of horizontal accountability in Latin America. *Political Studies, 66*(2), 356–375.

Ryan, H. (2016). From absent to present pasts: Civil society, democracy and the shifting place of memory in Brazil. *Journal of Civil Society, 12*(2), 158–177.

Schneider, N. (2011). Impunity in post-authoritarian Brazil: The Supreme Court's recent verdict on the amnesty law. *European Review of Latin American and Caribbean Studies, 90*(April), 39–54.

Schöpflin, G. (1993). *Politics in Eastern Europe: 1945–92*. Berghahn.

Seaton, P. A. (2007). *Japan's contested war memories: The 'memory rifts' in historical consciousness of World War II*. Routledge.

Selçuk, O. (2016). Strong presidents and weak institutions: Populism in Turkey, Venezuela and Ecuador. *Southeast European and Black Sea Studies, 16*(4), 571–589.

Seleny, A. (2007). Communism's many legacies in East-Central Europe. *Journal of Democracy, 18*(3), 156–170.

Simpser, A., Slater, D., & Wittenberg, J. (2018). Dead but not gone: Contemporary legacies of communism, imperialism, and authoritarianism. *Annual Review of Political Science, 21*, 419–439.

Stanley, B. (2016). Confrontation by default and confrontation by design: Strategic and institutional responses to Poland's populist coalition government. *Democratization, 23*(2), 263–282.

Stanyer, J., Salgado, S., & Strömbäck, J. (2017). Populist actors as communicators or political actors as populist communicators: Cross-national findings and perspectives. In T. Aalberg, F. Esser, C. Reinemann, J. Strömbäck, & C. de Vreese (Eds.), *Populist political communication* (pp. 353–364). Routledge.

Stavrakakis, Y., & Katsambekis, G. (2019). The populism/anti-populism frontier and its mediation in crisis-ridden Greece: From discursive divide to emerging cleavage? *European Political Science, 18*, 37–52.

Torcal, M., & Mainwaring, S. (2003). The political recrafting of social bases of party competition: Chile, 1973–95. *British Journal of Political Science, 33*(1), 55–84.

Urbinati, N. (1998). Democracy and populism. *Constellations, 5*(1), 110–124.

Valentino, N. A., & Sears, D. O. (2005). Old times there are not forgotten: Race and partisan realignment in the contemporary South. *American Journal of Political Science, 49*(3), 672–688.

Verovšek, P. J. (2016). Collective memory, politics, and the influence of the past: The politics of memory as a research paradigm. *Politics, Groups, and Identities, 4*(3), 529–543.

Voigtländer, N., & Voth, H.-J. (2012). Persecution perpetuated: The medieval origins of anti-Semitic violence in Nazi Germany. *The Quarterly Journal of Economics, 127*(3), 1339–1392.

Wilde, A. (1999). Irruptions of memory: Expressive politics in Chile's transition to democracy. *Journal of Latin American Studies, 31*(2), 473–500.

Wittenberg, J. (2015). Conceptualizing historical legacies. *East European Politics and Societies and Cultures, 29*(2), 366–378.

Wodak, R., & Forchtner, B. (2014). Embattled Vienna 1683/2010: Right-wing populism, collective memory and the fictionalisation of politics. *Visual Communication, 13*(2), 231–235.

Zubrzycki, G., & Woźny, A. (2020). The comparative politics of collective memory. *Annual Review of Sociology, 46*, 175–194.

Part IX

Populists in Office

CHAPTER 29

Populism in Southeast Asia

Paul D. Kenny

INTRODUCTION

Traditionally neglected in the comparative study of populism, Southeast Asia has in fact provided fertile territory for the emergence of populist campaigners and the consolidation of their power in office (Mizuno & Pasuk, 2009). Following the general surge in interest in populism in recent years, there has been a significant effort to apply concepts and theories derived from the study of populism in Europe and the Americas to states in the region, including the Philippines (Curato, 2017; Kenny & Holmes, 2020; McCoy, 2017; M. Thompson, 2020), Indonesia (Aspinall, 2015; Fossati & Mietzner, 2019; Gammon, 2020; Vedi R Hadiz & Robison, 2017; Mietzner, 2015), Malaysia (Azhari & Halim, 2019; Shah, 2015; Welsh, 2018) and Thailand (K. Hawkins & Selway, 2017; Hewison, 2017; Seo, 2019). There are also several comparative analyses of populism in the region, focusing especially on post-1990s Indonesia, the Philippines and Thailand (Case, 2017; Vedi R. Hadiz, 2016; Hellmann, 2017; Kenny, 2017, 2019a, 2019b; Pepinsky, 2017; M. R. Thompson, 2016). The appeal of populism in Southeast Asia has been attributed to various causes including the weakness of political parties

---

I would like to thank Oliver Friedmann and Nur Azizah for research assistance.

P. D. Kenny (✉)
Institute for Humanities and Social Sciences, Australian Catholic University, East Melbourne, VIC, Australia
e-mail: paul.kenny@anu.edu.au

(Gammon, 2020; Hicken & Self, 2018; Kenny, 2019b), lower class resentment of economic inequality (Vedi R Hadiz & Robison, 2017; M. R. Thompson, 2016), cleavages among the elite (Case, 2017), dissatisfaction with corruption and misgovernance (Mietzner, 2015; M. R. Thompson, 2010), fear of crime (Curato, 2017; Kenny, 2019a) and, in some cases, resurgent Islamism (Vedi R. Hadiz, 2016; Mietzner, 2018; Mietzner & Muhtadi, 2018).

The rapidly growing body of case studies and small-N comparisons on populism in Southeast Asia is full of insight but remains as yet poorly integrated. Although it is unlikely that there is any single explanation for the emergence of populism, the lack of agreement on an overarching paradigm for the Southeast Asian context is notable. One of the reasons for the lack of cohesion of this research program is the diversity of ways in which populism itself has been conceptualized. The meaning of populism remains contested in the broader literature, and this lack of consensus is especially evident when the concept has been applied to Southeast Asia. As with any popular topic, there has been a tendency towards conceptual inflation, as tangential or even unrelated cases are included within the populist fold (Sartori, 1970). Because populism has been understood in a variety of ways across this diverse body of case studies, we lack a good sense of which leaders or parties can be usefully compared within and beyond the region. To date, as a result, there are many more theories of populism in Southeast Asia than there are well executed empirical tests of rival hypotheses. There is, of course, a need to move beyond the issue of classification to an understanding of the causes of populist electoral success. However, the latter cannot proceed without the former. This chapter advocates a strategic conceptualization of populism, which results in a modest but non-trivial number of populists in modern Southeast Asia. Following a brief conceptual overview, the chapter enumerates all of the successful "full" and "partial" populists across the region from 1945 to the present. A final section illustrates how this exercise could facilitate future theory development and testing.

What Is Populism?

As is well known, the meaning of populism remains sharply contested (for a recent review, see Moffitt, 2020). A central aspect of the debate is whether populism should be understood primarily as a political ideology—the *ideational* approach—or as a type of political mobilization strategy—the *strategic* approach. Although there is no *true* definition of populism, there is good reason to believe that the strategic approach is more useful than its alternatives, not least in the Southeast Asian context (Kenny, 2019b). According to the ideational approach, populism is a thin political ideology in which politics is understood as a Manichean struggle between virtuous *people* and an illegitimate or corrupt *elite* (K. A. Hawkins & Kaltwasser, 2019; Mudde, 2004). An implication of this ideational approach is that although populism remains democratic in the sense that it purports to be rule by the people, it is illiberal in that it asserts that there is only one people—the majority—to represent. Indeed, for some political theorists, populism is thus directly opposed to liberalism or pluralism (Galston, 2018; Müller, 2016; Pappas, 2019; Riker, 1982).

Problematically, the proposition that populism is a people-centric ideology that guides political behavior rests on weak theoretical and empirical foundations in the region. There is very little evidence that a master people–elite cleavage works as a general description of politics in Asia (Hellmann, 2017). General appeals to the people are almost ubiquitous, thus providing little variation among political leaders. Indeed, recent survey research has shown that even in the region's two most democratic countries, the Philippines and Indonesia, populist attitudes fail to explain voters' candidate preferences (Fossati & Mietzner, 2019; Kenny & Holmes, 2020). Moreover, even if instead populism is understood as an illiberal democratic political ideology, it still remains unclear how the concept should be applied to a region in which liberalism itself has been only weakly established. Were we to take liberalism (instead of elitism) as the ideal opposite pole of populism, we would be left with the awkward result that almost every democratic or pseudo-democratic political movement or party in the region would also be populist. For example, the People's Action Party (PAP) of Singapore, which professes to be firmly democratic and majoritarian, but which is also quite illiberal, would have to be classified as populist according to this approach.

The main alternative conceptual approach sees populism as a distinct form of political strategy. Populism in this sense is understood as something that politicians do rather than something that they believe or say (Urbinati, 2019). According to the strategic approach, populist parties or movements can be conceived of as ones in which charismatic leaders seek to establish unmediated links with otherwise unattached mass constituencies in their quest to gain and retain power (Kenny, 2017, pp. 2, 28–30; 2021; Mouzelis, 1985, p. 334; Weyland, 2001, p. 14). Kurt Weyland (2001, p. 14) defines populism as "a political strategy through which a personalistic leader seeks or exercises government power based on direct, unmediated, and uninstitutionalized support from large numbers of mostly unorganized followers." Elsewhere, I simply define populism as the "charismatic mobilization of the people in pursuit of political power" (Kenny, 2021).

In this sense, populists organize the pursuit of power differently to the leaders of other types of political movements, most notably, those of programmatic and clientelist parties (Kenny, 2017; Kitschelt, 2000). The defining feature of programmatic parties is that they are based on stable institutionalized relationships with supporters, especially in the form of party membership or participation in aligned civil society organizations (e.g. unions and churches). Clientelist parties are ones that engage in a quid pro quo with supporters in which votes are exchanged for material benefits. Populist movements or parties in contrast rely heavily on the charisma—or personalized authority—of the party leader to establish direct linkages to supporters.

Utilizing the tools of mass communication (i.e. traditional media, social media, public rallies, etc.), populists minimize the costs associated with party building or the distribution of patronage. Under conditions of weak party institutionalization, populism thus represents a cost-effective political strategy.

Identifying Populists in Southeast Asia

Although the strategic approach is not the only valid one, it has the advantage of being able to account for the notable frequency of populism across the history of democratic Southeast Asia (1945–2020), but without falling into the trap of classifying every prominent political leader as a populist. To determine whether a party is populist or not, we can ask the following questions: Is the party or movement a newly created electoral vehicle of the party leader? Or to what degree has the party or movement leader substantially removed internal constraints on their power within the organization having otherwise gained control over it? And to what extent does the party or movement primarily rely on the mobilization of independent (or weakly attached) voters through the promotion of the charisma of the leader via direct means such as the media and mass rallies?

The Philippines

Within Southeast Asia, populists have been most prevalent and most successful in the Philippines. From the introduction of democracy under American tutelage in the 1920s, the Philippines developed a characteristically patronage-based form of politics. Landed elites mobilized their clienteles of dependents and divided the spoils of office amongst themselves. The campaign of Ramon Magsaysay in 1953 marked a departure from this clientelist mode of mobilization. Party identification remained almost non-existent. So free were party loyalties that both parties Liberals and Nacionalistas had attempted to nominate Magsaysay as their candidate before he ultimately defected from the Liberals to join with the Nacionalistas (Cullather, 1993, p. 321). The critical innovation of Magsaysay was to supplement "the traditional reliance on patron-client ties with direct campaign appeals to the people" (Hutchcroft & Rocamora, 2003, p. 273). Magsaysay campaigned across the country, seeking to establish direct personal contact with Filipino peasants (Kerkvliet, 1977, p. 238). As one academic commentator noted during the 1953 presidential campaign, Magsaysay's main strength came "not from a personal political machine, but rather from a groundswell of popular revolt against professional politicians" (Hart, 1953, p. 67). His campaign used slogans like "Magsaysay is My Guy" seeking to make the campaign about Magsaysay's personal character rather than about policy or mere distribution (Cullather, 1993, p. 305).

As with Magsaysay before him, Ferdinand Marcos also sought to link directly with voters in the Philippine countryside. In collaboration with his American political consultants, Marcos executed a sophisticated media campaign for the presidency in 1965. Radio remained the primary means of connecting with the masses but film images were also used, with his campaign team loading up projectors and screens and driving them to villages around the country (Johnson, 2016, p. 126). Once democracy was restored after Marcos's departure from power in 1986, populism was not long in returning. "Cory" Corazon Aquino, the widow of assassinated opposition leader Benigno "Ninoy" Acquino, became the figurehead of a mass movement to oust Marco and restore democracy. Cory's leadership of the pro-democracy movement had some clearly charismatic qualities as the movement was loosely organized and heavily associated with her personally. Yet, key anti-Marcos political factions were critical in propelling her to power. Cory indeed soon normalized, becoming entrenched in the clientelist and clan-based politics of the country. In contrast, Joseph Estrada, a presidential candidate in 2010 and president from 1998–2001, was the classic charismatic campaigner. A former actor, who often portrayed the role of the downtrodden hero, Estrada was the Force of the Filipino Masses' (PMP) first vice-presidential candidate in 1992 before winning the presidency in 1998 largely with the support of the country's poor. The Philippines has also seen unsuccessful presidential runs by a series of personalist candidates that also had many of the characteristics of populism. In particular, Miriam Defensor-Santiago of the People's Reform Party (PRP) and Eduardo Cojuangco Jr. of the Nationalist People's Coalition (NPC), were the 1992 presidential candidates of weakly institutionalized parties that relied mostly on their charisma to link with voters. The same can be said for Fernando Poe Jr. who ran as the United Opposition (KNP) candidate in 2004.

Current president (2016–), Rodrigo Duterte, meets the criteria comfortably. He is the absolute leader of what is otherwise an institutionally very weak party, the PDP-Laban (literally, the Philippine Democratic Party–People's Power). In 2016, PDP-Laban secured just three seats in Congress, even though Duterte won 39 percent of the national vote. Duterte hails from a minor political clan, and his mother's connections allowed him to secure an appointed position as vice mayor of Davao City in 1986. From this position, Duterte became mayor in 1988 when elections were reintroduced. In Davao, he was a controversial but popular mayor of one of the country's most populous cities, a position he effectively held—even though he had to step down occasionally to circumvent term limits—until his run for the presidency in 2016. Although Duterte was no stranger to old-style machine politics, his presidential campaign placed much greater emphasis on direct appeals to voters through the media, in part to transcend his provincial base of support. This mass media and social media populist campaign strategy allowed Duterte to appeal to Filipinos over the heads of powerful political clans. He centered his presidential campaign on anti-establishment and law-and-order messages, casting himself as the "man on horseback" who would challenge the elite or, as he characterized it, "Imperial Manila," which had dismally failed to address the country's drug problem. Duterte effectively used rallies, mass media and social media to deliver his message and build support, and has relentlessly personalized the administration since his election victory (Kenny, 2020).

Indonesia

In Indonesia, the first free national elections were held in 1955, five years after independence (Feith, 1957). The result was a fragmented parliament which was prorogued when President Sukarno adopted the concept of "guided democracy" from 1957; in 1959 he dissolved the parliament by decree (Mujani et al., 2018, p. 1). To the extent that Indonesia can be considered a democracy in this brief period, Sukarno is usefully classified as a populist. As the preeminent hero of the independence struggle, Sukarno styled himself as a nationalist and populist leader who could represent these competing local and organized factions with a fair hand. In spite of Sukarno's charisma, his party, the Indonesian National Party (PNI), won only a plurality but not a majority of votes in the 1955 election (Willner, 1984). Sukarno could neither fully incorporate the Communist Party of Indonesia (PKI) nor establish a sufficiently dominant patronage-based network of his own. The result of the 1955 election was a fragmented parliament and a stalemated constitutional assembly that presaged the effective suspension of democracy in 1957. Sukarno became stridently antiparty, expressed most clearly in a 1956 speech called "Let Us Bury the Parties" (Kenny, 2019b, p. 35). Sukarno was himself overthrown in a military coup in 1965 with General Suharto taking over and ruling for over 30 years.

Indonesia did not become a consolidated democracy again until 1999 as Suharto's military regime was ousted in the wake of the Asian Financial Crisis. Since then, in spite of electoral laws designed to mitigate the emergence of personalistic and regionalist parties, such as the requirement for parties to compete in all national constituencies, Indonesia has been host to several populist parties, most notably Partai Demokrat, the electoral vehicle of former president Susilo Bambang Yudhoyono. Other populist parties include Gerindra, the party of Prabowo Subianto and Hanura, the party of Wiranto. In some respects, Yudhoyono presents a challenging case. The relative lack of impact that he had on the institutional constraints on his authority, whether the courts, the media or others, has led most observers to conclude that he is not a populist at all. However, it is deeply problematic to determine whether a political candidate is populist based on their subsequent behavior. To do this is to reduce populism to a pejorative that is reserved for the most egregious political actors. His personal control over his party and the charismatic style of his campaign for office in 2004 are sufficient to classify him as a populist (Dagg, 2007).

There are other borderline cases in Indonesia. Most of the legacy parties in Indonesia are very clearly clientelist. This includes Golkar, the ruling party of the New Order regime that was able to retain much of its influence during the transition, and the Indonesian Democratic Party of Struggle (PDI-P), the main party to emerge from the fall of Suharto (Aspinall & Berenschot, 2019). The PDI-P, however, merits further discussion. Although classically clientelist in terms of a legislative party, remaining largely under the control of Megawati Sukarnoputri, it won the presidency in 2014 and retained it in 2019 in part thanks to the personal appeal of Joko Widodo ("Jokowi"). Jokowi owed his initial position in politics to oligarchic patronage, but more so than Prabowo, he came to be seen as a challenger to Indonesia's oligarchy and emerged as the most popular presidential candidate. His phenomenal popularity as governor of Jakarta forced Megawati to nominate him as the PDI-P's presidential candidate in spite of her own interest in the position. Although nominally a member of the PDI-P, Jokowi had little interest in or institutional ties to the party (Mietzner, 2015). Jokowi in turn went beyond the party leadership to establish direct connections with voters on the basis of a massive grassroots and social-media campaign (Tapsell, 2015). It is in these senses that Jokowi can be considered a populist (Mietzner, 2015). However, while I am sympathetic to this view, Jokowi lacks the kind of internal authority over the PDI-P possessed by other populists who have taken over an existing party. That is, Jokowi is externally populist but the PDI-P remains internally a fragmented and clientelist party over which Jokowi has limited control. Jokowi's second-term cabinet of 34 initially included 15 representatives from other parties, including his erstwhile rival, Prabowo Subianto. This leads me to treat Jokowi as a non-populist for the purposes of this chapter.

Similarly, I am skeptical of the argument that the Prosperous Justice Party (PKS) should be thought of as populist. Hadiz (2016), in his study of "Islamic populism" classifies the PKS as populist. While Hadiz adopts a conceptualization in which an amorphous "people" is strategically mobilized, he focuses on the class bases of the supporters rather than the organizational characteristics of the party. Patronage parties are also notoriously catch all parties. What is distinctive about populist parties is their structure and the role of charismatic leadership. The PKS is thus as close to a programmatic party as one gets in contemporary Indonesia.

Thailand

Thailand's regime history has been especially turbulent; it holds the unwanted distinction for having experienced the most military coups of any modern state. Thailand made its initial attempts at democracy in the early 1970s, but the experiment was quickly checked, with a coup restoring military rule in 1976. Although elections were held once again in 1979, a more sustained period of democracy did not begin until 1993. Although personalistic parties have been common in Thailand, full-blown populism has been relatively unusual. For instance, the Chart Pattana Party (CPP), Social Action and New Aspiration were all associated with particular party leaders—usually their founders. Yet most of them depended for their electoral support on building up coalitions of local rural notables, deploying patronage to mobilize the vote. The Prachakorn Thai (PTP) and Muan Chon (MCP) parties followed the same approach, but directed their particularistic appeals towards urban groups. Such parties are more appropriately classified as clientelist. The small Democrat Party and the Seritham and Solidarity parties are instead relatively programmatic (Murray, 1996, p. 36). The only parties in Thailand to count as populist according to the conceptualization used here are those of Thaksin Shinawatra, the Thai Rak Thai (TRT) and the Pheu Thai Party (PTP). What is different about Thaksin was not his rhetoric. Thaksin only began to deploy the language and imagery of a good "people" in competition with an evil "elite" several years into his Prime Ministership (Phongpaichit & Baker, 2008). What is different is the personalistic and direct appeal of Thaksin as leader of the TRT in its mobilization, which was evident from the beginning. Thaksin epitomized what McCargo (1997) called the "electoral professional party" that began to emerge in Thailand by the late 1990s. Such parties make direct appeals to the electorate, without any concern for formal party structures and depend primarily on "a highly marketable leader" (McCargo & Patthamānan, 2005, p. 77). The distinctiveness of the TRT stemmed from Thaksin's status as one of the country's most successful businessmen and his ability to appeal to voters directly. Fitting precisely the conceptualization of populist mobilization described above, the TRT "sought to bypass the existing linkages between ordinary voters and local politicians and MPs, creating a direct connection between the electorate and the government," personified by Thaksin (McCargo & Patthamānan, 2005, p. 110).

Beyond the Big Three

As the region's most consistently democratic states, The Philippines, Indonesia and Thailand have occupied most attention for populism scholars of the region. However, neither populism nor democracy are restricted to those cases. Although a potentially interesting case of populist mobilization, Timor Leste has been relatively neglected in the comparative literature. A small nation made up primarily of the eastern part of Timor Island and two smaller islands in the Indonesian archipelago, Timor Leste was a long-time colony of Portugal. The Timorese exploited the chaos of the fall of the Suharto dictatorship in 1999 to declare independence following a UN-sponsored referendum. Indonesia relinquished control to the UN in 1999 and the country became a fully sovereign state in 2002. The country held elections to a Constituent Assembly in 2001 and in 2002 the country was recognized by the UN (Feijó, 2016). The Constituent Assembly was then renamed as a parliament. A leader of the independence movement, Xanana Gusmão, who ran as an independent candidate in late 2001, was named as president. The main party, Fretelin, won 57% of the popular vote and a majority in the parliament, giving it control over the prime ministership. It has a mass membership base, a body of *militantes* or card-carrying members, marking it out as a remarkably bureaucratic party

(Aspinall et al., 2017). However, Fretelin did not remain effective for long, with government divided by Timor Leste's semi-presidential system. Under the new constitution, executive authority rested largely with the prime minster but the president remained an influent figurehead. In contrast to Fretelin, The National Congress for Timorese Reconstruction (CNRT) was more loosely organized and its electoral appeal was "intimately tied to that of its charismatic president," Gusmão, especially until 2007, after which it began to develop into a patronage-based party (Hynd, 2017, p. 3). For the 2007 election, however, we can consider Gusmão's CNRT populist. Fretelin regained a plurality in parliament in 2017, but has been unable to form a government on its own, raising the prospect of further populist mobilization.

After more than five decades of military rule, Myanmar recently began a partial transition to democracy in 2015. Although Myanmar was never quite a fully consolidated democracy, even prior to the return of military control, it would be reasonable to characterize the Aung San Suu Kyi-led National League for Democracy (NLD) as a populist party. Suu Kyi is the daughter of the country's independence leader, General Aung San, and was herself a political prisoner of the military government for over fifteen years between 1990 and 2010. Although prevented from engaging in overt political activity during that time, she remained a potent symbol of a democracy movement that had been violently repressed since an aborted opening in 1988. Since her release from house arrest in 2010, it has become clear that her authority over the party is immense and there is no questioning that supporters unequivocally identify her with the party. That is, the party's appeal is essentially based on Suu Kyi's charismatic appeal. In power, Suu Kyi has demonstrated a high level of comfort with a centralized and nationalistic approach to politics. The Nobel Peace Prize winner came under substantial criticism for the treatment of ethnic minorities in Myanmar.

Although elections have been consistently held in Malaysia since independence, most scholars classified the regime as only partially democratic or as "competitive authoritarian," until very recently. Gerrymandering and other restrictions had generally served to prevent the opposition from coming to power. The United Malays National Organization (UMNO) was the dominant political party in this period, leading the Barison National (BN) coalition to victory in every election from 1959 until its defeat at the hands of a new alliance called the Pakatan Harapan (PH) in 2018. Curiously, the figurehead of the PH-led coalition was then Mahathir Mohamad, the nonagenarian former prime minister and leader of UMNO. Although Mahathir is a unique political figure in Malaysian politics, having led the country from 1981 to 2003, few analysts would argue that the opposition PH in 2018 grounded its appeal on Mahathir's charisma. Rather, the relatively well-organized political parties that make up coalitions in Malaysia, both on the BN and PH sides, speak of a different pattern of political mobilization grounded in bureaucratic, if identarian, political parties. The fluidity of the political situation since 2020, however, raises the possibility of populist mobilization as an alternative.

All in all, we can identify eight relatively clear cases of populist success—that is, populists who've been elected to (de facto) executive office—in Southeast Asia. In the Philippines: Magsaysay, Marcos, Estrada and Duterte; in Indonesia: Yudhoyono; in Thailand, Thaksin; in East Timor, Gusmão; and in Myanmar, Suu Kyi. Sukarno and Jokowi in Indonesia are borderline or "partial" cases. In addition, there have been a substantial number of unsuccessful populists such as Prabowo Subianto in Indonesia.

Explaining Populism

When conceptualized as a type of strategy, an understanding of populism's causes can be found by probing the social, economic and political conditions that would favor populist rather than programmatic or clientelistic mobilization. Populism should thrive as a low-cost form of political mobilization where bureaucratic and centralized clientelistic party building is inhibited (2019b; Kenny, 2017). Of course, all political parties use mass communication to a degree. The difference is that populists rely *primarily* on these direct connections rather than party members, sympathizers or paid brokers to deliver votes for them. Critically this lowers the *cost* of populist mobilization when compared to other types of mobilization. Populist appeals may or may not include explicit references to "the people." Critically, however, they are organizationally based on direct appeals to broad constituencies that are relatively unattached to (or at least detachable from) parties at the national level. Unlike the leaders of patronage parties, populists do not need a nationwide system of brokers to mobilize votes. Analogously, unlike bureaucratic parties, populists do not need the deeply institutionalized links with supporters through interest groups and other civil society organizations that take many years to build. A single charismatic candidate like a Prabowo Subianto or a Joseph Estrada can utilize their personal connections or extant celebrity to build a position in the polls. In particularly weak party systems, voter choice often comes down to the trustworthiness of the individual candidate. Here populists' outsider status confers a distinct advantage, while being a "party man" can be a disadvantage. Even partial populist candidates like Jokowi, who come from mainstream clientelist parties, often pitch themselves as standing independent of the party machinery.

Critically, it turns out that a whole host of ostensibly rival theories can be subsumed within this general framework, providing possible causal mechanisms to account for the general relationship. A variety of social, economic and political phenomena influence the costs and benefits of different types of political organization and strategy. Mass political communication is likely to be much more effective under conditions that weaken or inhibit party building. Claims that populist success is precipitated by economic inequality, crime, Islamism, corruption, globalization, immigration or economic crisis all submit to this formula, as each in some way affects the costs of different political mobilization strategies. The social, political and economic causes of these conditions in Southeast Asia may well be different from those operating in Western Europe. But if populism is understood simply as a way of organizing the pursuit of power, inter-regional as well as intra-regional comparative analyses become possible.

Literature

Aspinall, E. (2015). Oligarchic populism: Prabowo Subianto's challenge to Indonesian democracy. *Indonesia, 99*(1), 1–28.

Aspinall, E., & Berenschot, W. (2019). *Democracy for sale: Elections, clientelism, and the state in Indonesia.* Cornell University Press.

Aspinall, E., Hicken, A., & Weiss, M. (2017). Election impressions from Timor L'Este. *New Mandala.* http://www.newmandala.org/9-notable-features-timor-leste-elections/

Azhari, A., & Halim, F. A. (2019). *The changing nature of populism in Malaysia.* Asia Democracy Research Network: Populism in Asia.

Case, W. (2017). *Populist threats and democracy's fate in Southeast Asia: Thailand, the Philippines, and Indonesia.* Routledge.

Cullather, N. (1993). America's Boy? Ramon Magsaysay and the illusion of influence. *Pacific Historical Review, 62*(3), 305–338. https://doi.org/10.2307/3640933

Curato, N. (2017). Politics of anxiety, politics of hope: Penal populism and Duterte's rise to power. *Journal of Current Southeast Asian Affairs, 35*(3), 91–109.

Dagg, C. J. (2007). The 2004 elections in Indonesia: Political reform and democratisation. *Asia Pacific Viewpoint, 48*(1), 47–59.

Feijó, R. (2016). *Dynamics of democracy in Timor-Leste: The birth of a democratic Nation, 1999–2012.* Amsterdam University Press, Distributed in the US and Canada by the University of Chicago Press.

Feith, H. (1957). *The Indonesian Elections of 1955.* Modern Indonesia Project, Southeast Asia Program, Cornell University.

Fossati, D., & Mietzner, M. (2019). Analyzing Indonesia's populist electorate: Demographic, ideological, and attitudinal trends. *Asian Survey, 59*(5), 769–794.

Galston, W. (2018). *Anti-Pluralism: The populist threat to liberal democracy.* Yale University Press.

Gammon, L. (2020). Is populism a threat to Indonesian democracy? In T. Power & E. Warburton (Eds.), *Democracy in Indonesia: From stagnation to regression?* (pp. 101–117). ISEAS.

Hadiz, V. R. (2016). *Islamic populism in Indonesia and the Middle East.* Cambridge University Press.

Hadiz, V. R., & Robison, R. (2017). Competing populisms in post-authoritarian Indonesia. *International Political Science Review, 38*(4), 488–502.

Hart, D. V. (1953). Magsaysay: Philippine Candidate. *Far Eastern Survey, 22*(6), 67–70. https://doi.org/10.2307/3024289

Hawkins, K., & Selway, J. (2017). Thaksin the populist? *Chinese Political Science Review,* 1–23.

Hawkins, K. A., & Kaltwasser, C. R. (2019). Introduction: The ideational approach. In K. A. Hawkins, R. E. Carlin, L. Littvay, & C. R. Kaltwasser (Eds.), *The ideational approach to populism: Concept, theory, and analysis.* Routledge.

Hellmann, O. (2017). Populism in East Asia. In C. Rovira Kaltwasser, P. Taggart, C. Mudde, & P. Ochoa Espejo (Eds.), *The Oxford handbook of populism*. Oxford University Press.

Hewison, K. (2017). Reluctant populists: Learning populism in Thailand. *International Political Science Review, 38*(4), 426–440.

Hicken, A., & Self, D. (2018). *Why populism? How parties shape the electoral fortune of populists*. V-Dem Working Paper.

Hutchcroft, P. D., & Rocamora, J. (2003). Strong demands and weak institutions: The origins and evolution of the democratic deficit in the Philippines. *Journal of East Asian Studies, 3*, 259–292.

Hynd, E. (2017). *Patterns of political party competition, dominance and institutionalism: The case of Timor-Leste* (PhD dissertation). Australian National University,

Johnson, D. W. (2016). *Democracy for hire : A history of American political consulting*. Oxford University Press.

Kenny, P. D. (2017). *Populism and patronage: Why populists win elections in India, Asia, and beyond*. Oxford University Press.

Kenny, P. D. (2019a). Populism and the war on drugs in Southeast Asia. *The Brown Journal of World Affairs, 25*(2), 121–136.

Kenny, P. D. (2019b). *Populism in Southeast Asia*. Cambridge University Press.

Kenny, P. D. (2020). Why is there no political polarization in the Philippines? In T. Carothers & A. O'Donahue (Eds.), *Old divisions, new dangers: Political polarization in South and Southeast Asia*. Carnegie Endowment for International Peace.

Kenny, P. D. (2021). The strategic approach to populism. In D. B. Subedi, T. Lynch, A. Scott, & H. Brasted (Eds.), *Handbook on populism in the Asia Pacific*. Routledge.

Kenny, P. D., & Holmes, R. (2020). A new penal populism? Rodrigo Duterte, public opinion, and the war on drugs in the Philippines. *Journal of East Asian Studies*.

Kerkvliet, B. J. (1977). *The Huk rebellion : A study of peasant revolt in the Philippines*. University of California Press.

Kitschelt, H. (2000). Linkages between citizens and politicians in democratic politics. *Comparative Political Studies, 33*(6), 7.

Mccargo, D. (1997). Thailand's political parties: Real, authentic, and actual. In K. Hewison (Ed.), *Political change in Thailand: Democracy and participation* (pp. xv, 301 p.). Routledge.

McCargo, D., & Patthamānan, U. (2005). *The thaksinization of Thailand*. NIAS Press.

McCoy, A. W. (2017). Global populism: A lineage of Filipino strongmen from Quezon to Marcos and Duterte. *Kasarinlan: Philippine Journal of Third World Studies, 32*(1–2), 7–54.

Mietzner, M. (2015). Reinventing Asian Populism: Jokowi's rise, democracy, and political contestation in Indonesia. *Policy Studies*(72), 0_1.

Mietzner, M. (2018). Fighting illiberalism with illiberalism: Islamist populism and democratic deconsolidation in Indonesia. *Pacific Affairs, 91*(2), 261–282. https://doi.org/10.5509/2018912261

Mietzner, M., & Muhtadi, B. (2018). Explaining the 2016 Islamist mobilisation in Indonesia: Religious intolerance, militant groups and the politics of accommodation. *Asian Studies Review*, 1–19. https://doi.org/10.1080/10357823.2018.1473335

Mizuno, K., & Pasuk, P. (Eds.). (2009). *Populism in Asia*. NUS Press in association with Kyoto University Press.

Moffitt, B. (2020). *Populism*. Polity.

Mouzelis, N. (1985). On the concept of populism: Populist and clientelist modes of incorporation in semiperipheral polities. *Politics & Society, 14*(3), 329–348. https://doi.org/10.1177/003232928501400303

Mudde, C. (2004). The populist zeitgeist. *Government and Opposition, 39*(4), 542–563.

Mujani, S., Liddle, R. W., & Ambardi, K. (2018). *Voting behavior in Indonesia since democratization: Critical democrats*. Cambridge University Press.

Müller, J.-W. (2016). *What is populism?* University of Pennsylvania Press.

Murray, D. (1996). The 1995 National Elections in Thailand: A step backward for democracy? *Asian Survey, 36*(4), 361–375.

Pappas, T. (2019). *Populism and liberal democracy: A comparative and theoretical analysis*. Oxford University Press.

Pepinsky, T. (2017). Southeast Asia: Voting against disorder. *Journal of Democracy, 28*(2), 120–131.

Phongpaichit, P., & Baker, C. (2008). Thaksin's populism. *Journal of Contemporary Asia, 38*(1), 62–83.

Riker, W. H. (1982). *Liberalism against populism : A confrontation between the theory of democracy and the theory of social choice*. W.H. Freeman.

Sartori, G. (1970). Concept misinformation in comparative politics. *American Political Science Review, 64*(4), 1033–1055.

Seo, B. K. (2019). Populist Becoming: The red shirt movement and political affliction in Thailand. *Cultural Anthropology, 34*(4), 555–579.

Shah, S. (2015). Populist politics in the new Malaysia. *New Diversities, 17*(1), 53.

Tapsell, R. (2015). Indonesia's media oligarchy and the "Jokowi Phenomenon." *Indonesia, 99*(1), 29–50.

Thompson, M. (2020). Duterte's violent populism: Mass murder, political legitimacy and the "death of development" in the Philippines. *Journal of Contemporary Asia*.

Thompson, M. R. (2010). Reformism vs. populism in the Philippines. *Journal of Democracy, 21*(4), 154–168.

Thompson, M. R. (2016). The moral economy of electoralism and the rise of populism in the Philippines and Thailand. *Journal of Developing Societies, 32*(3), 246–269.

Urbinati, N. (2019). *Me the people : How populism transforms democracy*. Harvard University Press.

Welsh, B. (2018). "Saviour" Politics and Malaysia's 2018 electoral democratic breakthrough: Rethinking explanatory narratives and implications. *Journal of Current Southeast Asian Affairs, 37*(3), 85–108.

Weyland, K. (2001). Clarifying a contested concept: Populism in the study of Latin American politics. *Comparative Politics, 34*(1), 1–22.

Willner, A. R. (1984). *The spellbinders: Charismatic political leadership*. Yale University Press.

CHAPTER 30

Populism in Africa and the Anti-Corruption Trope in Nigeria's Politics

Sylvester Odion Akhaine

Introduction

In 1980, the Nigerian Professor of Political Science, Peter Ekeh delivered his inaugural lecture "Colonialism and Social Structure", which rendered in the best tradition of that academic culture. The argument was somewhat dichotomized. The professor sought to answer the question: was colonialism in Africa episodic or epochal? Ekeh argued brilliantly that colonialism was epochal because it transformed substantially the social structure of Africa, in other words, colonialism's impact on the continent was total:

> Now that we have lived beyond colonial rule itself we must update our sociological conceptualization of colonialism over and above the colonial situation. We must search for the totality of colonialism as a reality sui generis, as a phenomenon in its own right. Fourthly, then, in addition to the disparate activities of the colonizers and the colonized, and in addition to the totality of colonial rule, that is, the colonial situation, colonialism may be considered to be a social movement of epochal dimensions whose enduring significance, beyond the life-span of the colonial situation, lies in the social formations of supra-individual entities and constructs. (Ekeh, 1983, p. 3)

Colonialism stopped the historical march of the continent and had grafted on it an alien culture that was opposed to Africa's way of life. The episodic or "... non-epochal, change is episodic and its direction cannot be fully predicted"

S. O. Akhaine (✉)
Department of Political Science, Lagos State University, Ojo, Nigeria
e-mail: sylvester.akhaine@lasu.edu.ng

© The Author(s), under exclusive license to Springer Nature Switzerland AG 2022
M. Oswald (ed.), *The Palgrave Handbook of Populism*,
https://doi.org/10.1007/978-3-030-80803-7_30

(Ekeh, 1983, p. 5). In the same way, historian, Professor Ade Ajayi captured the episodic perspective:

> In any long-term view of African history, European rule becomes just another episode. In relation to wars and conflicts of people, the rise and fall of empires, linguistic, cultural and religious change and the cultivation of new ideas and new ways of life, new economic orientations ... in relation to all these, colonialism must be seen not as a complete departure from the African past, but as one episode in the continuous flow of African history. (cited in Ekeh, 1983, p. 8)

For a continent with several years of history, colonial experience, barely a century old before the colonies gained formal independence, could not have been epochal. In other words, colonialism was a dot on the huge canvas of Africa's historical experience. However, Ajayi's argument does not vitiate Ekeh's epochal contention due to the dialectical nature of change. Furthermore, the enduring nature of the Westphalian nation-state structure has endured in post-colonial Africa.

In the analysis of populism in Africa, it is appropriate to begin and argue from Ekeh's epochal perspective. I argue that given the economic structure of society based on capitalist relations of production corruption would continue to dog society. The case of Africa is made worse by its peripheral position in the international capitalist system. Some of the economies, like Nigeria, are based on the extraction of oil resources; the state is the source of capital formation by social forces in society. Thus, corruption will remain a permanent feature of society while anti-corruption endeavor will retain its populist gloss. Many populism definitions highlight the contrast between corrupt political elites and those who claim to represent the interests of the people. Regarding Africa's reality, populism assumes the status of the language of politics and it is embedded in the power relations of social forces in society. This is also evident in populism's discursive continuity in the history of the liberation struggle in South Africa in the context of a post-apartheid vision and the statist articulations of nationalists and Africa's post-independence leadership (Halisi, 1994). It is from the above-mentioned perspective that we look at populism and the anti-corruption trope in Nigeria's politics.

This paper is structured into five sections. After the introduction, the second section overviews the populist trajectory in Africa. The third section traces the populist streak in Nigeria's politics while the fourth analyzes populism and the electoral interface. The fifth section concludes the paper.

Populism in Africa: An Overview

> Populist practices emerge out of the failure of existing social and political institutions to confine and regulate political subjects into a relatively stable social order. It is the language of politics when there can be no politics as usual: a

mode of identification characteristic of times of unsettlement and de-alignment, involving the radical redrawing of social borders along lines other than those that had previously structured society. It is a political appeal that seeks to change the terms of political discourse, articulate new social relations, redefine political frontiers and constitute new identities. (Panizza, 2005, p. 9)

The bifocal lens provided by Alli Mazrui and G. F. Engholm (1968) is useful in charting the trajectory of populism in Africa. The duo identifies two strands of populism in Africa, namely, empirical populism and intellectual populism. The former varied and "ranging from messianic movements and separatist popular churches in South Africa and Zambia to general rural discontent in, say, the Congo" and the latter as "intellectualized relationship of ideas" embedded in African political thought (Alli & Engholm, 1968, p. 20). Colonialism was central to the spawning of both the empirics and the theoretic of populism. In the modern history of Africa, colonialism being the direct domination of the colonial people's economic and political life by alien forces provided the moorings for intellection about the colonial situation and the corresponding quest for liberation.

Amilcar Cabral (1966) conceptualized colonialism and the imperative for freedom in terms that are overly populist. He acknowledged two aspects of imperial domination, namely, direct and indirect domination. The former is colonialism with direct control of a people by alien forces through a panoply of coercive agents while the latter is neo-colonialism operationalized largely by native agents of the former colonial powers. He then emphasized the imperative of liberation from colonial oppression:

> It is often said that national liberation is based on the right of every people to freely control its own destiny and that the objective of this liberation is national independence. Although we do not disagree with this vague and subjective way of expressing a complex reality, we prefer to be objective, since for us the basis of national liberation, whatever the formulas adopted on the level of international law, is the inalienable right of every people to have its own history, and the objective of national liberation is to regain this right usurped by imperialism, that is to say, to free the process of development of the national productive forces. (Cabral, 1966)

The nationalist leaders, whether of the plaintiff or the armed liberation movement hue, made the people the centerpiece of the liberation struggle. As Frantz Fanon (1967) has rightly noted in the Algerian context, education of the masses was key to the victory from forces of the colonial oppression. Therefore,

> To educate the masses politically does not mean making political speeches, what it means is to try, relentlessly and passionately, to teach the masses that everything depends on them; that we stagnate, it is their responsibility, and that if we go forward it is due to them too, that there is no such thing as a *demiurge*,

that there is no famous man who takes responsibility for everything, but that the *demiurge* is the people themselves and the magic hands are finally only the hands of the people. (Fanon, 1967, p. 159)

Elsewhere in the continent, especially South Africa, an intense intellectual engagement with the dynamics of the apartheid system by the leadership of the liberation movement occurred. The early leaders of the liberation struggle were concerned about how to convince other races, especially the Anglo-Afrikaner, that a democratic South Africa would not alienate them. Albert Luthuli (1963, pp. 207–216) leader of the African National Congress (ANC) conceived of a multi-racial South Africa that would be based on democratic rule. He denied "any-master race ambition". And Nelson Mandela's (1994, p. 317) deepest convictions were ANC's policy of democracy and non-racialism.

A democratic South Africa, of course, meant black majority rule. Clyde Halisi (1994) offered a useful insight into the trajectory of the development of African political thought in South Africa and the populist substance of the liberationists' engagement with the Apartheid system. He harnessed the complex and competing visions of the post-Apartheid social order while underlining the empirics and conceptual issues in the articulation of those visions and the embedded streak of populism. He concluded with an emphasis on the citizenship challenge which inheres in the transformation of citizenship in ways that transcend a mere address of racial domination to deal with the crucial issue of class in terms of economic equality.

Noticeable was the youth's hijack of leadership from the older generation of liberationists to accentuate populist nationalism as resistance against what Halisi (1994, p. 10) has called "liberal accommodation". The "black republicans" were preoccupied with theorizing "about the historic rights and nature of the African people. Africa and her people were virtuous, their degradation being a consequence of European intrusion and the imposition of alien cultural values" (Halisi, 1994, p. 16). They, therefore, envisioned a new South Africa based on the tenets of socialism or "black social democracy" conducive to the restoration of African's dignity (Halisi, 1994, p. 16). On the contrary the multi-racial unionists "advocate a territorial, and therefore multiracial, view of South African citizenship" (Halisi, 1994, pp. 15–16). This made possible the alliance of classes, races, and significantly the South African Communist Party (SACP) and the ANC cadres that worked for inclusive citizenship and a non-racial post-apartheid society (Halisi, 1994, p. 18). The emergence of Steve Biko's Black Consciousness Movement (BCM) did not constrain the populist intellectual tradition but buoyed it. The black consciousness philosophy encapsulates the pride of the blacks and the determination for self-actualization (Woods, 1987, p. 59). For this reason, the BCM introduced a subjective element into the liberation politics in contrast to the dominant focus on objective conditions by the black liberation movement (Halisi, 1994, p. 23). As Halisi (1994, p. 23) rightly put it: "As a subjective understanding of politics, populism provides a set of values for everyday life and readily lends itself to becoming a strand of thought within liberalism and socialism". As a radical racial populist theory, it created tension in the older generation who undermined it through "confrontation, containment, or co-optation" (Halisi, 1994, p. 24). However, Biko's philosophy raised the banner of liberation at a time lull had set in into the activities of the black organizations, ANC, and the Pan-African Congress (PAC). The populist interface bred "a body of syncretic ideas that evolve from the interaction of autochthonous social theory and formal Ideologies such as liberalism, socialism, and nationalism" underlined by populist emphasis on national, racial, ethnicity, and proletarian solidarity (Halisi, 1994, pp. 25–26).

If South Africa's experience evinces a robust intellectual dimension of populism, Julius Nyerere's (1969) politics approximates the unity of praxis and theory. *Ujamaa*, familyhood, articulates African socialism in opposition to capitalism's exploitation and doctrinaire socialism's class struggle. *Ujamaa* is an extension of the family's social security to the wider society and mankind in general. President Nyerere created village communities based on collectivized social production. Although the experiment failed, it did represent the objectification of the populist policy of *Ujamaa*.

In West Africa, Ghana and Burkina Faso trod the objectification path beyond rhetoric. Jerry Rawlings and Thomas Sankara were military officers and the objective conditions that spawned their intervention in politics were somewhat similar. Indeed, Donald Rothchild and Emmanuel Gyimah-Boadi (1989, p. 221) have noted that "In both countries, before the coup there was broad public resentment over evidence of extensive misuse of public office for private purposes and poverty and class inequality were widespread". The consequence was the appearance of the praetorian guards on the political scene. A form of reconstitutive anti-politics ensued along the line of their commitment to charting an authentic African development paradigm by eliminating class privileges, ensuring social inclusion, and building a new society. New popular structures were created that were seen to be functional and involved the people. However, these experiments were short-lived. In Ghana, the domestic economic condition and its external dimension forced a retreat. But as Rothchild and Gyimah-Boadi (1989, p. 242) have observed, populism was "alive and well, particularly at the rhetoric level. Rawlings continues to urge popular participation and people's power and administrative decentralization…".

Although Kenneth Roberts (2016, p. 69) notes the unqualified characterization of movements and leaders as populist, and sometimes with pejorative dimension, Sankara's commitment was not in doubt. His march in Burkina Faso was truncated by his assassination in a counterrevolutionary coup led by his bosom friend, Blasé Compaore. Indeed, "for the most part, Sankara persisted with his populist revolution, in both his rhetoric and his substantive commitments" (Rothchild & Gyimah-Boadi, 1989, p. 243). We now turn to the Nigerian context.

NIGERIA: IN SEARCH OF THE POPULIST STREAK

This section deals with populism in Nigeria. In the definitional complexity of populism, Bart Bonikowski and Noam Gidron (2016, p. 7) identified three traditions in populism research, namely, populism as a political strategy, ideology, and discursive style. As a political strategy, it is seen as a top-down political mass mobilization tool by personalist leaders who challenge entrenched political and economic elite usually on behalf of the popular forces of society. And as an ideology, the "ideas revolve around the Manichean contrast between the corrupt elite and the morally pure people" with the caveat that populism is not a comprehensive worldview but an appendage to some ideology like socialism or nationalism. In its discursive dimension, populism is based on the fundamental conflict between the corrupt elite and the people and conceived of as a rhetorical style used by political actors of diverse ideological persuasions (Bonikowski & Gidron, 2016, p. 9). Thus corruption fits into both the Manichean and discursive perspectives of populism and as a legitimizing means by diverse political regimes.

Nigeria has produced fourteen heads of state since independence in 1960. Some had made a comeback in the contradictory dynamics of the political process, a mixed bag of military autocrats and its civilian incarnate. Mode of succession has been largely through military coup d'états and "reluctant transitions". Recently, the country celebrated two decades of unbroken democratic practice. It is against this backdrop that we seek to highlight the populist trope of anti-corruption given more fervor following the inauguration of the fourth republic in 1999.

Anti-corruption rhetoric permeates each cycle of regime change. It is often a function of the quest for the legitimation of leadership change. In the democratic flip, after the-not-too free and fair election, the people are rallied into the inclusivity murmur of a government of national unity validating Jan-Werner Mueller's (2019) assertion that *"All populists claim to have unique knowledge of the real people and their will, and promise to serve as their 'voice'"* (Mueller, 2019). The putschists of January 15, 1966, in their dawn broadcast to the country, said:

> Our enemies are the political profiteers, the swindlers, the men in high and low places that seek bribes and demand 10 percent; those that seek to keep the country divided permanently so that they can remain in office as ministers or VIPs at least, the tribalists, the nepotists, those that make the country look big for nothing before international circles, those that have corrupted our society and put the Nigerian political calendar back by their words and deeds. (Nzeogwu, 1966)

The aftermath of the first coup, namely, the ascension to power of General Aguiyi Ironsi, the counter-coup, and the civil war are well documented (Ademoyega, 1981; Madiebo, 1980; Nzimiro, 1982). It is to be noted, however, that both Ironsi and General Yakubu Gowon who succeeded him were preoccupied with restoring the systemic equilibrium through brinkmanship, war diplomacy, and propaganda (Elaigwu, 1986). Nevertheless, the corruption strain made a comeback in the overthrow of the Gowon regime in 1975. The new head of state, General Murtala Mohammed told Nigerians that the military decided to topple the government because the deposed leader ignored:

> Responsible opinion, including advice by eminent Nigerians, traditional rulers, intellectuals, etcetera, was similarly discarded. The leadership, either by design or default, had become too insensitive to the true feelings and yearnings of the people. The nation was thus plunged inexorably into chaos...Fellow Countrymen, the task ahead of us calls for sacrifice and self-discipline at all levels of our society. This government will not tolerate indiscipline. The Government will not condone abuse of office. (Mohammed, 1975)

The Mohammed administration was short-lived. By February 1976, he was assassinated in a bloody coup and his successor, General Olusegun Obasanjo, stuck to the same anti-corruption trope as his predecessor. In his maiden broadcast, he emphasized:

> I expect every public officer indeed, every Nigerian to measure up to a high degree of efficiency, integrity and moral rectitude. The purge of the public service of undesirable elements was undertaken to revitalize the service...This objective has not been fully achieved. Those that are diligent and honest in their work need not fear. Indeed they would be rewarded. But those who continue to be indolent, inefficient or corrupt will be removed. These standards are set not only for public servants but for all Nigerians. (Obasanjo, 1976)

The military which had always regarded its incursion into politics as an aberration implemented a transition to civil rule that brought to power President Shehu Shagari. On October 1, 1979, the newly elected President Shagari stressed his government commitment "to building a united, stable and prosperous nation" (Shagari, 1979) over which he sought the cooperation and support of the citizens. Although the corruption trope did not quite feature in the speech, the populist thread was discernible in the appeal to the people as citizens and as a self-determining collective. The government was soon caught up in a cesspool of corruption and it became the rationale for a military comeback on December 31, 1983. In the maiden speech of the head of the military junta, General Mohammadu Buhari outlined his commitment to fighting corruption. In his words,

> While corruption and indiscipline have been associated with our state of underdevelopment, these two evils in our body politic have attained unprecedented height in the past few years. The corrupt, inept and insensitive leadership in the last four years has been the source of immorality and impropriety in our society. (Buhari, 1983)

The new military junta demonstrated extreme authoritarianism and sentenced many politicians on multiple counts to long prison terms. In its bid to address the symptoms of corruption rather than the structure that engendered it, a measure of anti-politics prevailed. The judiciary was hobbled with ouster clauses while the press was silenced. Authoritarian siege produced resentment and by August 1985, the junta was overthrown by the Army Chief of Staff, General Ibrahim Babangida. In his maiden speech, he acknowledged the degree of corruption in the civilian administration which the military had deposed. In redressing it, he said, a sense of natural justice should not be lost in a reference to the authoritarian methods of General Buhari (Babangida, 1985). General Babangida then began a prolonged transition which was inclined towards self-succession. While it produced a victor in the presidential election held on June 12, 1993, the mandate was annulled and as a result of mass resistance, the incumbent "stepped aside" and imposed an interim government. These developments formed the background of a civil society resistance and a consequent military coup led by General Sanni Abacha. Being one of brinkmanship or "a child of necessity", he was pre-occupied with restoring stability to a badly divided society. Even though he went after the financial institutions in his own war on corruption, politically, he began the same process of self-transmutation until his death in June of 1998. His exit paved the way for a short transition program under the leadership of General Abubakar Abdulsalami and power was transferred to a democratically elected president, a retired general and former military head of state, Obasanjo.

The elected president did not omit the corruption question in his first address to the nation; he acknowledged the depth of corruption and then promised that "Corruption, the greatest single bane of our society today, will be tackled head-on at all level" (Obasanjo, 1999). His successor, President Umaru Yar'Adua who was ill in office and died afterward, retained all the anti-corruption institutions created by President Obasanjo, namely, Economic and Financial Crime Commission (EFCC) and Independent Corrupt Practices and other Related Offences Commission (ICPC). Jonathan succeeded Yar'Adua and enhanced the institutional measures for combating by introducing Treasury Single Account (TSA), Integrated Personnel and Payroll Information System (IPPIS), and Bank Verification Number (BVN). Politics being the "only game" in town and the state being the source of capital formation and accumulation, corruption ran deep in the system under his watch. The next section of this paper analyzes the current trend expressed in the populism-electoral interface.

Buhari Administration, Populism and the Electoral Interface

> The question we should be asking ourselves now is, how and why is it that every coup plotter in Nigeria hung his colours on the mast of fighting corruption? How come that all successive governments have come in, accusing their predecessors of massive corruption only to turn around and do even worse or leave a similar legacy of rot? (Kukah, cited in Jonathan, 2015, p. 38)

The victors of the 2015 general election, before and after the election, stuck to the anti-corruption rhetoric as their trump card against an incumbent hedged by an overwhelming alliance of opposition parties and politicians. The All Progressive Congress (APC), crystallized from a handful of leading opposition parties in 2013, chose a presidential candidate, Mohammadu Buhari, who caught a messianic image mainly in his region of northern Nigeria and was regarded as *Mai Gaskiya* in Hausa, that is, "Mr. Honesty". The incumbent regime had been tainted with sundry corruption charges, prominent among which was the oil subsidy scam, which was subject of investigation of the lower house of the national parliament. An estimated $6 billion dollars was misappropriated through dubious oil subsidy payments. It became the ground for mass actions against the Jonathan administration. Given the widespread perception of a corrupt administration and despite its effort at enhancing the fight against corruption, a veritable platform was laid out in the public sphere for messianic fanfare and Mr. Honesty would be the protagonist. The APC with its broom, symbol of the party, was thus poised to sweep away the incumbent leadership and his Peoples Democratic Party (PDP) from power. The anti-corruption rhetoric echoes well the *Monterrey Concensus* (2002) which stressed that:

> fighting corruption at all levels is a priority. Corruption is a serious barrier to resource mobilization and allocation and diverts resources away from activities that are vital for poverty eradication and economic and sustainable development.

The consensus also emphasized sound economic policy, regulatory framework, and a competitive and predictable investment environment. The anti-corruption trope has an audience—the international community including international financial institutions (IFIs). Mr. Buhari got an audience in Chatham House to sell his party manifesto to the international audience. In a speech in which the word corruption repeatedly occurred seven times expressed his determination to sweep away a corrupt administration as well as fight corruption head-on in the country. As he put it:

> But I must emphasize that any war waged on corruption should not be misconstrued as settling old scores or a witch-hunt. I'm running for President to lead Nigeria to prosperity and not adversity...In reforming the economy, we will

use savings that arise from blocking these leakages and the proceeds recovered from corruption to fund our party's social investments programmes in education, health, and safety nets such as free school meals for children, emergency public works for unemployed youth and pensions for the elderly. (Buhari, 2015)

Buhari's statement approximates Francisco Panizza's (2005, p. 12) insight into the dynamics of populism to the extent that allegations of corruption and lack of accountability against incumbents are cast in antagonist terms resulting in a regime change.

Buoyed by its anti-corruption rhetoric, APC won the 2015 election against an incumbent whose party, the PDP, had boasted that it would govern nigeria for at least 60 years. However, four years down the line, the promised war against corruption has not seen any significant conviction. In the heat of the second-term campaign, the party chairman, Mr. Adams Oshiomhole, a former labor leader and governor of Edo State told opposition elements with corrupt credentials to join the ruling APC and their sins would be forgiven (Nwogu et al., 2019). A report in *The Guardian* of London would capture the tardy war on corruption as follows:

> Nigeria's president, who came to power with a pledge to tackle corruption, has said he needs more time to sort out the problem but has begun no successful prosecutions and has appeared to condone colleagues tainted by serious allegations. (Maclean & Egbejule, 2019)

The tardiness was accompanied by a significant measure of anti-politics as President Buhari strove to control the national parliament and evince an imperious tendency to the exercise of political power in ways that ignore the complex diversity of the polity. Having secured a second term in office, he then ramped up the politics of anti-politics in ways that have emasculated independent institutions of the state. Also, his party control of the leadership of the two houses of the national parliament undermines opposition voices. His administration's failure to address the issue of corruption in the last five years perhaps further underlines the contention of this paper that anti-corruption rhetoric in the Nigerian context lacks substance save for electoral leverage. The hollowness of the war against corruption compelled Luke Onyekakeyah (2013) to observe:

> Sometime last year, a cartoon in The Sun newspaper, depicted corruption in Nigeria as a huge elephant, lying firmly on the ground, while the Economic and Financial Crime Commission (EFCC), doggedly, scratched it expecting it to move. Since I saw that cartoon, I kept asking myself whether it means that the war against corruption can never be won. (Onyekakeyah, 2013, p. 292)

The failure of the war against corruption has a consequence, which is, promoting the discursive longevity of the phenomenon. And *The Guardian* of Nigeria was right in this regard:

But what must remain the concern of faithful citizens is continuing to take an objective and stark look at the phenomenon of corruption which, no matter the sophistry of the ruling elite, is still very much alive because it is woven into the very existence, corporate and material, of the nation. (*The Guardian*, 2018)

This lends credence to the point made at the inception of this paper that the structure of the economic, non-productive, and reliant on crude oil sales within a global capitalist system would always result in corrupt practices.

Conclusion: Beyond Rhetoric to Objectification

The author tried to capture the populist debate in Africa, especially its intellectual and empirical dimensions. In particular, he analyzed the recurring anti-corruption rhetoric in Nigeria's politics. In the African context, populist materiality has been exposed in the case of Nyerere's *Ujamaa* experiment in Tanzania; Rawlings's outing in Ghana; and Sankara's triumph in Burkina Faso. It is to be noted that only in Tanzania that the populist strain has survived after Nyerere typified by the incumbent President John Magufuli.

In the Nigerian context, populism has served as a legitimizing discourse in succession politics and with an electoral value that barely survives the day after polling. It has not taken the form of intellectual engagement that shapes the liberation struggle in South Africa; neither has it assumed the structural objectification as in Rawlings' Ghana and Sankara's Burkina Faso before the counter-revolution that truncated the processes in the two countries. Indeed, as the Nigerian case has shown, incumbent state actors are easily absorbed into the renting-seeking cycle of public office holders. For a country in the search of the appropriate state structure, and with an oil-based economy, the corruption scourge will most likely endure. The sometimes-skewed process of prosecution of corruption cases could easily inflame ethnic animosity and undermine the war on corruption. For this reason, anti-corruption rhetoric in the Nigerian case will remain an empty slogan without addressing the structural foundation of the scourge. The predatory character of the African ruling elite requires the mediation of popular democratic structures for accountability.

Literature

Abacha, S. (1993, November). *Maiden Broadcast to the Nation*. FRCN.
Ademoyega, A. (1981).*Why we struck*. Evans Brothers (Nigerian Publishers) Limited.
Babangida, I. B. (1985). *Portrait of a Nigerian Patriot, Selected Speeches of IBB*. Precision Press.
Bonikowski, B., & Gidron, N. (2016). Multiple traditions in populism research: Toward a theoretical synthesis by Bart Bonikowski & Noam Gidron. *Comparative Politics Newsletter*, 26(2), 7–14.
Buhari, M. (1983, December 31). *Maiden Broadcast to the Nation*. FRCN.

Buhari, M. (2015, February 26). *Prospects for Democratic Consolidation in Africa: Nigeria's Transition*. Paper presented at Chatham House, The Royal Institute of International Affairs, London, United Kingdom.

Cabral, A. (1966, January). *The weapon of theory*. Paper presented at the Tricontinental Conference of Peoples of Asia, Africa and Latin America, Havana.

Ekeh, P. (1983). *Colonialism and social structure*. University Press.

Elaigwu, J. I. (1986). *Gowon*. West Books Publishers Limited.

Frantz, F. (1967). *The Wretched of the Earth*. Penguin Books limited.

Halisi, C. R. D. (1994, July 13–15). *From liberation to citizenship: Identity and innovation in Black South African Political Thought*. Paper presented at University of the Witwatersrand History Workshop, Johannesburg.

Jonathan, G. E. (2018). *My transition hours*. Ezekiel Books.

Luthuli, A. 1963. *Let My People Go*. Collins.

Maclean, R., & Egbejule, E. (2019, February 11). Nigeria election: 'Mr Honesty' tainted by failure to tackle corruption, *The Guardian* (London). https://www.theguardian.com/world/2019/feb/11/nigeria-election-mr-honesty-muhammadu-buhari-tainted-by-failure-to-tackle-corruption.

Madiebo, A. (1980). *The Nigerian Revolution and the Biafran War*. Fourth Dimension Publishers.

Mandela, N. (1994). *Long walk to freedom*. Little, Brown and Company.

Mazrui, A. A., & Engholm, G. F. (1968). Rousseau and Intellectualized populism in Africa. *The Review of Politics*, 30(1), 19–32.

Mohammed, M. (1975, July 30). *Maiden Broadcast to the Nation*. FRCN.

Monterrey Consensus. (2002, March 21–22). *Communiqué of Summit of Heads of State and Government*.

Mueller, J-W. (2019, September). Can direct democracy defeat populism? *Project Syndicate*. https://www.project-syndicate.org/commentary/direct=democracy-weapon-against-populism-by-jan-warner-mueller-2019–09?utm_source=project+synd...

Nwogu, S., Onojeghen, T., & Peter. A. (2019, January 18). Oshiomhole: Once you join the APC your sins are forgiven, Oshiomhole declares. *Punch*. https://punchng.com/oshiomhole-once-you-join-the-apc-your-sins-are-forgiven/

Nyerere, J. (1969). *Freedom and unity*. Oxford University Press.

Nzeogwu, C. K. (1966, January 15). *Coup Broadcast*. Radio Nigeria.

Nzimiro, I. (1982). *Nigerian Civil War*. Frontline Publishers Company Ltd.

Obasanjo, O. (1976, February 13). *Maiden Broadcast to the Nation*. FRCN

Obasanjo. O. (1999, May 29). *Maiden Broadcast to the Nation*. FRCN.

Onyekakeyah, L. (2013). *The Crawling Giant*. Author House.

Panizza. F. (2005). *Populism and the mirror of democracy*. Verso.

Roberts, K. M. (2016). Populism as epithet and identity: The use and misuse of a contested concept. *Comparative Politics Newsletter*, 26(2), 69–72.

Rothchild, D., & Gyimah-Boadi, E. (1989). Populism in Ghana and Burkina Faso. *Current History*, 88(538), 221–244.

Shagari, A. (1979, October1). *Maiden Broadcast to the Nation*. FRCN.

The Guardian. (2018, December 11). Anti-corruption war beyond rhetoric. *The Guardian* (Lagos). https://guardian.ng/opinion/anti-corruption-war-beyond-rhetoric/

Woods, D. (1987). *Biko*. Penguin Books.

CHAPTER 31

Populism in Southern Africa Under Liberation Movements as Governments: The Cases of Namibia, South Africa and Zimbabwe

Henning Melber

Introduction

Populism in politics is not a new invention and anything but confined to African realities. It exists in a variety of historical settings and societies as well as ideological connotations in almost any part of the world. Beyond its particular substantive contents (if there are any), populism operates with a specific kind of rhetoric, addressing in a simple and direct way "the people." It creates the impression that it is them that matter, that they count more than access to political power by those acting in a populist mode. Populist forms of mobilization are not necessarily by definition despotic or authoritarian. At times, they deliberately take advantage of the understanding and practice of liberal democracy while being in their core utterly illiberal. This creates and testifies to a broad disparity between the propagated and claimed ideal and the reality, or between promises and deliveries (cf. Canovan, 1981, 1999). At a closer look, populists in most cases care mainly about their own interests, not those of the people and wider society.

Generally, there seems to be a close affinity between forms of populism and strong nationalist-oriented forms of governance and governments. Populism

H. Melber (✉)
Department of Political Sciences, University of Pretoria, Hatfield, South Africa
e-mail: Henning.Melber@nai.uu.se

Centre for Gender and Africa Studies, University of the Free State, Bloemfontein, South Africa

The Nordic Africa Institute, Uppsala, Sweden

© The Author(s), under exclusive license to Springer Nature Switzerland AG 2022
M. Oswald (ed.), *The Palgrave Handbook of Populism*,
https://doi.org/10.1007/978-3-030-80803-7_31

therefore not by accident is a widely shared phenomenon in African states. Following, at times, long battles for independence or as in the case of South African democracy, political self-determination cultivates strong nationalist tendencies as a substantial part of nation building. This occurs often in combination with individual rulers, symbolizing a "big chief" syndrome, leading dominant parties largely in control over public discourse and spheres.

This chapter engages with a specific genre and context of African populism. A particular blend which is strongly shaped by the history of armed struggle against settler-colonial minority rule and Apartheid. Interestingly so, while populism in (Southern) Africa has been a matter of analysis more recently, this constellation of anti-colonial movements as governments has so far hardly been considered a category of its own. Resnick (2010, 2017, 2018) as well as Cheeseman (2018), echoed by Nyadera and Agwanda (2019) use Michael Sata in Zambia, Raila Odinga in Kenya and Jacob Zuma in South Africa as most prominent individual examples for African populists. In contrast, this chapter mainly seeks to explore the extent to which particular political organizations, which as former liberation movements turned into governing parties in the course of nation building, resort to a narrative bearing the traits of populism as an integral part of the nature of governance. As a result of their anti-colonial resistance, they finally replaced white minority rule by seizing political control. These "movements turned into parties" are indeed rather succinct examples of utilizing a specific form of populist governance.

LIBERATION MOVEMENTS AS POPULIST GOVERNMENTS

While "liberation movements espoused ideologies prioritizing 'the capture of state power' as the means to transform societies structurally skewed," they created inevitable tensions between the values of liberal democracy and transformation (Southall, 2013, p. 330f.). The result was—in differing characters according to the specific trajectory of each of the societies—a party state, which "was simultaneously a 'party machine', a vehicle for the upward mobility of party elites and for material accumulation justified ideologically by reference to the historical rightness of transformation" (Southall, 2013, p. 247).

Such tendencies are not as new as the decolonization processes in the Southern African sub-region, which with the Independence of Zimbabwe in 1980, in Namibia in 1990 and the democratic elections in South Africa in 1994 paved the way for the erstwhile anti-colonial organizations seizing political control. Since then, the Zimbabwe African National Union (ZANU-PF), the South West Africa People's Organization (SWAPO of Namibia) and the African National Congress (ANC of South Africa) have remained in government, with differing degrees of support in general elections. But their track records remind of earlier warnings dating back 60 years.

Witnessing the emergence of sovereign governments and their policies in West African states during the late 1950s, Frantz Fanon presented in 1961 a scathing criticism of the rule of "liberators". In chapter three of his manifesto he characterized the performances as "The Pitfalls of National Consciousness" (Fanon, 2001, pp. 119–165). For Fanon the new state, instead of conveying a sense of security, trust and stability foists itself on the people, using mistreatment, intimidation and harassment as domesticating tools. The party in power "controls the masses ... to remind them constantly that the government expects from them obedience and discipline" (Fanon, 2001, p. 146). As he diagnosed:

> After Independence, the party sinks into an extraordinary lethargy. The militants are only called upon when so-called popular manifestations are afoot, or international conferences, or independence celebrations. The local party leaders are given administrative posts, the party becomes an administration, and the militants disappear into the crowd and take the empty title of citizen. (Fanon, 2001, p. 137)

The same applies for the leaders:

> The people who for years on end have seen this leader and heard him speak, who from a distance in a kind of dream have followed his contests with the colonial power, spontaneously put their trust in this patriot. Before independence, the leader generally embodies the aspirations of the people for independence, political liberty and national dignity. (...)
>
> The leader, who has behind him a lifetime of political action and devoted patriotism ... calls to mind his often heroic life, the struggles he has led in the name of the people and the victories in their name he has achieved, thereby intimating clearly to the masses that they ought to go on putting their confidence in him. ... The leader pacifies the people... we see him reassessing the history of independence and recalling the sacred unity of the struggle for liberation. (Fanon, 2001, pp. 133 and 135)

In Southern Africa, like elsewhere, current populist discourses are criticized as being anything but constructive in meeting the challenges and solving problems (Dikeni, 2017, p. 20). Notwithstanding such diagnosis, these discourses are an important element and ingredient in reproducing the continued influence of those maintaining political power. They are at times tailor-made messages to a wider audience revoking identification with the struggle narrative as well as utilizing and mobilizing sentiments deeply rooted in the settler-traumatic history and anything but aberrant forms of policymaking: "Populism, understood as an appeal to 'the people' (...) should not be dismissed as a pathological form of politics of no interest to the political theorist" (Canovan, 1999, p. 2). While liberation movements as well as governments need more than only a populist rhetoric, such appeals have been an integral part of their governance skills and techniques beyond the persons articulating them. There are many examples illustrating the forms and meaning of such features as an integral part of post-settler-colonial narratives in the region.

In more recent theoretical explorations of forms of democracy resembling features of a one-party dominance, systems such as those in Zimbabwe, Namibia and South Africa were classified as "competitive authoritarianism" (Levitsky & Way, 2002, 2010a). As the authors coining the term argue:

> The most durable party-based regimes are those that are organized around non-material sources of cohesion, such as ideology, ethnicity, or bonds of solidarity rooted in a shared experience of violent struggle. In particular, parties whose origins lie in war, violent anti-colonial struggle, revolution, or counter-insurgency are more likely to survive economic crisis, leadership succession, and opposition challenges without suffering debilitating effects. (Levitsky & Way, 2010b, p. 3)

As they conclude: "Revolutionary or liberation struggles also tend to produce a generation of leaders (...) that possesses the necessary legitimacy to impose discipline during crises." Hence "new ruling parties that emerged from violent struggle, such as SWAPO in Namibia, (...) appear to be more durable" (Levitsky & Way, 2010b, pp. 44 and 45).

Heroic-patriotic narratives designed formation building in former settler societies fell on fertile soil among the formerly colonized. The official discourses introduced were accompanied by the belief that the seizure of political power translates into a kind of "the end of history" in the sense that the form of governance is pre-determined once and for all: as from now on, there cannot exist any legitimate alternative to the liberation movements as governments, and changes in political control over the respective countries can only happen legitimately within those movements turned parties.

The right to self-determination by means of an at least formal democratic political system was among others achieved by the armed struggle as a contributing factor. The militant resistance and its sacrifices to overthrow white minority rule were combined with a promise for a better future. But the socio-political (much more than the economic) transfer of power and subsequent transformation was limited to handing over administration and governance to the erstwhile liberation movement. Such negotiated transitions, far from being fundamental socio-economic transformations, did not abandon or decisively reduce the structurally anchored discrepancies of a society based on institutionalized inequality. Instead, a new elite occupied the commanding heights of the state. It secured a similar status to those who under the old system were the privileged few. Meanwhile, large parts of the population remained marginalized. Beyond the formal civic rights for political participation anchored in a Constitution, such systems showed the narrow "limits to liberation" (Melber, 2003). It is not by coincidence that this has contributed to a renaissance in engaging with the writings of Fanon, with frequent references to the said chapter on "The Pitfalls of National Consciousness".

Zimbabwe: Mugabeism After Mugabe

Since the turn of the century, Mugabe and ZANU-PF lost legitimacy. They could only maintain power and control because of massive repression. This was tolerated if not supported by most other member states of the sub-region. Notwithstanding the loss of popular support, the image and claim of being the eternal liberator was perpetuated in the interpretations and perceptions of the regime. Those promoting such imaginations could rely on stereotypes that—while bordering on mystifications and mythologies—still be activated among parts of the population. This context:

> builds Mugabe into an abstract idea – the very embodiment of anti-colonial spirit. In this way, an attack on a Mugabe decision becomes not just an attack on him, but on the entire idea that black people deserve the right to self-determination. (Mpofu-Walsh, 2017, p. 96)

Robert Mugabe embodied the tenacious survival and cultivation of the status as heroes among the old men of the liberation struggle days. He underlined that "populism is not just a reaction *against* power structures but an appeal *to* a recognized authority," which illustrates "the tendency for heightened emotions to be focused on a charismatic leader" (Canovan, 1999, pp. 4 and 6; original emphasis).

The 93-year-old Mugabe could without any embarrassment publicly declare that he would never make room for a political opposition party by categorically stating that the Movement for Democratic Change (MDC) would never be allowed to govern the country and that only God, who has appointed him could remove him from office (Marx, 2017, p. 245). As president by God's will Mugabe felt not accountable to the people. His wife Grace could on several occasions suggest in all seriousness that her husband could also continue to reign from his grave (Jirihanga, 2017). Such phenomena of African gerontocracies underline that populism is effective and appealing to a wider audience. But beyond its outreach to "ordinary people", it is based on a group of compliant beneficiaries within the inner circle of state power. A profile of Mugabe therefore concludes that the really interesting phenomenon is not a man who stubbornly and ruthlessly accesses power but the political culture which produces such a form of personified rule. Marx (2017, p. 261) calls him a dictator. But populism and dictatorship are certainly not identical forms and the governance in Southern African states under former liberation movements is so far hardly translating into dictatorship.

That there are limits to such a rule showed the military intervention in Zimbabwean politics in mid-November 2017. As a "corrective measure", Mugabe was replaced by 75-year-old Emmerson Mnangagwa (dubbed "the crocodile"), his former confidante and another one from the first struggle generation. The aura of Mugabe, despite the countrywide celebrations of his ousting, remained largely untouched. He retained recognition beyond his fall from power. Ending in bitterness and isolation, feeling betrayed, his birthday was declared a national holiday. While Robert Gabriel Mugabe was forced to pass on the torch, "Mugabeism" (Ndlovu-Gatsheni, 2015) lives on in the forms of governance and the personified policies under ZANU-PF. Mnangagwa walks in the footsteps of his former mentor. He continues to intonate the *chimurenga* gospel (the Shona word for struggle): "Like Mugabe, Mnangagwa makes serious policy pronouncements at political rallies, taking everyone by surprise and would rather consolidate power to himself" (Muzulu, 2019). The case of Zimbabwe therefore raises the (so far inconclusive) question, at which stage forms of populist policy turn into a dictatorship.

NAMIBIA: NUJOMA'S LEGACY

The "big men" syndrome is an integral element of populism made in Southern Africa. Its impact continues to be inextricably linked with the history of the anti-colonial resistance whose mystification remains a central political element even today. Sam Nujoma (born 1929), since the founding of SWAPO in 1960 until 2007 its president and between 1990 and 2005 the first Namibian Head of State, was awarded at the end of his three terms in office by the National Assembly the official title "Father of the Namibian Nation". His biography (Nujoma, 2001) was published under the programmatic title "Where Others Wavered." It underlined the claim of uncompromising steadfastness.

Under Nujoma's reign, the new Namibian state came to be understood as a product of his nation building. This shaped and dominated national discourse. Nujoma's continued role since then underlines that in such an understanding a freedom fighter never retires but continues a lifelong mission (Melber, 2020). In 2010, he alerted the party's Youth League to "be on the full alert and remain vigilant against deceptive attempts by opportunists and unpatriotic elements that attempt to divide you." Only then, he asserted, would SWAPO "grow from strength to strength and continue to rule Namibia for the next ONE THOUSAND YEARS" (Nujoma undated; capital letters in the original).

Politics have also after Nujoma's presidency remained the domain of aging men (Melber, 2015). He had single-handedly imposed his loyal confidant Hifikepunye Pohamba (born 1936) as a successor for two terms from 2005 to 2015 at the price of a party division (Melber, 2006). Hage Geingob (born 1941), followed Pohamba with the latter's support. In the presidential elections of November 2019, he secured a second term in office from 2020 to 2025. He might be the last one holding office from the first generation of the liberation struggle, politically active since the early 1960s. Digressing from his predecessors, Geingob replaced the image of SWAPO as the family, home and nation by a wider formula. In his first State of the Nation Address in April 2015 he introduced the metaphor of the Namibian House, which according to him provides room for all Namibians. However, it remained open who is where and how accommodated in this Namibian House: who occupies the best rooms, who cooks, who washes dishes and takes care of the laundry and cleaning?

In April 2016, Geingob tabled the "Harambee Prosperity Plan" (HPP) (Office of the President, 2016). It replicated elements of the "Vision 2030" proclaimed by his predecessor Sam Nujoma prior to leaving office. The Vision's declared aim was a "prosperous and industralised Namibia" with less than 5% unemployment, no poverty and self-sufficient in food supply within the 25 years to come (Office of the President, 2004). HPP reinforces such unrealistic optimism not backed by any proper assessment of the socio-economic framework. It is based on an anticipated annual economic growth rate of seven percent and aims to eradicate poverty during Geingob's time in office. Such growth rate was at best wishful thinking. Instead, Namibia had already entered a recession. Since then the economy remained on a downward spiral. Rising unemployment and continued poverty were since then exacerbated by the impact of the Covid-19 pandemic. In as much as Vision 2030, HPP remains an illusion, but Geingob declared most goals remained a target. External factors were blamed for the miserable performance. Populists are never responsible for failures. Only others are, and circumstances beyond their control. Their promises of a better future are more wishful thinking than based on realistic assumptions. After 15 years of Vision 2030 and five years of the HPP, Namibia's annual per capita income has declined every year since 2016 (UNDP, 2019). Out of a total population of about 2.4 million, the number of those in formal employment declined from 365,703 in 2013 to 307,067 in 2018. If government employment (86,864) and employment in state-owned enterprises (30,654) is subtracted, the number of formally employed people in the private sector drops to 189,549 (Institute for Public Policy Research, 2019, p. 17). Not that any ordinary politician elsewhere would shy away from similar promises. It is part of their fabric. But populists seemingly tend to be even more generous with their claims.

South Africa: Zuma and Beyond

The "liberation movement syndrome" was diagnosed also for the ANC by De Jager and Steenekamp (2016, p. 928). They identified a self-conception of the party "as the leader, voice and embodiment of the people." It governs with a "pre-eminence of a liberationist culture, where group rather than individual responsibility is important" (De Jager & Steenekamp, 2016, p. 930). Brooks (2020) identified a tension between what she terms vanguardism and popular participation. She maintains that vanguardism prevents citizens from being empowered while keeping the party dominant. The difference between such vanguardism and populism is hardly existing, especially since "race-conscious populism is pulsating strongly within the ANC (…) feeding broader populist and Africanist thinking" (Ndlovu-Gatsheni, 2008, p. 80).

In contrast to the other two countries, however, the individual leaders played very different roles and the panorama ranges from the icon Nelson

Mandela to Jacob Zuma. The latter is a classic example of the category gradually losing support and trust through "bad governance" but resorting to conspiracy theories in a desperate effort to not surrender. Such leadership dismisses and ridicules any meaningful opposition even within the own ranks, as the power struggles inside the ANC documents. Accusations often suggest that opponents are remote-controlled agents of imperialism, seeking regime change as instruments of foreign agendas. When increasingly under pressure, Zuma even blamed "witches" inside the ANC being responsible for efforts to remove him from office (Politicsweb, 2016). In accordance with Robert Mugabe and Sam Nujoma, he also declared that the ANC rules forever (Mail & Guardian, 2014) and governs until the return of Jesus (Ngoepe, 2016).

As president in office, Zuma often intonated songs from the liberation struggle. This is a popular ritual to maintain the impression that the liberators are holding out in office. Such symbolism seeks to document solidarity with the masses and to confirm the belief that the political leadership sacrificed not only during the struggle days but relentlessly and selflessly continues to fight for a better future of the people. Since then, the ousted leader has even recorded an album (Nation, 2019). Zuma also appealed to primordial identities of a "Zulu warrior culture": at rallies he frequently intonated the struggle song "Bring me my machine gun" (Russell, 2009)—at a time when he was in court accused of rape.

Such mobilization signifies a popular and populist element: it creates the impression of a patriotic commitment, which seeks to cover its failures. It generates a timeline in which the protagonists feature as members of a struggle aristocracy. As a social movement activist diagnosed: "They want us to believe that the struggle is over, that all we have is remnants of the old order against whom our anger should be vented" (wa Bofelo, 2010). Efforts seeking distraction from the acute socio-economic crisis drew a distinction between the "real people" and its enemies—a foreign or fifth column, against which they claim a need to stand together. By doing so, they try to make use of a deeply entrenched, shared historic experience (Simkins, 2017, p. 36).

For the ultimate fall of Zuma—as in the case of Mugabe—populism alone is not enough. The anti-colonial movement as a party and government does not speak with one voice and has to observe the impact of governance on the electorate to remain in power. This at times motivates the replacement of populists who put the bigger interest at risk. The forms of state capture for personal gains made the Zuma-presidency untenable. The continued recourse to merits obtained during the liberation struggle was increasingly unpopular among the "born frees". The appeals to remain loyal to the liberators lost relevance. Together with the "struggle old-timers", the heroic narrative approached an expiry date and was dismissed as a self-serving invention:

> No leader – and no party – deserves a 'get out of jail free' card because of an intellectually shaky myth. To question that 'the ANC liberated us' is not only

a matter of historical accuracy, it's also a necessary, subversive political act, in a present crying out for historiographical honesty. (Mpofu-Walsh, 2017, p. 95)

This, however, does not signal an end to populism. Rather, as personified in Julius Malema and the Economic Freedom Fighters (EFF), it opens the playing field for new actors (Mbete, 2015). A mental offspring of his role model Zuma, the former leader of the ANC Youth League created a new and more aggressive form of populism in the public sphere (Posel, 2014), based "on performances to mobilize voters" (Resnick, 2018, p. 276). As a younger edition of Zuma, he does not stand in his former master's tradition and therefore represents the future—even if such future does not necessarily abide well. As observed by Ismael Lagardien (2018), social conditions in South Africa are a "fertile ground for fascist demagoguery and appeal." And Fölscher (2019, p. 110) alerted, "while South Africa does evince the contextual factors that are conducive to the manifestation of populist politics, only the EFF has consistently taken advantage of this condition." The discourses it triggered indicate a shift: torchbearers of hope are not any longer the aging veterans of the struggle days and their mindset. Zuma contributed to Malema's popularity by dismissing him from his own insider circle, thereby turning him into an alternative competing in terms of radical populism while "state capture" cumulating under Zuma into a deeply entrenched system of organized robbery was increasingly seen as an obstacle to progress. As much as he tried, he could no longer reinvent himself as a man of the people.

CONCLUSION: THE END OF BIG MEN?

The common engagement with populism tends to focus on the context of established democracies in which populists mobilize against an establishment and appeal to sentiments suspicious of those democrats in government, rallying "against both the established structure of power and the dominant ideas and values of the society" (Canovan, 1999, p. 3). The common assumption is that they are "of the people but not of the system" (Taggart, 1996, p. 32). This form of attack on established systems is not the point of departure for the kind of populism we are witnessing in Southern Africa. Rather, populism is a means to legitimize the continued governance of former liberation movements by appealing to the continued struggle against foreign domination and thereby marketing oneself as the only true alternative and promise of a better future. It is a kind of retrospectively applied populism vis-á-vis a colonial dominance. While this era is formally left behind and replaced by a local government in a sovereign state, it remains accused of efforts to regain power. This justifies an ongoing struggle led by the former liberation movement as the sole legitimate authority to represent the people freed from the colonial oppression. Liberation movements as governments retain a movement character and "often have more or less charismatic leaders, vivid individuals who can make politics personal and immediate instead of being remote and bureaucratic" (Canovan, 1999, p. 14).

The heroic narratives of liberation gospels were born in historical processes expected to achieve emancipation. Post-liberation, these processes elevated the anti-colonial movements into governments in firm social control. For Mugabe, Nujoma, Zuma and the like, including their offspring, authority is anchored in the struggle narrative. The "big men" syndrome is part of their populism. And by paying tribute to their peers, they applaud themselves. Namibia's current President Hage Geingob, for example, has praised Mugabe as his role model (Kwinika, 2015). Members of the new elite like to sing combat songs from the "struggle days" to show solidarity with the masses. They claim that they have not only sacrificed as liberation fighters but now work for a better future for all. Zambia's late President Michael Sata sang Zimbabwean *chimurenga* songs when Mugabe was criticized in closed meetings of the Southern Africa Development Community.

During the struggle for liberation, the aspiration for self-determination was associated with a better future for the formerly colonized. But, subsequently, social transformation was mainly limited to political control under which the new elite gained access to resources through the state. Such transition did not eliminate the colonial-era structural discrepancies. It privileged a few while the majority remained marginalized. A new compensatory ideology emerged, suggesting that the new injustice was purely the result of the colonial past. Populism, as a "universal mode of expression for unique national, cultural, class, ethnic, or racial identities of 'the people'" (Halisi, 1998, p. 424) came as a handy tool. But the times when leaders of the dominant parties could claim to be the alternative to the establishment are over. They are the established system. Their appeals to populist reminiscences of a bygone era of the "struggle days" sound increasingly hollow. Being escorted in the latest models of European limousines by motor cavalcades and flying in presidential jets to wine and dine with other leaders in the world are a mismatch with the liberation gospel.

Literature

Brooks, H. (2020). *The African National Congress and participatory democracy: From people's power to public policy*. Palgrave Macmillan.
Canovan, M. (1981). *Populism*. Harcourt Brace Jovanovich.
Canovan, M. (1999). Trust the People! Populism and the Two Faces of Democracy. *Political Studies, XLVII*, 2–16. https://doi.org/10.1111/1467-9248.00184
Cheeseman, N. (2018). Populism in Africa and the potential for "ethnically blind" politics. In C. de la Torre (Ed.), *Routledge handbook of global populism* (pp. 357–369). Routledge.
De Jager, N., & Steenekamp, C. L. (2016). The changing political culture of the African National Congress. *Democratization, 23*(5), 919–939. https://doi.org/10.1080/13510347.2015.1041382

Dikeni, L. M. (2017). Populism and Nationalism: Implications for South Africa. *Focus. The Journal of the Helen Suzman Foundation, 80*, 14–20. https://hsf.org.za/public ations/focus/focus-80-nationalism-and-populism-2/focus80-dikeni.pdf

Fanon, F. (2001). *The wretched of the Earth*. Penguin (originally 1963).

Fölscher, M. (2019). *The soft power of populist politics: A case study of the economic freedom fighters in the South African context* (MA Thesis). Department of Political Sciences, Stellenbosch University.

Halisi, C. R. D. (1998). Citizenship and Populism in the New South Africa. *Africa Today, 45*(3/4), 423–438. https://www.jstor.org/stable/4187237?seq=1#metadata_info_tab_contents

Institute for Public Policy Research. (2019, October–December). *Namibia Quarterly Economic Review*. https://ippr.org.na/publication/namibia-qer-quarter-4-2019/

Jirihanga, J. (2017, February 23). Will you let Mugabe rule from the grave? *New Zimbabwe*. http://www.newzimbabwe.com/opinion-34894-Will+you+let+Mugabe+rule+from+the+grave/opinion.aspx.

Kwinika, S. (2015, June 17). Africa Needs More Mugabes. *The Herald*. https://www.herald.co.zw/africa-needs-more-mugabes-2/

Lagardien, I. (2018, February 23). It's difficult but not impossible to see creeping fascism in the EFF. *Daily Maverick*. https://www.dailymaverick.co.za/opinionista/2018-02-23-its-difficult-but-not-impossible-to-see-creeping-fascism-in-the-eff/

Levitsky, S., & Way, L. A. (2002). Elections without democracy: The Rise of Competitive Authoritarianism. *Journal of Democracy, 13*(2), 51–65. https://scholar.harvard.edu/levitsky/files/SL_elections.pdf

Levitsky, S., & Way, L. A. (2010a). *Competitive authoritarianism: Hybrid regimes after the Cold War*. Cambridge University Press.

Levitsky, S., & Way, L. A. (2010b, September 2–5). *Beyond Patronage: Ruling Party Cohesion and Authoritarian Stability*. Paper prepared for the American Political Science Association Annual Meeting. Washington, DC.

Mail & Guardian. (2014, January 8). *Zuma: The ANC will rule until Jesus comes back*. https://mg.co.za/article/2014-01-08-zuma-the-anc-will-rule-forever

Marx, C. (2017). *Mugabe. Ein afrikanischer Tyrann*. C.H. Beck.

Mbete, S. (2015). The economic freedom fighters: South Africa's turn towards populism? *Journal of African Elections, 14*(1), 35–59. https://doi.org/10.20940/JAE/2015/v14i1a3

Melber, H. (Ed.). (2003). *Limits to liberation in Southern Africa: The unfinished business of democratic consolidation*. HSRC Press.

Melber, H. (2006). "Presidential indispensability" in Namibia: Moving out of office but staying in power? In R. Southall & H. Melber (Eds.), *Legacies of power: Leadership change and former presidents in African politics* (pp. 98–119). HSRC Press and Uppsala, The Nordic Africa Institute.

Melber, H. (2015). From Nujoma to Geingob: 25 years of presidential democracy. *Journal of Namibian Studies, 18*, 49–65.

Melber, H. (2020). Sam Nujoma: Lebenslänglich Freiheitskämpfer. In M. Epkenhans & E. Frie (Eds.), *Politiker ohne Amt. Von Metternich bis Helmut Schmidt* (pp. 239–256). Ferdinand Schöningh.

Mpofu-Walsh, S. (2017). *Democracy & delusion: 10 Myths in South African politics*. Tafelberg.

Muzulu, P. (2019, July 31). ED's big-man politics of populism. *Newsday*. https://www.newsday.co.zw/2019/07/eds-big-man-politics-of-populism/

Nation. (2019, January 3). *Jacob Zuma to release new struggle songs album*. https://nation.africa/kenya/news/africa/jacob-zuma-to-release-new-struggle-songs-album-124114

Ndlovu-Gatsheni, S. J. (2008). Black republican tradition, nativism and populist politics in South Africa. *Transformation, 68*, 53–86.

Ndlovu-Gatsheni, S. J. (Ed.). (2015). *Mugabeism? history, politics, and power in Zimbabwe*. Palgrave MacMillan.

Ngoepe, K. (2016, July 5). ANC will rule until Jesus comes, Zuma says again. *news 24*. http://www.news24.com/elections/news/anc-will-rule-until-jesus-comes-zuma-says-again-20160705

Nujoma, S. (2001). *Where others wavered: The autobiography of Sam Nujoma*. Panaf Books.

Nujoma, S. (undated). *Where we came from*. SWAPO Party web site. http://www.swapoparty.org/where_we_came_from.html

Nyadera, I. N., & Agwanda, B. (2019). The emergence and evolution of populism in Sub-Saharan Africa: Party politics and personalities. *International Journal of Political Studies, 5*(2), 76–91.

Politicsweb. (2016, November 19). *I know who are the witches at work—Jacob Zuma*. http://www.politicsweb.co.za/news-and-analysis/i-know-who-are-the-witches-at-work--jacob-zuma

Office of the President. (2004). *Namibia Vision 2030: Policy Framework for Long-Term National Development*. Government of the Republic of Namibia.

Office of the President. (2016). *Harambee Prosperity Plan 2016/17–2019/20. Namibian Government's Action Plan towards Prosperity for All*. Government of the Republic of Namibia.

Posel, D. (2014). Julius Malema and the post-apartheid public sphere. *Acta Academica, 46*(1), 31–52. http://scholar.ufs.ac.za:8080/bitstream/handle/11660/2997/academ_v46_n1_a5.pdf?sequence=1&isAllowed=y

Resnick, D. (2010). *Populist strategies in African democracies*. UNU-WIDER. https://www.wider.unu.edu/publication/populist-strategies-african-democracies

Resnick, D. E. (2017). Populism in Africa. In C. R. Kaltwasser, P. Taggart, P. O. Espejo, & P. Ostiguy (Eds.), *The Oxford handbook of populism* (pp. 101–119). Oxford Handbooks Online.

Resnick, D. E. (2018). The influence of populist leaders on African democracy. In C. de la Torre (Ed.), *Routledge handbook of global populism* (pp. 267–279). Routledge.

Russell, A. (2009). *Bring me my machine gun: The Battle for the Soul of South Africa From Mandela to Zuma*. Public Affairs.

Simkins, C. (2017). The crisis of African Nationalism. *Focus. The Journal of the Helen Suzman Foundation, 80*, 35–41. https://hsf.org.za/publications/focus/focus-80-nationalism-and-populism-2/focus80-simkins.pdf

Southall, R. (2013). *Liberation movements in power: Party and State in Southern Africa*. James Currey and Pietermaritzburg, South Africa: University of KwaZulu-Natal Press.

Taggart, P. A. (1996). *The new populism and the new politics: New Protest parties in Sweden in a comparative perspective*. Macmillan.

UNDP. (2019). *Briefing note on Namibia for 2019 Human Development Report*. http://hdr.undp.org/sites/all/themes/hdr_theme/country-notes/NAM.pdf

wa Bofelo, M. (2010, March 25). "Shoot the Boers!" Deflecting attention from new songs of protest. *Pambazuka News*, 475. https://www.pambazuka.org/governance/%E2%80%98shoot-boers%E2%80%99-deflecting-attention-new-songs-protest

Venezuela: The Institutionalization of Authoritarian Populism

Thomas Kestler and Miguel Latouche

Introduction

In late 1998, Hugo Chávez, a former military officer who had come to prominence by staging a failed coup in 1992, surprisingly won the presidential election in Venezuela. His rise from an obscure conspirator to the presidency marked the end of a decade-long party democracy and the start of a new political era, which can be regarded as a populist regime by any given standard (Hawkins, 2010). Instead of using populism just as an outsider strategy of mobilization, Chávez turned it into the guiding principle of his government and established a regime marked by extreme personalism, continuous mobilization and direct rule.[1] This renders his regime a crucial case for studying populism in power. Moreover, the fact that *Chavismo* has become the dominant force in Venezuelan politics even up until the present day draws attention to the forms and conditions of populist institutionalization.

This research was supported by a grant from the Bavarian University Center for Latin America (BAYLAT).

T. Kestler (✉)
Institute of Political Science and Sociology, University of Würzburg, Würzburg, Germany
e-mail: thomas.kestler@uni-wuerzburg.de

M. Latouche
University of Rostock, Rostock, Germany
e-mail: miguel.latouche@ucv.ve

© The Author(s), under exclusive license to Springer Nature Switzerland AG 2022
M. Oswald (ed.), *The Palgrave Handbook of Populism*,
https://doi.org/10.1007/978-3-030-80803-7_32

After initial challenges from established political and economic elites, Chávez successively strengthened his grip on power. He sponsored the drafting of a new constitution, reversed the preceding process of decentralization, increased control of the judiciary and reduced the scope of opposition media (Brewer-Carías, 2010; García-Guadilla & Mallen, 2018; Ramos Jiménez, 2011). A commodity boom starting in 2003 poured hundreds of billions of dollars into the government's coffers and allowed lavish patronage spending (Mazzuca, 2013). Not least, Chávez also benefitted from his extraordinary charismatic qualities, which were outstanding even by the standards of a region where many colorful, personalist rulers have made their appearance (Conniff, 2012).

Over time, Venezuelan populism turned more authoritarian, especially after Chávez's death in 2013, when his hand-picked successor, the former union leader and foreign minister Nicolás Maduro, took the helm of the regime (Levitsky & Loxton, 2018; López Maya, 2014). Faced not only with low personal approval but also with collapsing oil prices, Maduro stepped up repression and removed the last remnants of institutional checks and balances (Buxton, 2018; Corrales & Penfold, 2015). In May 2018, he was re-elected in a rigged presidential election which many countries refused to recognize, and which marked the country's final descent into open authoritarianism (Pantoulas & McCoy, 2019).

However, Maduro not only recurred to authoritarian means for securing his power, he also pursued a legitimation strategy based on the charismatic legacy of his predecessor. He further entrenched Chávez's personal myth and, thereby, provided an institutional underpinning to his regime. This aspect of Venezuelan populism has so far received little attention, supposedly because both, populism and authoritarianism, are often regarded as antithetical to institutionalization. This, however, is not necessarily the case. In the following section, we will discuss the relationship between populism, authoritarianism and institutionalism to identify ways of integrating these seemingly antagonistic concepts. Specifically, we focus on the ideational level and introduce a concept of institutionalization from above. In section three we will show how Chávez, from his position of power, laid the foundations for a persistent personalist myth during his presidency. In section four, we turn to the presidency of Maduro and his efforts at further institutionalizing this myth. The article concludes with a summary of our observations.

Reconciling the Concepts of Institutionalization, Populism and Authoritarianism

Institutions are defined by Richard Scott (2008, p. 48) as 'regulative, normative and cultural-cognitive elements that, together with associated activities and resources, provide stability and meaning to social life'. Once established, institutions are marked by path dependence following from self-reinforcing mechanisms such as learning effects, coordination effects and adaptive expectations (North, 1990, p. 94). On the regime-level, institutionalization means, in very general terms, the emergence and reproduction of institutional structures sustaining a regime (Lauth, 2007).

The concept of institutionalization is mostly applied to liberal institutional contexts—open markets and democratic polities. In these contexts, institutions are supposed to reduce transaction costs in social and economic interaction and, therefore, emerge from the voluntary exchange between actors in pursuance of their interest (e.g. Weingast, 1997; Williamson, 2000).[2] Conceived in this way, institutionalization stands in contradiction to authoritarianism which is, by definition, based on power asymmetries, not on 'structure-induced equilibria', as institutionalists call a state in which everybody is better off abiding by the rules (Shepsle, 1979). In addition, institutionalization appears to be hard to reconcile with populism, too. According to Benjamin Moffitt (2016), populism is defined by its performative, aesthetic and relational elements, which are, by their very nature, difficult to institutionalize. Moreover, populism often goes hand in hand with charismatic leadership and, therefore, a type of rule completely antithetical to institutionalization. While institutions are structures of impersonal, rule-based exchange, the defining principle of charismatic leadership is the supreme will of the leader, which leads Paul Taggart (2000, p. 99) to speak of a 'populist institutional dilemma'. The inherent tension between populism and institutionalization is further aggravated when populists gain power. When the governing elite cannot be blamed for persistent adversities anymore, when promises of progress and well-being fail to materialize and when corruption afflicts the very advocates of the 'little guy' himself, populists have a hard time surviving in government. This is why populists in power usually face an unpleasant choice: either they shed their populist tendencies, thereby provoking the wrath of their followers and renouncing their messianic calling, or they plunge their government into turmoil and risk losing power, as happened, for example, to Abdalá Bucaram in Ecuador or Thaksin Shinawatra in Thailand. Accordingly, Yves Mény and Yves Surel (2002, p. 18) assume that 'populist parties are by nature neither durable nor sustainable parties of government. Their fate is to be integrated into the mainstream, to disappear, or to remain permanently in opposition'.

However, a considerable range of empirical examples shows that populism in power is not necessarily short-lived (e.g. Albertazzi, 2015). To the contrary, some historical populist figures like Juan Domingo Perón in Argentina or Getulio Vargas in Brazil left a lasting legacy and shaped their country's political landscape for decades. To resolve this paradox, Takis Pappas (2019) carves out a range of mechanisms employed by populists to compensate for their deficiencies and the contradictions of populist rule: Populist regimes undermine institutional checks and balances, concentrate power in a charismatic leader, employ patronage to win elections, use an aggressive discourse to mobilize resentful voters, manipulate public communication and, eventually, resort to repression to fend off opposition. Yet, these tools are costly and difficult to sustain. Open violations of democratic norms provoke international rebuke while repression exacerbates internal conflicts and exposes a ruler's lack of legitimacy (Levitsky & Way, 2010). This leads us to introduce the aspect of institutionalization into the equation of regime durability and to look for possibilities of institutionalizing some features of populism. In fact, the anti-institutionalism of populists referred to for example by Margaret Canovan (1999) only applies to a specific set of institutions, namely 'intermediary bodies' like political parties, media and the courts (Urbinati, 2015). It does not extend to structures reflecting the populist logic and reproducing the populist style. When it comes to organize their own mass base, for example, populists often overcome their anti-institutional inclinations (see e.g. Roberts, 2006). Recent examples like Silvio Berlusconi in Italy show that even charisma is not generally antithetical to processes of institutionalization—it can be artificially created and reproduced through the media (Schlemmer, 2019).

But still, one question remains: How can institutionalization be reconciled with authoritarianism which has become a dominant trait of populism in Venezuela? To resolve this puzzle, the concept of institutions as equilibria emerging from a bottom-up process of voluntary exchange has to be modified, or rather, complemented by a power-based approach to institutionalization. According to Terry Moe (2005), institutional structures can also be created from above, through the use of power. From government position populists and authoritarian leaders can employ the resources at their disposal not only for compensatory means such as repression and patronage, but also for establishing institutional structures that reproduce and reinforce their position of power. This applies especially to the 'third face of power' (Lukes, 1974), which Paul Pierson (2016) associates with mass beliefs and ideas about what is possible and what is desirable. Indeed, examples from Post-Soviet countries show that authoritarian regimes frequently rely on ideational structures—symbols, discourse and mass beliefs—to stabilize their rule (see e.g. Soest & Grauvogel, 2015). Such ideational structures created from above can be expected in populist-authoritarian regimes, too.

One outstanding example is Juan Domingo Perón in Argentina. Explanations of Perón's lasting influence on Argentine politics usually focus on the role of the unions (e.g. McGuire, 1997). However, Perón built his power not only on organizational structures but also on ideas. Starting in the late 1940s, he established the so-called *Justicialismo* as guiding ideational framework, which integrated elements of corporatism, nationalism and socialism with typical populist motifs (Waldmann, 1974). A crucial step toward institutionalizing this 'doctrine' was the foundation of the *Escuela Superior Peronista* (ESP) in 1950, which, according to Perón, was supposed to maintain the movement's ideational foundations, disseminate it among the public and educate future Peronist leaders. Perón also made efforts to entrench the myth around his first wife, Eva Perón, who died in 1952. Her autobiographical book 'La razón de mi vida' was made compulsory reading in all Argentine schools and her birthday became a fixed holiday in the Peronist calendar (Taylor, 1981). Perón therefore used his position of power to establish durable structures not only on the organizational level but also on the level of symbols, discourse and mass beliefs—with the latter turning out to be even more durable than the former.

From the foregoing considerations and the prototypical example of Peronism, three conclusions can be drawn regarding the conditions and patterns of populist institutionalization. First, neither populism, nor authoritarianism need to be an impediment to institutionalization. Some crucial features of populism like the personal myth of the populist leader can be reproduced from above. Second, institutionalization in populist and authoritarian contexts is to be expected mainly on the ideational level and takes the form of symbolic structures, narratives and mass beliefs. These structures become entrenched through institutes, libraries, think tanks and educational entities. This means, thirdly, that control of public discourse plays a crucial role not only for silencing criticism, as Pappas (2019) observed, but also for strengthening and reproducing the regimes 'third face of power' through symbolic and narrative structures. In the following sections, we will show that this was indeed the case in Venezuela. Although Hugo Chávez represented a prototypical example of a personalist, charismatic leader, there are important aspects of institutionalization which helped stabilize his rule and explain the enduring dominance of *Chavismo* until the present day.

ESTABLISHING A PERSONALIST MYTH: THE POPULIST REGIME OF HUGO CHÁVEZ, 1999–2013

Between re-democratization in 1958 and the collapse of the party system in the 1990s, Venezuela was regarded as a 'partidocrazia'—a system dominated by two clientelist mass parties and based on an elite consensus about state-led modernization through the use of the country's enormous petroleum wealth (Coppedge, 1994; Coronil, 1997). This model was shattered when oil prices plummeted and citizens started to rebel against liberal reforms, corruption and growing inequalities (Gil Yepes, 2015; Latouche, 2006). The concomitant delegitimation of the established parties over the course of two decades set the stage for Hugo Chávez's rise to power—a man who not only represented an antidote to the ossification and cartelization of the Venezuelan party state, but to liberal democracy itself (Corrales & Penfold, 2015; Monaldi & Penfold, 2014).

Chávez promised to install an alternative model through what he called his 'Bolivarian Revolution', which turned out as a populist regime marked by an extreme kind of direct rule (Urbinati, 2015). The consequence was erratic decision-making, poor governance quality, waste of resources and rampant corruption. Once the oil boom abated, inflation picked up while the economy entered a downward spiral. Nonetheless, Chávez enjoyed continued support, even when economic and social indicators started to deteriorate in 2010. The question, therefore, is how Chávez could maintain his position of power for more than 14 years and remain the dominant factor in Venezuelan politics even after his death. How could it be that such an extremely personalist regime became so firmly entrenched, despite the corruption and the economic disaster it produced?

A first approximation to answer this question leads to the mechanisms described by Pappas (2019): Patronage, personalism and concentration of power in the executive. These mechanisms, however, only provide a partial explanation because they largely depend on the availability of resources. Between 2004 and 2009, when Chávez benefited from an oil boom of unprecedented dimensions, amble resources were available, but when the boom turned into a bust, one would expect the populist leader to be drawn into the abyss, too. Still, Chávez gained 55.1 percent of the vote in 2012, when poverty and inflation were markedly on the rise—despite the fact that, according to a survey, only 10 percent of the population benefitted directly from social programs (España, 2015; Hidalgo, 2014). Thus, patronage provides an insufficient explanation for Chávez's strong grip on power.

Another potential explanation is organizational support (see e.g. Handlin, 2016). Especially during his first few years in office, when the regime's hegemony had not yet been firmly established and the scope for distributive policies was limited, Chávez encouraged the establishment of a base organization, a Bolivarian union movement and the consolidation of the government party, the *Movimiento Quinta República* (MVR). However, given the personalist character of the regime, these efforts largely failed. In the face of continuing corruption and factionalism, the MVR was dissolved in 2007 only to be refounded as *Partido Socialista Unido de Venezuela* (PSUV) (Bergen Granell, 2016; Kestler, 2009). Still, as all relevant decisions ultimately depended on Chávez, there was little room for the emergence of autonomous organizational structures. Thus, the tensions and contradictions between the authoritarian need for control and the direct representational logic of populism, on the one hand, and the mechanisms of institutionalization, on the other, became clearly visible on the level of formal and organizational structures.

This did not mean, however, that *Chavismo* remained uninstitutionalized. While organizational efforts failed, the regime became successively entrenched on the level of discourse, symbols and mass beliefs. The government used its resources also to strengthen the third face of power and to create durable ideational structures. This strategy, however, was conditioned upon communicational hegemony. To entrench the regime's narrative and to establish a personalist myth, Chávez needed to connect with his base through a continuous stream of discourse and images. Public communication, therefore, became a central battlefield for the entire period of Chávez's presidency. From the start, private media became subject to restraints and menaces; a number of radio and television stations were bought by governmental agents and oppositional newspapers were put under economic and judicial pressure. More importantly, oppositional TV stations were brought, one by one, under government control, with the last communicational bastion of the opposition, *Globovision*, being silenced in 2013. Moreover, the government legally obliged all TV and radio stations to transmit government broadcasts, so-called *Cadenas*, which could interrupt the running program at any time and without temporal limitations. According to Elisabeth Safar (2016, p. 233), during Chávez's presidency the number of *Cadenas* totaled 2,274, covering a broadcasting time of 1,650 hours. Chávez also created his own personal TV show called *Aló Presidente*, which featured the president attending to citizen's concerns personally. Starting in the year 1999, this show became a weekly ritual, run by all broadcasting stations of the country simultaneously and lasting up to seven hours. Through this media presence, Chávez conveyed a notion of identity and the impression of direct communication between him and the community of the 'faithful' (Michelutti, 2016).

Beyond performative aspects, including singing and dancing interludes by the president, communicational hegemony was used to build a stable ideational base. Despite his tendency toward eclecticism and improvisation, Chávez's discourse revealed a certain degree of continuity or, rather, a kind of ideational evolution, in whose course a stable framework of symbols, narratives and attitudinal patterns emerged. Initially, Chávez referred almost exclusively to historical motifs, especially to the hero of Venezuelan independence, Simón Bolívar, after whom he named his movement and his 'revolution'. The cult of Bolivar had a long tradition in Venezuela, but Chávez used it more intensely and he significantly changed the way this figure was represented aesthetically and symbolically (Boeckh & Graf, 2007). As part of what may be called a process of symbolic resignification, the exhumed remnants of Bolívar were subjected to a 'scientific' investigation and, after a reconstruction of his face, the government presented a new image of Bolivar with mixed or 'mestizo' characteristics (Angosto-Ferrández, 2016).[3] These features appealed to large sectors of Venezuelan society that, like Chávez himself, shared these ethnic characteristics. Thus, the deeply rooted cult of Bolívar was reinterpreted and used to install and to reproduce a sense of identification with Chávez and his government. For that purpose, Chávez also frequently referred to a genealogical line between himself and historical figures from the nineteenth century (Gott & Bartoli, 2005; Krauze, 2012).

Generally, the appreciation of Venezuela's cultural and ethnic heterogeneity became a mainstay of *chavista* discourse and symbolism. It was given institutional underpinning through the formal recognition of the rights of indigenous people in the 1999 constitution as well as through the support of research and teaching in the field of African and diaspora studies. Chávez also used popular tales like 'Florentino and the Devil', in which a cowboy defeats the devil in a singing contest, to transmit the idea of a virtuous and authentic people (Hawkins, 2010). Against this backdrop, the social missions, that were introduced by Chávez in 2004 and named after heroes of independence, were not just tools of patronage. Rather, they gave substance to his discourse of appreciating and re-valorizing the so-called 'popular classes' (Zúquete, 2008).

Thus, the term 'the people' was not just invoked on a general level, but subjected to a fundamental reinterpretation based on motifs from Venezuelan history and culture. These motifs were reproduced in Chávez's discourse and entrenched symbolically, mainly through the social missions, but also through symbolic acts like re-naming the republic, adding an additional star to the country's flag and redesigning the horse in the national emblem.

By the year 2005, Chávez introduced the term socialism linking it to Bolívar whom he declared to be the first socialist: 'If he had lived a few decades longer, I am absolutely sure he would have become a Socialist', Chávez asserted in one of his speeches (Brown, 2009, p. xiv). From that point on, the term socialism turned into a centerpiece of *chavista* discourse, passing through different varieties like 'twenty-first century socialism' or 'petroleum socialism'. While Chávez himself remained rather vague regarding the concrete content of these terms, intellectuals from his surroundings such as the sociologist Heinz Dieterich tried to develop a more elaborate concept of 'twenty-first century socialism' (Dieterich, 2006). Such efforts, however, were inconsequential. In 2010, the ruling PSUV in an apparent allusion to the Maoist example, issued a 'Red Book', which substituted the term twenty-first-century socialism with 'Bolivarian socialism', but it failed to provide it with substance (PSUV, 2010). Thus, unlike other charismatic leaders, Chávez did not lay down his ideas in a 'revolutionary bible', except for a programmatic book written between the years of 1992 and 1994, the so-called *Libro Azul*, which went largely unnoticed during his presidency. The production and reproduction of ideas remained symbolic and performative in nature, with the person of the president being the main symbol and interpreter of the *Bolivarian Revolution*.

Still, it would be inadequate to speak with Ernesto Laclau (2005) of an empty signifier. In fact, Chávez embodied and symbolically represented important aspects of Venezuelan culture and social reality, while at the same time reshaping this reality. This can be best observed on the level of public attitudes, which underwent a substantial and lasting transformation. For example, Venezuelans' attitudes toward the United States turned negative, while the *chavista* movement still enjoys astonishingly high support (e.g. Azpuru & Zechmeister, 2013; El Universal, 2020). Moreover, Chávez created a strong sense of attachment to himself and a deeply ingrained belief in his charismatic leadership (Merolla & Zechmeister, 2011).

Given the centrality of his personal appeal, Chávez's death in 2013 presented an existential challenge to the regime. As Margarita López Maya (2014, p. 68) notes, his death 'left an immense political vacuum' and threatened the legitimacy of the regime. The following reaction was twofold: On the one hand, repression was stepped up to compensate for the loss of legitimacy. On the other hand, the regime put major efforts in creating a *Chavismo sin Chávez* by recovering and entrenching the myth left by the populist leader. Thus, the institutionalization of populism took a markedly different turn after 2013.

The Institutionalization of the Charismatic Legacy After 2013

Even after his death, Chávez remained the focus of identification for his followers. During his funeral, they proclaimed the slogan 'Chávez, I swear to you: I will vote for Maduro' (Muñoz, 2013) and, accordingly, Maduro presented himself as Chávez's 'son' and 'apostle' and he even tried to emulate the style of his predecessor. However, in the face of a rather narrow victory in the presidential election of April 2013 and an opposition victory in the parliamentary elections of 2015, it became apparent that more solid structures were needed to sustain the regime.

At first, the government focused on consolidating its power base by enhancing the use of force and legal means against the opposition and dissidence within its own ranks. The armed forces were further built up and positions of command were filled with loyalists. The official party, the PSUV was subjected to internal purges and turned into a more cohesive tool of mobilization and control. The implementation of the so-called *Carnet de la Patria*, a document necessary to access subsidized food, medicine and other social benefits, was established as a mechanism of social control (Salmerón & Salmerón, 2019). Moreover, internal dissent was dissipated by distributing spoils and providing a share of power to potential rivals (EIU, 2018).

Thus, the reactions of the regime to the loss of its charismatic leader and to declining revenues largely corresponded to the patterns described by Pappas (2019). However, the regime not only recurred to compensatory tools of repression and co-optation, but it also made efforts at further institutionalizing the personalist myth established by Chávez. Already in 2013, the government had announced the publication of a new edition of Chávez's *Libro Azul*, prefaced by Maduro. Similar to Muammar Gaddafi's *Green Book*, the *Libro Azul* was converted into an official regime bible to be distributed and studied in all governmental and military facilities (Meza, 2013). In 2014, the government also distributed a new collection of books for all levels of the educational system, praising the rule of Chávez and conveying a highly ideological interpretation of recent Venezuelan history (Ore, 2014).

At its third Congress in 2014, the PSUV decided to recognize Chávez officially as the party's 'eternal leader and foundational president' and to establish his legacy as the 'fourth root of the Bolivarian revolution', next to the historical figures Simón Bolívar, Simón Rodríguez and Ezequiel Zamora. The PSUV also decided to 'guarantee the preservation, compilation, organization and systematization of the whole documentary base (written and audio-visual material) which in its entirety constitutes the doctrinal legacy of thought and action' left by Chávez (PSUV, 2014). In 2016, the government launched the website 'todochavez.gob.ve', which provides access to thousands of documents and sources from Chávez's life. To physically represent this legacy, the government created an 'Institute for Higher Studies of the Thinking of Hugo

Chávez', located at Chávez's birthplace in the state of Barinas and presided over by his brother Adán.

With these efforts, the regime was arrogating for itself the role of guardian of *Chavismo*'s foundational ideas, which helped prevent competing factions from claiming Chávez's legacy. In this way it became easier to label internal opponents as traitors and to legitimize repression against any manifestation of dissidence. To underpin its association with Chávez, the government also introduced a range of TV programs featuring government members who present quotations, pictures and speeches of Chávez. Thereby, the performative aspects of populist rule were partly recovered and reproduced. While television had previously served to establish a direct relationship between Chávez and his followers, now it is used to entrench and solidify his memory and the myth based on it.

Chávez not only appears constantly on television, but his pictures are also ubiquitous in public spaces and his name is frequently referred to in official discourse. As Franz Manuel von Bergen Granell (2016, p. 201) observes, 'Chávez came to be transformed into a kind of Venezuelan Big Brother who has to be admired with loyalty and who serves as a guide'. Thereby, the memory of Chávez serves as a unifying idea to the point that he has even displaced Bolívar as the main political reference. In a certain way, 'Chávez is now to Maduro what Bolívar was to Chávez', as Lucia Michelutti (2016, p. 245) notes. With the sacralized figure of Hugo Chávez at its center, government discourse revolves around motifs like the 'survival of the revolution' and the 'construction of socialism'. It strongly relies on dichotomies like 'the people' vs. the 'bourgeoisie', 'independence' vs. 'imperialism' or 'socialism' vs. 'capitalism'. Therefore, the discursive patterns established by Chávez have solidified into a stable legitimizing narrative, which leaves no room between the government as defender of the people and the revolution, on the one hand, and its domestic and external enemies, on the other (Arenas, 2016).

The process of institutionalizing the populist regime was also enhanced on the symbolic level, starting with Chávez's funeral in March 2013. Chávez was buried in a mausoleum, the so-called 'Cuartel de la Montaña', specifically erected for that purpose on the symbolic site of the former military museum. There, Chávez had conceded the failure of an attempted coup in 1992 in a short televised interview, which had gained him national prominence. As early as 2002, this site was turned into a museum of the *Bolivarian Revolution*, but only in 2013 did it become the center of the *chavista* imaginary. The whole place was designed to represent Chávez as a central figure in Venezuelan history and to symbolically express his continued status as the country's president. The mausoleum became a place of worship, where adherents of the regime gather to render homage and to be 'in touch' with the dead leader. A chapel was even erected near the grave, which has an image of Chávez next to Christ and the Virgin Mary (Angosto-Ferrández, 2016). Thus, the personalist myth established by Chávez was transformed into recurring rituals and material, permanent symbols.

While these efforts may be regarded mainly as government propaganda, the sacralization of Chávez's legacy also developed 'from the bottom up', starting already during his lifetime. In fact, religious motifs and attributions associated with Chávez sprang up immediately after the military insurrection of 1992. During his presidency, he was the object of multiple forms of personal veneration. After his death, Chávez took a firm place within a specific variety of popular religiosity in Venezuelan, the so-called María Lionza cult, which combines elements of Afro-Caribbean religions, indigenous beliefs and Catholicism (Pollak-Eltz, 2004). Chávez joined the array of spirits and saints used in this cult. His image is now found in places of popular worship as well as in altars of many Venezuelan homes. According to testimonies cited by Luis Hernández (2018), people not only pray to Chávez, but they also petition him and attribute miracles to him. These beliefs and practices are fairly common among government followers and they are similar to those found in the case of Simón Bolívar, Eva Perón or, to a somewhat lesser degree, Ernesto Ché Guevara. Institutionalization of charismatic leadership through practices of sacralization, thus, seems to be a more general pattern, at least in Latin America (Krauze, 2012).

Taken together, these observations point to a process of institutionalization on the level of discourse, symbols and mass beliefs that have been taking place since 2013. To compensate for the loss of charismatic legitimacy, the government of Nicolás Maduro made efforts to restore some elements of direct, charismatic rule through the media, to turn Chávez's legacy into material structures and to establish ritualized forms of memorializing the supreme leader. To be sure, these efforts have yielded modest results insofar as most Venezuelans still refuse to recognize Maduro as Chávez's direct heir and blame him for the economic disaster the country is going through. However, veneration for Chávez is widespread and deeply entrenched. Thus, while Maduro has failed to establish a direct identification between himself and his predecessor, he has succeeded in reproducing and entrenching *Chavismo* as a civil religion based on the myth around Chávez. The populist regime established by Chávez has solidified into ideational structures, including the identification of large sectors of the Venezuelan population with *Chavismo*.

Conclusion

The concepts of populism and authoritarianism, on the one hand, and institutionalization, on the other, are usually regarded to be strange bed-fellows. Institutionalization seems to contradict certain aspects of both populism and authoritarianism. However, as the foregoing considerations and observations from the Venezuelan case have shown, this need not necessarily be the case. On the conceptual level, the contradictions seem less severe when the focus is shifted from formal, organizational structures and intermediary bodies of representation to the 'third face of power'—to discourse, symbols and mass beliefs. On the ideational level, important aspects of populism can be reproduced and structurally entrenched through the educational system, research institutes and, above all, the media. Authoritarianism need not necessarily stand in the way of such a process, to the contrary. Once institutionalization is not seen exclusively as a bottom-up process of routinization leading into a state of equilibrium, authoritarian means can be regarded as supportive of a process of institutionalization from above.

The Venezuelan case showed that even an extreme variety of populism like the one established by Hugo Chávez can include a mechanism of institutionalization. A key factor for entrenching populist rule on the ideational level is communicational hegemony. Once the direct link between the populist leader and her followers becomes routinized by everyday practices and experiences, it solidifies into stable beliefs and expectations. This process is frequently supported by the establishment of symbolic structures and mechanisms of reproduction. In the Venezuelan case, two distinct periods of populist institutionalization could be identified. Until 2013, populism remained largely performative in kind, with Chávez himself acting as the central symbol and embodiment of the *Bolivarian Revolution*. The civic religion established during his regime remained centered on his person and the myth created around him. After Chávez's death, the process of institutionalization took a markedly different direction. Given Maduro's lacking capabilities of assuming the role of a charismatic leader, the regime recurred to measures of entrenching the personalist myth from above, through the symbolic representation of Chávez's legacy, its reproduction through the media and its inculcation through the educational system. Not least as a result of these efforts, *Chavismo* is now deeply entrenched as a kind of civil religion and it will with all probability remain the dominating factor of Venezuelan politics for the foreseeable future. Although Maduro's attempts at establishing an identification of his government with Chávez have been largely unsuccessful, the opposition's failure to oust him and to mobilize noteworthy support for a regime change is indicative of the firm institutionalization of populism in Venezuela.

Notes

1. It is commonplace to refer to populism as a contested concept (see e.g. Weyland, 2001). Nonetheless, we refrain from a discussion of the varying definitions of populism, which can be found elsewhere (see Chapter 1 in this volume). Here, we rely on a family resemblance concept of populism as proposed by Rogers Brubaker (2017), who conceptualizes populism as a discursive and stylistic repertoire centering around the notion of the common people and including features such as anti-elitism, anti-intellectualism, protectionism and 'direct rule' (see also Urbinati, 2015).
2. As Avner Greif and Christopher Kingston (2011, p. 25) put it: 'The core idea in the institutions-as-equilibria approach is that it is ultimately the behavior and

the expected behavior of others rather than prescriptive rules of behavior that induce people to behave (or not to behave) in a particular way'.
3. 'Mestizo' is a Spanish term referring to a person of mixed ethnicity, especially one having European and indigenous descent.

Literature

Albertazzi, D. (2015). *Populists in power*. Routledge.
Angosto-Ferrández, L. F. (2016). The afterlives of Hugo Chávez as political symbol. *Anthropology Today, 32*(5), 8–12.
Arenas, N. (2016). Nicolás Maduro: ¿populismo sin carisma? *Cuadernos Del Cendes, 33*(92), 113–128.
Azpuru, D., & Zechmeister, E. (2013, June 24). Latin Americans' perceptions of the United States and China. *Americas Quarterly*. https://www.vanderbilt.edu/lapop/news/062413.AB-AmericasQuarterly.pdf
Bergen Granell, F. M. v. (2016). *Auge y declive de la hegemonía chavista. Colección Visión Venezuela*. UCAB Ediciones.
Boeckh, A., & Graf, P. (2007). El comandante en su laberinto: el ideario bolivariano de Hugo Chávez. In G. Maihold (Ed.), *Venezuela en retrospectiva: Los pasos hacia el régimen chavista* (pp. 151–178). Vervuert.
Brewer-Carías, A. R. (2010). *Dismantling democracy in Venezuela: The Chávez Authoritarian Experiment*. Cambridge University Press.
Brown, M. (Ed.). (2009). *The Bolívarian Revolution. Simón Bolívar: Introduction by Hugo Chávez*. Verso.
Brubaker, R. (2017). Why populism? *Theory and Society, 46*(5), 357–385. https://doi.org/10.1007/s11186-017-9301-7
Buxton, J. (2018). Venezuela: Deeper into the Abyss. *Revista De Ciencia Política, 38*(2), 409–428.
Canovan, M. (1999). Trust the people! Populism and the two faces of democracy. *Political Studies, 47*(2), 2–16.
Conniff, M. L. (Ed.). (2012). *Populism in Latin America* (2nd ed.). University of Alabama Press. http://site.ebrary.com/lib/uniregensburg/Doc?id=10603216
Coppedge, M. (1994). *Strong Parties and Lame Ducks: Presidential Partyarchy and Factionalism in Venezuela*. Stanford University Press.
Coronil, F. (1997). *The magical state: Nature, money, and modernity in Venezuela*. University of Chicago Press.
Corrales, J., & Penfold, M. (2015). *Dragon in the Tropics: The Legacy of Hugo Chávez* (2nd ed.). Brookings Institution Press.
Dieterich, H. (2006). *El socialismo del siglo XXI: La democracia participativa*. Gara Egunkaria.
EIU [Economist Intelligence Unit]. (2018, June 25). *Maduro attempts to secure regime's internal stability*. https://country.eiu.com/article.aspx?articleid=1216866705&Country=Venezu
El Universal. (2020). *Hinterlaces: 36% de los venezolanos apoya al PSUV*. https://www.eluniversal.com/politica/62018/hinterlaces-36-de-los-venezolanos-apoya-al-psuv
España, L. P. (2015). Aumento de la pobreza y acciones para su superación. In A. Freitez Landaeta, M. J. González, & R. G. Zúñiga Álvarez (Eds.), *Una mirada*

a la situación social de la población venezolana (pp. 23–33). Universidad Católica Andrés Bello.

García-Guadilla, M. P., & Mallen, A. (2018). Polarization, participatory democracy, and democratic erosion in Venezuela's twenty-first century socialism. *The Annals of the American Academy of Political and Social Science, 681*(1), 62–77. https://doi.org/10.1177/0002716218817733

Gil Yepes, J. A. (2015). *Poder, petróleo y pobreza*. Editorial Libros Marcados.

Gott, R., & Bartoli, G. (2005). *Hugo Chávez and the Bolivarian Revolution*. Verso.

Greif, A., & Kingston, C. (2011). Institutions: Rules or Equilibria. In N. Schofield (Ed.), *Political economy of institutions, democracy and voting* (pp. 13–43). Springer.

Handlin, S. (2016). Mass organization and the durability of competitive authoritarian regimes. *Comparative Political Studies, 49*(9), 1238–1269. https://doi.org/10.1177/0010414016628186

Hawkins, K. A. (2010). *Venezuela's Chavismo and populism in comparative perspective*. Cambridge University Press.

Hernández, L. A. (2018). El culto a Hugo Chávez en Venezuela: ¿Santo, ser vergatario o muerto poderoso? *Ciências Sociais E Religião, 20*(28), 114–128.

Hidalgo, M. (2014). The 2012 and 2013 presidential elections in Venezuela. *Electoral Studies, 34*, 315–321. https://doi.org/10.1016/j.electstud.2013.12.007

Kestler, T. (2009). *Parteien in Venezuela: Repräsentation, Partizipation und der politische Prozess* (Dissertation). Katholische Universität Eichstätt-Ingolstadt, Nomos.

Krauze, E. (2012). *Redeemers: Ideas and power in Latin America* (H. Heifetz & N. Wimmer, Trans.). Harper Perennial.

Laclau, E. (2005). *On populist reason*. Verso.

Latouche, M. A. (2006). Los dilemas de la representación: Hacia una revisión de la crisis del sistema político venezolano contemporáneo. *Revista Venezolana De Análisis De Coyuntura, 12*(2), 11–27.

Lauth, H.-J. (2007). Transformation. In A. Benz, S. Lütz, U. Schimank, & G. Simonis (Eds.), *Handbuch Governance: Theoretische Grundlagen und empirische Anwendungsfelder* (pp. 144–157). VS Verlag für Sozialwissenschaften. https://doi.org/10.1007/978-3-531-90407-8_11

Levitsky, S., & Loxton, J. (2018). Populism and competitive authoritarianism in Latin America. In C. de La Torre (Ed.), *Routledge International Handbooks. The Routledge Handbook of Global Populism* (pp. 334–350). Routledge.

Levitsky, S., & Way, L. A. (2010). *Competitive authoritarianism: Hybrid regimes after the Cold War*. Cambridge University Press. https://doi.org/10.1017/CBO9780511781353

López Maya, M. (2014). Venezuela: The political crisis of Post-Chavismo. *Social Justice, 40*(4), 68–87.

Lukes, S. (1974). *Power: A radical view*. Macmillan.

Mazzuca, S. L. (2013). The rise of rentier populism. *Journal of Democracy, 24*(2), 108–122. https://doi.org/10.1353/jod.2013.0034

McGuire, J. W. (1997). *Peronism without Perón: Unions, parties, and democracy in Argentina*. Stanford University Press.

Mény, Y., & Surel, Y. (2002). The Constitutive ambiguity of populism. In Y. Mény & Y. Surel (Eds.), *Democracies and the populist challenge* (pp. 1–21). Palgrave Macmillan.

Merolla, J. L., & Zechmeister, E. J. (2011). The nature, determinants, and consequences of Chávez's Charisma: Evidence From a study of Venezuelan public opinion. *Comparative Political Studies, 44*(1), 28–54. https://doi.org/10.1177/0010414010381076

Meza, A. (2013, November 23). El profeta Chávez. *El País*. https://elpais.com/internacional/2013/11/23/actualidad/1385161969_472312.html

Michelutti, L. (2016). We are all Chávez. *Latin American Perspectives, 44*(1), 232–250. https://doi.org/10.1177/0094582X16666023

Moe, T. M. (2005). Power and political institutions. *Perspectives on Politics, 3*(2), 215–233.

Moffitt, B. (2016). *The global rise of populism: Performance, political style, and representation*. Stanford University Press.

Monaldi, F., & Penfold, M. (2014). Institutional collapse: The rise and decline of democratic governance in Venezuela. In F. Rodríguez & R. Hausmann (Eds.), *Venezuela before Chávez: Anatomy of an economic collapse* (pp. 285–320). Pennsylvania State University Press.

Muñoz, B. (2013, July 13). *Después de Chávez*. https://gatopardo.com/reportajes/la-muerte-de-chavez-en-venezuela/

North, D. C. (1990). *Institutions, institutional change and economic performance*. Cambridge University Press.

Ore, D. (2014). *'Chavista' school books stoke passions in Venezuela*. https://www.reuters.com/article/us-venezuela-education/chavista-school-books-stoke-passions-in-venezuela-idUSKBN0ED1OM20140602

Pantoulas, D., & McCoy, J. (2019). Venezuela: An unstable equilibrium. *Revista De Ciencia Política (Santiago), 39*(2), 391–408. https://doi.org/10.4067/S0718-090X2019000200391

Pappas, T. S. (2019). *Populism and liberal democracy: A comparative and theoretical analysis* (1st ed.).

Pierson, P. (2016). Power in historical institutionalism. In O. Fioretos, T. G. Falleti, & A. Sheingate (Eds.), *The Oxford handbook of historical institutionalism* (pp. 124–141). Oxford University Press.

Pollak-Eltz, A. (2004). *Maria Lionza: Mito y culto venezolano ayer y hoy* (3rd ed.). Universidad Católica Andrés Bello.

PSUV [Partido Socialista Unido de Venezuela]. (2010). *Libro rojo - Documentos fundamentales del PSUV*. http://www.PSUV.org.ve/temas/biblioteca/libro-rojo/

PSUV [Partido Socialista Unido de Venezuela]. (2014). *III Congreso: Por el legado del Comandante Supremo Hugo Chávez la militancia psuvista entra en debate*. https://issuu.com/alexismejias5/docs/psuv_iii_congreso_acta_de_decisione

Ramos Jiménez, A. (2011, January–June). La 'revolución' que no fue. Desgobierno y autoritarismo en la Venezuela de Chávez. *Estudios Políticos, 38*, 69–91.

Roberts, K. M. (2006). Populism, political conflict, and grass-roots organization in Latin America. *Comparative Politics, 38*(2), 127–148.

Safar, E. (2016). El Aló Presidente y las cadenas de radio y televisión: Espejos de la pasión autoritaria del presidente Chávez. In M. Bisbal (Ed.), *La comunicación bajo asedio: Balance de 17 años* (pp. 226–249). Universidad Católica Andrés Bello.

Salmerón, M., & Salmerón, C. (2019). *¿Por qué Nicolás Maduro sigue en el poder pese al colapso de Venezuela?* https://www.cidob.org/es/content/download/72131/2265645/version/6/file/NOTES%20211_MELISSA%20SALMER%C3%93N%20%26%20CARLOS%20SALMER%C3%93N_CAST.pdf

Schlemmer, T. (2019). Die Macht der Populisten – Populisten an der Macht. *Vierteljahrshefte Für Zeitgeschichte*, *67*(3), 486–498. https://doi.org/10.1515/vfzg-2019-0031

Scott, W. R. (2008). *Institutions and organizations: Ideas and interests* (3rd ed.). Sage.

Shepsle, K. A. (1979). Institutional arrangements and equilibrium in multidimensional voting models. *American Journal of Political Science*, *23*(1), 27. https://doi.org/10.2307/2110770

von Soest, C., & Grauvogel, J. (2015). *How do non-democratic regimes claim legitimacy? Comparative insights from post-Soviet countries* (GIGA Working Paper No. 277).

Taggart, P. A. (2000). *Populism. Concepts in the Social Sciences*. Open University Press. http://www.loc.gov/catdir/description/mh051/99086747.html

Taylor, J. M. (1981). *Eva Perón, the Myths of a Woman* (Pbk). University of Chicago Press.

Urbinati, N. (2015). A Revolt against Intermediary Bodies. *Constellations*, *22*(4), 477–486. https://doi.org/10.1111/1467-8675.12188

Waldmann, P. (1974). *Der Peronismus 1943–1955*. Saarbrücken, University, Habil.-Schr., 1973, Hoffmann und Campe.

Weingast, B. R. (1997). The political foundations of democracy and the rule of law. *American Political Science Review*, *91*(2), 245–263.

Weyland, K. (2001). Clarifying a contested concept: Populism in the study of Latin American politics. *Comparative Politics*, *34*(1), 1–22. https://doi.org/10.2307/422412

Williamson, O. E. (2000). The new institutional economics: Taking stock, looking ahead. *Journal of Economic Literature*, *38*(3), 595–613.

Zúquete, J. P. (2008). The missionary politics of Hugo Chávez. *Latin American Politics and Society*, *50*(1), 91–121.

CHAPTER 33

Populist Neo-Imperialism: A New Take on Populist Foreign Policy

Ole Frahm and Dirk Lehmkuhl

INTRODUCTION

Right-wing populists abhor all things foreign. Yet, right-wing populists still need a foreign policy, especially once they reach or are close to the levers of power. In this analysis of Turkey and a selection of right-wing populist parties from former imperial countries, we identify consistent policies across cases. This set of foreign policies which we call populist neo-imperialism testifies to an ideological thickness in populist foreign policy that mirrors similar findings from the Global South (Dodson & Dorraj, 2008; Plagemann & Destradi, 2018, 16) but defies the widespread conception of populism as a thin ideology (e.g., Hadiz & Chryssogelos, 2017; Kriesi, 2012; Mudde, 2004).

POPULIST FOREIGN POLICY AND RIGHT-WING POPULISM

For the purposes of our analysis, we understand populism as the rhetorical juxtaposition of an out-of-touch elite with the genuine people. Populism is thus "an anti-status quo discourse that simplifies the political space by symbolically dividing society between 'the people' (as the 'underdogs') and its 'other'" (Panizza, 2005, 3), with populists claiming to represent the genuine people

---

O. Frahm (✉) · D. Lehmkuhl
School of Economics and Political Science, University of St. Gallen, St. Gallen, Switzerland
e-mail: ole.frahm@unisg.ch

D. Lehmkuhl
e-mail: dirk.lehmkuhl@unisg.ch

© The Author(s), under exclusive license to Springer Nature Switzerland AG 2022
M. Oswald (ed.), *The Palgrave Handbook of Populism*,
https://doi.org/10.1007/978-3-030-80803-7_33

and thus the popular will neglected by the incumbent elites (Mudde, 2004). Crucially, populism is commonly conceived as a *thin* ideology that "is unable to stand alone as a practical political ideology" (Stanley, 2008, 95), meaning that the content of policy is both flexible and secondary to the style and overall posturing of populist politicians (e.g., Canovan, 2002; Mudde, 2004). This thin ideology builds on and borrows from stronger, *thicker* ideological traditions and reformulates them along a presumed elite vs. people divide (Chryssogelos, 2010).

Given the policy void allegedly at the core of populist parties, it is an open question whether a populist foreign policy exists, i.e., whether there are foreign policies pursued by populist parties that transcend the individual country case. Inductive theoretical models of populist foreign policy postulate, among other things, that populists oppose restrictions on national sovereignty such as multilateral institutions (Drezner, 2017), exhibit a "compromise deficit" vis-à-vis other state leaders (Magcamit, 2017) and show a preference for the politics of securitization and isolationism (Verbeek & Zaslove, 2017) which along with their inexperience may result in more unpredictable and crisis-prone foreign policies (Kane & McCulloch, 2017). The only systematic *empirical* typologies of contemporary populist foreign policy, however, have been advanced for European right-wing populist parties (Balfour, et al., 2016; Dennison & Pardijs, 2016) and point to the existence of a core of *right-wing* populist foreign policy principles. Despite differences in what they actively strive for (Chryssogelos, 2010), European right-wing populists concur on a number of issues and policies they consistently oppose (Schori Liang, 2007). Three features stand out. Right-wing populists are

(a) against free trade and in favor of protectionist measures for national markets;
(b) against immigration and in favor of restrictive border and visa regimes;
(c) against multilateral organizations, especially the EU but also other organizations such as the UN or NATO while favoring a bilateral conduct of foreign relations.

Given that right-wing populism is increasingly a global phenomenon, we sought to establish whether these foreign policy principles also held for cases outside of Western and Central Europe.

Research Puzzle and the Case for Populist Neo-Imperialism

Analyzing contemporary Turkey, we find that the foreign policy pursued by the right-wing populist Justice and Development Party (*Adalet ve Kalkınma Partisi* (AKP)) does not match this set of foreign policy principles. In fact, in the three areas of trade, immigration and regional integration the AKP directly contradicts the foreign policy principles characteristic of its European right-wing populist counterparts. The theoretical argument we propose is that the AKP's foreign policy deviates from the model of European right-wing populist foreign policy not only because it is in government (Albertazzi & McDonnell, 2015) but because of the Turkish government's emphasis on reinterpreting and utilizing the country's Ottoman imperial past. We hypothesize that Turkish foreign policy at the time of our research (2017–2019) differed from other right-wing populists in Europe because its historical rooting and self-placement is not a glorified *national* past but a glorified *imperial* past (Yilmaz & Bashirov, 2018, 1822).

What is more, based on an exploratory look at other post-imperial countries, we argue that these findings from Turkey are transferable, i.e., there is a distinct class of countries with an imperial past whose populist parties' foreign policy differs from other right-wing populists whose focus is solely on the nation-state precisely *because of* their focus on the imperial as opposed to national past.

Moreover, we show that the claim that populism is a thin ideology is not tenable for this class of cases that share specific *thick* features in their foreign policy outlook. This outlook which we call populist neo-imperialism is however only a viable choice for populist parties and movements that are in government and in cases where the imperial past is not already being utilized effectively by mainstream parties.[1]

TURKEY'S RIGHT-WING POPULISTS FALL OUT OF LINE

The Turkish government has undergone a substantial shift toward a more and more populist discourse throughout the ruling AKP's time in power (2002–2021). This shift is reflected in the Global Populism Database's analysis of selected speeches by the President and former Prime Minister Recep Tayyip Erdoğan who went from not populist in 2003–2007, to somewhat populist in 2007–2014 and very populist in 2014–2018. The AKP's nativist, nationalist and religiously exclusionary stance places it firmly in the right-wing populist camp (Arat-Koç, 2018). Foreign policy making has meanwhile become highly centralized as decision-making rests with the president and a very small group of close advisors (Park, 2014, 163–164).[2] The diplomatic corps and the foreign policy communities in Turkey have been systematically pushed aside[3] in a maneuver characteristic of populist governments that seek to take away decision-making and agenda-setting powers from incumbent foreign policy elites (Plagemann & Destradi, 2018). "Having purged the Kemalist and secular establishment from the ranks of the bureaucracy, judiciary and the military" (Yabanci, 2016, 599) and with docile mainstream media owned by AKP-supporters (Corke et al., 2014), the government can push through its foreign policy agenda largely uninhibited by other domestic actors.

The neo-imperial focus of Turkey's foreign policy accordingly fits into Turkey's domestic political dynamics as the rehabilitation of Turkey's Ottoman past is a direct attack against the preceding generations of secularist elites (Ongur, 2015; Özpek & Yaşar, 2018, 204). Hence, it is fitting that former Foreign Minister Ahmet Davutoğlu (2010) publicly lamented the fact that Turkey had to rediscover the neighboring regions with which it shared a long common history. Ever since Atatürk's reform process and the founding of the Turkish Republic in 1923, the Ottoman past had been used as a foil that represented the backwardness and failures of the past that had to be overcome. The Turkish Republic was explicitly conceived as a nationalist as opposed to an imperial or multinational project as it sought to create a nation-state for the Turks and the Turks only (Hanioğlu, 2017)—a proposition the AKP has worked to repeal by rejecting the ethnicization of national identity centered around Turkishness (Uzer, 2018, 342).

A recurring theme in President Erdoğan's speeches is thus the claim that "this nation, we are the heirs to those that ruled over 23 million square kilometers and spread justice over three continents and seven climate zones" (Erdoğan, 2019). The president's closest foreign policy adviser Ibrahim Kalin (2010, 99) explicitly framed the country's foreign policy as transcending the nation-state: "Not surprisingly, as Turkey eyes a post-nation-state strategic outlook it comes back to its past experiences, dreams and aspiration in its greater hinterland. Turkey's post-modernity seems to be embedded in its Ottoman past." The AKP's domestic vision of the nation as neo-Ottoman is thus reproduced in the country's foreign policy (Saraçoğlu & Demirkol, 2015, 302–303) as this wider frame of reference explains the special foreign policy focus on the Balkans and on Crimea, on Syria and on Libya as these regions at one point belonged to the Ottoman Empire.

Turning to populist neo-imperialism therefore had a dual advantage as the ruling party "both exploited the post-imperial inferiority complex of the Turks and easily demonized the opposition circles by employing a banal anti-imperialist discourse" (Özpek & Yaşar, 2018, 210). Accusing the opposition that "according to them, the Turkish Republic is a newly created rootless state without history" (Erdoğan, 2018a), President Erdoğan with the help of popular soap operas like *Payitaht Abdülhamit* has sought to change the image of the last Sultan Abdulhamid II from that of a bloodthirsty tyrant and enemy of the Republic to a benevolent forefather of contemporary Turkey. Importantly, policymakers and analysts in neighboring countries perceive TV series such as *Muhteşem Yüzyil* or *Diriliş: Ertuğrul* about the rise and glory days of the Ottoman Empire as sending subliminal messages about the Turkish government's renewed regional ambitions.[4]

The economic and domestic political conditions throughout the majority of the AKP's time in power have been favorable for populist neo-imperialism. In the economic realm, Turkey experienced nearly uninterrupted economic growth which enabled the AKP's brand of domestic "neoliberal populism" (Akcay, 2018). The government has responded to the deepening economic crisis since 2018 with interventionist measures toward price controls that defy the liberal creed. To date, however, a similar reversal in *foreign* economic policy cannot be observed. This may indicate the higher tolerance of populist parties and regimes to stay the course in the international arena compared to a much greater sensitivity to popular sentiments in domestic politics.

When it comes to the substance of contemporary Turkey's foreign policy, several policies diverge from what a typical European right-wing populist party would espouse. For one, the Turkish government has throughout the AKP's time in government endorsed the principles of market liberalism (Özbay et al., 2016). In the international realm this has found its expression in the active promotion of free-trade agreements with regional neighbors and work toward visa liberalization, to the point that one of the country's foremost academics considered Turkey on the road toward becoming a "trading state" (Kirişci, 2009).

Secondly, in spite of a domestic audience that has become markedly critical of the presence of millions of Syrian refugees (International Crisis Group, 2016; Makovsky, 2019) and a long history of isolationist and partly xenophobic nationalism that has become deeply ingrained in the national psyche (Özkırımlı, 2011), the government has maintained a policy of relative openness and welcoming toward these same refugees. The fact that the policy of generosity toward Syrian refugees is not only placed in contrast to the reluctance of Western countries to receive refugees (Erdoğan, 2018b) but also publicly portrayed as standing in the legacy of the Ottoman Empire as a haven for persecuted groups (Hürriyet Daily News, 2012) highlights the thick ideological nature of this policy.

The third aspect is that Turkey's government follows both a regionalist and a global agenda and is far from an isolationist stance. Under the AKP, Turkey has consistently sought a larger role in the world (Davutoğlu, 2011), embodied by membership of the G20, persistent calls for a reform of the UN Security Council and ad hoc alliances with other emerging powers such as Russia or Brazil (Öniş, 2011). To realize this ambition of becoming a global actor, Turkey intended to utilize historical, cultural and economic ties to adjacent regions (Davutoğlu, 2013). While the heyday of enthusiasm for integration into the European Union in the mid-2000s is today but a distant memory, Turkey continues to push for closer ties to several of its surrounding regions (Frahm & Hoffmann, 2020).

This includes the aspiration to play a dominant and influential role in the territories of the former Ottoman Empire (Murinson, 2006).[5] There, Turkey acts as a benevolent protector of the weak against unjust external forces from Kosovo (Demirtaş, 2013) to Somalia, from the Crimean Tatars to Syria, which allows the government to transpose the elites-versus-the-people trope to the international theater.

The Three Pillars of Neo-Imperial Populist Foreign Policy

Based on deductions from the case of Turkey, our hypothesis is that in the areas of (a) immigration, (b) trade and (c) the multilateral conduct of international relations, populist neo-imperialists pursue more liberal positions than their non-imperial and purely nationally oriented right-wing populist counterparts. In the area of immigration, the neo-imperial sense of regional or continental mission leads to a more generous and welcoming environment for refugees and migrants from the former imperial territories and countries that are associated to the reimagined idea of the contemporary state's supranational reach. In the field of trade, the same sense of international importance drives a preference for free-trade agreements and a liberalization of trading regimes with the regional and/or former imperial territories with which a special—and in many cases asymmetrical—relationship is thought to exist. And in spite of a frequent rejection of the current *global* multilateral system, populist neo-imperialists are proponents of *regional* integration and regional multilateral organizations. This is linked to the expectation that these fora will be led by themselves and thus present a vehicle for regional leadership. Hence, in contrast to the instrumental logic employed by Sandra Destradi and Johannes Plagemann (2019, 13) who claim that right-wing populists in the Global South advance regional economic integration "where predatory elites are explicitly associated with 'neo-imperialism'," we see this policy as an emanation of the populists' own "thick" ideology.

Testing for Populist Neo-Imperialism in Three Former Imperial Countries

To see whether this typology of what we call populist neo-imperialism transcends the singular case of Turkey, we test the extent to which these features also apply to the foreign policy principles espoused by right-wing populists in other countries with an imperial past. The three countries we chose to test our model on are Russia, the United Kingdom and France. The reason for this choice is that all three possess strong right-wing populist parties, the imperial past continues to play an important part in the national consciousness and in public debates and there are persistent political, economic and cultural links to the now independent former imperial possessions. In addition, like Turkey, all three countries have the capacity and the willingness to pursue an active regional or even global foreign policy. On the other hand, the electoral position of these parties differs substantially, from dominance in Russia (United Russia) to a narrow majority (Torys) to a large opposition party (Rassemblement National). Moreover, each country has a different approach to publicly remembering its imperial past which should allow for an insightful comparison of the factors that lead right-wing populists to either favor or discard a neo-imperialist approach.

In the field of migration, the Russian government systematically resorts to anti-immigration rhetoric and migrants from the countries of the former Soviet Union often face social and racial stigmatization but they can nonetheless enter the country without a visa and receive preferential treatment when it comes to work permits and therefore constitute an important link to the former Soviet republics (Malakhov, 2014). British right-wing populists, on the other hand, run *primarily* on an anti-immigration platform. Opposition to immigration from former colonies among right-wing populists dates to the late 1970s (Fella, 2007) and the same sentiment informed then-Home Secretary Theresa May when in 2012 she publicly stated her aim to create a hostile environment for migrants. The French RN likewise runs on an ethno-socialist platform that links nationalist anti-immigration with pro-welfare positions (Reynié, 2011).

In the realm of free trade, Russia has long sought to maintain close economic ties to former Soviet republics and to this effect formed a customs union with Belarus and Kazakhstan in 2010 and in 2015 founded the Eurasian Economic Union (EAEU) (Vieira, 2017). Free trade is meanwhile considered a crucial part of the imperial legacy and a priority of the Tory government's Global Britain agenda (Połońska-Kimunguyi & Kimunguyi, 2017; Wellings, 2017). In France, on the other hand, the RN has moved away from its formerly postcolonial revisionist stance (Flood & Frey, 1998) and opposes both the EU and special economic links embodied by *Françafrique*.

In the area of regional integration and multilateral governance, the Eurasian Union has been devised as a Russian-led counter-project of regional integration to the European Union as "there is a widespread belief among at least some factions of the Russian elite and epistemic communities that the EAEU performs as a tool protecting Russia's influence in post-Soviet Eurasia and, even more, that a regional organization is a necessary attribute of a Great Power in the modern world" (Libman & Obydenkova, 2018, 1044). The Tory government's "Global Britain" agenda illustrates that British right-wing populists seek to expand and maintain the influence of the UK as the defender of a liberal-cosmopolitan world order, notably in their former spheres of influence (Wellings, 2017), with intergovernmental cooperation within an "Anglosphere" of Commonwealth countries portrayed as a desirable alternative (Daddow, 2019).

NECESSARY CONDITIONS FOR POPULIST NEO-IMPERIALISM

What transpires from this juxtaposition of different foreign policies pursued by right-wing populists from Turkey, Russia, the UK and France is that not all right-wing populists propagate populist neo-imperialism. We argue that three factors are crucial in determining the opportunity structure for a right-wing populist movement's choice to opt for or against a neo-imperial foreign policy outlook. One, previous elites must have neglected or scorned the imperial past. Two, the economy has to be robust and growing. And, most importantly, three, the party or movement's domestic political position has to be dominant.

The first condition is that previous elites must have left the imperial past a barren soil, an ideological wasteland that was not deemed worthy of investing political capital into. If prior elites neglected or even vilified the imperial past, this opens political space for right-wing populist challengers to rehabilitate what they deem a glorious period of national history. Importantly, presenting their own interpretation of national history and thus clawing back opinion leadership from cosmopolitan elites that supposedly lack an appreciation of the nation's place in the world transposes the elite-versus-the-people dynamic from the domestic arena to the realm of foreign policy. What is more, by directing its gaze at the behavior of prior elites and turning present-day neo-imperial foreign policy into a symbolic struggle over the past, populist right-wing parties can continue to exploit the people-vs-elite dichotomy even when they are already in government and should normally find it harder to act as the outsider or the underdog.

This condition is clearly fulfilled in the case of Turkey but also Russia where antagonistic rhetoric toward the leaders that preceded Vladimir Putin, Mikhail Gorbachev and Boris Yeltsin, is common as both are condemned for dismantling the Soviet Union and in the process showing no concern for the Soviet and Czarist imperial legacy (Bershidsky, 2018). However, the situation is quite different in the UK and France. In France, revisionism and neo-colonialist engagement in French spheres of influence have been the domain of mainstream Conservatives, framed economically under *Françafrique* and culturally under the *Francophonie* (Gegout, 2017) and both Conservative and Socialist governments have not shied away from using military force in former African colonies. As such, the RN has nothing to gain from endorsing a neo-imperialist foreign policy that mimics the incumbent elites the party decries. In the UK, meanwhile, the imperial legacy has remained relevant in mainstream politics as even "New Labour" leaders drew on imperial sentiments to defend interventionist and at times revisionist positions (Kenny, 2017). Nostalgically idealizing the imperial past in a form of nationalist "retrotopia" (Beaumont, 2017) is thus a common element of British politics used by mainstream politicians *and* right-wing populists alike.

The second condition for right-wing populists to be able to choose a neo-imperial foreign policy is that the country finds itself in a position of economic strength. Since reaching out to the former imperial territories and providing for refugees and migrants from said territories comes with a considerable price tag, such endeavors can only be countenanced during an economic boom or with deep coffers of financial reserves. The salience of this factor of affordability can best be seen during economic downturns experienced by a populist government. At a certain point, the costs of pursuing populist neo-imperialism outweigh the benefits. This does not only apply to the economic circumstances but also to political costs.

Thus, *the third condition* which is often closely intertwined with economic strength is that a populist party's domestic political position has to be dominant for it to be able to pursue a neo-imperialist foreign policy. The reason is that populist neo-imperialism is a deviation from the existing foreign policy. In order to overcome institutional bias and the force of path dependency, a right-wing populist party must be in such a strong electoral position to overcome institutional inertia and resistance from within the foreign policy establishment. This is the case in both Turkey and Russia where Putin's Eurasian conceptualization of the Russian nation disregards the Russian Federation's present-day borders (Tipaldou & Casula, 2018) and contemporary Russian elites "see themselves as continuing the Russian empire, albeit with some distinctly Soviet features" (Trenin, 2011, 212).

Crucially, populist neo-imperialism does not work like chauvinist nationalism in rallying public opinion. In times of weakness—an economic downturn or a political crisis—a populist movement is likely to shift away from populist neo-imperialism rather than double-down on the policy. With its control of mainstream media and deep financial reserves, the Russian government was able to compensate for the economic fallout of Western sanctions imposed after the annexation of Crimea and maintain a neo-imperial foreign policy in spite of growing domestic discontent (Balzer, 2019; Sherlock, 2019). In contrast, with its popularity on the wane and the economy in decline, the Turkish government has increasingly turned toward a classic rally-around-the-flag foreign policy with its military assault on Afrin in Syria in 2019 (Özkırımlı, 2019) and attacks on Northern Iraq in 2020. The reason for these diverging paths is that establishing populist neo-imperialism comes with potential costs in popularity as not all parts of the populist coalition will support the reach to a target group that transcends the more narrowly defined nation and its territory. For example, AKP voters that supported Turkey's regional ambitions during the economic boom may feel quite differently during an economic crisis when there appears to be a trade-off between spending on Syrian refugees and spending on their own parochial interests. Therefore, we only see a turn to populist neo-imperialism in situations of domestic dominance.

IDEOLOGY AS THE SUFFICIENT CONDITION: THE "THICKNESS" OF POPULIST NEO-IMPERIALISM

The fact that populist neo-imperialism comes with very real costs in terms of political and economic resources highlights the *thick* ideological motivations that inspire this policy. Rather than being mere accidental topics chosen to appeal to one's followers, populist neo-imperialism comes from a very particular ideological orientation of right-wing movements with a project to rehabilitate a specific transnational idea of the national past. Foreign policy populism in its neo-imperial guise is thus anything but random or unpredictable. The conditions developed above are necessary but not sufficient for a neo-imperial foreign policy to be chosen. The key factor is that every right-wing populist movement in a country with an imperial past will contain a faction that believes in a neo-imperial vision irrespective of whether the conditions for its implementation are met. If and when all necessary conditions are met, this enables the neo-imperial faction to gain the upper hand and to realize its thick but up to this point only latent ideology of populist neo-imperialism.

Conclusion

Populist neo-imperialism marks a distinct class of populist foreign policy and challenges the established wisdom that populism is by necessity a thin ideology or, in Michael Freeden's (2017, 2–3) words, "ideologically too scrawny even to be thin." Going by the analysis of populist neo-imperialism, there appears to be a clear core of foreign policy principles, a protruding belly so to speak, that right-wing populists from former imperial powers strive for, irrespective of their differences in domestic politics. This *thick* neo-imperial foreign policy consists of a liberal immigration regime for people from the former empire as well as a preference for free-trade agreements and for regional multilateral organizations.

Both Turkey and Russia fully comply with this model, the United Kingdom only adheres to some facets of populist neo-imperialism while France's right-wing populists go into a different direction altogether. The way to incorporate deviating cases into our model of populist neo-imperialism is by conceiving of it as a continuum. The necessary conditions—elites neglecting the imperial past, a strong economy and a dominant political position for the populist right-wing party—determine whether a populist party follows through with pursuing populist neo-imperialism or chooses a different foreign policy mix. A shift in conditions in one of the fields we identify as decisive for whether populist neo-imperialism is chosen is likely to lead to a concomitant shift in policy.

We also identify the paradox of populist neo-imperialism. The pursuit of a neo-imperial foreign policy is not necessarily a vote-winner; in some cases, quite the opposite. Thus, the foreign policy pursued by these populist parties could be seen to contradict the strategies they employ to gain domestic popularity. We argue, on the contrary, that while their hope to win domestic popularity certainly plays a part in choosing a neo-imperial foreign policy, the fact that these populist governments are up to a point willing to stomach losses to their domestic popularity speaks to the genuinely ideological nature of populist neo-imperialism. In foreign policy at least, ideology can indeed trump the populist impulse to maximize popular appeal.

As such, it is fascinating to study the inflection points at which the costs for each regime become too burdensome to continue to adhere to a neo-imperial foreign policy. What remains to be analyzed is whether and how a shift away from populist neo-imperialism during adverse conditions—a process we can observe in Turkey's shift in immigration policy (Içduygu & Ayaşlı, 2019, 12)—is reversed when conditions once again become more favorable. The UK government's decision in June 2020 to fuse the Department for International Development with the Foreign Office, widely interpreted as a nod to those who want less spending on foreign aid, is an early indication that the

Covid-19 pandemic may well put a lasting dent into populist neo-imperialism's popularity.

Notes

1. This study relies on a mix of methods to substantiate and provide evidence for the model of populist neo-imperialism. For the case study of Turkey's foreign policy, we triangulate an Atlas.ti-based analysis of primary data such as speeches and policy documents with approximately 120 expert interviews in Turkey and neighboring countries conducted in 2018 and secondary literature. For the classification of populist governments and parties we relied on the indices provided by *The PopuList* (Rooduijn et al., 2019), the *Global Populism Database* (Hawkins et al., 2019) and the *Populists in Power Around the World* project (Kyle & Gultchin, 2019).
2. Interviews with an expert in Istanbul, 21 February 2018, and an analyst in Ankara, 10 May 2018.
3. Interview with three analysts in Ankara, 10 May 2018, and with a former high-ranking politician in Istanbul, 16 May 2018.
4. Interviews with an expert in Baku on 30 January 2018, with analysts in Kyiv on 21 and 22 April 2018 and with a businessperson in Tbilisi on 2 April 2018.
5. Interview with an expert in Istanbul, 23 February 2018.

Literature

Akcay, Ü. (2018). *Neoliberal populism in Turkey and its crisis* (Working Paper 100). Institute for International Political Economy, Berlin School of Economics and Law.

Albertazzi, D., & McDonnell, D. (2015). *Populists in power*. Routledge.

Arat-Koç, S. (2018). Culturalizing politics, hyper-politicizing 'culture': 'White' vs. 'Black Turks' and the making of authoritarian populism in Turkey. *Dialectical Anthropology, 42*(4), 391–408.

Balfour, R., Emmanouilidis, J. A., Fieschi, C., Grabbe, H., Hill, C., Lochocki, T., Mendras, M., Mudde, C., Niemi, M. K., Schmidt, J., & Stratulat, C. (2016). *Europe's troublemakers. The populist challenge to foreign policy*. European Policy Centre. https://wms.flexious.be/editor/plugins/imagemanager/content/2140/PDF/2016/Europe_s_troublemakers_complete_book.pdf

Balzer, H. (2019). *Public opinion paradoxes? Russians are increasingly dubious about the costs of Putin's foreign policies* (PONARS Eurasia Policy Memo 595). http://www.ponarseurasia.org/sites/default/files/policy-memos-

Beaumont, P. (2017). Brexit, Retrotopia and the perils of post-colonial delusions. *Global Affairs, 3*(4–5), 379–390.

Bershidsky, L. (2018, August 22). Russians get a revisionist view of Soviet Union's end. *Bloomberg*. https://www.bloomberg.com/opinion/articles/2018-08-22/yeltsin-s-role-in-soviet-union-gets-the-revisionist-treatment

Canovan, M. (2002). Taking politics to the people: Populism as the ideology of democracy. In Y. Mény & Y. Surel (Eds.), *Democracies and the populist challenge* (pp. 25–44). Palgrave Macmillan.

Chryssogelos, A.-S. (2010). Undermining the west from within: European populists, the US and Russia. *European View, 9*(2), 267–277.

Corke, S., Finkel, A., Kramer, D. J., Robbins, C. A., & Schenkkan, N. (2014). *Democracy in crisis: Corruption, media, and power in Turkey*. Freedom House.

Daddow, O. (2019). GlobalBritain™: The discursive construction of Britain's post-Brexit world role. *Global Affairs*, 5(1), 5–22.

Davutoğlu, A. (2013, March 9). *Speech at the meeting organized by the foreign economic relations board*. http://www.mfa.gov.tr/disisleri-bakani-sayin-ahmet-davutoglu_nun-dis-ekonomik-iliskiler-kurulu-tarafindan-duzenlenen-toplantida-yaptiklari-konusma_-9.tr.mfa

Davutoğlu, A. (2010, January 4). *Speech at the Opening of the 2nd Ambassadors' Conference*. http://www.mfa.gov.tr/disisleri-bakani-sayin-ahmet-davutoglu_nun-ikinci-buyukelciler-konferansi-acilis-oturumunda-yaptigi-konusm-_-4-ocak-2010_-ankara.tr.mfa

Davutoğlu, A. (2011, December 23). *Speech at the Opening of the 4th Ambassadors' Conference*. http://www.mfa.gov.tr/disisleri-bakani-sn_-ahmet-davutoglu_nun-iv_-buyukelciler-konferansi-acis-konusmasi_-23-aralik-2011.tr.mfa

Demirtaş, B. (2013). Turkey and the Balkans: Overcoming prejudices, building bridges, and constructing a common future. *Perceptions*, 18(2), 163–184.

Dennison, S., & Pardijs, D. (2016). *The World according to Europe's insurgent parties: Putin, migration and people power*. European Council on Foreign Relations.

Destradi, S., & Plagemann, J. (2019). Populism and International Relations: (Un)predictability, personalisation, and the reinforcement of existing trends in world politics. *Review of International Studies*, 45(5), 711–730.

Dodson, M., & Dorraj, M. (2008). Populism and foreign policy in Venezuela and Iran. *Whitehead Journal of Diplomacy & International Relations*, 9, 71–87.

Drezner, D. W. (2017). The angry populist as foreign policy leader: Real change or just hot air. *Fletcher Forum of World Affairs*, 41, 23–44.

Erdoğan, R. T. (2018a, February 10). *Speech at the Conference "Commemorating the 100th anniversary of the death of Sultan Abdulhamid"*. https://www.tccb.gov.tr/konusmalar/353/90385/vefatinin-100-yilinda-sultan-abdulhamidi-anlamak-konulu-konferansta-yaptiklari-konusma

Erdoğan, R. T. (2018b, September 25). *Speech at the United Nations General Assembly*. https://www.tccb.gov.tr/konusmalar/353/98783/73-birlesmis-milletler-genel-kurulunda-yaptiklari-konusma

Erdoğan, R. T. (2019, March 19). *Speech at an AKP campaign rally in Kocaeli*. https://www.tccb.gov.tr/haberler/410/102567/-turkiye-dunyanin-bir-ucundaki-milyonlar-icin-baris-huzur-ve-guvenin-semboludur-

Fella, S. (2007). Britain: Imperial legacies, institutional constraints and new political opportunities. In D. Albertazzi & D. McDonnell (Eds.), *Twenty-first century populism: The spectre of Western European democracy* (pp. 181–197). Palgrave Macmillan.

Flood, C., & Frey, H. (1998). Questions of decolonization and post-colonialism in the ideology of the French extreme right. *Journal of European Studies*, 28(109–110), 69–88.

Frahm, O., & Hoffmann, K. (2020). Dual agent of transition: How Turkey perpetuates and challenges neo-patrimonial patterns in its post-Soviet neighbourhood. *East European Politics*. https://doi.org/10.1080/21599165.2020.1733982

Freeden, M. (2017). After the Brexit referendum: Revisiting populism as an ideology. *Journal of Political Ideologies*, 22(1), 1–11.

Gegout, C. (2017). The persistence of the French Pré-Carré. In C. Gegout (Ed.), *Why Europe intervenes in Africa: Security, prestige and the legacy of colonialism* (pp. 135–207). Oxford University Press.

Hadiz, V. R., & Chryssogelos, A. (2017). Populism in world politics: A comparative cross-regional perspective. *International Political Science Review, 38*(4), 399–411.

Hanioğlu, M. Ş. (2017). *Nationalism and Kemalism*. Princeton University Press.

Hawkins, K. A., Aguilar, R., Jenne, E., Kocijan, B., Rovira Kaltwasser, C., & Castanho Silva, B. (2019). *Global Populism Database: Populism Dataset for Leaders 1.0*. http://populism.byu.edu

Hürriyet Daily News. (2012, September 6). Premier vows to pray in Damascus mosque 'soon'. http://www.hurriyetdailynews.com/premier-vows-to-pray-in-damascus-mosque-soon-29505

İçduygu, A., & Ayaşlı, E. (2019). *Geri Dönüş Siyaseti: Suriyeli Mültecilerin Dönüş Göçü İhtimali ve Gelecek Senaryoları*. MiReKoc Working Papers.

International Crisis Group. (2016, November 30). *Turkey's Refugee Crisis: The Politics of Permanence* (Europe Report 241). https://d2071andvip0wj.cloudfront.net/241-turkey-s-refugee-crisis-the-politics-of-permanence_0.pdf

Kalin, I. (2010). US–Turkish relations under Obama: Promise, challenge and opportunity in the 21st century. *Journal of Balkan and near Eastern Studies, 12*(1), 93–108.

Kane, C., & McCulloch, C. (2017). Populism and foreign policy: Deepening divisions and decreasing efficiency. *Global Politics Review, 3*(2), 39–52.

Kenny, M. (2017). Back to the populist future? Understanding nostalgia in contemporary ideological discourse. *Journal of Political Ideologies, 22*(3), 256–273.

Kirişci, K. (2009). The transformation of Turkish foreign policy: The rise of the trading state. *New Perspectives on Turkey, 40*, 29–56.

Kriesi, H.-P. (2012). *Populism as an ideology*. University of Zurich.

Kyle, J., & Gultchin, L. (2019). *Populists in power around the World*. Tony Blair Institute for Global Change. https://institute.global/insight/renewing-centre/populists-power-around-world

Libman, A., & Obydenkova, A. V. (2018). Regional international organizations as a strategy of autocracy: The Eurasian Economic Union and Russian foreign policy. *International Affairs, 94*(5), 1037–1058.

Magcamit, M. (2017). Explaining the three-way linkage between populism, securitization, and realist foreign policies: President Donald Trump and the pursuit of "America first" doctrine. *World Affairs, 180*(3), 6–35.

Makovsky, A. (2019, March 13). *Turkey's Refugee Dilemma: Tiptoeing Toward Integration*. Center for American Progress. https://www.americanprogress.org/issues/security/reports/2019/03/13/467183/turkeys-refugee-dilemma/

Malakhov, V. S. (2014). Russia as a new immigration country: Policy response and public debate. *Europe-Asia Studies, 66*(7), 1062–1079.

Mudde, C. (2004). The populist zeitgeist. *Government and Opposition, 39*(4), 541–563.

Murinson, A. (2006). The strategic depth doctrine of Turkish foreign policy. *Middle Eastern Studies, 42*(6), 945–964.

Ongur, H. O. (2015). Identifying Ottomanisms: The discursive evolution of Ottoman pasts in the Turkish presents. *Middle Eastern Studies, 51*(3), 416–432.

Öniş, Z. (2011). Multiple faces of the "New" Turkish foreign policy: Underlying dynamics and a critique. *Insight Turkey, 13*(1), 47–65.

Özbay, C., Erol, M., Terzioglu, A., & Umut Türem, Z. U. (Eds.). (2016). *The making of neoliberal Turkey*. Routledge.

Özkırımlı, U. (2011). The changing nature of nationalism in Turkey: Actors, discourses, and the struggle for hegemony. In A. Kadıoğlu & E. F. Keyman (Eds.), *Symbiotic antagonisms: Competing nationalisms in Turkey* (pp. 82–100). University of Utah Press.

Özkırımlı, U. (2019, January 23). *Turkey's Afrin offensive an instrument of domestic politics*. Ahval News. https://ahvalnews.com/afrin/turkeys-afrin-offensive-instrument-domestic-politics

Özpek, B. B., & Yaşar, N. T. (2018). Populism and foreign policy in Turkey under the AKP rule. *Turkish Studies, 19*(2), 198–216.

Panizza, F. (2005). Introduction: Populism and the mirror of democracy. In F. Panizza (Ed.), *Populism and the mirror of democracy* (pp. 1–31). Verso.

Park, B. (2014). Turkey's 'New' foreign policy: Newly influential or just over-active? *Mediterranean Politics, 19*(2), 161–164.

Plagemann, J., & Destradi, S. (2018). Populism and foreign policy: The case of India. *Foreign Policy Analysis, 15*(2), 283–301.

Połońska-Kimunguyi, E., & Kimunguyi, P. (2017). 'Gunboats of soft power': Boris on Africa and post-Brexit 'Global Britain. *Cambridge Review of International Affairs, 30*(4), 325–349.

Reynié, D. (2011). The ethnosocialist transition of the national front in France. *Études, 415*(11), 463–472.

Rooduijn, M., Kessel, S. van, Froio, C., Pirro, A., Lange, S. de, Halikiopoulou, D., Lewis, P., Mudde, C., & Taggart, P. (2019). *The PopuList: An overview of populist, far right, far left and Eurosceptic parties in Europe*. http://www.popu-list.org

Saraçoğlu, C., & Demirkol, Ö. (2015). Nationalism and foreign policy discourse in Turkey under the AKP rule: Geography, history and national identity. *British Journal of Middle Eastern Studies, 42*(3), 301–319.

Sayarı, S. (2016). Back to a predominant party system: The November 2015 snap election in Turkey. *South European Society and Politics, 21*(2), 263–280.

Schori Liang, C. (2007). *Europe for the Europeans: The foreign and security policy of the populist radical right*. Ashgate.

Sherlock, T. (2019). Russian society and foreign policy: Mass and Elite orientations After crimea. *Problems of Post-Communism*.

Stanley, B. (2008). The thin ideology of populism. *Journal of Political Ideologies, 13*(1), 95–110.

Tipaldou, S., & Casula, P. (2018). Populist justifications for war? The Russian intervention in eastern Ukraine. *Revista CIDOB D'afers Internacionals, 119*, 135–159.

Trenin, D. V. (2011). *Post-Imperium: A Eurasian Story*. Carnegie Endowment.

Uzer, U. (2018). Glorification of the past as a political tool: Ottoman history in contemporary Turkish politics. *The Journal of the Middle East and Africa, 9*(4), 339–357.

Verbeek, B., & Zaslove, A. (2017). Populism and foreign policy. In C. Rovira Kaltwasser, P. A. Taggart, P. Ochoa Espejo, & P. Ostiguy, (Eds.), *The Oxford handbook of populism*. Oxford University Press.

Vieira, A. (2017). A tale of two unions: Russia-Belarus integration experience and its lessons for the Eurasian Economic Union. *Journal of Borderlands Studies, 32*(1), 41–53.

Wellings, B. (2017). The Anglosphere in the Brexit Referendum. *Revue Française de Civilisation Britannique. French Journal of British Studies, 22*(2), 1–14.

Yabanci, B. (2016). Populism as the problem child of democracy: The AKP's enduring appeal and the use of meso-level actors. *Southeast European and Black Sea Studies, 16*(4), 591–617.

Yilmaz, I., & Bashirov, G. (2018). The AKP after 15 years: Emergence of Erdoganism in Turkey. *Third World Quarterly, 39*(9), 1812–1830.

Part X

Strategic Populism & Societal Support

CHAPTER 34

Populism as an Implementation of National Biopolitics: The Case of Poland

Szymon Wróbel

THEORETICAL PREMISES

Let's start with a few conceptual corrections. The wave of populism that has flooded the modern world requires precise and unbiased thinking. Perhaps it also requires a new dictionary to understand the technique of populism in the world of new media and new digital technologies but also requires reflections on the new political subject articulating new demands. The return of populism can certainly be associated with the threat of blurring collective identities, employment, loss of social security, the migration crisis, etc. Populism has always been associated with a dangerous excess that undermines clear forms of a rational society. Today, however, this 'irrationality' of populism has become the mainstream of all 'rational' politics. This is the fundamental challenge of our time.

In this text I will try to understand who is the addressee of the new populist policy; therefore I will, first of all, ask about a new political entity who, as I claim, is no longer 'people,' 'sovereign nation,' but also not a 'lonely crowd,' 'mass,' 'plebs,' 'proletariat' but 'population.' Ernesto Laclau writes, in *On Populist Reason*, in a completely open style—"My attempt has not been to find the *true* referent of populism, but to do the opposite: to show that populism has no referential unity because it is ascribed not to a delimitable phenomenon but to a social logic whose effects cut across many phenomena. Populism is, quite simply, a way of constructing the political" (Laclau, 2005, p. XII).

S. Wróbel (✉)
Institute of Philosophy and Sociology of the Polish Academy of Sciences,
University of Warsaw, Warsaw, Poland

© The Author(s), under exclusive license to Springer Nature
Switzerland AG 2022
M. Oswald (ed.), *The Palgrave Handbook of Populism*,
https://doi.org/10.1007/978-3-030-80803-7_34

Yes, one must agree with Laclau that "populism is a way of constructing the political," but this does not mean that its 'object of reference' remains 'empty,' 'unclear,' or 'difficult to identify,' 'fuzzy' or 'devoid of unity.' On the contrary, such style of thinking limits populism to 'populist logic,' that is, depriving populism of 'ideological content' and 'clear reference,' risks equating populism with politics at all. In such an approach, there is no policy other than populist policy. In this paper, I argue that the key subject of populist rhetoric is a population that is only declaratively presented as 'sovereign union of people.' In fact, however, this 'sovereign people' is relegated to the role of a bare 'material, biological resource' on which politics is working.

In the first volume of *The History of Sexuality*, Michel Foucault noted a significant new quality of modern politics. One of the innovations in the techniques of power in the eighteenth century was the emergence of the population as an economic and political problem. "Governments perceived that they were not dealing simply with subjects, or even with a 'people,' but with a 'population,' with its specific phenomena and its peculiar variables: birth and death rates, life expectancy, fertility, state of health, frequency of illnesses, patterns of diet and habitation" (Foucault, 1978, p. 25). A few chapters later, Foucault adds, in his prophetic style, an important generalization—"For millennia, man remained what he was for Aristotle: a living animal with the additional capacity for a political existence; modern man is an animal whose politics places his existence as a living being in question" (Foucault, 1978, p. 118).

Many years have passed since this declaration, which did not help to clarify the meaning of the concept of biopolitics. As interpreted by Foucault, the concept of biopolitics gave rise to numerous neologisms—biopower, thanatopolitics, necropolitics, positive and negative forms of bio-power, and neuropolitics (Foucault, 1978, 2003, 2007, 2008). Jacques Derrida, Donna Haraway, and Rosi Braidotti argued that biopolitics should be studied from the point of view of the concept of immunization and autoimmunity (Braidotti, 2007; Derrida, 2009; Haraway, 1989). Giorgio Agamben, referring at the same time to the idea of 'camps without biopolitics' in Hannah Arendt and 'biopolitics without camps' in Foucault, postulates that the beginnings of the emergence of biopolitics should be extended to Greek and Roman times (Agamben, 1998, 2015).

Roberto Esposito, trying to counteract the negative, i.e., the thanatopolitics of Agamben, and the positive interpretations of the productive and new revolutionary class—the multitude—of Antonio Negri and Michael Hardt, argued that biopolitics should be read more widely in the context of community, nihilism, the right to possession, and the policy of the non-personal (Esposito, 2008, 2010, 2012). Hardt and Negri's concept of biopolitics concerns only immaterial life, while physiological or biological life is exiled to the oppressive and fatal realm of transcendent biopower. The authors of *Assembly* seem to introduce innovation into the standard accounts of biopower and biopolitics, by conceiving of life as both biological (the object of biopolitics) and immaterial (the object of biopower) (Negri & Hardt, 2004, 2017).

Furthermore, Foucault's concept of biopolitics was also criticized by Dipesh Chakrabarty, who accused it of being 'narcissistic provincial,' arguing that it was impossible to write a history of genocide that begins and ends in Europe, for example, even if Europe is assumed to be the distinguished point of reference (Chakrabarty, 2007). Finally, Achille Mbembe supplements that German Nazism was genealogically related to the era of European colonialism and therefore cannot be abstracted from this broader context. Therefore, it must be stated that we do not know what precise meaning should be assigned to the term 'biopolitics' (Mbembe, 2003).

The very concept of biopolitics does not imply a new quality of modern politics because biopolitics has always existed and defined the West's political horizon. The meaning of the term should therefore not so much be expanded as it should be sharpened. In a new, more precise sense, biopolitics is responsible for the regulation of political populations and constitutes a significant element in nation-building, state sovereignty, capable of producing various collective identities. The subject of biopolitics is still the population, but its technique is a set of practices and devices to control human and inhuman bodies and the world's materiality in general. Finally, and importantly, biopolitics can serve diverse, also, conservative purposes.

In this sense, I would like to go beyond the theoretical framework set by Foucault, Agamben, and Esposito: biopolitics is more than just a technique for executing and legitimizing power relations over life. I argue that the biopolitical practices of constructing normativity and the mechanisms of social surveillance and social inclusion and exclusion techniques are powerful tools for creating what I would call a 'biopolitical community.' I refer to this concept for clarification—how biopolitical investments shape specific populations as belonging to specific communities—national, religious, linguistic, class and gender and the like. To put it bluntly, I believe that the strategy of biopolitical thinking in Foucault's style should be combined with the tactics of populist thinkers like Ernesto Laclau and Chantal Mouffe (Laclau, 2005; Mouffe, 2018).

Populism in the Question

When it comes to populism, let's start with a similar finding like the one that opened the discourse on biopolitics: populism has many names (Babones, 2018; Bill & Stanley, 2020; Crouch, 2005; Mudde, 2007; Müller, 2016; Mounk, 2018; Panizza, 2005). Certainly, such concepts as 'democratic decay,' 'radical right political movements,' 'post-democracy,' 'the new authoritarianism,' 'not liberal-minded,' 'neo-Nazi,' 'national-radical front,' 'fundamentalist,' 'anti-constitutional political regime' do not have the same meaning, nor even the same content. Populism is a vague and contested concept.

There are many understandings of 'populism,' some of which simply identify it with popular governmental initiatives; others, with state interventionism in the economy, or with a focus on closeness to working people, 'blue-collar workers,' farmers, and other lower or lower middle classes. In recent years the most influential understanding is offered by Jan-Werner Müller who identifies populism with anti-pluralism, and more specifically, with making the "claim to exclusive moral representation of the people" (Müller, 2016, p. 48). Populists, Müller adds, attempt "to speak in the name of the people as a whole" and to morally delegitimate those who contest that claim, which is to say: those who contest their involuntary inclusion in a 'We the People'; such resisters to populism are effectively saying: 'not in our name.'

Perhaps the most comprehensive concept of populism was proposed by Ernesto Laclau. For Laclau, populism is not just a collection of anti-system movements, but the logic of political action itself. Mouffe supplements this general thesis by implementing it in a specific political context: we are witnessing, in Europe, a 'populist moment' that signals the crisis of neoliberal hegemony. By establishing a frontier between 'the people' and 'the oligarchy,' a left-populist strategy could bring together the manifold struggles against subordination, oppression, and discrimination. Right-wing populism, on the other hand, contrasts the oligarchic system of privileged and well-educated people with a 'common man' who did not get a chance to occupy a privileged position in society and success (Mouffe, 2018). This populist moment points to a 'return of the political' after years of 'liberal post-politics.' Can biopolitics help deepen the conception of populism understood in this way?

To apply biopolitical ideas to understand the current demand for populism, I will attempt to go beyond the opposition formulated by Foucault himself, which opposes biopolitics with the logic of sovereignty. I do this largely by showing that sovereignty is a highly biopolitical concept in the sense that different strategies of sovereign power place the issues of the body and 'man as species' at the center of their concerns. Elizabeth A. Povinelli argues that the modern world is full of political events pointing to the return of the logic of sovereign power. These expressions of new sovereign power are deeply rooted in the practice of biopower (Povinelli, 2016). Therefore, there is no gap separating modern regimes of biopower from the ancient order of sovereignty.

Reading Foucault, we have been told that disciplinary power works through 'subjugation techniques' directed at bodies and persons. Sovereign power operates through 'elimination techniques' directed toward the death side, and biopolitical power manifests itself through 'medical and demographic techniques' directed toward the multiplication of life in the population. These divisions have now become insufficient. Sovereignty does not develop dialectically toward disciplinary power, and disciplinary power does not cross the biopolitical threshold. On the contrary, all three of these formations are always co-present, although they are distributed and positioned relative to each other according to time and place. All three power formations—sovereign, disciplinary, and biopower, act as mechanisms of regulating life and distinguishing life from non-life.

Such a biopolitical, and, at the same time populist orientation allows us to understand why old practices so often reproduce in modern societies, despite the existence of an institutional framework intended to produce 'liberal effects' opposing nativism, nationalism, racism, and authoritarian tendencies. Perhaps this direction of thinking between the 'modern population' and the 'pre-modern commoners' allows us to understand the revival of nationalist traditions in the liberal world.

What constitutes the still unexplained political paradox of our times is contained in the question: how is it possible that in the twenty-first century, in the era of globalization, that the most primitive temptations of building political communities are based on the bodily and genetic characteristics of human existence such as gender, race, and ethnicity? We cannot be content with expressing formulas like—bare life, immunitas, panoptic apparatus, population, state of exception, control, surveillance, threshold, apparatus, government, or disposition. Each time, we must retrack the implementation of these concepts in a specific territory and at a specific time (Makarychev & Yatsyk, 2019). Biopolitics might be part of nation-building, a force that produces collective identities grounded in accepting the sets of corporeal practices of control over human bodies. Even more—modern medicine and molecular biology make it possible to refine the physical characteristics that enable more precise, advanced methods of distinguishing enemy from friend.

So, what is populism in the light of biopolitics? Populism is characterized by a central paradox: constant lip service to the power of the people but ultimate control and decision-making by a small clique of politicians. In this respect left populism and right populism are too often uncomfortably close. Populism, in this framework, retains strategy in the hands of leadership and limits the movements to tactical actions. After creating deep political divisions, populist logic makes a sudden turnaround toward regaining unity. We need to understand what the main promise of biopolitical populism is. It is not only about the promise of regaining symbolic unity; it is about something more, regaining a unity of the species, purely biological. The novelty of biological populism stems not from 'embodied philosophy' or 'embodied ideology' but from embodied and fully realized 'biology' (Esposito, 2012).

There are strong arguments for the thesis that biopolitics is less and less able to exist and function as Foucault described it. On the one hand, most of its functions are taken over by the modern enterprise and its managerial logic, as the coronavirus crisis is showing today. On the other hand, throughout the twentieth century, political movements have functioned oppositely to biopolitics, which translates historical processes into biological ones. Today, public health sectors are not governed by the biopolitical logic of 'taking care of the population' or by the equally generic 'necropolitics' (biopolitics of death, or eugenics). Rather, they are ruled by a meticulous, pervasive, rational, and violent mode of production driven by profit and rent.

POPULISM AND THE RIGHT TO PROPERTY

To say that populism is grounded in the claim of identity is undoubtedly true, but behind identity lurks property. Sovereignty and racialized property are the stigmata that mark the body of right-wing populisms. Right-wing movements are reactionary in that they seek to restore a past social order and borrow the protest repertoires, vocabularies, and even goals of left resistance and liberation movements (Negri & Hardt, 2004, 2017). This is especially evident in right-wing populist movements that mobilize the poor and subordinated segments of society to protest against elites in the people's name but serve to maintain or restore social hierarchies. That is the task of right-wing populism: to appeal to the masses without disrupting the power of elites or, more precisely, to bind the energy of the masses to reinforce the power of elites. Right-wing populisms serve to reinforce the power of some elites but to make sense of this we have to distinguish among different kinds of social hierarchies and, in fact, different forms of property.

Populist politics often expresses indignation against the rule of property, a form that is disembodied, mobile, and unattached to identity. The power of money, global markets, and even national central banks that depreciate currency are particular objects of criticism. On the other hand, populists, in seeking to defend the people, especially defined in racial, religious, gender, or civilizational terms, affirm another kind of property: immobile and embodied property, and ultimately property that is tied to identity. Land rights are thus a recurring theme as is the constancy of monetary values.

This relationship between identity and property takes two primary forms. First, identity is meant to provide privileged rights and access to property. A primary appeal of populist movements is to restore the economic power and social prestige they imagine to have lost, most often conceived, explicitly or implicitly, in terms of racial identity. Conceptions of a superior race, as Hannah Arendt observes, take the aristocratic experience of pride in privilege without individual effort and merit, simply by virtue of birth and make it accessible to ordinary people said to share a common nature (Arendt, 1976). In the populist anti-migrant movements that have expanded throughout Europe, the people's identity—sometimes defined explicitly in terms of whiteness and Christianity and at other times in 'civilizational' terms centered on liberal values—is strongly mixed with promises of property.

For both the criminal movements that violently attack migrants, such as Golden Dawn in Greece and Casa Pound in Italy and their more 'respectable' counterparts, such as the Front National and the Sweden Democrats and last but not least, Law and Justice in Poland, the racist, anti-migrant rhetoric is backed by the promise to restore the social position they believe they have lost, specifically the race privilege of working-class whites. Unfortunately, it became very visible in Poland's last presidential election, during which President Andrzej Duda (representative of the 'Law and Justice' party) used openly illiberal messages in the summer campaign, contesting the rights of sexual minorities related to the LGBTQ movement. People belonging to this movement were stripped of their humanity and treated as the effect of the LGBTQ ideology. During the election rallies, President Duda shouted: "We are told that these are people, but this is ideology!" (Reuters News Agency, 2020). Speaking to his supporters at the campaign rally in Brzeg, in southern Poland, president Duda said that, "parents are responsible for the sexual education of their children… no institutions can interfere in the way parents raise their children" (Reuters News Agency, 2020). As part of his run-up to the elections, President Duda signed a 'Family Charter' on June 10, 2020, in which he pledged to prevent gay couples from being able to get married or adopt children. The bill will also see the outlawing of teaching LGBT issues in schools.

The link between populism and the promise of a right of ownership to some indigenous citizens is no different in Poland, where the success of the Law and Justice party is based on the promise of 'regaining dignity' by a simple (read: uneducated) Pole, an ordinary man who was deceived and rejected by liberal and modernist political agendas. A simple Polish worker, who is a 'zealous Christian,' not only has to regain the right to his property, land, and means of production but above all, he has to 'get up from his knees.' Which means that during the last years of Polish modernization, a significant part of the population was lying in humiliation and rejection, watching only the growing success of the few "foreign-educated, pro-European elite" that have succeeded.

The democratic and liberal forces in Poland gathered, in vain, in mass marches on the streets of 2017, where the people shouted—"Free courts, free elections, free Poland"—against the current 'power of counterrevolution,' 'conservative revolution,' aimed at managing the life of the population, which in the mind of the ruling party, only expects the return of the *nomos* that allows the understanding of the unjust liberal order of things. The victories of the conservative bloc were not only an expression of rebellion against global financial capitalism, but also—to use the concept coined by Nancy Fraser— 'progressive neoliberalism,' i.e., an alliance of emancipatory social movements (Fraser, 2017)—feminism, anti-racism, multiculturalism, and LGBTQ rights, and a well-educated class of intellectual workers which supported the liberal 'Civic Platform' party led by Donald Tusk and found its apparatus of ideological articulation in 'Gazeta Wyborcza' newspaper and the independent television station TVN.

In conservative propaganda, the alliance of 'progressive forces' has been effectively linked to the "forces of cognitive capitalism," and 'progress' with 'meritocracy' instead of 'equality,' and 'emancipation' with the formation of a 'new elite' of talented women and all sorts of 'minorities,' well-installed in corporations. Perhaps it is correct, then, to also conclude that the future of Democrats representing the precariat will have to give up the comforting but false myth that the Left has lost to the 'defective' racists, misogynists, and homophobes, and will have to rethink how the political economy of capitalism can be changed, renewing the slogan 'common institution' and reflecting on what it can mean in the twenty-first century.

Populism and Extremism

So is there any fundamental difference between extremism and populism? Does extremism have clear indicators or clues of political presence that would take it significantly away from populism, particularly populism, which is focused on protecting populations? Golden Dawn in Greece and the Casa Pound party in Italy, for example, are clearly an extremist party, which might use a populist style, but it is foremost xenophobic; hence the question of the difference between extremism and populism is so important.

Well, my thesis would be like this: extremism can become part of populist logic, but never the other way. Extremism is always local, contingent, impermanent, and devoid of a clear political subject. Populism, on the contrary, has a clearly defined subject and goals. Populism is an enduring political technique that merely creates the constellation for various local and transient extremisms. Extremism is idiosyncratic, populism is never ephemeral, and it always targets biological indicators of the population or the population's well-being as a whole. As a result, there is no rationality for extremism. There is an autonomous logic of populism. Extremism could be described merely in vagueness, imprecision, intellectual poverty, radicalism, and manipulative procedures; there is no way of determining its *differentia specifica* in positive terms. Extremism is heterogeneous, multiple articulations of dissatisfaction with the moderate politics of institutions and parliamentarism. On the contrary, when it comes to populism. In this case, „the question 'what is populism?' should be replaced by a different one: "to what social and ideological reality does populism apply?" (Laclau 2005, p. 17). Just again: by 'populism' we do not understand a *type* of movement but a *political logic* concentrated on one population's interest.

To put it another way, I would say that extremism has its 'tools of expression' but is devoid of its 'enduring rhetoric' which is at the service of populism. This is why extremism is mainly based on the radicalization of sentiments, demands, expectations, beliefs, etc. On the other hand, populism does more than just radicalize it: it indicates solutions, it judgesit puts the accused, calls for other economic solutions, it breaks with the impossibilism of the existing policy. As a result, populism cannot be derived from group suggestion, collective hypnosis, group contagion, imitation, or even escape disposition, not even a process of deindividuation. Extremism is always violent, populism, on the contrary, is based on very complex rhetoric and the promise of regaining unity. The category of 'population as people' is a strictly politically produced category in the process of producing unity. In extremism, 'people' are rather a datum of the social structure. As a result, populism seeks to achieve lasting changes in political representation and the political structure itself. Extremism is satisfied with performative effects. Populism aims to achieve a permanent new political hegemony; extremism is satisfied with temporary effects and has no systemic aspirations.

If we assume that the construction of the 'people' is always a radical construction, we must assume that there is always an element of radicalism in populism. However, this is the 'radicalism of operations,' not the radicalism of demands or 'pure expressions.' The radicalism of populism tends to close the population state radically. It is the radicalism of the 'nationalization of society' (population), not the radicalism of the liberal rationalization and new reorganization of the state.

Legal Populism

The argument about the link between populism and the economy focused on national population growth, and rising national income is reinforced by the analysis carried out by Katharina Pistor. In *The Code of Capital. How the Law Creates Wealth and Inequality,* she argues in favor of the thesis that "capital is coded in law" (Pistor, 2019). Ordinary assets are just that—a plot of land, a promise to be paid in the future, the pooled resources from friends and family to set up a new business, or individual skills and know-how. Yet every one of these assets can be transformed into capital by cloaking them in the legal modules used to code asset-backed securities and their derivatives, which were at the core of the rise of finance in recent decades. These 'legal modules,' namely—contract, property rights, collateral, trust, corporate, and bankruptcy law, can be used to give the holders of some assets a comparative advantage over others. For centuries, private attorneys have molded and adapted these legal modules to a changing roster of assets, thereby enhancing their clients' wealth. States have supported the coding of capital by offering their coercive law powers to enforce the legal rights that have been bestowed on capital.

The classic way of thinking and the empire of law made us think that this is the realm of wild capitalism regulation. From the time of Motesquieus to the times of the German ordo-liberals, we were told that the empire of law is a collection of regulations, statutes, ordinances, and other legal acts that are to regulate the market, control human entrepreneurship and profit, administratively, establish a list of permitted forms of ownership and property exchange. From Pistor's point of view, however, this is not true. The empire of law is rather a set of regulations that strengthen some forms of ownership and eliminate others.

The Code of Capital tells a story of the legal coding of capital from the asset's perspective: land, business organizations, private debt, and knowledge, even nature's genetic code (Pistor, 2019). Pistor has tried to make the legal institutions accessible and interesting and relevant for current debates about inequality, democracy, and governance. The law is a powerful tool for social ordering and, if used wisely, has the potential to serve a broad range of social objectives. The law has been placed firmly in the service of capital.

In regard to the question about the genesis of capital—how is wealth created in the first place?—we hear the simple answer: capital power lies in its legal code. Fundamentally, capital is made from two ingredients: an asset, and the legal code. It should be immediately added that Pistor uses the term 'asset' broadly to denote any object, claim, skill, or idea, regardless of its form. In their unadulterated appearance, these simple assets are just that: a piece of dirt, a building, a promise to receive payment at a future date, an idea for a new drug, or a string of digital code (Pistor, 2019). With the right legal coding, any of these assets can be turned into capital, thereby, increasing its propensity to create wealth for its holder(s). How does this legal capital code work in a specific case?

Let's look at the scandal of the so-called 'two towers' in Poland, which the ruling PiS party (the Law and Justice Party) wanted to build in the center of Warsaw as its main capital investment. The most important element in this affair turned out to be the testimony of the Austrian businessman, Gerald Birgfellner, regarding Fr. Rafał Sawicz, member of the board of the Institute Lech Kaczyński. According to the businessman, the PiS president was to persuade him to give Sawicz 50,000 PLN in cash in February 2018. It was supposed to be a form of payment for the priest's signature on the resolution of the foundation council. Without this signature, as a foundation council member, it was impossible to start building the skyscrapers.

Two days before the elections—October 11, 2019, the Prosecutor's Office in Warsaw refused to start an investigation into the building of the two towers. How did the prosecution justify the refusal to investigate? First, it concluded that the Lech Kaczyński Institute Foundation, which is the owner of the main investor—Srebrna Company, whose council is Jarosław Kaczyński, does not conduct any economic activity. 'Only a person who performs a managerial function in an entity carrying out economic activity may be the subject of a crime'—we read, in the justification. Secondly, according to the prosecutor's office, the priest is only a member of the collective body, which takes resolutions, statements, and other decisions by a simple majority of votes. According to the prosecutor, the dispute between the parties is purely civil law and may be resolved through civil proceedings.

As a result of a far-reaching journalistic investigation, complex connections between prominent politicians of the 'Law and Justice' party, investment companies and the construction industry were revealed. The real estate on Srebrna Street—two office buildings with plots of land—is the 'assets' of the Solidarity Press Foundation. This Foundation was established in the early 1990s as an instrument of the 'Porozumienie Centrum' (Center Agreement), the first party of Jarosław Kaczyński. Based on the Foundation, Kaczyński wanted to create a media concern in opposition to the liberal'Gazeta Wyborcza'.

I mention the 'Srebrna affair' because it has become symbolic in Poland. Jarosław Kaczyński, who earlier was considered the Maximilien de Robespierre of Polish politics, the father of the nation, deprived of the accumulative drive and cunning of people promoted during the modernization process, the king of the poor, revealed his new face of a rational and aggressive capitalist, who perfectly understands that ideas must be valued by capital. The subordination of the judiciary branch and the courts to the political will also allow for the blocking of all investigations in cases that could harm the unblemished public image and reputation of the Robin Hood of the Polish political scene.

Procreative Policy

However, the subject of subordinating legal institutions to politics in the service of capital does not end with the twin tower affair. Wojciech Sadurski, in his important book *Poland's Constitutional Breakdown*, highlights how Poland, once the great success example of the post-1989 new world order, has been brought to the brink of authoritarianism (Sadurski, 2019). Without tanks in the streets or dissidents imprisoned, Poland's legal institutions are being commandeered to crush the democratic opposition. This is the most careful account of how democracy is undermined from within, by the most insightful constitutional scholar on contemporary Eastern Europe. According to Sadurski, in just a few years, Poland has been transformed from a model state to a pariah, and his account shows how and why in ethnographic and legal detail (Sadurski, 2019).

After 2015, a dramatic change in Polish politics occurred, not as a result of a coup but through a takeover by democratically elected politicians, by and large playing by the democratic rules of the game. It started with two national elections. The first was the presidential election on the 10th and 24th of May, 2015, which the Law and Justice party candidate Andrzej Duda won—a young and largely unknown political newcomer. Andrzej Duda is the Martyniuk of Polish politics. There is no doubt about that; the second step occurred soon after: in the parliamentary elections of the 27th of October 2015. PiS won with an absolute majority of five seats, giving them the authority to govern single-handedly. It ended the two-term, eight-year domination by the centrist-liberal PO, ruling in coalition with the politically moderate 'Polish Peasants' Party (Polskie Stronnictwo Ludowe).

Victorious populism in Poland is part of a broader surge of populism worldwide, and more specifically in Europe, with populism being, in turn, a species of a broader phenomenon of general global discontent with liberal democracy in recent years (Sadurski, 2019). But the Polish case is different. Nowhere else in Europe did populist parties manage to dismantle the institutional system of checks and balances. In some countries—such as the UK Independence Party in the United Kingdom or the Freedom Party in Austria, populists did not even display any particular illiberalism when it came to the constitutional structure of government. The Polish assault upon constitutional checks and balances is exceptional, and more specifically, Poland is unique in its ostentatious disregard for its own formal constitutional rules.

According to Sadurski, the essence of the political developments in Poland after the 2015 elections, is "anti-constitutional populist backsliding," and all three ingredients are equally important (Sadurski, 2019, pp. 6–29). The important dimension of the anti-constitutional character of PiS power is governance through multiple breaches of the Constitution. The first instance of the constitutional breakdown was the president's refusal to swear in elected judges correctly. The constitution does not give the president any such role in designing the composition of the Constitutional Tribunal. The notion of populism emphasizes that what is going on in Poland is not authoritarianism simpliciter, but that it is an illiberal condition whereby the rulers care about popular support.

The concept of 'backsliding' is the third feature central to the characterization of Polish developments in recent years. The trajectory of backsliding has to be distinguished from the absence of democratic progress in countries that have not achieved a satisfactory level of democracy in the first place. The use of the notion of backsliding emphasizes a temporal dimension and highlights a retrogression that is not visible in a time-slice account. The word 'backsliding' accurately describes the process of reversal and the fact that there is no rapid, immediate rupture, as in a coup. It also emphasizes a process as opposed to a state of affairs (Sadurski, 2019). What is important to us in the recent history of the non-liberal mind is that dismantling separation of powers, constitutional checks, and democratic rights, undermine democracy itself.

At the moment, we do not have time to precisely analyze all the consequences of this new legal order related to Poland's Constitutional Breakdown; we will focus only on the last piece of the puzzle, i.e.,the decision of the Constitutional Tribunal on abortion. This decision is so important to us because it most clearly shows the link between populism and biopolitics. On October 22nd, 2020, the Constitutional Tribunal, chaired by Julia Przyłębska, a person closely associated with the PiS community, ruled that the right to abortion in the event of severe and irreversible fetal impairment is inconsistent with the constitution. In connection with this decision, demonstrations are being held all over the country against the tightening of the anti-abortion law.

The problem is that protests against the abortion interdict are taking place during a pandemic, and therefore a time of restrictions on civil liberties. As a result, the participants of these protests are being accused of contributing to the creation of a life-threatening situation. The public media has repeatedly presented the protests as anarchist riots by feminists and left-wing youth in the streets, intended only to disturb social peace, not to restore the constitutional, lawful order. Protesters were systematically accused of vandalism, the vulgarization of the language, aggressive behavior, and lack of respect for the public good. Despite this, a wave of protests against the sentence passed on October 22, continues on the streets of all big cities across Poland. There is a discussion in Parliament on how to silence these anxieties. "Those who call for protests after the judgment of the Constitutional Tribunal, and those who participate in them, bring about a common danger, and thus commit a serious crime"—said Jarosław Kaczyński, PiS president. He also called on PiS members to "defend the Church" (Barteczko & Florkiewicz, 2020).

"I think, feel, decide!"—such a slogan is heard in front of the Polish Parliament in autumn 2020. The strike in defense of women's right to legal abortion is sweeping through Poland like a new generation of rebellion. This protest is gaining huge support from both men and older women. Perhaps it is a symbol of cultural change, a kind of counterrevolution to the conservative PiS counterrevolution. In the spirit of our intellectual conduct, we only need to note that this rebellion is also biopolitical in a threefold sense. First, it takes place during a pandemic, and despite the protesters marching in face masks, there is no doubt that they come into conflict with the law restricting the right to collective demonstrations. Second, it is a biopolitical issue because it concerns the body and the reproductive process. This protest is a reaction to the political temptation to "nationalize the body." To the question—"to whom does the body belong?" the protesters reply: to women, to the individual! What is surprising about this answer is that the liberal category of 'person' and 'individual' returns from oblivion. Thirdly, it is a biopolitical protest, because on the streets of Polish cities, the PiS's 'family-oriented' procreative policy with the flagship '500-plus project' ahead, according to which every family receives a financial allowance for a second and subsequent child, reaches the bottom here. It seems that young people want to decide for themselves about the process of reproduction and are faced with an absurd morally shaming choice: either you are for the civilization of death with euthanasia and abortion and a free narcissistic will to self-determination, or you are for the civilization of life, the duty to the state, and for the protection of the unborn life, they choose this first civilization. Polish young people no longer want to defend the church.

Perhaps the novelty of Polish biopolitics is not the focus on "life that does not deserve to live" or "life unworthy of being lived" "life devoid of value." The novelty of Polish biopolitics is rather 'forcing life' and "giving birth to life" against the will of the woman who is responsible for giving this life a 'human dimension.' Agamben argued that the novelty of modern biopolitics lies in the fact that the biological given is, as such, immediately political, and the political is, as such, immediately the biological given (Agamben, 1998). This is exactly what is happening in Poland. In some sense, it is a kind of 'upside-down euthanasia.' 'Upside down euthanasia' is no longer 'mercy killing' or 'death by grace,' but a 'blessed life,' which is to be the grace of the state, by a sovereign decision the leader of the nation.

Instead of the End

What kind of conclusions are we to draw from our brief history of populism as a concern for the national population's future? Are we doomed, in the future, to the development of this kind of populism and the fall of liberal democracies, disappointed with the subordination of the value of all things to the authority of the market as the only measure of the real value of goods, disappointed with the idea of the free play of competition as the only guarantee of good economy, and finally, disappointed with the institution of sovereign judicial power as the only guarantee of justice as impartiality and fairness?

To answer this difficult question, let us return once again to the idea of biopolitics. It seems that we have two paradigms in understanding this concept. In the first sense, the goal of biopolitics is the control of life in its biological sense. For Foucault and Agamben, the state's essential function is to take control of life, manage it, compensate for its aleatory nature, explore and reduce biological accidents and possibilities. In the second sense, biopolitics means control of life in its immaterial work. On the other hand, for Hardt and Negri, biopolitics concerns only immaterial (and hence immortal) life, while physiological or biological (and hence mortal) life is exiled to the oppressive and fatal realm of transcendent biopower. However, both paradigms share a common denominator. They both operate within a dualism that attributes biological life to transcendence and immaterial life to immanence. Thereby producing the further political dualism between the subjection of the material aspects of life to an oppressive power (biopower), and the attribution of revolutionary potential (biopolitics) to the immanent and immaterial aspect of life. The question is: can we trust this convenient distinction between oppressive transcendence and revolutionary immanence? Moreover, can this dualism help us grasp the actual workings of the politics of biopower?

A. Kiarina Kordela, author of *Being, Time, Bios: Capitalism and Ontology*, calls biopolitics the production, management, administration, and control of the presence or absence of gazes that allow the subject to experience itself as mortal or immortal (Kordela, 2013). What does this mean? It means that the central biopolitical mechanism is "secular administration of the illusion of immortality – a kind of Faustian pact in which subjects give up their ethical dimension in exchange for immortality" (Kordela, 2013, p. 150). Does the essence of biopolitics concern the regulation of our perception of mortality and immortality?

For Kordela, biopolitical order is not limited to the symbolic order, understood as a given society with its ideological systems, laws, rules of kinship, principles of economic exchange, technologies of empowerment, as in many scholars like Slavoj Žižek's or Ernesto Laclau and Chantal Mouffe's argue. No society is ever given in its totality as an object to be perceived by an empirical subject. By that token, we can say that empirically 'society' is impossible as a whole. But for Kordela, 'secular' does not mean the simple elimination of transcendence; rather, the 'unconscious' is a term for indicating the enfolding of transcendence within immanence. The true formula of atheism is not *God is dead,* but *God is unconscious* (Kordela, 2013, p. 11).

But what conclusions we are to draw from this displacement of the element of immortality? Does shifting God's place into unconscious positions result in an unconscious belief in the body's mortality and a conscious image of the mortality of the self (soul)? A. Kiarina Kordela offers a completely independent interpretation of biopolitics. In Kardela's interpretation, what we have so far called the "biological unity of the population," which did not know the division into an individual and society, singularity and collective, she calls "the sense of immortality of the body." It is not the body under the biopolitical regime that is mortal, and it is not the soul that is immortal, but rather the "illusion of the immortality of the body" is the main object of biopolitical strategies. How is this illusion even possible? To explain to us this 'biopolitical manipulation,' Kordela turns to the famous distinction proposed by Hans Kelsen into two distinct systems of representation, double representation of bios—*Darstellung* and *Vertretung*. How does this distinction work?

Kordela refers to Hans Kelsen's observation that the idea of the parliament as a simple representative (proxy or placeholder) of the people is the fiction of representation since the appointed members of the parliament are not obliged to follow any binding instructions from their voters (Kelsen, 2013, pp. 47–67). The advent of the parliamentary system replaced in politics *Vertretung*—as was practiced in the *Ständeversammlungen*, in which the represeners (*Stellvertreter*) were bound to reflect the interests of the caste or profession of their voters—with *Darstellung*. What does this conversion really mean? Whereas *Vertretung* involved an organic link between represented and their representatives, *Darstellung* is an arbitrary representation system. Whereas the representation (*Vertretung*) is based on an *organic link* determined by its specific kind and the cultural and moral norms of the society in which it is performed; its representation (*Darstellung*) is purely 'fictitious', that is, it involves no apodictic rapport between the representer and the represented.

It follows that *Vertretung* is a pre-secular mode of representation, as was, at least conceptually and structurally, also the *Ständeversammlung*. For *Vertretung* is based on ternary signs: the thing, the mark, and the similitude ('moral' and other historically determined judgments) that provides the 'organic' bond between the mark and the thing. By contrast, *Darstellung* is a secular system of representation. It consists of binary, differential signs: the thing and the mark with no 'apodictic rapport' or 'organic' bond but only an 'arbitrary' or 'fictitious' connection. In short: *Vertretung is a scandal* within the realm of liberal democracy for this political order is that Vertretung remains its repressed (Kelsen, 2013, pp. 47–67).

As a result, we get a new formula of biopolitical mechanisms which involve arrangements and administrations of representation in such a way that the persistent perpetuation of *Vertretung* within secular order of modernity is hidden, so that everything appears as abstract, immortal, differential, arbitrary, and autonomous value—as if there were no bodies whose labor bears an organic link with the money that remunerates it.

My last thesis in this text is: the strength of biopolitical populism results from the reversal of modernity's liberal formula, i.e., recalling and trying to recreate and reactivate the representation understood as *Vertretung*. Biopolitical populists promise a return to the world without abstract and contractual, arbitrary representation, they promise a return to an organic order that gives a sense of an unqualified relationship between representation and what is represented. This is a formidable promise that we should fear. It is a false promise that no one can fulfill. It is a promise of a return to the archaic times before modernity. In history, such returns always end in tragedy or tragicomedy.

The analysis of A. Kiarina Kordela should be completed and expanded. At present, what we are concerned with is not the transformation of the end of History into the Age of Imitation or even the transformation of the Age of Imitation into the end of the Liberal Mind (Krastev & Holmes, 2020), but the metamorphosis of the Ant-Liberal Mind into something that does not yet have a unique name. Seventy years after the publication of Theodor W. Adorno's authoritarian personality, we are still trying to rethink the fascism of everyday life, fascism not outside of democracy, but in democracy.

Adorno writes about people in America 'ready for fascism' but thinking of themselves in conservative or even liberal terms. Thus, he diagnoses the chances of a potential triumph of fascism in America. *The Authoritarian Personality* is a book on the birth of fascism *in* a democracy, not *after* or *against* democracy (Adorno et al., 1950). This brings Adorno's work closer to the subtle analysis of Alexis de Tocqueville's *Democracy in America*, although the latter was obviously not talking about fascism, but about anti-democratic tendencies in radical democracy itself (Tocqueville, 2000). Adorno explicitly declares that the focal point of his interest is a potentially fascist individual, that is, an individual with a personality structure that makes him particularly vulnerable to anti-democratic propaganda.

People who are ready for fascism are people who would be willing to accept fascism if it turned into a strong and acceptable social movement. The main premise for the return of fascism is that democracy has never become a 'real democracy.' We live in apparent democracies, i.e., democracies by name only, legitimized by referring to election procedures. For Adorno, not a single real democracy in the socioeconomic sense has developed to this day. Democracies are only formally present, and in this sense, fascist movements could be described as 'wounds' or 'scars of democracy,' which until today has not been able to satisfy its own concept (Adorno et al., 1950). The concept of fascism would, therefore, be closely related to the concept of democracy. The enigmatic nature of the concept of democracy would make the concept of fascism enigmatic.

The loss of Donald Trump in the last US presidential election will not allow us to sleep. This is not a failure of populism or, much less, politics of populism. Donald Trump did not lose the elections because of populism, but he almost won the elections again for the simple reason that the most important category for voters was not the pandemic and COVID-19, or even racial politics, but the economy and economic growth rates. Populism is not a strategy alongside economics or biopolitics; it is a strategy embedded in both issues, it is a kind of managing of life and its biological parameters by managing the brain and its cognitive or affective states. A few months before Trump's defeat in the United States, Andrzej Duda wins Poland's elections using xenophobic, anti-LGBTQ, and overtly populist rhetoric. The promise of a holiday supplement' and the launch of new social programs resulted in the oblivion of attacks on the rule of law, the separation of powers, and the destruction of the Constitutional Tribunal, which took place during the three-year rule of PiS.

Literature

Adorno, T. W., Frenkel-Brunswik, E., Levinson, D. J., & Sanford, R. N. (1950). *The authoritarian personality*. Harper & Row.
Agamben, G. (1998). *Homo sacer: Sovereign power and bare life*. Stanford University Press.
Agamben, G. (2015). *The use of bodies: Homo sacer IV*, 2. (A. Kotsko, Trans.). Stanford University Press.
Arendt, H. (1976). *The origins of totalitarianism*. A Harvest Book.
Babones, S. (2018). *The new authoritarianism: Trump, populism, and the tyranny of experts*. Polity Press.
Barteczko, A., & Florkiewicz, P. (2020, October 27). Poland's Kaczynski demands Poles defend patriotism amid abortion backlash. *Reuters*. Available at: https://www.reuters.com/article/poland-abortion/update-3-polands-kaczynski-demands-poles-defend-patriotism-amid-abortion-backlash-idINL1N2HI0OU?edition-redirect=in. Accessed 25 January 2021.
Bill, S., & Stanley, B. (2020). Whose Poland is it to be? The struggle between monism and pluralism in democratic Poland. *East European Politics*, Early Access.
Braidotti, R. (2007). Bio-power and Necro-politics: Reflections on an ethics of sustainability. *Springerin, 2*(7), 18–23.
Chakrabarty, D. (2007). *Provincializing Europe: Postcolonial thought and historical difference*. Princeton University Press.
Crouch, C. (2005). *Post-democracy*. Polity Press.
Derrida, J. (2009). *The Beast and the Sovereign, Volume 1* (G. Benjamin, Trans.). University of Chicago Press.
de Tocqueville, A. (2000). *Democracy in America*. ed. and trans. H. C. Mansfield & D. Winthrop. University of Chicago Press.
Esposito, R. (2008). *Bios: Biopolitics and philosophy* (T. Campbell, Trans.). Minnesota University Press.
Esposito, R. (2010). *Communitas: The origin and destiny of community* (T. Campbell, Trans.). Stanford: Stanford University Press.
Esposito R. (2012). *Third person: Politics of life and philosophy of the impersonal* (Z. Hanafi, Trans.). Polity Press.
Foucault, M. (1978). *The history of sexuality, Volume 1: An introduction* (R. Hurley, Trans.). Pantheon Books.
Foucault, M. (2003). *Society must be defended* (Lectures at the College de France, 1975–76). (D. Macey, Trans.). Picador.
Foucault, M. (2007). *Security, territory, population* (Lectures at the Collège de France, 1977–1978) (G. Burchell, Trans.). Palgrave Macmillan.

Foucault, M. (2008). *The birth of biopolitics* (Lectures at the Collège de France, 1978–1979) (G. Burchell, Trans.). Palgrave Macmillan.

Fraser, N. (2017, January 2). *The end of progressive neoliberalism*, [w:] *Dissent*.

Haraway, D. (1989). The biopolitics of postmodern bodies: Determinations of self in immune system discourse. In D. Harawa (Ed.), *Simians, cyborgs, and women: The reinvention of nature* (pp. 203–230). Routledge.

Kelsen, H. (2013). *The essence and value of democracy*, trans. B. Graf, N. Urbinati, & A. C. Invernizzi (Eds.). Rowman & Littlefield.

Kordela, A. K. (2013). *Being, time, bios: Capitalism and ontology*. Suny Press.

Krastev, I., & Holmes, S. (2020). *The light that failed: Why the west is losing the fight for democracy* (p. 2020). Pegasus Books.

Laclau, E. (2005). *On populist reason*. Verso.

Makarychev, A., & Yatsyk, A. (2019). *Critical biopolitics of the post-Soviet: From populations to nations*. Lexington Books.

Mbembe, A. (2003). *Necropolitics* (L. Meintjes, Trans.). *Public Culture, 15*(1), 11–40.

Mouffe, C. (2018). *For a left populism*. Verso.

Mounk, Y. (2018). *The people vs democracy*. Harvard University Press.

Mudde, C. (2007). *Populist radical right parties in Europe*. Cambridge University Press.

Müller, J.-W. (2016) *What is populism?* University of Pennsylvania.

Negri, A., & Hardt, M. (2004). *Multitude: War and democracy in the age of empire*. Penguin Books.

Negri, A., & Hardt, M. (2017). *Assembly*. Oxford University Press.

Panizza, F. (Ed.). (2005). *Populism and the mirror of democracy*. Verso.

Pistor, K. (2019). *The code of capital*. Princeton University Press.

Povinelli, E. A. (2016). *Geontologies: A requiem to late liberalism*. Duke University Press.

Reuters News Agency. (2020, August 6). Polish opposition shows rainbow LGBT solidarity at president's swearing-in. *Reuters*. Available at: https://www.reuters.com/article/uk-poland-politics-idUKKCN25228V. Accessed 25 January 2021.

Sadurski, W. (2019). *Poland's constitutional breakdown*. Oxford University Press.

CHAPTER 35

Understanding the Support of Right-Wing Populist Positions Within Unsuspected Groups: The Case of Professional Social Workers in Italy

Luca Fazzi and Urban Nothdurfter

INTRODUCTION

The rise of right-wing populist parties is a global phenomenon that scholars from a variety of disciplines have been trying to explain for years (Camus & Lebourg, 2017; Judis, 2016; Muis & Immerzeel, 2017; Ron & Nadesan, 2020; Rooduijn, 2019; Wodak et al., 2013). Most widely accepted theories converge in explaining the success of right-wing populist parties by the fact that at times of great economic and social uncertainties, populists offer simplified solutions to the causes of these crises by using propaganda intended to emphasize the primacy of the native population against the 'predatory' interests of outsiders and elites (Clarke et al., 2016; Vliegenthart et al., 2012). In particular, right-wing populism uses communications to leverage content that polarizes political positions even further (Müller et al., 2017). This way, populist parties gather support above all from among people who have fewer cultural tools and antibodies to assess the soundness and rationality of populist programs, and who demand greater security in the face of economic and cultural uncertainties (Inglehart & Norris, 2016; Wirz et al., 2018). The new media play a crucial role as a sounding board for populist positions enabling

L. Fazzi
Department of Sociology and Social Research, University of Trento, Trento, Italy
e-mail: luca.fazzi@unitn.it

U. Nothdurfter (✉)
Faculty of Education, Free University of Bozen-Bolzano, Bolzano, Italy
e-mail: urban.nothdurfter2@unibz.it

© The Author(s), under exclusive license to Springer Nature Switzerland AG 2022
M. Oswald (ed.), *The Palgrave Handbook of Populism*,
https://doi.org/10.1007/978-3-030-80803-7_35

and encouraging forms of communication that can select information and manipulate the public opinion with ease (Heiss & Matthes, 2020).

This analytical perspective on the spread of populism undoubtedly covers a significant part of the phenomenon. There is, however, a growing body of literature suggesting that supporters of right-wing populist positions cannot be fully identified as falling within a clear profile of more easily manipulable voters (Akkerman et al., 2014; Van Hauwaert & Van Kessel, 2018). Studies are also taking an increasing interest in ideological motivations and the various psychosocial factors that explain support for right-wing populism (Spruyt et al., 2016; see also Lilleker and Weidhase & Betz and Oswald in this volume).

As an interesting example, this chapter focuses on a social and professional group that should, in theory, be especially resistant to the siren call of populism, namely, welfare professionals. Their social identity is based on ethical and professional principles such as social justice, universalism, and respect for diversity seen as antithetical to right-wing populism. Notwithstanding these value driven premises, empirical research has shown that political preferences and expressions of support for right-wing populists can also develop among welfare professionals (Fazzi, 2015; Milbrandt & Wagner, 2017; Radvan & Schäuble, 2019). How can this be the case? What factors drive certain social workers to look on right-wing populist parties with favor? Is it simply a result of the information spread in populist propaganda? Or are we facing the outcome of more complex processes that need to be understood through more in-depth and qualitative analyzes and interpretations?

The aim of this chapter is to contribute to the debate on these issues by means of a qualitative study conducted on a group of Italian social workers who expressly state their support for the programs proposed by right-wing populist parties. The first section of the chapter describes the context and methodology of the study, while the second illustrates its main findings. The conclusion discusses dynamics and factors that help to understand the spread of right-wing populism among unexpected groups as well as steps to be taken to counter this phenomenon.

Right-Wing Populism and Social Work in Italy

This study was conducted in Italy, which is one of the countries in which the phenomenon of right-wing populist and its capacity to manipulate public opinion have manifested themselves in the most prominent way (Bobba & Legnante, 2016). The rise of the new right-wing populism in Italy has been traced back to the end of the so-called First Republic in the early 1990s. The crisis of confidence in the historical political parties created a favorable climate for the birth of new populist political movements such as the magnate Silvio Berlusconi's Forza Italia and the Northern League, which attracted votes as a result of a popular feeling of dissatisfaction with the old-established institutions (Albertazzi & McDonnell, 2010; Ignazi, 2014). More recently, right-wing populism began to be transformed into sovereignism concurrently with increasing inflows of migrants from North Africa. The Secretary of the Northern League, Matteo Salvini, who had taken on the role of media leader of the center-right after the scandals that overtook Berlusconi, immediately rode the wave of the concerns and dislike of large sections of the population, who had in part already been adversely affected by the persistence of the economic crisis, regarding large number of migrants landing on the shores of the Southern regions (Albertazzi et al., 2018). In the 2018 national elections, the League took 18% of the vote and became a member of the government, together with the 5 Stars Movement, the anti-establishment party led by former comedian Beppe Grillo. Over the twelve-month period when Salvini was a member of the government, acting as Minister of Interior, the League's positions became increasingly populist and sovereignist, and it won all the regional elections one by one during this period.

An unexpected government crisis in September 2019 led to the formation of a government between the center-left Democratic Party and the 5 Stars Movement. However, support for the League is still high and constantly confirming its pole position in opinion polling for the next general elections. As to popularity of political leaders, after Prime Minister Conte who gained large support particularly during the first phase of the COVID-19 pandemic, Italians mostly like Giorgia Meloni, the President of the ex-Fascist party Brothers of Italy whom *The Times* identified as one of 2020s twenty most influential women worldwide. Even though government participation of right-wing populist parties on both the national and regional level has resulted above all in policies with a powerful emotional impact but limited practical results, the ongoing propaganda against migrants as well as against national and European political elites continue to attract impressive consensus.

Social workers are largely considered to be one of the professional categories that have remained immune to right-wing populism (Noble & Ottmann, 2018). Social work has its professional origins in the various responses to the social problems of modern societies and so, it cannot operate without a societal anchoring of its founding values and principles and its legitimacy within a welfare consensus. Social work as a profession is, therefore, not only legitimized by its own professional autonomy and ethics but operates and finds its legitimation based on a social mandate deriving from a political consensus on how social rights are configured and what the boundaries of state mediated solidarity are. A broad welfare state consensus, at least in the European context, has not just provided a framework for the development of social policies and services but also been the basis for the development and establishment of social work as a profession. Notwithstanding the differences in the various welfare regimes and the profound transformations that have taken place in all European welfare systems, social work continues to be based on the idea that inclusive public welfare is a constitutive element of its legitimacy and identity. These powerful ties between the welfare system and the profession's identity have remained a central feature of social work as a pro-welfare profession with a strong public connotation. This is also reflected in a collective image of social workers as representatives and guardians of the welfare system that has perhaps been taken too much for granted for many years, also by the profession itself.

Social work in Italy operates in accordance with formal welfare policies defining assistance to be provided to citizens in need, regardless of their religious, ethnic or political affiliations (Facchini & Lorenz, 2013). Social workers also respond to an ethical code emphasizing professional responsibilities based on principles such as universalism, human rights, social justice and respect for diversity and personal dignity. Until a few years ago, the profession was highly respected by institutions and society. Recently, however, various studies have shown that the working conditions of social workers have been adversely affected by cuts in social spending and the reorganization of social services abetting also processes of professional delegitimization (Garrett & Bertotti, 2017; Tousijn & Dellavalle, 2017). The workload has increased disproportionately in many areas and there are fewer social workers than there is demand. In addition, the system of social services has been increasingly partitioned, with planning and purchase departments being rigidly separated from those providing the services, thereby creating increasing problems with coordination and integrated interventions. In this framework, social workers frequently become subject to what Jane Fenton (2016) has termed 'ethical stress,' a situation in which working conditions enter into strong conflict with the founding principles of the profession.

Despite these changes, the idea that the profession is inspired by universalist and inclusive principles of solidarity and social justice has historically made it possible to catalogue social workers as 'unsusceptible,' i.e., as individuals whose professional commitment, ethical values, and political preferences should per se identify them as antagonists of right-wing populist parties' programs. Recent studies have shown, however, that this assumption is currently less solid than assumed in the past (Fazzi, 2015; Fazzi & Nothdurfter, 2020). In the context of growing right-wing populism, there are also social workers who are beginning to show sympathy and support for right-wing populist parties and positions. What induces these social workers to express political preferences that conflict with the values of their profession? Are they only aberrated outliers or individuals who are thinking unknowingly or irrationally? Or are we witnessing a more profound process of transformation of consolidated social identities, even of unsusceptible professional groups?

The Study: Objectives and Methods

Exploring the phenomenon of support for right-wing populist positions by social workers is difficult because of the reluctance to talk about a topic that is rather awkward in mainstream debates of the professional community. In order to overcome this problem, this study was carried out by means of in-depth interviews with a group of social workers recruited via Facebook where they had publicly supported positions in favor of right-wing populist parties' programs and positions during the previous twelve months.

Notwithstanding its wide-scale availability, the use of Facebook as a tool for recruiting the interviewees has its limits regarding the representativeness of the recruitment process. Many individuals do either not have a public profile for confidentiality reasons or do not wish to use social networks for sharing private information. However, various researchers have shown that social networks can be a very useful tool for recruiting interviewees from among so-called difficult to reach populations (Sikkens et al., 2017). One major initial advantage of Facebook is that it offers a representation of the ideas of potential interviewees, thereby making detectable to researchers features and characteristics of a population that would otherwise remain hidden or invisible (Masson et al., 2013). A second advantage of using Facebook for research especially on delicate topics is the ease of making potential responders participate. People who express public opinions on a social network are generally more willing to argue their positions, even though they may be socially objectionable. Because of these features, Facebook is a very good means to contact individuals with more extremist political preferences who would otherwise be almost impossible to identify, all the more within an 'unsuspected' professional group.

The group of social workers to be interviewed was identified by using two strategies: (i) by identifying users of discussion groups on social work topics that publish comments supporting the positions of right-wing populist parties, and (ii) by gathering information from among social workers with representative roles in the professional community on colleagues who were active in their public support for right-wing populist positions on Facebook. The interviewees were first contacted by means of a private message, and then by a telephone call in which the aims of the study were explained and guarantees of privacy and anonymity were given in order to get the informed consent for participation. A total of 26 social workers were contacted. Five turned down the invitation, while 21 accepted to take part in the study. Interviews were conducted using a flexible guideline of open questions to deepen the following aspects: (i) professional training, role, and experiences, (ii) expectations with respect to the professional mandate and the professional community, (iii) political orientation and commitment, (iv) general personal value orientation, (v) professional values, (vi) job satisfaction and well-being, (vii) perception of the social role of the profession, (viii) forms and reasons of support toward right-wing populist positions and parties, (xi) experiences and relationships with immigrants and other non-conventional or marginalized groups. The interviews lasted an average of almost two hours and were conducted both face to face and via Skype. The analysis of the transcribed interview data started with thematic coding and the categorization of data in order to come up, eventually, with an interpretative model reconstructing four ideal-typical profiles of social workers supporting right-wing populist positions.

Who Are the Right-Wing Populist Social Workers?

'Right-wing populism' itself is an umbrella term and although dominant approaches tend to depict an identifiable profile of the typical voter of right-wing parties, its supporters embrace heterogeneous groups of individuals. This study on members of a professional group provides more qualitative insights in different positions and reasonings behind such sympathy and support. These findings are summarized in a model of four different ideal types of right-wing populist (supporting) social workers.

A first group of interviewed social workers presented the typical profile of a conservative voter. They were professionals with stable jobs and a traditional family. They had an average age of 45 years, and medium to long work experience. Although only discussed to a limited extent, the fact that there is a consistent group of social workers with conservative political preferences has been noted in the literature (Rosenwald, 2006). While agreeing with the principles and values of social work as protecting the most vulnerable persons, many social workers interpret these values from a politically conservative perspective. Accordingly, these interviewees favored the traditional family and social order, and expressed support for markedly non-liberal positions. Their religious stance was conservative Catholic and linked to their mistrust or even hostility particularly toward Islamic migrants, whom they considered to be a threat to the traditional religious values of the native population in the Christian West. The conservative interviewees did not totally align their ideas and preferences with those of right-wing populist parties, and also strongly opposed certain radical positions. However, their attitudes toward topics such as the family, social order, controlling crime, and protecting Christian values were sufficient reasons for expressing support for right-wing populist parties. The organizational context in which the conservatives worked is characterized by a certain amount of work pressure, but only one of them said that they were under stress. The other interviewees did not express any particular dissatisfaction with their working conditions and did not expect any changes from the populist parties in this regard. Their suspicious attitude toward migrants does also not directly derive from concrete working experiences or professional conflicts. What makes these social workers support some aspects of right-wing populism is their strong commitment to conservative values and their view of right-wing populist parties as the last defenders of these values. This position is well illustrated by the following interview quote: "*For me there is a normality that needs to be protected. It is the one of the family made up of father, mother and children. I don't care that there are homosexual couples or anything else as long as we don't want to question the role of the normal family*" *(from interview 5).*

A second group of right-wing populist social workers can ideal-typically be described as militants. They actively participate in party campaigning and activities sharing objectives and values of right-wing populism, although they in turn mitigate the more extreme positions by virtue of their profession. They are, however, convinced that groups of persons who do not share the values and traditions of the native population must not equally come to the benefit of solidarity. These groups are even depicted as endangering the prospects of being able to help autochthonous people in need. They do not consider that giving priority to native-born individuals on the scale of need is contrary to the ethical principles of social work. The idea of social justice and universalism is nationally framed, by the way in a national context whose welfare system has historically given weak guarantees even for the most marginalized groups of the native population. Against this background and in face of increasing social issues such as the aging population, unemployment, poverty, and the fragmentation of social ties, militants share the idea of 'Italians first' while 'others' come later and the solution advocated for helping migrants and refugees is to 'help them at home.' Regarding civil rights and individual choices, the militants were on average more tolerant than the conservatives. For example, they did not express negative opinions about same-sex couples or the adoption of children by non-traditional families. Right-wing populism was viewed above all as a way to defend the native population against a presumed invasion of migrants who would be responsible for a reduction in services that affects the native population. With one single exception, the militants had permanent employment contracts. The organizational context in which they worked, however, was characterized by pressures to ration resources, and this had induced some of them to use political activism as a space in which to advocate for individuals considered to have been unjustly excluded from welfare benefits. Their position is summed up by the following quote: "*Then you'd have to turn over billions to welcome strangers you don't know where they are coming from or what they're coming to do. This is not ok for me. When we say our people first, this means that before them there are the problems of normal Italian people. It's not that they disappear just because there is no fancy journalist from the lefty newspaper who puts them on the front page*" *(from interview 2).*

A third group of social workers supporting right-wing populist positions, labelled as the angry, fell within the group of losers from globalization and neoliberal policies standing rather on the margins of the professional community. Although they had received the same education and training, they differed from the other interviewees in that they had insecure and precarious jobs that only partly matched their qualifications and aspirations as well as very uncertain future employment prospects. They were mainly younger social workers belonging to the 'workfare generation' grown up in a period when public welfare was being dismantled amid powerful pressure for individualization and depoliticization. The ethical and value-based purposes of the profession were shared at an abstract level, but they were far more relative and fluid points of reference than is the case with the older generations of social workers. Their support for right-wing populist parties consisted above all in their agreement with criticism of the elites as responsible for the economic and employment crisis and with the identification of migrants and foreigners as enemies intent on taking the remaining resources away from the native population and, as one interviewee pointed out, increasingly also as concurrence in the segment of lower paid jobs in the social care work sector. The position of the angry is put straight to the point by the following statement: "*What does it mean rights for everyone? Who is in there? Me, for example, as a precarious social worker who in three months must start again to find a job, where am I? Isn't that a question, too?*" *(from interview 1)*.

A last group of supporters of right-wing populist positions, labelled as the frustrated, consisted of social workers who represented the typical image of welfare professionals. They were mostly trained during the period when public welfare was still growing, and shared the typical values of social work, such as social inclusion, justice, and universalism. Their attitude toward ethical issues was prevalently liberal. They were in favor of or at any rate not hostile to—new types of family, they defended civil and social rights, and were culturally open to diversity, individual lifestyle choices, political orientations, and religious beliefs. Unlike their younger colleagues, these interviewees had stable jobs and did not have to worry about their working futures. What induced them to express their support for right-wing populism was above all an expectation that the conditions that made their work difficult might improve. Many of them were extremely frustrated about working in a context of scarce resources, a bureaucracy that reduced professional autonomy, and in a climate in which their profession was strongly disregarded. One of these social workers made the point: "*Today the climate is heavier, and the job is more difficult. But above all I have the impression that nobody or almost nobody cares anymore about what we do. Social services have become the last resort of the most desperate people, as if the belief that what we do is useful for something had disappeared*" *(from interview 17)*. This resulted in a high sense of frustration that led these social workers to identify migrants as having demands that made it even more difficult to do their everyday work and pursue their professional goals of justice and equity. Their encounters with migrants often took place in a very difficult climate in which the high level of formalization and bureaucracy of services and the lack of resources made highly discordant the demands for assistance from people whose main interest was to acquire material benefits rather than implement active pathways of change and social integration. In the eyes of these social workers it is hard to reconcile the efforts required to interact with welfare claimants with their extremely heavy workload and a welfare organization that provides increasingly segmented services and poor resources in spite of increasing and more complex social needs. The overall result of such frustrations is a tendency for migrants to become scapegoats for impoverishment of welfare services that place social workers in the schizophrenic position of wanting to defend the principles of universalism and inclusion while at the same time working against them.

Betraying or Betrayed?

The issue of betrayal of the founding values of social work is central to understanding why these professionals adopt positions in favor of right-wing populism. Social work is imbued with ethical principles that collide head-on with populist ideologies. How is it possible, in practice, for these founding values of the profession to be concealed to leave room for positions that are antithetical to them? What are the underlying processes and trajectories that make these members of unsusceptible group supporters of right-wing populism?

A first trajectory is the one followed by conservatives who adopt a very elementary cognitive strategy in order to make their support for populist programs cognitively compatible with the founding principles of social work. On the one hand, they downgrade the more extreme positions of populism. As one interviewee stated indignantly, for example: *"You can't talk about sinking migrant boats; this can't be accepted"* (from interview 8). This way, a demarcation line is drawn that outlines a moral perimeter in which conservative social workers distance themselves from positions that are incompatible with the profession's principles. At the same time, they have a charitable concept of welfare based on the idea of doing good that does not lend itself to deeper considerations on citizenship, rights, and the value of individual freedoms. The overlapping of benevolence and the spirit of the profession thereby enables this group of social workers to take the subject of the betrayal of the values of social work into only superficial consideration. Conservatives are therefore part of a broader group of people who express their support for populism by virtue of the compatibility of their conservative values with the content of the new political messages that tap into a fear of cultural uncertainty and change (Jason, 2015).

A second trajectory leads to the type of support given by the militants. This is the group that most openly rejected the values and principles of universalistic and inclusive principles of welfare. The issue that various interviewees raised in response to the question of whether they believed they were betrayers of the founding values of social work was the provocative counterquestion: *"Are the progressive parties pro-welfare?"* It is mainly the progressive parties in Italy that have taken a position in favor of welcoming migrants and of civil rights promotion. In the day-to-day experiences of social workers, however, these pro-rights and pro-welfare positions have been contradicted by cuts in spending on social services and measures of reorganizing welfare to which progressive parties have contributed both at the national and the local level. These measures have created not only a deterioration in working conditions, but also increasing problems in responding to the needs of those groups whose protection populist social workers believe take priority over those of migrants. The reasoning used by the militants to justify their political position is that when welfare coverage is lacking, the concept of justice inevitably loses its universalistic tension. Why should assisting the migrants first and not caring for the needs of the elderly—the militants' political argument goes—be a fairer policy whereas giving to the elderly first and then to the migrants is not? When put in these terms, the question of the betrayal of the ideals of social work irrevocably enters the context of the relativism of these values and allows the militants to avoid the moral weight of their position. The militants even state that they are remaining loyal to the ideal matrix of social work as a profession that cares for the weakest and perceive themselves as individuals fighting for rights and a better national society.

A third trajectory to support right-wing populist positions is typical for younger social workers who cannot find a job or are in precarious employment. They belong to the new generation of social workers who grew up in a political climate very different from that of the expansion of welfare and social rights. Their professional values are imbued with changes that have characterized welfare models over the past twenty years. Principles such as welfare conditionality and the selected provision of services go hand in hand with the depoliticization of social work and with the identification of the profession in terms of expert knowledge and evidence-based practice. For this generation of social workers, the sense of identification with a professional community that expresses the values of welfare is therefore already weaker in principle compared with previous generations. *'Betraying what?'* is their counterquestion that sums up the attitude of these social workers to the call to respect principles and values that have already been eroded and transformed in the work practices that they have learned. In this case, adhesion to populist programs can be defined as the outcome of a long-term process in which the foundations of welfare, such as universalism, the right of access to services, and the funding of welfare have been reformulated and reorganized one after the other, thereby gradually modifying the very structure to which the values of social work applied. These young social workers are less politicized and less attentive to the topics of inclusion and universalism simply because it is the very system in which they have grown that has slackened the pursuit of these values. Their encounter with populism therefore has a dual significance: on the one hand, it enshrines what the official political system does not wish to say explicitly, i.e., that the process of reformulation and reorganization of welfare is creating an army of 'losers' who find it increasingly difficult to cope with their uncertain social role and employment situation. On the other hand, populism offers what Margaret Canovan (1999) calls a 'redemptive' perspective, which in the minds of these social workers means that their situation is at last being politically considered.

The final trajectory found is that followed by professionals who are highly frustrated by the constant cuts in resources and the constant reorganization of their professional work. They could probably represent the largest category of right-wing populism supporters within the professional community. The condition of these professionals is the most conflicting. On the one hand, they feel that they are required to guarantee the principles of social justice and inclusion, while on the other hand, they are personally experiencing the problems involved in working according to these principles in a climate in which resources are being rationed, they are increasingly overworked and suffering from confusion about their identities. This problem is not an imaginary one, it is very real for the interviewed social workers. Their perception was that they are like soldiers left at the front without supplies who must look for solutions for themselves in order to survive. One of these social workers put it: "*I assure you that contradictions are explosive here, because of the difficulties of the job, the reorganization and the continuous cuts. I say frontline not by chance. Do you know the image of the caravan in the middle of the desert? Well, it's that thing here*" *(from interview 11)*. In the field of social work, direct contact with service users give rise to relationships very far from the Weberian ideal of administrative impersonality. Social workers faced with tensions between limited resources and high demand use their discretion as normative choice (Maynard-Moody & Portillo, 2010), which leads them to categorize the most difficult clients in defensive, self-absolving terms. The very powerful contrast experienced by these social workers is frequently described using the war rhetoric of the heroic combatants in the trenches and the treacherous generals who have sent them for slaughter at the frontline. The frustration over these conditions puts to blame mainly the progressive parties. There is a very simple explanation for why these parties are blamed more than the other parties that have also substantially contributed to weakening social services over the past ten years. The loss of appreciation and respect for traitors is classically more serious the more trust had been placed in them previously. Therefore, the breakdown of trust in the progressive parties is much heavier among these social workers grown up with the ideas of strong social rights and an open society. This aspect of the emotional reaction to a betrayal on the part of social workers who feel that their ideals and social role have been betrayed is probably the most important and most underestimated entry point for right-wing populism into this unsuspected professional group.

Conclusions

This study contributes to more nuanced qualitative analyses on the demand side of populism as it is one of the first studies to explore experience and trajectories that lead to support of right-wing populism within a professional group deemed as being by definition in favor of universalism and inclusive welfare and, accordingly, immune to the siren calls of right-wing populists. The findings suggest that there is a risk that right-wing populism as a political ideology might take solid root also within non-marginal fringes of unsuspected groups. While the explorative study involved a limited group of professionals who openly expressed their opinions on social media, their experiences and attitudes as well as the reasons they provided to justify their support for populist programs strongly suggest that this group of professionals might actually be only the most visible tip of a larger iceberg below the surface.

Undoubtedly, the simplistic populist messages that divide the world into threatened in-groups and threatening out-groups might be appealing also in the perceptive framework of those social workers more prone to populist propaganda. The findings of this study, however, suggest that for a significant section of social workers it is the working conditions that they experience on a daily basis, the cuts in social services, the waiting lists of people to whom they cannot provide an answer, and the precarious nature of their own professional and employment status that evidence very concretely the ambiguity and lack of interest on a large part of the political class toward the needs of the most must vulnerable groups and the dignity of welfare workers. Who is betraying and who is being betrayed therefore becomes a matter of perspective. From one standpoint, those who are betraying welfare ideals are the social workers who welcome ideas proposed by right-wing populist parties on how to redefine political priorities and welfare agendas in favor of an exclusive welfare for the native population. From another point of view, however, various interviewees also invited reflection on the responsibility that should be borne by those who have allowed welfare policies to become gradually weakened and who have contributed toward making professions upholding welfare ideals increasingly difficult, precarious, and delegitimized.

From this perspective, the phenomenon of right-wing populism cannot simply be explained as falling into a propaganda trap aimed at exploiting the feelings of the easily seduced. As the findings of this study on social workers suggest, support for right-wing populism also stems from more profound processes and ambiguous dynamics of identity construction in various social and professional groups during an extremely uncertain historical phase. Most of the interviewed social workers continued to believe that their work is a means to help vulnerable groups. What many of them identified as a problem, however, is that the welfare blanket has become short, and pulling from one side inevitably means leaving someone on the other side uncovered. Faced with this dilemma, support for right-wing populism becomes a way of sticking a knife into the wound of open questions to which even progressive politics have not been able to provide a response. What needs should be satisfied as a priority in a regime with limited resources? And does the collective answer to social needs still have political value, or is it a topic that has lost its relevance and dignity?

In this sense, support for populism might be conceptualized not only as a symptom of the disease, but also as an (albeit reckless) attempt on the part of a social body debilitated by exhaustion and years of uncertainty to cure itself. Many of the interviews showed that there is an unsatisfied and unheard demand for meaning that has accumulated in part as a result of policies that have weakened the structures and solutions that hold the political and social system together. To combat the spread of right-wing populism, it is not enough to denounce the propaganda used to take advantage of the fears of public opinion. The results of the study indicate that for building an effective barrier to the spread of populism, it is fundamentally important to intervene in the factors and processes that have led to the weakening of the institutions that guarantee the security and welfare of the community by modifying structural conditions that fuel the demand for new answers and social identities of a large segment of the population.

This means that a political class that wishes to respond to the siren call of populism has to listen to people's needs and demands for meaning, return to making investments in structures and processes that offer social security and services and sacrifice the objective of maximizing economic growth, thereby reviving the fabric of basic social relations that makes up the architectural backbone of a society. Politicians also need to provide greater visibility to and explanations of the decisions to be taken to face social and economic problems, to enable citizens to understand the reasons behind the various decisions, and to be oriented toward an evaluation of the various measures in order to understand their consequences in good time. New social infrastructures of the idea of citizenship and justice based on participation among the various representative groups are needed to give value to the sense of belonging, on the one hand, and to respect for diversity, dialogue and the inclusion of minority groups on the other.

In a nutshell, the lesson to be learned from the presented insights in social workers' support for right-wing populism is twofold. First, the findings suggest the importance to think of a new welfare agenda as a crucial arena in which to contrast the spread of right-wing populism. Going beyond the nostalgic retrospective on the better days of the welfare state, progressive parties must regain terrain in taking social questions seriously and in coming up with effective and sustainable welfare policies adapted to current conditions and challenges. In the aftermath of the COVID-19 pandemic such opportunities will not be lacking. Secondly, as to the research agenda on populism, the findings suggest paying more attention to the need for better studying and understanding the qualitative momentum and the various trajectories that in the face of real, ignored problems might increase support for right-wing populism from groups that had previously been held to be largely above suspicion.

LITERATURE

Akkerman, A., Mudde, C., & Zaslove, A. (2014). How populist are the people? Measuring populist attitudes in voters. *Comparative Political Studies, 47*(9), 1324–1353.

Albertazzi, D., & McDonnell, D. (2010). The Lega Nord back in government. *West European Politics, 33*(6), 1318–1340.

Albertazzi, D., Giovannini, A., & Seddone, A. (2018). 'No regionalism please, we are Leghisti !' The transformation of the Italian Lega Nord under the leadership of Matteo Salvini. *Regional & Federal Studies, 28*(5), 645–671.

Bobba, G., & Legnante, G. (2016). Italy. A breeding ground for populist political communication. In T. Aalberg, F. Esser, C. Reinemann, J. Strömbäck, & C. H. de Vreese (Eds.), *Populist political communication in Europe* (pp. 222–234). Routledge.

Camus, J.-Y., & Lebourg, N. (2017). *Far-right politics in Europe*. The Belknap Press of Harvard University Press.

Canovan, M. (1999). Trust the people! Populism and the two faces of democracy. *Political Studies, 47*(1), 2–16.

Clarke, H., Whiteley, P., Borges, W., Sanders, D., & Stewart, M. (2016). Modelling the dynamics of support for a right-wing populist party: The case of UKIP. *Journal of Elections, Public Opinion and Parties, 26*(2), 135–154.

Facchini, C., & Lorenz, W. (2013). Between differences and common features: The work of social workers in Italy. *International Social Work, 56*(4), 439–454.

Fazzi, L. (2015). Social work, exclusionary populism and xenophobia in Italy. *International Social Work, 58*(4), 595–605.

Fazzi, L. & Nothdurfter U. (2020). The multifaceted challenges of new right-wing populism to social work: Towards the professional's swansong or the re-birth of activism? In G. Ottmann & C. Noble (Eds.), *The challenge of nationalist populism for social work: A human rights approach*. Routledge.

Fenton, J. (2016). *Values in social work: Reconnecting with social justice*. Palgrave.

Garrett, P. M., & Bertotti, T. (2017). Social work and the politics of 'austerity': Ireland and Italy. *European Journal of Social Work, 20*(1), 29–41.

Heiss, R., & Matthes, J. (2020). Stuck in a nativist spiral: Content, selection, and effects of right-wing populists' communication on Facebook. *Political Communication, 37*(3), 303–328.

Ignazi, P. (2014). *Vent'anni dopo. La parabola del berlusconismo*. Il Mulino.

Inglehart, R. F., & Norris, P. (2016). *Trump, Brexit, and the rise of populism: Economic have-nots and cultural backlash* (HKS Working Paper No. RWP16-026). Available at: https://doi.org/10.2139/ssrn.2818659.

Jason, K. (2015). The demand side of support for radical right parties. *Comparative European Politics, 13*(5), 553–576.

Judis, J. B. (2016). *The populist explosion: How the great recession transformed American and European politics*. Columbia Global Reports.

Masson, H., Balfe, M., Hackett, S., & Phillips, J. (2013). Lost without a trace? Social networking and social research with a hard-to-reach population. *British Journal of Social Work, 43*(1), 24–40.

Maynard-Moody, S., & Portillo, S. (2010). Street-level bureaucracy theory. In R. F. Durant (Ed.), *The Oxford handbook of American bureaucracy* (pp. 255–277). Oxford University Press.

Milbrandt, B., & Wagner, L. (2017). Rechtpopulistische Bewegungen und die Folgen für die Soziale Arbeit. *Soziale Passagen, 8*(2), 275–291.

Muis, J., & Immerzeel, T. (2017). Causes and consequences of the rise of populist radical right parties and movements in Europe. *Current Sociology, 65*(6), 909–930.

Müller, P., Schemer, C., Wettstein, M., Schulz, A., Wirz, D. S., Engesser, S., & Wirth, W. (2017). The polarizing impact of news coverage on populist attitudes in the public: Evidence from a panel study in four European democracies. *Journal of Communication, 67*(6), 968–992.

Noble, C., & Ottmann, G. (2018). Nationalist populism and social work. *Journal of Human Rights and Social Work, 3*(3), 112–120.

Radvan, H., & Schäuble, B. (2019). Rechtsextrem orientierte und organisierte Studierende –. Umgangsweisen in Hochschulen Sozialer Arbeit. In M. Kötting, M. & D. Röh, D. (Eds.), *Soziale Arbeit in der Demokratie – Demokratieförderung in der Sozialen Arbeit: Theoretische Analysen, gesellschaftliche Herausforderungen und Reflexionen zur Demokratieförderung und Partizipation* (pp. 216–227). Verlag Barbara Budrich.

Ron, A., & Nadesan, M. (Eds.). (2020). *Mapping populism: Approaches and methods.* Routlegde.

Rooduijn, M. (2019). State of the field: How to study populism and adjacent topics? A plea for both more and less focus. *European Journal of Political Research, 58*(1), 362–372.

Rosenwald, M. (2006). Exploring the political diversity of social workers. *Social Work Research, 30*(2), 121–126.

Sikkens, E., van San, M., Sieckelinck, S., Boeije, H., & de Winter, M. (2017). Participant recruitment through social media: Lessons learned from a qualitative radicalization study using Facebook. *Field Methods, 29*(2), 130–139.

Spruyt, B., Keppens, G., & Van Droogenbroeck, F. (2016). Who supports populism and *what* attracts people to it? *Political Research Quarterly, 69*(2), 335–346.

Tousijn, W. & Dellavalle, M. (Eds.) (2017). *Logica professionale e logica manageriale: Una ricerca sulle professioni sociali.* Il Mulino.

Van Hauwaert, S. M., & Van Kessel, S. (2018). Beyond protest and discontent: A cross-national analysis of the effect of populist attitudes and issue positions on populist party support. *European Journal of Political Research, 57*(1), 68–92.

Vliegenthart, R., Boomgaarden, H. G., & Van Spanje, J. (2012). Anti-immigrant party support and media visibility: A cross-party, over-time perspective. *Journal of Elections, Public Opinion and Parties, 22*(3), 315–358.

Wirz, D. S., Wettstein, M., Schulz, A., Müller, P., Schemer, C., Ernst, N., Esser, F., & Wirth, W. (2018). The effects of right-wing populist communication on emotions and cognitions toward immigrants. *International Journal of Press/politics, 23*(4), 496–516.

Wodak, R., KhosraviNik, M., & Mral, B. (Eds.). (2013). *Right-wing populism in Europe: Politics and discourse.* Bloomsbury.

CHAPTER 36

Clarifying Our Populist Moment(s): Right-Wing and Left-Wing Populism in the 2016 Presidential Election

Edward G. Carmines, Eric R. Schmidt, and Matthew R. Fowler

INTRODUCTION

This chapter finds that while Americans are divided in their support for populist attitudes, these attitudes are two-dimensional—reflecting the distinction between *right-wing populism* and *left-wing populism*. Using an original survey index fielded on the 2017 Cooperative Congressional Election Study (CCES), we document what Americans believe about the issues that scholars (e.g., Inglehart & Norris, 2017; Oliver & Rahn, 2016) associate with populism: immigration, multiculturalism, and income inequality. We document that citizens take distinct positions on two domains: first, how government should prioritize and respond to immigration; and second, what the proper response should be to economic inequality. Our findings indicate that right-wing populism describes how Republican identifiers think about politics, while left-wing populism is the province of Democratic identifiers. In other words, Republican and Democratic identifiers have polarized not just on long-standing policy differences (Abramowitz & Saunders, 2008; Campbell, 2016) and racial attitudes (Tesler, 2016; Westwood & Peterson,

E. G. Carmines (✉) · E. R. Schmidt
Department of Political Science, Indiana University, Bloomington, IN, USA
e-mail: carmines@indiana.edu

M. R. Fowler
Center for the Study of Race, Politics, and Culture, University of Chicago, Chicago, IL, USA
e-mail: mrfowler@uchicago.edu

© The Author(s), under exclusive license to Springer Nature Switzerland AG 2022
M. Oswald (ed.), *The Palgrave Handbook of Populism*,
https://doi.org/10.1007/978-3-030-80803-7_36

2020). Rather, the parties-in-the-electorate have fundamentally different interpretations of populist ideology—even as the *logic* of populism exerts similar influence on Republican and Democratic identifiers alike.

Moreover, these dimensions were a significant factor in the 2016 presidential election. Among Republican identifiers and independents, right-wing populism was associated with support for Donald Trump. These effects were robust to controls for negative racial attitudes; partisan strength; ideological self-identification; and socioeconomic status. Meanwhile, the effects of left-wing populism on Republican identifiers' and independents' voting behavior were especially sensitive to model specification. In the case of Democratic identifiers, moreover, left-wing populism had a negligible effect on support for Hillary Clinton. By failing to nominate a credible left-wing populist as Trump's opponent, the Democratic Party may have overlooked the prevalence of left-wing populism among the Democratic rank-of-file.

Our analysis proceeds as follows. First, we detail reasons for discussing populism in terms of left-wing and right-wing belief systems. In particular, we are interested in the hawkish immigration attitudes that Donald Trump championed; the economic concerns of Bernie Sanders' failed campaign for the Democratic nomination; and the degree to which these attitudes influenced voting behavior in 2016. We derive hypotheses about the nature of populist attitudes in U.S. public opinion, and their connection to presidential vote choice.

Second, we introduce an original survey index piloted on the 2017 CCES. Confirmatory factor analysis shows that right-wing and left-wing populism are empirically distinct, anchored by different policy concerns, and differentiated by disagreements about the importance of multiculturalism and the appropriateness of deporting undocumented children. Third, we analyze the determinants of right-wing and left-wing populism. This helps to both validate our index and guide model specification for predicting voting behavior.

Finally, we explore whether right-wing and left-wing populism explained voting behavior in 2016. We conclude that right-wing populism was an especially strong determinant of whether Republican identifiers voted for Donald Trump, rather than abstained from voting or supported Hillary Clinton instead; the effect of right-wing populism on Trump support also extends to partisan independents. However, while left-wing populism decreased the likelihood that independents would support Donald Trump, its effects were otherwise muted. Indeed, even Democratic identifiers showed a null relationship between left-wing populism and voting behavior—with left-wing populism making no difference (*ceteris paribus*) for whether Democratic identifiers supported Clinton on Election Day. This suggests that while left-wing populism *is* emblematic of Democrats' political attitudes, Clinton was not as forceful an advocate for left-wing populism as Senator Bernie Sanders (I –VT).

While others have called attention to the resurgence of populism in American politics (Azari & Hetherington, 2016; Inglehart & Norris, 2017; Levitsky & Ziblatt, 2018; Müller, 2016), our analysis is among the first to show that this extends beyond partisan responses to Donald Trump. It is not just that Donald Trump reshaped Republican politics, prompting a response from Democrats bewildered at his improbable rise. Rather, *mass populism is reshaping the nature and terms of partisan conflict in the United States*. Republican and Democratic identifiers have gravitated toward different, stylized interpretations of political conflict—developing, in essence, populist narratives compatible with their parties' ideological priorities. While it is too early to tell how dramatically populism will reshape American politics, we document forces in motion that cannot be easily ignored.

THE TWO POPULISMS OF 2016

Among political scientists, to discuss the 2016 presidential election is to confront the question of populism. It seems more than coincidental that *The Oxford Handbook of Populism* (2017) appeared in its first edition shortly after Trump's election (and British voters' decision to leave the European Union). Political theorists (e.g., Isaac, 2017; Müller, 2016) are debating how Trump's election (and radical right-wing movements throughout Western Europe; see Kitschelt & McGann, 1995) compare to traditional understandings of populism—as a political philosophy in which "the people," opposing an illegitimate elite, proclaim their right to popular rule (Mudde, 2013; Mudde & Kaltwasser, 2013; see Urbinati, 2019). For comparative and American politics scholars, Trump's election parallels right-wing populism in Western Europe (Inglehart & Norris, 2017) and (perhaps) populism in the late-1890s United States (Azari & Hetherington, 2016).

We approach this question as scholars of long-term partisan change in American politics (for a review, see Carmines & Schmidt, 2019). Yet we also approach it as citizens interested in current events, for whom reading the newspaper is as routine as eating breakfast or making coffee. One cannot help but notice that the *New York Times* and *Washington Post* often use the term "populist" to refer not only to President Trump, but to some of his Democratic opponents: politicians who advocate welfare-state expansions comparable in scope to the New Deal or Great Society.

Indeed, presidential politics in 2016 involved two figures deemed populists by the mainstream media (Kazin, 2016). For his part, Donald Trump advanced an anti-immigration agenda that draws comparison with European variants of right-wing populism (Inglehart & Norris, 2017; see also Reny et al., 2019). Trump pledged to construct a 2000-mile wall on the U.S.–Mexico border, ban all Muslims from entering the United States and deport undocumented immigrants *en masse*. He characterized illegal immigration as a national security threat and used racially charged language to make these appeals (Hajnal & Abrajano, 2016; Sides et al., 2018).

Trump represented a shock to Republican politics-as-usual. His success departed from conventional wisdom about how the GOP—which depends disproportionately on whites for its electoral success (see Mason, 2018)—might remain relevant to racial and ethnic minorities that compose an increasingly larger percentage of the population. Long before Trump's candidacy was a serious threat, Republican strategists worried Trump would alienate Latino voters and cost the GOP the White House (Gabriel & Preston, 2015). Perhaps recognizing that immigration was a stronger source of partisan conflict (Abrajano & Hajnal, 2015; Wong, 2017) than often assumed, Trump ignored these concerns.

The second (potential) populist in 2016 was Senator Bernie Sanders, who lost the Democratic nomination to Hillary Clinton but accumulated far more delegates than expected. Sanders' derision of great wealth in American society draws comparisons with the agrarian populist revolt of the late 1800s (see Kazin, 2016). Indeed, Sanders identifies as a democratic socialist, and routinely seeks to differentiate his socialism from planned economies in undemocratic, authoritarian states. Of course, Sanders failed to secure the Democratic Party's nomination for president in 2020. However, unlike in 2016, he seemed briefly poised to win the nomination outright—receiving the majority of votes in initial nominating contests, and only losing ground to Joe Biden after the COVID-19 pandemic prompted Democratic leaders to coalesce around a traditional nominee.

In perhaps the clearest signal of Sanders' influence, Democratic Party officials voted in 2018 to limit the influence of "superdelegates" at the 2020 Democratic National Convention (Herndon, 2018). Superdelegates (elected or high-profile Democrats whose convention votes are unbound by primary or caucus results) were instituted in the early 1980s, as a check on the whims of primary voters (Miller & Jennings, 1986). However, superdelegates at the 2020 DNC were unable to vote on their party's nominee unless no candidate secured nomination on the first ballot—an outcome that had not occurred since 1952 (see Shafer, 1988) and did not occur in 2020 either (Olorunnipa et al., 2020). Thus, whether or not Sanders *is* a populist (for an opposing viewpoint, see Müller, 2016), the anti-establishment energies he unleashed encouraged the Democratic Party to scale back its unease concerning popular control of presidential nominations.

While Trump's influence is more obvious than Sanders', both have challenged the terms of discussion within their respective parties. Consider that if Sanders and Trump had each won their respective parties' nominations in 2016, both major party candidates would have boasted almost no history of identifying with the parties under whose banner they ran. This outcome would have occurred, moreover, within a party system already marked by ideological polarization (McCarty et al., 2008), accustomed to preventing insurgents from winning nomination to the presidency (Cohen et al., 2009). As this is hardly an extreme counterfactual, it serves as inspiration for our analysis. To analyze populism in U.S. public opinion, we must pay equal attention to what Trump and Sanders have brought to American politics.

Right-Wing and Left-Wing Populism

During the 2016 presidential primaries, there was some common ground between Trump's and Sanders's candidacies. For example, then-candidate Trump echoed some of Sanders' appeals to working-class Whites. While Trump's economic policies were disorganized and contradictory, Trump blamed Democrats for brokering unfair trade agreements (Sargent, 2017) and promised to restore jobs for displaced American workers (White, 2016). Where Sanders criticized Hillary Clinton for her paid speeches at large financial institutions, Trump had a similar choice of words for Wall Street bankers (Confessore & Horowitz, 2016).

Yet the comparisons between Trump and Sanders only extend so far. Instead, their rhetoric showcases the distinction between *right-wing populism* and *left-wing populism* in the United States. According to Joseph Lowndes (2017), U.S. populism "can be roughly divided between left-wing and right-wing variants *according to how each defines the principal foe of the people*: for left populists it is economic elites; for right populists it is non-white others and by extension the state itself" (233, emphasis ours). The distinction, then, turns not on policy proposals, but on the stylized narratives that right and left-wing populists weave: narratives that distinguish "the people"—worthy of popular sovereignty—from their common enemies (Mudde, 2013; Mudde & Kaltwasser, 2013).

This framework is consistent with the distinction between Donald Trump and Bernie Sanders. Trump identified clear enemies, responsible for economic and cultural distress: not only undocumented immigrants, but also the countries that encouraged them to flee to the United States, the companies that hired them, and the cities that refused to report them to Immigrations and Customs Enforcement.

The most generous interpretation of Trumpism is that it excludes non-citizens from the right to be counted among "the people." Less generously, but with unfortunate empirical support (Reny et al., 2019; Schaffner et al., 2018), Trump found success through flagrant racial appeals: favoring Whites over non-Whites and Christians over non-Christians. Historians will need to decide which prejudices Trump was most interested in fomenting. For our purposes, it suffices that his populism was preoccupied with the distinction between citizens and undocumented immigrants.

Bernie Sanders, however, embraced a different narrative—one consistent with left-wing populism. His narrative retained the zero-sum logic of Trumpism but featured different heroes and villains. Drawing attention to the U.S. Supreme Court's relaxation of campaign finance regulations in *Citizens United v. F.E.C.* (2010), Sanders decried the influence of "millionaires and billionaires," and described income inequality as an existential threat. To the extent Sanders advocated clear policies ("Medicare-for-all," progressive tax reform, and free college education), these echoed his pledge to wrest popular control from economic elites.

Yet unlike Trump, there was no room in Sanders' rhetoric for anti-immigration sentiments, nor for authoritarian attitudes that might dovetail with populism. While Trump's ascent has been likened to an "authoritarian spring" (MacWilliams, 2016)—with ominous implications for the stability of democracy (Levitsky & Ziblatt, 2018; Oswald & Robertson, 2020)—we cannot say the same for Sanders' success. Rather, Sanders condemned Trump's racism, xenophobia, and bullying—identifying his movement with the "99 percent" of Americans that lacked extreme wealth. For Sanders, the ultra-rich—not immigrants—were the enemies of fairness and decency. Sanders' disavowal of racism and xenophobia, identification of wealthy elites (rather than immigrants) as a common enemy, and endorsement of redistributive policies are all compatible with left-wing populism.

Crucially, the populisms of Sanders and Trump found expression at a time when neither were considered serious candidates for president. This suggests that for a time, they made independent contributions to public discourse. As (respective) advocates of left-wing and right-wing populism, Sanders and Trump did not enter the race with an obvious need to distinguish their messages from one another. Nor were the Republican and Democratic parties—at least in the early stages of the 2016 nominating contests—necessarily aware of the threat Trump and Sanders posed to politics-as-usual. As Frances Lee (2020) notes, party organizations may not fully grasp the disruptive potential of populist candidates—not least because the intensity of mass partisanship belies citizens' frustration with the choices parties offer and the representation they provide.

For this reason, we hypothesize that right- and left-wing populism are distinct dimensions in U.S. public opinion: *right-wing populism*, as an *anti-immigrant* ideology associated with hawkish immigration attitudes; and *left-wing populism*, as an *anti-economic-elite* ideology concerned with income inequality.

Hypothesis 1: Among eligible voters in the United States, populist attitudes have two empirically distinct dimensions: *right-wing populism*, anchored by hawkish immigration attitudes; and *left-wing populism*, anchored by support for addressing economic inequality.

Further, if right- and left-wing populism took shape among Republican and Democratic identifiers (respectively), this has implications for voting behavior. We explored whether in 2016, voters were cross-pressured between these two dimensions of populist attitudes. To do this, we derived hypotheses about the voting behavior of Republicans, Democrats, and independents.

Yet except for independents, we were not interested in simply modeling the influence of populism on presidential vote *choice*. After all, the number of "floating voters"—Republicans and Democrats open to casting a presidential ballot for the opposing-party candidate—has plummeted in recent years (Bafumi & Shapiro, 2009; Smidt, 2017). Rather than attempt to convince opposing party supporters to support their candidates instead, party organizations have adopted a different strategy: highlight differences that opposing party supporters might have with their own parties' nominees, and indirectly encourage these supporters to stay home on Election Day (Leege et al., 2002). For our purposes, generic "vote-choice" models were unlikely to do more than reaffirm the importance of party ID and the demographic differences between the parties.

Instead, we assessed the degree to which right- and left-wing populism increased or decreased the likelihood that partisan identifiers would turn out for their party's candidate, rather than stay home or (much less frequently) support someone else for president. Of course, we derived similar expectations for the 17% of our sample that identified as political independents (neither "leaning" Republican nor Democratic). Our expectations were expressed in Hypotheses 2–4.

Hypothesis 2: Right-wing populism made *Republican identifiers* more likely to vote for Donald Trump—while left-wing populism made them more likely to abstain from voting or vote against Trump.

Hypothesis 3: Right-wing populism made *Democratic identifiers* more likely to abstain from voting or vote against Hillary Clinton—while left-wing populism made them more likely to vote for Hillary Clinton.

Hypothesis 4: Right-wing populism made *partisan independents* more likely to vote for Donald Trump, rather than abstain from voting or vote against Trump—while left-wing populism made them more likely to vote for Hillary Clinton, rather than abstain from voting or vote against Clinton.

These hypotheses carried the same logic: to the degree that voters had plausible choices in 2016, right-wing and left-wing populism should have informed these choices. For Republican and Democratic identifiers, the populist dimension most compatible with their party's presidential nominee should have pushed them toward that candidate; the alternative dimension, toward abstinence from voting instead. Since both major party candidates were plausible choices for independents, right-wing populism should have pushed these disenchanted voters toward Trump; and left-wing populism, toward Clinton.

We turn now to the items used to measure right- and left-wing populism, along with analysis of their determinants and performance across the partisan subgroups. Much of this analysis was exploratory, driven by an open-minded interest in how the response structure (especially the covariance between both dimensions of populism) differed between subgroups. Our analysis was sufficient to demonstrate H1, and factor scores aggregating our measures helped to test their effects on Republican (H2), Democratic (H3), and independent (H4) voting behavior.

Data and Methods

To assess the dimensionality of mass populism in the United States, we initially developed an eight-item survey index. In late July 2017, we pretested items on Amazon's Mechanical Turk service (Berinsky et al., 2012). Items were selected that (1) exemplified our dichotomy, (2) showed covariance with similar pretested items, and (3) demonstrated variance across response options. Our index was then launched on a module ($n = 1000$) of the 2017 Cooperative Congressional Election Study, sponsored by Indiana University's Center on American Politics.[1] All items were five-point Likert scales, with response options ranging from "strongly agree" to "strongly disagree." The items read as follows:

1. Reducing income inequality is one of the most important things government can do right now (*Income Inequality*; reverse-coded).
2. It's unfair that the wealthy pay less in taxes than most Americans (*Unfair Taxes*; reverse-coded).
3. Multiculturalism and diversity should be celebrated (*Diversity*).
4. We should deport the children of undocumented immigrants instead of giving them special treatment (*Deport Children of Immigrants*; reverse-coded).
5. Our economy will never recover completely until we stop hiring immigrants (*Stop Hiring Immigrants*; reverse-coded).
6. Companies should stop hiring immigrants and prioritize hiring American citizens (*Hire American Citizens*; reverse-coded).
7. The government should intervene in the economy to bring manufacturing jobs back to the United States (*Manufacturing Jobs*; reverse-coded).
8. Until America returns to its traditional values, it's impossible to be proud of this country (*Traditionalism*; reverse-coded).

These items captured our distinction between right-wing and left-wing populism. In addition, they typified the differences between Bernie Sanders and Donald Trump—indicating values, grievances or policy positions expressed in the 2016 campaign. Three solicited attitudes about how government (and the private sector) should respond to immigration (*Deport Children, Stop Hiring Immigrants, Hire American Citizens*). Three dealt with whether government should be proactive in addressing economic inequality, either by intervening to protect American jobs (*Manufacturing Jobs*) or prioritizing structural concerns (*Unfair Taxes, Income Inequality*). Finally, two items asked about America's role in a changing society (*Traditionalism, Diversity*).

Except for *Traditionalism* and *Diversity*, these were newer concerns. That is, post-war policymaking has not revolved around either immigration or a broad-sweeping critique of capitalism and wealth (see Claggett & Shafer,

2010). This made them especially useful indicators of right-wing and left-wing populism, distinguishing populism from long-standing divisions between Republicans and Democrats.

H1 suggested that responses would be consistent with two empirically distinct dimensions: one reflecting right-wing populism; the other, left-wing populism. Nevertheless, we doubted these dimensions would be completely orthogonal; instead, we expected the dimensions to covary in any two-dimensional structure that emerged. Moreover, we assumed that some (but not all) items would cross-load in inversely signed directions. Thus, while H1 required that these data reflect a distinction between right-wing and left-wing populism, we were agnostic about which two-factor specification would give the clearest account of the data-generating process. We proceeded first with exploratory (EFA) and then confirmatory factor analysis (CFA). Below, we document the entire process (from EFA to CFA) used to determine the best-fitting specification.

A Two-Factor Solution: EFA and CFA

97.3% of our sample answered all eight items. An EFA of complete cases (see Table 36.1) suggested two factors with eigenvalues greater than 1. However, after applying promax rotation to this two-factor EFA, we concluded that two items had poorer measurement properties than pre-testing had led us to believe. First, support for economic interventionism (*Manufacturing Jobs*) loaded positively onto both factors, indicating this was an item about which most respondents expressed agreement—rather than one that differentiates left-wing and right-wing populism. Further, *Traditionalism* had a much higher uniqueness statistic (u2) than the remaining items. That is, after accounting for

Table 36.1 Exploratory factor analysis with two retained factors, eight initial items in populism index

Indicator variable	Factor 1	Factor 2	u^2
Stop hiring immigrants	**0.77**	0.03	0.42
Hire American	**0.80**	−0.06	0.33
Income inequality	−0.10	**0.73**	0.41
Unfair taxes	0.02	**0.75**	0.45
Diversity	**0.31**	**−0.57**	0.48
Deport children	**0.67**	−0.30	0.34
Traditionalism	**0.42**	0.00	0.83
Manufacturing jobs	**0.45**	**0.38**	0.75
Eigenvalue	2.86	1.13	

$c^2_{(28)} = 2884.71$, $p < 0.0001$. Data from the 2017 Cooperative Congressional Election Study. All items rescaled so that more "populist" responses have higher scores. Matrix generated using exploratory factor analysis (EFA) with two retained factors and promax rotation. Factor loadings greater than or equal to 0.30 in bold two latent factors, there was too much-unexplained variance in *Traditionalism* to warrant its inclusion in our index (see Carmines & Zeller, 1979). Consequently, we dropped *Manufacturing Jobs* and *Traditionalism*, reanalyzing the covariance matrix with six items instead.[2]

Using only our six retained items, a respecified exploratory factor analysis (EFA) still recommended a two-factor solution. This time, only the first factor had an eigenvalue higher than the informal, 1.0 threshold ($l_1 = 2.69$). Nevertheless, the eigenvalue for the second factor was not dramatically lower than 1.0 ($l_2 = 0.83$); all additional factors had eigenvalues indistinguishable from zero; and the covariance pattern seen in our eight-item EFA was undisturbed. Table 36.2 shows the results of a two-factor EFA (with promax rotation) on the six retained items.

The EFA results in Table 36.2 remained consistent with our dichotomy between right-wing and left-wing populism. On the first factor, we saw strong positive loadings for *Stop Hiring Immigrants*, *Deport Children of Immigrants*, and *Hire American Citizens*. On the second factor, we saw comparable loadings for *Unfair Taxes* and *Income Inequality*.

In other words, the first dimension constituted hawkish attitudes about immigration—with higher scores indicating support for uncompromising, punitive measures. Meanwhile, the second dimension assessed respondents' feelings about structural economic inequality. *Unfair Taxes* and *Income Inequality* were as ideologically potent as the immigration items, but they identified a different villain: not immigrants and Americans that shelter them, but wealthy interests and (perhaps) capitalism itself. With strong positive loadings onto their respective factors, these items *anchored* the two dimensions of populism.

Table 36.2 Exploratory factor analysis with two retained factors, six items (Dropping *Traditionalism* and *Manufacturing Jobs*)

Indicator variable	Factor 1	Factor 2	u^2
Stop hiring Immigrants	**0.80**	0.11	0.42
Hire American	**0.81**	0.02	0.35
Income inequality	0.00	**0.78**	0.40
Unfair taxes	0.09	**0.76**	0.47
Diversity	0.24	**−0.57**	0.49
Deport children	**0.65**	−0.26	0.34
Eigenvalue	2.69	0.83	

$c^2_{(15)} = 2516.38$, $p < 0.0001$. Data from the 2017 Cooperative Congressional Election Study. All items rescaled so that more "populist" responses have higher scores. Matrix generated using exploratory factor analysis (EFA) with two retained factors and promax rotation. Factor loadings greater than or equal to 0.30 in bold. Subsequent analyzes are not substantively changed if analysis is conducted with eight or six items; we use the six-item CFA specification recommended by this model

As Table 36.2 shows, some items cross-loaded onto both factors, with alternately positive and negative loadings. Where items cross-loaded, these were consistent with the friction between Trump's and Sanders's populist visions. One of our anchoring items already exposed this tension. While *Deport Children* loaded positively onto the first (*right-wing populism*) factor, it had a weaker negative loading onto the second (*left-wing populism*). Thus, left-wing populist attitudes covaried with opposition to one of right-wing populism's harshest tenets: deporting undocumented children rather than offering them a path to citizenship.

Similarly, *Diversity* functioned as a differentiating item. On the first factor, discomfort with multiculturalism loaded alongside hawkish immigration attitudes—a pattern consistent with the racial and cultural appeals Trump made in his public discussion of immigration (Hajnal & Abrajano, 2016; Wong, 2017). Meanwhile, we saw a strong negative loading for *Diversity* on the dimension representing left-wing populism. Thus, where citizens wanted government to prioritize and remedy economic inequality (*Unfair Taxes* and *Income Inequality*), they preferred to celebrate *Diversity* rather than deport undocumented children (*Deport Children*).

These results indicated (1) a right-wing populist dimension anchored by hawkish immigration attitudes and (2) a left-wing populist dimension anchored by demands for economic justice. The performance of these items in an EFA specification gave preliminary evidence for H1. They indicated that the electorate viewed anti-immigration attitudes and calls for economic justice not as a single populist vision, but as distinct considerations.

With EFA offering preliminary support for H_1, we turned to confirmatory factor analysis (CFA), modeling each dimension only in terms of the *anchoring* and *differentiating* indicators recommended by EFA. This meant specifying a *right-wing populism* dimension that included the three immigration attitudes (*Hire American, Stop Hiring Immigrants, Deport Children*) as anchors and a *left-wing populism* dimension with the economic justice items (*Unfair Taxes, Income Inequality*) as anchors. Since EFA recommended *Deport Children* and *Diversity* as differentiating items, we allowed these indicators to cross-load onto both dimensions. As Table 36.3 documents, CFA indicated a well-fitting model.[3]

Figure 36.1 plots standardized factor scores (for *right-wing* and *left-wing populism*) for Republican identifiers, Democratic identifiers, and independents.[4] The scatterplots indicate that the electorate in 2017 (despite some between-group asymmetries) saw left-wing and right-wing populism as antithetical. For all three groups, majorities of respondents were found in the "off-diagonal" quadrants—indicating higher scores on one form of populism and lower scores on the other. Moreover, for Republican and Democratic identifiers, majorities of respondents were consolidated in the quadrant most compatible with their partisan-ideological commitments. Republican identifiers tended to be right-wing but not left-wing populists; Democratic identifiers, left-wing populists but not right-wing populists.

Table 36.3 Confirmatory factor analysis, right-wing populism and left-wing populism, 2017 cooperative congressional election study

Indicator	Dimension	
	Right populism	Left populism
Stop hiring immigrants	0.78 (0.03)	
Hire American	0.85 (0.02)	
Income inequality		0.85 (0.02)
Unfair taxes		0.74 (0.03)
Diversity	0.28 (0.04)	−0.57 (0.04)
Deport children	0.67 (0.03)	−0.30 (0.04)
CD	0.972	
N	1000	

Data from the 2017 Cooperative Congressional Election Study. Standard errors in parentheses. Model estimated using full-information maximum likelihood (FIML) in Stata 16.0; incomplete cases composed 2.7% of the sample

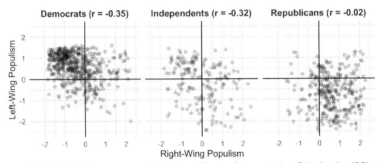

Standardized factor scores computed using confirmatory factor analysis in Stata (version 16.0); see Table 3 for details. Data are from the 2017 Cooperative Congressional Election Study.

RIGHT-WING POPULISM involves (1) agreement that 'Companies should stop hiring immigrants and prioritize hiring American citizens'; (2) agreement that 'Our economy will never recover completely until we stop hiring immigrants'; (3) agreement that 'We should deport the children of illegal immigrants instead of giving them special treatment'; and (4) disagreement that 'Diversity and multiculturalism should be celebrated.'

LEFT-WING POPULISM involves (1) agreement that 'It's unfair that the wealthy pay less in taxes than most Americans'; (2) agreement that 'Reducing income inequality is one of the most important things government can do right now'; (3) agreement that 'Diversity and multiculturalism should be celebrated'; and disagreement that 'We should deport the children of illegal immigrants instead of giving them special treatment.'

Fig. 36.1 Right-wing and left-wing populism by party identification 2017 cooperative congressional election study

However, it is noteworthy that Republican identifiers showed more ambivalence than other respondents. On balance, they landed in the quadrant where we would expect to find them. Yet their views were more heterogeneous and their attitudes on right- and left-wing populism were uncorrelated ($r = -0.02$). It is beyond the scope of this piece to reflect on this asymmetry. Nonetheless, it may reflect Republicans' lingering disagreements about whether Trump was an appropriate standard-bearer and whether his immigration proposals went too far.

This modest asymmetry did nothing to dislodge our evidence for H1. CFA demonstrated our anticipated dimensions of populist attitudes. The majority of respondents were either right-wing populists or left-wing populists, but not both. Moreover, the distribution of populist attitudes indicated that these broke along partisan lines—with Democrats consolidating around left-wing populism, and Republicans trending toward right-wing populism.

Who Are the Right-Wing and Left-Wing Populists?

Before testing our hypotheses about populist attitudes and presidential voting behavior (H_2), we explored the factors associated with right- and left-wing populism. We did this for two reasons: first, to be transparent about the correlation between our measures and other predictors of vote choice; and second, to determine whether these correlations helped validate our index. Using ordinary least-squares (OLS) regression, we modeled right- and left-wing populism as a function of relevant covariates: negative racial attitudes, the strength of partisan identification, ideological self-identification, and socioeconomic status. We estimated separate models (see Tables 36.4, 36.5, and 36.6) for Republican identifiers, Democratic identifiers, and independents—using as dependent variables the standardized factor scores from CFA.

On the right-hand side of these models, we controlled for an additive index of three *Negative Racial Attitudes* (see DeSante & Smith, 2020), included in the Common Content of the 2017 CCES. These items assessed the degree to which respondents (1) were not angered that racism exists; (2) denied the existence of White privilege; and (3) believed that racial incidents were isolated rather than systemic problems.[5] Because these measures primarily dealt with whites' racial attitudes, we interacted *Negative Racial Attitudes* with *White* (non-Hispanic) race/ethnicity.

In addition, the models controlled for partisan strength, using dummy variables (where appropriate) to indicate *Strong Partisans* and *Weak Partisans* (with partisan "leaners" as the omitted group). Dummy-variable controls indicated self-identified *Conservative* or *Liberal* respondents, based on answers to the traditional seven-point measure of ideological self-identification.[6] Standard demographic controls indicated *Married* respondents; attainment of a *Four-Year Degree*; *Family Income* (16-point scale; 0 = less than $5,000, 15 = more than $500,000) and respondents with *Income Unreported*[7]; *Age* (in years); residence in the *South*; *Female* gender identity; and identification as a *Born-again Christian*. Results are found in Tables 36.4, 36.5, and 36.6; they can be summarized in three basic observations.

First, across all three subgroups, *Negative Racial Attitudes* were associated with higher levels of right-wing populism and lower levels of left-wing populism. These strong, consistent effects were useful for validating our measures. It would have been odd if right-wing populism were not associated

Table 36.4 Republican identifiers: Determinants of right-wing and left-wing populism

Variables	(1) Right populism	(2) Left populism
Negative racial attitudes	1.64***	−2.30***
	(0.57)	(0.45)
White	0.46	−0.54**
	(0.28)	(0.25)
Negative racial attitudes x White	−1.15*	0.97*
	(0.61)	(0.52)
Strong Partisan	0.11	0.14
	(0.11)	(0.12)
Weak Partisan	−0.17	0.23*
	(0.13)	(0.14)
Conservative	−0.04	−0.36***
	(0.14)	(0.12)
Four-Year degree	−0.31***	−0.18*
	(0.10)	(0.10)
Family income	−0.68***	−0.43*
	(0.26)	(0.26)
Income unreported	−0.16	−0.27**
	(0.14)	(0.12)
Age (in years)	0.00	−0.01***
	(0.00)	(0.00)
Married	0.10	−0.02
	(0.10)	(0.11)
Born-again Christian	0.19*	0.02
	(0.10)	(0.09)
South	0.18*	0.11
	(0.10)	(0.09)
Female	0.07	0.14
	(0.10)	(0.09)
Constant	−0.01	1.11***
	(0.34)	(0.29)
Observations	304	304
R-squared	0.19	0.31

Ordinary least squares regression; robust standard errors in parentheses. Data from the 2017 Cooperative Congressional Election Study. ***$p < 0.01$, **$p < 0.05$, *$p < 0.1$

with negative racial attitudes. Hawkish immigration measures, exemplified by Trump, coexist with racially charged rhetoric (Hajnal & Abrajano, 2016).

Likewise, it made sense that left-wing populism was associated with greater awareness and anger about racial injustice. Consistent with Lowndes' (2017) distinction between left-wing and right-wing populism in U.S. history, left-wing populists should demonize "economic elites" rather than immigrants.

Table 36.5 Democratic identifiers: Determinants of right-wing and left-wing populism

Variables	(1) Right populism	(2) Left populism
Negative racial attitudes	1.29***	−1.35***
	(0.36)	(0.27)
White	−0.28***	0.05
	(0.09)	(0.07)
Negative racial attitudes x White	1.12***	−0.07
	(0.41)	(0.31)
Strong Partisan	−0.02	0.04
	(0.08)	(0.06)
Weak Partisan	0.14	−0.11
	(0.09)	(0.08)
Liberal	−0.08	0.21***
	(0.09)	(0.07)
Four-Year degree	−0.13*	−0.05
	(0.07)	(0.06)
Family income	−0.25	0.42***
	(0.20)	(0.14)
Income unreported	0.13	0.02
	(0.09)	(0.07)
Age (in years)	0.01***	0.00
	(0.00)	(0.00)
Married	0.01	−0.09*
	(0.08)	(0.05)
Born-again Christian	0.30***	−0.08
	(0.11)	(0.07)
South	0.05	−0.04
	(0.07)	(0.05)
Female	0.13*	−0.16***
	(0.07)	(0.05)
Constant	−0.96***	0.63***
	(0.17)	(0.15)
Observations	492	492
R-squared	0.34	0.33

Ordinary least squares regression; robust standard errors in parentheses. Data from the 2017 Cooperative Congressional Election Study. ***$p < 0.01$, **$p < 0.05$, *$p < 0.1$

Given that our indicators of left-wing populism included concerns about income inequality and regressive taxation—as well as support for diversity and multiculturalism—we were unsurprised to discover that left-wing populists were more likely to acknowledge structural racism.

Second, the dimensions' relationship with self-reported ideology was consistent with the indicators in our CFA model. Our models suggested

Table 36.6 Partisan independents: Determinants of right-wing and left-wing populism

Variables	(1) Right populism	(2) Left populism
Negative racial attitudes	1.65***	−1.87***
	(0.56)	(0.36)
White	−0.20	0.10
	(0.22)	(0.17)
Negative racial attitudes x White	0.52	−0.08
	(0.59)	(0.41)
Conservative	−0.21	−0.74***
	(0.17)	(0.15)
Liberal	−0.24	0.37***
	(0.17)	(0.12)
Four-Year degree	−0.32**	−0.20
	(0.14)	(0.13)
Family income	−0.25	0.13
	(0.39)	(0.34)
Income unreported	0.06	−0.21
	(0.15)	(0.15)
Age (in years)	0.01*	−0.00
	(0.00)	(0.00)
Married	−0.19	−0.21*
	(0.14)	(0.12)
Born-again Christian	0.13	0.02
	(0.17)	(0.15)
South	−0.21	0.02
	(0.14)	(0.11)
Female	0.14	0.08
	(0.14)	(0.11)
Constant	−0.57*	0.65**
	(0.33)	(0.28)
Observations	169	169
R-squared	0.35	0.61

Ordinary least squares regression; robust standard errors in parentheses. Data from the 2017 Cooperative Congressional Election Study. ***$p < 0.01$, **$p < 0.05$, *$p < 0.1$

that ideological self-identification was associated with left-wing but not right-wing populism. Republicans and independents had lower levels of left-wing populism if they identified as *Conservative*; Democrats and independents had higher levels of left-wing populism if they identified as *Liberal*. Yet self-reported ideology had no independent effect on right-wing populism.

It made sense that *Conservative* and *Liberal* respondents were no more or less likely to endorse right-wing populism, but that they (respectively) opposed or endorsed left-wing populism. In an exhaustive longitudinal study, Caughey et al. (2019) showed that "immigration conservatism" constitutes a distinct dimension of public opinion in European democracies, not fully captured by citizens' self-placement on the liberal-conservatism spectrum. Thus, if immigration is a new source of partisan conflict in the United States, it may not be captured by terminology familiar to other debates.

Moreover, unlike left-wing populists' vaguer concerns about economic inequality, the immigration items in our index translated more readily into substantive policies. As Ellis and Stimson (2012) suggest, self-reported ideology is often symbolic in nature—reflecting not policy preferences, but vaguer notions of what it means to be a good citizen. For these reasons, we should have expected that self-reported ideology would show minimal association with right-wing populism, despite predictable covariance with left-wing populism.

Finally, we noted the relationships (or lack thereof) between socioeconomic status and populist attitudes. Among Republicans, Democrats and independents alike, those with four-year degrees showed lower levels of right-wing populism (*ceteris paribus*); among Republican identifiers, right-wing populism showed a further, negative association with higher income. This was consistent with Donald Trump's resonance among working-class Whites (Williams, 2017).

Across the board, however, we saw inconsistent effects of socioeconomic status on left-wing populism. Among independents, left-wing populism was associated with neither educational attainment nor family income. Yet while Democrats with higher income levels showed stronger support for left-wing populism, Republicans with higher incomes showed the opposite effect. These inconsistent associations between populism and socioeconomic status shed additional light on the nature of our populist moment. Despite the economic salience of (at least) four of our populism indicators, the resonance of populist attitudes clearly went beyond socioeconomic disadvantage (see also Green & McElwee, 2019; Mutz, 2018).

By modeling the determinants of populist attitudes, we gained clarity about what *was* and *was not* represented by our measures. First, we saw a strong relationship between both dimensions of populism and racial attitudes; negative racial attitudes were associated with right-wing populism; positive racial attitudes, with left-wing populism. At minimum, this finding recommended we test H_2-H_4 by taking racial attitudes into account. Second, of the two dimensions, only left-wing populism was associated with self-reported ideology. Since self-reported ideology overlaps with symbolic rather than programmatic concerns (Ellis & Stimson, 2012) and since our indicators of left-wing populism were disproportionately symbolic, this asymmetry was not critical for our analysis. Finally, the inconsistent relationship between socioeconomic status and populist attitudes suggested that support for right- and left-wing populism was not necessarily tethered to socioeconomic disadvantage. Rather, our measures captured a distinctly ideological feature of public opinion: *right-wing populists*' endorsement of hawkish immigration attitudes; and *left-wing populists*' concerns about economic inequality.

Effects on Presidential Voting Behavior

Our final task, then, was to test whether right and left-wing populism were associated with voting behavior in the 2016 presidential election. According to our hypotheses, right-wing populism should have increased the likelihood that Republican identifiers voted for Donald Trump, but left-wing populism should have influenced them to stay home (H_2). The reverse should have held true for Democratic identifiers (H_3). Left-wing populism should have increased the likelihood that Democrats voted for Hillary Clinton, while right-wing populism should have promoted abstention by the Democratic rank and file. Finally, populist attitudes should have pulled independents toward different major party candidates: right-wing populism, toward Trump; and left-wing populism, toward Clinton (H_4).

We modeled Republican identifiers' support for Trump (Table 36.7); Democratic identifiers' support for Clinton (Table 36.8); and independents' support for both Trump (Table 36.9) and Clinton (Table 36.10).[8] For each subgroup and dependent variable, we performed stepwise logistic regressions. In each case, the initial model used only right and left-wing populism as explanatory variables. Then, for each subsample, a second model added negative racial attitudes. Next, where appropriate, we introduced dummy variables controlling for strong and weak partisanship. In all cases, the final model controlled for ideological self-identification, socioeconomic status, and other demographics.

Looking first at Table 36.7, we found partial support for H_2. Right-wing populism—even after controlling for negative racial attitudes, partisan strength, and other confounding variables—increased the likelihood that Republican identifiers voted for Donald Trump. Indeed, the magnitude and significance of the coefficient on *Right-Wing Populism* was almost undisturbed across the specifications. However, while left-wing populism exerted the reverse effect in our baseline model—inducing Republicans to abstain or vote against Trump—this effect was fully mediated by demographic controls (Column 4). Thus, we can claim (with confidence) that right-wing populism made Republican identifiers more likely to vote for Donald Trump in 2016. Nevertheless, while left-wing populism may have had the opposite effect, this conclusion was more sensitive to model specification.

H_3 suggested that for Democratic identifiers, right-wing populism would decrease (and left-wing populism increase) the likelihood of voting for Hillary Clinton. However, Table 36.8 suggests that any effects from right- and left-wing populism were fully mediated by other determinants of voting behavior. Among Democrats, left-wing populism had the hypothesized effects in our initial, baseline model. Yet this effect lost significance once we controlled for

Table 36.7 Republican identifiers: determinants of voting for Donald Trump in 2016

Variables	(1) Model 1	(2) Model 2	(3) Model 3	(4) Model 4
Right-wing populism	0.65***	0.58***	0.53***	0.56**
	(0.18)	(0.18)	(0.20)	(0.24)
Left-wing populism	−0.64***	−0.46***	−0.47***	−0.31
	(0.17)	(0.17)	(0.18)	(0.20)
Negative racial attitudes		0.82	0.52	0.54
		(1.54)	(1.58)	(1.87)
White		0.47	0.34	−0.02
		(0.77)	(0.76)	(0.86)
Negative racial attitudes x White		0.70	1.07	0.76
		(1.78)	(1.80)	(2.01)
Strong Partisan			1.07***	1.10***
			(0.37)	(0.39)
Weak Partisan			0.20	0.37
			(0.37)	(0.41)
Conservative				0.43
				(0.40)
Four-Year degree				−0.18
				(0.36)
Family Income				1.00
				(1.01)
Income unreported				0.43
				(0.54)
Age (in years)				0.04***
				(0.01)
Married				0.51
				(0.38)
Born-again Christian				0.31
				(0.36)
South				0.52
				(0.33)
Female				−0.66**
				(0.33)
Constant	0.33*	−0.42	−0.77	−3.45***
	(0.19)	(0.66)	(0.68)	(1.13)
Observations	302	302	302	302

Logistic regression; standard errors in parentheses. Data from the 2017 Cooperative Congressional Election Study. Dependent variable coded 1 if the respondent indicated they voted for Donald Trump in the 2016 presidential election; and 0 if they supported a different candidate or abstained from voting. ***$p < 0.01$, **$p < 0.05$, *$p < 0.10$

Table 36.8 Democratic identifiers: determinants of voting for Hillary Clinton in 2016

Variables	(1) Model 1	(2) Model 2	(3) Model 3	(4) Model 4
Right-wing populism	−0.19	0.06	0.07	0.02
	(0.13)	(0.16)	(0.17)	(0.18)
Left-wing populism	0.60***	0.39**	0.25	0.12
	(0.18)	(0.19)	(0.20)	(0.21)
Negative racial attitudes		0.18	−0.18	0.36
		(0.92)	(0.89)	(0.97)
White		1.20***	1.25***	0.69*
		(0.31)	(0.32)	(0.36)
Negative racial attitudes x White		−3.77***	−3.35***	−3.19***
		(1.14)	(1.13)	(1.23)
Strong Partisan			1.54***	1.57***
			(0.30)	(0.33)
Weak Partisan			0.10	0.35
			(0.30)	(0.33)
Liberal				0.55**
				(0.28)
Four-Year degree				0.78***
				(0.30)
Family income				1.73**
				(0.77)
Income unreported				0.25
				(0.38)
Age (in years)				0.03***
				(0.01)
Married				−0.33
				(0.29)
Born-again Christian				0.24
				(0.33)
South				0.15
				(0.26)
Female				0.01
				(0.27)
Constant	0.69***	0.59**	−0.06	−2.36***
	(0.13)	(0.25)	(0.35)	(0.62)
Observations	481	481	481	479

Logistic regression; standard errors in parentheses. Data from the 2017 Cooperative Congressional Election Study. Dependent variable coded 1 if the respondent indicated they voted for Hillary Clinton in the 2016 presidential election; and 0 if they supported a different candidate or abstained from voting. ***$p < 0.01$, **$p < 0.05$, *$p < 0.10$

Table 36.9 Partisan independents: determinants of voting for Donald Trump in 2016

Variables	(1) Model 1	(2) Model 2	(3) Model 3
Right-wing populism	1.24***	1.35***	1.63***
	(0.29)	(0.36)	(0.50)
Left-wing populism	−1.28***	−1.37***	−1.12***
	(0.25)	(0.30)	(0.37)
Negative racial attitudes		4.11**	4.36*
		(2.08)	(2.36)
White		3.68***	3.62**
		(1.27)	(1.46)
Negative racial attitudes x White		−5.74**	−5.77**
		(2.44)	(2.68)
Liberal			0.48
			(0.95)
Conservative			0.45
			(0.71)
Four-Year degree			−0.10
			(0.67)
Family income			2.00
			(1.81)
Income unreported			0.61
			(0.65)
Married			0.51
			(0.58)
South			−0.29
			(0.53)
Age (in years)			0.00
			(0.02)
Female			−0.55
			(0.69)
Born-again Christian			0.47
			(0.60)
Constant	−1.72***	−4.45***	−5.52***
	(0.26)	(1.14)	(2.11)
Observations	164	164	164

Logistic regression; standard errors in parentheses. Data from the 2017 Cooperative Congressional Election Study. Dependent variable coded 1 if the respondent indicated they voted for Donald Trump in the 2016 presidential election; and 0 if they supported a different candidate or abstained from voting. ***$p < 0.01$, **$p < 0.05$, *$p < 0.10$

Table 36.10 Partisan independents: determinants of voting for Hillary Clinton in 2016

Variables	(1) Model 1	(2) Model 2	(3) Model 3
Right-wing populism	−0.66***	−0.52**	−0.47
	(0.22)	(0.25)	(0.31)
Left-wing populism	0.88***	0.69**	0.50
	(0.24)	(0.30)	(0.36)
Negative racial attitudes		−4.20*	−5.47*
		(2.54)	(3.15)
White		−0.51	−0.53
		(0.70)	(0.77)
Negative racial attitudes x White		3.32	4.00
		(2.52)	(2.91)
Liberal			−0.28
			(0.48)
Conservative			−1.93*
			(1.00)
Four-Year degree			0.54
			(0.49)
Family income			1.49
			(1.39)
Income unreported			0.56
			(0.51)
Married			−0.34
			(0.49)
South			−0.34
			(0.52)
Age (in years)			0.00
			(0.01)
Female			−0.54
			(0.48)
Born-again Christian			0.45
			(0.75)
Constant	−1.45***	−0.59	−0.50
	(0.22)	(0.69)	(1.46)
Observations	164	164	164

Logistic regression; standard errors in parentheses. Data from the 2017 Cooperative Congressional Election Study. Dependent variable coded 1 if the respondent indicated they voted for Hillary Clinton in the 2016 presidential election; and 0 if they supported a different candidate or abstained from voting. ***$p < 0.01$, **$p < 0.05$, *$p < 0.10$

the strength of Democrats' partisan attachment and the addition of further controls did nothing to change this conclusion. In other words, we found no indication that Democrats in 2016 voted on the basis of populist attitudes—whether right-wing or left-wing. We reflect on these null findings in the next section; they contrast with the sharp effect of right-wing populism on Republicans' support for Donald Trump.

Finally, we found our strongest effects on voting behavior among partisan independents (offering partial confirmation of H_4).[9] In Tables 36.9 and 36.10, we applied the same stepwise procedure to examine independents' voting decisions—either to vote for Trump (Table 36.9) or Clinton (Table 36.10). As Table 36.9 illustrates, right-wing populism made independents more likely to vote for Trump, while left-wing populism made them more likely to abstain or vote against Trump. Given the smaller number of independents, this finding was remarkably robust. However, these effects did not necessarily translate into Clinton's support on Election Day. As Table 36.10 shows, the effects of populist attitudes on independents' support for Clinton were fully mediated by controls for self-reported ideology and demographic indicators.

To be sure, there was more uncertainty around the predicted effects for independents, as the wide confidence bands in Fig. 36.2 suggest. However, since independents abstain from voting in large numbers, our models suggested that right- and left-wing populism made the difference between *near-guaranteed* abstention and non-zero likelihood that independents would pull the lever for Donald Trump. Given the razor-thin margins by which Trump secured his Electoral College majority, the nudge independents received from populist attitudes should not be ignored.

Figure 36.2 visualizes the results of the fully specified versions of each model in Tables 36.7, 36.8, 36.9, and 36.10; the figure was produced using the *ggplot2* (Wickham, 2009) package in R (R Development Core Team, 2008). The graphs show predicted probabilities of candidate support (with 95% confidence intervals) associated with a −2 to 2 (i.e., 4 s.*d.*) increase in populist attitudes. To reiterate, Republican identifiers' likelihood of voting for Donald Trump was associated with higher levels of right-wing populism, while the reverse effect from left-wing populism was less robust. Among independents, we found especially strong effects from both dimensions of populism; right-wing populism increased the likelihood that independents would vote for Trump and left-wing populism dampened support for Trump.

However, left-wing populism had no meaningful effect on whether Democratic identifiers or independents voted for Hillary Clinton. Rather than mobilize Democratic identifiers in 2016, then, the main effect of left-wing populism on the election outcome was far more modest. Left-wing populism seems only to have confirmed political independents' decision to stay home. As we suggest next, this discrepancy offers valuable direction for future research.

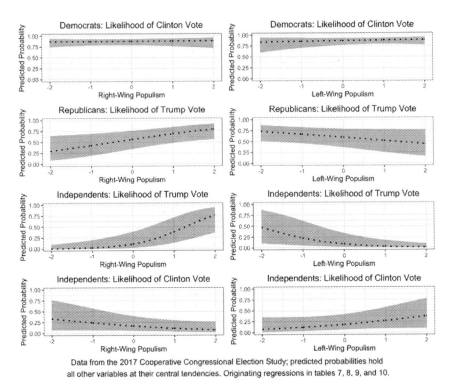

Fig. 36.2 Predicted effects of right and left-wing populism on Trump or Clinton voting in 2016, by partisan subgroup

Null Effects for Democrats: Why?

Our analysis indicated that in 2016, right-wing populism made both Republican identifiers and independents more likely to vote for Donald Trump. In addition, left-wing populism made independents more likely to abstain from voting or vote against Trump, rather than support Trump on Election Day. As these effects were robust to a bevy of control variables, they suggest that populism *was* relevant for voting behavior in 2016. Although these effects did not hold for Democrats, they held for Republicans, and for the non-negligible proportion of voters that identified with neither of the major parties.

Results suggest that political scientists should not overstate the degree to which 2016 confirms existing explanations of voting behavior. To be sure, Trump's election illustrated the importance of party identification (Bartels, 2018). As Larry Bartels (2018) documents, the election did little to dislodge the existing issue divides between Republican and Democratic identifiers. Yet our findings indicate that despite being relative newcomers to the political landscape, right- and left-wing populism influenced voting behavior, too. Populism made a difference among voters with no partisan allegiance and it made a difference among Republican identifiers who swept President Trump into office.

However, populism—whether left-wing or right-wing—did not influence whether Democratic identifiers turned out for Hillary Clinton. Juxtaposed against the strong effect of right-wing populism on Republican support for Trump, this finding has an obvious interpretation: While Donald Trump was a right-wing populist, Hillary Clinton had no credible claim to be a left-wing populist. Had Bernie Sanders instead won the Democratic nomination in 2016, left-wing populism might indeed have influenced Democrats to turn out for their party's nominee.

This thought experiment does not require that the differences between Clinton and Sanders were as stark as their campaigns suggested. Nor does it require us to defend the premise that Bernie Sanders *is* a populist in every sense of the term (for an opposing take, see Müller, 2016). Rather, our data speak for themselves: in response to our measures, Democratic identifiers articulated opposition to right-wing populism and support for left-wing populism. To the extent our Democratic identifiers were left-wing populists, they expressed concern about excessive wealth and income inequality. These echoed the rhetorical appeals of the Sanders campaign.

Sanders's failure to secure the Democratic nomination, then, potentially explains why populism did not influence Democrats' voting behavior. Had Sanders been nominated, would left-wing populism have influenced whether Democrats turned out for their party's candidate? We cannot know. But Clinton's nomination cannot have helped the matter.

Indeed, this asymmetry clarifies rather than obscures the intensity of our populist moment. First, right-wing and left-wing populism—as our factor analysis documented—are now one more manner in which polarization manifests among Republican and Democratic identifiers. Second, in 2016 only the Republican Party nominated a candidate understood to embrace the version of populism most compatible with their party's preexisting ideological commitments. The Democrats, for their part, *failed* to nominate the candidate—Bernie Sanders—responsible for reintroducing the language of left-wing populism to the Democratic Party.

Yet Sanders's failure as a candidate belies his influence on how Democratic identifiers think and reason about issues of economic inequality. Indeed, Sanders's rise and fall may have left Democratic identifiers in a curious position: not only without a left-wing populist as their nominee, but relatively consolidated in their support for what that left-wing populist might have offered as Trump's opponent. By contrast, the influence of right-wing populism on Republican identifiers' support for Trump likely reflects the GOP's nomination of a right-wing populist as its presidential candidate. In the long run, however, we expect the electorate to consolidate further in its perception that right and left-wing populism are incompatible.

Conclusion

In this analysis, we piloted and validated an original index of populist attitudes in the United States: documenting Americans' beliefs about concerns associated with populism in public discourse. We hypothesized that populist attitudes would have two distinct dimensions: one right-wing, motivated by anti-immigration attitudes; the other left-wing, motivated by ideologically potent but vaguer concerns about economic inequality.

To justify our two-dimensional framework, we drew upon the candidacies of Donald Trump and Bernie Sanders in the 2016 presidential primaries. Trump and Sanders embodied *right-wing populism* and *left-wing populism*. At least in the early stages of the presidential nominating contest, these visions were presented by equally long-shot candidates, each with minimal support from the party organizations. Lacking the immediate backlash that serious candidacies would have prompted, Trump's and Sanders's frameworks perhaps had time to take root on opposing sides of the partisan–ideological divide. We contended that Trump's and Sanders's visions would be treated as incompatible by many citizens—not just because right- and left-wing populism offer different narratives (Lowndes, 2017), but because Trump and Sanders made their appeals to primary voters in different parties.

In general, this is what we found. Exploratory factor analysis (EFA) suggested a structure consistent with our typology, and confirmatory factor analysis (CFA) suggested that the dichotomy held for Republicans, Democrats and independents alike. Survey responses were consistent with two latent factors: *right-wing populism*, anchored by hawkish immigration attitudes, and *left-wing populism*, anchored by concern over economic unfairness.

Moreover, we tested the effects of right-wing and left-wing populism on presidential vote choice in 2016. We found that right-wing populism made Republican identifiers and independents more likely to vote for Donald Trump. However, neither populist dimension helped explain why Democratic identifiers turned out for Hillary Clinton. Where our measures could not explain Democratic voting behavior, we suggested that Bernie Sanders' failure to win the Democratic nomination had a more profound effect than scholars have realized—diluting the electoral potency of left-wing populism among Democratic voters. In future work, we intend to explore whether Joe Biden—despite defeating Trump in the 2020 presidential election—underperformed among left-wing populists that would have preferred Sanders as the Democratic nominee.

These findings suggest an opening for scholars interested in contextualizing populism in the U.S. context. Post-2016, two dimensions of populist attitudes—drawing on distinct currents of populism in American history—have grafted onto opposing party platforms. They have done so at a time of far-reaching elite polarization (Campbell, 2016; McCarty et al., 2008) and they find expression among the parties' rank and file. Republican identifiers, whether in response to Trump or in tandem with him, now speak the language of right-wing populism. Democratic identifiers are perhaps even more unified in their embrace of left-wing populism. To the extent independents can be induced to select from the choices on offer, the availability of an amenable, major party populist candidate matters a great deal.

Most important, if right-wing populism seems more relevant to the 2016 presidential election and its aftermath, this is likely due to the outcome of the Democratic nominating contest. As our data showed, Democrats' commitment to the populism of Bernie Sanders is just as profound as Republicans' commitment to the populism of Donald Trump. If mass populism continues to reshape the nature of partisan conflict, we anticipate no shortage of opportunities to test this premise further.

Notes

1. The CCES is a nationally representative, annual survey of the American public. The 2017 survey was conducted in a single wave by YouGov from November 8, 2017 to December 12, 2017. Indiana University's team module of the 2017 CCES is available on the CCES Dataverse, hosted by Harvard University (see Schmidt, 2020).
2. However, when we calculated factor scores using a confirmatory factor analysis (CFA) with all eight items (and the structure recommended in Table 36.1), our conclusions about the determinants and effects of populist attitudes remained substantively unchanged.
3. Our confirmatory factor analysis (CFA) used full information maximum likelihood (FIML), to include the small number ($n = 27$) of incomplete cases in the sample.
4. We counted citizens that "lean" toward the Republican and Democratic parties as partisan identifiers.
5. Among the measures of negative racial attitudes included on the CCES, a fourth item asked whether respondents are "often fearful of people of other races." This item had a weaker correlation with the three items we used in our additive index. In addition, while DeSante and Smith (2020) suggest that these items should be used as individual control variables, non-Hispanic whites' responses to these items loaded onto a single factor, as did the responses of the full sample.
6. There were too few self-identified liberal Republicans or conservative Democrats (see Levendusky, 2009) to justify controlling for these ideological self-identifications in models involving those partisan subgroups.
7. *Income Unreported* indicated whether respondents "preferred not to say" when asked their income ($1 = $ yes; $0 = $ no); these respondents were provisionally coded at the mean of the *Family Income* distribution.
8. Our measure of respondents' vote choice is based on self-reports of voting in the 2016 presidential election. We coded respondents as having abstained from voting if they indicated on the 2017 CCES that they were not registered to vote (and thus were not asked about their vote choice in 2016); if they were registered to vote but indicated that they did not vote in the 2016 presidential election; or if they reported voting in 2016 but indicated they did not cast a vote for president. Respondents were treated as missing data if they did not know whether they were registered to vote; were registered but could not recall

who they supported in 2016; said that they voted for president but could not recall which presidential candidate they supported; or indicated they voted but did not answer the question about presidential vote choice. Missing data on presidential vote choice applied to only 25 of our 1000 respondents.
9. In an era of increasingly polarized policy attitudes (Abramowitz, 2010; Campbell, 2016) and partisan animus (Mason, 2018), it is easy to forget that partisan independents still exist. They constituted nearly 17 percent of our sample, and their voting behavior suggested a choice between voting for Trump (n = 37), voting for Clinton (n = 48), or either abstaining from voting or supporting minor-party candidates (n = 84). While abstaining from voting was the modal behavior for partisan independents, there was enough support for both major-party candidates to test whether right-wing and left-wing populism exerted their predicted effects (H_4).

Literature

Abrajano, M., & Hajnal, Z. L. (2015). *White backlash: Immigration, race, and American politics*. Princeton University Press.
Abramowitz, A. I. (2010). *The disappearing center: Engaged citizens, polarization, and American democracy*. Yale University Press.
Abramowitz, A. I., & Saunders, K. (2008). Is polarization a myth. *Journal of Politics, 70*(2), 542–555.
Azari, J., & Hetherington, M. J. (2016). Back to the future? What the politics of the late nineteenth century can tell us about the 2016 election. *The ANNALS of the American Academy of Political and Social Science, 667*, 92–109.
Bafumi, J., & Shapiro, R. Y. (2009). A new partisan voter. *Journal of Politics, 71*(1), 1–24.
Bartels, L. M. (2018). Partisanship in the Trump era. *Journal of Politics, 80*(4), 1483–1494.
Berinsky, A. J., Huber, G. A., & Lenz, G. S. (2012). Evaluating online labor markets for experimental research: Amazon.com's Mechanical Turk. *Political Analysis, 20*(3), 351–368.
Campbell, J. E. (2016). *Polarized: Making sense of a divided America*. Princeton University Press.
Carmines, E. G., & Schmidt, E. R. (2019). Critical elections, partisan realignment, and long-term electoral change in American politics. *Oxford Bibliographies Online*. https://doi.org/10.1093/obo/9780199756223-0246.
Carmines, E. G., & Zeller, R. A. (1979). *Reliability and validity assessment*. Sage.
Caughey, D., O'Grady, T., & Warshaw, C. (2019). Policy ideology in European mass publics, 1981–2016. *American Political Science Review, 113*(3), 674–693.
Claggett, W. J. M., & Shafer, B. E. (2010). *The American public mind: The issue structure of mass politics in the postwar United States*. Cambridge University Press.
Cohen, M., Karol, D., Noel, H., & Zaller, J. (2009). *The party decides: Presidential nominations before and after reform*. University of Chicago Press.
Confessore, N., & Horowitz, J. (2016, January 21). Hillary Clinton's paid speeches to Wall Street animate her opponents. *New York Times*. Retrieved from https://www.nytimes.com/2016/01/22/us/politics/in-race-defined-byincome-gap-hillary-clintons-wall-street-ties-incite-rivals.html.

DeSante, C. D., & Smith, C. W. (2020). Fear, institutionalized racism, and empathy: The two dimensions of whites' racial attitudes. *P.S.: Political Science & Politics*, forthcoming. Retrieved from https://doi.org/10.1017/S1049096520000414.

Ellis, C., & Stimson, J. A. (2012). *Ideology in America*. Cambridge University Press.

Gabriel, T., & Preston, J. (2015, August 18). Donald Trump paints Republicans into corner with Hispanics. *New York Times*. Retrieved from https://www.nytimes.com/2015/08/19/us/politics/with-tough-immigration-talk-gop-again-risks-losing-latinos.html.

Green, J., & McElwee, S. (2019). The differential effects of economic conditions and racial attitudes in the election of Donald Trump. *Perspectives on Politics*, *17*(2), 358–379.

Hajnal, Z., & Abrajano, M. (2016). Trump's all too familiar strategy and its future in the GOP. *The Forum*, *14*(3), 295–309.

Herndon, A. W. (2018, August 25). Democrats overhaul controversial superdelegate system. *New York Times*. Retrieved from https://www.nytimes.com/2018/08/25/us/politics/superdelegates-democrats-dnc.html.

Inglehart, R., & Norris, P. (2017). Trump and the xenophobic populist parties: The silent revolution in reverse. *Perspectives on Politics*, *15*(2), 443–454.

Isaac, J. C. (2017). Liberal democracy in question? *Perspectives on Politics*, *15*(1), 1–5.

Kazin, M. (2016, March 22). How can Donald Trump and Bernie Sanders both be populists? *The New York Times Magazine*. Retrieved from https://www.nytimes.com/2016/03/27/magazine/how-can-donald-trump-and-bernie-sanders-both-be-populist.html.

Kitschelt, H., & McGann, A. J. (1995). *The radical right in western Europe*. University of Michigan Press.

Lee, F. E. (2020). Populism and the American party system: Opportunities and constraints. *Perspectives on Politics*, *18*(2), 370–388.

Leege, D. C., Wald, K. D., Krueger, B. S., & Mueller, P. D. (2002). *The politics of cultural differences: Social change and voter mobilization strategies in the post-New Deal period*. Princeton University Press.

Levendusky, M. (2009). *The Partisan sort*. University of Chicago Press.

Levitsky, S., & Ziblatt, D. (2018). *How democracies die*. Crown Publishing Group.

Lowndes, J. (2017). Populism in the United States. In C. R. Kaltwasser, P. Taggart, P. O. Espejo, & P. Ostiguy (Eds.), *The Oxford handbook of populism* (pp. 232–247). New York: Oxford University Press.

MacWilliams, M. C. (2016). Who decides when the party doesn't? Authoritarian voters and the rise of Donald Trump. *P.S.: Political Science and Politics*, *49*(4), 716–721.

Mason, L. (2018). *Uncivil agreement: How politics became our identity*. University of Chicago Press.

McCarty, N., Poole, K. T., & Rosenthal, H. (2008). *Polarized America: The dance of ideology and unequal riches*. The MIT Press.

Miller, W. E., & Jennings, M. K. (1986). *Parties in transition: A longitudinal study of party elites and party supporters*. Russell Sage.

Mudde, C. (2013). Three decades of populist radical right parties in Western Europe. *European Journal of Political Research*, *52*, 1–19.

Mudde, C., & Kaltwasser, C. R. (2013). Populism. In M. Freeden & M. Stears (Eds.), *The Oxford handbook of political ideologies*. Oxford University Press.

Müller, J.-W. (2016). *What is populism?* University of Pennsylvania Press.

Mutz, D. C. (2018). Status threat, not economic hardship, explains the 2016 presidential vote. *Proceedings of the National Academy of Sciences (PNAS)*.

Oliver, J. E., & Rahn, W. M. (2016). Rise of the trumpenvolk: Populism in the 2016 election. *The ANNALS of the American Academy of Political and Social Science, 667*, 189–206.

Olorunnipa, T., Janes, C., Sonmez, F., Itkowitz, C., & Wagner, J. (2020, August 18). Joe Biden officially becomes the Democratic Party's nominee on the convention's second night. *Washington Post*. Retrieved from https://www.washingtonpost.com/elections/2020/08/18/democratic-national-convention-live-updates/.

Oswald, M., & Robertson, J. (2020). A constitutional crisis, Norm derogation and the broader impact of partisan polarization in contemporary American politics'. In M. Oswald (Ed.), *Mobilization, representation and responsiveness in the American democracy* (pp. 3–36). Palgrave Macmillan.

R Development Core Team. (2008). R: A language and environment for statistical computing. *R Foundation for Statistical Computing*. ISBN 3-900051-07-0. http://www.R-project.org

Reny, T., Collingwood, L., & Valenzuela, A. A. (2019). Vote switching in the 2016 election: How racial and immigration attitudes, not economics, explain shifts in White voting. *Public Opinion Quarterly, 83*(1), 91–113.

Sargent, G. (2017). 'Feel the Bern': Hillary's agonizing loss and the future of the Democratic Party. In L. J. Sabato, K. Kondik, & G. Skelley (Eds.), *Trumped: The 2016 Election that broke all the rules* (1st ed., pp. 112–122). Rowman and Littlefield.

Schaffner, B., MacWilliams, M., & Nteta, T. (2018). Understanding white polarization in the 2016 vote for president: The sobering role of racism and sexism. *Political Science Quarterly, 133*(1), 9–34.

Schmidt, E. (2020). CCES 2017, team module of Indiana University (IU). Retrieved from https://doi.org/10.7910/DVN/HOQOIF, Harvard Dataverse, V1, UNF:6:acHXpibx3TbbBKL8lopaUg==.

Shafer, B. E. (1988). *Bifurcated politics*. Oxford University Press.

Sides, J., Tesler, M., & Vavreck, L. (2018). *Identity crisis: The 2016 presidential campaign and the battle for the meaning of America*. Princeton University Press.

Smidt, C. D. (2017). Polarization and the decline of the American floating voter. *American Journal of Political Science, 61*(2), 365–381.

Tesler, M. (2016). *Post-racial or most-racial? Race and politics in the Obama era*. University of Chicago Press.

Urbinati, N. (2019). Political theory of populism. *Annual Review of Political Science, 22*, 111–127.

Westwood, S. J., & Peterson, E. (2020). The inseparability of race and partisanship in the United States. *Political Behavior*, forthcoming. Available https://doi.org/10.1007/s11109-020-09648-9.

White, J. K. (2016). Donald Trump and the scourge of populism. *The Forum, 14*(3), 265–279.

Wickham, H. (2009). *ggplot2: Elegant graphics for data analysis*. Springer. http://ggplot2.org.

Williams, J. C. (2017). *White working class: Overcoming class cluelessness in America*. Harvard Business Review Press.

Wong, T. K. (2017). *The politics of immigration: Partisanship, demographic change, and American national identity*. Oxford University Press.

Part XI

Consequences of Populism & Anti-Populist Discourse

CHAPTER 37

New Parties, Populism, and Parliamentary Polarization: Evidence from Plenary Debates in the German *Bundestag*

Marcel Lewandowsky, Julia Schwanholz, Christoph Leonhardt, and Andreas Blätte

INTRODUCTION

The relationship between populism and representative democracy is ambiguous. Populists display hostility towards the actors and institutions of representative democracy, accusing them of limiting, if not contradicting, the people's will. The challenge they present to the established parties of the political mainstream is twofold. First, populists claim to support 'niche' issues that might appeal to a significant share of mainstream voters. Second, populists criticize the established parties, calling into question their legitimacy to speak for the citizens, accusing them of corruption, and portraying them as disconnected. Yet populism is not limited to a distinct group of parties, nor are new parties necessarily populist. While many new parties are indeed populist (Hobolt & Tilley, 2016), new parties generally present themselves as an alternative to the establishment, oftentimes claiming to speak up for those who

---

M. Lewandowsky (✉)
Center for European Studies, University of Florida, Gainesville, FL, USA
e-mail: mlewandowsky@ufl.edu

J. Schwanholz · C. Leonhardt · A. Blätte
Institute of Political Science, University of Duisburg-Essen, Duisburg, Germany
e-mail: julia.schwanholz@uni-due.de

C. Leonhardt
e-mail: christoph.leonhardt@uni-due.de

A. Blätte
e-mail: andreas.blaette@uni-due.de

© The Author(s), under exclusive license to Springer Nature Switzerland AG 2022
M. Oswald (ed.), *The Palgrave Handbook of Populism*,
https://doi.org/10.1007/978-3-030-80803-7_37

are not represented (Lucardie, 2000), and therefore transporting this aspect of populism into the political discourse. Not all parties, however, claim to represent the will of the 'homogenous' people and are therefore populist in the full sense as the concept contains both anti-elitism and people-centrism (Mudde, 2004). In turn, mainstream parties have a number of reactions at their disposal, such as engaging or disengaging their populist contesters; or seeking proximity or distance from the issues championed by populists (Heinze, 2018, 2020).

When parties that make extensive use of populist rhetoric join legislative bodies, this shapes the parliamentary party systems in two ways. First, they address the mainstream parties, forcing them either to copy the anti-establishment profile of the former or to distance themselves from it. Second, depending on the position of mainstream parties on the issues, the populist presence can lead to increasing polarization; as some mainstream parties shift closer to the populists' position and others reject it, the distance between them increases and discourse becomes more divided. The advent of populism in parliament would hence make the core institution of parliamentary democracy a site of political division.

This analysis therefore addresses how populism shapes parliamentary discourse when new parties, populists and non-populists, enter the stage. It does so by investigating the following aspects of plenary debate: (1) the use of populist rhetoric, (2) the overall level of polarization on the populists' core issues before and after they were represented, and (3) the distance of the other parties on this issue, respectively. The Federal Republic of Germany is a particularly interesting context in this regard, which had a highly stable and concentrated party system between 1961 and 1980 and then witnessed new parties successively arriving in the *Bundestag*: the Greens in 1983, the Party of Democratic Socialism (PDS) in 1990, the Left in 2005,[1] and the Alternative for Germany (AfD) in 2017. The Greens and the PDS have made use of anti-establishment rhetoric but are not considered populist; the Left and the AfD, however, represent left and right populist parties.[2] Germany is thus a case where both new populists and non-populists have emerged, allowing for a comparison of both scenarios and for conclusions to be drawn on the extent to which populism has altered parliamentary discourse. The focus on parliamentary discourse reflects its importance for democracy. Parliament is the primary arena of debates between government and opposition, in which parties, according to their share of support in the population, articulate their position and represent the interests of their constituents (Sarcinelli & Tenscher, 2000). All communication in parliament is therefore located at the 'heart' of representative democracy.

Methodically, we employed a quantitative text analysis of parliamentary speeches to measure both populism and issue-based polarization. The quantitative approach to text rendered it possible to cover periods of time that could not be analyzed by qualitative means. By observing three legislative periods for each party (except for the AfD, which only entered the *Bundestag* in 2017), we were able to examine parliamentary discourse in the legislative period before and after the party in question had entered parliament. The data base for this analysis is the GermaParl corpus of parliamentary debates (Blätte & Blessing, 2018) that has been extended for the purpose of this analysis to cover debates relevant here.

In the next section, we will overview the interplay of new populist parties and polarization in parliament before briefly sketching how the formerly 'hyper-stable' German party system has been characterized by the arrival of anti-establishment and populist contenders. After explaining our methodology and data in the subsequent section, we will extensively discuss polarization and populism in the German *Bundestag* before interpreting and contextualizing the results in the final part.

Populism, New Parties, and Polarization

In the past several decades, new parties, many of them populists, have made their way into the parliaments of almost all European countries (Hobolt & Tilley, 2016). Despite numerous definitions—and lively academic debate about the nature of populism (e.g., Aslanidis, 2016)—it is safe to say that populism has a 'Manichean outlook, in which there are only friends and foes', and considers society to be 'ultimately separated into two homogeneous and antagonistic groups, "the pure people" versus "the corrupt elite". Populists argue that politics should be an expression of the volonté générale (general will) of the people' (Mudde, 2004, pp. 544, 562). They claim to be the only legitimate representatives of the people, with whom they form an 'organic' relationship, embodying the voice of a politically homogenous *Volksgeist* (Müller, 2016, p. 186). In this sense, populism is both a set of ideas (Hawkins & Rovira Kaltwasser, 2017), which manifests in party ideologies (Rooduijn & Pauwels, 2011), and parties' political communication (Franzmann, 2016). At the same time, it is a political style in which populists seek to embody the *vox populi* through bad manners, direct appeals to the people, and a portrayal of democracy in crisis (Moffitt & Tormey, 2014).

These characteristics shape the behavior of populist parties in parliament in two ways. First, they represent niche issues—that is, issues that have not been emphasized by the political mainstream (Wagner & Meyer, 2017)—and increase the visibility of these issues by discussing them in the legislative body. Populist radical left parties often highlight the welfare state issue; populist radical right parties, on the other hand, focus on the topic of migration and integration. Second, populist parties focus on the parliamentary functions of scrutiny (e.g., through written and oral questions) and communication (by performing anti-establishment attitudes), with less focus on the tools available to them for policymaking compared to mainstream parties (Louwerse & Otjes, 2019). While anti-elitism and people-centrism are defining features of the ideology of populist parties (Rooduijn & Pauwels, 2011), the populist appeal as a feature of political communication is not restricted to them. Anti-elitism, for example, is also a defining feature of many new parties, who present themselves as alternatives to the establishment as a source of their self-proclaimed legitimacy (Lucardie, 2000).

When challenged by populists, mainstream parties face a twofold threat. First, the newcomers often deal with issues neglected by the mainstream. As a result, the latter is forced to recalibrate their strategy regarding 'niche' issues by either changing their own position (towards or against it) or attempting to either decrease or increase the salience of the issue (Meguid, 2005). For example, the success of radical right parties encourages mainstream right parties to adopt the position of the populists on the issue of immigration (Han, 2015). Yet this effect is not limited to mainstream right parties. Center-left parties tend to struggle with the strategic implications of successful populist radical right competitors. Whereas in some cases, they have rejected the positions of the radical right, they even have embraced more restrictive positions on immigration in others (Bale et al., 2010). Second, mainstream parties are put on the defensive when populists accuse the political establishment of corruption and further claim to defend the 'genuine will of the people' against the elite. Since the populist appeal directly addresses the mainstream parties, it forces a reaction, either engaging or disengaging the populist contender (Heinze, 2018, 2020). Research has shown, however, that unlike issue positions, populism is not 'contagious' and mainstream parties do not embrace a more populist profile to imitate successful challengers (Rooduijn et al., 2014).

The impact of populism on mainstream parties on (non-parliamentary) party competition aside, little is known about how populism shapes the legislative discourse. Based on the previous considerations, four hypotheses can be formulated. First, all new parties, not only genuine populists, employ anti-establishment rhetoric before and after they enter parliament. Second, populist rhetoric is likely to remain a feature of the new parties as mainstream parties would rather avoid it. Third, the entry of new parties into parliament leads to increasing polarization on their core issues. This is due to the variance in ideological proximity among the mainstream parties; while some will seek to shift towards the position of the populists, others will distance themselves from them (Enyedi, 2008, p. 288).[3] Finally, the impact of populist parties is dynamic. A newly successful populist party, whether left or right, will have a more substantial effect on the mainstream parties than a populist party that has been around for some time. New populist parties threaten the electoral domains of mainstream parties and drive them to strategic responses. Furthermore, with the new party having existed for a certain amount of time, the mainstream parties might have adapted to the situation. In general, populist parties represent a significant change in the strategic environment and thus might lead to rapid adjustment. Over time, a reformation of the party system in terms of the acceptance or rejection of positions of the populists by the mainstream parties is likely. Populist parties, in particular, might adapt to the institutions they operate in through learning and training, and their populist appeal might deteriorate the longer they remain in parliament.

NEW POPULIST AND NON-POPULIST PARTIES IN GERMANY

For decades, Germany represented one of the most stable party systems in western Europe. Between 1957 and 1983, it consisted of three major parties: the center-right Christian Democratic Union (CDU/CSU),[4] the center-left Social Democratic Party (SPD), and the market-liberal Free Democratic Party (FDP). In its heyday, around 90% of the votes went to Union and SPD, with the FDP functioning as a coalition partner to form minimal winning coalitions with the Liberals as a junior partner.

Although radical and niche parties existed, they did not manage to cross the 5% electoral threshold. Nonetheless, the 'hyper stable' and concentrated phase of the German party system came to an end with the appearance of the Greens (*Die Grünen*) in the late 1970s. The Greens emerged from the environmental, anti-nuclear, and peace movements, as well as the women's movement, all of which were the result of a postmaterialist transformation of the German political spectrum that took place from the late 1960s onwards. These 'new values' were not represented by the established parties. This electoral niche carried the Greens into the *Bundestag* in the 1983 election. Although mistrust of political elites was not (yet) a major feature in the German electorate in the late 1970s and early 1980s (Müller-Rommel, 1993, p. 194), the political style of the Greens was characterized by an anti-establishment attitude, which they expressed through their outer appearance, wearing beards, sneakers, and sweaters, and knitting during parliamentary debates. Rhetorically, they described themselves as the 'anti-party party'. Their anti-elitist outlook notwithstanding, they lacked the people-centered appeal that is typical of populist parties.[5]

With the reunification of Germany, the Party of Democratic Socialism (PDS) entered the *Bundestag*. As a post-Marxist successor party of the SED (*Sozialistische Einheitspartei Deutschlands*)—the former ruling party of the German Democratic Republic (GDR)—the PDS was a radical left, but not a populist, party. It had too many ties with the elites of the former GDR to be considered populist, and it operated on a Marxist–Leninist ideological profile, or at least what was left of it after 1990. Nevertheless, it claimed to speak for the 'forgotten' citizens of the former German Democratic Republic as well as to represent the interests of former supporters of the GDR (Decker & Hartleb, 2007). However, the party remained insignificant in the West until the introduction of the controversial welfare reforms by the SPD/Green federal government in 2003. The Agenda 2010, which embraced a more liberal welfare state agenda, led to the emergence of Labor and Social Justice— The Electoral Alternative (WASG) in 2004. In the 2005 federal election, PDS and WASG competed under one banner, and, in 2007, the two parties merged, resulting in the Left (*Die Linke*), which focused on the defense of the welfare state against 'neoliberalism'. While there was no PDS party group between 2002 and 2005—despite two direct mandates—the party has been constantly represented in the *Bundestag* since 2005. In contrast to its predecessor, the

PDS, the Left embraces a strong anti-establishment attitude and resembles the profile of a populist radical left party (Olsen, 2018).

Populism is a latecomer in the Federal Republic of Germany. In the party systems of some of its neighbor countries, such as Denmark, Austria, France, and Switzerland, populist parties successfully established themselves as early as the 1980s; Germany, however, represents an exceptional case in this regard (Berbuir et al., 2015, pp. 158–161). The Federal Republic's immunity against the populist radical right came to an end when the Alternative for Germany (AfD) managed to gain seats in parliament in the 2017 federal election. Founded in 2013, the AfD originally promoted a Eurosceptical, but not yet far-right agenda (Arzheimer, 2015); eventually, however, the AfD turned into a populist radical right party, especially in the course of the so-called 'refugee crisis' in 2015 and 2016. In the 2017 federal election, the AfD emerged as the largest opposition party in parliament, combining an anti-immigrant agenda with a harsh populist profile (Art, 2018). With the electoral success of the AfD, the party system became even more segmented, this time towards the right side of the spectrum.

In sum, since the 1980s, the German party system has witnessed the arrival of four new parties. Approximately every ten years, a new party has established itself: the Greens in the early 1980s, the PDS in the early 1990s, the left-wing populist Left in the mid-2000s, and the right-wing populist AfD in 2017. The two early new arrivals were non-populist. The Greens embraced an anti-establishment profile in the first ten years of their existence but did side with the 'pure people'. Moreover, the PDS was too closely associated with the old elites of the GDR to be considered truly populist. The post-millennium new parties, the AfD and the Left, are considered genuinely populist parties. Therefore, we are able to observe the effects of four different parties at four different points in time. In the next section, we will elaborate on our methodology.

Data and Method

We analyzed two phenomena, polarization and populism as expressed in parliament, utilizing a quantitative text analysis. The analysis is based on a corpus of parliamentary debates from the German *Bundestag*, the *GermaParl* corpus created within the PolMine project (Blätte & Blessing, 2018), which has been extended for the purpose of this analysis to cover all legislative periods relevant here. The period of investigation was limited to legislative periods 9–19 (1980–2020). We only considered speeches delivered by members of parliament. Speakers not belonging to a parliamentary group—the president or ministers without a parliamentary seat—were excluded. To measure parliamentary polarization on new parties' core issues, we only included speeches to which we could assign a substantial topic using a topic modelling approach before employing the scaling approach. Thus, the analysis of polarization was based on a subset of about 113,000 speeches. The analysis of the use of populist language was based on all speeches delivered by members of parliament in the period of interest (about 190,000 speeches).

Measuring Populist Speech

Following previous research, we understand populist speech-making as the relative usage of respective language in a parliamentary speech (Rooduijn & Pauwels, 2011). This approach has been employed previously by the authors and has been described by Julia Schwanholz et al. (2020). To capture the occurrences of populist speech in a text, we used a dictionary-based approach. Starting from a word list suggested by Matthijs Rooduijn and Teun Pauwels (2011, p. 1283), we created a lexicon of key terms that indicated the use of populist references. Based on these occurrences, it was possible to calculate the frequency of populist terms relative to the length of a speech. To increase the validity and reliability of the approach (Grimmer & Stewart, 2013, p. 275), we examined the context in which the identified keywords occurred (using a keyword-in-context analysis) on a sample basis and defined context words which must or must not occur in the vicinity of the key term.[6]

Measuring Polarization

We operationalized polarization as the maximum ideological distance between parliamentary groups in the German Bundestag in a given legislative period. Following Sven-Oliver Proksch and Jonathan Slapin, who argued that "parliamentary speech is primarily an act of position-taking" (2015, p. 17), we assumed that speeches reflect the ideological positions of political actors and therefore serve as an appropriate basis for measuring ideological positions. Measuring preference variance or ideological position based on text has emerged as a long-standing interest in the discipline (Lowe, 2016, p. 2).[7] The Wordfish algorithm proposed by Slapin and Proksch has established itself as the de facto standard to measure such positions.

The central assumption is that the relative word usage of parties provides insight into their political positions (Slapin & Proksch, 2008, p. 708). Wordfish is based on several additional assumptions, the first of which is the stability of word meaning (Slapin & Proksch, 2008, p. 711). This assumption presents a potential challenge when new vocabulary is introduced since the model cannot distinguish between an agenda shift and ideological change (Proksch & Slapin, 2009a, p. 332; Slapin & Proksch, 2008, p. 711;). Furthermore, Wordfish 'assumes the principle dimension extracted from texts captures the political content of those texts' (Slapin & Proksch, 2008, p. 711). It estimates a position for each document on a single dimension that is dependent on the selection of the documents (Proksch & Slapin, 2009a, p. 331, cp. Goet, 2019, p. 525).[8]

Working with Wordfish thus requires documents that are (a) relatively stable in word meaning and that are (b) on the same principle dimension (i.e., thematically similar to each other). Accordingly, we subsetted all speeches of the corpus along three dimensions: the parliamentary group, the primary topic of the speech, and the legislative period the speech was made in. We were interested in the legislative period before, during, and—whenever possible—after a party's entry into the Bundestag. We attempted to keep word meanings relatively stable by restricting the maximum number of years covered to 12 (the duration of three full legislative periods) and by limiting the analysis to one single topic, assuming that this satisfied the need to 'carefully select the words that enter the analysis' as Proksch and Slapin have suggested (2009a, p. 332).

This topical selection process significantly influenced the empirical analysis. We clustered all speeches of a single parliamentary group in a given legislative period about a single topic. While preparing the input data, we applied only some soft vocabulary reduction (Denny & Spirling, 2018). Details of this process, as well as some validation steps, can be found in the online appendix.

Parliamentary Debates and New (Populist) Parties in Germany

In this section, we will compare the impact of the four new parties on parliamentary discourse in Germany. We analyzed the extent to which parliamentary debates have become more polarized after these parties entered the *Bundestag*.

First, we display the salience of the new parties' core issues—the 'niche' they represent—across all election periods (1–19) through the share of speeches with this topic (Fig. 37.1). For the Greens, we observe environmental politics, with the PDS representing one end of the issue of German re-unification. Its de facto successor, the Left, embraced the welfare state issue and the AfD,

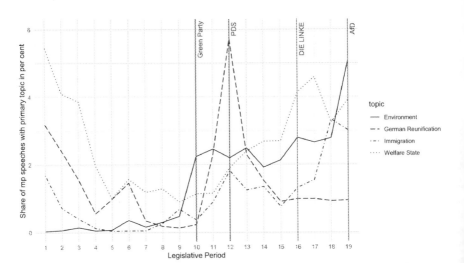

Fig. 37.1 Salience of selected issues in *Bundestag* speeches

in particular, emphasized the topic of immigration. Although different trends can be identified over time, at no point in time could these four political fields be considered fringe issues. Nevertheless, we observe an increase in salience in the respective issue whenever the 'owning' party entered parliament. The environmental issue increased significantly when the Greens gained seats in the 10th period. Similar findings applied to re-unification (PDS; 12th period) and the welfare state (the Left; 16th period). Only the salience of the immigration issue slightly decreased after the AfD entered the *Bundestag* in the 19th period, most likely due to the emergence of the refugee crisis in the summer of 2015, when the AfD was not yet represented in parliament but the salience of the issue was already high.

Our measurement of the level of polarization in parliament on the respective issues is shown in Fig. 37.2. The issues are observed over three election periods each, with the first bar indicating the level of polarization in the last term before the party was elected into parliament. The second and the third bar show polarization in the first and the second term in which the party was in parliament. Since the last federal election occurred in 2017, we only included two terms for the AfD.

When the Greens entered the *Bundestag* in the 10th term, polarization on the environmental issue clearly increased compared to the 9th period and even more so in the subsequent term. Before the PDS entered parliament in the 12th period, the debate on re-unification was highly polarized but saw a decrease afterwards. When the Left joined the *Bundestag* in the 16th period, the degree of polarization in debates on the welfare state slightly increased compared to the preceding term. With their reformation and subsequent re-election to the 17th *Bundestag*, the polarization in this issue slightly increased

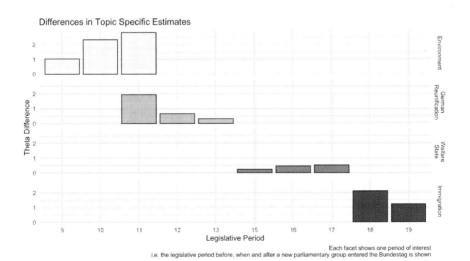

Fig. 37.2 Polarization in selected issues in *Bundestag* speeches

again. Finally, debates on migration were already polarized even before the AfD joined parliament, likely due to the 2015 refugee crisis. When the AfD joined in the 19th period, polarization decreased only slightly.

Overall, no clear pattern emerged showing that polarization increased with the advent of new parties, either populist or non-populist. In the following section, we will examine the positions of the other parliamentary groups and populism considering the four parties in question.

We first consider the legislative periods 9, 10, and 11 (Fig. 37.3). Before the Greens were in parliament, the parties' polarization on environmental issues was relatively low, with CDU/CSU and FDP close together and the SPD in a more distant position. This changed, however, after the Greens entered the *Bundestag* in 1983. While Union and Liberals somewhat retained their position, the Greens occupied the other extreme point, with the SPD in the center. In the 11th term, the SPD shifted closer to the Greens, which resulted in a strongly polarized parliament between two blocs. Populist language was mostly present in speeches from CDU/CSU and SPD members of parliament and rarely articulated by liberal MPs in the 9th period. Upon the arrival of the Greens, the newcomers' speeches displayed a distinct populist profile, followed by CDU/CSU, SPD, and FDP. In the subsequent period, after the Greens had been re-elected, they remained the most populist parliamentary group, but the SPD, which seemed to have embraced its oppositional role, followed suit as second. Moreover, the CDU/CSU made greater use of populism in their speeches than they had in previous terms.

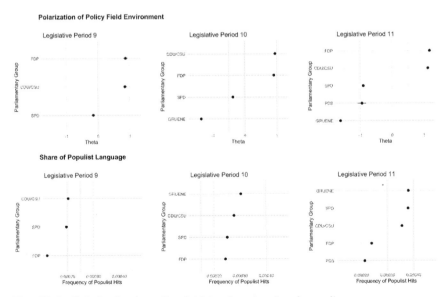

Fig. 37.3 Polarization in policy field 'environment' and populism

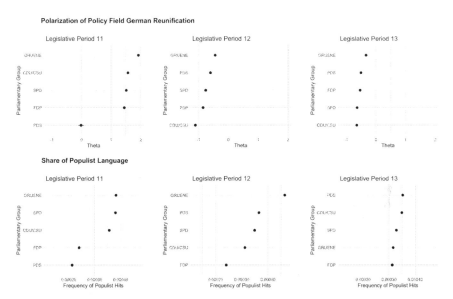

Fig. 37.4 Polarization in policy field 'reunification' and populism

Figure 37.4 conveys how, in the last legislative term of divided Germany, opinions on re-unification were highly uniform across party lines, with the exception of the East German PDS, whose members of the People's Chamber (*Volkskammer*) joined the *Bundestag* for the last two months of the term. This changed, however, with the re-unified parliament in the 12th period when all parties, including the PDS, embraced similar positions, a picture which remained the same in the subsequent term. Afterall, re-unification itself was hardly controversial. While the PDS People's Chamber deputies took a fundamentally different position, after 1990 they were simply faced with historical facts they could not undo. Moreover, at the time, the PDS in re-unified Germany was not a populist party; in the first years, the PDS represented the old regime of the GDR, advocating for the interests of its former citizens but also the rehabilitation of its elites (Gapper, 2003: 66). Consequently, the PDS did not make more use of populist language in the 12th term, and its speeches were only slightly more populist than those of the other parties in the 13th *Bundestag*.

When the PDS and the WASG joined forces in 2004/2005, the characteristics of the party changed (Fig. 37.5). Formerly an East German party of the old regime in the 1990s, the Left evolved into a populist left party that emphasized the welfare state issue in the first decade of the new millennium. The change of the Left, however, is not immediately reflected in its behavior in parliament. It was not until the 17th legislative period that the speeches of the Left became the most populist ones in parliament, followed by the Greens by some distance. The governing parties CDU/CSU and FDP as well as the

Fig. 37.5 Polarization in policy field 'welfare state' and populism

SPD used populist wording to a much lesser degree. Regarding polarization on the welfare state issue, the differences between the parties became slightly more pronounced over time, while the parties had been relatively close to each other in the 16th *Bundestag*. In the 17th period, the Left represented one extreme point on the welfare state issue, followed by the Greens, while Christian Democrats and Liberals as well as the SPD took a more moderate position. Yet overall, the positions of the parties were relatively close to each other, so that polarization remained low on this issue.

The most recent new party to gain seats in German parliament was the populist radical right AfD. Previously, the Left was by far the most populist parliamentary group (Fig. 37.6). This was still the case in the subsequent term after 2017, but the AfD MPs embraced populism in their speeches to almost the same degree, while all other parties remained on the other side of the scale (Schwanholz et al., 2020, p. 192). Furthermore, the pattern for the immigration issue is relatively clear cut. Before the AfD joined the Bundestag, the governing parties CDU/CSU and SPD and the opposing Greens and Left were close to each other, respectively. In the subsequent term, the distances between the parties were more fine-grained, with the CDU/CSU and AfD representing the extreme points of the scale.

Overall, the findings from the *Bundestag* show that first, both the degree of populist language and the uniqueness of the position on the respective core issue vary with the party in question. With regard to the 'contagiousness' of populism, different patterns appeared. After the Greens joined the *Bundestag*, they made slightly more use of populist wording than the other

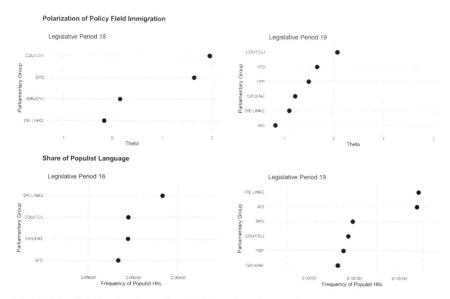

Fig. 37.6 Polarization in policy field 'immigration' and populism

parties. Whereas the PDS did not stand out in terms of populism, it became more populist after it re-entered parliament as the Left. The clearest separation between parliamentary groups that make strong use of populist language and those who do not was found before and immediately after the AfD gained seats in the 2017 election. Speeches by the Left and AfD MPs were clearly populist, those of all other parties to a much lesser extent. Second, only when the Greens and, to a lesser degree, the Left (re-)entered parliament, the overall level of polarization in their core issues increased. The other two topics—reunification and immigration—saw a lower level of polarization. While in all issues, with the exception of re-unification, differences between the new contenders and the other parties could be seen, it was only on environmental issues that the new party took a significantly distanced position.

Summary

In this chapter, we examined how populism shaped German parliamentary discourse. We accounted for two genuine left and right populist parties (The Left and the AfD) and two non-populist parties, one of which previously embraced anti-establishment stances (the Greens and the PDS).

Once in parliament, all new contenders, with the exception of the PDS, made some use of populist language, whether they were genuine populists or not. In the case of the Greens, this has changed over time, with the party eventually embracing a more mainstream profile. The Left and the AfD on the other hand have remained populist. With the arrival of genuine populist parties both on the left and on the right, established parties in the German parliament employed more exclusionary tactics, rather than trying to cultivate their populist appeal. This indicates that the overall profile of the populists is more likely to encourage the other parties to distance themselves from their contenders. Comparative studies would have to demonstrate whether this finding holds in other countries.

New parties, populists or not, neither increase the general level of polarization nor do the other parties react to their arrival with distinct pattern of shifts in core issues. In fact, the impact of new and populist parties on plenary polarization varies according to the topic in question. Overall, their impact does not take place on the issue they champion but appears in how they present themselves as contesters of the establishment. True populists, in particular, thus shape the parliamentary debate through their appeal, yet not by 'pulling' the others to their side, but by 'pushing' them in the other direction. In the German *Bundestag*, the populist/non-populist divide is growing. Populism in parliament is thus not necessarily contagious; rather, it appears to function as a strategic option that new actors make use of and that is occasionally mimicked by the mainstream parties. With the arrival of genuine populists, the divide has become much clearer, and the mainstream parties appear to opt for demarcation rather than imitation.

Notes

1. Formally, the Left was a reformation of the PDS; yet due to the fact that it resulted from a merger with another party (WASG), we consider it a new party.
2. Whether the PDS is a populist party is contested in the literature. For instance, Decker and Hartleb (2006) classify the party as populist. However, we agree with Neu (2003), who refers to the complexity of the party, noting that while the party often embraces populist communication, it is not genuinely populist in regard to its history and ideology. For the Greens, there is no examination or conflict on this issue in the literature, and they have never been classified as populist to begin with (e.g., van Haute, 2016).
3. For example, when the populist radical right Party for Freedom (PVV) entered parliament, the Christian Democrats (CDA) in part adopted their positions on immigration, while the Labor Party (PvdA) rejected this shift to the right (de Lange, 2018).
4. The Union is composed of the CDU and the Christian Social Union (CSU), the latter being an organizationally autonomous Bavarian party, yet closely associated with the CDU.
5. After German reunification in 1990, the West German Greens failed to gain seats in parliament and were represented only by the eight MPs of the Eastern Electoral Alliance 90. In 1993, Alliance 90 and the Greens merged into one nationwide party which, from 1994 on, has been represented continuously in the Bundestag. It was also in the early 1990s when the Greens developed a more moderate profile and turned from an anti-establishment to an ecological reformist party (Mende, 2012). From 1998 to 2005, the party was the smaller partner of an SPD/Green coalition.

6. The dictionary used is available in the online appendix of this paper: https://polmine.github.io/populism_and_polarisation/index.html.
7. There is a growing number of extensions of and alternatives to the Wordfish algorithm used here. Wordshoal extends Wordfish with "within-debate scaling" (Lauderdale & Herzog, 2016, p. 375). Using classifier accuracy (Goet, 2019; Peterson & Spirling, 2018) or word embeddings (Rheault & Cochrane, 2020) utilizes machine learning approaches to identify the distinctiveness or ideological placement of parties in speech.
8. An additional concern is that Wordfish as well as other statistical scaling models were developed with manifestos in mind. These can be very different from political speeches, given the latter's' limited scope in both substance and length (Proksch & Slapin, 2009b, p. 595). According to Goet (2019, p. 520), speeches can be described as 'much messier', presented in a less polished format and with speakers often going off-topic.

Literature

Art, D. (2018). The AfD and the end of containment in Germany? *German Politics and Society, 36*(2), 76–86.

Arzheimer, K. (2015). The AfD: Finally a successful right-wing populist Eurosceptic party for Germany? *West European Politics, 38*(3), 535–556.

Aslanidis, P. (2016). Is populism an ideology? A refutation and a new perspective. *Political Studies, 64*(1), 88–104.

Bale, T., Green-Pedersen, C., Krouwel, A., Luther, K. R., & Sitter, N. (2010). If you can't beat them, join them? Explaining social democratic responses to the challenge from the populist radical right in western Europe. *Political Studies, 58*(3), 410–426.

Berbuir, N., Lewandowsky, M., & Siri, J. (2015). The AfD and its sympathisers: Finally a right-wing populist movement in Germany? *German Politics, 24*(2), 154–178.

Blätte, A., & Blessing, A. (2018). The GermaParl corpus of parliamentary protocols. *Proceedings of the Eleventh International Conference on Language Resources and Evaluation* (LREC 2018). ELRA = European Language Resources Association.

Decker, F., & Hartleb, F. (2006). Populismus auf schwierigem Terrain. Die rechten und linken Herausfordererparteien in der Bundesrepublik. In F. Decker (Ed.), *Populismus. Gefahr für die Demokratie oder nützliches Korrektiv?* (pp. 191–215). Springer VS.

Decker, F., & Hartleb, F. (2007). Populism on difficult terrain: The right- and left-wing challenger parties in the Federal Republic of Germany. *German Politics, 16*(4), 434–454.

de Lange, S. L. (2018). From limited multipartism to extended multipartism? The impact of the Lijst Pim Fortuyn, the Partij voor de Vrijheid and the Socialistische Partij on the Dutch party system. In S. Wolinetz & A. Zaslove (Eds.), *Absorbing the blow. Populist parties and their impact on parties and party systems* (pp. 55–82). ECPR Press.

Denny, M. J., & Spirling, A. (2018). Text preprocessing for unsupervised learning: Why it matters, when it misleads, and what to do about it. *Political Analysis, 26*, 168–189.

Enyedi, Z. (2008). The social and attitudinal basis of political parties: Cleavage politics revisited. *European Review*, *16*(3), 287–304.

Franzmann, S. T. (2016). Calling the ghost of populism: The AfD's strategic and tactical agendas until the EP election 2014. *German Politics*, *25*(4), 457–479.

Gapper, S. (2003). The rise and fall of Germany's party of democratic socialism. *German Politics*, *12*(2), 65–85.

Goet, N. D. (2019). Measuring polarisation with text analysis: Evidence from the UK House of Commons, 1811–2015. *Political Analysis*, *27*(4), 518–539.

Grimmer, J., & Stewart, B. M. (2013). Text as data: The promise and pitfalls of automatic content analysis methods for political texts. *Political Analysis*, *21*(3), 267–297.

Han, K. J. (2015). The impact of radical right-wing parties on the positions of mainstream parties regarding multiculturalism. *West European Politics*, *38*(3), 557–576.

Hawkins, K., & Rovira Kaltwasser, C. (2017). What the ideational study of populism can teach us, and what it can't. *Swiss Political Science Review*, *23*(4), 526–542.

Heinze, A.-S. (2018). Strategies of mainstream parties towards their right-wing populist challengers: Denmark, Norway, Sweden and Finland in comparison. *West European Politics*, *41*(2), 387–409.

Heinze, A.-S. (2020). *Strategien gegen Rechtspopulismus? Der Umgang mit der AfD in Landesparlamenten*. Nomos.

Hobolt, S., & Tilley, J. (2016). Fleeing the centre: The rise of challenger parties in the aftermath of the euro crisis. *West European Politics*, *39*(5), 971–991.

Lauderdale, B. E., & Herzog, A. (2016). Measuring political positions from legislative speech. *Political Analysis*, *24*(3), 374–394.

Louwerse, T., & Otjes, S. (2019). How populists wage opposition: Parliamentary opposition behaviour and populism in Netherlands. *Political Studies*, *67*(2), 479–495.

Lowe, W. (2016). *Putting it all on the line: Some unified theory for text scaling (formerly 'scaling things we can count' and 'there's (basically) only one way to do: Some unifying theory for text scaling models')*. Paper Prepared for the American Political Science Association Meeting September 2013, Chicago. Draft April 2016.

Lucardie, P. (2000). Prophets, purifiers and prolocutors. Towards a theory on the emergence of new parties. *Party Politics*, *6*(2), 175–185.

Meguid, B. M. (2005). Competition between unequals: The role of mainstream party strategy in Niche Party Success. *American Political Science Review*, *99*(3), 347–359.

Mende, S. (2012). Von der „Anti-Parteien-Partei" zur „ökologischen Reformpartei". Die Grünen und der Wandel des Politischen. *Archiv Für Sozialgeschichte*, *52*, 273–315.

Moffitt, B., & Tormey, S. (2014). Rethinking populism: Politics, mediatisation and political style. *Political Studies*, *62*(2), 31–397.

Mudde, C. (2004). The populist Zeitgeist. *Government and Opposition*, *39*(3), 541–563.

Müller, J.-W. (2016). Was ist Populismus? *Zeitschrift Für Politische Theorie*, *7*(2), 187–201.

Müller-Rommel, F. (1993). *Grüne Parteien in Westeuropa*. Springer VS.

Neu, V. (2003). Die PDS: Eine populistische Partei? In N. Werz (Ed.), *Populismus. Populisten in Übersee und Europa* (pp. 263–277). VS Verlag für Sozialwissenschaften.

Olsen, J. (2018). The left party and the AfD. Populist competitors in Eastern Germany. *German Politics and Society, 36*(1), 70–83.

Peterson, A., & Spirling, A. (2018). Classification accuracy as a substantive quantity of interest: Measuring Polarisation in westminster systems. *Political Analysis, 26*, 120–128.

Proksch, S.-O., & Slapin, J. B. (2009a). How to avoid pitfalls in statistical analysis of political texts: The Case of Germany. *German Politics, 18*(3), 323–344.

Proksch, S.-O., & Slapin, J. B. (2009b). Position taking in European parliament speeches. *British Journal of Political Science, 40*(3), 587–611.

Proksch, S.-O., & Slapin, J. B. (2015). *The politics of parliamentary debate. parties, rebels and representation*. Cambridge University Press.

Rheault, L., & Cochrane, C. (2020). Word embeddings for the analysis of ideological placement in parliamentary corpora. *Political Analysis, 28*, 112–133.

Rooduijn, M., de Lange, S. L., & van der Brug, W. (2014). A populist Zeitgeist? Programmatic contagion by populist parties in Western Europe. *Party Politics, 20*(4), 563–575.

Rooduijn, M., & Pauwels, T. (2011). Measuring populism: Comparing two methods of content analysis. *West European Politics, 34*(6), 1272–2123.

Sarcinelli, U., & Tenscher, J. (2000). Vom repräsentativen zum präsentativen Parlamentarismus? Entwurf eines Arenenmodells parlamentarischer Kommunikation. In O. Jarren, K. Imhoff, & R. Blum (Eds.), *Zerfall der Öffentlichkeit?* (pp. 74–96). Westdeutscher Verlag.

Schwanholz, J., Lewandowsky, M., Leonhardt, C., & Blätte, A. (2020). The upsurge of right-wing populism in Germany. In I. Khmelko, F. Stapenhurst, & M. L. Mezey (Eds.), *The rise of populism and the decline of legislatures?* (pp. 184–197). Routledge.

Slapin, J. B., & Proksch, S.-O. (2008). A scaling model for estimating time-series party positions from texts. *American Journal of Political Science, 52*(3), 705–722.

van Haute, E. (2016). *Green parties in Europe*. Routledge.

Wagner, M., & Meyer, T. M. (2017). The radical right as niche parties? The ideological landscape of party systems in Western Europe, 1980–2014. *Political Studies, 65*(1), 84–107.

CHAPTER 38

The Enemy in My House: How Right-Wing Populism Radicalized the Debate About Citizenship in France

Elena Dück and Sebastian Glassner

Introduction

Relief swept European liberals, when Emmanuel Macron won the French presidential election against the right-wing populist Marine Le Pen in 2017. The victory of Macron symbolized hope: Not all was lost, populism would not sweep the European Union (EU) unhampered. However, in May 2019, the Rassemblement national (RN) slightly overtook Macron's République en Marche (LREM) in the European Parliament election, showing that the RN's attraction was rising rather than shrinking. Moreover, the election of populist leaders such as Jair Bolsonaro in Brazil, Donald Trump in the US, Boris Johnson in the UK or the success of the Lega Nord in Italy indicate that the success of nationalist and right-wing populism is an international rather than a regional phenomenon.

While some have argued that populists would be tamed by institutional constraints once in office (Roubini, 2016), others have warned that populists permanently "shifted the bonds of the legitimate discursive space and rendered ideas previously associated with the extreme right acceptable" (Art, 2006, p. 203).[1] Exploring such a discursive shift, in this article we focus on discussions about citizenship and its revocation in France. Our thesis is that narratives that originated within the right-wing populist Front national

---

E. Dück (✉) · S. Glassner
Professorship of International Politics, University of Passau, Passau, Germany
e-mail: elena.dueck@uni-passau.de

S. Glassner
e-mail: sebastian.glassner@uni-passau.de

© The Author(s), under exclusive license to Springer Nature Switzerland AG 2022
M. Oswald (ed.), *The Palgrave Handbook of Populism*,
https://doi.org/10.1007/978-3-030-80803-7_38

FN/RN were adopted by more moderate politicians in security discourses and thus became the new "normal". Furthermore, securitizations, i.e. the construction of a certain issue as a security threat, act as catalysts for these discursive shifts.

We chose to focus on citizenship as, due to its exclusionary nature, citizenship and especially naturalization and denaturalization are ideal topics for nationalist politicians. We conduct a diachronic comparison of the debates about the revocation of citizenship before and after the terrorist attacks in 2015 and the following securitization of the War on Terror (WoT). In so doing, we show that the loss of citizenship is a warranted form of punishment for certain crimes spread form the far-right political spectrum to the left, thus becoming "normalized".

The last extensive debate about citizenship before 2015 took place in 2010, after Sarkozy's "Discours de Grenoble". In this speech, the French President reacted to unrests in the outskirts of Grenoble. He reinforced his "tough-on-crime" policies and called for more expulsions and the reintroduction of a law that would broaden the legal grounds for the revocation of citizenship. In a second step, we analyze the debate about the revocation of citizenship after the terrorist attacks in 2015. We are especially interested in the reactions to this demand, as they allow us to detect if this demand was perceived as being part of the "normal" political positions or considered to be extreme and/or populist. Hence, we conducted a qualitative content analysis. We inductively analyzed eighty documents: parliamentary sessions, articles in *Le Figaro* and *Le Monde* from July to October 2010, respectively, November 2014 to March 2015; and statements by official representatives of the Parti socialiste (PS) and the FN/RN.

In the following, we briefly outline our theoretical assumption about populism and Securitization Theory. Secondly, we summarize the development of citizenship in France. We then turn to the comparison and the results of our empirical analysis. Finally, we discuss the implications of our findings and their relevance in the context of populism, security and citizenship studies.

THEORETICAL FRAMEWORK

Definition of Populism

As the previous contributions show, populism can be conceptualized in different ways, be it strategic (e.g. Jansen, 2011; Roberts, 2006; Weyland, 2017) or ideational (e.g. Moffitt & Tormey, 2014a; Mudde, 2004; Stavrakakis & Katsambekis, 2014). In the following, we consider populism as a thin-centered ideology according to Mudde (2004, p. 543). This is arguably a controversial approach (see Aslanidis, 2016; Freeden, 2017). Yet, we chose the ideological perspective due to our research question and design. The approach allows us to include more than one ideology and thus makes it possible to categorize the various populist movements (Hawkins & Rovira Kaltwasser, 2017,

p. 2; Mudde, 2017, pp. 36–38). Moreover, the ideological approach calls for a qualitative analysis of populist discourses. Thus, we are able to trace elements of right-wing populist core ideology in the French discourse on citizenship.

Mudde's (2004, p. 543) definition implies three central, normative principles of populism:

1. *Anti-institutional*: As the people are the sovereign and the only legitimate source of state action, populism rejects all representative democratic institutions (Skenderovic, 2017, p. 55).
2. *Anti-elite*: As the corrupt elite impedes the realization of the true will of the people, it consequently also impedes good politics in general (Mudde, 2004, p. 547).
3. *Anti-pluralistic*: As populists claim to be the only true representatives of the people, they reject diversity of opinions and special protection of minority rights (Poier et al., 2017, p. 55).

Anti-pluralism is an especially important feature of populism—and even more so of radical right-wing populism—as it highlights the fundamental belief in a homogenous nation or people that can be clearly defined. Following this belief, not all people living in a country are members of the *heartland*. This heartland is an "idealised conception of the community" (Taggart, 2004, p. 274). In the new European populist movements, this community is often connected to the idea of ethnically and culturally homogenous nations.

As populism itself cannot fill "its empty heart", the meaning of "the people" arises from its connection to other ideologies. In the case of the FN/RN this ideology is right-wing nationalism. Right-wing populists in liberal countries draw on nativist values, which are shared by parts of the population. Hence, they (re-)establish the notion that "states should be inhabited exclusively by members of the native group ('the nation') and that non-native elements (persons and ideas) are fundamentally threatening to the homogenous nation-state" (Mudde, 2007, p. 19).

Nativism is dependent on *othering* and the drawing of boundaries between in- and out-groups. Thus, those members of society that stand against the will of the people are, following the populist logic, the enemies of the people (Mudde, 2004, p. 544). There are two dimensions along which these populist divisions operate: On the one hand, they establish a vertical division against the elite, and on the other hand, against other minorities and groups that are – in their view – unduly favored (Poier et al., 2017, p. 52). Therefore, right-wing populism is always identity politics (Müller, 2016, p. 3). While the vertical differentiation is a feature of all forms of populism, the horizontal one is a special characteristic of right-wing populism (March, 2017, pp. 284–285). By drawing this horizontal division, right-wing populists position themselves against those part of the population that are not part of the heartland and therefore do not really belong.

In the case of France, this can be exemplified by the idea (or conspiracy theory) that the country is threatened by an on-going Islamization due to mass immigration and greater acceptance of Muslim customs (horizontal) and that this Islamization is promoted by the liberal establishment (vertical) (Nilsson, 2018, p. 2).[2] The debate about what "makes" a person French (or any other nationality) and when somebody should be able to enter this national community is very apt to implement horizontal division. Furthermore, it creates the illusion of the heartland and its true inhabitants. Thus, following the idea of the heartland, some essentially belong to a nation and others do not. Those who are not *truly* members of this imagined community must—in the right-wing populist logic—earn this privilege. As citizenship is hence not a right of those not truly belonging to the heartland, but a privilege, this privilege should be lost again if an individual fails to prove themselves worthy of it.

Therefore, it is not surprising that the FN has argued in favor of citizenship revocation for criminal offenders, especially if they or their ancestors recently immigrated to France, for almost thirty years and continues to do so. Moreover, by constantly linking crime and migration, the FN/RN is constantly *securitizing* migration and non-white persons.

Securitization Theory

Securitization Theory (ST) originated in the 1980s (Buzan, 1983) and was developed further in the 1990s (Buzan et al., 1998), sparking a debate about the concept of security itself. It has since produced a rich body of work that further develops the theory (Albert & Buzan, 2011; Floyd, 2016, 2019; Huysmans, 2011; Roe, 2008; Stritzel, 2011; Wæver, 1995, 1999, 2011; Williams, 2011) and thorough case studies (Aradau & van Munster, 2009; Bigo, 2002; Buzan, 2006; Huysman, 2006; Salter, 2011). In a nutshell: ST highlights the importance of language in defining what constitutes a threat and hence should be protected against.

During a securitization, a collective is presented as being existentially threatened by a *referent subject* (Balzacq, 2005, p. 177). In terms of ST, this collective is the *referent object*. The *securitizing actor* is the person or group who declares the referent object as existentially threatened (Buzan et al., 1998, p. 21). We consider a securitization to be successful if the audience accepts the notion that the referent object is existentially threatened and that "it is accepted that some rules must be broken" (Bright, 2012, p. 871) in order to resolve the problem.

Following Stritzel (2011, p. 351), we assume that securitization can occur in "waves", with Grenoble being the first wave[3] and the WoT discourse being the second wave in our analysis of an ongoing securitization of "others". These waves are marked by discussion about changing the constitution in order to make citizenship revocation easier and hence by the attempts to institutionalize the securitization.

Securitizing Populist Divide

We argue that under certain circumstances, securitization draws on populist anti-pluralism. By carrying the populist divide into the political discourse, the divide is reinforced and normalized. This catalytic effect of ST occurs when the perceived threat comes from within a society, and social groups excluded by right-wing populism become the referent subject (Fig. 38.1).

If securitization takes place in times of domestic threats, a social divide is established between the part of society in need of protection and the part from which the threat emanates. Already established division lines, e.g. the populist divide between the heartland and the domestic enemies of the heartland, may serve as a discursive resource. We argue that in France this populist divide has been adopted by the security actors in both cases. The referent subject is securitized in order to legitimize the security act. This establishes and strengthens the populist divide in political discourse, regardless of the success of securitization. By portraying certain social groups as an existential threat to society, their belonging to this very society—their citizenship—is doubted. As Guillaume and Huysman (2013, p. 1) have pointed out, security and citizenship are closely connected. This nexus becomes especially visible in the context of the WoT and the ensuing debates about denaturalization in several European countries (for many: Beauchamps, 2017; Engle, 2004; Joppke, 2016).

CITIZENSHIP IN FRANCE

In order to situate the two waves of securitization in their historical context, the following section provides a brief overview of the historical development of the concepts of and laws on citizenship in France. According to a cardinal principle of the French republic, the French are not a *Volk*.

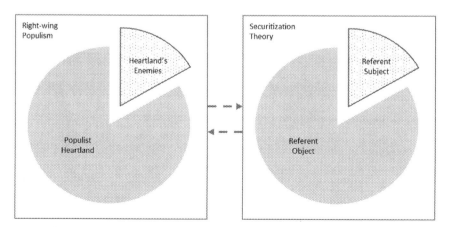

Fig. 38.1 Interaction between right-wing populism and Securitization Theory. (*Source* Own illustration)

> [...] bound together by the ties of blood, but a body of citizens who had come together at the French revolution to establish a new social contract that would guarantee the rights of man and the citizens. (Gildea, 2002, p. 132)

Articles 17 to 33 of the Civil Code define French nationality, which can be obtained either by attribution or by acquisition. Articles 18 and 19 lay down the principles for citizenship attribution via parentage (*ius sanguinis*) and birth place (*ius soli*) (Legifrance, 2019a, 2019b). The principle of acquisition, i.e. naturalization, on the other hand, applies by declaration, decree or operation of law and is clarified in article 21 of the Civil Code (Legifrance, 2019c).

In practice, this means that everybody born to at least one parent holding French citizenship receives French citizenship. In addition, everybody born in France with at least one parent who was also born in France receives French citizenship. Moreover, due to its colonial history, France grants citizenship to persons born in France before 1994 to a parent who was born in a French oversea territory before it became independent. Finally, persons born in France after 1962 with a parent born in Algeria prior to its independence are also French citizens (France Diplomatie, 2016a). The possession of two or more nationalities is in general compatible with French law, which allows bi- or plurinationality (France Diplomatie, 2016b).

While the French concept of citizenship seems to be more inclusive and apt to adopt to migration influxes than a *völkische* idea of national identity, Gildea (2002) points out that

> [...] though in theory it was possible to acquire French nationality by an act of will, in practice the French refused to consider that anyone could be properly French if they were foreign in origin, spoke a different language or threatened the idea of the secular state by demanding public recognition of their religion. (p. 133)

Besides, the notion that being a French citizen means joining a social contract that is based on liberal values and secular statehood leaves room for the exclusion of individuals and groups that do not share these values, even though they might meet other criteria such as being born on French soil, having a French parent or speaking French. Thus, against the backdrop of this conception of citizenship the idea that somebody can cease to be French or is "not really French" if she acts in ways that indicates that she has left this social contract becomes plausible—even if one does not agree with revocations of citizenship or the concept of nationality in the first place. During the 1980s, citizenship law was much debated in the context of migration and national identity. Nationalist criticized citizenship acquisition by immigrants as "turning foreigners into Frenchmen on paper without making sure that they were 'French at heart' (*Français de coeur*)" (Brubaker, 1992, p. 143). Moreover, the far right attacked *ius soli* as the FN proclaimed that "to be

French, you have to deserve it" (*Être Français, cela se mérite*) (Brubaker, 1992, p. 138).[4]

When it comes to capitalizing on the exclusionary potential of citizenship and belonging, the French extreme right has identified numerous internal enemies over the decades: Jews, Protestants, Freemasons and migrants in general (Hazareesingh, 1994, p. 134). Starting in the 1980s, the FN further advanced the social exclusion of those it described as "Arabs". The FN particularly emphasized the alleged threat that Islamic religion posed to French political cohesion (Hazareesingh, 1994, p. 135). Wolfreys (2018) argues that "[t]he notion of a clash of civilization did not emerge in France with the 'war on terror', [but] [...] had long been an integral part of the French colonial project justified in terms of France's 'civilising mission'" (p. 14). There is also a long history of securitizing North African migrants, especially migrants from Algeria as "terrorists and traitors" (Gildea, 2002, p.172).

The possibility to lose citizenship has been inscribed in French legislation since the First World War (Beauchamps, 2017, p. 49).[5] Today, Article 25 of the Code Civil regulates denaturalization as a means of sanction under the rule of law. From 1993 to 2006, article 25 was subject to several amendments. First, law n°96–647 added crimes or misdemeanors related to a terrorist act to the first sentence of the article (Legifrance, 2019d). Thus, terrorism for the first time became a legal reason for the deprivation of nationality. The article was modified by law n°98–170 according to the European Convention on Nationality ratified by France in 1997 (Legifrance, 2019e). In Article 7(3), the latter prohibits the creation of stateless individuals as a consequence of a deprivation of nationality: (Council of Europe, 1997).France made the last amendment (law n°2006–64) to the legislative text in 2006 by eliminating the time limit on the possibility of deprivation of nationality. Taking this historical development of the last 25 years into account, the current text of the law reads as follows:

> An individual who has acquired the status of French may, by decree issued after obtaining the assent of the Council of State, be deprived of French nationality, unless the result of the deprivation is to render him stateless:
>
> 1° If he is convicted of an act qualified as a crime or offence constituting an attack on the fundamental interests of the Nation or for a crime or offence constituting an act of terrorism;
>
> 2° If he is convicted of an act qualified as a crime or misdemeanor provided for and punished by Chapter II of Title III of Book IV of the Criminal Code;
>
> 3° If he is convicted of evading the obligations resulting for him from the national service code;
>
> 4° If he has engaged in acts for the benefit of a foreign State that are incompatible with the status of Frenchman and prejudicial to the interests of France.
>
> Deprivation shall be incurred only if the acts alleged against the person concerned and referred to in article 25 occurred before the acquisition of

French nationality or within ten years of the date of such acquisition. It may be pronounced only within ten years of the commission of the said acts. If the facts alleged against the person concerned are referred to in 1° of Article 25, the time limits referred to in the two preceding paragraphs shall be extended to fifteen years. (Legifrance, 2019f)

Hence, denaturalization applies only to naturalized citizens with at least one other nationality, whose naturalization dates back not more than 10 years and who were judged to have committed one of the acts described above. As Beauchamps (2017, p. 49) points out, this law is particularly problematic, "because instead of equally applying to all French citizens, it solely applies to nationals by acquisition". This problematic effect of unequal treatment of French citizens would be amplified, if the possibility of denaturalization for certain crimes was implemented on the constitutional level. However, the constitutional change proposed in 2015 would have allowed for the revocation of citizenship of French-born, bi-national French citizens.

Empirical Analysis

First Wave of Securitization: Grenoble

The debate about citizenship revocation in 2010 was triggered by riots in response to police violence in Villeneuve, a disadvantaged suburb (*banlieu*) of Grenoble. During the night of the July 15 to 16, 2010, an officer had shot 27-year old Karim Bodouda who was trying to escape after having committed an armed robbery (Bordenave, 2010). In Saint-Aignan, people from a local Roma community attacked a police station with hatchets and iron bars on July 18, 2010 after a 22-year old man from a French-Roma community was shot dead. He was killed after driving through a police checkpoint, hitting a police officer and fleeing the police (BBC News, 2010). In response to these events and the escalating violence in Villeneuve and Saint-Aignan, President Sarkozy (Union pour un mouvement populaire [UMP]) held a speech in Grenoble on July 30, 2010.

Sarkozy's speech strongly focused on criminality, especially youth delinquency, and criminal migrants. He announced that he had "decided to wage a war against drug dealers, against thugs" (Sarkozy, 2010). Likewise, his Interior Minister, Brice Hortefeux, called for "a national war against insecurity" (cited from Leclerc, 2010). The speech shows features of securitization such as the notion that France is at some kind of war. Moreover, a strong connection between crime, youth criminality, and immigration is constructed. Sarkozy (2010) claimed: "What happened is not a social problem, it is a gangster problem, values are vanishing". The president thus moved the issue from the realm of social and economic problems into that of security and policing. The solution to this alleged "gangster problem", in his view, were increased support for the police and tougher laws, including the possibility of citizenship revocation. According to Sarkozy (2010) "[t]he French citizenship must be earned and one has to prove oneself worthy of it!" Sarkozy, in his role as securitizing actor, literally adopted Jean-Marie Le Pen's stance on citizenship, and therefore drew on populist divide with his securitizing move. The president went on to scrutinize the alleged neglect of the parents of young delinquents; then turning to illegal immigration and the "lawless zones" (Sarkozy, 2010) of Roma campsites, establishing a triad of crime-migration-Roma.

As a result, the former Minister for Immigration, Integration and National Identity, Éric Besson, proposed a bill extending the grounds for the deprivation of citizenship (Article 25). It included persons who have injured the life of a person holding public authority, in particular police officers (Ministère de l'Intérieur, 2010). The proposal to expand the grounds for withdrawal of citizenship and Sarkozy's general response to the situation was met with a wide array of criticism. However, some party and cabinet members, most prominently the Minister of the Interior Brice Hortefeux, called for an even broader reform, including polygamy into the offenses that could be punished with the loss of citizenship (Gabizon, 2010). This reflects the underlying assumption that there are people in the French nation state that are a security threat and do not really belong, as they are criminals and do not adhere to French values. In contrast, Francois Hollande argued that Sarkozy's idea was an infringement of the republican tradition (cited from BFMTV, 2016) and in no way apt to protect civilians—an opinion that he would apparently change in the years to come. Ségolène Royal, who had lost the presidential election against Sarkozy in 2007, called it "a new dangerous step in a populist and xenophobic overbid" (cited from Le Figaro, 2010). Marine Le Pen commented on Sarkozy's proposition as "having only one merit, that of officially confirming the criminal character of certain immigrants, a truth for which le Front national has been persecuted for three decades" (cited from Leparmentier, 2010).

In an editorial on August 3, 2010, Le Monde scrutinized Sarkozy for his conflation of crime and immigration (Le Monde, 2010). In contrast, coverage in Le Figaro was less harsh, with some articles arguing that foreign Roma posed a real problem in France and that Sarkozy was right to address it (Ferry, 2010). Furthermore, some of its authors were arguing that the left was overreacting, especially when it came to comparisons with the Vichy Regime[6] (Ferry, 2010; Klarsfeld, 2010) which had been employed by several critics (Rocard cited from Ferry, 2010; Chemin, 2010; Human Rights League cited from L'OBS, 2010). Some argued that it was important to raise the issue of illegal immigration as otherwise the FN would be the only party addressing the problem (Jaigu & Bourmaud, 2010). In contrast, members of the PS accused Sarkozy of "having a sub-category of French citizens in his mind, which does not deserve the same rights as native French citizens" (Moscovici cited from Le Figaro, 2010).

Second Wave of Securitization: Paris

The second debate about citizenship revocation emerged in the aftermath of the terrorist attacks in Paris in November 2015. In a series of attacks in Paris on November 13 and 14, 2015, the perpetrators killed 130 people and injured 350 persons. The attackers belonged to an Islamic terrorist cell in Brussels; the majority of them were EU citizens with either French or Belgian nationalities (CNN, 2018). Hollande first voiced his idea of reforming citizenship law in front of the Congrès on November 16, 2015, two days after the murders, stating:

> This revision of the Constitution must be accompanied by other measures. The issue at stake is the deprivation of nationality. The deprivation of nationality should not result in making someone stateless, but we need to be able to strip French nationality from an individual found guilty of a terrorist act or other acts against a country's fundamental interests *even if he was born a French person* [emphasis added], if he has another nationality. In the same way, we must be able to prohibit dual nationals from returning to our country if they constitute a terrorist threat, unless they agree to be closely monitored, as is the case in Britain. (Hollande, 2015)

Hollande's speeches and statements were clearly part of an on-going securitization of terrorism in France at the time (Dück & Robin, 2019, p. 18) which is not surprising, given the deadly attacks in Paris as well as the previous attack on the satire magazine "Charlie Hebdo" in January 2015. While terrorism had not played a crucial role in the debate in 2010, and was only referred to within historical references (i.e. the introduction of terrorism as a cause for denaturalization in the Code Civil), it was obliviously a dominant topic in 2015. In contrast, crime was hardly mentioned at all—with the exception of terrorism, which was, however, mostly treated as a horrid phenomenon sui generis or an "act of war" (Hollande, 2015).

While the security measures taken by the French government in order to address to terrorist threat were mostly accepted, such as the state of emergency that followed the attack and lasted for two years and a new anti-terrorism law that granted law enforcement significantly more competences, Holland's proposal to reform citizenship law was contested. He proposed a legislative amendment to Article 34 of the French Constitution, whereby all bi- or plurinational French citizens (including those by attribution) could be deprived of their citizenship if they committed an act of terrorism (Legifrance, 2020). However, even after giving up the addition "binational", the proposal sparked a heated debate about the principal of equality before the law (Assemblée nationale, 2016a).

The parliamentary debate on the constitutional amendment vote (November 10, 2016) revealed inner-party dividing lines that ran through both the political left and the right. Parties of the conservative spectrum, above all the UMP, largely supported the amendment to Article 34 (Assemblée nationale, 2016b). The PS was deeply divided into a pro and a con camp (Le Parisien, 2016). The Greens and the Radical Left, on the other hand, opposed the deprivation of citizenship in general (Assemblée nationale, 2016b).

Like in 2010, the opponents focused mainly on the following aspects: Equality of citizens, the values of the French republic, usefulness of the reform, the dangers of adapting extreme right-wing positions and of rendering individuals stateless.

In 2015, it was argued again that the reform was anti-republican and established an undesired distinction between two types of citizens:

> Last but not least, denaturalization is an affront against the republican values. It implies that there are two types of French: the citizens born in France, who the extreme right likes to call 'native French' and the others, who are not and who have to behave properly day after day that they are worthy to stay French. (Le Monde, 2015)

In contrast, others now argued that in order to avoid such an "unfair" distinction, it would be necessary to extend the law to all French citizens, even if this might lead to rendering people stateless (Lozès, 2016), a position irreconcilable with EU law. Nevertheless, according to its proponents it would allow to define the boundaries of the national community more clearly:

> The withdrawal of nationality and its extension to binational French-born terrorist allows to limit the conditions of belonging to the national community and contributes to the definition of what is compatible with French nationality. (Lozès, 2016)

Le Monde further stressed that it was also worried about the adaptation of positions from the far right:

> The president's decision is a double and heavy mistake. On the one hand, it directly damages the principle of equality between the citizens [...] Like the Republic, the citizenry is indivisible. One the other hand, by adapting a measure that has long been claimed by the Front national, the head of state takes major responsibility for downplaying this detestable xenophobic logic. (Nouchi, 2016)

Other members of the PS were strongly alienated by the proposal and Justice Minister Christiane Taubira even stepped down over the proposed constitutional change (BBC News, 2016). In contrast, Florian Philippot, the vice president of the FN, applauded Holland's proposal and added: "Once the principle is rehabilitated through Francois Hollande, we will enter the second stage, that is, we will build pressure in order to use this denaturalization far more widely" (Philippot cited from Thierry, 2015).

Hollande's reform plan entered the legislative process in spite of the strong contestation within even his own party. Although the constitutional amendment to Article 34 was abandoned, the parliamentary debates on the proposed amendment (e.g. Assemblée nationale, 2016a, 2016b) clearly showed the entry of populist positions into the political mainstream.

Discussion of Our Findings

While neither Sarkozy nor Hollande were ultimately able to gain support for their legal reform, our case studies show that the call to expand the withdrawal of citizenship traveled form the FN/RN to the UMP to the PS. While both Sarkozy's and Holland's proposal sparked criticism within their own party, they nevertheless felt comfortable proposing said reforms. In both cases, the discussion can be summarized along the lines of the group that is perceived as dangerous, the questions of the legality of the proposed changes in the laws regarding citizenship, the usefulness of the reform in pragmatic terms, French values and the adoption of right-wing positions by the PS. The most obvious difference between the two discourses were the circumstances from which the debate emerged and the group that was perceived as threatening the French state. In the 2010 case, we observe a clear targeting of immigrant Roma communities and criminal migrants in general. While Klarsfeld (2010) and Ferry (2010) draw a clear line between French and foreign Roma in their articles in Le Monde and Le Figaro, this line was rather blurred in Sarkozy's speech, arguably on purpose. Although the unrests were not caused by an incident with a foreign Roma, but with a French citizen, he strongly emphasized the issue of migration, linking it to crime and security concerns. In 2015, Muslims (even those born and raised in France) were the target of the reform. Again, security issues were linked to migration and a debate about "real" Frenchness and hence about the true heartland. The discourse was strongly influenced by the adaption of the securitization of the WoT in general and the othering of terrorist offenders as coward, uncivilized and barbaric (Hollande, 2015). Concerning the legality and legitimacy of the reforms, its critics argued in both cases that it would create second-class citizens and a division within society. In regard to the usefulness of the proposed reforms, Valls (2016) openly admitted that he considered the proposed reforms as "symbolic" rather than as deterrence. Overall, our analysis shows that at the core of the debate was the question of what republican and French values were and how they related to citizenship, rather than the concrete effect of any reform on actual crime rates. This confirms the in-, respectively, excluding nature of the debate. It also sheds some light on the evolution of the French notion of citizenship. It seems that the notion of France being a state-centered nation (Brubaker, 1992, 14) is coming under pressure and is increasingly challenged by the counter discourse of France being a cultural nation. The symbolic dimension of the debate is very much in line with the right-wing populist idea of the heartland as well as their vision of an anti-pluralistic view of society.

Conclusion

In the 1980s, Jean-Marie Le Pen's slogan "La nationalité française, ça se mérité" (French nationality has to be earned) was still considered a fringe position. Thirty years later, waves of securitizing migration and othering of minority communities have swept this populist divide into the political mainstream. While citizenship right reforms have not been able to gain a majority in parliament in both chambers yet, this is a concerning finding.

The case of France shows that in both cases the securitization which accompanied the discussion about nationality led to strong othering of groups that already experience racism and discrimination. In 2010, foreign-born Roma, one of the most vulnerable groups in the French—and arguably the European Union—society, were targeted. The clear line that some authors drew between French and foreign-born Roma, while more accurately depicting the events, inherently reproduces the idea of the true French heartland in which some travelers can live—as the "natural" outsiders in the French society—while there are others that due to their foreignness are threating and should be deported. The demand to also include polygamy into the reasons for citizenship withdrawal further emphasized the symbolic character of the planned reforms and shows a strong link to the right-wing notion of cultural war waging in Europe.

In the case of the terrorist attacks of 2015, the PS leadership failed to find political answers to the threat of terrorism and instead of taking a root-cause approach, opted for increased surveillance and a new debate about citizenship reform. An intersectionality of vulnerabilities emerges from these different securitizations and the establishment of the migration-crime and migration-terrorism, Muslim-terrorism nexus. In the end, people (especially male) with dark skin are held to be more dangerous than others and must endure increased policing. People living in poor communities with higher crime rates also undergo increased surveillance, but often not as a measure of protecting them, but rather because they are (by their very "nature") suspect. These marginalized persons are often aware that—in the right-wing populist logic—they can never truly belong or become part of the heartland. This feeling is amplified by increased policing, hence contributing to an estrangement from liberal mainstream society. At the same time, the rise of the FN/RN clearly shows that a strategy of adapting right-wing narratives and policies does not diminish their attractiveness, but rather normalizes their positions, thus preparing the ground for their future success.

The danger of right-wing populism is hence not limited to the worst-case scenario of its representatives becoming part or even head of a government. It also lies in the more subtle change to our societies as whole, as populist and anti-pluralistic ideas become normalized in the discursive realm. Thus, the shift of the discourse of all parties erodes those positions that once countered populist and racist narratives and political positions once unthinkable enter into the programs of even those parties that supposedly fight right-wing and populist narratives. Moreover, the strong division within the PS in 2015, as illustrated by the resignation of Christiane Taubira, might indicate a dissolution of the right–left patterns in French party politics. The rise of populist discourses might have a corrosive effect on this pattern and further research should investigate this connection.

Notes

1. Art's statement is based on an analysis of narratives of the Nazi past in Austria.
2. While horizontal differentiation is especially prone to produce racist othering, while the vertical differentiation is likely to bring forward conspiracy theories. These are often connected to antisemitic tropes. This antisemitism is, for instance, expressed in resentments against "Globalist" Jews that are destroying cultural identity or the notion that Jews are pulling the strings behind Muslim immigration (Rensmann, 2017, p. 129).
3. This does not mean that we assume that there was no securitization of migration in discourses on citizenship before 2010. Therefore, "first wave" and "second wave" refer to our analysis and not to the absolute number of securitizations of migration/terror in France.
4. At the same time, the Socialist criticized *ius soli* for turning "second-generation immigrants into French citizens without their knowledge and, in some cases, against their will" (Brubaker, 1992, p. 142).
5. Beauchamps (2017, p. 49) points out that the English translation "denaturalization" fails to convey the strong moral connotation of the French term "déchéance de la nationalité".
6. Under the Vichy regime during the Second World War, the deprivation of citizenship was used as a strategic instrument to get rid of political opponents. Fifteen thousand French citizens (including 7.000 of Jewish origin) were deprived of their citizenship. As Carroll put it: "Under Vichy law, to be French meant not only that one had met the standard minimum criteria for citizenship but also and primarily that one could legally 'prove' that one was not Jewish" (1998, p. 39). Therefore, the political practice of deprivation of citizenship has an anti-democratic connotation in France (Chemin, 2010).

Literature

Albert, M., & Buzan, B. (2011). Securitization, sectors and functional differentiation. *Security Dialogue, 42*(4–5), 413–425. https://doi.org/10.1177/0967010611418710.

Aradau, C., & van Munster R. (2009). Exceptionalism and the 'War on Terror'. Criminology meets international relations. *The British Journal of Criminology, 49*(5), 686–701. https://doi.org/10.1093/bjc/azp036.

Art, D. (2006). Reacting to the radical right. Lessons from Germany and Austria. *Party Politics, 13*(3), 331–349. https://doi.org/10.1177/1354068807075939.

Aslanidis, P. (2016). Is populism an ideology? A refutation and a new perspective. *Political Studies, 64*(1), 88–104. https://doi.org/10.1111/1467-9248.12224.

Assemblée nationale (2016a, février 5). *Compte rendu integral. Priemière séance du vendredi* . Retrieved from http://www.assemblee-nationale.fr/14/cri/2015-2016/20160122.asp. Last accessed 22 June 2020.

Assemblée nationale. (2016b, février 10). *Compte rendu integral. Séance du mercredi*. Retrieved from http://www.assemblee-nationale.fr/14/cri/2015-2016/20160128.asp#P725749. Last accessed 22 June 2020.

Balzacq, T. (2005). The three faces of securitization: Political agency, audience and context. *European Journal of International Relations, 11*(2), 171–201. https://doi.org/10.1177/1354066105052960.

BBC News. (2010, July 19). *Troops patrol French village of Saint-Aignan after riot*. Retrieved from https://www.bbc.co.uk/news/mobile/world-europe-10681796#sa-link_location=morestory1&intlink_from_url=https%3A%2F%2Fwww.bbc.com%2Fnews%2Fworld-europe-10798440&intlink_ts=1567177098452&story_slot=1-sa. Last accessed 30 August 2019.

BBC News. (2016, January 27). *French Minister Christiane Taubira resigns amid terror row*. Retrieved from https://www.bbc.com/news/world-europe-35417732. Last accessed 21 June 2020.

Beauchamps, M. (2017). Perverse tactics: 'Terrorism' and national identity in France. *Culture, Theory and Critique, 58*(1), 48–61. https://doi.org/10.1080/14735784.2015.1137480.

BFMTV. (2016, January 13). *Quand Valls et Hollande étaient contre la déchéance de nationalité*. Retrieved from https://www.bfmtv.com/politique/quand-valls-et-hollande-etaient-contre-la-decheance-de-nationalite-943233.html. Last accessed 30 August 2019.

Bigo, D. (2002). Security and immigration: Towards a critique of the government of unease. *Alternatives: Global, Local, Political, 27*(1), 63–92. https://doi.org/10.1177/03043754020270S105.

Bordenave, Y. (2010). *La jeunesse perdue de Karim Boudouda, enfant déscolarisé devenu caïd des cites*. Retrieved from https://www.lemonde.fr/societe/article/2010/07/24/la-jeunesse-perdue-de-karim-boudouda-enfant-descolarise-devenu-caid-des-cites_1391792_3224.html. Last accessed 30 August 2019.

Bright, J. (2012). Securitization, terror, and control: Towards a theory of the breaking point. *Review of International Studies, 38*(4), 861–879. https://doi.org/10.1017/S0260210511000726.

Brubaker, R. (1992). *Citizenship and nationhood in France and Germany*. Havard University Press.

Buzan, B. (1983). *People, states and fear: The national security problem in international relations*. University of North Carolina Press.

Buzan, B. (2006). Will the 'global war on terrorism' be the new Cold War? *International Affairs, 82*(6), 1101–1118. https://doi.org/10.1111/j.1468-2346.2006.00590.x.

Buzan, B., Wæver, O., & de Wilde, J. (1998). *Security: A new framework for analysis*. Lynne Rienner.

Carroll, D. (1998). What it meant to be "a Jew" in Vichy France: Xavier Vallat, state anti-semitism, and the question of assimilation. *SubStance, Special Issue: The Occupation, 27*(3), 36–54. https://doi.org/10.2307/3685578.

Chemin, A. (2010, August 13). Décodage, Peur-on créer de nouveaux cas de déchéance de la Nationalité? *Le Monde*, p. 10.

CNN (2018). *2015 Paris terror attacks fast facts*. Retrieved from https://edition.cnn.com/2015/12/08/europe/2015-paris-terror-attacks-fast-facts/index.html. Last accessed 30 August 2019.

Council of Europe. (1997, 6 November). *European convention on nationality*. Strasbourg. Retrieved from https://www.coe.int/de/web/conventions/full-list/-/conventions/rms/090000168007f2c8. Last accessed 29 August 2019.

Dück, E., & Robin, L. (2019). Same old (macro-)securitization? A comparison of political reactions to major terrorist attacks in the United States and France. *Croatian International Relations Review, 25*(84), 6–35. https://doi.org/10.2478/cirr-2019-0001.

Engle, K. (2004). Constructing good aliens and good citizens: Legitimizing the war on terror(ism). *University of Colorado Law Review, 75*(1), 59–114.

Ferry, L. (2010, September 2). La France de Sarkozy au bord du fascisme? Quelle ânerie! *Le Figaro*, p. 15.

Floyd, R. (2016). Extraordinary or ordinary emergency measures: What, and who defines the 'success' of securitization? *Cambridge Review of International Affairs, 29*(2), 677–694. https://doi.org/10.1080/09557571.2015.1077651.

Floyd, R. (2019). *The morality of security: A theory of just securitization*. Cambridge University Press.

France Diplomatie. (2016a). *L'acquisition de la nationalité française*. Retrieved from https://www.diplomatie.gouv.fr/fr/services-aux-francais/etat-civil-et-nationalite-francaise/nationalite-francaise/article/l-acquisition-de-la-nationalite-francaise. Last accessed 22 June 2020.

France Diplomatie. (2016b). *Nationalité française. Qu'est-ce que la nationalité française?* Retrieved from https://www.diplomatie.gouv.fr/fr/services-aux-citoyens/etat-civil-et-nationalite-francaise/nationalite-francaise/. Last accessed 29 August 2019.

Freeden, M. (2017). After the Brexit referendum: Revisiting populism as an ideology. *Journal of Political Ideologies, 22*(1), 1–11. https://doi.org/10.1080/13569317.2016.1260813.

Gabizon, C. (2010, July 31). Le président veut durcir les conditions d'accès à la nationalité. *Le Figaro*, p. 3.

Gildea, R. (2002). *France since 1945*. Oxford University Press.

Guillaume, X., & Huysman, J. (Eds.). (2013). *Citizenship and security. The constitution of political being*. Routledge.

Hawkins, K., & Rovira Kaltwasser, C. (2017). The ideational approach to populism. *Latin American Research Review, 52*(4), 1–16. https://doi.org/10.25222/larr.85.

Hazareesingh, S. (1994). *Political traditions in modern France*. Oxford University Press.

Heinisch, R. C., Holtz-Bacha, C., & Mazzoleni, O. (2017). *Political populism*. Nomos.

Hollande, F. (2015). *Déclaration de M. François Hollande, Président de la République, devant le Parlement réuni en Congrès à la suite des attaques terroristes perpétrées à Paris et en Seine-Saint-Denis, Versailles le 16 novembre 2015*. Retrieved from http://discours.vie-publique.fr/notices/157002982.html. Last accessed 30 August 2019.

Huysmans, J. (2006). *The politics of insecurity: Fear, migration and asylum in the EU*. Routledge.

Huysmans, J. (2011). What's in an act? On security speech acts and little security nothings. *Security Dialogue, 42*(4–5), 371–383. https://doi.org/10.1177/0967010611418713.

Jansen, R. S. (2011). Populist mobilization: A new theoretical approach to populism. *Sociological Theory, 29*(2), 75–96. https://doi.org/10.1111/j.1467-9558.2011.01388.x.

Jaigu, C., & Bourmaud, F. (2010, August 3). Sécurité: le PS esquive le débat, Nicolas Sarkozy estime que ses declaration sont en phase avec l'opinion des Français. *Le Figaro*, p. 3.

Joppke, C. (2016). Terror and the loss of citizenship. *Citizenship Studies, 20*(6–7), 728–748. https://doi.org/10.1080/13621025.2016.1191435.

Kaya, A. (2009). *Islam, migration and integration. The age of securitization.* Palgrave Macmillan.

Klarsfeld, A. (2010, August 20). La sécurité ne s'oppose pas à la morale. *Le Figaro*, p. 17.

Leclerc, J. (2010, August 2): La majorité multiplie les propositions sur le thème de la sécurité; L'UMP déposera à la rentrée une proposition de loi visant à menacer d'une peine de prison les parents de mineurs délinquants. *Le Figaro*, p. 3.

Le Figaro. (2010, August 1). *Délinquance : Aubry dénonce une « dérive antirépublicaine ».* Retrieved from http://www.lefigaro.fr/politique/2010/07/30/01002-20100730ARTFIG00632-un-discours-contraire-aux-principes-d-egalite.php. Last accessed 30 August 2019.

Legifrance. (2019a). *Chapitre II: De la nationalité française d'origine. Section 1 : Des Français par filiation.* Retrieved from https://www.legifrance.gouv.fr/affichCode.do?idArticle=LEGIARTI000006419373&idSectionTA=LEGISCTA000006149907&cidTexte=LEGITEXT000006070721&dateTexte=20060701. Last accessed 29 August 2019.

Legifrance (2019b). *Chapitre II : De la nationalité française d'origine. Section 2 : Des Français par la naissance en France.* Retrieved from https://www.legifrance.gouv.fr/affichCode.do;jsessionid=3D643EACBB611C51631F2B9F98D3220D.tplgfr35s_2?idSectionTA=LEGISCTA000006149908&cidTexte=LEGITEXT000006070721&dateTexte=20060701 (last accessed 29 August 2019).

Legifrance. (2019c). *Chapitre III : De l'acquisition de la nationalité française. Section 1: Des modes d'acquisition de la nationalité française.* Retrieved from https://www.legifrance.gouv.fr/affichCode.do?idArticle=LEGIARTI000006419548&idSectionTA=LEGISCTA000006165433&cidTexte=LEGITEXT000006070721&dateTexte=20060701. Last accessed 29 August 2019.

Legifrance. (2019d). *Chapitre IV: De la perte, de la déchéance et de la réintégration dans la nationalité française. Section 3: De la déchéance de la nationalité française. Version en vigueur du 23 juillet 1996 au 1 septembre 1998.* Retrieved from https://www.legifrance.gouv.fr/affichCodeArticle.do;jsessionid=3D643EACBB611C51631F2B9F98D3220D.tplgfr35s_2?idArticle=LEGIARTI000006420132&cidTexte=LEGITEXT000006070721&categorieLien=id&dateTexte=19980831. Last accessed 29 August 2019.

Legifrance. (2019e). *Chapitre IV : De la perte, de la déchéance et de la réintégration dans la nationalité française. Section 3 : De la déchéance de la nationalité française. Version en vigueur au 1 septembre 1998.* Retrieved from https://www.legifrance.gouv.fr/affichCodeArticle.do;jsessionid=3D643EACBB611C51631F2B9F98D3220D.tplgfr35s_2?idArticle=LEGIARTI000006420133&cidTexte=LEGITEXT000006070721&categorieLien=id&dateTexte. Last accessed 29 August 2019.

Legifrance. (2019f). *Chapitre IV : De la perte, de la déchéance et de la réintégration dans la nationalité française. Section 3 : De la déchéance de la nationalité française.*

Retrieved from https://www.legifrance.gouv.fr/affichCode.do;jsessionid=2BEA13DF1523E2AA3103319491997002.tplgfr35s_2?idSectionTA=LEGISCTA000006150513&cidTexte=LEGITEXT000006070721&dateTexte=20190829. Last accessed 29 August 2019.

Legifrance. (2020). *Projet de loi constitutionnelle de protection de la Nation (PRMX1529429L), conseil des ministres du 23 décembre 2015*. Retrieved from https://www.legifrance.gouv.fr/Droit-francais/Les-avis-du-Conseil-d-Etat-rendus-sur-les-projets-de-loi/2015/Projet-de-loi-constitutionnelle-de-protection-de-la-Nation-PRMX1529429L-23-12-2015. Last accessed 21 June 2020.

Leparmentier, A. (2010, August 3). *Sécurité: la gauche réticente à polémpiquer avec Nicolas Sarkozy*, 1.

Le Monde. (2010, August 3). *Editorial: Le président, l'escalade et l'amalgame*, 1.

Le Monde. (2015, December 3). *Déchéance de nationalité : attention, danger*, 29.

L'OBS. (2010, July 31). *Tollé contre le discours sécuritaire de Nicolas Sarkozy*. Retrieved from https://www.nouvelobs.com/politique/20100731.OBS7905/tolle-contre-le-discours-securitaire-de-nicolas-sarkozy.html. Last accessed 31 August 2019.

Le Parisien. (2016, February 3). *Déchéance de nationalité: on n'y comprend plus rien!* Retrieved from https://www.leparisien.fr/politique/decheance-de-nationalite-on-n-y-comprend-plus-rien-03-02-2016-5510461.php. Last accessed 11 November 2019.

Lozès, P. (2016, January 8). Mieux vaudrait une déchéance pour tous. *Le Monde*, 15.

March, L. (2017). Left and right populism compared: The British case. *The British Journal of Politics and International Relations, 19*(2), 282–303. https://doi.org/10.1177/1369148117701753.

Ministère de l'Intérieur. (2010). *Présentation du projet de loi relatif à l'immigration, à l'intégration et à la nationalité devant la Commission des lois de L'Assemblée nationale, Discours d'Éric BESSON*. Retrieved from https://www.immigration.interieur.gouv.fr/Archives/Les-archives-du-Cabinet-de-M.-Eric-Besson-2009-2010/Les-discours-du-Cabinet-de-M.-Eric-Besson-2009-2010/Septembre-2010/Presentation-du-projet-de-loi-relatif-a-l-immigration-a-l-integration-et-a-la-nationalite-devant-la-Commission-des-lois-de-l-Assemblee-Nationale-le-8-septembre-2010-Discours-d-Eric-BESSON. Last accessed 21 June 2020.

Moffitt, B., & Tormey, S. (2014). Rethinking populism: Politics, mediatisation and political style. *Political Studies, 62*(2), 381–397. https://doi.org/0.1111/1467-9248.12032.

Mudde, C. (2004). The populist zeitgeist. *Government and Opposition, 39*(4), 542–563. https://doi.org/10.1111/j.1477-7053.2004.00135.x.

Mudde, C. (2007). *Populist radical right parties in Europe*. Cambridge University Press.

Mudde, C. (2017). Populism: An ideational approach. In C. Rovira Kaltwasser, P. Taggart, P. Ochoa Espejo & P. Ostiguy, *The Oxford handbook of populism* (pp. 27–47). Oxford University Press.

Mudde, C., & Rovira Kaltwasser, C. (2018). Studying populism in comparative perspective: Reflections on the contemporary and future research agenda. *Comparative Political Studies, 51*(13), 1667–1693. https://doi.org/10.1177/0010414018789490.

Müller, J. (2016). *What is populism*. Univeristy of Pennsylvania Press.

Nilsson, P. (2018). *French populism and discourses on secularism*. Bloomsbury.

Nouchi, F. (2016, January 10). Déchéance : la boîte de Pandore. *Le Monde*, 17.

Poier, K., Saywald-Wedl, S. & Unger, H. (2017). *Die Themen der "Populisten". Mit einer Medienanalyse von Wahlkämpfen in Österreich, Deutschland, der Schweiz, Dänemark und Polen*. Nomos.

Roberts, K. M. (2006). Populism, political conflict, and grass-roots organization in Latin America. *Comparative Politics, 38*(2), 127–148. https://doi.org/10.2307/20433986.

Roe, P. (2008). Actor, audience(s) and emergency measures: Securitization and the UK's decision to invade Iraq. *Security Dialogue, 39*(6), 615–635. https://doi.org/10.1177/0967010608098212.

Rensmann, L. (2017). The noisy counter-revolution: Understanding the cultural conditions and dynamics of populist politics in Europe in the digital age. *Politics and Governance., 5*(4), 123–135. https://doi.org/10.17645/pag.v5i4.1123.

Roubini, N. (2016, November, 11). *The oval office will tame President Donald Trump*. Retrieved from https://www.theguardian.com/business/2016/nov/11/oval-office-will-tame-us-president-donald-trump. Last accessed 21 June 2020.

Salter, M. B. (2011). When securitization fails: The hard case of counter-terrorism programs. In T. Balzacq (Ed.), *Securitization theory: How security problems emerge and dissolve* (pp. 116–132). Routledge.

Sarkozy, N. (2010). *Le discours de Grenoble de Nicolas Sarkozy*. Retrieved from http://www.lefigaro.fr/politique/le-scan/2014/03/27/25001-20140327ARTFIG00084-le-discours-de-grenoble-de-nicolas-sarkozy.php. Last accessed 30 August 2019.

Skenderovic, D. (2017). Populism: A History of the Concept. In R. C. Heinisch, C. Holtz-Bacha & O. Mazzoleni (Eds.), *Political populism: A handbook*. (pp. 39–58). Nomos.

Stavrakakis, Y., & Katsambekis, G. (2014). Left-wing populism in the European periphery: The case of SYRIZA. *Journal of Political Ideologies, 19*(2), 119–142. https://doi.org/10.1080/13569317.2014.909266.

Stritzel, H. (2011). Security, the translation. *Security Dialogue, 42*(4–5), 343–355. https://doi.org/10.1177/0967010611418998.

Taggart, P. (2004). Populism and representative politics in contemporary Europe. *JoUrnal of Political Ideologies, 9*(3), 269–288. https://doi.org/10.1080/1356931042000263528.

Thierry, M. (2015). *Quand le FN proposait la déchéance de nationalité pour de simples "faits délictuels"*. Retrieved from https://www.nouvelobs.com/politique/20151231.OBS2111/quand-le-fn-proposait-la-decheance-de-nationalite-pour-de-simples-faits-delictuels.html. Last accessed 2 September 2019.

Valls, M. (2016). *Déclaration de M. Manuel Valls, Premier ministre, sur le projet de loi visant l'inscription de l'état d'urgence et la déchéance de la nationalité dans la Constitution, à l'Assemblée nationale le 27 janvier 2016*. Retrieved from https://www.vie-publique.fr/discours/197763-declaration-de-m-manuel-valls-premier-ministre-sur-le-projet-de-loi-v. Last accessed 22 June 2020.

Wæver, O. (1995). Securitization and desecuritization. In R. D. Lipschutz (Ed.), *On security* (pp. 46–87). Columbia University Press.

Wæver, O. (1999). Securitizing sectors? Reply to Eriksson: *Cooperation and Conflict, 34*(3), 334–340. https://doi.org/10.1177/00108369921961906.

Wæver, O. (2011). Politics, security, theory. *Security Dialogue, 42*(4–5), 465–480. https://doi.org/10.1177/0967010611418718.

Weil, P. (2005). *Qu'est-ce qu'un Français ? Histoire de la nationalité fançaise depuis la Révolution.* Gallimard.

Weyland, K. (2017). Populism: A political-strategic approach. In C. Rovira Kaltwasser, P. Taggart, P. Ochoa Espejo & P. Ostiguy (Eds.), *The Oxford handbook of populism* (pp. 48–72). Oxford University Press.

Williams, M. C. (2011). The continuing evolution of securitization theory. In T. Balzacq (Ed.), *Securitization theory: How security problems emerge and dissolve* (pp. 212–222). Routledge.

Wolfrey, J. (2018). *Republic of Islamophobia: The rise of respectable racism in France.* Hurst & Company.

CHAPTER 39

Can Right-Wing Populist Parties Solve the "Democratic Dilemma"?

Martin Althoff

Introduction

In many European countries the voter turnout at elections has declined over time (Blais, 2006, 2007). On average, in Europe in the 1970s and 1980s, the electoral turnout was close to 85%. During the 1990s the decline started and nowadays it is solely close to 65% (IDEA, 2021). The question why such a large share of the population does not use their right to vote is puzzling political scientists. Some people do not vote because they are dissatisfied with the political parties. Some do not vote because they think they are not represented by the mainstream parties, or feel forsaken by the politicians. Yet other voters do not participate because they have even become estranged from democratic institutions and the political elite. Studies show that these people can often be assigned to one social class: the less well-educated with a low socio-economic status and low incomes (Gallego, 2015; Wolfinger & Rosenstone, 1980).

Could the low turnout be a problem for our democratic society? The answer is probably yes. Researchers found that the lower the participation and thus voter turnout is, the higher is the inequality against the less privileged citizens (Gallego, 2015; Rosenstone & Hansen, 1993; Solt, 2008, 2010). If the less privileged citizens fail to vote, governments and legislators do not take into account their needs and views in policy-making. As a result, one could call it a serious dilemma for representative democracies (Lijphart, 1997).

M. Althoff (✉)
NSI—University of Applied Sciences, Hannover, Germany
e-mail: martin.althoff@nsi-hsvn.de

This is where right-wing populist parties come into play. Some authors argue that right-wing populist parties are primarily targeting the less privileged citizens with their election programs and their public appearance. In the 1970s and 1980s, they were only of minor relevance in Western European countries. However, since the beginning of the 1990s after the fall of the iron curtain this has changed and numerous successes for right-wing populist parties could be observed in both Western and Eastern European countries. Since the 2010s right-wing populist parties have grown significantly and today they are more successful than ever before. In 2018 in European countries the electoral support for right-wing populist parties was almost at 16% (Timbro & The Foundation for Free Enterprise, 2019).

In addition, it appears that in some countries, with the rise of right-wing populist parties, the average turnout has also grown. In Germany, for example, between the 2013 and 2017 national elections, both the voter turnout increased by 4.7% and the right-wing populist parties' share of the vote rose by 7.9 percent. In the UK, between 2001 and 2015 both the voter turnout increased by 7% and the proportion of right-wing populist votes rose by 11.1% and it looks very similar in Sweden. Also in Poland it seems like the two values are related. From 2011, both the voter turnout and the proportion of votes by right-wing populist parties increased significantly.

The question if there is a (causal) relationship between the right-wing populist vote shares and voter turnout seems to be a lacuna in scholarly work. Although vast academic research investigated the electorate of right-wing populist parties (Arzheimer, 2009, 2018; Mudde, 2007) as well as voter turnout (Blais, 2006, 2007; Geys, 2006; Jackman, 1987; Smets & van Ham, 2013; Wolfinger & Rosenstone, 1980), the relationship between both remains unclear. A recently published study provided interesting findings. The authors stated that the electoral success of right-wing populist parties enhance the electoral participation in Western European countries, especially among higher educated citizens. Further it could also be shown that in Eastern European countries the right-wing populist parties electoral success lowers the turnout rates mainly among the young citizens with positive attitudes towards immigration. But the main finding was that there is no general positive effect of right-wing populist parties on voter turnout. Unfortunately, the explanatory power of this study is limited, because the authors only use individual data of the European Social Survey for the years 2002–2012 (Immerzeel & Pickup, 2015). Other scholars found in their study that populist parties do not boost voter turnout, but the authors mainly focus on the moderating effect of populist parties on the relationship between income inequality on voter turnout (Schwander et al., 2020). Thus, it can be stated that there is no systematical research on the relationship between the electoral success of right-wing populist parties and voter turnout.

This contribution aims at reducing that theoretical and empirical gap. To achieve this, a dataset of 31 European countries and 387 parliamentary elections was created for the period from 1960 to 2018 and a comprehensive analysis of the relationship between the electoral success of right-wing populist parties and voter turnout was carried out. A series of analyses shows that the election success of right-wing populist parties does not have a clear positive influence on voter turnout. Most of the coefficients in the analyses models either do not point in the expected direction or do not achieve statistical significance. The electoral success of right-wing populist parties does not matter a great deal for voter turnout.

Theory

A large group of the society in European democracies has left the process of political participation, resulting in an immense decline of voter turnout. This question has puzzled political scientists and the reasons for the trend in turnout decline became subject of a controversial debate (Blais, 2006, 2007; Geys, 2006; Lijphart, 1997; Smets & van Ham, 2013).

According to the electoral context school (Franklin, 2004; Franklin et al., 2004), the nature of elections has changed over time. They became less relevant and politicians and parties aim at consensus and want to avoid conflicts. The polarization of mainstream parties has decreased and due to the converging of ideological positions it gets increasingly harder for voters to distinguish the different parties, which fosters non-voting.

Another argument indicates that people do not vote because they are dissatisfied with politicians and parties (Armingeon & Guthmann, 2014; Hooghe & Marien, 2013). Furthermore, people feel lower levels of political efficacy and think that it is impossible for them to influence legislative processes (Karp & Banducci, 2008). This leads to turnout decline, too.

As reported by various researchers of the generation-school and the civic voluntarism model, this trend is caused by the decrease of the involvement in traditional civic organizations such as labor unions, the church or political parties. These organizations promote the acquisition of the necessary resources to better understand political processes and stimulate social trust and foster civic norms as, for example, the duty to vote in elections. However, modernization processes and increasing individualization prevent (younger) people from internalizing the act of voting as a civic duty (Armingeon & Schädel, 2015; Blais, 2000; Brady et al., 1995; Dalton, 1984; Inglehart, 1977; Inglehart & Flanagan, 1987).

How can the role of right-wing populist parties in this context be conceptualized? Research reveals at least two arguments why people vote for right-wing populist parties: Political dissatisfaction and agreement (with right-wing populist parties) on how political issues are dealt with.

The first argument maintains that voters do not cast their ballot for right-wing populist parties because of issue preferences. Rather they want to express their dissatisfaction with mainstream parties and other democratic actors and institutions (Bowler et al., 2017; Franklin, 2004). Right-wing populist parties are most likely to benefit from 'anti-mainstream-tendencies' because they constitute themselves as 'anti-establishment-alternatives' and outsiders of 'the' system. This group of voters may feel forsaken by the political elites and think that decision-making is to complex for them and non-transparent. Since right-wing populist parties promise to destroy the 'corrupt' elite system, they could be interpreted as some kind of 'watchdog', as a 'democratic corrective' in the political system (Immerzeel & Pickup, 2015). Consequently, right-wing populist parties can pull political dissatisfied and uninterested voters, who feel lost and forsaken, to the polls again.

The second one indicates that electoral choices are based on ideological closeness and the assumed competence of the parties regarding certain issues. According to this view some scholars highlight the importance of sociocultural value preferences like attitudes toward immigration and ethnic diversity for right-wing populist parties votes (Arzheimer, 2018; Sorensen, 2016). Other researchers emphasize the role of subjective feelings of economic insecurity and the competition for limited resources with immigrants (Burgoon et al., 2019). This group of voters is also the group with fewer material and cognitive resources and in absence of a right-wing populist parties this group would be less likely to vote in elections (Brady et al., 1995). In sum, this school of thought considers that the assumed competence of the parties and ideological closeness between the issue preferences of the voter and the party positions fosters voting for right-wing populist parties.

Another point of view in the literature indicates that the success of right-wing populist parties causes a notable mobilization of people 'from the other side' who think that right-wing populist parties are a threat to democracy. The political positions of right-wing populist parties are often perceived as incorrect and harmful for the society by mainstream parties and a large part of the public. This group of voters has opposite sociodemographic characteristics and political attitudes than voters of right-wing populist parties: Higher material and cognitive resources, higher political satisfaction and positive attitudes towards immigration (Arzheimer, 2018; Lubbers & Coenders, 2017). Accordingly, this group of voters could feel alerted and turn out to vote more likely than otherwise (when there were no right-wing populist parties) to prevent the electoral success of right-wing populist parties.

To sum it up, the arguments outlined above suggest that the presence of right-wing populist parties fosters voter turnout. This assumption will be examined in the following sections.

EMPIRICAL STRATEGY

Data and Measurement

The dataset covers 31 European countries and the time period from 1960 to 2018. 11 Eastern European countries of the sample are post-communist. Allover, the dataset covers 387 parliamentary elections. Due to the availability of data and the inclusion of data on post-communist countries from the first democratic election in 1991, the dataset is unbalanced (in some countries more elections took place compared to others). For each election, the dataset contains information on voter turnout and election results of right-wing populist parties. Additionally, the data contains variables that are commonly found to affect voter turnout.[1] These are compulsory voting, unemployment, GDP per capita (the logarithm), proportionality, presidentialism and the effective number of parties (Blais, 2006, 2007; Cancela & Geys, 2016; Geys, 2006; Smets & van Ham, 2013; Stockemer, 2017). A time variable to control for general trends in turnout decline and electoral success of right-wing populist parties is also included. Several sources were used to create the dataset. For instance, the voter turnout database from the International Institute for Democracy and Electoral Assistance (IDEA, 2021) and the Comparative Political Data Set 1960–2017 (Armingeon et al., 2019). Voter turnout is operationalized as the number of voters who cast their ballot to all registered voters in parliamentary elections. The electoral results of right-wing populist parties are measured as the vote share for right-wing populist parties in percent. The classification and vote shares of right-wing populist parties are based on Mudde (2007), Armingeon et al. (2019) and the Timbro Authoritarian Populism Index (2019).

Because the Western European countries have longer experiences with democracy and free electoral competitions it is assumed that these different contexts also have different effects on voting behavior and turnout (Immerzeel & Pickup, 2015). As a result, the analyses are not only carried out and compared for all countries in the dataset, but also separately for the Western European and Eastern European countries.

Methods

Due to the variation both between and within the countries, methods are needed that can handle the so-called time-series cross-sectional data (Baltagi, 2005; Fortin-Rittberger, 2015; Wooldridge, 2010). Frequently used strategies to deal with this kind of data and the problem of autocorrelation are employing the method of ordinary least squares in combination with a lagged dependent variable and panel corrected standard errors (Beck & Katz, 1995). But this highly cited approach has some downsides and is controversially debated in the methodological literature (Achen, 2001; Plümper et al., 2005). Other scholars prefer Prais–Winsten-transformations in combination with panel corrected standard errors. Another, particular in economics commonly used technique are fixed effects models. With this approach, researchers assume that the unobserved heterogeneity (the effect of omitted variables) may be correlated with the included variables. For example, one could claim that factors like the political context or the electoral system could be able to account for the relationship between right-wing populist parties' electoral success and voter turnout. Fixed effects can control for these (fixed) differences between countries. Fixed effects models are particularly useful when analyzing causal relationships between variables. One disadvantage is that time-constant variables are abbreviated due to the calculation from the model. Another disadvantage is that the variation between countries can no longer be analyzed. This could be counterproductive for many questions in political science, since it is precisely the variation between countries that is of interest. Under the assumption that the unobserved effect is uncorrelated with the explanatory variables, one could also use a random effects approach. In this research strategy, time-invariant factors are allowed to remain in the equation (Wooldridge, 2010, p. 281 ff.). Because it cannot be assumed that the residuals at the country level are uncorrelated, an important assumption for the calculation of regression analyses is violated. As a result, the standard errors are clustered on the country level.[2]

As it is common that scientists report results out of different strategies, this approach is used in the next section. But first it is checked whether the descriptive analysis reveals anything about the connection between voter turnout and the success of right-wing populist parties.

Results and Discussion

To recall, it is suspected that the election success of right-wing populist parties leads to an increase in voter turnout. Do the data suggest a positive correlation? The answer is yes. As Table 39.1 reveals that both voter turnout has fallen on average and right-wing populist parties have become more successful in

Table 39.1 Voter turnout and vote shares for right-wing populist parties in European Countries

Western European Countries	1960	1970	1980	1990	2000	2010	Overall
Turnout	84.7	84.3	82.1	78.9	77.2	72.9	80.2
	63.8	48.1	46.2	42.2	45.2	45.5	42.2
	65.1	95.1	96.1	97.2	96.9	93	97.2
Share of votes by right-wing populist parties Vote Share	0.4	0.7	1	5.2	5.6	9	3.5
	0	0	0	0	0	0	0
	5.1	8.7	9.8	26.9	28.9	29.4	29.4
Eastern European Countries							
Turnout	–	–	–	72.5	59.5	56.4	63.3
				38.2	39.2	39.8	38.2
				96.8	72.2	65.6	96.8
Share of votes by right-wing populist parties Vote Share	–	–	–	9.6	8.1	8.9	8.9
				0	0	0	0
				45.2	32.1	37.6	45.2

From top to bottom: Mean; minimum and maximum, each in percent elections. However, there is a lot of variation between and within the different countries.

Table 39.1 shows that in the Western European countries (in this dataset) the participation rates in elections have decreased over the years. While more than 80% of all eligible voters went to vote between the 1960s and 1990s, it was only around 77% at the beginning of the 2000s. From 2010 this value fell to just over 70%.[3] It can also be seen that right-wing populist parties have become more successful over the years. Until the end of the 1980s, the proportion was less than one percent, and from 2010 onwards they could get an average of 9% of the votes. The trend in the Eastern European countries is similar, but somewhat more pronounced. While an average of 72% of eligible voters cast their vote from the first free elections in the early 1990s, this figure has steadily decreased over the years. As of 2010, only about 52% of those eligible to vote cast their ballot. What is also noticeable is that the proportion of votes for right-wing populist parties has not grown over the years, as in Western European countries. This has remained relatively the same at around 9%.

Due to the variation between and within the individual countries, Figs. 39.1 and 39.2 provide a more detailed overview of the relationship between the electoral success of right-wing populist parties and the level of voter turnout in Eastern and Western European countries.

The top line shows the average turnout. The bottom line shows the success of right-wing populist parties. The figures confirm that turnout has declined and right-wing populist parties have grown significantly in many countries. The figures also show that there is a large variance within and between countries. In some countries (e.g. Belgium and Luxembourg) the turnout rates are very high as a result of compulsory voting. In other countries (e.g. Switzerland, Poland and Lithuania) the voter turnout is rather low. In Austria, Switzerland and Poland, the right-wing populist parties' share of votes is relatively high, and in Portugal and Spain right-wing populist parties do not seem to play a major role.[4] The assumed direction and strength of the bivariate relationship between the election success of right-wing populist parties and average turnout also differ. In Western countries (Fig. 39.1), both variables mostly are negatively related (e.g. in France and Austria). In Eastern countries (Fig. 39.2), the influence of the election success of right-wing populist parties is predominantly positive (e.g. in Poland, Romania and Slovakia).

Because a more detailed look through the multivariate analysis is necessary, Table 39.2 shows the results of the time-series cross-sectional analysis.

Do the analyses indicate a positive influence of right-wing populist parties on voter turnout? The results are only mixed and ambiguous. It can be stated that the positive influence of right-wing populist parties on voter turnout assumed from the literature cannot be confirmed on the basis of the analyses.

First, all countries are analyzed in the entire dataset. Then the Western European and Eastern European countries are examined separately. The entire dataset is examined first. The results of the fixed and random effects models

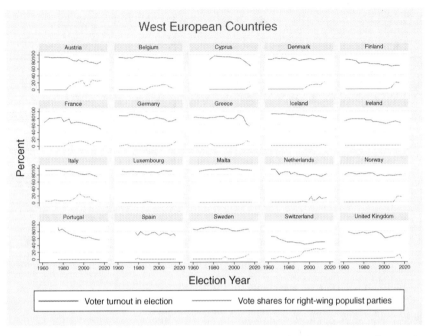

Fig. 39.1 Relationship between the electoral success of right-wing populist parties and the level of voter turnout in Western European countries

suggest that turnout is positively influenced by right-wing populist parties and that the effect is rather weak. The positive direction corresponds to the expectations from the literature and the assumption that right-wing populist parties boost voter turnout. However, the model with panel corrected standard errors indicates a negative connection. This contradicts the expected positive direction. Furthermore, only the model with panel corrected standard errors shows a significant coefficient of right-wing populist vote shares. The fixed and random effects models provide p-values that are above the conventional threshold. The results in Western European countries differ somewhat. The influence of the right-wing populist parties share of votes on voter turnout is also a negative one in all of the three models. Again, only in the model with panel corrected standard errors the coefficient is statistically significant. It looks a little different in the Eastern countries. The positive signs correspond to the expectations from the literature. However, only the coefficient in the fixed effects model is statistically significant.

The effects of the control variables mostly meet the expectations derived from the literature. The obligation to vote increases the turnout considerably. Because the formulation of models with fixed effects absorbs time-constant variables, the coefficient of compulsory voting in models with fixed effects cannot be estimated. Presidential systems have significant negative coefficients in a few models. GDP per capita and proportionality only have significant

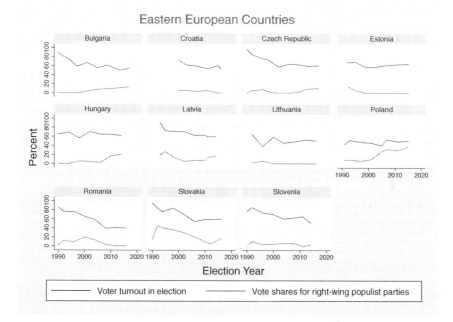

Fig. 39.2 Relationship between the electoral success of right-wing populist parties and the level of voter turnout in Eastern European countries

statistical effects in some models as well. The effective number of parties, apart from two models, does not meet the usual statistical significance levels.

How can the results be interpreted? The results are partly contrary to the results from the literature. Researchers note a positive relationship in Western European countries (due to the mobilization of the better-educated) and negative effects in Eastern European countries and justify this with demobilization, especially of younger people with positive attitudes towards migration (Immerzeel & Pickup, 2015). The analyses in this contribution reveal, however, negative effects in the entire sample and in Western European countries. The negative coefficients indicate that right-wing populist parties do not mobilize voters to vote. Can it be concluded from this that right-wing populist parties have a demobilizing effect? Scholars found this for a group of voters who, due to the negative campaign of right-wing populist parties, were demobilized and intimidated did not vote (Immerzeel & Pickup, 2015).[5] However, the relatively small effect would also have to be taken into account in this context. A slight mobilization effect can be derived from the positive and statistically significant effect of the fixed effects model in Eastern Europe. Because the fixed effects model controls all time-invariant variables and thus differences between the countries, the coefficient only shows the variation over time, which is explained by the success of right-wing populist parties. As a result, this suggests that right-wing populist parties have little mobilization

Table 39.2 Regression models (dependent variable: voter turnout)

	Complete sample—fixed effects	Complete sample—random effects	Complete sample PCSE	Western European countries—fixed effects	Western European countries—random effects	Western European countries—PCSE	Eastern European countries—fixed effects	Eastern European countries—random effects	Eastern European countries—PCSE
Right-wing populist parties vote share	0.123 (0.110)	0.0906 (0.100)	−0.223* (0.0990)	−0.0678 (0.102)	−0.0801 (0.0931)	−0.258* (0.115)	0.334* (0.145)	0.0810 (0.173)	0.0851 (0.146)
Unemployment rate	0.228 (0.176)	0.135 (0.170)	−0.622*** (0.137)	0.0963 (0.190)	0.0647 (0.182)	−0.531*** (0.122)	0.0242 (0.494)	0.0229 (0.506)	0.0340 (0.299)
Compulsory Voting	— (.)	15.71*** (3.715)	12.24** (1.501)	— (.)	9.067** (3.456)	9.631** (1.193)	—	—	—
(Log.) GDP	0.425 (0.262)	0.308 (0.276)	−1.047+ (0.630)	0.374 (0.278)	0.380 (0.280)	0.424 (0.603)	−1.683 (1.452)	−1.651 (1.698)	−1.742 (1.679)
Proportionality	3.513+ (1.959)	3.270* (1.603)	3.404*** (0.991)	2.922 (1.975)	3.169* (1.547)	3.804*** (0.979)	−2.065 (2.096)	8.634+ (4.792)	8.605+ (5.093)
Presidentialism	−2.972 (2.374)	3.469+ (1.788)	−4.582*** (0.798)	−1.829*** (0.687)	−2.484*** (0.827)	4.520*** (0.810)	−7.826 (4.931)	−8.808*** (2.871)	8.780*** (1.924)
Effective number of Parties	−0.0504	−0.172	−0.830*	0.103	0.0226	0.643+	−0.446	0.358	0.195
Constant	631.3*** (116.8)	604.6*** (118.9)	487.3*** (88.83)	506.0*** (117.5)	484.7*** (115.2)	183.0* (85.71)	1638.4** (457.1)	1181.8* (596.8)	1206.9*** (358.3)
N	301	301	301	245	245	245	56	56	56
R^2	0.369	0.375	0.630	0.426	0.375	0.643	0.505	0.361	0.467

Standard errors in parentheses. N: Number of Elections; PCSE: Panel Corrected Standard Errors in combination with Prais-Winsten-Transformation; Country/Time Fixed Effects included. +p <0.10, *p <0.05, **p <0.01, ***p <0.001

effect on voter turnout in Eastern European countries. However, one should take into account the small number of cases (56 elections). Moreover, the effect appears to be relatively weak.

The results are robust against various modifications of the empirical strategy (Neumayer & Plümper, 2017). A lagged dependent variable was included for the calculation of the models with panel corrected standard errors. In addition, a lagged variable for the right-wing populist vote shares has been included to take into account the general mobilization effects caused by the increasing election campaign. Further, the models were executed with Driscoll–Kraay standard errors in order to take account of the cross-sectional dependency. In some countries, the electoral success of right-wing populist parties does not seem to be a big issue (e.g. Portugal and Spain). These countries were excluded and the analysis were carried out again. As the robustness checks show, the results do not differ significantly. Ultimately, the data used in this study do not confirm the phrase that the election success of right-wing populist parties represent a democratic corrective in terms of higher voter turnout.

Conclusion

The main result of this analysis is that right-wing populist parties do not lead to an increase in voter turnout. There are slight differences between Western European and Eastern European Countries, but the differences are only small.

What are the implications of this contribution? One implication is that the democratic dilemma related to inequality in voter turnout remains unsolved. Even right-wing populist parties cannot mobilize to vote. This means that a large part of society no longer takes part in political decision-making processes related to the simplest way: Voting. This fact coincides with the research literature, according to which the typical voters of right-wing populist parties on the one hand want parties that represent their views, but do not want to be active themselves in the form of participation in elections (Mudde, 2007). In addition, voters could vote for right-wing populist parties, primarily because of economic fears for the future. Consequently, it would mean that right-wing populist parties cannot mobilize people simply because they are socially disadvantaged. In this case, economic fears for the future would be more decisive than the current socially disadvantaged situation (Schwander et al., 2020). It can be assumed that the group of non-voters will increase in the future. Education will play a key role in this. Just like voting as an internalized civic duty. A recently published study has shown that socially disadvantaged people in particular benefit from the educational reforms by narrowing the social gap in terms of voter turnout (Lindgren et al., 2019). Compulsory voting would significantly reduce inequality in voter turnout, too. Compulsory voting has been established by law in some countries and the pro and contra arguments are controversially discussed in the literature. The main counter-argument is the loss of individual freedom to choose to go to the polls or not (Brennan & Hill, 2014; Lever, 2010; Lijphart, 1997).

Further research should focus on differences between Eastern and Western European countries and take a closer look at them. Because the results of this study are based only on European data, further studies should use data from other democracies such as the USA or countries in South America and Asia. Future studies should focus on contextual factors that influence the relationship between right-wing populist parties and voter turnout. In addition, it is unclear whether the success of right-wing populist parties might influence other forms of political participation. Scientists claim that the number of people taking part in protests has increased significantly (Dalton, 2008). It would be conceivable that right-wing populist parties promote protest participation even more.

Notes

1. The research literature reveals that voter turnout is influenced by a vast number of factors. All of these factors are not the focus of this study and cannot or should not be considered for the analysis. At this point, reference is made in particular to the meta-studies of Geys (2006) and Smets and van Ham (2013).
2. For a critical discussion: (King & Roberts, 2015).
3. At this point, one should take into account countries with compulsory voting whose high values distort the average values.
4. In 2019, the Vox party in Spain received around 15% of the votes. However, the year 2019 is not part of the dataset and is therefore excluded from the calculation.
5. It is important to note that these results were achieved by individual data whereas this contribution relates on aggregated election data. The relationships observed by aggregated data do not necessarily hold for individuals (and vice versa). Furthermore, such statements would only be valid to a limited extent.

Literature

Achen, C. H. (2001). *Why lagged dependent variables can supress the explanatory power of other Indepenten variables*. Retrieved from https://www.princeton.edu/scdp/events/Achen121201/achen.pdf.

Armingeon, K., & Guthmann, K. (2014). Democracy in crisis? The declining support for national democracy in European countries, 2007–2011. *European Journal of Political Research, 53*(3), 423–442. https://doi.org/10.1111/1475-6765.12046.

Armingeon, K., & Schädel, L. (2015). Social inequality in political participation: The dark sides of individualisation. *West European Politics, 38*(1), 1–27. https://doi.org/10.1080/01402382.2014.929341.

Armingeon, K., Wenger, V., Wiedemeier, F., Isler, C., Knöpfel, L., Weisstanner, D., & Engler, S. (2019). *Comparative political data set 1960–2017*. Zurich: Institute of Political Science, University of Zurich.

Arzheimer, K. (2009). Contextual factors and the extreme right vote in Western Europe, 1980–2002. *American Journal of Political Science, 53*(2), 259–275.

Arzheimer, K. (2018). Explaining electoral support for the radical right. In R. Jens (Ed.), *The oxford handbook of the radical right* (pp. 143–165). Oxford University Press. https://doi.org/10.1093/oxfordhb/9780190274559.013.8.

Baltagi, B. H. (2008). *Econometric analysis of panel data.* Chichester, UK: John Wiley & Sons.

Beck, N., & Katz, J. N. (1995). What To Do (and not to do) with time-series cross-section data. *American Political Science Review, 89*(3), 634–647. https://doi.org/10.2307/2082979.

Blais, A. (2000). *To vote or not to vote: The merits and limits of rational choice theory.* Pittsburgh: University of Pittsburgh Press.

Blais, A. (2006). What affects voter turnout? *Annual Review of Political Science, 9*(1), 111–125. https://doi.org/10.1146/annurev.polisci.9.070204.105121.

Blais, A. (2007). Turnout in elections. In R. J. Dalton & H.-D. Klingemann (Eds.), *The Oxford handbook of political behavior* (pp. 621–635). Oxford University Press.

Bowler, S., Denemark, D., Donovan, T., & McDONNELL, D. (2017). Right-wing populist party supporters: Dissatisfied but not direct democrats: RIGHT-WING POPULIST PARTY SUPPORTERS. *European Journal of Political Research, 56*(1), 70–91. https://doi.org/10.1111/1475-6765.12166.

Brady, H. E., Verba, S., & Schlozman, K. L. (1995). Beyond SES: A resource model of political participation. *American Political Science Review, 89*(2), 271–294.

Brennan, J., & Hill, L. (2014). *Compulsory voting: For and against.* Cambridge University Press.

Burgoon, B., van Noort, S., Rooduijn, M., & Underhill, G. (2019). Positional deprivation and support for radical right and radical left parties*. *Economic Policy, 34*(97), 49–93. https://doi.org/10.1093/epolic/eiy017.

Cancela, J., & Geys, B. (2016). Explaining voter turnout: A meta-analysis of national and subnational elections. *Electoral Studies, 42,* 264–275. https://doi.org/10.1016/j.electstud.2016.03.005.

Dalton, R. J. (1984). Cognitive mobilization and partisan dealignment in advanced industrial democracies. *The Journal of Politics, 46,* 264–284.

Fortin-Rittberger, J. (2015). "Time-Series Cross-Section" in Henning Best and Christof Wolf (Eds.), *The Sage handbook of regression and causal inference* Sage Publishers.

Franklin, M. N. (2004). *Voter turnout and the dynamics of electoral competition in established democracies since 1945.* Cambridge: Cambridge University Press.

Franklin, M. N., Lyons, P., & Marsh, M. (2004). Generational basis of turnout decline in established democracies. *Acta Politica, 39*(2), 115–151. https://doi.org/10.1057/palgrave.ap.5500060.

Gallego, A. (2015). *Unequal political participation worldwide.* Cambridge University Press.

Geys, B. (2006). Explaining voter turnout: A review of aggregate-level research. *Electoral Studies, 25*(4), 637–663. https://doi.org/10.1016/j.electstud.2005.09.002.

Heinö, A. J. (2019). "*Timbro Authoritarian Populism Index 2019*". Timbro (blog). https://timbro.se/allmant/timbro-authoritarianpopulism-index-2019/.

Hooghe, M., & Marien, S. (2013). A Comparative analysis of the relation between political trust and forms of political participation in Europe. *European Societies, 15*(1), 131–152. https://doi.org/10.1080/14616696.2012.692807.

IDEA. (2021). *International Institute for Democracy and Electoral Assistance (International IDEA).* https://www.idea.int/data-tools/data/voter-turnout.

Immerzeel, T., & Pickup, M. (2015). Populist radical right parties mobilizing 'the people'? The role of populist radical right success in voter turnout. *Electoral Studies, 40*, 347–360. https://doi.org/10.1016/j.electstud.2015.10.007.

Inglehart, R. (1977). *The silent revolution: Changing values and political styles among Western publics*. Princeton: Princeton University Press.

Inglehart, R., & Flanagan, S. C. (1987). Value change in industrial societies. *American Political Science Review, 81*(4), 1289–1319.

Jackman, R. W. (1987). Political institutions and voter turnout in the industrial democracies. *American Political Science Review, 81*(2), 405–424.

Jahn, D. (2009). Die Aggregatdatenanalyse in der vergleichenden Politikwissenschaft. In S. Pickel, G. Pickel, H.-J. Lauth, & D. Jahn (Hrsg.), *Methoden der vergleichenden Politik-und Sozialwissenschaft: Neue Entwicklungen und Anwendungen* (S. 173–196). VS Verlag für Sozialwissenschaften.

Karp, J. A., & Banducci, S. A. (2008). Political efficacy and participation in twenty-seven democracies: How electoral systems shape political behaviour. *British Journal of Political Science, 38*(2). https://doi.org/10.1017/S0007123408000161.

King, G., & Roberts, M. E. (2015). How Robust standard errors expose methodological problems they do not fix, and what to do about it. *Political Analysis, 23*(2), 159–179. https://doi.org/10.1093/pan/mpu015

Lever, A. (2010). Compulsory voting: A critical perspective. *British Journal of Political Science, 40*(4), 897–915. https://doi.org/10.1017/S0007123410000050.

Lijphart, A. (1997). Unequal participation: Democracy's unresolved dilemma. *American Political Science Review, 91*(1), 1–14.

Lindgren, K.-O., Oskarsson, S., & Persson, M. (2019). Enhancing electoral equality: Can education compensate for family background differences in voting participation? *American Political Science Review, 113*(1), 108–122. https://doi.org/10.1017/S0003055418000746.

Lubbers, M., & Coenders, M. (2017). Nationalistic attitudes and voting for the radical right in Europe. *European Union Politics, 18*(1), 98–118. https://doi.org/10.1177/1465116516678932.

Mudde, C. (2007). *Populist radical right parties in Europe*. Cambridge University Press.

Plümper, T., Troeger, V. E., & Manow, P. (2005). Panel data analysis in comparative politics: Linking method to theory. *European Journal of Political Research, 44*(2), 327–354. https://doi.org/10.1111/j.1475-6765.2005.00230.x.

Rosenstone, S. J., & Hansen, J. M. (1993). *Mobilization, participation, and democracy in America*. New York: Macmillan Pub. Co.

Schwander, H., Gohla, D., & Schäfer, A. (2020). Fighting fire with fire? Inequality, populism and voter turnout. *Politische Vierteljahresschrift, 61*(2), 261–283. https://doi.org/10.1007/s11615-020-00247-1.

Smets, K., & van Ham, C. (2013). The embarrassment of riches? A meta-analysis of individual-level research on voter turnout. *Electoral Studies, 32*(2), 344–359. https://doi.org/10.1016/j.electstud.2012.12.006.

Solt, F. (2008). Economic inequality and democratic political engagement: Economic inequality and political engagement. *American Journal of Political Science, 52*(1), 48–60. https://doi.org/10.1111/j.1540-5907.2007.00298.x.

Solt, F. (2010). Does economic inequality depress electoral participation? *Testing the Schattschneider hypothesis: Political behavior, 32*(2), 285–301. https://doi.org/10.1007/s11109-010-9106-0.

Sorensen, R. J. (2016). After the immigration shock. *Electoral Studies, 44*, 1–14. https://doi.org/10.1016/j.electstud.2016.06.009.

Stockemer, D. (2017). What affects voter turnout? A review article/meta-analysis of aggregate eesearch. *Government and Opposition, 52*(4), 698–722. https://doi.org/10.1017/gov.2016.30.

Wolfinger, R. E., & Rosenstone, S. J. (1980). *Who votes?* New Haven: Yale University Press.

Wooldridge, J. M. (2010). *Econometric analysis of cross section and panel data.* Cambridge, Mass: MIT Press.

CHAPTER 40

Searching for the Philosopher's Stone: Counterstrategies Against Populism

Mario Schäfer and Florian Hartleb

POPULIST MOVEMENTS AS SERIOUS THREATS FOR LIBERAL DEMOCRACY

In "How Democracy Ends", David Runciman (Runciman, 2018) discusses a watershed of political events in recent years. These include, inter alia, the election of President Donald Trump in the United States (Weyland & Madrid, 2019), combined with Trump's refutation of his electoral defeat; the Brexit referendum; the electoral success of Italy's Lega; Brazil's sudden lurch to the right with the election of President Jair Bolsonaro (Feres Júnior & Gagliardi, 2021); and the increasing support for populist parties across Europe (Guth & Nelsen, 2019). Altogether they have brought the word "populism" into media headlines (Kyle & Gultchin, 2018) around the globe (Hartleb, 2021a)—the "trumpetisation of politics" has thus become a global trend (Weyland & Madrid, 2019). These political events have weakened both democratic norms and institutions (Levitsky & Ziblatt, 2018).

The last decades were ground shaking for liberal democracies not only in terms of the rise of right-wing populist movements, but also in the rise of left-wing populist movements. Although left-wing populism is not an entirely new phenomenon—in Latin America, a range of countries have been

M. Schäfer (✉)
International Politics, University of Passau, Passau, Germany
e-mail: mario.schaefer@uni-passau.de

F. Hartleb
Hanse Advice Tallin, Tallin, Estonia

or are currently ruled by populist left-wing leaders—and political science research has increasingly become aware of left-wing populism (Agustín, 2020; Damiani, 2020; Mouffe, 2018) and left-wing populist parties in Europe such as Podemos in Spain or the Five Stars Movement in Italy (Kioupkiolis, 2016; Mudde & Kaltwasser, 2017; Roodujin et al., 2019). Nevertheless, the mainstream research on these matters is conducted in respect of right-wing populism (Mudde & Kaltwasser, 2017; Kaltwasser et. al., 2017; Moffitt, 2020; Müller, 2016; Rooduijn, 2019).

Researchers investigate the sources for the rise of populism (Cox, 2018; Fukuyama, 2017; Hawkins, 2017; Margalit, 2019; Moffitt, 2020), but there is no unitary answer to this question: Is it the crisis and the system of democracy itself that causally lead to global populism (De la Torre, 2019), or is populism both a deceptive symptom and cause of an oncoming crisis? In the historical context of the USA, even a general populist momentum is debated (Goodwyn, 1976). Indeed, we are currently facing widespread disillusion with the Western model of liberal democracy (Inglehart & Norris, 2016).

Populism at the beginning of the twenty-first century is neither a mere style of communication nor a rigid ideology (in the sense of socialism, liberalism, conservatism or even fascism). This chapter follows the definition of Florian Hartleb (2004), who understands populism as strategy ensembled of four core elements (Hartleb, 2004, p. 68): first, the technique of drawing rigid boundaries; second, the orchestration of an apparently authentic "people's voice"; third, an anti-liberal stance; and fourth, mistrust of traditional media. Based on these considerations, the authors propose to analyze populism along three dimensions: First, in terms of a technique: constructing the "people" and an "other". Second, regarding content: positioning against status quo and identity issues. Third, concerning media: using new communication channels and Social-Media while blaming traditional media as disinformation channels and state agents (Table 40.1).

Table 40.1 The three dimensions of populism

Dimensions	Description
Technique-related	Construction of the "people", style of simplification and polarization; "us" versus "them" dichotomy; sometimes based on centralized leadership
Content-related	Against the status-quo; focus on identity topics addressing the dangers of globalization and effects such as globalization and Europeanization; nostalgic elements (reference to the national state)
Media-related	Focuses especially on tabloid media's scandalization habit; show elements; communication via alternative media and echo chambers; creating and spreading disinformation and attacking established media for creating such "fake news"

Updated Table based on Florian Hartleb (2004, p. 68)

Yet, despite some research has been undertaken already, the scientific landscape lacks some analyses on counterstrategies to populism: the philosopher's stone has not been found yet and further research in this field is clearly needed. The philosopher's stone was the central symbol of the mystical terminology of alchemy and a place of longing for the solution of mostly monetary problems. As the centuries passed, the search for this stone became synonymous with the search for all solutions. Thus, we ask: Can the philosopher's stone be found to conduct a counterstrategy[1] against populism in party competition?

However, next to the scientific relevance, there is also a societal relevance to conduct further research: combatting populism empty-handed can either fuel populists' own distinct "there is no alternative" agenda (Krastev, 2014, p. 75) or lead to adopting the populist agenda due to a lack of one's own forward frameworks and narratives—thus, the populist "identity". Mainstream politics has taken a defensive position due to recent crisis moments. If Europe cannot find common solutions to these crises—economy in 2009/2010, migration in 2015/2016 and the ongoing pandemic started in 2020—joint counterstrategies on a European level cannot be implemented.

In this chapter, we analyze the aforementioned dimensions and discuss possible counterstrategies against the rising left- and right-wing populism challenge. Each counterstrategy is approached in a threefold way: (1) counterstrategy description, (2) application examples and (3) success evaluation. As further explained below, the authors distinguish between actor-related and supporter-related response strategies and their respective core elements.

COUNTERSTRATEGIES ALONG THE THREE DIMENSIONS OF POPULISM

The further considerations on counterstrategies to populism are preceded by two basic assumptions: (1) The electoral majority does not want to vote for a populist party and (2) the supporters of populist parties differ from politicians, respectively, members of populist parties (Wuthrich & Ingleby, 2020, pp. 33–34). General counterstrategies[2] have to account for both domestic actors (such as political parties, civil society organizations and social movements, legal instruments and the media) and domestic supporters (the electorate that votes for populist parties form part of movements, shares the populist rhetoric—also via the media—and believes in the authenticity of the parties/movements). The actor- and supporter-based reactions can be short or long-term (Mudde & Kaltwasser, 2017). According to this analytical differentiation, we firstly display the actor-related counterstrategies ("Actor-Related Counterstrategies: Combating the Symptoms of Populism" section) and secondly the supporter-related ones ("Supporter-Related Counterstrategies: Combating the Causes of Populism" section).

Parties do not necessarily change their strategies homogeneously en bloc. Instead, they change positions independently, leaving the political system fragmented in terms of counterstrategies (Fallend & Heinisch, 2016, pp. 328–330). Additionally, as multiple examples show, counterstrategies might shift on the time axis as well. In Austria, for instance, established parties changed their position towards the FPÖ (Fallend & Heinisch, 2016, pp. 327–328). According to William M. Downs' (2012; Goodwin 2011, p. 23) two axes model, beginning by the most exclusive strategy and ending by the most inclusive one as well as disengagement and engagement, we address the selected counterstrategies. This axes model suits well to analytically order the corresponding strategies. Downs developed his model as a tool to analyze extremism. Although some scholars use extremism and populism almost interchangeably, we follow the populist strand of research to distinguish between the two terms strictly. Extremists might use populist strategies, but populists are no extremists, and thus they should not be labeled as such (von Beyme, 2019, pp. 57–61; see in this Volume Oswald, Schäfer, Broda). We include counterstrategies commonly used by established parties, and the observed counter-strategic claims of established political parties. Most of the strategies failed in various contexts during their application. That is why we propose a broader counterstrategy to combat populism sustainably.

Actor-Related Counterstrategies: Combating the Symptoms of Populism

When it comes to the question of how the symptoms of populism have been combatted so far, research identified several actor-related counterstrategies, seven of which will be introduced below (see Table 40.2).

Claiming a Ban and Forming a Cordon Sanitaire *on Populism*
Banning is the most aggressive exclusionary claim against populism and seeks to counter all three dimensions of populism. This strategy comprises all "legal attempts to isolate, restrict, repress, and even ban the offending pariah" (Downs, 2012, p. 31). It comprises legal restrictions on party names, symbols, slogans and publications and implies imposing legal restrictions on expression, assembly and financing (ibid., p. 37). This strategy seems well-suited to combat populist parties long-term without engaging them. So, mainstream politicians claimed that the Alternative for Germany (AfD) should be banned since they were "mental arsonists" (Bavarian Minister of the Interior, 2020). The Bavarian Minister of the Interior, Joachim Herrmann, demanded the ban of the party with regards to right-wing terrorist attacks (Hartleb, 2020) in Germany (Halle 9th October 2019; Hanau 19th February 2020).

However, the contrary is true. As Downs (2012) mentions, if the legal means for a constitutional/political ban exists, e.g. in Germany, France or Turkey (Backes, 2019; Karvonen, 2007), it aims to ban extremist parties operating against the constitutional order and oppose the system as such. Populist parties might pursue to build an illiberal democracy (Kuisz & Wigura, 2020, pp. 41–42), but they do not want to burn down the democratic system—if

Table 40.2 The exclusionary–inclusionary axis of counterstrategies actor-related (Combating the symptoms)

Claiming a Ban and forming a *cordon sanitaire*	– Using legal measures and options to isolate, restrict
	– Altering the rules of the games
	– Abstaining cooperation (*cordon sanitaire*)
Ignore	– Ignore it and hope that it may vanish (internal struggles of populists, disappointing electorate, etc.)
	– Position themselves as superior to populist parties (experienced in politics, believing in old routines)
Maintain the status quo	– Keeping the smile and holding established parties' own positions
	– Believe in own strength (taking voters back)
Tolerate	– Tolerating the new approaching force in parliament or government
	– Treating populists as other politicians
	– No change at all, but being sceptic about behavior/style/content
Adopt	– Changing their own positions/strategy/rhetoric
Cooperate	– Pressing the "power button" (coalition building with populist parties)
	– Using the embracing-strategy
	– Trying to "roll back"
Collaborate	– Cooperation on all levels (coalition on government level, toleration model, common force or bloc)

Own table with modifications based on Downs (2012)

they would, they must be declared extremists, not populists. Thus, the rhetorical strategy by established parties fails and could be even counterproductive, a failure of a party exclusion could reinforce populist parties' already strong and successful self-victimization strategy (Haller, 2015).

Instead, a more appropriate strategy against populism would be quarantine populist parties aiming at a technique- and content-related counterstrategy. This exclusionary approach is aimed long-term and obligates parties to disengage with populist parties. A conscious political quarantine of the parties in question means that mainstream parties actively decide that they are unwilling to accept populist parties as participants in the political playing field. Such an agreement, sometimes in the form of a contract, states that all agreeing parties reject cooperation with populist parties. The idea of quarantining is to make populist parties lose voting shares since the party has limited opportunities to obtain power. A *cordon sanitaire* of established parties has been undertaken in European countries such as Sweden, France, Belgium, Austria and Germany. In Sweden, for instance, the right-wing Swedish Democrats (SD) were excluded from advertising in media and participating in democratic discourse which caused massive demonstrations (Klein, 2013). For Belgium, Teun Pauwels sees a positive outcome of the *cordon sanitaire*, even though this attracted protest voters to vote for populist parties, "it seems that it also scares away large groups of voters in the long run" (Pauwels, 2013, p. 97) and the populist party Vlaams Belang (former Vlaams Bloc, VB) has never been in power. Despite the *cordon sanitaire's* positive effect, the stigmatization of being a party that needs to be quarantined again reinforces populists' self-portrayal as victims of the system (Pauwels, 2013, p. 97). Additionally, the parties need to respect the agreement and, as the French example regarding the Front National (today National Rally, FN) shows, party politics sometimes alter the code of conduct. So, in some departments, the French Republicans collaborated with the FN and arranged favorable agreements about their respective candidates for electoral districts (Balent, 2013, pp. 179–180).

Such a quarantine measure could also change the rules of party politics (Downs, 2012, p. 34). The most common instruments are, therefore, to restrict a party's participation in elections or parliament. This may include issues related to ballot access, eligibility for state campaign funding, deposit requirements and/ or entitlement to media time (ibid., p. 35). For instance, after the general elections in 2017, the Vice-President of the federal parliament "Bundestag" nominated from AfD was rejected several times irrespective of the consensual rules commonly applied in other times (Patton, 2019, p. 179). The strategy, however, was not successful in combating populism in parliament. It merely demonstrated to voters that the established parties would not even grant the rights they have been given to the biggest opposition party for decades. Still, it was an effective symbol that the *cordon sanitaire* stands strong.

A political quarantine imposed on a populist party by mainstream political actors can also send a message to the electorate that anyone wishing to be part of the political center should avoid supporting populism—as Pauwel (2013) suggests. On the contrary, the established political parties quarantine legally elected representatives and, as a result, exclude votes from the political arena.

Ignore Populism
Another counterstrategy to combat populism is the *ignoreit* approach, which is less exclusionary than the strategies mentioned above but just as disengaged as those, because established parties do not actively respond to populist parties. Ignoration can be characterized as combating all three dimensions of right-wing populism, technique-related, content-related and media-related. Established parties continue with business as usual without paying further attention to populists. Convinced that populist parties will disappear with time passing on the medium- or long-term due to internal struggles or shifts in

electoral support, established parties wait without applying additional countermeasures. Therefore, one cannot expect a change in media-strategic behavior or changes in party content strategy.

The ignore it approach was applied in the Netherlands during the 1990s when the Dutch Center Democrats were represented in the national parliament. Being framed as undemocratic populists, the leading figures were "usually ignored and never taken seriously by his colleagues in the other parties" (van Spanje & van der Brug, 2007, p. 1030). By that time, the DCD was a marginal party and thus not even taken seriously as a whole.

The ignore it strategy might work when the party is small and has an insignificant voting share. However, the larger the populist party gets, the less practical and capable the strategy is since it would mean ignoring larger parts of the electorate (Downs, 2012, pp. 46–47). It therefore could also have the contrary effect; ignoring populist parties and sticking to old routines may give the impression of intangibility and fuel populist movements.

Considering the present success of populism, the ignore it approach appears to be far from a successful remedy. Given that populists generally articulate real problems—albeit via oversimplification and scrupulous elements of discourse or action—ignoring them would be strategically shortsighted (Heinze, 2018). In addition to the ignoration of the political figures, established parties need to convince their supporters that established parties are aware of their needs and demands.

Maintain the Status Quo and Tolerance
Similar, but less exclusionary to the ignoration approach and more a possible tactical behavior than a strategy would be to *maintain the status quo and tolerate* the populist party, which would tackle the technique- and content-related dimension of right-wing populism. Established parties maintain the status quo as it is without any change as if there were no threat of populist parties. Thus, they do not change their own positions and continue with business as usual without any alarmist or activist behavior. The focus here is more on the party's own strength and their conviction that voters can be re-gained through proceeding with their long-term policies, taking into account short-term electoral losses. To put it in the words of Ann-Sophie Heinze: "Although it is often the first strategy to be attempted, its success is unlikely if the other mainstream parties adopt the RPP's position" (Heinze, 2018, p. 290).

In Norway, established parties used the strategy to maintain the status quo and to hold their own positions against the electoral success of the Progress Party (FrP) in 1989. The newcomer acted responsible and supportive of the budgetary negotiations over many decades and was therefore tolerated by the other political forces until a general shift in the party system throve other parties towards a more right-wing orientation in the 1990s and the FrP formed part of the government (Heinze, 2018, p. 296). Here, the established parties diffused the immigration topic for a long time. The contrary happened in Finland. Although the governing parties in Finland dishonored The Finns, they added immigration into political discourse (Raunio, 2013, p. 137). These examples demonstrate that maintaining the status quo and holding their own positions does not necessarily lead to a successful defeat of populist parties.

Toleration must not be equated with acceptance. While tolerance includes possible opposition to some issues or the whole party, acceptance is the formal recognition and legitimization of another party (cf. Hjerm et al., 2020, p. 904; Van Quaquebeke et al., 2007, pp. 189–193). Maintaining the status quo and tolerating populist parties can also result in the respective toleration of minority governments—backed by populist parties.

In Denmark, the established parties tolerated the Dansk Folkeparti (DF) after the DF was represented in the Danish parliament. Andreas Klein argues that even "[i]n this way, the DF enjoyed more freedom than it would have been allowed had it been directly involved in the government" (Klein, 2013, p. 115). In 2001, the DF backed the liberal–conservative government by not opposing them. They were not represented in the cabinet but did also not formally counteract the government. Thus, the DF became a kingmaker in Danish politics. Doing so, Prime Minister Anders Fogh Rasmussen was re-elected in 2005 and 2007 (Klein, 2013, p. 108).

This approach seems somewhat problematic: Oliver Geden (2007, p. 24) dissuade from deriding (right-wing) populist parties and exclude or only tolerate. If one considers populism as a result of a crisis, the latter is neither tackled nor defeated, and populist arguments are not delegitimized. Consequently, the cause remains, perhaps even pushing more voters towards the populist camp. So, this strategy seems more short-term and neither engaged nor disengaged with populist actors.

Adapt the Concerns and Rhetoric of Populists
Putting aside any moral considerations, the most salient political solution for neutralizing populism is to integrate populist themes and agendas into mainstream discourse (Lucardie & Voerman, 2013, p. 226). Thus, this counterstrategy is content- and media-related since established parties change their content and their media strategy. Most strikingly in Denmark, even the Social Democrats adopted much of the Danish People's Party's anti-migrant rhetoric, risking a betrayal of liberal core values. Whether causally related or not, the Social Democrats won the election in June 2019 with 25.9% of the votes (Statistics Denmark, 2021). For the Netherlands, Paul Lucardie and Gerrit Voerman conclude that "[i]t would seem exaggerated to conclude that Dutch politics as a whole has become more populist, if we use populism in the ideological sense and not as a rhetorical style" (Lucardie & Voerman, 2013, p. 200). Thus, the political rhetoric has shifted as a result of populist parties in parliament. For instance, the refugee crisis of 2015/16 has shifted discourse not only in Poland but in many European countries. As in the Polish case, populist parties were the drivers for shifting the discourse (Krzyzanowski, 2018).

Could the philosopher's stone be found in the *adaptation of populist rhetoric* or content for a longer term? In an attempt to re-gain voting shares, mainstream parties sharpen their political agenda to incorporate populist topic attractivity (Goodwin, 2011, p. 24). Changing their agenda, established parties risk losing voters' trust and decreasing party's core constituency. As a result, intra-party discussions might polarize and instead of re-gaining voters, the legitimacy of populist positions might increase (Heinze, 2018, p. 290). The adaptation strategy is certainly risky as mainstream parties are ultimately imposters in this game; and thus only imposter of the original. The effects can be long-lasting: Chancellor Sebastian Kurz's ÖVP was not the only party that failed to re-adapt center-right positions in the past. Taking into account their share of votes of 37.46% in 2019—5.99% points more than in 2017— (Nationalratswahl, 2019. (n.d.)), one could argue that they should not even do so. Similar evidence can be found, for instance, in the refugee crisis when other countries failed to shift back party positions (Grabow & Hartleb, 2013, p. 402; 2014). A more general effect that can be observed is that mainstream parties try to counter the anti-elitism of populists with slogans such as "we are not ordinary politicians". Parties such as La République en Marche labeled themselves not as parties, instead they preferred the term "movement" or "social movement", a strategy by populists to separate themselves from the establishment (Hartleb, 2004; Raunio, 2013, p. 134; Wodak, 2019). Even the ÖVP re-labeled them as "List Sebastian Kurz – the new People's Party" in the same manner (Wolkenstein, 2019). The strength of anti-establishment parties could enforce the tendency to trivialize politics (in a "fast food" format), for example, by offering simple solutions to complex problems. Adaption, on the other hand, may contribute to retroactively legitimizing populist's positions (Goodwin 2011, p. 24) and setting the political agenda (Roodujn et al. 2014, p. 563ff., Mudde, 2004, p. 563, Downs, 2012, p. 44f., 63).

Cooperating and Collaborating
Downs concludes that policies "of isolation, ostracism and demonization prove surprisingly ineffective at rolling back or even containing threats to the democratic order from party-based extremism" (Downs, 2012, p. 20). Even though he refers to extremist parties and not to populist parties, the same conclusion applies to populist parties. To combat populism, parties use even more substantial and more inclusionary strategies than adapting the concerns and rhetoric of right-wing populists. Some parties cooperate or even take populists as coalition partners in government.

Cooperation and collaboration both account for countering all three dimensions of populism. If democratic parties, regardless of their actual ideological orientation, adopt ring-wing populist demands by signing a coalition treaty based on compromise, they run a number of severe risks. One of them is a potential loss of credibility, both among their voters and the wider public. In Estonia, the consequences of right-wing populist participation in government (from April 2019 till the government split in January 2021) can be seen as if under a magnifying glass: they were dividing society (Hartleb, 2021b). After all, the Conservative People's Party of Estonia (EKRE) is now mainstream in society and a remaining factor in politics. In contrast, in Finland The Finns destroyed themselves discursively when they first entered the government. The polarization gap led to the separation of two independent movements (Jungar, 2016).

Collaboration means actively and tolerantly working together as—more or less—equal partners who can form coalition governments together. Through the close relationship and trust-building measures that collaboration encompasses, established parties expect populist parties to show incompetence in office and, thus, to disenchant themselves. Furthermore, the collaboration should deepen the internal conflicts between a more radical wing and a more moderate wing (van Spanje & van der Brug, 2007, p. 1023).

In Austria, for instance, the FPÖ was first isolated by a *cordon sanitaire* in the 1990s. While the party successively gained larger voting shares, the ÖVP loosened its quarantine and began to build coalitions, first on a regional level, later the national level. In 2000, the ÖVP formed a formal coalition with the FPÖ making the FPÖ concede parts of its program—the ÖVP pushed through a pro-European course, as well as a commitment against anti-Semitism. As a result, the FPÖ become deradicalized to shift towards more moderate positions. In the process, the gap between the political wings—those willing and those unwilling to form a coalition—widened. The result was a schism of the party and a clear containment of their political power (Fallend & Heinisch, 2016, pp. 328–329).

Even though no incontrovertible proof can be found that demystification through participation in government is an effective strategy for successfully combating politically right-wing populists in the long-term, there is no doubt that this allows populists to directly exert influence on a country's political decision-making with being directly held accountable for it. Instead of more exclusionary approaches, such a strategy uncovers whether populists continue to exploit the public disquietly and mobilize dissatisfied voters against the "establishment". Heinze concluded: Being in office, populist movements lose their movement character and could be "tamed" by "de-radicalise its position and rhetoric" (Heinze, 2018, p. 290). Today, Podemos and the 5 Star Movement demonstrate that "taming" is not a self-fulfilling prophecy. Although ruling in coalitions, they remain populist—Podemos' changed towards Mouffe's agonism model (Franzé, 2017). Additionally, the fear remains that populist parties "become legitimised, to emerge from their marginalised position, and gain influence in politics without being held responsible" (Heinze, 2018, p. 290).

Supporter-Related Counterstrategies—Combating the Causes of Populism

Having introduced into actor-related counterstrategies, we now look at counterstrategies that address the supporters of populist parties. Five of such

Table 40.3 Countering the roots of populism—supporter-related

Confront	– Debating concretely and actively with right-wing populists
	– Finding arguments why populists fail the reality tests (especially the aspect countering simplification and generalization)
Debate	– Addressing aspects of political (debate) culture
	– Stimulating debates in the organized civil society (NGOs etc.)
Increasing participation (democraticdeliberation)	– Offering established participation tools (e.g. referenda)
	– Using digital technologies
	– Applying inclusion and intergenerational aspects
	– Creating new opportunities for participation
Pushing forward *media awareness and education*	– Educating media competences and developing means for it
	– Fighting against the spread of misinformation and disinformation
Boosting socio-economic welfare and addressing cultural needs	– Diminishing the gap of distribution within societies (output-legitimation)
	– Addressing cultural issues
	– Finding integrativ tabBODYe tools society as a whole (against parallel societies)

Own table

strategies will be displayed below (see Table 40.3). The authors make no claim to completeness of this supporter-related strategies, and many more are thinkable. These examples are either currently performed or our own suggestion.

Confrontation

The first supporter-related counterstrategy *confronting populism* accounts for the content-related dimension of populism. It seeks to confront populists and, foremost, their supporters with populists' scandals and contradictions to show that populist parties are not reliable or competent to obtain power. For instance, in the case of Fidesz, scandals and internal contradictions became obvious: Being a loyal party member, Member of the European Parliament and cofounder of the party, Joszef Sajer wrote parts of the new Hungarian constitution, which encompasses paragraphs against homosexuality and the sanctity of the marriage. During the pandemic-related lockdown in Brussels, he attended a gay sex party and was caught by the police due to social-distancing measures, such a party was not allowed (Kaszás, 2020).

This event put Fidesz in a problematic self-defending situation, since Sajer contradicted apparently party principles. Such inconsistencies are manifold within populist rhetoric and behavior. Thus, making them public and exposing populist parties to criticism is a strategy to convince voters that these parties are not as sacrosanct as they seem. However—thanks to the populists' tactic to portray themselves as victims—this does not necessarily end populist politician's careers; although Sajer left the Fidesz party after 30 years not completely voluntarily.

Active Discussion
The most harmonious solution in terms of democratic principles is when populists are engaged in *active discussion* about the existing problems they address (Hubacher Haerle & Beckstein, 2019). Thus, this counterstrategy is technique- and content-related, highly engaging and long-term. The counterstrategy active discussion presumes that the political system is in a kind of crisis and accordingly that populists seek to address a society's hopes and fears that exist in society. Through active discussion, politicians of established parties distinguish ideological claims from actual necessities and begin to speak directly or indirectly with the supporter of populist parties (Biskamp, 2019, p. 100).

This way, populist argumentation is confronted with reality, and their exaggerations are corrected, while at the same time policy solutions are developed (Hubacher Haerle & Beckstein, 2019, pp. 173–174). Pluralistic democracies require engagement in dialog, especially when individual opinions diverge (p. 173). This idealistic approach, however, is not straightforward in practice, and it demands a particularly high level of competence, rhetorical agility and "soft skills" on part of the dialogue partners; indeed, the democratic deficit which fueled the success of populism also occurred under the watch of the same elite (Hubacher Haerle & Beckstein, 2019, pp. 174–175). Even if communication is improved and more satisfactory policy solutions are put in place, a section of society with preference for populists would likely remain, since populist attitudes are likely to persist (Geurkink et. al., 2020).

Increasing Deliberative Political Participation
A rethinking of political participation could focus on an inclusive rather than an exclusive approach. This counterstrategy concerns all three dimensions of populist strategy and accounts for a more deliberative manner of combating populism. Thus, it is long-term and less engaging with direct populist movements. The strategy takes into account deliberation in the sense of Jürgen Habermas (1992). Referenda, for instance, would be probate means to include the public if they are used to counter populist parties' desires (van Crombrugge, 2020). In Ecuador, Lenín Moreno obtained government from the populist president Rafael Correa, and used referenda to secure the political system against populist rules (de Lara & de la Torre, 2020, p. 70). To the detriment of the Ecuadorian liberal democracy, he misused this means to gain

more political power, just as a number of Latin American populists did before him (ibid., p. 69; 79). The result of this understanding of deliberation is a possible backfire and increase in populism, as seen in the Ecuadorian example, where populism re-gained popularity (ibid., p. 79).

In the world of digital politics, e-participation offers new possibilities, such as webcasts and podcasts, surveys, participation in web-portals, chat rooms, polls and decision-making games, e-petitioning and e-voting. Across Europe, many e-participation projects have been funded in recent years, but their effects and impacts are difficult to ascertain.

However, studies often show mixed results, with digital technologies facilitating reinforcement and mobilization only among particular user groups of digital platforms (Nam, 2012). Nevertheless, changes will be less striking than some party strategists and academics claim because parties can reform or transform their organizational patterns only to a certain extent. The use of e-voting (in Estonia on the national level since 2005) does not increase participation, and it did not prevent populists from being kept out of parliament (Krimmer, 2012; Lanko, 2015). Participation-maximizing reforms assume that the locus of political reform should be to strengthen ties between individual voters and individual politicians. This can lead to the effect, intended or not, of weakening intermediating influences and institutions, such as parties and fragmentize politics, although Ian Budge rather rebuts this argument, since he found evidence on the contrary development (Budge, 2001, 2006).

Media Awareness and Education

A long-term strategy to combat populists' technique- and media-related dimensions, less engaging but long-term, promotes media awareness and education. We are aware that not all populists believe in conspiracy theories or share misinformation or disinformation. In (right-wing) populist circles, however, the belief and the frequency to share such theories or disinformation is, generally speaking, higher than in majority society (van Kessel & Van Hauwaert, 2021). Additionally, populists often simplify information or frame messages to polarize society. At the beginning of the digital era, mainstream media lost its gatekeeping function because stories and information can be published and distributed freely on the internet or social-media platforms such as Facebook, Instagram or Youtube (Peter & Koch, 2019, p. 436). Even for a well-equipped citizen, it can be hard work to differentiate between facts and fiction (Bergmann, 2020). Bergmann examines Russia, the U.S. and the U.K. and clearly illustrates the problem. He concludes: The current world is filled with over-information, where we can lose track of which data we can trust or how to distinguish fake from fact. If everything is true, then in the end, nothing is true at all (Bergmann, 2020, p. 262). Especially for democratic discourse, this can be poisonous.

Therefore, media competence and awareness are crucial in countering populist strategies. If applied successfully, this strategy facilitates ordinary citizens to evaluate information and classify its quality as well as serosity of media sources. This means "to reinforce and stabilize the basic procedures and values of the democratic system – [...], to help its consolidation" (Capoccia, 2005, p. 49). Citizenship education aims at enabling citizens to critically interact with the political system, media and information. Thus, education prevents authoritarianism, xenophobia and leads to more toleration and acceptance (Hagendoorn & Nekuee, 2018; Johnsson, 2013).

Since the so-called refugee crisis in 2015/16, fake news, disinformation and moralistic manipulation via social channels has accelerated in Europe (Humprecht, 2019). Facebook itself has published a detailed and precise study on civic engagement that discusses possible countermeasures. The company states:

> The networks of politically-motivated false amplifiers and financially-motivated fake accounts have sometimes been observed commingling and can exhibit similar behaviours; in all cases, however, the shared attribute is the inauthenticity of the accounts. [...] In some instances, dedicated, professional groups attempt to influence political opinions on social media with large numbers of sparsely populated fake accounts that are used to share and engage with content at high volumes. (Weeden et al., 2017)

According to Facebook, the spread of disinformation is accelerated and professionalized by certain groups and, thus, not negligible and needs to be countered. At the beginning of 2017, then Czech Prime Minister Bohuslav Sobotka announced his government's intention to modify the school curriculum in order to teach children how to assess the credibility of information (Prague Daily Monitor, 2017). However, presenting people facts could have the reverse effect of making them adhere even more strongly to their own beliefs. Recent research suggests that backfire effects are unlikely to happen (Haglin, 2017). Nevertheless, contrasting rival information imposes unrealistic and often unfair burdens on people's time and cognitive capacities. The training of digital and media competencies seems to be an increasingly important counterstrategy in times of disinformation, big data and information overload.

To the dismay of sincere and well-principled societies, truthfulness is often not of high value to populists. On the contrary, populists aim to scandalize what directly affects mainstream media and is diffused even more (Bergmann, 2020 p. 252).

Secure Socio-economic Welfare and Incorporate Cultural Issues
While other counterstrategies fail or require a high level of training, we suggest a new approach to combat populism more fundamentally, accounting for all three dimensions of populist strategies.

More interaction and comprehension are needed between the privileged and the more vulnerable non-privileged. Instead of treating the symptoms of populist rise, politics and society need to address the social, economic and, above all, cultural needs of the supporters of populism. The first part of that strategy is to carefully listen and take supporters' fears seriously. Second, established parties need to account for the emotions of the people. Populism strikingly mobilizes emotions, whereas established parties rather communicate in a rational way (Kuisz & Wigura, 2020, p. 46). What these parties need is a new vision in today's world, with a sustainable economy and society. To counter populist arguments, established parties must appeal to an emotional-narrative counterargument (ibid., pp. 46–47). Its long-lasting positive effects might be a reduction of polarization, more equality and more equal opportunities for most of the population combined with a more robust economic development based on inclusion instead of the exclusionary narrative of populists. That way, the needs for socio-economic security (based on the proud preservation of the ideals of the welfare state (Jungar, 2016) and cultural issues must not be neglected but incorporated to leave the track towards identity politics (Fukuyama, 2018; Inglehart & Norris, 2016).

Concluding Remarks

To tackle the various populist strategies, numerous counterstrategies are being applied by established political actors. As displayed above, these can be traced along the technique-related, the content-related and the media-related dimension of populism. Following the previous discussion and evaluation of these strategies, one can say: Neither is there a uniform counterstrategy against populism, nor is there a single "model" that can be applied across markedly different cases and regions. The factors fueling populism are likely to persist. Populism will be a fixture of politics for the foreseeable future teasing established political parties with their technique, content and media dimensional strategies. This does not mean, however, that the formation or establishment of right-wing or left-wing populist parties must be seen as inevitable. Yet, a more comprehensive approach that takes into account the various dimensions of populist strategies is needed to effectively combat populism.

While the presented evaluations concentrated mostly on right-wing populism, further research is needed that considers the various societal effects of left-wing populism on societies.

We have not found many examples that these counterstrategies were applied to left-wing populist parties. We suspect that it is the case because left-wing populism is perceived as more inclusionary—especially in Latin America—than the exclusionary right-wing populism we see in Europe. In other parts of the world, left-wing populism is not even considered dangerous to liberal party systems (Mudde & Kaltwasser, 2013).

In Europe, liberal democratic actors must learn to compete responsibly and to contain the adverse effects that populism can have on liberal democracies. From time to time, it seems as if politicians assumed that political topics would be too complicated for many voters to digest. If this rather elitist argument was true, democratic parties must not shy away from patiently explaining publicly their goals or means. Additionally, they need to develop and articulate visions.

In this respect, populist agenda setting may help them to identify areas of policy that are causing dissatisfaction or concern among the public. These areas must be addressed in a clear, targeted way by the established mainstream parties. In any way, the growth of populist parties should be seen as an early-warning system whose signals must be interpreted correctly by the established democratic parties. Effective and sustainable counterstrategies must devitalize the criticism brought up by populists, regarding a premature, neoliberal spurt of modernization that casts the model of the nation-state into question. The fragmentation of the established media and its disintegration by virtue of social media renders it almost impossible to attain a societal consensus that can deconstruct and delegitimize the illusions of authenticity presented by populists. Therefore, we suggest ensuring socio-economic security and address cultural issues. More equal distribution of wealth and equal opportunities, plus a new emotional narrative culminating in a new vision might help cure a possible cause for populist movements: Polarization of society and disenfranchisement. Nevertheless, the search for the philosophers' stone continues. We provided some starting points for further engagement and a possible new counterstrategy. Whether the philosophers' stone to combat populism can be found, the future will show.

Notes

1. We are convinced that the summary by Ann-Sophie Heinze is fitting: "As each strategy is a conceptual calculation of actors, based on their perceived goals and resources, it cannot be directly observed but can only be interpreted through their political actions" (Heinze, 2018, p. 291). Thus, we interpret the concrete actions of established parties to combat populism.
2. Current approaches of Chantal Mouffe (2018) of others promote left-wing populism in opposition to right-wing populism, thus, conceptualizing populism more as a style and a logic than a strategy. Therefore, the authors do not refer to left-wing populism as a counterstrategy on right-wing populism. Additionally, the authors have not found many examples of counterstrategies applied to left-wing populist parties. This might be the case because in some parts of the world- for example South America-, left-wing populism is not even considered dangerous to liberal party systems (Mudde & Kaltwasser, 2013). Thus, the paper is more focused on counter-strategies for right-wing populist parties.

Bibliography

Agustín, Ó. G. (2020). *The left-wing populist wave in Europe*. Emerald Publishing Limited.

Backes, U. (2019). Banning political parties in a democratic constitutional state: The second NPD ban proceedings in a comparative perspective. *Patterns of Prejudice, 53*(2), 136–151.

Balent, M. (2013). The French national front from Jean-Marie to Marine Le pen: Between change and continuity. *Exposing the Demagogues. Right-wing and National*

Populist Parties in Europe. Joint publication of CES and Konrad Adenauer Stiftung. Belgium: Drukkerij Jo Vandenbulcke, 161–187.

Bavarian Minister of the Interior Herrmann Blames AfD for Being Joint Guilty for the Terror Attacks of Hanau. (2020, February 21). *BR24*. https://www.br.de/nachrichten/meldung/bayerns-innenminister-herrmann-gibt-afd-mitschuld-am-terroranschlag-von-hanau,30029d02e.

Bergmann, E. (2020). Populism and the politics of misinformation. *Safundi, 21*(3), 251–265.

Biskamp, F. (2019). Six theories and sic strategies concerning right-wing populism. In P. Bevelander, & R. Wodak (Eds.), *Europe at the crossroads: Confronting populist, nationalist and global challenges* (pp. 93–112.). Nordic Academic Press.

Budge, I. (2001). Political parties in direct democracy. In *Referendum democracy* (pp. 67–87). Palgrave Macmillan.

Budge, I. (2006). Direct and representative democracy: Are they necessarily opposed? *Representation, 42*(1), 1–12.

Capoccia, G. (2005). *Defending democracy: Reactions to extremism in interwar Europe.* JHU Press.

Cox, M. (2018). *Understanding the global rise of populism.*

Damiani, M. (2020). *Populist radical left parties in Western Europe: Equality and sovereignty.* Routledge.

De Lara, F. B., & de la Torre, C. (2020). The pushback against populism: Why Ecuador's referendums backfired. *Journal of Democracy, 31*(2), 69–80.

De la Torre, C. (Ed.). (2019). *Routledge handbook of global populism.* Routledge.

Downs, W. M. (2012). *Political extremism in democracies.* Palgrave Macmillan.

Fallend, F., & Heinisch, R. (2016). Collaboration as successful strategy against right-wing populism? The case of the centre-right coalition in Austria, 2000–2007. *Democratization, 23*(2), 324–344.

Feres Júnior, J., & Gagliardi, J. (2021). Populism and the media in Brazil: The case of Jair Bolsonaro. In *The politics of authenticity and populist discourses: Media and education in Brazil, India and Ukraine* (pp. 83–104).

Franzé, J. (2017). La trayectoria del discurso de Podemos: Del antagonismo al agonismo. *Revista Española De Ciencia Política, 44*, 219–246.

Fukuyama, F. (2017). *What is populism?.* Tempus Corporate.

Fukuyama, F. (2018). *Identity: The demand for dignity and the politics of resentment.* Farrar, Straus and Giroux.

Geden, O. (2007). Rechtspopulismus: Funktionslogiken-Gelegenheitsstrukturen-Gegenstrategien.

Geurkink, B., Zaslove, A., Sluiter, R., & Jacobs, K. (2020). Populist attitudes, political trust, and external political efficacy: Old wine in new bottles? *Political Studies, 68*(1), 247–267. https://doi.org/10.1177/0032321719842768

Goodwyn, L. (1976). *Democratic promise: The populist moment in America.* Oxford University Press.

Goodwin, M. (2011). *Right response. Understanding and countering populist extremism in Europe.* Chatham House.

Grabow, K., & Hartleb, F. (2013). Strategic responses to the populists' advance: Options for Christian democratic and conservative parties. In F. Hartleb, & K. Grabow (Eds.), *Exposing the demagogues: Right-wing and national populist parties in Europe* (pp. 399–410). CES Centre for European Studies and Konrad-Adenauer-Stiftung.

Grabow, K., & Hartleb, F. (2014). '*Europa – No, thanks? Study on the rise of right-wing and nationalist populist parties*. CES Centre for European Studies and Konrad-Adenauer-Stiftung.

Guth, J. L., & Nelsen, B. F. (2019). Party choice in Europe: Social cleavages and the rise of populist parties. *Party Politics*. https://doi.org/10.1177/1354068819853965

Habermas, J. (1992). Drei normative Modelle der Demokratie: Zum Begriff deliberativer Demokratie. In H. Münkler (Ed.), Die *Chancen der Freiheit. Grundprobleme der Demokratie* (pp. 11–24).

Hagendoorn, L., & Nekuee, S. (2018). *Education and racism: A cross national inventory of positive effects of education on ethnic tolerance*. Routledge.

Haglin, K. (2017). The limitations of the backfire effect. *Research & Politics*. https://doi.org/10.1177/2053168017716547

Haller, A. (2015). How to deal with the Black Sheep? An evaluation of journalists' reactions towards intentional selfscandalization by politicians. *Journal of Applied Journalism & Media Studies*, 4(3), 435–451 (17).

Hartleb, F. (2004). *Rechts- und Linkspopulismus: Eine Fallstudie anhand von Schill-Partei und PDS*. VS Verlag für Sozialwissenschaften.

Hartleb, F. (2020). *Lone wolves. The new terrorism of right-wing single actors*. Springer.

Hartleb, F. (2021a). Materalizations of populism in today's politics: Global perspectives. In B. Christophe, H. Liebau, C. Kohl, A. Saupe (Eds.), *The politics of authenticity and populist discourses: Media and education in Brazil, India and Ukraine* (pp. 31–52). Palgrave Macmillan.

Hartleb, F. (2021b). Estland: Rechtsradikale im Mainstream. *Blätter für deutsche und internationale Politik*, 66(3), 33–36.

Hawkins, K., Read, M., & Pauwels, T. (2017). Populism and its causes. *The Oxford handbook of populism* (pp. 267–286).

Heinze, A.-S. (2018). Strategies of mainstream parties towards their right-wing populist challengers: Denmark Norway, Sweden and Finland in comparison. *West European Politics*, 41(2), 287–309. https://doi.org/10.1080/01402382.2017.1389440

Hjerm, M., Eger, M. A., Bohman, A., & Connolly, F. F. (2020). A new approach to the study of tolerance: Conceptualizing and measuring acceptance, respect, and appreciation of difference. *Social Indicators Research*, 147(3), 897–919.

Hubacher Haerle, P., & Beckstein, M. (2019). Das Paradox der Toleranz zwischen politischer Theorie und zivilgesellschaftlicher Praxis. Soll man PopulistInnen zu Podiumsdiskussionen einladen?. *ZPTh – Zeitschrift für Politische Theorie*, 2, 169–192.

Humprecht, E. (2019). Where 'fake news' flourishes: A comparison across four Western democracies. *Information, Communication & Society*, 22(13), 1973–1988.

Inglehart, R., & Norris, P. (2016, August). *Trump, Brexit and the rise of populism. Economic have-Nots and Cultural Backlash*. Harvard Kennedy School, Working Paper, Cambridge/Massachusetts. https://papers.ssrn.com/sol3/papers.cfm?abstract_id=2818659. Accessed on 4st March 2021).

Johansson, S. (2013). Innovative methods and models of collaboration in the field of pedagogical prevention of xenophobia, anti-Semitism and right-wing extremism: Chances and perspectives for a better cooperation between formal and non-formal education in Germany. *Socialinė Teorija, Empirija, Politika Ir Praktika*, 7, 119–132.

Jungar, A.-C. (2016). From the mainstream to the margin? The radicalization of the True Finns. In T. Akkerman, S. de Lange, & M. Rooduijn (Eds.), *Radical right-wing populist parties in Western Europe. Into the Mainstream?* (pp. 113–143).

Kaltwasser, C. R., Taggart, P. A., Espejo, P. O., & Ostiguy, P. (Eds.). (2017). *The Oxford handbook of populism*. Oxford University Press.

Karvonen, L. (2007). Legislation on political parties: A global comparison. *Party Politics, 13*(4), 437–455. https://doi.org/10.1177/1354068807077955

Kaszás, F. K. (2020, December 2). Szájer scandal: opposition criticizes Fidesz for 'Shallow Christian conservative values.' *Hungary Today*. https://hungarytoday.hu/szajer-scandal-opposition-fidesz-reaction/.

Kioupkiolis, A. (2016). Podemos: The ambiguous promises of left-wing populism in contemporary Spain. *Journal of Political Ideologies, 21*(2), 99–120.

Klein, A. (2013). The end of solidarity? On the development of right-wing populist parties in Denmark and Sweden. In F. Hartleb, & K. Grabow (Eds.), *Exposing the demagogues: Right-wing and national populist parties in Europe* (pp. 105–132) CES Centre for European Studies and Konrad-Adenauer-Stiftung.

Krimmer, R. (2012). *The evolution of E-voting: Why voting technology is used and how it affects democracy*. Tallinn.

Krastev, I. (2014). Chapter 3. Exit politics. In *Democracy disrupted* (pp. 63–78). University of Pennsylvania Press. https://doi.org/10.9783/9780812290745.63.

Krzyzanowski, M. (2018). Discursive shifts in ethno-nationalist politics: On politicization and mediatization of the "refugee crisis" in Poland. *Journal of Immigrant and Refugee Studies, 16*(1–2), 76–96.

Kuisz, J., & Wigura, K. (2020). The pushback against populism: Reclaiming the politics of emotion. *Journal of Democracy, 2*, 41–53.

Kyle, J., & Gultchin, L. (2018). *Populists in power around the world*. https://institute.global/insight/renewing-centre/populists-power-around-world. Accessed 13 March 2021.

Lanko, D. (2015). Estonian political parties in the mid-2010s. *Baltic Region, 2*, 50–57.

Levitsky, S., & Ziblatt, D. (2018). *How democracies die: What history reveals about our future*. Crown.

Lucardie, P., & Voernman, G. (2013). Geert wilders and the party for freedom in the Netherlands: A political entrepreneur in the polder. In F. Hartleb, & K. Grabow (Eds.), *Exposing the demagogues: Right-wing and national populist parties in Europe* (pp. 187–204). CES Centre for European Studies and Konrad-Adenauer-Stiftung.

Moffitt, B. (2020). *The global rise of populism*. Stanford University Press.

Margalit, Y. (2019). Economic insecurity and the causes of populism, reconsidered. *Journal of Economic Perspectives, 33*(4), 152–170.

Mouffe, C. (2018). *For a left populism*. Verso.

Mudde, C. (2004). The populist zeitgeist. *Government and Opposition, 39*(4), 542–563.

Mudde, C., & Rovira Kaltwasser, C. (2013). Exclusionary vs. inclusionary populism: Comparing contemporary Europe and Latin America. *Government and Opposition, 48*(2), 147–174. doi:https://doi.org/10.1017/gov.2012.11.

Mudde, C., & Kaltwasser, C. R. (2017). *Populism: A very short introduction*. Oxford University Press.

Müller, Jan-Werner. (2016). *What is populism?* Pennsylvania: University of Pennsylvania Press.

Nam, T. (2012). Dual effects of the internet on political activism: Reinforcing and mobilizing. *Government Information Quarterly, 29*(1), 90–97.

Nationalratswahl 2019. (n.d.). Retrieved April 26, 2021, from Bmi.gv.at website: https://bmi.gv.at/412/Nationalratswahlen/Nationalratswahl_2019/.

Patton, D. (2019). The race for third: Small parties in the 2017 Bundestag election. In E. Langenbacher (Ed.), *Twilight of the Merkel Era: Power and politics in Germany after the 2017 Bundestag Election* (pp. 173–190). Berghahn Books. doi: https://doi.org/10.2307/j.ctv1850gvc.12.

Pauwels, T. (2013). Belgium: Decline of national populism? In F. Hartleb, K. Grabow (Eds.), *Exposing the demagogues: Right-wing and national populist parties in Europe* (pp. 81–104). CES Centre for European Studies and Konrad-Adenauer-Stiftung.

Peter, C., & Koch, T. (2019). Countering misinformation: Strategies, challenges, and uncertainties. *SCM Studies in Communication and Media, 8*(4), 431–445.

Prague Daily Monitor. (2017, January 25). 'Týden: Gov't to teach children how to face propaganda'. *Prague Daily Monitor.* http://praguemonitor.com/2017/01/25/t%C3%BDden-govt-teach-children-how-face-propaganda. Accessed on 7th March 2021.

Raunio, T. (2013). The Finns: Filling a gap in the party system. In F. Hartleb, & K. Grabow (Eds.), *Exposing the demagogues: Right-wing and national populist parties in Europe* (pp. 133–160). CES Centre for European Studies and Konrad-Adenauer-Stiftung.

Rooduijn, M. (2019). State of the field: How to study populism and adjacent topics? A plea for both more and less focus. *European Journal of Political Research, 58*(1), 362–372.

Rooduijn, M., De Lange, S. L., & Van der Brug, W. (2014). A populist zeitgeist? Programmatic contagion by populist parties in Western Europe. *Party Politics, 20*(4), 563–575.

Rooduijn, M., Van Kessel, S., Froio, C., Pirro, A., De Lange, S., Halikiopoulou, D., & Taggart, P. (2019). The PopuList: An overview of populist, far right, far left and Eurosceptic parties in Europe.

Runciman, D. (2018). *How democracy ends.* Profile Books.

Statistics Denmark. (2021). *Folketingsvalg Onsdag 5. Juni 2019.* http://www.dst.dk/valg/Valg1684447/valgopgmid/valgopgHL.htm.

Van Kessel, S., Sajuria, J., & Van Hauwaert, S. M. (2021). Informed, uninformed or misinformed? A cross-national analysis of populist party supporters across European democracies. *West European Politics, 44*(3), 585–610.

Van Quaquebeke, N., Henrich, D. C., & Eckloff, T. (2007). "It's not tolerance I'm asking for, it's respect!" A conceptual framework to differentiate between tolerance, acceptance and (two types of) respect. Gruppe. Interaktion. Organisation. *Zeitschrift für Angewandte Organisationspsychologie (GIO), 38*(2), 185–200.

Van Spanje, J., & Van Der Brug, W. (2007). The party as pariah: The exclusion of anti-immigration parties and its effect on their ideological positions. *West European Politics, 30*(5), 1022–1040. https://doi.org/10.1080/01402380701617431

Von Beyme, K. (2019). Populism, right-wing extremism and neo-nationalism. In *Rightwing populism* (pp. 57–64). Springer.

Van Crombrugge, R. (2020). Are referendums necessarily populist? Countering the populist interpretation of referendums through institutional design. *Representation,* 1–22.

Weeden, J., Nuland, W., & Stamos, A. (2017). *Information operations and Facebook*. https://fbnewsroomus.files.wordpress.com/2017/04/facebook-and-information-operations-v1.pdf. Accessed 28 February 2021.

Weyland, K., & Madrid, R. (Eds.). (2019). *When populism Trumps populism: European and Latin American lessons for the United States*. Cambridge University Press.

Wodak, R. (2019). Entering the "post-shame era": The rise of illiberal democracy, populism and neo-authoritarianism in Europe. *Global Discourse: An Interdisciplinary Journal of Current Affairs, 9*(1), 195–213.

Wolkenstein, F. (2019). *Rethinking party reform*. Oxford University Press.

Wuthrich, F., & Ingleby, M. (2020). The pushback against populism: Running on "radical love" in Turkey XE "Turkey." *Journal of Democracy, 2*, 24–40.

Index

A

Abacha, Sanni, 492
Absolutism, 218
A charismatic leader, 18, 70, 473, 477, 501, 505, 513, 515, 518, 519, 521, 522
Actor-related, 667–669, 674
Adalet ve Kalkınma Partisi (AKP), 395, 396, 398–400, 528–531, 535
Adorno, Theodor, 86, 89, 90, 92–97, 201, 560
Affect/affective style, 4, 12, 14, 19, 23, 76, 88, 89, 91–96, 98, 110, 111, 123, 124, 126, 129, 130, 134, 136, 147, 150, 151, 155, 204, 209, 268, 278, 281, 282, 293–295, 298, 306, 311, 322, 328, 333, 352, 355, 358, 360, 372, 375, 379, 393, 395, 396, 398, 414, 415, 439–443, 445, 453, 456, 457, 461, 462, 480, 561, 565, 566, 569, 653, 678
Africa, 180, 485–488, 495, 498
African National Congress (ANC), 62, 488, 489, 498, 503–505
All Progressive Congress (APC), 493, 494
Alternative für Deutschland (AfD), 106, 109, 291, 389, 437
Althusser, Louis, 49, 50
Americanism, 187, 425
American politics, 35, 42, 474, 580–582

Anger, 15, 104, 117, 120–123, 125, 126, 129, 133–135, 146–149, 151–157, 270, 282, 422, 439, 444, 446, 504, 592
Anomie, 60–62, 165
Antagonism, 6, 50, 56, 59, 65, 87, 91, 167, 199, 201, 206, 214, 230, 323, 357, 370, 416, 461
Anthropology, 216, 221, 230, 233, 439
Anti-democratic/antidemocratic, 16, 17, 19, 20, 23, 44, 86, 197, 201, 214, 218, 221, 560, 642
Anti-elitism, 14, 17, 44, 69, 70, 74, 75, 103, 120, 198, 199, 201, 229, 234, 236, 322, 323, 327, 330, 331, 360, 447, 522, 612, 613, 615, 631, 673
Anti-establishment, 6, 8, 13, 111, 119, 136, 323, 343, 379, 380, 441, 455, 463, 475, 565, 582, 612–616, 623, 624, 652, 673
Anti-feminism, 175, 278, 281
Anti-government, 446
Anti-intellectualism, 173, 343, 522
Anti-liberal, 86, 163, 165, 206, 666
Antipluralist/anti-pluralistic, 17, 21, 42, 237, 360, 631, 640, 641
Antipodean populism, 69–71, 77, 79, 80
Anti-populist, 35, 39, 199, 258, 411–413, 418
Anti-semitic, 11, 76, 206, 453, 642
Anxiety, 117, 122–124, 130, 133, 151, 173, 264, 283, 380, 390, 408, 446

© The Editor(s) (if applicable) and The Author(s), under exclusive license to Springer Nature Switzerland AG 2022
M. Oswald (ed.), *The Palgrave Handbook of Populism*,
https://doi.org/10.1007/978-3-030-80803-7

Apartheid, 62, 453, 486, 488, 498
Arab Spring, 395, 400
Argentina, 54, 163, 164, 170, 248, 250, 251, 253–256, 284, 292, 455, 460, 463, 513, 514
Aristotle, 407, 408, 416, 546
Austria, 14, 115, 116, 128, 215, 282, 284, 326, 331, 332, 376, 457, 555, 616, 642, 655, 668, 670, 674
Authoritarianism, 17, 19, 20, 164, 169, 177, 191, 196, 200, 201, 229, 230, 371, 453, 455, 459, 492, 500, 512–515, 521, 522, 547, 555, 556, 678
Authoritarian populism, 177–179, 191, 195, 196, 200, 201, 205–208, 266
Autochthonous, 280, 283, 292, 489, 569
Automation, 124, 128–130, 133, 134, 232, 269

B

Bangladesh, 344, 393
Bann, 332, 346, 395, 668
Bannon, Steve, 174
Belgium, 14, 116, 453, 462, 655, 670
Belief systems, 60, 401, 580
Benjamin, Walter, 66
Berlusconi, Silvio, 66, 458, 514, 564, 565
Bharatiya Janata Party (BJP), 126, 393, 394, 398
Biden, Joe, 163, 174, 582, 604
Biopolitics, 293, 546–549, 556–560
Birtherism, 280
Black Lives Matter, 297, 462
Blue Party, 440, 441, 445, 447
Bolivarian Revolution, 309, 515, 518–520, 522
Bolívar, Simón, 170, 517–521
Bolivia, 54, 55, 255, 259, 328, 332, 455
Bolsonaro, Jair, 163, 174, 175, 291, 297, 322, 331, 343, 348, 460, 461, 629, 665
Boulanger, Georges/Boulangism, 65, 66
Bourgeoise, 165

Brazil, 163, 165, 174, 175, 248, 253, 254, 291, 292, 322, 333, 343, 455, 460, 461, 513, 531, 629, 665
Breitbart, 174
Brexit, 32, 109, 115, 128, 132, 133, 207, 213, 236, 264, 351, 359, 389, 407, 408, 414, 418, 447, 665
Bulgaria, 459
Burkina Faso, 489, 495
Butler, Judith, 283, 298

C

Calculated ambivalence, 278, 282
Canovan, Margaret, 8, 11, 18, 20, 50, 61, 66, 70, 200, 292, 323, 423, 438, 497, 499, 501, 505, 506, 514, 528, 572
Capitalism, 42, 59, 77, 89–91, 166, 231, 254, 297–299, 321, 328, 379, 391, 489, 520, 551–553, 586, 588
Catholic, 174, 292, 296, 521, 568
Champetie, Charles, 173
Chávez, Hugo, 54, 55, 170, 172, 303, 309, 310, 312, 316, 455, 511, 512, 515–522
Chavismo, 303, 304, 308–310, 312, 314–316, 511, 515, 516, 518, 520–522
Chavista pueblo, 303
Checks and balances, 12, 34, 38, 55, 179, 190, 191, 200, 206, 208, 432, 455, 512, 513, 555, 556
Ché Guevara, Ernesto, 521
Chile, 54, 62, 253, 254, 458, 460, 464
Christian Right, 425
Citizenship, 16, 36, 37, 75, 107, 171, 182, 280, 293, 298, 309, 310, 312, 313, 423, 488, 571, 575, 589, 629–642, 678
Civil rights, 11, 32, 40, 322, 383, 569, 571
Cleavages, 59, 128, 131, 135, 146, 147, 149, 151, 197, 332, 369–375, 381, 410, 431, 446, 460, 472, 473
Climate change, 321, 322, 326–333, 375, 383

INDEX 689

Clinton, Hillary, 174, 187, 268, 417, 580, 582, 583, 585, 596, 598, 600, 601, 603, 604
Cold War, 42, 53, 216, 245, 246
Collective memories/collective memory, 195, 196, 202, 203, 206, 208, 209, 451–458, 460–463
Collor de Mello, Fernando, 254, 455
Colonialism, 72, 207, 453, 461, 485–487, 547
Commonwealth countries, 533
Communism, 41, 438, 457, 459
Communist totalitarianism, 172
Conservative/conservatism, 70, 74, 78, 104, 109, 130, 180, 214–216, 221, 255, 264, 282, 295, 296, 298, 299, 326, 330, 333, 370–374, 381, 398, 455, 460, 534, 547, 551, 557, 560, 568, 569, 571, 591, 592, 594, 597, 599, 600, 638, 672, 674
Conservative Revolution, 218
Cordon sanitaire, 116, 668–670, 674
Correa, Rafael, 55, 255, 332, 455, 676
Corruption, 36, 60, 76, 78, 174, 181, 232, 348, 380, 412, 456, 472, 480, 486, 490–495, 513, 515, 516, 611, 614
Cosmopolitanism and communitarianism, 370–372
Couches populaires, 127
Coughlin (Father), 11, 40, 425
Council of Europe, 181, 635
Counterstrategy, 667–670, 672, 675, 676, 678–680
COVID-19 pandemic, 175, 270, 341–348, 358, 360, 362, 503, 537, 560, 565, 582
Creative-class workers, 131
Crimea, 530, 535
Crimean Tatars, 531
Critical materialism, 90
Critical theory, 86
Cultural backlash, 263, 265
Cultural conflicts, 373, 375, 376
Cultural political economy (CPE), 390
Cultural Revolution, 125

D
Danish People's Party (DPP), 441, 672
Dansk Folkeparti (DF), 128, 672
de Benoist, Alain, 173
Decolonial feminism, 304, 306
Deficit spending, 245, 252, 253, 257
Deliberative democracy, 183, 186, 189
Demagogy, 412, 413
Democratic, 5, 10, 12, 16, 17, 19, 22, 23, 33, 34, 37, 38, 40, 41, 51, 52, 56, 59, 61, 63, 79, 85, 86, 94, 95, 116, 120, 127, 163, 165, 167–169, 171–173, 175, 177–182, 185, 187, 188, 190, 191, 197–201, 206, 208, 214, 217, 230, 237, 266, 268, 304, 305, 309, 310, 330, 333, 353, 360, 370, 371, 380, 381, 391, 393, 408, 413, 424, 426, 429, 432, 438, 454, 456–462, 472–474, 478, 479, 488, 490, 492, 495, 498, 500, 513, 514, 547, 551, 555, 556, 579–582, 584, 585, 589, 591, 593, 596, 598, 601–605, 631, 649, 651–653, 659, 665, 668, 670, 673, 675–680
Democratic Party, 39, 41, 311, 381, 397, 428, 475, 565, 580, 582, 584, 603, 679
Democratic Party of Struggle (PDI-P), 476, 477
Depoliticized democracy, 199
Deport, 580, 581, 586–590, 641
de Tocqueville, Alexis, 37, 560
#120dezibel, 282
Diamand, Marcelo, 248–252
Dichotomy, 13, 14, 22, 59, 86, 184, 264, 325, 348, 383, 407, 412, 427, 534, 586, 588, 604, 666
Die Linke, 10, 119, 133, 462, 615
Difference, 16, 32, 33, 38, 40, 51, 52, 56, 58, 64, 70–72, 79, 106, 120, 132–134, 150, 154, 164, 166, 191, 216, 249, 267, 278, 283, 295, 306, 308, 326, 329, 332, 334, 352, 373, 390, 395, 399, 400, 422, 423, 425, 427, 428, 431, 438, 480, 528, 536, 552, 565, 579, 580, 585, 586, 601–603, 622, 623, 640, 653, 657, 659, 660
di Lampedusa, Giuseppe, 51

Disadvantage, 14, 15, 129, 130, 373, 454, 480, 595, 636, 654, 659
Discourse, 4–6, 9–11, 19, 50, 58, 59, 70, 72–75, 79, 87, 88, 123, 126, 127, 129, 136, 145–147, 149–152, 157, 165, 167, 168, 182, 195, 196, 198, 200, 202, 203, 207, 208, 214, 228, 229, 254, 264, 271, 278, 281, 292–294, 298, 299, 311–313, 321, 323, 324, 326–329, 331, 332, 342, 347, 353, 361, 392, 393, 395, 408, 409, 411–414, 416–418, 422, 423, 425, 431, 439, 441, 452–457, 460, 487, 495, 498–500, 502, 505, 513–518, 520, 521, 527, 529, 530, 547, 584, 604, 612–614, 618, 623, 630–633, 640–642, 670–672, 677
Discursive level, 455
Disenfranchisement, 231, 232, 264, 680
Disinformation, 392, 666, 675, 677, 678
Diversity, 16, 134, 135, 230, 264, 265, 294, 296, 313, 372, 395, 423, 472, 494, 564, 566, 570, 575, 586–590, 593, 631, 652
Divide, 51, 59, 69, 70, 105, 118, 131, 132, 172, 174, 199, 228, 232, 255, 265, 268, 307, 370, 371, 376, 383, 408, 425, 438, 446, 452, 459, 460, 474, 479, 490, 492, 502, 528, 574, 579, 583, 602, 604, 612, 621, 624, 633, 637, 639, 641
Duterte, Rodrigo, 177, 180, 182, 184, 185, 187, 191, 344, 348, 475, 480

E
Early-warning system, 680
Economic populism, 227–233, 235, 238, 245–248, 250–253, 255, 256, 258, 259
Ecuador, 55, 255, 332, 455, 513, 676, 677
Egalitarians/egalitarianism, 17, 96, 134, 216, 325, 373
Egypt, 54, 390–392, 395, 397–401
Electoral success, 73, 74, 79, 106, 131, 182, 332, 438, 452, 472, 582, 616, 650–653, 655, 659, 665, 671

#EleNão, 292
Elite/elitist/elitism, 6, 8, 11, 13–15, 17–20, 22, 32, 39, 61, 70, 71, 75, 76, 79, 85, 86, 88–92, 94, 95, 97, 103, 108, 117, 118, 120, 123, 133, 135, 150, 151, 167, 170, 173, 178, 179, 182, 184, 197, 199, 200, 205–207, 213–221, 228–230, 237, 258, 269, 294, 304, 305, 309, 311, 312, 316, 322–325, 330, 346–348, 351, 354, 356, 357, 359, 371, 376, 380, 389–394, 398, 400, 408, 410, 418, 422–424, 426, 429, 438, 452, 455, 462, 463, 472–475, 478, 486, 490, 495, 498, 500, 506, 512, 513, 515, 527–536, 550, 551, 563, 565, 569, 581, 583, 584, 592, 604, 613–616, 621, 631, 649, 652, 676, 679
Emancipation, 12, 89, 93, 96, 200, 271, 416, 506, 551
Emancipation fatigue, 278
Embitterment, 122, 126
Emotion/emotions, 4, 19, 70, 109, 110, 117, 120–126, 128, 133–136, 145–157, 166, 167, 198, 281, 293, 294, 407, 414, 415, 438, 439, 442, 445, 446, 501, 565, 573, 679, 680
Enlightenment, 121, 307, 314, 326, 413, 417
Erdogan, Recep Tayyip, 393, 396
Errejón, Iñigo, 55, 87, 91
Escuela Superior Peronista (ESP), 514
Establishment, 5, 11, 13, 22, 52, 74, 77, 116, 117, 120, 134, 135, 167, 173, 187, 200, 213, 219, 228, 234, 256, 322, 329, 330, 342, 343, 346, 393, 409, 410, 421, 424, 427, 429, 431, 432, 454, 505, 506, 516, 522, 529, 535, 565, 611, 614, 624, 632, 641, 673, 674, 679
Ethnic homogeneity, 53
Ethnocracy, 135
Ethnosexism, 298
EU Commission stimulus packages, 205
Eurasian Economic Union (EAEU), 533
European Central Bank policies, 205
European integration, 196, 204, 359, 374

European Stability Mechanism, 205
European Union (EU), 31, 104, 132, 181, 231, 235, 238, 239, 283, 296, 415, 528, 531, 533, 581, 629, 638, 639, 641
Eurosceptic/eurosceptical, 20, 106, 154, 359, 616
Evola, Julius, 214, 216, 217, 221
Exclusionary, 16, 17, 21, 42, 44, 136, 263, 292–294, 298, 322, 395, 409, 461, 529, 624, 630, 635, 668–671, 674, 679

F

Facebook, 111, 184, 356, 566, 567, 677, 678
Fake news, 181, 291, 294, 347, 408, 409, 411, 414, 415, 418, 666, 678
Farmers' Alliance, 35, 39
Fascism, 163–167, 169–175, 200, 214, 215, 217, 218, 220, 221, 258, 326, 456, 457, 460, 560, 666
Fear, 14, 15, 19, 73, 76, 104–107, 117, 120–125, 130, 131, 135, 136, 146–149, 151–157, 177, 178, 184, 188, 207, 208, 269, 270, 279–281, 294, 297, 329–331, 343, 345, 376, 383, 408, 425, 431, 439, 441, 442, 444, 445, 472, 491, 560, 571, 574, 659, 674, 676, 679
Ferrer, Aldo, 250, 251, 253, 254
Fiatal Demokratak Szovetsege (Fidesz), 180–182, 459, 675, 676
Financial crisis, 105, 115, 116, 177, 178, 180, 204, 232, 264, 266, 268, 270, 380, 411
5 Stars Movement, 565
Forum voor Democratie, 118
Forza Italia, 325, 564
Framing, 125, 197, 200, 202, 207, 309, 315, 329, 411, 422, 426, 438–443, 445, 446
Françafrique, 533, 534
France, 43, 65, 115, 116, 132, 173, 197, 277, 284, 326, 327, 330, 331, 333, 379, 446, 463, 532–534, 536, 616, 629, 630, 632–642, 655, 668, 670

Freedom, 34, 77, 92, 168, 181, 308, 314, 316, 360, 487, 502, 571, 660, 672
Freedom House, 180
Freedom Party of Austria (FPÖ), 116, 453, 447
Free markets, 229, 230, 254, 255, 325, 327, 331, 373, 376, 379, 381, 382, 393
Free speech, 15, 376, 455
Freiheitliche Partei Österreich (FPÖ), 127, 326, 332, 453, 454, 668, 674
Fremskrittspartiet, 116, 119
French revolution (1789), 381
Freudian, 54, 91, 96
Freud, Sigmund, 50, 53, 87, 92–96
Front national (FN), 33, 43, 116, 127, 132, 135, 233, 550, 630–632, 634, 635, 637, 639–641, 670
Frustrations, 15, 71, 92, 93, 122, 133, 256, 270, 354, 422, 432, 446, 570, 573, 584
Fujimori, Alberto, 55, 254, 255, 455

G

Gatopardismo, 51
Gauck, Joachim, 213
Gauland, Alexander, 220
Gellner, Ernest, 50
Gender, 41, 59, 115, 117, 146, 148, 155, 174, 269, 270, 277–284, 291–299, 308, 333, 373, 547, 549, 550, 591
Gender equality, 295–297, 381, 455
Gender gap, 277
Génération Identitaire, 173
Germany, 10, 14, 18, 31, 106, 107, 116, 117, 123, 125, 130, 132–134, 149, 152, 154, 157, 165, 170, 213–219, 221, 257, 278–280, 282, 284, 291, 299, 323, 326, 328, 331, 333, 370, 376, 389, 417, 437, 438, 440–447, 453, 457, 462, 463, 547, 553, 612, 613, 615–618, 621–624, 650, 668, 670
Gerrymandered/gerrymandering, 172, 181, 479
Ghana, 489, 495

Global Britain agenda, 533
Globalism/globalization, 14, 15, 71, 74, 75, 112, 120, 122, 124–134, 147, 174, 200, 229, 230, 232, 233, 235, 238, 264, 279, 280, 293, 322, 328–330, 353, 356, 359, 370, 375, 379, 381, 383, 393, 409, 416, 437, 480, 549, 569, 642, 666
Global populism, 32, 279, 351–354, 360–362, 537, 666
Global South, 296, 328–330, 352, 356, 390, 395, 527, 532
Goldwater, Barry, 40
Goodwin, Matthew, 32, 132, 228, 229, 323, 668, 673
Gorbachev, Mikhail, 534
Gramsci, Antonio, 50, 51, 56, 59, 64, 87, 89, 90, 218, 391
Great Depression, 169, 204, 269
Greece, 31, 328, 354, 410–413, 415, 418, 458, 550, 552
Greens, 79, 370, 376, 444, 612, 615, 616, 618–624, 639
Gridlock, 268, 332
Grillo, Beppe, 565

H
Haider, Jörg, 116
Hanson, Pauline, 69–77, 79, 119, 133
Harambee Prosperity Plan (HPP), 503
Harris, Kamala, 280
Health crises, 342, 343, 346–348
Hegemony, 50, 51, 56–59, 64–66, 87, 89, 90, 97, 197, 279, 298, 299, 306, 359, 408, 416, 458, 516, 517, 522, 548, 553
Hindu nationalist, 392
Hindutva, 390, 391, 393, 398
Hitler, Adolf, 164, 172, 459
Hobbes, Thomas, 53
Höcke, Björn, 213, 214, 218–221, 291, 299
Hofstadter, Richard, 11, 42–44, 228, 236
Homogeneity, 133, 293, 297, 316, 423
Horkheimer, Max, 86, 90, 92–96
Horthy, Miklós, 459
Humala, 255

Hungary, 177, 180–183, 185, 190, 191, 207, 283, 284, 432, 455, 459, 464
Hyperdiscursive, 86, 87

I
Identity, 33, 51, 52, 54, 56–59, 64, 65, 70, 72, 74, 78, 79, 86, 88, 91, 92, 94–96, 98, 103–106, 108, 111, 124–126, 131, 135, 136, 148, 149, 167, 168, 171–173, 202, 203, 205, 263, 264, 268, 283, 295, 296, 299, 306, 311, 322, 383, 390, 393, 395, 399, 400, 415, 429, 451, 452, 461, 517, 530, 550, 564, 565, 574, 591, 631, 634, 637, 642, 666, 667, 679
Iglesias, Pablo, 55
Ignore, 70, 86, 96, 120, 134, 166, 167, 188, 200, 204, 206–208, 214, 232, 245, 265, 453, 462, 491, 494, 575, 581, 582, 601, 669–671
Illiberalism, 16, 168, 180, 230, 265, 555
Immanent critique, 86, 88, 89
Import Substitution Industrialization (ISI), 248, 259
Income inequality, 247, 269, 579, 583, 584, 586–590, 593, 603, 650
Indonesia, 345, 390–401, 471, 473, 476–478, 480
Inequality/inequalities, 79, 130, 136, 152, 184, 185, 187, 216, 229, 232, 238, 268, 269, 279, 294, 297–299, 330, 333, 373, 383, 390, 391, 393, 395, 397, 398, 408, 472, 480, 489, 500, 515, 553, 579, 584, 586, 588, 589, 595, 596, 603, 604, 649, 659
Injustice, 36, 90, 91, 95, 122, 129, 148, 203, 204, 229–232, 506, 592
Insecurity, 105, 108, 121, 123, 128, 132, 147–149, 201, 232, 264, 379, 380, 391, 636, 652
Institute for Global Change, 180
Institut für Staatspolitik, 214, 215, 218
Institutionalization, 61, 201, 228, 237, 314, 328, 473–475, 478, 480, 500, 511–516, 518, 519, 521, 522
International Monetary Fund (IMF), 180, 245

Ionescu, Ghita, 50
Iraq, 266, 535
Islamic populism, 390, 391, 393–398, 400, 477
Islamization, 106, 632
Islamophobia, 74, 76, 77, 229
Isolationist, 204, 355, 531
Italy, 14, 31, 66, 115, 116, 128, 131, 134, 164, 165, 170, 284, 342, 354, 458, 514, 550, 552, 564–566, 571, 629, 665, 666

J

Jefferson/Jeffersonians, 35–38, 41, 42, 125
Johnson, Boris, 109, 110, 629
Justice and Development Party, 396, 528
Justicialismo, 514

K

Kaltenbrunner, Gerd-Klaus, 215–221
Kampfbegriff, 5, 10
Kenya, 498
Keynes/Keynesians, 248, 258
Kirchner, Carlos Kirchner, 255
Know-Nothing Party, 236
Kosovo, 531

L

Laclau, Ernesto, 6, 9, 12, 20, 32, 33, 49–67, 85–92, 94–96, 98, 120, 135, 150, 165, 178, 199, 229, 304, 306, 308, 354, 380, 411, 413, 414, 416, 423, 454, 518, 545–548, 552, 558
Laissez-faire, 229, 254
Latin America, 4, 53, 55, 169, 170, 179, 180, 197, 245–248, 250–252, 254, 255, 259, 279, 296, 303, 306, 311, 328, 332, 352–354, 356, 359, 362, 390, 453, 455–457, 460, 461, 463, 521, 665, 677, 679
Le Bon, Gustave, 50, 214
Lefort, Claude, 56, 171, 172
Left-right (divide), 372, 373, 381, 383
Left-wing populism, 17, 85–89, 91, 92, 94–97, 179, 229, 328, 579, 580, 583–605, 665, 666, 679, 680
Lega/Lega Nord, 116, 119, 131, 173, 629, 665
Legacies, 11, 44, 297, 298, 309, 438, 453–463, 476, 493, 502, 512, 513, 519–522, 531, 533, 534
Legal populism, 553
Leitkultur, 107
Le Pen, Marine, 44, 116, 127, 132, 135, 173, 277, 327, 629, 637
LGBT/LGTBQ/LGBTQI, 278, 297, 381, 551, 561
Liberalism, 16, 34, 41, 116, 166, 209, 230, 250, 251, 322, 324, 330, 331, 381, 382, 409, 432, 473, 489, 666
Liberal values, 265, 455, 550, 634
Libertarian, 372
Lionza, María, 521
Long, Huey, 40, 425, 582
Longing, 123, 198, 667
Losers of modernization, 116, 127
Loss of status, 14, 437
Loss-perspective, 330
Low incomes, 649
Lukashenko, Alexander, 345
Luxembourg, 655

M

Machiavelli, Niccolò, 218
Macroeconomic populism, 246, 247, 253, 257
Maduro, Nicolás, 55, 256, 346, 512, 519–522
Malaysia, 471, 479
Maori, 70–80
March on Rome, 220
Marielle Presente!, 297
Market integration, 379
Market liberalism, 250, 324, 325, 327, 328, 372, 376, 383, 531
Marxism/Marxist Theory, 43, 53, 62, 86, 87, 89, 90, 94, 96, 97, 166, 215, 216, 221, 248, 615
Mass and social media, 390, 395, 399
Masses, 42, 50, 92, 104, 165, 197, 214, 215, 219–221, 229, 305, 391, 398,

414, 418, 475, 487, 499, 504, 506, 550
Mass psychology, 91, 92, 96, 216, 221, 414
May, Theresa, 109, 533
Mbeki, Thabo, 343
Menem, Carlos, 254, 255, 455
#MeToo, 282
Michels, Robert, 214, 218, 219
Middle East, 180, 353, 399
Midwest, 39, 128
Migrants/migration, 15, 104, 111, 116, 126, 128, 132, 135, 181, 182, 184, 188, 206, 251, 279, 280, 292, 324, 341, 346, 353, 354, 375, 440–442, 447, 454, 532–534, 545, 550, 565, 568–572, 613, 620, 632, 634–637, 640, 641, 667, 672
Minogue, Kenneth, 50
Minorities, 14, 18, 70, 130, 148–151, 187, 190, 199, 201, 216, 217, 229, 230, 265, 295, 296, 311, 333, 334, 343, 357, 373, 375, 393, 398, 399, 455, 459, 460, 463, 479, 498, 500, 551, 575, 582, 631, 641, 672
Misogynist, 121, 185, 281, 295, 552
Mobilization, 6, 19, 51, 61, 63, 87, 88, 92, 93, 95, 97, 110, 116, 117, 120, 122, 130, 134–136, 146, 147, 179, 201, 207, 264–266, 268, 270, 283, 294, 305, 324, 345, 356, 357, 379, 380, 383, 389, 390, 393, 398, 400, 424, 439, 445, 446, 454, 472–474, 478–480, 490, 493, 497, 504, 511, 519, 652, 657, 659, 677
Modernization/modernization theory, 15, 116, 120, 124, 125, 127, 147, 166, 201, 294, 369, 392, 395, 412, 437, 515, 551, 555, 651, 680
Modi, Narendra, 126, 345, 393
Mohler, Armin, 214
Monetarists, 248, 252, 258
Monistic, 33
Morales, Evo, 55, 255, 332, 455
Moralization/moralism, 18, 19, 21, 44, 190, 198, 199, 203, 207, 208, 237, 329, 399, 678
Moreno, Lenín, 676

Movimiento Quinta República (MVR), 516
Mubarak, Husni, 395, 397–399
Mugabeism, 501, 502
Mugabe, Robert, 501, 502, 504, 506
Multiculturalism, 72, 107, 131, 135, 188, 233, 265, 372, 399, 551, 579, 580, 586, 589, 593
Multivariate analysis, 655
Muslim, 71, 74, 77, 135, 149, 174, 182, 187, 188, 229, 279, 282, 292, 295, 297, 346, 381, 392–400, 454, 581, 632, 640, 641
Muslim Brotherhood, 395, 397, 398, 400
Mussolini, Benito, 164, 218, 220, 458

N
Narodnichestvo, 197
Narrative/narratives, 51, 58, 59, 64, 66, 80, 95, 104, 105, 108, 117, 124, 126, 184, 185, 203, 205–207, 213, 250, 251, 258, 280, 281, 292, 294, 296–298, 304, 308, 316, 322, 326, 347, 355, 356, 359, 392, 394, 397–400, 418, 421, 427, 431, 432, 438, 439, 441, 445, 446, 462, 498–500, 504, 506, 515–517, 520, 581, 583, 604, 629, 641, 642, 667, 679, 680
Nationalism, 91, 97, 109, 119, 126, 166, 198–201, 209, 229, 230, 252, 279, 282, 324–327, 342, 383, 393, 453, 459, 488–490, 514, 531, 535, 549, 631
Nationalist People's Coalition (NPC), 475
National League for Democracy (NLD), 479
Nativism, 20, 71, 80, 118, 119, 126, 135, 178, 207, 325, 549, 631
Nativist attitudes, 360
Nazism, 165, 218, 463, 547
Neo-colonialism, 487, 534
Neo-imperialism, 527–530, 532–537
Neoliberal/neoliberalism, 15, 71, 74, 76–80, 88, 95, 97, 110, 149, 197, 255, 278–280, 293, 297, 298, 309,

311, 328, 379, 381–383, 391, 395, 396, 398, 400, 455, 530, 548, 551, 569, 615, 680
New Labour, 534
New Order, 60, 392, 394, 396, 397, 476
New Reflections, 50, 56
New Right, 148, 173, 214, 215, 293, 373, 374, 564
New Zealand First (NZF), 69–71, 73–80
Nietzsche, Friedrich, 214
Nigeria, 346, 486, 489–491, 493–495
1989, 106, 246, 247, 249, 253, 254, 257, 258, 311, 316, 417, 418, 427, 440, 443, 459, 463, 489, 546, 555, 671
#NiUnaMas, 297
#NiUnaMenos, 284, 292, 297
Non-voters, 659
Normative attachment, 5, 10, 23
Norms, 5, 19, 22, 33, 34, 53, 60, 111, 179, 188, 190, 191, 201, 411, 432, 514, 559, 651, 665
Nostalgia, 43, 75, 106, 117, 122–126, 136, 163, 174, 188, 203, 205, 207, 214, 228, 230, 399, 439
Not My President, 292

O

Obama, Barack, 31, 32, 40, 44, 108, 269, 280, 333
Obasanjo, Olusegun, 491, 492
Occupy Wall Street (OWS), 54, 63
Ochlocracy, 219, 220
Odinga, Raila, 498
Oligarchy, 88, 91, 199, 219, 228, 267, 477, 548
Omaha Platform, 35, 36, 231, 233
One Nation (ON), 69–71, 73–75, 77, 79
Ontological/ontology, 56, 60, 86, 87, 89, 94–97, 124, 126, 303, 304, 306, 308, 313, 315, 325, 415
Opitz, Reinhard, 215, 217
Opportunity-risk, 383
Opportunity structures, 456, 457, 462, 533
Ortega y Gasset, José, 214

Orthodox economists, 249, 254, 256
Ostalgie, 125
Österreichische Volkspartei (ÖVP), 128, 673, 674
Othering, 106, 280, 297, 631, 640, 641
Ottoman Empire, 530, 531

P

Pan-African Congress (PAC), 431, 489
Pareto, Vilfredo, 214, 215, 218
Partidocrazia, 515
Partido Socialista Unido de Venezuela (PSUV), 516, 518, 519
Partisan, 105, 108, 217, 235, 237, 258, 268, 333, 381, 580–582, 584, 585, 589, 591–602, 604, 605
Patriotische Europäer gegen die Islamisierung des Abendlandes (PEGIDA), 106, 121, 299
Patronage, 357, 397, 474, 476–480, 512–514, 516, 517
People's Action Party (PAP) of Singapore, 473
Peoples Democratic Party (PDP), 493
People's Party of Estonia (EKRE), 674
People's Party/United States People's Party, 11, 33, 35, 39, 197, 231, 234, 425
People's Reform Party (PRP), 475
Perón, Eva, 514, 515, 521
Peronismo, 248
Perón, Juan, 164, 165, 169, 170, 172, 513, 514
Perot, Ross, 425
Peru, 55, 253–255, 259, 345, 455
Peters, Winston, 69–72, 74–79
Pheu Thai Party (PTP), 478
Philippines, 182, 184–186, 344, 474, 475
Philippot, Florian, 639
Plebs, 51–55, 58, 59, 61, 64, 66, 545
Pluralism, 16, 37, 107, 188, 199, 201, 237, 408, 423, 457, 460, 473, 548, 631, 633
Podemos, 33, 54, 55, 119, 325, 328, 666, 674

Poland, 207, 283, 284, 292, 297, 326, 432, 459, 464, 550, 551, 554–557, 561, 650, 655, 672
Polarization, 128, 129, 131, 135, 168, 191, 266–268, 331–333, 359, 375, 409, 411, 421, 429, 582, 603, 604, 612–614, 616, 617, 619–624, 651, 666, 674, 679, 680
Political extremism, 174
Political language, 34, 304, 390–392, 400
Political logic, 20, 21, 32, 57, 167, 549, 552
Political stability, 311, 408
Political strategy, 4, 6, 32, 86, 97, 254, 473, 474, 490
Polybios, 219
Popular sovereignty, 17, 34, 38, 167, 171, 190, 199, 200, 327, 328, 355, 356, 414, 423, 456, 583
Population, 13, 14, 16, 18, 22, 32, 34, 73, 104, 107, 108, 111, 117, 118, 121, 130, 131, 133, 135, 136, 146, 148, 149, 152, 167, 168, 171, 184, 264–267, 269, 270, 280, 298, 310, 326, 341, 347, 357, 375, 394, 425, 439–442, 445, 446, 500, 501, 503, 516, 521, 545–549, 551–553, 557, 559, 563, 565, 567–570, 574, 575, 582, 612, 631, 649, 679
Populist cycle, 235, 245, 247–249, 251, 253, 256, 257, 259
Populist moment, 35, 86, 197, 351, 548, 595, 603, 666
Populist parties, 10, 12, 14, 17, 39, 40, 70, 79, 97, 115–119, 121, 127, 128, 135, 136, 145–149, 152–154, 156, 157, 170, 173, 178, 179, 233, 234, 255, 264, 265, 270, 277, 295, 324, 328, 330–334, 369, 375, 437–440, 442–447, 458, 459, 462, 464, 473, 476, 477, 479, 513, 527–529, 531, 532, 534–536, 555, 563–569, 574, 612–616, 621, 623, 624, 650–657, 659, 660, 665–676, 679, 680
Populist Reason/*On Populist Reason (OPR)*, 50, 56–60, 66, 91, 413, 545

Populist rhetoric, 40, 61, 104, 107, 108, 122, 123, 182, 185, 255, 299, 328, 421, 422, 424–432, 438, 439, 441, 442, 447, 499, 546, 561, 612, 614, 667, 673, 676
Populus, 51–53, 58, 59, 66
Portugal, 379, 458, 478, 655, 659
Post-democracy, 199, 547
Postfascism/post-fascist, 163, 172, 174, 198, 214, 458
Post-Marxism/post-Marxist, 87, 89, 90, 94, 96, 97, 615
Postmaterialism, 373
Post-politics, 199, 415, 418, 548
Post-structuralism, 87
Post-truth, 331, 347, 407–416, 418
Poujadists, 119
Precarity, 379, 380, 383, 390
Presente, Marielle, 292
Privilege, 13, 33, 37, 41, 56, 62, 66, 90, 103, 112, 131, 132, 135, 169, 269, 270, 278, 296, 305, 408, 489, 500, 506, 548, 550, 591, 632, 649, 650, 678
Progress Party (FrP), 671
Proletarization, 127
Protectionism, 148, 252, 325, 381
Protecto ergo obligo, 53
Proto-totalitarian, 455
Proudhon, Pierre-Joseph, 37, 38
Public opinion, 12, 407, 415, 457, 461, 535, 564, 567, 574, 580, 582, 584, 595, 596
Pure people, 8, 110, 178, 199, 206, 323, 422, 490, 613, 616
Putin, Vladimir, 44, 534, 535

Q

QAnon, 174
Quarantine, 345, 669, 670, 674
Queer, 282, 284

R

Racism, 71, 73, 74, 85, 165, 174, 175, 187, 201, 264, 265, 270, 278–280, 282, 284, 333, 453, 461, 549, 551, 584, 591, 593, 641

Rancière, Jacques, 52, 60, 62, 408
Rasmussen, Anders Fogh, 672
Rassemblement National (RN), 119, 127, 129, 532–534, 629–632, 640, 641
Reagan, Ronald, 246, 257, 425
Reconocimiento, 304, 312–316
Reconstruction, 37, 60, 86, 91, 202, 205, 216, 310, 311, 517
Reflection, 10, 88–90, 93, 94, 96, 111, 313, 314, 342, 453, 545, 574
Refugee crisis, 106, 616, 619, 620, 672, 673, 678
Refugees, 104, 106, 148, 206, 292, 370, 375, 376, 440, 447, 531, 532, 534, 535, 569
Religious/religious symbols, 59, 105, 107, 135, 149, 171, 281, 292–296, 346, 357, 369, 371, 372, 390, 391, 393, 395, 397, 399, 455, 459, 486, 521, 529, 547, 550, 566, 568, 570
Republican, 34–37, 39, 42, 131, 174, 188, 218, 268, 347, 383, 398, 426, 428–430, 461, 488, 579–582, 584, 585, 587, 589–592, 594–597, 601–605, 637, 639, 640, 670
République en Marche (LREM), 629, 673
Resentment, 14, 17, 107, 117, 120–123, 126, 129, 130, 133, 134, 136, 146–149, 151, 216, 220, 229, 263, 268–271, 346, 439, 441, 442, 446, 472, 489, 492, 642
Resonance, 110, 124, 125, 146, 219, 221, 296, 400, 431, 440, 595
Retrotopia, 278, 534
Reunification, 443, 615, 621, 623
Revanchism, 265, 268
Reverse anti-colonialism, 293, 294, 296
Rhetoric, 8, 13, 31, 40, 57, 74, 76, 77, 79, 103–107, 109, 111, 120, 127, 136, 146, 151, 168, 169, 182, 187, 188, 190, 197–199, 201, 207, 208, 220, 228, 229, 254, 297, 343, 345, 357, 383, 407, 408, 421, 422, 424–427, 431, 438, 439, 447, 478, 489, 490, 493–495, 497, 527, 533, 534, 550, 552, 573, 583, 584, 592, 603, 612, 614, 615, 669, 672–674, 676
Right, political, 120, 200, 213, 214, 220, 547, 630
Right to property, 550
Right-wing populism (RWP), 5, 10, 14, 17, 19, 86, 88, 89, 96, 97, 115–119, 122, 126, 133, 135, 136, 146, 147, 152, 213–215, 218, 221, 229, 252, 255, 269, 277–284, 291, 292, 294, 297, 298, 333, 370, 371, 374, 375, 438–440, 457, 527, 528, 548, 550, 563–566, 568–575, 579–581, 583–585, 587, 589–592, 594–605, 629, 631, 633, 641, 666, 667, 670, 671, 679
Right-wing populist complex, 281, 292, 296, 298, 299
Right-wing populists, 14, 15, 17, 70, 97, 115–119, 121, 123, 124, 127, 128, 130, 131, 134–136, 145–149, 152–154, 156, 157, 213, 215, 218, 221, 229, 264, 277, 282–284, 291–295, 297–299, 322, 331, 333, 334, 369–371, 373, 375, 437–441, 447, 453, 458, 459, 527–529, 531–536, 550, 563–570, 572–574, 589, 591, 596, 603, 616, 629, 631, 632, 640, 641, 650–657, 659, 660, 665, 673–675
Romania, 459, 655
Royal, Ségolène, 637
Russia, 10, 42, 125, 197, 205, 208, 323, 345, 531–536, 677

S

Sajer, Joszef, 675, 676
Salvini, Matteo, 34, 116, 131, 173, 565
Sanders, Bernie, 580, 582–584, 586, 589, 603–605
Sankara, Thomas, 489, 495
Sata, Michael, 498, 506
Schmitt, Carl, 53, 61, 87, 170, 217, 220
Sexism/sexual misconduct, 188, 280, 282, 294, 297
Sexual exceptionalism, 282, 294, 295
Simplification, 18, 22, 343–345, 348, 666, 675

Slovakia, 459, 655
Sobotka, Bohuslav, 678
Social class, 105, 123, 213, 649
Social justice, 32, 53, 54, 131, 330, 395, 564, 566, 569, 572, 615
Social media, 111, 121, 184, 185, 294, 342, 392, 394, 395, 399, 474–476, 573, 678, 680
Social-psychological critique, 86, 91
Social psychology, 86, 94, 96, 117, 203
Social workers, 564–575
Societal cohesion, 66, 360, 413
Socio-economic status, 129, 649
Solidarity, 50, 64, 65, 70, 108, 118, 280, 284, 297–299, 314, 328, 393, 399, 459, 478, 489, 500, 504, 506, 554, 565, 566, 569
Somalia, 531
South Africa, 343, 345, 453, 486–489, 495, 498–500, 502, 503, 505
Southeast Asia, 344, 353, 471–474, 480, 481
Southern Tenant Farmers' Union, 40
South West Africa People's Organization (SWAPO of Namibia), 498, 500, 502
Spain, 31, 54, 55, 116, 117, 284, 328, 458, 463, 655, 659, 660, 666
Spectacularization, 344, 345, 347, 348
Spengler, Oswald, 220
Stigma, 5, 147, 201, 236, 280, 292, 346, 422, 444, 451, 455, 458, 460–462, 533, 550, 670
Strache, Heinz-Christian, 116
Strategy, 6, 32, 50, 56, 94, 106, 125, 127, 149, 150, 153, 167, 220, 255, 258, 282, 283, 293, 296, 322, 358, 361, 411, 415, 422, 423, 441, 445, 472, 475, 480, 511, 512, 516, 547–549, 560, 571, 585, 614, 641, 652, 654, 659, 666, 668–674, 676, 677, 679
Structuralist/structuralism, 64, 166, 246, 248–250, 252, 329, 358
Style, 4, 5, 7, 18, 42, 69–72, 79, 103, 105, 108–111, 146, 149–151, 156, 157, 164, 167, 168, 184, 198, 228, 321, 342, 343, 348, 355, 358, 421, 422, 424, 425, 431, 445, 447, 475,
476, 490, 514, 519, 528, 545–547, 552, 613, 615, 666, 669, 672
Subversive, 53, 60–62, 64, 65, 505
Supporter-related, 667, 674, 675
Supranational institutions, 206, 296
Sverigedemokraterna, 128, 135
Swamp, 73, 187, 357
Swedish Democrats (SD), 670
Swiss People's Party (SVP), 127
Switzerland, Poland and Lithuania, 655

T
Tanzania, 344, 495
Taubira, Christiane, 639, 642
Tea Party, 268, 278, 425, 426
Technocratic populism, 347
Terrorism, 148, 174, 177, 178, 354, 635, 638, 641
Terrorist attacks, 383, 630, 638, 641, 668
Thai Chart Pattana (CPP), 477
Thailand, 471, 477, 478, 480, 513
Thai Rak Thai (TRT), 478
Thatcher, Margaret, 217
The Finns, 671, 674
The National Congress for Timorese Reconstruction (CNRT), 479
The Philippines, 177, 180, 182, 184, 185, 187, 190, 191, 342, 345, 347, 455, 471, 473–475, 478, 480
Thin ideology, 22, 229, 322, 422, 423, 527–529, 536
Threat representations, 85, 95, 103, 130, 187
Timbro's Authoritarian Populism Index, 179
Tolerance, 17, 76, 188, 200, 372, 394, 531, 671, 672
Torys, 532
Trade agreements, 228, 238, 239, 381, 531, 532, 536, 583
Traditionalism, 125, 216, 325, 382, 586–588
Transitional justice, 456, 457
Trump, Donald, 12, 31, 32, 34, 44, 109, 110, 115, 120, 121, 124, 126, 128, 130, 132, 133, 163, 172–175, 177, 180, 187, 188, 190, 191, 232,

233, 236, 238, 257, 264, 265, 268–270, 280, 281, 291, 297, 322, 325, 331, 341, 342, 344–346, 348, 351, 407, 408, 414, 417, 418, 421, 426, 432, 442, 447, 461, 493, 536, 560, 561, 580–586, 589, 591, 592, 595–597, 599, 601–605, 629, 665
Trumpism, 389, 583
Trust, 5, 105, 108, 232, 234, 266, 267, 347, 380, 426, 431, 444, 499, 504, 553, 558, 573, 651, 673, 674, 677
Truth, 11, 56, 70, 119, 171, 294, 307, 407–410, 412–418, 445, 456, 457, 461, 637, 678
Truth wars, 410, 418
Turkey, 255, 390–393, 395, 396, 398–400, 455, 463, 527–537, 668
2016 Presidential election, 130, 265, 580, 581, 596–600, 605
21st century socialism, 518

U

Ujamaa, 489, 495
UKIP, 107, 151, 152, 233
Underprivileged, 52, 205, 374
United Kingdom (UK), 78, 104, 107, 109, 128, 132, 278, 284, 331, 380, 389, 407, 532–534, 536, 555, 629, 650
United Opposition (KNP), 475
United Russia, 532
U.S. National Bureau of Economic Research (NBER), 246, 247, 252, 254

V

Values, 4, 11, 17, 21–23, 51, 73, 75, 76, 92, 94, 104, 106–108, 110, 121, 125, 128, 133, 149, 151, 165, 167, 170, 173, 181, 188, 190, 202, 214, 220, 235, 255–257, 264, 265, 278, 295, 296, 322, 323, 326, 330, 371–376, 381, 395, 399, 415, 416, 427, 432, 452, 458, 462, 488, 489, 495, 498, 505, 550, 555, 557–559, 564–572, 574, 575, 586, 615, 631, 634, 636, 637, 639, 640, 650, 652, 655, 656, 660, 672, 678

van Rompuy, Herman, 31, 34, 40
Vargas, Getulio, 165, 248, 252, 513
Varguismo, 248
Venezuela, 54, 255, 256, 303, 304, 309, 310, 312, 316, 346, 455, 511, 512, 514–522
Vergangenheitsbewältigung, 457, 460, 462
Vichy regime, 637, 642
Vietnam War, 266
Visuals/images, 53, 60, 103, 106, 109–111, 122, 124, 127, 146, 171, 173, 174, 202, 204, 315, 345, 359, 396, 399, 414, 455, 461, 475, 478, 493, 501, 502, 516, 517, 519–521, 530, 555, 559, 566, 570, 573, 601
Vlaams Belang (VB), 117, 119, 670
Völkisch, 219, 293, 634
Volksgeist, 613
Volonté Générale, 8, 17, 296, 423, 613
Voting/voter turnout, 12, 32, 34, 41, 104, 121, 133, 134, 152, 172, 180, 267, 268, 277, 279, 381, 438, 444, 446, 452, 580, 584, 585, 591, 596–604, 649–656, 659, 660, 669, 671, 673, 674, 677
Vox populi, 17, 329, 357, 613

W

Wagenknecht, Sahra, 119
Wallace, George, 40, 425
Weber, Max, 34, 205, 380, 573
Welfare/welfare-state, 71, 76, 108, 117, 118, 134, 135, 146–148, 151, 173, 228, 235, 236, 256, 278, 280, 360, 370, 373, 375, 376, 380, 398, 447, 533, 564–566, 569–575, 581, 613, 615, 618, 619, 621, 622, 675, 678, 679
White supremacy, 174, 311
Women's March, 292, 297
Women, appeal to, 41, 278
Working class, 105, 110, 127, 134, 164, 165, 217, 371
World Health Organization (WHO), 346
World Trade Organization (WTO), 238, 239
World War I (WWI), 169, 324

World War II (WWII), 196, 204, 216, 264, 269, 455

X
Xenophobia, 111, 155, 156, 187, 199, 201, 229, 584, 678

Y
Yeltsin, Boris, 534

#YoSoy132, 54
YouTube, 342, 677
Yugoslavia, 459

Z
Zambia, 487, 498, 506
Zeitgeist, 206, 216, 230
Zimbabwe African National Union (ZANU-PF), 498, 501, 502
Zuma, Jacob, 498, 503–506

Printed in the United States
by Baker & Taylor Publisher Services